Political Economy and Global Affairs

Political Economy and Global Affairs

ANDREW C. SOBEL

Washington University in St. Louis

CQ PRESS

A Division of Congressional Quarterly Inc.

Washington, D.C.

CQ Press
1255 22nd Street, NW, Suite 400
Washington, DC 20037

Phone: 202-729-1900; toll-free, 1-866-427-7737 (1-866-4CQ-PRESS)
Web: www.cqpress.com

Cover design, interior design, and composition: Auburn Associates, Inc.
Photo credits appear on page 485.

⊚ The paper used in this publication exceeds the requirements of the American National Standard for Information Sciences—Permanence of Paper for Printed Library Materials, ANSI Z39.48-1992.

Printed and bound in the United States of America

09 08 07 06 05   1 2 3 4 5

Library of Congress Cataloging-in-Publication Data
Sobel, Andrew C.
  Political economy and global affairs/Andrew C. Sobel.
    p. cm.
  Includes bibliographical references and index.
  ISBN 1-56802-861-X (alk. paper)
  1. Economics—Political aspects. 2. Globalization. 3. International economic relations. 4. National state. 5. World politics. I. Title

  HB74.P65S63 2006
  337—dc22

2005027075

~ To Pam, Donna, and Amy ~

Brief Contents

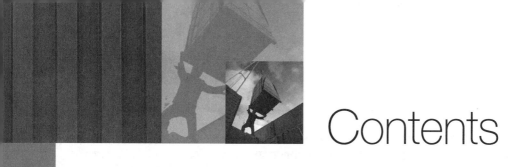

Contents

Figures, Tables, and Maps

FIGURES

TABLES

MAPS

Preface

Positioned at the nexus of politics and economics, international relations and international political economy involve broad and diverse subjects that significantly touch all our lives. By definition, any introductory text is incomplete. It can, at best, provide a solid foundation for more advanced study and stir student interest in further study of its subject matter. Constructing *Political Economy and Global Affairs* presented many challenges: what to include and what to exclude; what approaches to adopt and which ones to omit; how much history and contextual detail to include versus how much theoretical abstraction is needed; how much economics versus how much political science; whether to approach the topic with macro or micro tools; whether to afford primacy to the structure of relations between nation-states or to open up nation-states to consider the mechanisms of domestic politics. Another challenge involved how to develop students' empathy for the difficulties that policymakers face in selecting policies in a complex social system where seemingly sound choices can turn bad and produce unexpected outcomes. The many pitfalls encountered in constructing *Political Economy and Global Affairs* reflect how limited we are in understanding how the pieces fit together in international affairs and how much more work we must do.

Many in political science separate international relations from international political economy, applying distinctions such as the "high politics" of security versus the "low politics" of economic relations. I find this separation to be a false, misleading, and intellectually damaging dichotomy. Because their field of study is a science, political scientists must look for explanations and processes that generalize from one setting to others. If man is "a political animal," we should establish what we mean by *political* and how the mechanisms of politics work. The theories and explanations that help us make sense of political behavior are likely to be similar across domestic and international arenas and across issue areas, whether security, economic, or social. Separating the study of security and conflict from the study of economic relations in the international arena suggests that politics works completely differently in one sphere than in another. Others have made this dichotomy and suffered serious consequences. Napoleon, a warrior, dismissed England as a "nation of shopkeepers," and Mao Zedong ("all power comes from the barrel of a gun") called the United States a "paper tiger." The shopkeepers and the paper tiger eventually prevailed in the political-military sphere because of their activities and capabilities in the political-economic arena. The Soviet Union amassed an impressive military but lost the cold war to the economic prowess of the U.S.-led global capitalist political economy. The United Kingdom and the United States dominated international affairs during the 1800s and 1900s, respectively, becoming hegemons through the strength of their economies and their policy choices in the political-economic arena.

Success in political-economic affairs spills over to the security sphere. Creating a false dichotomy between substantive spheres of political activity and neglecting connections across them is therefore dangerous not only in terms of policy, but also in terms of our understanding of political behavior.

Questions of pedagogy and ontology are often ignored by students being introduced to the study of a social science. The genesis of this project, however, offers important insights into this volume's approach, which is different enough from other texts in international relations and international political economy to merit some attention. I have adopted a political economy approach in this text, but students should note that, in general, competing approaches exist in the study and analysis of international political and economic relations, even if one analytic approach dominates a text. Students should question and challenge ideas and frameworks, continually assessing the power and validity of all approaches. In laying out the pedagogy of the approach that dominates this text, I hope to help them do so intelligently, productively, and with healthy skepticism.

WHY THIS TEXT?

For many years I was frustrated with the introductory texts in international political economy and international relations. Many do an excellent job at describing an array of important topics—whether giving details about international conflict, the International Monetary Fund and the World Bank, international monetary and trade arrangements, the activities of multinational corporations, or the problems of development. They tend, however, toward atheoretical, nonanalytical, and nonpolitical descriptions of events. Although in some cases they offer excellent descriptions of *what* has occurred, they make little attempt to develop explicit theoretical frameworks explaining *why* things happen in global political and economic relations. What analysis does appear in most of these texts takes the form of macro theory, which relies upon system structure and monolithic nation-states to account for behavior in the global arena. Individual decision makers and subnational actors are missing from such accounts, or, at best, they are presented as automatons reacting in a deterministic fashion to the vicissitudes of the international system. Many of my friends in microeconomics find the very notion of macro theory implausible because of the relative absence of individuals as decision makers, but it is an appropriate description of a causal argument built upon a perception of monolithic nation-states acting within a particular global context. I include aspects of those macro approaches—liberalism and realism—in this text as a means of demonstrating their weaknesses and arguing the need for examination of micro foundations in the domestic political economy to explain international political and economic relations.

These macro approaches failed to resonate with me during my intellectual development, as I had difficulty placing myself in a decision maker's shoes as required in making the calculations and choices demanded by these approaches. Indeed, when I placed myself in that context, I often made choices that conflicted with what was prescribed by the macro approaches. This contradiction seems to characterize real policymakers' choices as well, for all too often their decisions conflict with those anticipated by macro approaches to political and economic behavior.

This point was brought home to me when al-Qaida attacked on September 11, 2001. I was teaching a large class on introduction to international relations, and as expected, the attack sparked frequent questions and debates, as students tried to make sense of world affairs. The events of 9/11 highlighted the role of individuals and nonstate actors in global affairs, and the difficulties of understanding the actions of terrorists within the boundaries of the macro frameworks underscored the weaknesses and limitations of those approaches. In fact, I had plenty of theory and tools that helped students better understand the events of 9/11 and those after, but those tools came from micro political economy, which was on the syllabus for later in the course. These micro tools focused on individual preferences, constraints on individual choice, incentives and disincentives to individuals, and strategic interactions of individual choice and calculations. I saw clearly that a text such as *Political Economy and Global Affairs* was needed, and my frustration that semester intersected with the persistence and persuasiveness of Charisse Kiino, an editor at CQ Press. At a conference several years earlier, she had approached me about writing a text for international political economy. I initially resisted, because I thought the project would interfere with my research program on globalization, risk, and the changing role of the state. Circumstances and Charisse's persistence eventually converged to convince me that I should accept her offer.

EXPLANATORY FRAMEWORK AND ORGANIZATION

Of necessity, I made several working assumptions that define the boundaries of what this text does and does not do. First, it is meant for a course in analytical political science, not politics or current events. It is designed to help students to probe, dissect, and analyze political behavior, not to promote memorization and regurgitation of facts and events. Some beginning students know a lot about politics, which is of great use for those interested in political science, but such knowledge is not to be confused with political science. They may be history buffs, political "junkies," or well-informed on current events, but they probably comprehend little political science despite knowing a lot of "stuff" about day-to-day politics. Students may have tremendous native abilities, but they are diamonds in the rough until they have developed and honed their skills. The process of education is a technological transformation of human labor and abilities. This text focuses on developing a particular set of systematic tools for explanation or exploration of the phenomena we study in political science. It emphasizes explanatory frameworks for social behavior that are based on the rational choice approach to political economy.

Second, I assume that a text students read is better than one they do not read, even if the text they neglect covers more material more thoroughly. My experience on a university campus continually reminds me that time is a scarce resource that students must allocate between multiple courses and community life. I appropriately adjusted my expectations for this text by limiting the material to be presented, but without sacrificing the comprehensiveness of core topics that instructors will want to cover. I constrained the boundaries of the text in the belief that accomplishing a few key objectives well is better than a diffuse effort covering a broader area. In the spirit of lowering the barriers to students' success at grasping and playing with the frameworks in this text, I limited the use of footnotes and references to other sources. Such cites are useful in more advanced undergraduate and graduate courses, where students are expected to develop depth and expertise, but at this level they can only distract from the big ideas. For those students who want to move beyond this text, I include suggestions for further reading at the end of each chapter. These supplementary reading lists can also guide instructors as they tailor the text to their needs and objectives.

Third, I assume that students can absorb, digest, and process news and events available through the media and histories. As a consequence, I focus on theories, frameworks, information, and tools that are harder to grasp on one's own. I do not attempt to provide extensive factual background or details about the world beyond what is necessary to support the core objective of the text, which is to develop a set of systematic tools that help make sense of the facts, construct stories about relationships, and test interpretations. How much contextual background and history to include is a difficult balance to strike: too much can distract from the text's primary focus on theoretical tools and perversely encourage students to spend time memorizing details, but developing such tools in the absence of sufficient background and history is pointless and potentially pathological. Context matters! Details and facts are potentially useful, but not independent of explanatory frameworks. Reading and analyzing other texts, periodicals, magazines, and newspapers in conjunction with reading this volume is necessary and worthwhile.

In addition to serving as a core text for a range of courses in international political economy, this book can be used as a core or complementary text in an introductory international politics course to teach the microfoundations of political behavior and underscore the role of global exchange (not conflict) in that curriculum. The political processes highlighted should be the same across substantive areas—domestic or international, security or economics. Textbooks reflect the teaching strategies of their authors, but teachers inevitably take different approaches to their courses and materials. Ten political scientists asked to design a particular course will create ten different syllabi with some important similarities and some important differences; often similar topics will be covered, but in a different order and from different perspectives. This volume reflects my general approach to teaching international affairs, but I tried to design a text that could be used in a number of courses, in a variety of approaches, and at various levels of instruction.

This flexibility requires that instructors thoughtfully integrate the text into their courses in the manner most complementary to their own approaches. For example, chapters 3 through 6 focus on the core ideas of realism and liberal market exchange, two macro frameworks typically covered in most introductory courses in international relations and international political economy. I include these chapters because they serve as foils to the micro approach favored elsewhere in this text. Likewise, in chapter 1, I provide an introduction to the process of science as a framework for social analysis, because I hope it will serve as a reminder throughout the text that the goal is explanation, not simply description. The instructor of an upper-level course—especially one who examines only micro political economy foundations to behavior—might move quickly through these chapters as students are likely to have already seen and mastered these materials. However, for those who have previously studied these topics, the early chapters are a good refresher and can help orient them toward key assumptions operative throughout the remainder of the text.

Some teachers prefer to emphasize history over theory—a valuable endeavor, especially given many students' underdeveloped knowledge of history and its importance for understanding the present and future. A course that targets the construction of a good historical foundation might emphasize chapters 7 through 11, which look at the historical evolution of globalization and international political economic relations from the 1800s to the present.

Instructors choosing to focus on the microfoundations of behavior in international relations and international political economy will find major theoretical tools developed extensively in chapter 2, in parts of chapters 5 and 6, and in chapters 12 through 15. These chapters explore individual rationality, market failure, social traps, collective action, interest groups and political cleavages, and the role of institutions, or rules of the game. Throughout the text, examples are offered that employ the logic of the micro tools developed in these chapters.

ACKNOWLEDGMENTS

I have been lucky to teach at Washington University in St. Louis, where I have taught students with strong analytical capabilities. Their feedback has improved the content and design of this text. My graduate teaching and research assistants have made valuable contributions to this project: Zdravka Brunkova, Gyung-ho Jeong, Michael Popovic, Scott Schmidt, and Jianmin Zhang read and commented on several chapters, and Paul Scharre provided tremendous assistance in developing the exercises, outlines, and presentations on the ancillary CD for instructors. I also roped several undergraduate research assistants into the project: Amelia Boone, Zahra Egal, Seema Kanwar, Sagar Ravi, and David Rogier read drafts, researched facts, and helped to construct tables and the exercises at the end of chapters. Several other undergraduates provided significant assistance: Jonathan Caplis, Maggie Hughes, Stephen Quinn, and Shelby Wolff. The Murray Weidenbaum Center on the Economy, Government, and Public Policy and the College of Arts and Sciences at

Washington University provided resources and means by which I could include these talented undergraduates in this project.

My involvement traces to Charisse Kiino, who is a persistent, convincing, and supportive editor at CQ Press. The project is a result of her vision. Also at CQ Press, Michael Kerns offered thoughtful, useful feedback and strict deadlines as the development editor. Katharine Miller improved the quality of writing immeasurably in her responsibilities as copyeditor. Joan Gossett, the production editor at CQ Press, tracked down photos and visuals and nurtured the project in its final stages. I really enjoyed writing this book, and just when I thought I had it right after repeatedly writing and rewriting chapters, the editorial staff at CQ made additional suggestions that improved the organization of the text and its prose. My colleagues at institutions around the country who served as reviewers for CQ Press—among them, J. Lawrence Broz, University of California, San Diego; Scott Gates, International Peace Research Institute, Oslo; David Leblang, University of Colorado; Quan Li, Pennsylvania State University; Eloise Malone, United States Naval Academy; Waltraud Q. Morales, University of Central Florida; and Beth Simmons, Harvard University—dedicated substantial time to provide excellent feedback and suggestions. Their comments have greatly improved the text.

I thank Pam Lokken for reading and rereading draft upon draft of this book and all my other projects. She has provided tremendous support and encouragement over the years, and I look forward to more of the same. Finally, I want to thank the folks at Einstein's Bagels, Sharky's Grill, the Beach Break, and Gary's Dewey Beach Grill for providing much-needed sustenance during my intensive writing periods. To all those named here and those who wish to remain anonymous, I extend my thanks and appreciation. As always, any remaining problems are solely the responsibility of this author.

1

Introduction: Concepts, History, and Social Science

The history of the American tariff is the story of a dubious economic policy turned into a great political success. The very tendencies that have made the legislation bad have made it politically invincible.

E.E. Schattschneider, Politics, Pressures and the Tariff *(1935, 283)*

A PUZZLE AND AN AGENDA

In 1930 Congress passed the Smoot-Hawley Act, the last general tariff adopted and implemented in the United States. Almost since the founding days of the Republic, *tariffs,* a particular form of trade barrier that increases the cost of imports by imposing a tax on them, had been a focus of much congressional activity. Debates and divisions over trade policy colored early U.S. history. Shortly after the country's founding, Alexander Hamilton endorsed trade protections as a tool to stimulate economic activity in nascent American industries. In the latter 1800s, the issue of tariffs became a significant source of conflict between Republicans and Democrats, with the Republicans generally favoring tariffs and the Democrats pushing to lower trade barriers.

The depression-era bill, named after Senator Reed Smoot (R-Utah) and Representative Willis Hawley (R-Oregon), imposed tariffs on over twenty thousand imported goods and raised tariff rates to their highest level in U.S. history. Economists, particularly trade economists, view the Smoot-Hawley Act as among the most damaging interventions by government into the economy—and one of the worst pieces of legislation—in U.S. political-economic history. Many political scientists and historians argue that the Smoot-Hawley tariffs added to the depth and duration of the Great Depression. Due to the position of the United States in the global economy, domestic policy choices such as Smoot-Hawley spilled across national boundaries and influenced economic activity in other countries, in this case causing unemployment and economic distress among other nations' laborers and producers.

Other governments retaliated by raising their tariff rates and trade barriers, and over the next several years, the volume of world trade declined drastically. As imports and exports fell, the economic activity associated with those imports and exports also declined. The decline in trade slowed economic activity, cut off avenues for expansion and recovery, and fed the social and political dislocations of the depression years.

Political parties on both the extreme right and the extreme left took advantage of the economic distress to build support among the disaffected and so advance their political agendas. Hitler, Mussolini, Franco, and others mobilized widespread popular discontent to take command of their respective governments; World War II followed. Certainly other factors contributed as well, but the breakdown in the processes of international trade abetted by the Smoot-Hawley tariffs played a major role in the progression of events leading up to the war.

Why would two Republican members of Congress propose legislation that produced such damaging outcomes? Why would other Republicans support this legislation? Why would a Republican president, Hoover, sign it into law? And why would U.S. society tolerate such antitrade practices, which would predictably damage the social welfare? Why would the United States—a country that professed a belief in market exchange and the mechanisms of capitalism—adopt such high levels of tariff protection when such policies intervened in market exchange, reduced the efficiency and gains from market exchange, and threatened the welfare of its own people?

We cannot claim that the Republican supporters of Smoot-Hawley were ignorant of these economic arguments against government intervention in market exchange and against their legislation in particular. After all, the Republican Party represented the business and economic elites that strenuously resisted government intervention in their domestic economic activities. With some exceptions, such as Teddy Roosevelt, the Republican Party reliably championed corporate capitalism against the interests of labor and small enterprise, as Republican business elites fondly embraced the tenets of social Darwinism and the survival of the fittest in economic affairs. And in case these Republican legislators had forgotten the connection of trade to market exchange, more than one thousand economists, including all the top experts, signed a letter imploring Congress to reject Smoot-Hawley and asking President Hoover to veto the legislation. Drawing on David Ricardo's insights into trade in the early 1800s, economists had come to accept as law the pure utilitarian gains that trade provided: overall, societies benefited from more—not less—trade, regardless of the circumstances. Why, then, would policymakers favor policies that they knew would limit the gains to their society, and even potentially harm it? Did Senator Smoot and Representative Hawley set out to damage the national economy and destroy the global economy, prolong the Great Depression, and generate conditions conducive to another world war? Unlikely!

Yet Republican support for tariffs had a long history. Following the Civil War, a partisan divide had emerged over tariffs, with Republicans generally supportive of and Democrats usually opposed to such measures. We cannot argue that Democrats actually understood market economics and the purported benefits of capitalist market exchange better than Republicans did during this period. As mentioned earlier, many influential Republicans had long been forceful proponents of laissez-faire capitalism and social Darwinism—whereby the discipline of free-market exchange created economic winners and losers, rewarding the winners and forcing the losers to adjust their economic activity. In contrast, many leading Democrats had advanced a progressive agenda, which advocated using the tools of government to constrain laissez-faire and corporate capitalism. Given this history, Democrats would seem more likely than Republicans to advocate government intervention to rein in the harshness of social Darwinism and to cushion workers and small businesses from the potential violence of the rapid adjustments generated by market exchange.

In the epigraph provided at the beginning of this section, E.E. Schattschneider, a young political scientist, wrote in the early 1930s that the conditions surrounding bad economic policy such as the tariff actually made such policy "politically invincible," or undefeatable. Schattschneider argued that the institutional makeup of the U.S. political system promoted the tariff despite its poor economic policy prospects; U.S. political institutions—"the rules of the game"—structured political bargaining and the partisan divide in such a way as to make elected representatives amenable to flawed public policy such as Smoot-Hawley. This argument suggests that we would still be burdened by these poor policy choices if the rules of the game, the political institutions, had not changed. And in 1934, Congress did indeed pass legislation that changed the rules of the game, despite their seeming invincibility: the Reciprocal Trade and Tariff Act (RTTA) was an institutional reform that shifted some responsibility for U.S. tariff levels to the executive branch. Congress gave the president the ability to unilaterally negotiate and adopt reductions of up to 50 percent in existing tariffs without consulting lawmakers. The president could not impose new tariffs, for that prerogative rests constitutionally in the power of the House of Representatives to create taxes, but the president could now reduce existing tariffs within the guidelines established by Congress. This new rule started a long decline in U.S. tariff levels and a liberalization of access to U.S. markets. Given the size of the U.S. economy and its position in the global economy, this trend helped promote an expansion in international exchange and contributed to an increase in global social welfare. Within the space of four years, the United States had adopted diametrically opposed policies.

In this historical example, we encounter many of the broader topics that are to be the focus of this book. First, a democratic government enacts a policy—Smoot-Hawley—that is inconsistent with its society's long-term welfare, although another policy would produce a better outcome for society as a whole. This dysfunctional policymaking in a democratic political economy produces a suboptimal collective outcome: we call this occurrence a *social trap* or *political market failure*. Second, there is breakdown in economic market exchange as international trade declines precipitously: we call this effect *economic market failure*. Third, as we noted, the U.S. government is divided along partisan lines, and these lines reflect *cleavages* in domestic society. Fourth, we see the importance of the rules of the political game: we call these *institutions*. A dramatic change in the rules of the game from the 1930 Smoot-Hawley Act to the 1934 RTTA provided an opportunity to observe the consequences of institutional change, as Schattschneider's politically invincible tariff became vulnerable. Finally, all of these observations concern activities and actions that originate within a specific political economy, and yet their consequences spill across borders to influence other political economies and the global arena itself. We will return to these topics again and again in the following pages.

GLOBALIZATION AND GLOBAL CAPITALISM

Global relations of various kinds play a growing and important role in our day-to-day lives. Economic and political relations within and across nations have shifted dramatically over the past two centuries, and they continue to change at a rapid rate. These transformations contribute to a process called **globalization,** which colors social relations between and within nation-states. Globalization consists of multiple processes by which people in one society become culturally, economically, politically, strategically, and ecologically closer to peoples in geographically distant societies. These processes include the expansion of cross-border trade, the production of goods and services via the multinational corporation, the movement of peoples, the exchange of ideas and popular culture, the flow of environmental degradation and disease from one nation to another, and the routine transfer of billions of dollars across borders in a nanosecond. They connect communities, cultures, national markets for goods and services, and national markets for labor and capital. The food we consume, the clothes we wear, the jobs we perform, the air we breathe and the water we drink, the cars we drive, the transport that delivers our goods, the information we access, the capital that powers our economies, the services and computers we use, the places we travel to, the education we seek, the diseases we contract, and just about every aspect of day-to-day life has some international component. This book seeks to help students develop a toolkit for understanding why policymakers, public and private, make the choices they make in an era of increasing globalization.

One characteristic of globalization is convergence across nations as markets and societies become increasingly exposed to each other and increasingly integrated. The more integrated economies become, the more closely prices for commodities and labor in those economies should converge. Still, there is little reason to expect complete—or even near—convergence in many arenas of social life. A continued divergence in commodity and labor prices across markets demonstrates the persistence and stickiness of distinct national political economies in the face of globalizing pressures. The modern nation-state is far from dead or from being brushed aside by the trend toward globalization.

One factor that has contributed to economic convergence is the advance of **global capitalism,** which is a particular form of social and economic relations connecting national economies. After the collapse of the communist regimes of the Eastern bloc in the late twen-

The signs of globalization abound in the Akihabara shopping district of Tokyo, as they do in other cities worldwide. The opening of national boundaries to multinational corporations means that whether in London, New York, Shanghai, or Tel Aviv, purchasers have easy access to the same consumer, financial, and information products. Although some find this expansion of economic opportunity a positive development, others oppose the homogenization of economic sectors and the effects of globalization on local businesses.

tieth century, it emerged as the unchallenged form of social and economic organization in the global political economy. In global capitalism, exchange across nations occurs primarily in markets, where consumption choices are voluntary, determined by supply and demand, and coordinated by a price mechanism. Markets can be located in physical structures such as buildings, on docks, in town squares, in any physical setting where merchants and consumers gather, and also in digital accounting programs where exchanges are conducted in cyberspace via computer keystroke.

Markets aggregate individual activities and produce a collective outcome. They are relatively **decentralized** mechanisms for allocating goods, capital, and services within and across societies. This mode of exchange differs from more **centralized means of allocation** such as government-administered distribution mechanisms that are more hierarchical and authoritative than the voluntary, consensual nature of a market. In this book, we extend the framework of market exchange beyond the boundaries of economic exchange to encompass political exchange as well. When economic and political markets work well, they are a wonderful means of aggregating and conveying tremendous amounts of information. They tell us about the preferences of consumers and voters in society, about the productive capabilities of producers and policymakers given the distribution of resources in society, and about the most efficient ways to coordinate the choices of consumers and voters with those of producers and policymakers.

The expansion of globalization means that economic production and consumption choices in one nation are increasingly influenced by similar choices in other nations. For many years, economists used **closed-economy models** to examine economic conditions in a society: they ignored economic factors and conditions external to a nation, thinking about the nation's economy as if it were a secluded island. But with the transformation of national capitalist relations into increasingly global capitalist relations, closed-economy frameworks have given way to **open-economy models,** in which connections across national economies become important factors to consider when exploring a nation's economic and social welfare, and the politics that surround it.

The extent of global influence on our lives may vary depending upon where we live, our nationality, our income, our profession, and the openness and strength of our national political economy. However, the world is figuratively shrinking, as activities in one nation spill over to influence activities in other nations with greater and greater frequency. Almost certainly, the connection of economic markets across borders will influence choices and actions in national political markets. The shifts in global economic activity spawn debate about the changing role of markets and states, about the risks individuals face in this changing state of affairs, and about whether those risks can be managed and by whom. At the heart of these debates rests an extraordinary tension between economic and political forms of social organization. Economic life under global capitalism is based upon market exchange that spans national borders; with globalization, economic relations are increasingly formed and shaped by global market forces. In theory, these forces do not recognize the political boundaries of nation-states, yet national borders define political arenas in theory and in practice. Political relations are defined by the modern nation-state system. Thus, national boundaries organize political life, but economic life spans those boundaries. Political organization, authority, and geography do not overlap with the economic geography of globalization. This tension between sovereignty and interdependence will return again and again in our study of modern international affairs. As billionaire currency trader George Soros noted, "we can have a market economy, but we cannot have a market society."

Creating such connections across national boundaries brings good and bad consequences: it improves the well-being of many, but it also creates new risks and problems for societies. Globalization and global capitalism can blur the economic boundaries of the nation-state, spill over into noneconomic areas of social activity, and challenge the policy autonomy of national governments. In this shifting arena, significant challenges, perils, and opportunities confront governments, societies, firms, policymakers, and individuals. Many praise globalization; others rail against it; yet others see both its good and bad consequences and argue for managing the negatives while promoting the positives. This divisive effect goes beyond academic debate to visceral public arguments that evoke conflicting passions and fears. Demonstrators at the World Trade Organization meetings in Seattle in 2001, at economic conferences in Davos, Switzerland, and Genoa, Italy, in that same year, and at the regular World Bank and International Monetary Fund meetings in Washington, D.C., have protested globalization and the transformations in global capitalism, sometimes violently.

Many fear the potential for increasing income inequality and wealth concentration that accompanies market exchange—even if individuals are better off than they were the year before, and the year before that. But concern about globalization extends beyond the economic consequences: many fear its homogenizing effect on the distinct identities and cultures of different societies, as Nike, McDonalds, and other symbols of global capitalism insinuate themselves into national economies and consciousness. Perhaps worried about the fate of the classic French bistro in the face of competitive pressures from McDonalds and other fast-food chains, Jack Lang, a former French minister of culture warned:

> The disappearance of languages and cultural forms is the great risk today. Diversity threatens to be replaced by an international mass culture without roots, soul, color, or taste.[1]

These debates, protestations, and concerns will continue, both because globalization and international political-economic relations are complex and incompletely understood phenomena and because the dominant form of political organization does not mesh with the dominant form of economic organization in the global political economy.

Despite such worries about globalization and its consequences, societies and governments rarely seek complete isolation from the global economy—a status called **autarky,** or self-sufficiency. Both autarky and isolationism are sure paths to retarding the future growth and welfare of a society. To be sure, potential risks to some individuals, families, and communities do accompany the significant societal payoffs to be expected from interacting with the global political economy, and we should not be naively optimistic about the dislocations that it is likely to cause. Most of these effects will be short-term, but they will nevertheless be costly to those who suffer them. This is true of any major social transformation, regardless of how beneficial for society the change may be in the long term. Change is inherently costly to anyone who prefers the status quo or who fears the uncertainty of the future. Here we see the roots of the conflicted politics of globalization: many stand to benefit from the transformations it will bring, but some legitimately fear the potential costs to them, their families, and their communities.

At the societal level, the potential gains from the global exchange of goods, services, capital, and ideas far outweigh the benefits of self-sufficiency and isolationism, even if such strategies were plausible. Hiding our national heads in the global sand or retreating behind xenophobic national barriers based on fear of foreigners cannot be advanced as a plausible policy for dealing with the world unless we want to consign our economies, polities, and societies to second-class status. Policymakers are confronted with the challenge of reaping the rewards of globalization for the majority in their societies while managing the disloca-

---

[1] Quoted in Walter LaFeber, *Michael Jordan and the New Global Capitalism* (New York: Norton, 1999).

tion to the few. On the international front, they may resort to either unilateral or multilateral strategies to manage the effects of globalization upon their societies—either adopting policies without the cooperation and coordination of other governments or attempting to coordinate policies with those of other governments. On the domestic front, policymakers must decide how to manage the inevitable dislocations (hopefully short-term) to the minority who will be negatively affected, for this minority could deny or dampen the benefits of globalization to the majority if they are effective at political action.

THE PAST AS PROLOGUE

Despite recent fascination with globalization, the transformations in global political-economic relations of the later decades of the twentieth century are not unique in the history of human affairs. Bits and pieces of cross-border market exchange have existed for many centuries, but the full-blown emergence of global capitalism as a dominant form of international exchange dates to the early 1800s. It has been a halting transformation, plagued with breakdowns, interludes, and reversals along the way.

The Nineteenth Century

Unlike the international affairs of the eighteenth century and of the first half of the twentieth century, those of the nineteenth century were notable for the relative absence of cross-border conflict and a tremendous increase in cooperation between nation-states. Expanding international trade and exchange went hand in hand with this period of calm. It was the first great era of globalization, wherein a revolutionary and rapid transformation in the movement of capital, goods, services, information, and people across national boundaries produced a skeletal framework for the global political economy. This transformation also allowed dramatic shifts in the relationships between governments and their peoples, between polities and their economies, and between the national political economies of different states.

In the early 1800s, those national political economies were more similar than dissimilar—in their forms of political and economic organization, in their manner of economic production, in their distribution of wealth and opportunity, in the gaps between the wealthy and the poor in domestic society, and in the relative per capita incomes across nations. At the beginning of the nineteenth century, the world's political economies were dominated by agricultural forms of production. Politics was controlled by agrarian elites, and democracy was extremely limited, if existent at all. Even in those nations that we regard as the birthplace of modern democracy (England, France, and the United States), suffrage proved extremely limited, as voting rights were related to **property rights** (the rules defining the ownership of property), as well as to characteristics such as gender and religion. The preferences of ruling lords and elites dominated the patterns of trade and exchange across borders, for such exchange was in the service and the interests of the sovereign or king—or in the interests of the elites that the sovereign represented.

This form of international political economic relations became known as **mercantilism.** Mercantilism produced interesting but odd patterns of international interaction, as politics, not economics, dominated the rationale for exchange across borders. Neighbors might not trade with neighbors even though geographic proximity would make such exchange easy or the nature of the goods produced in the adjacent nations would make the potential gains from such trade attractive. Sovereigns viewed other nations and their sovereigns as competitors in what is called a **zero-sum game.** In such situations, one's gain translates into another's loss.

As the century progressed, a form of global political-economic relations called **liberalism** became increasingly prevalent. Liberalism, which is addressed more thoroughly in chapter 5, is a form of economic interaction based upon voluntary exchange in market settings, where the consumption and production of goods and services are coordinated by a mechanism called **price.** Internationally, liberalism involves exchange that is based upon the economic choices of consumers and producers across boundaries and not manipulated via the intervention of political actors. This form of exchange is at the heart of the processes of global capitalism.

The most significant global shifts of the nineteenth century occurred within and across what has been called the **Atlantic economy.** This loose aggregation includes the political economies of western and southern Europe, North America, Australia, and Japan—today the core members of the Organization for Economic Cooperation and Development (OECD). These political economies underwent tremendous political consolidation, social transformation, and economic expansion, involving fundamental changes in the nature of the state, state-society relations, political rights and liberties, and domestic forms of economic production. Meanwhile, changes in international trade, migration, and expansion of international capital flows contributed significantly to these internal transitions. The resulting political and economic transformation was deep and wide, affecting all parts of these societies as they underwent the changeover from agricultural elites and rural labor (then called peasants) to urban elites and labor.

Political and economic power began to shift from rural areas to urban areas, rearranging political cleavages and coalitions, affecting policy debates, and altering the demands upon politicians and governments. A burgeoning middle class—labeled the bourgeoisie—emerged as an influential force and pushed for expanded political and economic rights. Rural workers moved to the cities, where they provided the labor to fuel industrial transformation but also created new demands upon management and government. As political leaders began to extend suffrage in response to these changes, labor too began to emerge as a political force within the nations comprising the Atlantic economy, altering politics within and across nations.

By the late nineteenth century, such changes in the political and economic conditions in a few nations led to a massive transformation in the distribution of wealth and power in the international arena as a whole. Nations were no longer more alike than unalike; huge discrepancies emerged across boundaries in terms of economic capacity, forms of political organization, and political influence. The emerging distinction between the "haves" (those nations with relative plenty and opportunity) and the "have-nots" (those defined by low per capita income and economic output) was rooted in the fact that these changes were experienced by the "haves" and not experienced by the "have-nots."

By the century's end, Western Europe—the "haves"—sat perched on the edge of a golden age of enlightenment and cooperation that grew from a period of long peace, extension of political rights, economic transformation and expansion, and increasing international trade. The participants in this age of enlightenment, or *belle époque*, celebrated rational and liberal civilization, respected constitutionalism, developed representative government, encouraged the rule of law, and advanced the demise of monarchical rule.

The Twentieth Century

The twentieth century, in contrast, turned out to be a turbulent and momentous era. Yet it began optimistically, with great hope for the continued expansion of political and economic opportunity. Globalization of economic relations stood fairly developed and growing. Mass migration complemented movements of goods, services, and capital. However, the advance of prosperity, suffrage, and global economic relations was soon interrupted by a world war, a devastating economic depression, and then another world war.

The onset of World War I launched Europe into one of most violent, wasteful, and tragic conflicts in human history, gutting an economically, politically, and socially advancing continent. It was a tragedy of monumental proportions that was grounded in the stupidity of kings, politicians, and generals who feared the future and naively incited the conflict without appreciating the destructiveness of modern warfare. In 1914 the world embarked upon global conflict as if primping for a party: stylish uniforms, dress parades, too much male testosterone and bravado, too much female admiration, and too much belief in the invincibility and immortality of youth glamorized the armies that marched off to war with the promise to return before the leaves fell.

The four years of horrific combat that ensued left 10 million dead, many more mangled and maimed, and even more tortured emotionally and psychologically. Entire generations of men in the prime of their lives were lost to the conflict, depriving European nations for years to come of the labor that is a key factor of economic production. Who knows what ideas and creativity, what opportunities for these societies, were lost among the casualties? And the foolishness of the negotiated peace that ended World War I only compounded the losses. The Treaty of Versailles imposed a harsh settlement upon the vanquished, helped undermine economic recovery in Europe, generated a legacy of political rancor among the losers, and opened the door to fascist and socialist malcontents in societies experiencing economic hardship. The fascist political leaders who rose to power then implemented the policies that led to World War II. Authoritarian political relations extinguished the roots of economic liberalism and political constitutionalism in Italy after 1922, in Germany in 1933, and in Spain after 1936. Totalitarianism deprived citizens of electoral rights, excited nationalistic political instincts, and limited political debate by attacking internal opposition.

In hindsight, the resolution of the first world war almost ensured the outbreak of the second, despite an intermission of about twenty years. World War I introduced the manufacture of mass death to the world and the twentieth century, but World War II raised it to a new level of technological consummation, producing atrocities beyond experience or imagination: 55 million dead, 35 million wounded, some 3 million more lost and unaccounted for, and 30 million civilian deaths. The concentration camps at Auschwitz, Belsen, and Treblinka; the war-ravaged cities of Leningrad, Stalingrad, Warsaw, London, Berlin, and Rotterdam—all were the legacy of decades of conflict between the "civilized" Western nations. The destruction that had begun on the World War I battlefields at the Somme, Verdun, Champagne, and the Marne, ended in the devastation of Berlin, Hiroshima, and Nagasaki.

In terms of international conflict, the first half of the twentieth century was a violent episode that interrupted and reversed the trend toward globalization and the progressive trajectory established in the mid- to late nineteenth century. And the second half of the twentieth century could have been even deadlier, given the escalation in military technology with the advent of nuclear weapons. But the primary antagonists—the United States and the Soviet Union—restrained themselves from meeting in active combat, instead competing in a so-called cold war, which ended with the breakup of the Soviet Union and its sphere of influence. By the end of the century, democratization and the globalization of capitalist economic activity emerged as the apparent winners of a struggle between competing forms of political-economic organization—the centralized and decentralized mechanisms mentioned earlier. The twentieth century had witnessed major shifts in the geopolitical-economic landscape, generating conflicts across major ideologies over the manner of organizing political-economic relations within societies and within the global arena.

Given the prevalence of international conflict throughout the twentieth century, many courses and texts about international relations following World War II focus on political-military relations, war, and national security. This narrow focus on wartime politics neglects the tremendous flow of goods, services, information, and people that characterized the global political economy during different periods of the twentieth century and the years preceding it. The politics of war is just one aspect of global affairs; the politics of the absence of war—and engagement in exchange—constitute another, equally important component. Peace and prosperity, war and destruction are two parts of the same puzzle as we try to understand relations across national boundaries. The study of international affairs becomes increasingly pressing, not only because of the growing destructiveness of weapons and militaries, but also because of the increasing demand for economic and social exchange within and across borders to promote growth and development, in order to advance the human condition and attack the problems that plague policymakers—problems that often spill over into international conflict.

As we go about examining and explicating world affairs of the past, present, and possible futures, we need systematic tools and frameworks to assist our efforts. We do not want to rely on one-shot, ad hoc explanations, because without frameworks to help us anticipate and understand international relations, we will always be surprised by events. The specific tools and frameworks that we develop and employ to understand global affairs will influence our understanding of those affairs. We will also come to appreciate both the robustness of these tools in the face of competing understandings and their adaptability to new events, settings, and scenarios. In this volume we approach the study of international affairs as a science—a social science—which has an explicit meaning in terms of the processes by which we generate and assess knowledge.

AN APPROACH TO SOCIAL RESEARCH: GOALS, ASSUMPTIONS, AND FRAMEWORKS

In the study of global affairs, social scientists focus upon a spectrum of behavior that ranges from the most violent conflict to the most productive cooperation across national boundaries. This book tends to focus on the political mechanisms of international political-economic relations, not on war. But cooperation and conflict are related as two sides of the same coin. The choice to focus on international political-economic relations reflects a preference for what we seek to explain. I assume that the explanatory frameworks or mechanisms of political behavior are similar regardless of the differences in the phenomenon we want to understand. If politics are politics, then the same explanatory frameworks should operate in a variety of situations, domestic or international, in war or peace. The setting may shift, but the theories and tools we use to account for political behavior should remain constant. This approach explicitly assumes that similar processes and mechanisms are at work across the different fields of political science and that the boundaries separating the different fields— such as comparative politics and international relations—are organizational artifacts, not differences in explanatory mechanisms.

Goals and Methods

Social scientists engage in a variety of activities: description, explanation, prediction, and prescription. They employ a variety of theoretical frameworks as they explore the range of human activity. No single unified framework has prevailed; multiple, or competing, approaches robustly coexist. This text relies predominantly on an approach called political economy. A variety of approaches fall into the category of political economy—as we will see in the next chapter—but our approach emphasizes the rationality, preferences, capabilities, calculations, strategies, and choices of individual political-economic actors in social settings where their choices interact with the choices of others to produce the social outcomes we observe. This approach seeks to investigate and construct the *micro* foundations of *macro* outcomes. Individual choices aggregate to produce macro outcomes, but we need to understand why individuals make the choices they make if we are to understand and thus be able to influence broader social outcomes in the world. Hopefully, we can use these micro foundations to explain why decision makers make the choices they make and how context affects their individual-level calculations. Chapter 2 provides a foundation to this framework, laying out key assumptions about how individuals behave.

But in any science, explanatory approaches become more prominent or fade only in relation to alternative approaches. It is useful to compare the micro approach favored in this text with other approaches. Chapters 3–6 in the first part of this book introduce several alternative approaches that are influential in the study of international affairs, particularly in introductory courses. These are macro approaches that rely primarily upon the structure of social relations, emphasizing states and their positions in the international system to explain social behavior. Individual action is viewed as fairly deterministic in these approaches, which ignore the political activity and strategic manipulation between individuals. Such structural approaches offer useful comparisons to the micro approach, and they can be useful as a first cut at understanding behavior, but they have fairly substantial limitations if individuals' behavior is not purely determined by the structure of social affairs. We need to consider these structural approaches in order to assess the shortcomings in what they can explain and to help demonstrate the value of focusing instead on the micro foundations of macro outcomes.

In developing this social science toolkit to explore the micro foundations of global political-economic relations, I emphasize the endeavor of explanation, use description, and largely ignore prediction or prescription. Social scientists engage in all these activities as part of their discipline, but they tend to specialize and focus more heavily upon one activity over the others. First, let's consider what I mean by *science* in this book, and then proceed to define the activities that constitute its practice.

Social Analysis as Science

Science is about the process of research. Despite underlying similarities, the superficial process of science in the social sciences looks different from how we think about the process of science in the physical and life sciences. Social scientists do not wear lab coats. Day-to-day activities in the world and history serve as their dominant laboratories. They rarely have the luxury enjoyed by the physical sciences to conduct experiments in controlled laboratory settings where all inputs are carefully measured and a scientist can vary one input (called an intervention) at a time and then look for a change in outcomes that can be attributed to the change in the input. A controlled laboratory setting thus allows the scientist to insulate the experiment from other inputs that could affect the outcome. This control of the experimental environment and of the intervention allows for more comfortable assessments about **causality,** or whether the change in the input *A* actually caused a change in the outcome *B*, and if so, how much change and why. If the physical scientist worries about control of the intervention and about potential threats to causal claims, she can design experiments involving multiple groups whose members are randomly assigned; one group (the treatment group) receives the intervention, and the other group (the control group) does not. Random assignment helps to disperse preexisting characteristics in the experimental population that could influence the outcome independent of the intervention. Randomizing ensures that such characteristics are unsystematically distributed across the different groups, thus equalizing the groups and negating the ability of such characteristics to threaten the causal test of the experiment.

Controlled experiments and random assignment are powerful tools in the design of research, but they are tools that are often unavailable to social scientists. Unfortunately, relatively small portions of the phenomena that the social sciences seek to understand are conducive to experimental research settings, and, even then, questions remain about the applicability of the research findings to the nonexperimental world. These limitations can affect the strength and confidence of our causal claims. Instead of sterile and controlled experimental settings, the world and history serve as the laboratories where political scientists test their theories. Political scientists obtain some of their data from controlled laboratory settings, but most of their data come from uncontrolled research settings such as the forensic probing of past events, elite and mass interviews, opinion surveys, historical archives, examination of government reports of economic and social statistics, analyses of media reporting, consideration of legislative voting behavior, and other activities that occur outside the laboratory.

The absence of control by the researcher means that she cannot assign an intervention to a particular group and not to another, nor does she get to distribute the subjects being studied (governments, decision makers, voters, businesses, etc.) among the different groups. For example, political scientists do not designate some people to live under authoritarian regimes and others to live under democratic regimes in order to evaluate the effects of regime type upon citizen behavior; they do not assign war to some nations and not to others in an effort to determine the effects of war upon society; they do not impose economic recession on some societies and not on others so as to examine the influence of economic downturns on political behavior; nor can they lower barriers to international trade in some societies and not in others in order to evaluate the impact of free trade on domestic politics.

The lack of control and assignment by the researcher creates tremendous obstacles for analyzing and testing causal relationships. Unlike the laboratory researcher who can control or manage most outside forces that might affect an experiment, the political scientist generally has no such control—which makes it far more difficult to confidently assert that *A* causes *B*. Generally social scientists must take greater leaps of faith in making their causal claims than physical scientists do. Noting this absence of control does not belittle the endeavor of the social scientists or the results of their research, but it highlights the greater obstacles that social scientists encounter as they undertake their tasks.

Already a tough challenge due to the lack of control over the research setting, the process of social science is further complicated by an additional uncontrolled factor: the subjects of social science research, human beings, exercise choice. At least on the surface, they change their minds. One day a person eats fish, another day, chicken, and another day, meat. In one election a person votes Republican; in another, Democratic. A policymaker who claims to be a proponent of free trade may promote freer trade in one industry but advocate trade protections in another. Physical laws governing the bonding of chemical elements, chemical reactions, movement of objects through space, behavior of neutrons and electrons, or genetic patterns appear immutable—or at least the physical scientist can specify under what conditions the relationships dictated by the laws of nature do not hold. Social scientists are far from being as successful as physical scientists at creating general laws of behavior in their fields, or in specifying under what conditions those laws do or do not hold. Ironically, perhaps the only successful overarching law of behavior in the social sciences is the one that states how difficult it would be to generate such laws.

Despite the differences separating the physical and life sciences from the social sciences, there are tremendous similarities across the two spheres that make them sciences and separate them from the humanities. I emphasize four key similarities here: *the is versus the ought, systematic and rigorous exploration, cumulative progress,* and *generalizability versus uniqueness.* The difference between the *is* and the *ought* is simply the difference between how the world works and how we want it to work—between the real and ideal. How we desire the world to work is a normative statement: our individual visions of an ideal world are loaded with our individual values. How the world actually operates is a positivist statement, regardless of whether we like the outcomes or not. The *ought,* the ideal, can and will vary from person to person, but how the world does work, the *is,* does not—although as individuals we may have different interpretations of that reality. This contrast underpins the difference between **positive** and **normative theory.** Physical and social scientists both care about the normative state of the world—they have preferences about how the world should be—but their basic research generally attempts to explain what does happen, not what ought to happen. Sometimes this distinction can be uncomfortable for investigators, as they discover that the world operates in a manner contrary to their normative preferences or values. But to change such undesired outcomes in the world requires understanding the mechanisms that produce those outcomes. Normative philosophers emphasize the *ought;* although they too may care deeply about an ideal, scientists engaged in basic research strive to uncover the *is.*

Both physical and social scientists seek to systematically and rigorously explore the world in an attempt to develop causal understanding of physical and social phenomena, respectively. They seek to build and test causal explanations about how the world works in their particular areas of interest. Systematic, rigorous exploration involves clear and explicit statements about how one set of factors known as **independent variables** relates to another factor called the **dependent variable,** or how and why change in the independent variables may cause shifts in the dependent variable. This systematic positing of relationships differs significantly from simply asserting or demonstrating a relationship. It involves construction of a logical formulation of how one set of factors relates to another—a causal path. There are crucial differences between establishing causality and discovering an association or correlation between one set of factors and another. *Correlation* suggests only a connection between different factors: it tells us that factors co-vary in relation to each other, but not why they co-vary. *Causality* requires more than demonstration of a covariance: it is an attempt to tell *why* factors covary in relation to each.

Claims of causality require a story, a theory, that links the independent and dependent variables. For example, since the end of World War II, the expansion of international trade is positively associated with economic growth. This is a descriptive statement that tells us that trade covaries with economic growth, but it does not tell us why. Within this simple statement of association, we lack a story that explains whether trade causes economic growth, whether growth causes trade, or whether, perhaps, the relationship is simply **spurious**—the two factors really are not related, and just by happenstance they covary. Now, if we say that the connections of trade encourage economic specialization and economies of scale, which lead to more effective employment of skills and the different distribution of inputs to production in national economies, then we have a plausible causal story that tells us why trade contributes to economic growth.

A scientist, physical or social, has the responsibility of developing and considering competing explanations, alternative theories, and causal paths. Positing a causal relationship is only part of the process; another part is the systematic and rigorous empirical testing of those posited relationships. This testing is critical for evaluating the validity of the posited causal explanations—for evaluating the *is* versus the *ought*—and for selecting among a variety of plausible but competing explanations of the same behavior. Rigorous design of empirical tests helps to rule out some explanations and increases confidence in others. Such rigor is clearly more difficult for social scientists, for the reasons discussed earlier.

Both physical and social scientists seek to develop cumulative bodies of knowledge and understanding that build and improve upon previous work. This focus reflects the fact that science is an ongoing, progressive enterprise. New generations of scientists build upon the foundations and work of past researchers, developing a body of knowledge that contributes to future research and understanding. This cumulative effort differs from the endeavors of the arts and humanities. For example, our drama is not better than Shakespeare's, nor our art better than that of Rembrandt or Michelangelo, just because we have had centuries to build upon their work. But if we are successful as scientists, our physical science is better than that of Galileo Galilee, a seventeenth-century astronomer, and our social science is better than that of Max Weber, a German sociologist of the late nineteenth and early twentieth centuries, even if they might prove to be better investigators than we are if we could transport them through time to the present.

Finally, physical and social scientists concern themselves with the generalizability of the relationships and phenomena they study, as opposed to their uniqueness. A social scientist may study a particular case, but she does so in the hope that by understanding the specific case she can generalize the findings and so extend her understanding to other cases and settings. Social scientists seek to be able to generalize from one setting to another. Theory provides the backbone of this process. Social scientists engage in empirical testing of theories in multiple settings, seeking to reproduce their findings in support or rejection of a theory, but always with the goal of finding robust explanations of human behavior that work in a variety of settings. Students of the arts and humanities may revel in the uniqueness of a phenomenon, but social scientists relish the discovery of characteristics that undermine claims of uniqueness and distinctiveness.

Tasks of Inquiry

Now let's turn to the four tasks of social science: description, explanation, prediction, and prescription. *Description* is the process of telling *what* happened; it is a recounting of events. Those engaged in description act as storytellers and perform a great service. Without description we do not have a history of our past or a good understanding of the contexts in which we operate. Without such understanding, our choices are more likely to prove dysfunctional, even pathological. Those engaged in the endeavor of description may implicitly convey a story about *why* something happened or the causality of the event in question, but the process of description does not explicitly provide or require an explanation of why something occurred. Descriptions in world politics tend toward highly detailed accounts of how the participants behave. By their focus on particular events, descriptions often emphasize the uniqueness of events and behavior; journalistic accounts of world affairs generally fall into the category of description. This text engages in some description of global political economic relations, particularly in chapters 7–11, to provide a context for evaluating and using tools of explanation.

Introducing tools of *explanation* is the goal of this text. As political scientists interested in global affairs, we want to know *why* certain phenomena occur—such as war, peace, growth, development, democracy, financial distress, trade barriers, alliances, international investment, migration, and environmental decay—not simply *what* occurs. Explanation is the process of trying to understand the causal relationship between independent and dependent variables. We hope to understand why and how changes in the independent variables will produce changes in the dependent variable.

Simply asserting a relationship between independent and dependent variables does not constitute an explanation, only an association. Explanation is the goal of theories that link the dependent variable to the independent variables. They are attempts to make sense of why people behave the way they do in specified settings, or why they make the choices they make under specified conditions. Such theories are logically constructed, which means that each step of a theory, a step along a causal path, attempts to follow rigorously, logically, and consistently from the previous step. This deliberate progress contrasts with ad hoc or off-the-cuff argumentation, which amounts to assertion, even if intelligent assertion.

Another term for theory is **model.** By definition, models or theories are not real but simplified intellectual constructions that propose relationships. By simplifying or extracting core, primitive relationships among variables, models provide tools for recognizing similarities across social behavior. This process may enable us to generalize our discoveries about social behavior in one setting to understand similar behavior another setting. In an incredibly complex world, loaded with information and noise, models help us determine where to look, what to ignore, and what to expect. They establish frameworks for collecting, connecting, and evaluating information, and then interpreting events. They become devices for sampling information about the world and interpreting that information. They help us distinguish important from trivial information. Sometimes our models are wrong and we overlook or misinterpret important information. If our models prove consistently inaccurate and unhelpful, then we seek to construct new models. But if our models prove useful and stand the text of continual reexamination and application, then we gain confidence in them.

Multiple explanations are plausible and likely for almost any interesting social behavior. How do we choose among competing explanations, particularly if several seem plausible? Political scientists evaluate models of political behavior by examining their theoretical characteristics and construction, and also empirically. At a theoretical level, we assess the plausibility and usefulness of a model's assumptions, and its internal consistency and logic. Empirically, we test a model's **validity,** or how accurately the model reflects the actual relationship, in the laboratory of the world. As mentioned earlier, this is generally a more difficult laboratory than the typical physical scientist confronts in her controlled laboratory setting. The social scientist rarely has direct control over the setting or the range of factors that can influence human behavior. Consequently, in most cases the social scientist's conclusions about causality are necessarily weaker than those of physical scientists. Within the constraints of such lower expectations, does a model do well at explaining what it claims to explain? How does a model fare in comparison with other models? Good theories produce **testable hypotheses** or conjectures about behavior that can be evaluated with information, which we call data, from the empirical world. Data can be quantitative or qualitative. Investigators can compare expectations produced by the different models and then use empirical tests to select among competing explanations. If successful, other researchers can build upon those findings, creating a cumulative body of research and knowledge.

Whereas description is a process of telling what happened and explanation the task of telling why it happened, *prediction* is the process of telling what will happen. Prediction is a primary concern for those engaged in policymaking. Policymakers want to know what is going to happen, with the goal of being able to affect what happens or at least gain some warning to better prepare to manage the consequences. Soothsaying, fortune-telling, and divine prognostication are forms of prediction, but not the type meant here. Prediction for a social scientist is more than a random, unsystematic, mystical gaze into the future. For a social scientist, prediction is based upon systematic frameworks or models of human behavior. Like the logically and systematically derived hypotheses used to test models of explanation, predictions derive from such models—implicitly or explicitly. The testing of models of explanation can engender confidence that translates into predictive capabilities of the successful models. Yet, this does not mean that good predictions tell us why things happen. Nor does understanding why things happen necessarily produce good predictions. E.B. White wrote,

> The so-called science of polling *(a favorite activity of many political scientists)* is not a science at all but mere necromancy. People are unpredictable by nature *(the effect of choice)*, and although you can take a nation's pulse, you can't be sure that the nation hasn't just run up a flight of stairs, and although you can take a nation's pulse, you can't be sure that if you came back in twenty minutes you'd get the same reading. This is a damn fine thing.[2]

Finally, some social scientists engage in *prescription,* or advocating specific policies for implementation. This activity separates those social scientists engaged in basic research from those in applied work, distinguishing those who try primarily to understand why things happen from those who work to change what happens in the near term. These tasks are not independent, but collegial. The most effective prescription builds on understandings of causal processes that are illuminated by those engaged in the task of explanation. Knowing why things happen, the causal path, can give applied social scientists and policymakers valuable insight to where and how best to intervene to alter social outcomes, where and how to use scarce resources to change behavior in societies. Prescribing policy without some systematic notion of the underlying processes is little more than random prescription, or throwing money at problems. Yet this may be the best a policymaker can do in some situations, given the difficulty of uncovering the root causes and mechanisms of complex social behavior.

PLAN OF THE BOOK

This text is divided into three parts. First, chapters 1–6 begin by introducing some basic building blocks, both materials essential to a micro political economy approach to global affairs and some materials that reflect macro or structural approaches to behavior, such as realism and liberalism. The next section, chapters 7–11, provides some history about the

---

[2] E.B. White, *New Yorker,* November 13, 1948. (Italics added.)

evolution of globalization and international political and economic relations that helps to demonstrate the strengths or weaknesses of those building blocks. The final part, chapters 12–15, develops a more sophisticated kit of micro tools for examining social behavior in the global arena that help to address the weaknesses uncovered in the historical section.

Developing the building blocks of the micro political economy approach of this text, chapter 2 lays out several core assumptions about rationality, the motivation of political actors, and constraints on their choices. The process of rationality is foundational to the approach that runs throughout this text. Chapters 3–6 continue with the process of building a foundation for the analysis of world affairs, but they shift the focus from micro foundations to macro frameworks. Macro approaches rely upon the structure of social relations in the international arena to account for behavior in that arena. Individuals are essentially missing from such accounts, which focus, instead, on monolithic nation-states and governments. Such macro approaches lack a theoretical means for recognizing differences in policy preferences within domestic political arenas and using those differences to help systematically explain the outcomes we observe in the international arena. They fail to account for bargains or compromises within domestic political arenas, cleavages or coalitions in domestic societies, interest groups, political parties, and institutional differences playing important roles in determining government policy selection. But, this is the stuff of politics. Any reliance macro explanations have upon these matters—the calculations of individual decision makers or domestic political arenas—to account for political economic relations between nations amounts to an ad hoc addition rather than a fundamental component. These influences may be cited to help resolve inconsistencies between macro explanations and empirical behavior, but they are undefined within the boundaries of macro theories.

Chapter 3 introduces several basic macro-level concepts related to the structure of international affairs, such as nation-states, sovereignty, and anarchy. Continuing with the macro building blocks, chapter 4 examines concepts of power and hierarchy. Power is the currency of political science. It contributes to the formation of hierarchy in international affairs, which can structure international political and economic relations in what we call a state of anarchy. Chapter 5 provides a baseline model for economic liberalism and market exchange, the dominant economic framework underpinning modern globalization and international economic relations. Economic liberalism assumes market exchange. How closely do global relations correspond to the expectations of this baseline model, how much does behavior deviate from its expectations? If behavior deviates significantly and persistently enough, how can we explain such activity? Chapter 6 takes many of the ideas of market exchange and applies them to political behavior, providing a baseline for understanding the functioning of political markets and political exchange.

The historical chapters, 7–11, engage heavily in the process of description, offering a solid historical foundation for understanding the ebb and flow of globalization. Considered thoughtfully, they demonstrate the shortcomings of structural and macro approaches. Policymakers sometimes select policies consistent with the expectations of the macro or structural frameworks, but all too frequently they select policies that are at odds with or inexplicable by those frameworks. Like the example from the beginning of this chapter, the historical record shows such inconsistencies. The bargains, compromises, cleavages, coalitions, interest groups, partisanship, and institutional differences of domestic political arenas influence government policy choices in international affairs. The stuff of politics within domestic arenas motivates and constrains policymakers as they interact with their counterparts in other nations. I use this progression through the text—from the baseline macro models through the historical context of globalization showing those models' shortcomings—to help motivate a shift to micro-level tools of explanation.

Chapter 7 introduces the development of modern globalization based upon capitalism, the resulting expansion of economic opportunity, and the extension of political rights in the nineteenth century. It also introduces the notion of collective goods, a central and recurring theme throughout the remainder of the book. Chapter 8 discusses the breakdown of the globalization that characterized the Atlantic economy by the end of the 1800s, the discomforting legacy of World War I, the drift into economic nationalism and protectionism, the resulting rise of economic hardship, and the rise of political extremism that led into World War II. This chapter is singularly important in the historical flow, for it demonstrates that globalization and the advance of political rights are not inexorable. As we discussed earlier in this chapter, the processes of economic and political advance unleashed in the nineteenth century broke down and were even reversed. Chapter 8 contrasts a world with more limited international exchange against a world with more open global exchange (chapters 7, 9, and 10) and so provides important variation on the key dependent variable of globalization. Without such variation, analysts face a more difficult task in assessing causality and the impact of a variety of potential independent factors, or variables. Chapter 8 highlights a puzzle that cannot be addressed within the boundaries of structural explanations: if globalization and the expansion of political rights are such good societal outcomes, why do governments and societies adopt policies that reject those gains and undermine the greater social welfare?

Chapter 9 looks at the efforts of policymakers to avoid the mistakes of the dysfunctional interwar years as they sought to develop international and domestic institutional frameworks to help restore and protect the processes of globalization. Their efforts produced what is known as the Bretton Woods system. Through institutional design, the Bretton Woods system sought to create an environment conducive to expanding liberal economic relations, which lasted until the early 1970s. Chapter 10 explores the post–Bretton Woods international political economy, focusing on changes in financial globalization. Chapter 11 considers the shifts in East-West relations that eventually led to stunning transformations in Eastern Europe, the Soviet Union, and China.

The remainder of the book then turns to micro tools of explanation that can help shed light on the puzzle raised most explicitly by chapter 8: If cooperation, globalization, and the expansion of political rights are such good societal outcomes, why do governments and societies adopt policies that detract from those outcomes and undermine the greater social welfare? Chapters 12–15 examine the incentives of individual political actors and how those incentives are conditioned, influenced, and manipulated. Choices in political arenas produce gains and losses across different actors in societies, or differences in the amount of gains and losses. Such distributional differences become sources of political competition and conflict if the manipulation of the political arena can influence distributional outcomes, produce bigger winners or bigger losers, rearrange the gains among the winners, or reallocate the losses among the losers. Chapter 12 considers the phenomenon of market failure. The history depicted in chapters 7–11 suggests that social behavior can deviate, sometimes significantly, from the expectations of the baseline economic and political models of chapters 5 and 6. As appealing and elegant as they may appear, the reality of economic and political market exchange often falls short of these expectations. Within its theoretical framework, classical economic liberalism cannot account for the breakdown in globalization, and it cannot suggest policy strategies to avoid and manage such breakdowns. Elegant democratic theory often overlooks the potential pitfalls of democratic governance—social traps that motivate rational political actors to make choices that appear individually sound in the short-run but are socially dysfunctional in the long-run. This does not mean that economic liberalism and political democracy are wrong and useless, but it does raise challenges and highlight the theoretical limitations of liberal economic exchange and democratic political exchange. This is good, for discovering limitations and advancing possible solutions is progress in science, even if it frustrates us. Chapter 12 serves as an entrée to the remaining chapters of the book, which are intended to help students understand the mechanisms that account for economic and political market failures; hopefully, better understanding can help limit those failures.

Chapter 13 introduces the idea of collective action to help account for why some interests in society become mobilized for political action, while others remain latent. This concept is critical for understanding why some forces in society succeed in placing their interests on the policymakers' agendas and other forces fail to do so. This chapter also introduces an approach called "hegemonic stability theory," which advances a macro framework to address the shortcomings of economic liberalism as an explanation for international affairs. Hegemonic stability theory uses hierarchy in international affairs, the presence of a dominant political economy, to explain how governments overcome barriers to the expansion of liberal economic relations in a social context that presents dilemmas for liberal relations. Yet, this theory also presents empirical problems: significant activities occur that cannot be explained within the boundaries of its theoretical framework. These problems are consistent, instead, with the framework of collective action.

Chapter 14 considers international sources of potential political division, or cleavage, in domestic political arenas. Some people gain from international exchange and some lose, or some gain disproportionately versus others and some lose disproportionately. Winners and losers are systematically predictable within the frameworks of international trade models, and this predictability provides systematic leverage for anticipating divisions and coalitions in societies. Finally, chapter 15 looks at the role of institutions in affecting social behavior. Institutions are the rules of the game that provide political and economic actors with incentives or disincentives, helping to create winners and losers in society and, consequently, becoming targets of political competition and motivators of political action. Policymakers are faced with the challenge of developing rules of the game that allow them to manage discrepancies between short-term and long-term pressures. Ideally, we would like policymakers to pursue policies in the short-run that are consistent with long-term societal interests; we call such policies "time consistent."

Now, as Holmes said to Watson, "the game is afoot . . . ."

EXERCISES

1. What is the difference between an independent variable and a dependent variable? Give one example each of an independent and a dependent variable pair.

2. Which of the following are variables?
   - Foreign aid levels   George Bush
   - 3% growth   Birth rates

3. Assess whether each of the following statements is a claim of causality or of correlation:

   a. Economic growth almost always accompanies population increase.
   b. Trade promotes peace because it increases the costs from war.
   c. Tourism rises all over the world during the years that the Olympics are held.

4. Identify the independent and dependent variable in each of the following statements:

   a. Knowledge is advanced by systematic research.
   b. The more foreign aid a country receives from the United States, the more likely that country is to vote consistently with the U.S. position at the United Nations.
   c. Low labor costs encourage the construction of U.S.–owned factories in Southeast Asia.
   d. Authoritarian regimes discourage international investment.
   e. The more educated a nation, the larger the voter turnout in national elections.

5. What is globalization? Give an example of global integration.

6. Why are some societies and peoples resistant to globalization?

7. What are the four similarities across the physical and social sciences that distinguish them from the humanities?

8. Why do social scientists emphasize cumulative knowledge, and how does this differ from the humanities?

9. What are the four primary activities of social scientists?

Assumptions, Rationality, and Context

"You mean, the theory of games like chess." "No, no," he said. "Chess is not a game. Chess is a well-defined form of computation. You may not be able to work out all the answers, but in theory there must be a solution, a right procedure in any position. Now real games are not like that at all. Real life is not like that. Real life consists of bluffing, of little tactics of deception, of asking yourself what is the other man going to think I mean to do."

John von Neumann, in William Poundstone,
Prisoner's Dilemma *(1992)*

WHAT IS POLITICAL ECONOMY?

Let's turn to the primary task of this book: developing a political economy approach to help us examine international relations and international political economy. First, what is political economy? The term encompasses a variety of approaches. For some, description of macro political-economic activities constitutes political economy. Macro political-economy investigates associations between political activities and substantive performance of an economy. Macro economic numbers such as gross national product (GNP), gross domestic product (GDP), national debt and deficit, inflation, unemployment, exchange rates, size of the public sector, balance of trade, central bank interest rates, investment, money supply, and productivity describe the state of the national political economy, supplying information about a nation's welfare. We use such descriptive characteristics to infer how well or poorly governments are performing in managing their economies, and what areas governments need to target for improvement. From a macro political-economic perspective, these descriptions can serve as dependent variables that are influenced by government policy choices, or they can be considered as independent variables that motivate and influence government's choice of policies. In either case, the substantive questions revolve around the nexus of government and economic behavior: how do government actions affect the state of the economy, or how does the state of the economy affect government actions? Many approaches to international political economy focus on such macro depictions. These depictions are important at both the domestic and international levels, and they can be a component of our discussion of political economy, but they differ from the micro approach that we emphasize throughout this book.

Our micro political economy approach focuses on the processes that influence, motivate, and constrain the choices of individual political actors. In this approach, political economy describes the processes of choice that lead to government policies and to social, economic, and political outcomes. These processes are just as relevant to understanding decisions about war and conflict as they are to understanding why governments implement some economic policies and not others. Conceptualizing political economy in this way, we attempt to discover the inner workings, or causal foundations, of actions in political arenas by focusing on the calculations and choices of individuals in social settings, the incentives that influence these calculations and choices, and the processes by which individuals interact, compete, bargain, compromise, and even fight over policies, elections, regulations, and rules. These processes affect the allocation of gains and losses in society, creating winners and losers. Such choices interact and aggregate to produce the social, economic, and political outcomes that are reflected in the macro political economy depictions. From our micro perspective, political economy is a story about the processes and means by which members of society decide on policies and rules of the game that allocate gains, losses, and risks.

So why is this micro approach to politics considered political economy, and not political anthropology, political sociology, or some other strategy of analysis? Simply, we assume that political actors use a specific form of logic—an economic logic—when evaluating alternatives as they engage in the processes of producing decisions and political behavior. This approach to human decision making compares the costs and benefits of alternative strategies and the likelihood of different outcomes given the possible actions of others. In this text, we apply this political economy approach to understanding our primary topic, global political-economic relations, but it can be used to gain insight to social phenomena that are not exclusively economic, such as war, migration, voting decisions and rules, judicial activity, political and civil liberties, ethnic conflict, discrimination, gender rights, and other political activities.

THREE CORE ASSUMPTIONS

Three powerful assumptions underpin the tools of explanation developed in this book. First, *we live in a world of scarce resources.* Second, *political actors seek to survive.* Third, *decision makers act as if they are rational.* Let's consider each of these more carefully, for the logic of our micro political economy approach builds on these assumptions.

Scarcity

Scarcity is a key assumption, as it generates the conditions for competition, cooperation, and conflict over the distribution of resources and opportunities. It creates the possibility for relative winners and losers to emerge. In a world of plenty—a world absent scarcity—men and women could consume whatever they wanted and whenever they wanted without impinging on the choices of others. No competition or conflict over the distribution of resources would exist, nor would there be a need for compromise or cooperation to overcome barriers to the distribution or allocation of resources. Selfish actors—gluttons—could consume as much as they wanted without diminishing the supply of resources for others. Hunger, impoverishment, jealousy, and want would not exist or make sense. In such a world, envy and *egoistic* (selfish) actions would be meaningless, as they would create no costs for others and would not affect one's own opportunities or those available to others. Neither money nor any other medium of exchange would have value, for we all could consume what we wanted without concern for the rules of supply and demand. **Costs,** those things that we forgo when we choose to consume a particular item, become meaningless, as no costs would exist. We would not have to forgo consumption of some items because we elected to consume other items. A world without scarcity would translate into an absence of constraints on our consumption, as well as an absence of the conditions that spawn distributional conflict, competition, and cooperation. A world without scarcity would be literally a Garden of Eden.

Unfortunately, we do not live in such a garden of unlimited resources. All items we consume—those produced by man and those produced by nature—exist in some finite amount, regardless of the demand for those items. In a world of scarce resources, items in high demand and low supply become expensive and valuable relative to items in high supply and low demand. Scarcity may appear as a budgetary constraint, such as how much money is in one's wallet; as a resource constraint, such as height and strength; or as an information constraint, such as incomplete information or limited ability to process information. In a world of scarcity, mechanisms of exchange become important. A world of plenty would be a world devoid of political squabbling over the distribution of resources, but a world of scarcity creates the conditions for politics, which is a use of coercive means to allocate resources, to divide the proverbial pie, to decide who gets what, why, and how. Unlike economic exchange in a market, where the **property rights** (ownership) of one commodity are voluntarily exchanged for the property rights of another commodity, politics imposes a nonvoluntary component upon exchange and allocation. For example, if you vote for the Democrat but the Republican wins, you still must consume the political policies enacted by the Republican.

Politics helps create rules—for social, economic, and political exchange and allocation within and across communities—which, if violated, can trigger penalties and punishment. We call such rules **institutions,** a concept that we examine more carefully in chapter 15. These rules may be formal or informal. Examples of formal institutions include constitutions, statutory laws, and regulations; informal institutions can arise from a variety of sources, such as common beliefs and practices, differences in power, the emergence of societal norms, religious prescriptions, folklore, and voluntary cooperation. Informal rules are nonstatutory, but they may prove just as forceful as formal rules in motivating and constraining human activity. The use of threats, penalties, and punishment is by definition

Anti-globalization protestors voiced their concerns in June 2002 in Calgary during a Group of Eight summit of world leaders held in Canada. Such demonstrations have become regular occurrences at G-8 gatherings, evincing the intensity of opposition among critics of globalization and the pressures that policymakers must confront and manage in formulating policies and laws related to the processes of globalization.

coercive, as these measures constrain human choice (that is, without such constraints a person would choose differently), but they may be necessary to encourage social, economic, and political exchange that can be socially beneficial within and across national boundaries. The rules of exchange and allocation produced in political arenas create relative winners and losers in political economies. Constructing a law, rule, or regulation, or invoking a social practice one way versus another, affects the distribution of resources and influence in societies. Altering laws moves the boundaries of distribution and allocation; therefore, laws and regulations themselves can become targets of fierce competition, sometimes leading to cooperation and compromise, sometimes to conflict.

Political Survival

The second assumption on which the tools in this book build is that political actors and governments want to survive—to stay in office and in power—and will act to survive. In democratic electoral systems, these actors work to enhance their prospects for reelection; in less democratic systems, they may instead work to build a constituency among those groups that can protect them, such as the military. The assumption that survival is an important goal helps us to analyze the choices made by policymakers, by asking how political actors view such choices as affecting their prospects for political survival. This assumption does not imply that politicians have no preferences about the state of the world or about the public policies that affect the state of the world, but it does suggest that they evaluate policies for achieving those preferences within a context that involves assessing how their choices will affect their ability to survive politically and whom they must satisfy to survive. A politician who finds her policy preferences in conflict with her ability to survive faces difficult choices and trade-offs. Such conflict is very common, and it underpins much of the cynicism about politics that is generated when politicians seem to compromise their policy preferences in order to stay in office. However, if selecting policies independent of considerations about reelection and political survival should lead to her political demise, the politician would not be able to promote her policy preferences in the future, whereas her opponent, who has different policy preferences, would. Compromising on policy preferences to improve the odds of political survival is thus akin to retreating in order to fight another day.

Rationality

Our third assumption is that people behave as if they were rational. This is not to claim that people really are rational beings, but that they behave and make choices *as if* they were. Explicitly assuming that people behave as if they were rational, regardless of whether they really are, embeds decision making within a particular logic that can be applied to politicians, policymakers, and interested parties. This logic is key to systematic and consistent investigation of the actions of such actors within political economies, for it provides a powerful and explicit lever for analyzing behavior and understanding decision making. Making this assumption explicit also creates better opportunities to challenge it. Unstated assumptions prove more difficult to challenge because they offer greater wiggle room, whereas more explicit approaches encourage rigorous testing and build a healthy skepticism into the process of investigation. Good scientific investigation requires constant reexamination—creating opportunities to be proven wrong. Testing and retesting the same logic across multiple settings helps to construct robust explanations for social behavior that are cumulative and advance our understanding, even if we find the logic wanting.

What do we mean by *rationality,* and why is it such a useful tool? Rationality describes a particular process of choice. The focus on the choices of individuals is called **methodological individualism,** and it amounts to a claim that individuals—not larger units of aggregation such as nations or societies—make choices. A variety of approaches exist to investigate the choices of individuals: anthropologists place their primary focus upon the effects of culture upon individual choice; sociologists emphasize the influence of group dynamics upon individual choice; and psychologists look primarily at psychological, emotional, and subliminal constraints on individual choice. The assumption of rationality in this book on political economy focuses our attention on a particular means by which individuals choose among alternatives under constraints of scarcity.

RATIONALITY, PREFERENCES, AND SELF-INTEREST EXPLORED

Because the assumption of rationality is central to the micro political economy approach of this text, we need to take a closer look at some mechanics of this assumption and how it interacts with the first two assumptions about scarcity and political survival. Assuming that political-economic actors behave as if they are rational means that we assume they can systematically order their **preferences** over the state of the world, along with the expected outcomes of their choices, and that the ordering will be consistent over time and in their **self-interest.** Preferences can be ordered randomly, as in drawing them blindly from a hat; or they can be ordered alphabetically or by some other scheme. The rationality assumption assumes that preferences are ordered in terms of self-interest.

Ordering Preferences

To understand the ordering principle that underpins rationality and our approach to individual choice, we first must ask, what are preferences and self-interest? At the level of the individual, *preferences* are simply individual wants such as food, wealth, entertainment, security, community, justice, status, respect, influence, fairness, liberty, and so on. These preferences include material wants as well as social and spiritual wants; a want can be a preference over the state of the world, as the state of the world is instrumental in affecting the distribution of other wants. *Self-interest* is simply a statement about how an individual's preferences affect her interpretation of her position in the world. Economists call this utility, which is shorthand for everything that affects an individual's expected satisfaction. Will a particular choice increase or decrease an individual's utility? Self-interest assumes that individuals will select choices by seeking to improve their utility, or expected satisfaction. Remember, we have assumed that decision makers, or political actors, will seek to survive and to advance their interests. So one criterion for evaluating and comparing preferences is determining how they affect the survival and status of the decision maker.

This approach to investigating decision making involves the following assumptions:

- People act as if they can discriminate among their preferences.
- People act as if they can order their preferences in terms of most to least desirable.
- People can evaluate and rank possible outcomes of their choices in terms of their preferences because they recognize that there may be some discontinuity between a choice based on a preference and the actual outcome.
- People will choose to obtain an expected outcome that is higher in their ranking rather than a lower one.
- People will be fairly consistent in their choices and preferences over time and, if presented with the same list of preferences and outcomes at different times, will rank them similarly.

Assuming that people behave *as if* rational and can place their preferences along a single dimension based upon their self-interest—thus creating a hierarchy of preferences from most to least preferred—is a vast simplification and potentially a tenuous one, but it is nonetheless useful as the first step in adopting rationality as an analytic tool. It supplies a systematic way of discriminating across preferences and alternative outcomes and of evaluating different courses of action. We can employ this assumption of rationality to understand why a decision maker might choose one action over another. It enables investigators to examine alternative courses of action or strategies for achieving the actor's objectives and to evaluate those strategies in terms of their potential to produce the preferred objectives and of their likely costs. This tool allows investigators and individuals to evaluate the trade-offs between costs and benefits, to weigh disadvantages and advantages.

Rationality under Scarcity and Political Survival

Our three core assumptions work together to shape our inquiry. Understanding the assumption of rationality returns us to the scarcity and political survival assumptions. In a world of plenty, we would not have to consider the criteria that guide individual choices, because decisions would not matter in terms of consumption opportunities. Irrelevant to the distribution of resources, political survival would also be meaningless. But scarcity places costs on decision making because making choices involves forgoing other possibilities, affects distributional outcomes in society, and makes political survival relevant. The assumption of scarcity creates both a need for decision criteria to make trade-offs and a demand upon politicians to act in their self-interest in terms of political survival. Rationality is one such decision criterion, and it is constrained by scarcity. Decision makers' time and energy are scarce resources. They may need to make choices with incomplete information, limited by the demands of time and handicapped by the dilemmas of trying to forecast an uncertain future. Such constraints can affect a decision maker's process of choice and force her to allocate more time and effort to some decisions than to others. Together, these assumptions help us to investigate why a political actor may focus on one objective over another, by making it clear that a decision-maker does not value all objectives equally but discriminates across a wide range of objectives as she allocates her limited time and energy.

Rationality prescribes the most efficient choice, determining which strategy can be expected to deliver the largest payoff, given a preference ordering, at the least cost. When the expected costs of obtaining the most preferred objective are too high, the assumption of rationality allows us to evaluate the trade-offs between secondary objectives, strategies to obtain those objectives, and the cost of each strategy. For example, despite a general trend toward trade liberalization—which is consistent with their own dominant preference for free trade over government intervention in trade—policymakers in the United States occasionally create and maintain barriers to trade. Such barriers have been imposed on products such as textiles, shoes, steel, and automobiles. At first glance, this practice appears nonrational, because it seems to conflict with the preference ordering of policymakers. But policymakers also want to survive, and we can assume that this preference generally dominates other preferences. If supporting free trade in a particular sector, such as textiles or shoes, would severely threaten a politician's ability to survive because it would produce dislocated and unhappy voters, we should expect that politician to support a less costly policy. And if enough politicians were threatened in this way, we would find an explanation based on rationality for the adoption of trade barriers in particular sectors. The assumption of rationality means that we expect decision makers to choose the course of action that is most likely to produce the best outcome given costs and benefits.

Putting our three core assumptions together suggests that as policymakers operate in a world of scarcity, they will act to further their policy preferences within the limits of their ability to survive, and they will follow a logic based upon rationality to do so. This means that they will act in their self-interest—broadly defined as a calculation of how their choices will affect their ability to survive and prosper, given the alternatives. Ideally, their self-interest will be compatible with societal welfare, but there are no guarantees that the interests of policymakers and those of the broader society will overlap significantly.

Two Properties of Preference Ordering: Completeness and Transitivity

Next we consider two important properties that are involved in using preferences and rationality to examine behavior: completeness and transitivity. **Completeness** establishes that two alternatives are comparable and can be placed in a hierarchy. If you can say that an individual prefers one alternative over another (or vice versa) or is indifferent between the two, we are establishing qualities about the alternatives that constitute completeness. **Indifference** means, quite literally, that an individual is indifferent between alternatives, that they are equal but still comparable. Completeness is a useful concept because it allows us to study an individual and say that she prefers one alternative to another or is indifferent, and then to expect her to behave according to that preference ordering.

Transitivity extends the logic of comparability that is reflected in completeness to more than two alternatives. Transitivity means that three or more alternatives are comparable and can be placed in a hierarchy of preference. For example, imagine that an individual has to choose among three alternatives for dinner: steak, chicken, and fish. She begins by first looking for completeness, or comparability between two alternatives, by comparing each pair of alternatives: steak and chicken, chicken and fish, and steak and fish. Her preferences are transitive if she prefers steak to chicken, chicken to fish, and steak to fish, because this pattern permits a strict ordering, or **hierarchy of preferences.** If we were trying to understand her preferences so that we could take her to dinner for her birthday, determining that she has a strict hierarchy of preferences would make our task easier. Even if she were indifferent between several alternatives, her preferences would still be transitive if they could be arranged in order, and we could therefore anticipate what restaurants would give her the greatest satisfaction for her birthday celebration.

Unfortunately, not all choice situations are this simple. In relatively rare cases, individuals display complete but intransitive preferences. For example, our birthday celebrant may prefer steak to chicken, chicken to fish, but fish to steak. Every alternative is comparable, which satisfies completeness, but we cannot build a strict hierarchy across the three alternatives. This leaves us with the dilemma of where to take her for her birthday dinner if we want

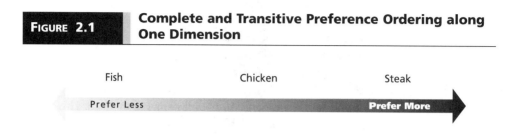

FIGURE 2.1   **Complete and Transitive Preference Ordering along One Dimension**

to provide her with the greatest expected satisfaction. We might say that individuals who can fulfill a condition of completeness but not transitivity are nonrational or confused, or perhaps that life is complicated and rational people can have preferences that fall along more than a single dimension. Both life and the investigation of choices are much simpler when we can establish a preference ordering that falls along a single dimension, as in figure 2.1; then we can simply anticipate choices being made for more preferred over less preferred alternatives, given the constraints of resource scarcity. But if we add another dimension to the choice of food—such as the ambience of the restaurant, whether it is quiet or loud, as in figure 2.2—both the investigation of individual choice and the choices themselves become far more complicated. This added complexity creates uncertainty about individual choice and interjects considerations of costs or trade-offs into the selection of one alternative over another. Figures 2.1 and 2.2 offer useful visual tools for examining the distribution of preferences over outcomes. Each is a spatial depiction, or what is called a **spatial model** of an individual's preferences.

In reality, this problem is relatively rare for individuals. When forced to select between alternatives, individuals can usually produce a complete and transitive preference ordering—they are able to force their individual preferences into a strict hierarchy. But the dilemma of intransitive preferences is quite likely to arise in constructing the preference orderings of collectivities such as a group, a society, or an electorate by means of some democratic voting rule or market exchange mechanism. The aggregation of individual preferences by such means can often produce an **intransitive collective outcome,** even if all the individuals voting have expressed complete and transitive preferences. This possibility opens the door to troubling questions about whether democratic and market processes of choice in economic and political exchange can actually maximize the social welfare function of society—whether individuals voting in accordance with their complete and transitive preference orderings can indeed produce a complete and transitive collective preference ordering that optimizes the social welfare of society. If individuals and groups confronted with three or more alternatives satisfy the condition of completeness but not that of transitivity, this ele-

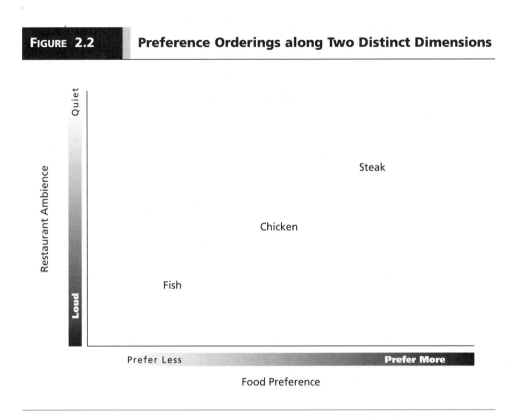

FIGURE 2.2   **Preference Orderings along Two Distinct Dimensions**

ment of uncertainty presents potential hindrances to our use of rationality as an analytical tool. The next section offers examples of individual and collective preferences in the political arena that are complete but intransitive.

This conceptualization of preference ordering describes a particular logic that assumes rationality and a specific process by which individuals select among alternatives. Even if individuals have intransitive preferences, we can use this logic as a tool to investigate choices in politics, economics, and other avenues of life. This logic allows us to consider the trade-offs and costs across alternatives, and to evaluate the preference orderings of individuals over the range of alternatives they consider. This process amounts to a cost-benefit analysis of possible alternative choices, in which we consider the preference ordering of outcomes, whether these outcomes satisfy conditions of completeness and transitivity, the likelihood of obtaining each alternative outcome given our available strategies and resources, and the cost of obtaining each alternative outcome. This type of analysis offers a strategy for understanding past choices and anticipating future choices. We can anticipate that decision makers will select a course of action that is most likely to produce the best outcome on their hierarchy of preferences, given cost constraints. This logic provides the foundation for a systematic strategy to examine why decision makers make the choices they do.

Examples of Complete and Intransitive Preferences

Let's examine completeness and transitivity in two scenarios, looking at preference ordering over outcomes, first, by an individual, and second, by a collectivity or group. The latter is the more interesting and important case for societies relying on elections and markets to determine public preferences and produce social outcomes, and, as we will see, it is a problematic case for democratic societies. Since the properties of completeness and transitivity are logically consistent, relatively straightforward, and fairly easy to grasp in terms of rationality, we will intentionally construct cases wherein the preference orderings in the individual and collective scenarios are complete but intransitive. This is actually quite difficult in the individual case, but it happens fairly easily and often in the case of collectivities.

Why is this pattern of completeness plus intransitivity so difficult to illustrate in the individual case? When forced by constraints such as scarcity, individuals can usually construct a preference ordering between two alternatives that fulfills the condition of completeness, or among three or more alternatives that satisfies the condition of transitivity. This ordering process requires several simplifying presumptions that might be considered heroic. The first presumption is that individuals are well informed about the differences between alternatives and can distinguish those differences. This is a demanding criterion, but it is important for our use of rationality to examine social behavior and for the recognition of potential pitfalls of the rationality assumption. When we relax this presumption, individuals can still be rational yet make choices that appear inconsistent with rationality due to their being poorly informed or confused; they are still rational, but they are working with incomplete information. This recognition will focus our attention on the constraints of information in decision-making contexts.

For example, a wine expert should be easily able to rank-order two wines based on taste, and if a third wine were added to the tasting, the expert should be able to rank it vis-à-vis each of the other wines, so that the ordering would be transitive. If another wine were to be added, again a paired comparison could be made to establish completeness of preferences. The wines would all be comparable pair by pair, and when all the choices were put together, the property of completeness would also be consistent with the property of transitivity. We assume that a fully informed wine expert could produce such complete and transitive preferences. In reality, however, few individuals are master sommeliers. Most people would probably be able to do a paired comparison, comparing any two wines against each other and thereby establishing completeness, but they would likely falter on creating a transitive ranking of preferences over a large number of wines. Are these nonexperts nonrational, or do they just have insufficient knowledge and experience with wine? The latter is more likely the case. If so, they are still rational, but confused by their informational shortcomings—no doubt an accurate assessment for most of us.

Our second presumption—also quite rigid—is that preferences do not change. We know empirically that tastes do change and evolve, but presuming fixed preferences is a simplifying condition that provides us with analytical leverage to examine choices. By holding this one component of the decision process constant, we can look at variations in other parts of the process and attribute variations in behavior, in choice, to those inconstant components. Presuming that preferences are constant means that the moving parts in this approach to choice are information and context. As a consequence, we look for variations in those parts to explain choices that look inconsistent with a rational decision maker's assumed preference ordering.

We can construct a situation in which an individual political actor—for instance, a judge in the European Court of Justice, the high court of the European Union (EU)—has complete but intransitive preferences. In her deliberations, the judge weighs how her decisions affect three different outcomes: the legal process, justice for individuals, and European integration. We can examine her preferences over outcomes for completeness by conducting a paired comparison of the weighting she gives each outcome in her deliberations. When comparing the importance of the legal process to justice for individuals, she values the process of law more than justice for individuals; we can say that legal process defeats justice. When comparing justice for individuals to European integration, her preference for justice defeats EU integration. Finally, when comparing her weighting of the legal process and European integration, we discover that EU integration defeats the legal process. We've established completeness, as each pair is comparable. To summarize her paired comparisons:

legal process > justice

justice > EU integration

EU integration > legal process

Yet, if we look closely at her paired comparisons, we discover that her preferences are intransitive. Rationality and the property of transitivity dictate that if she prefers process to justice, and justice to EU integration, she should prefer process to EU integration. But she actually weights EU integration over legal process in her deliberations, which means that her judicial decisions may cycle across alternatives if her deliberations involve considering the effects upon all three outcomes. To her colleagues on the bench and to observers of the court who makes strict assumptions about rationality, her decisions appear nonrational, poorly informed, or confused—not a good way to build a consistent and coherent body of law that will help guide social behavior. An informed observer may consider this problem manageable, however, as long as the judge's deliberations involve making a decision that will affect only two of the alternatives. This situation of intransitive preferences can be problematic for those trying to observe and understand social behavior, but it is actually quite rare at the individual level.

Unfortunately, the problem of complete and intransitive preferences can occur regularly when examining collective decision making such as elections and markets, which aggregate the preferences of many individuals to produce a collective preference ordering. Therefore the second scenario, involving a collectivity's preference orderings, is much more relevant for our study of political behavior. Every democratic society adopts voting rules to aggregate individual preferences among alternatives. There are a variety of voting rules, such as unanimity, majority, plurality, proportionality, and other rules that can transform individual preferences over outcomes into a social preference. For simplicity's sake, we use a simple majority rule—or winner-take-all—but another choice of voting rule would not make a difference in our example.

Also for the sake of simplicity, the society in our example is made up of three individuals. These three members of society, or voters, evaluate their choices among particular policies according to how the policies influence three big social outcomes: social justice, democratic rule, and economic growth. Each voter makes a complete and transitive preference ordering over these outcomes.

Voter 1 values: social justice (A) to democratic rule (B);
democratic rule (B) to growth (C);
and social justice (A) to growth (C).

Voter 2 values: growth (C) to social justice (A);
social justice (A) to democratic rule (B);
and growth (C) to democratic rule (B).

Voter 3 values: democratic rule (B) to growth (C);
growth (C) to social justice (A);
and democratic rule (B) to social justice (A).

These paired comparisons produce an individual transitive ordering as follows:

Voter 1: social justice > democratic rule > growth
Voter 2: growth > social justice > democratic rule
Voter 3: democratic rule > growth > social justice

An election decided by a majority rule transforms these individual preferences into a social or collective preference. We find that social justice is preferred to democratic rule (A defeats B) by 2 to 1. Democratic rule is preferred to growth (B defeats C) by 2 to 1. So far, so good, but growth is preferred to social justice (C defeats A), also by 2 to 1. If our collective preference ordering were to be transitive, social justice would have defeated growth (A defeats C). However, the collective's preference ordering is intransitive; the outcomes of elections can cycle across the three alternatives.

The lack of a fixed hierarchy of preferences makes society look confused or nonrational, but it is produced by individually rational behavior. This problem, known as the **Condorcet Paradox,** can occur under any voting rule in a democratic society. Kenneth Arrow, a Nobel Prize–winner, proved that except in a dictatorship, where only one individual decides, any voting rule to create a social ordering among alternatives can produce an intransitive ordering even though the individuals making up the social group have complete and transitive preferences. This dilemma means that it is impossible for democratic societies to construct a social welfare function from individual preference functions. This realization opens a chink in the normative appeal of democracy, if we value democratic voting rules solely for their ability to accurately map individual preferences into a social welfare function that maximizes collective welfare. Democracy has many other appeals, though.

CONTEXT AND THE INTERDEPENDENCE OF CHOICES

We must be careful in building upon the assumption of rationality. Even after ordering preferences and determining whether they have properties of completeness and transitivity that fall along a single dimension and so produce a consistent ordering, choice may not be straightforward. We should consider two primary reasons why: *choice is not independent of context*; and *choice is not independent of the actions of others*.

Choices occur within contexts. Taken independent of context, rationality becomes a trivial—or worse, pathological—assumption. Context influences costs and the likelihood of obtaining particular outcomes. The same rational decision maker may select one strategy in one context and another strategy in another context. This does not mean that the decision maker behaves nonrationally, but that a change in context can affect her evaluation of the trade-offs, costs, and gains involved with different strategies. The policymaker who decides to lower trade barriers during a period of economic expansion may resist such a policy change during a period of economic contraction. The policymaker who advocates military intervention in Iraq or Serbia for humanitarian reasons may resist such intervention in Rwanda or North Korea. Politicians who advocate placing limits on whaling in order to protect a species from risk of extinction may not be so inclined in order to protect other fishing stocks. A shift in context produces this change, not a shift in rationality. Rational action is embedded in context; it only makes sense given context. Therefore it is important to study decisions within context, for context informs us about the options and constraints that decision makers encounter.

The second reason for apparent inconsistency is that choice is not independent of the actions of others. This complication is a function of the structure of context, of who the other parties are within a context, and the preferences of those different parties over outcomes. Interesting outcomes in social settings are generally consequences of the interaction of multiple individuals' choices and actions. Most social outcomes, depending upon the actions of more than a single person, are produced by an interaction of multiple individuals and their strategies, and this interdependence raises the opportunity for strategic behavior, whereby individuals are aware that an outcome depends upon the interaction of their strategy with others' strategies, and so they try to select a strategy that anticipates what others may do. If my most preferred outcome depends upon my choice of strategy and a specific choice of strategy by another person, but that person would never make that specific choice, then my selecting a strategy to obtain that preferred outcome is fruitless. It might even prove perverse, if the interaction of such choices should produce a far worse outcome than if I had compensated for the other person's likely choice by making another choice accordingly.

GAME THEORY: MODELING CONTEXT AND INTERDEPENDENT CHOICES

Game theory, the systematic study of rational choice in strategic settings, is a useful tool for modeling and investigating such problems. Strategic settings are those situations in which outcomes depend upon the interaction of the choices of two or more individuals. Decision makers must consider the strategies of others in this decision context, their likely choices, and how those choices interact to produce individual and collective outcomes. Figure 2.3 uses several simple games to illustrate how individual choices interact to produce an outcome, and how the same rational individuals may behave differently if the context varies. The games in figure 2-3 are models of decision settings or contexts in which two decision makers must decide among alternative strategies. By definition these models are simplifications, but they capture some important underlying dynamics of a choice situation.

In these games, each decision maker, or player, has a choice of two strategies, A or B. The payoffs that each decision maker will obtain if their choices intersect are located in each cell. The payoffs for Player 1 are listed before the comma and those for Player 2 are after the comma. For example, in Game A, if Player 1 and Player 2 both select Strategy A, Player 1 will receive 20 and Player 2 will receive 10. If we assume that the decision makers will act as if they are rational, we can rank all the outcomes or payoffs in terms of the players' preferences (more is better in this example): given the possible outcomes in Game A, Player 1 prefers 20 to 5 to 0 to -1 ($20 > 5 > 0 > -1$) and Player 2 prefers 10 to 5 to 0 to -1 ($10 > 5 > 0 > -1$). These preference orderings are complete and transitive. Now, each player must consider the other player's expected behavior given her preferences and choice of strategies, and then select the strategy that can be expected to produce the greatest benefit contingent upon the other player's choice of strategy.

This is a nice game, as both players can obtain their best outcomes by selecting Strategy A. Player 1 knows that Player 2 prefers the outcome produced by Strategy A, and Player 2 knows that Player 1 prefers the outcome produced by Strategy A. There is no tension or con-

FIGURE 2.3	**Strategy and Choice in Different Contexts**

GAME A

	Player 2's Choice	
Player 1's Choice	Strategy *A*	Strategy *B*
Strategy *A*	20, 10	5, −1
Strategy *B*	−1, 5	0, 0

GAME B

	Player 2's Choice	
Player 1's Choice	Strategy *A*	Strategy *B*
Strategy *A*	20, 10	5, 15
Strategy *B*	10, 20	−5, −5

flict in this game because both players can select their preferred strategies and obtain their preferred outcomes. Each has a **dominant strategy,** which is the one she would select regardless of what the other player does. In this case, the dominant strategy produces the best collective outcome, 20 + 10, and everyone is happy! This is the situation that eighteenth-century economist and philosopher Adam Smith envisioned in *The Wealth of Nations* with his argument about the functioning of the **invisible hand** in efficient markets. In such settings, individuals only need to act sincerely, choosing their most preferred outcomes to obtain the best possible collective outcome.

In Game A, a dominant strategy exists for both players, whereby the intersection of their choices—their payoffs—is stable, and neither player can improve her payoff by unilaterally selecting another strategy. This is called a **stable equilibrium,** or, in game theory terms, a **Nash equilibrium,** named after its inventor John Nash (who was the subject of the book and award-winning film, *A Beautiful Mind*). This idea transformed microeconomics, and Nash won a Nobel Prize in Economics for its invention. An **equilibrium** is nothing more than a situation in which activity has stopped; there is no switching of strategies. Aside from this quality of stability and its value for predicting and explaining behavior, there is nothing inherently special or attractive about equilibrium, which may be normatively good or normatively bad.

An international agreement about fishing rights that allocates catch shares and ensures survival of a fishing stock would be a normatively good equilibrium if you think species preservation is a good outcome. Being locked in ethnic conflict or a civil war might also be an equilibrium, if neither side could improve its prospects for survival by unilaterally selecting another strategy. But we would likely consider this situation as normatively perverse, for the equilibrium promotes continued killing and destruction.

Game B changes the context or structure of the interaction between the same decision makers. In terms of payoffs, Player 1 prefers 20 to 10 to 5 to −5 ($20 > 10 > 5 > -5$), while Player 2 prefers 20 to 15 to 10 to −5 ($20 > 15 > 10 > -5$). Again, these preference orderings are complete and transitive. In this situation, Player 1 has a dominant strategy, Strategy A, which she will select regardless of Player 2's choices. Player 1 prefers 20 to 10 and 5 to −5, which are the different outcomes she can expect between Strategies A and B, dependent upon Player 2's choice of strategy. So Player 1 will always select Strategy A in this game. If Player 2 recognizes that Player 1 has a dominant strategy of A, she can make her decision contingent on that knowledge. If she wanted to maximize her payoff without any knowledge of Player 1's strategy, she would choose Strategy A, with the expectation of obtaining 20 should Player 1 choose Strategy B. But, as Player 2's payoff results from the intersection of her choice with Player 1's choice, she would receive only 10 instead of the expected 20, because Player 1 will have selected Strategy A. What a disappointment! There is no way Player 2 can obtain 20 because Player 1 has no incentive to shift strategy. But if she recognizes that Player 1 will always choose Strategy A, Player 2 can do better for herself by choosing Strategy B and obtaining a payoff of 15, which is much better than 10. By acting strategically—selecting a strategy that does not reflect her most preferred outcome in an absolute sense but represents her best choice given the structure of her interaction with Player 1—she will do better.

In both games, we had rational decision makers, but their choices changed with the shift in context. Context is not trivial; in fact, it is critical to understanding choices, as social settings can influence payoffs by determining how choices interact. We return to game theory models in chapter 12 to illustrate how contexts can produce **social traps** in economic and political markets. A social trap is a situation in which what appears to be an individual's maximizing, self-interested choice to obtain a preferred outcome actually results in a subpar outcome both for the individual and for the larger group or society. This unexpected outcome occurs because of the structure of interactions of the choices made by multiple individuals.

OUTCOMES VERSUS CHOICE

The previous section highlights an important distinction between choices and outcomes. One might reasonably ask why, if policymakers behave as if they are rational, their choices sometimes produce costly and seemingly perverse outcomes. Should we not expect rational decision makers to be reasonably successful in attaining their preferences, and only occasionally to fail in their efforts? And if their choices fail to attain their preferred outcomes, shouldn't they be able to avoid extremely costly and perverse outcomes? When we observe bad outcomes—such as the destructiveness of total war, the failure of a trade policy, an international financial crisis, or the extinction of a fish species due to overfishing in international waters—does this mean that policymakers intended to produce such outcomes through the careful and rational comparison of alternatives and strategies?

Did the leaders of European nations in 1914 rationally intend to reduce the population of Europe by approximately 10 million people when they entered into World War I? Did Hitler rationally seek the outcome of 55 million dead, 35 million wounded, some 3 million more lost and unaccounted for, his own death, and the complete destruction of his Germany when he took the steps that would embroil much of the globe in World War II? When Congress enacted the Smoot-Hawley Act in 1930, dramatically raising tariffs on U.S. imports and provoking other nations to raise their tariff rates, did Smoot, Hawley, and the other legislators who voted in favor really want to torpedo the global economy? Did President Herbert Hoover, as a rational decision maker, known for his humanitarian efforts in Europe after World War I, consciously elect to promote economic disarray and human suffering when he decided to sign the Smoot-Hawley Act against the advice of over one thousand economists? The answer to all these questions is, unequivocally, No! But, then, how can rationality help us to understand choices that produce such perverse outcomes?

Backward Induction

These examples illustrate a very important lesson for how we use the rationality assumption to investigate human behavior: *the consequences of choice differ from the motivations of choice.* It may seem obvious, but it is important to understand that a decision differs from an outcome. As the simple games in figure 2.3 illustrate, in social settings (those that involve more than one person) outcomes result from the interaction of choices but are not the choices themselves. Otherwise, one's choice to play a lottery game would be equivalent to winning. The rationality assumption helps us to investigate the individual motivations leading to decisions, but it does not necessarily explain the consequences of those decisions. If we assume that people operate as if they were rational, we can look at a decision situation and work backward to try to understand the rational calculations that could lead to the decision under examination. This process, which is called **backward induction,** is a very powerful tool for probing history and understanding politics.

Backward induction places the primary focus of analysis on the decision rather than on the outcome of that decision. It involves starting with a decision—not its outcome—and asking what the decision maker hoped to accomplish with her choice, what were her objectives, how did she rank those objectives, and how did she understand the preferences and likely choices of others that could impinge on her actions? How does her choice of a particular strategy allow us to evaluate her understanding of the trade-offs between objectives and the cost of the strategies to obtain those objectives? The assumption of rationality means that we expect decision makers to choose a course of action most likely to produce the best outcome given costs and benefits. This expectation gives us a tool to help us recreate the scenario of a decision we hope to understand, even if the outcome of that choice appears nonrational. We try to put ourselves in the decision maker's shoes. We look for supporting evidence in the historical record, in archives, in interviews with participants to an event, and in any data that provides a glimpse of the context in which the decision was made. The assumption of rationality provides a logical framework in which to evaluate that information. Under the rationality assumption, we do not expect decision makers to make random choices or to select their second or third preferences if their first choices have equal or lesser costs. Consequently, we seek to understand how a decision maker came to view her choice as the best option given her understanding of the costs and benefits of alternative strategies.

Focusing on an outcome is very different from focusing on motivation when we investigate the choices that have produced an outcome. Outcomes attract our attention because we hope to understand what causes crises and disasters, as well as what promotes good and fruitful outcomes in the global political economy. But to focus on an outcome as we try to understand the choices leading to that outcome represents a potential trap that ensnares many investigators. Outcomes result from the interaction of choices made in a world where decision makers are limited in the time and energy they can devote to any single choice, are not fully aware of other decision makers' understandings of the world, and are not equipped with functioning crystal balls. An outcome may occur as expected and predicted, it may be unanticipated, it may produce unintentional consequences, or it may be just one of many possible outcomes that could have occurred—but decision makers have weighted all those possible outcomes with a probabilistic evaluation that has proven to be accurate or faulty.

An Example of Backward Induction

Let's return to the Smoot-Hawley Act of 1930 as an example. Smoot-Hawley raised U.S. tariff barriers to heights not seen before or since. In retrospect and with 20/20 hindsight, Smoot-Hawley looks like one of the worst, most destructive policies ever implemented in American politics. Were Smoot and Hawley seeking such infamy when they introduced their legislation and nurtured its passage through Congress? If we were to begin with the outcome of worldwide economic depression and contraction that followed Smoot-Hawley and employ the rationality assumption and backward induction, we would be assuming that policymakers wanted to encourage a worldwide economic catastrophe.

A more appropriate research strategy to understand the passage of Smoot-Hawley, however, would ask under what conditions legislators would view the Smoot-Hawley Act as a rational strategy or a best choice given their understanding of the costs and benefits of different strategies. What did Smoot and Hawley and the supporting members of Congress expect to accomplish when they passed the legislation? Clearly they did not expect what happened, or we would have to call them crazy or sick. More likely, they were civil servants seeking to promote the welfare of their constituents and to enhance their own prospects for reelection. These goals required cushioning their constituents during a time of economic downturn and uncertainty. Jobs, livelihoods, and communities were being threatened, creating a situation that could easily translate into disgruntled voters. In response to this situation, the Smoot-Hawley legislation sought to transfer the costs of the economic downturn—job losses and other dislocations—to workers and producers in other countries by erecting barriers to their access to U.S. markets. Protecting U.S. markets for U.S.–produced products by raising the costs of imported products, Smoot-Hawley was an attempt to shift the costs of economic hardship overseas.

Senator Smoot and Congressman Hawley had good reason to believe in the soundness of their strategy, for it had worked numerous times in the past. Indeed, the U.S. economy grew up as a highly protected economy with high barriers to entry in particular sectors, and the U.S. Congress had raised tariff protections in the agricultural sector as recently as 1922 without destroying the global economy. But the context and position of the U.S. economy in the global context had changed by 1930, so that their actions instead contributed to a process of impoverishment, which ensured their electoral demise.

An outcome may attract us to a particular problem, but the focus on choice permits us to seek out the motivations and expectations underpinning the choice, to conduct an autopsy in order to learn what went wrong or what went right. Asking what decision makers expected to achieve is the first step toward understanding the micro foundations of the macro outcomes that we observe in the world. This approach offers a useful strategy for analysis of the decision-making process. Often we do not have access to decision makers at the time of their choices—we cannot be flies on the wall, or parties to their mental musings and policy deliberations. Sometimes these political actors are dead, sometimes they are retired, with selective and retrospective memories that rearrange history to make them look better, and sometimes they are leaders in other countries, about whose motivations we have limited information. Ultimately, we want to have some means of inferring why policymakers did what they did, or what they will do. Retracing the process of rationality, along with our other core assumptions, provides us with tools to help us in our attempts to explicate and anticipate choices.

CONCLUSION AND SOME OTHER PITFALLS

We have discussed the three assumptions that lie at the heart of a micro political economy approach, offering powerful and elegant tools to leverage our investigation and understanding of political behavior. We must remember that they are simplifications. We do not know whether political actors actually are rational and actually want to survive, but these assumptions are useful. Even with such powerful assumptions and tools, the analysis of political behavior is difficult. Strategic settings complicate the dilemma of connecting preferences, choices, and outcomes in the social world.

Several other problems hamper this process, both for investigators trying to understand choices and for policymakers trying to make choices in strategic settings. Two problems warrant mention. First, decision makers generally operate under some degree of uncertainty: they have incomplete information about the world, about their possible choices, about the preferences and possible choices of others, and about how multiple decision makers' choices will interact. The games represented in figure 2.3 model interactions of complete information, in which all players know the payoffs and possible strategies; this omniscience greatly simplifies the search for preferences and dominant strategies. Dilemmas exist for decision makers even in such simple interactions, but the game becomes infinitely more complicated when a decision maker encounters a real-world strategic challenge armed with incomplete information about her choices, the preferences of others, and the structure of her interaction with others.

Second, we cannot assume that choices in strategic settings interact in linear fashion. This means that we cannot just add individual choices together to arrive at an outcome, for they may not interact additively. An outcome may be different than simply the sum of individual choices. In this situation, which we call a **fallacy of composition,** the outcome is different than the sum of the parts: perhaps greater, perhaps less, but different. These two problems—incomplete information and the fallacy of composition—raise the possibility of unanticipated outcomes, which are unintentional consequences of choice. No policymaker is capable of looking down a decision path and fully anticipating the consequences of her choices and those of others. Some uncertainty about the future, some risk, always remains.

EXERCISES

1. What do we call the analytical strategy that focuses upon individual choice?

2. What do we call the state of a decision maker's preference if she must choose between two alternatives that are comparable, but she does not prefer one alternative or the other? What kind of behavior might this account for?

3. In game theory, what do we call the situation in which no player in a social interaction can improve her outcome by unilaterally choosing another strategy?

4. Consider the following game:

	Player 2's Choice	
Player 1's Choice	Strategy A	Strategy B
Strategy A	2,1	0,0
Strategy B	0,0	1,2

Does a dominant strategy exist for either or both players? If so, what is it for Player 1? for Player 2?

5. Explain what a Nash equilibrium is. Give examples of good and bad equilibria.

6. Why do political scientists use backward induction? Why is it more beneficial to look at the desired outcome rather than the actual outcome?

7. Equilibria are appealing for understanding social behavior, but are they inherently good normatively? Why or why not?

8. Assume Iran and Kuwait are (the only) members of an oil cartel. Each may choose to expand or restrict its output of oil. The table below shows each side's profits (in $ billions) for these possible outcomes. (Iran's profits are in bold.)

	Kuwait	
Iran	Expand	Restrict
Expand	**$50**, $25	**$65**, $15
Restrict	**$30**, $40	**$60**, $35

a. What is Kuwait's dominant strategy: expand, restrict, or depends on what Iran chooses?

b. Which of these outcomes is the Nash equilibrium: both expand oil production, both restrict oil production, Iran expands oil production and Kuwait restricts, or Iran restricts oil production and Kuwait expands?

c. Is any one of the following outcomes better for both than the Nash equilibrium: both expand oil production, both restrict oil production, Iran expands oil production and Kuwait restricts, or Iran restricts oil production and Kuwait expands?

FURTHER READING

Axelrod, Robert. 1984. *The Evolution of Cooperation*. New York: Basic Books.

Dixit, Avinash, and Barry Nalebuff. 1991. *Thinking Strategically: The Competitive Edge in Business, Politics, and Everyday Life*. New York: Norton.

Lave, Charles, and James March. 1975. *An Introduction to Models in the Social Sciences*. New York: Harper & Row.

Poundstone, William. 1992. *Prisoner's Dilemma: John Von Neumann, Game Theory, and the Puzzle of the Bomb*. New York: Doubleday.

Riker, William. 1986. *The Art of Political Manipulation*. New Haven: Yale University Press.

Schelling, Thomas C. 1978. *Micromotives and Macrobehavior*. New York: Norton.

———. 1980. *The Strategy of Conflict*. Cambridge, Mass.: Harvard University Press.

3 Structure of the International System

L'État, c'est moi

Louis XIV

THE CONTEXT OF INTERNATIONAL VERSUS DOMESTIC POLITICAL ARENAS

The previous chapter began to raise the issue of how context can affect the choices of rational policymakers. Context can transform a social interaction, alter beliefs about what might be a more appropriate strategy, influence evaluations of what others' choices might be in a situation, and affect perceptions of possible benefits and possible costs. In this chapter we look at some structural characteristics of the international system that help to define the context within which policymakers operate. Although our focus in this book is on global political economy, the tools and the approach we develop here are applicable in a wide variety of political settings. We can apply the logic of rational self-interested decision makers operating in an environment of scarcity to both domestic and international political arenas. There is, however, an important structural distinction between the study of politics in international arenas and the study of politics in domestic arenas. This difference, which reflects the current international context, colors our analyses of global affairs, international politics, and international political economy by adding another independent variable to our explanations.

International politics and international political economy take place in an arena that lacks a central overarching authority—there is no central government as in domestic political arenas. Although some domestic political arenas have more effective, fairer, more capable, less corrupt, more just, and more legitimate governments than others, domestic political arenas are nonetheless generally characterized by the presence of a central, overarching authority. But there is no central or world government with legitimate governing authority over the actions of all those living on the planet; no world government with binding authority to implement and enforce international laws presides over national governments. Because the absence of a supranational government is important to our understanding of global political-economic relations, this distinction between political arenas with central authority and those with no central authority must be included as an independent variable in our analyses.

For centuries, the nation-state has been the dominant unit of political aggregation in world affairs. This explains the term *international relations*, or relations between nations. As the key defining unit of world politics, nation-states must be considered from several angles: what are their origins, what makes them similar and what differentiates them, what makes some more capable than others, why as investigators of global political economy do we care about nation-states, and how does a system of nation-states affect world politics? As we begin to explore the concept and history of nation-states and the nation-state system, we will encounter key terms, such as *legitimate authority, identity, nationalism, sovereignty, anarchy, self-help, power,* and *influence.* All represent concepts that are central to our understanding of the influence of context upon world politics.

NATION-STATES

A **nation-state** is a form of political organization. In the past, other forms of political organization have been influential in the global arena: city-states, empires, feudal kingdoms, commonwealths, leagues, and others. In the future, new forms may emerge to supplant the state as the primary unit of political aggregation in world affairs; some new forms of political aggregation are emerging already, such as the supranational governmental structure of the European Union (EU). Currently, the EU appears subordinate to its member states, but its structure and reach are evolving and may someday challenge—perhaps supplant—the governmental structures, reach, and authority of its members. We can divide the term *nation-state* into its two components: *nation* and *state.*

States and Their Defining Characteristics

A state is a legal entity, which can undertake and accept legal commitments such as treaties and other legal obligations via its representative authority or government. Much as an individual can enter into contracts and other commitments, a state can also make such contractual commitments. From this perspective, a state is a legal abstraction that can assume the same responsibility under law that individuals can. A state can enter into contracts within its national boundaries or across national boundaries. This premise sits at the heart of constitutions and bodies of domestic law and regulation, which are contracts between states and their citizens; it also underpins international law, international organizations, and international treaties. In the agreements that create international governmental organizations—those organizations whose members are nation-states—or anchor international treaties, the basic assumption is that states, like individuals and firms, can accept binding legal commitments. Of course, states may renege on their agreements, just as individuals and firms sometimes fail to live up to their commitments. Nevertheless, such agreements are viewed as contracts similar to those that individuals, firms, and other organizations undertake within national political arenas. However, as we will shortly see, because of the structure of modern international relations, such contracts or treaties between states are not backed with the same weight of law as contracts and agreements made within national boundaries.

Aside from their function as legal entities, states have several other very important characteristics. First, a state has a defined geographic territory. In the modern nation-state system, states are the only international actors that technically control territory. Of course, private property ownership does exist in most states around the world—individuals may own their homes and companies may own buildings and land, but the ability to exercise property rights over a defined geographic area is determined by the state. Through law, states define property rights and delegate them to others. States may follow different practices in defining private property and assigning property rights. Some states retain greater control of property than others, which explains why notions of private property vary from one country to another.

Second, a state has a population that inhabits its geographic territory. The characteristics of populations may vary from state to state: they may be rich or poor, old or young, highly educated or not, healthy or unhealthy, diverse or homogeneous, or identified by some other feature or quality. But each state has a population that is connected to its territory. These are the people who provide revenues to the state, staff its militaries, and propel the economy.

Third, every state has a government to represent some component of the people who inhabit its territory. Governments vary in this notion of representation, and such differences in representation help explain some of the differences in government activities from nation to nation. A government may represent a broad swath of society, as democratic governments do, or it may represent some more parochial and narrow segments in society, as patronage or authoritarian regimes do. The state apparatus of a government is considered the source of legitimate coercion within a society. Governments use police forces to enforce their laws, regardless of whether or not those laws are fairly constructed and enforced. The government may not be the only possible source of coercion and violence in a society, but it is the only legitimate source. Of course, that very legitimacy is often a matter of conflict and dispute.

Functional Equality and Specialization

Within the current nation-state system, all states are functionally equal. Does this mean that all states are equal? Are the United States and Ecuador equal? Clearly they are not equal on most dimensions. The United States has a much bigger economy, more extensive territory and a larger population, a more capable military, a higher per capita income, longer life expectancies, and so on. So what does **functional equality** mean and why is it relevant? Functional equality is a comparative statement about what states do—what functions states undertake—rather than a statement about how well they perform those functions. Regardless of their abilities, all states attempt to perform similar essential functions, such as defining notions of property, extracting taxes, providing for the common defense, developing legal systems to impose order on social relations within state boundaries, devising means such as courts and regulators to adjudicate disputes in society, creating police agencies to enforce both the legal structure and judicial resolutions, and representing some interests (however defined and implemented) in the society.

Again, all states are equal not in how they perform such functions—only in that they all do attempt to perform them. This functional equality means that governments and their societies do not take advantage of specialization in the international arena in terms of the activities of government. For example, the French government may excel at tax collection, the Swedish government at provision of social services, the Russian and Chinese governments at domestic spying and surveillance, the Japanese government at managing industrial policy, and the United States government at the provision of national security. Yet, governments and societies do not purchase such public commodities from the government that is the better producer. The Soviet and Chinese governments do not hire the U.S. government to provide for their common defense, nor do the Mexican and Nigerian governments contract with the French government for tax collection. Governments do not engage in exchange relations with other governments to implement the functions of government. They all perform the same basic functions, regardless of their capabilities and effectiveness.

The functional equality of states and their lack of particular expertise in the provision of government commodities differ dramatically from the global economic arena, where international trade and market exchange enable consumers and producers to take advantage of **specialization** in the production of nongovernment commodities. With specialization, a producer does not attempt to produce the entire range of commodities she desires, but instead relies upon her community to supplement her production of some commodities with other commodities she may want. Producers concentrate on the production of particular commodities and trade for others they do not produce. Perhaps when mankind was in its hunter-gatherer stage of economic activity, or even during the early stages of the transformation from hunter-gather communities to pastoral-agricultural communities, we might have observed a high degree of functional equality from producer to producer. With economic advance, however, individual producers began to specialize in production, trading the output of their labors for commodities they did not produce.

Efficiencies of the Market and Fragmentation of Government Services

Factors that we call **economies of scale** and **economies of knowledge** can increase the efficiency of production of a commodity. Economies of scale occur with the concentration of resources in that production—producing more of a commodity may be more efficient due to the aggregation of activities and resources that are required to produce it. Economies of knowledge occur with gains from learning about how to produce a product—the more we do something, the better and more efficient we may become at doing it. **Efficiency** is simply a statement about how much is produced for a fixed amount of labor. More efficient producers produce more with the same amount of labor than less efficient producers do. All other things being equal, specialization in production generally produces efficiency gains. In economic life, we can develop specialization in our productive activities, which focuses our individual efforts on producing a narrow range of products, and then exchange our products for a wide variety of other products we desire. Such specialization allows us to produce and consume more commodities than if we individually had to produce all the products we wanted.

We live in domestic and global political economies in which economic actors take advantage of specialization. As we see in future chapters, market mechanisms in the global political economy condition production, promote specialization, and generate gains in efficiency in economic arenas. But states do not take advantage of possible gains in efficiency from specialization in production of governmental goods. This characteristic of functional equality in terms of government activities, which occurs across national governments, can present formidable dilemmas for the well-being of communities. The resulting fragmentation in provision of governmental services can lead to inefficient governance, producing redundancies in management of such services and a lack of economies from scale and knowledge, as well as an unwillingness to share governmental resources with those who live in communities under different governmental arrangements.

National Autonomy and Interdependence

This difference between the functional equality of government activities in the nation-state system and the specialization that characterizes the production of economic commodities across nation-states highlights an interesting and important component of modern international relations. We live in a global political economy wherein the dominant production of political commodities—defense goods, social welfare goods, and other government services—is structured and conditioned *within* national polities, but the production of economic commodities is increasingly structured *across* national economies. This difference in setting raises the possibility of tensions between the production of political and economic goods, since the mechanisms that condition and discipline the production of government and nongovernment goods diverge dramatically. In one arena, the domestic polity acts as the disciplinary mechanism, while in the other arena, economic processes that do not recognize national boundaries act as the disciplinarian. This difference is at the crux of the tension between **interdependence**—the connections across nations—and **national policy autonomy**—the production of political commodities for local consumption—and it helps to account for the production of political commodities that may impinge on the production of economic commodities.

For example, take the international production and trade in steel. With trade, the global market rewards efficient and competitive producers of steel and penalizes less efficient producers. Consumers will prefer to purchase steel from more efficient and competitive producers because their product, at any given quality, will be less expensive. Less efficient producers of steel must transform their production capabilities to meet the challenge of global competition, or they will lose business, falter, and possibly fail. This is the discipline of the global market: those penalized by trade must find a way to use their productive resources more efficiently. Of course, the less competitive steel producers (and their labor force) may appeal to their politicians for some form of government intervention in the economic arena to protect their enterprise—a tariff, a quota, or a subsidy—that alters either the supply or the price of foreign steel in the domestic market or the cost of producing domestic steel. Here, a government has intervened in international trade to affect the price and, consequently, the production of steel. National government is the disciplinarian on steel production. Workers and companies in the domestic steel industry evade the discipline of the global market, but foreign producers of steel face the discipline imposed by the government that has made the intervention. Here economic producers respond to government incentives, and not to the efficiency demands of the market.

Equality and Effectiveness

Despite the characteristic of functional equality, in reality some states are more effective than others, more capable at performing their functions. Some governments are better than others at tax collection, provision of social services, national security tasks, and building an infrastructure that is conducive to economic activity. Governments that are effective in one arena are often effective in multiple arenas. Theoretically, we could rank-order states from most to least capable in terms of their effectiveness and capabilities, thus sketching a **hierarchy** in the international arena based upon capabilities. Many of us already do this informally, on a case-by-case basis, when an international dispute arises between states. Whether we observe a trade dispute, a dispute over fishing rights, an international negotiation about pollution, an extradition dispute, a disagreement between governments over information-sharing in the process of a criminal investigation, or a war, we often project the outcome based simply on our estimation of the differences in the capabilities of states, of governments and their societies. We call this a difference in power; we will examine power and hierarchy more thoroughly in the next chapter.

Nation and Collective Identity

Let's turn to the other part of the term *nation-state*. A **nation** is a form of collective identity or community identification that is based on some common or shared knowledge. Unlike the physical, geographic entity of the state, it is an abstraction, for neither this common knowledge nor the collective identity itself can be seen or touched. It is thus more difficult to measure or observe than the physical entity of the state. Yet the conception of nation is critically important, as it reflects a highly potent form of collective affinity that can motivate individuals to engage in extraordinary activities. Policymakers can enlist this collective identification to influence their societies to participate in collective action. The common knowledge that underlies the identity of nation builds upon a grouping of individuals who share one or more characteristics that help to define who is a member of the specific community and who is not. By definition, the idea of community is based upon recognizing boundaries between members and nonmembers of the community. Common characteristics that make individuals feel part of the same grouping can thus serve as a basis for the construction of identity and community.

A nation is a grouping, but not all groupings are nations. Each of us belongs to a variety of groups that contribute to our identities. The difficulty in observing and measuring the characteristic of nation arises from the fact that we live in social settings that are filled with clubs, associations, religions, community groups, and other organizations that contribute to identities. You might be a member of a fraternity or sorority, a labor union, a political party, a business or professional association, or a specific profession; a follower of a particular faith; an emigrant from a particular country; a person of one gender or the other, of a particular race, of a particular class, or of some other grouping. Such collective associations help form the basis of our identities, but they are not all part of the collective identity called nation, which is a social institution that political elites can mobilize and manipulate in pursuit of collective action.

How do we distinguish between a nation and some other grouping that contributes to collective identity? This is not a simple or straightforward task, but some general characteristics do help. First, most people self-identify their attachment to a grouping called nation. One might reply Russian, American, British, Indian, Cuban, or Palestinian when asked about nationality, but one would not say the American Medical Association, Al-Qaeda, or Pi Sigma Alpha. Second, national identity is more all-encompassing than most other collective groupings. Third, individuals may have hierarchies of group identification, making it possible to rank our group associations in terms of their importance to our individual identities. We may be members of multiple groups, but some motivate us more than others. When the identity of nation is activated and elevated in importance during times of strife and state crisis, an individual's other collective identities tend to take a subordinate role. Fourth, nation is one of the few identities that large numbers of men seem willing to kill and die for. This characteristic is what makes nation as an identity so powerful a force—if this concept of identity can inspire large numbers of people to make the ultimate sacrifice, it can surely be a strong motivation for other endeavors. Religion, as another such source of identity, can motivate in the same way. But it would be rather hard to believe that many members of a college fraternity, the American Bar Association, or the United Auto Workers would be willing to kill and die for these associations.

Unlike state, nation is not necessarily tied to physical geography. People can share the collective identity of a nation although they do not have a territory or a government that is recognized under the tenets of international law. Before 1947, the Jewish nation existed, but not the state of Israel. The Palestinian nation is currently fighting for the right to be a state. The Kurdish people in northern Iraq, southeastern Turkey, and northern Iran constitute a nation and want to become a state. In Spain, Basque nationalists fight for statehood and independence. The Navajo, Mohicans, Sioux, and Comanche may have lost their territory in wars with the United States, but they still remain nations. Vietnamese nationalists resisted Chinese domination, later French colonialism, and then American political-military intervention to fight for the creation and preservation of the Vietnamese state. Biafran nationalists tried to secede from Nigeria in the early 1970s, but two other nations, the Hausa and Fulani, fought the dissolution of Nigeria, resulting in a bloody civil war. Bangladeshi nationalists in East Pakistan sought, and finally obtained, independence from Pakistan; they created the state of Bangladesh. With the demise of the Soviet bloc in 1989–1991, independence movements based on national identity arose all over Eastern Europe and Central Asia, transforming the political map as new states emerged: the new countries of Bosnia and Herzegovina, Croatia, Macedonia, Serbia and Montenegro, and Slovenia were part of the former state of Yugoslavia; Czechoslovakia split into the Czech and Slovak Republics; Estonia, Lithuania, Latvia, Georgia, Ukraine, Armenia, and other nations demanded independence and obtained statehood.

Some of these transformations from nation to nation-state occurred relatively peacefully, but others followed brutal conflicts of national unification and independence, terrorism, and abuse of individual political and civil liberties. Not all attempts to create state boundaries that coincide with the boundaries of national identification succeed. The persistence of nationalist civil conflict in many states shows the potential incongruence between states and nations. Since the breakup of the Soviet Union, most combat deaths have occurred in civil wars, which represent battles over the concept of nation, rather than in interstate conflicts.

Moreover, states can exist without nations. State boundaries in Europe emerged from centuries of conflict and state-building, which drew upon the construction of national identities that were based on the state and the allegiance of individuals to the state. But the drawing of state boundaries in Africa took place in European capitals. These boundaries are legacies of colonialism, and they do not necessarily coincide with the emergence of particular national identities within those boundaries. The people living within those boundaries may not share a collective identity that coincides with the state, or the state may place several national identities in conflict, which can result in civil war, ethnic cleansing, and discrimination—as in Rwanda, Zimbabwe, and Sudan. Even the Western European states, the United States, and other modern nation-states were not spared this dilemma of incongruence

A Palestinian celebrates in the Gaza Strip in August 2005 in anticipation of the withdrawal by Israel from Palestinian territories it had occupied since 1967. Behind him is Neve Dekalim, a Jewish settlement established like many others to strengthen Israeli claims to the land by creating facts on the ground. The Palestinians remain a nation without a fully formed state, as Jews were before the creation of the State of Israel in Palestine. The Palestinian-Israeli conflict is, at its core, a dispute between two nationalities staking claim to the same piece of land.

between nation and state, for the evolutionary nation-building they experienced was also marked by a history of violence and civil conflict. Indeed, violence is often a part of nation-building—just ask any American Indian, the ancestors of men who served in the U.S. Civil War, or the men and women of Iraq today!

Building National Identity

Successful construction of a sense of nation, or *nationalism,* amounts to the evolution of individuals into a group with an extraordinarily potent form of common identity. How do large masses of individuals come to identify themselves with a nation? How do individuals develop a collective identity that is aligned with a nation and that is stronger than their personal ambitions? What integrative forces contribute to the development of a nation? Let's first consider the influence of the key characteristics of a state—common territory and common government—upon the evolution of national identity. A common territory can be integrative if individuals transfer their emotional ties to territory to a collective identity attached to that territory. A common government, whereby people live under common political institutions, can also be integrative. Physical territory and common government can be integrative, but they can also be divisive, if the groups within that territory have competing collective identities. Moreover, we listed earlier some examples of nations that exist without congruent states, territories, or governments. Thus common territory and government are not necessary conditions for the development of nation. If nation is the dependent variable, common territory and government are not the critical independent variables for its development.

What other forces might be integrative, helping to weave a group of individuals into a grouping called a nation? A common economy, in which individuals share a common medium of exchange and participate in a web of interconnected economic relations might prove helpful. State-issued currencies (monies) are mediums of exchange that can store value, serve as units of accounting and exchange, and help create a bond between users of those currencies and their states. Government-issued money, often covered with decorations evocative of state identity, is itself a symbol of the state: U.S. currency features past presidents, while British currency has a place for the queen and other state symbols. Every time a person uses her state currency, she employs a symbol of the state in an economic transaction. Implicitly, she is validating the state symbol and integrating it into her daily life. If using a state-issued currency endows a state with some legitimacy or authority, this activity amounts to voting with your wallet for the state. Economic interactions carried out within a state's boundaries are often more frequent and more intricate than those that extend across state boundaries, and this factor can be integrative if more frequent and more intricate interactions help to form a common identity.

But if nation is the dependent variable, a common economy is not the critical independent variable for development of nation, for it is not a necessary condition for development of a national identity. The Kurds have rarely, if ever, lived within a common economic framework, but they share a strong bond of national identity. Between the time when they were driven from Jerusalem many centuries ago and the formation of the modern state of Israel, Jews were scattered across many state territories and did not share a common economy, yet they retained a common identity as a nation. Other nations are spread across a variety of states and hence come under a variety of economic arrangements. Moreover, merely living under a set of common economic arrangements may fail to be a compelling integrative force. The inhabitants of the Basque regions of Spain operate within the Spanish economy, employ the euro, and accept that their economic futures are strongly influenced by Spanish economic institutions, yet the Basques strongly resist becoming Spanish. In the European Union, many countries have converted their currency to the euro, but they do not consider themselves part of a single nation called Europe. So far, they have maintained their distinct national identities even as they adopt some common economic tools.

A common culture, common religion, or common language may perhaps contribute significantly to the evolution of a group into a nation. Individuals who eat the same foods, wear similar dress, listen to similar music, appreciate and revere similar art, speak the same language, employ similar expressions and slang, practice the same religion, and engage in similar social practices share a common culture, and this sharing can be integrative and help to develop a common identity. After all, people who share common cultural characteristics tend to be more alike than not. However, although Australians, Brits, Americans, Canadians, and New Zealanders share a common language, they do not consider themselves part of a single nation. Argentines, Chileans, Spaniards, Mexicans, and Costa Ricans speak a common language and practice a common religion, but they do not identify themselves as belonging to a single nation. In Miami and Los Angeles, significant portions of the population use Spanish as their primary language, but they identify with the nation of people making up the United States, despite this preference for a language that is not dominant outside of their local communities. English serves as the secondary language in many Chinese-American, Japanese-American, Serbian-American, Croatian-American, and other ethnic American households and neighborhoods, yet those households and neighborhoods are vital parts of the U.S. nation. Japanese-Americans and German-Americans served valiantly in the U.S. armed forces during World War II even though Japan and Germany were the enemies. Again, if nation is the dependent variable, common culture, common religion, and common language are not the critical independent variables for the development of nation. They can help, but they are not necessary or sufficient conditions.

Perhaps sharing a common political ideology can serve as the integrative force that promotes the development of nation? A common political ideology is a shared set of beliefs about the relationship between governments and their peoples, about the role of government in society, about what people can expect from government and what government can demand from people. Common political ideology differs from common government, which is a key component of a state, for people can live under a common government and yet hold distinctive political ideologies—including those that contradict their government. Moreover, people who live in many different states can share a common political ideology. Does this mean that they are part of the same nation, yet part of different states? Possibly, but in most of these cases, these linked ideologues are not part of the same nation or of the same state. During the Great Depression and for many years thereafter, some Americans held socialist and communist political ideologies even though they lived under governing structures that rejected such ideologies. And many of them shared an American national identity with those who supported another political ideology—same nation, different political ideology. In authoritarian states as well, there may be groups that support political ideologies that differ from those held by the governing regime. These examples suggest that common political ideology, while potentially a force for integration into a common national identity, is not a necessary condition. People can belong to a nation and yet hold different political ideologies.

What about a common history? Does sharing a common past ensure the development of nation? Consider states that have experienced large immigrations. During the 1800s and early 1900s, several large waves of immigrants arrived in the United States and other parts of the New World from a variety of Old World countries. People emigrated from Norway, Sweden, Ireland, the United Kingdom, Germany, Russia, the Baltic Republics, Italy, China, and other places to become U.S., Canadian, Argentine, Chilean, or Australian residents. Many of these immigrants sought to become members of those states' nations, to share in the common knowledge and common national identity of the people of their destination state. They did not share a common history, but they sought to share the common identity of belonging to the same nation. Some of these New World destinations developed strong nations and integrated new members into those nations despite the lack of common shared histories. Governments can use the teaching of a common history to foster an integrative common knowledge and identity, but it is not a necessary condition.

Common territory, government, political ideology, culture, religion, language, or history can be integrative forces, but a nation may emerge absent these integrative forces, or they may be present where a nation does not exist. If none of these shared characteristics is a necessary and sufficient condition for the development of a nation, what, then, is? A shared sense of common destiny or common future is the critical component. The past, where people have been, is less important than where people are going. Linking individual destinies together to develop a group destiny sits at the heart of the concept of nation. Israelis, Palestinians, Kurds, French, Americans, Mexicans, and Hutus become members of their respective nations when they share an identity based upon future, not past, hopes and associations. As in the Horatio Alger story, which emphasizes the opportunities for success that await those coming to American shores with little or nothing and regardless of their past, the successful nation-states of the New World built impressive collective national identities in a relatively short period of time. Those nation-building success stories were based upon the emergence of a sense of a common destiny shared among people looking to the future, without extensive common pasts, without much accumulated culture, often with several different languages and religions, and sometimes under changing governmental arrangements and state-society bargains.

The Importance of Nation in World Affairs

This abstract concept of national identity can work to governments' advantage in terms of extracting and mobilizing resources for state activities, promoting responsible community behavior and participation, and constraining threats to community and government authority. The combination of an abstract nation with a concrete state—the development of a nation-state—is an extremely powerful phenomenon. The governments of states whose people enjoy common knowledge about their national identity can manipulate that knowledge to increase their own authority over their peoples and their territories. Such governments can exploit the sense of national identity to ask more of their citizens than can governments whose populations have not developed this quality of nationalism, and they can extract greater individual sacrifice for the welfare of the larger group or nation. The governments of nation-states can draw more resources from their populations per capita than can the governments of mere states; they are more successful at collecting taxes, as those being governed are willing to contribute larger portions of their personal wealth if they believe in a shared national destiny. Governments can thus take advantage of the social institution of identity to motivate the actions of individuals in their societies, for people with a collective sense of the future are more willing to invest in the future, to forgo current consumption. They are less likely to hide their revenues from their governments, more likely to voluntarily ante up to the state coffers, and more likely to contribute their energies and those of their children to societal endeavors. This same pattern of voluntary activity is repeated across strong nation-states, where national identity overlays the people's physical residence.

Nation-states are also better at getting their youth to contribute several years of their lives to national service. Consider the effect of national identity upon eighteen-year-olds in nation-states, who are generally more willing to risk their lives in the service of their nations than are those in states that have not developed a sense of nation. This same feeling of nationalism can also increase a government's effectiveness at managing affairs in the domestic political arena. The governments of nation-states can ask more of their people for domestic programs, even for redistributive programs that are designed to benefit other members of the society.

Entrepreneurial governments may seek to promote the development of national identity in order to create a responsive citizenry and to reduce divisive localism. Many, if not all, governments face the dilemma of governing populations made up of diverse groups. Diversity may be more apparent in states with heterogeneous racial, religious, or ethnic makeups, but even apparently homogeneous societies are composed of assorted groups that impose competing demands upon individual identity. Such separate demands place cross-cutting pressures—pressures that overlap and compete—upon individuals, which can lead to community divisiveness and undermine the collective purpose of the larger group.

The Rise of Modern Nationalism

States and nations have existed for centuries, but as more distinct than connected phenomena. The linkage of nationalism to the state is a relatively new trend. The American and French Revolutions, Napoleon, and the Napoleonic Wars ushered in modern nationalism, which represents a transformation from an elite to a mass form of collective identity and the development of mass attachments to the state. Prior to the Napoleonic Wars, only small elite groups identified with the power and policies of their states; mass loyalty was, instead, directed toward the monarch. Most of a state's inhabitants had no significant attachment to the state or the government of the state. One lord of the manor looked similar to any other feudal king to peasants, serfs, and those with no political rights or identity. Armies were predominantly professional armies, composed of mercenaries.

The rise of nationalism and national identification with the state coincided with the huge growth in the size of militaries, broad conscription to fill the ranks, and the expansion of rights of citizens in exchange for their contributions to national service. Napoleon invented the civilian army with the *levée en masse,* which led to a dramatic increase in the size of militaries as governments drew upon their inhabitants for military service. The boundaries of citizenship were expanded as the quid pro quo—an exchange between the state and the people for the participation of the masses in the military. This form of conscription differed from the press gangs and coerced service of those seeking to avoid prison that were the traditional means of forcing an unfortunate minority, those apprehended in the wrong place at the wrong time, into the military service of the government. In contrast, the mass conscriptions, begun under Napoleon and soon adopted throughout Western Europe and later the

United States, applied to large segments of males in societies, rich and poor, regardless of religion.

To expand the base of conscription beyond the limited numbers who volunteered required an upgrading of public records and better accounting within societies. Many of the states becoming modern nation-states began to take national census counts in the early to mid-1800s. These national accountings gathered information for the state about the number of citizens, where they lived, and their approximate well-being. This data provided the records necessary both to implement universal conscription for military service and also to know whom to tax.

Serving together, training together, and living together helped to develop bonds among the conscripts, whose lives (and futures) depended upon one another. Successful political leaders then sought to transfer this bond of loyalty from the small group to the larger nation-state. The military became a school for embedding a modern national identity in the mass population. Broad-based conscription contributed to a dramatic increase in the number of people who identified with the state's power and policies, and in their willingness to sacrifice for the state. The recasting of identity and of the bargains made between the state and its residents transformed the state's capabilities, which changed the nature of warfare. Wars became more deadly as governments mobilized larger and larger armies made up of their everyday citizens.

Governments of states can seek to develop common knowledge about collective national identity in order to expand the capabilities of the state, but national movements can also press for the creation of new states. The nineteenth century saw the rise of national movements that advocated statehood and independence. Territorial consolidations and unification in Germany, Italy, and the United States merged fragments into large states and also built national identities congruent with the physical state. Nationalists overcame significant barriers to building nation-states. Activities of Italian nationalists such as Joseph Mazzini, Camillo di Cavour, and Guiseppe Garibaldi led to the making of Italy by 1870. Count Otto von Bismarck, the Prussian leader, succeeded in unifying distinct German entities into a single German state by the Franco-Prussian War in 1870. In the United States, President Abraham Lincoln led a war to preserve and cement national union; one result of the U.S. Civil War was to elevate central government and national identity over state government and more localized identity.

By the late 1800s, the more successful states were those whose governments had somehow managed to expand their support from a small cadre of elites to the masses, which shared in the collective identity. Then and today, *failed states* are partly defined by the failure of their governments to create common knowledge about collective identity, which enshrines a bargain between the state and mass society that encourages allegiance and sacrifice by the masses for the state.

If history provides any insight, conflicts over nation-building can prove extremely deadly. This is an important lesson to remember as we watch contemporary conflicts over nation-building in places such as Sri Lanka, Indonesia, Central Asia, Georgia, Rwanda, the Philippines, and the fragments of the former Yugoslavia. Today, those in the advanced industrialized states may be aghast at the violence that characterizes many of these modern nation-building efforts, but they need only look to their own histories to see examples of the violence and destruction that can occur during the process of territorial consolidation and construction of national identity.

Often, however, a national identity tied to the state that can dominate competing identities fails to emerge. The former Yugoslavia is an example of the difficulties a government faces in managing the tensions between local and national identities. For almost fifty years after World War II, the government of Yugoslavia appeared to have successfully managed the cross-cutting pressures of a handful of strong and diverse local ethnic identities—Serbian, Croatian, Bosnian, and others. But the death in 1980 of Marshal Tito, the Yugoslav leader, the dissolution of Soviet control over the Eastern bloc nations at the end of that decade, and the ensuing manipulation of ethnic identities by local political leadership eventually revealed that those regional ethnic identities were stronger than Yugoslav nationalism. Yugoslavia fragmented under such pressures, producing militarized conflict between Bosnians, Serbs, Croatians, and inhabitants of the region surrounding Kosovo.

What do governments do to promote common knowledge about national identity? Educational systems provide exceptional vehicles for socializing a sense of broader community and national identity. The expansion of public education and the mandating of required schooling for youth was seen as a device to improve the quality of the workforce by early training of skills, but it was also a tool for embedding a sense of community, national civics, and respect for the processes of government. In the 1870s, the Germans started singing *Deutschland über Alles*. Students in American classrooms began reciting the Pledge of Allegiance in the 1890s. Most U.S. students take classes in American civics and government during their K–12 training, and sometimes at higher educational levels regardless of whether the schools are public or private. This practice of training in the model of the national government is repeated around the world. What better way to develop an attachment to the state than to inculcate beliefs and knowledge through the educational mechanisms of society?

Other tools exist aside from the formal institutional setting of schools to build common knowledge about identity. Required military and public service can help build broad national identity and attachment to the state. Public holidays, parades, and folklore help build civil mythologies that contribute to a sense of group identification. Some of these efforts advance attachment and identity to groups smaller than a nation, but many contribute to the development of national identity. Manifest destiny, Horatio Alger and the American Dream, the 1000-year Reich, George Washington and the cherry tree, Lord Nelson and the Battle of Trafalgar, the rise of republican government and the French Revolution, Napoleon's military success, and other military exploits are examples of the mythologies that are promoted to overcome cross-cutting allegiances and contribute to a sense of belonging to a community that extends beyond the boundaries of individual, family, or other smaller group associations.

Origins of the State System: Empire and Fragmentation

What are the roots of the state system that, together with markets, dominates relations in today's global political economy? The modern state is a relatively new form of political organization, dating from the Treaty of Westphalia in 1648, which ended the Thirty Years' War in Europe. Before that extended continental conflict, the political map of Europe displayed a vast mixture of empires and feudal kingdoms or entities, where networks of transactions and authority relationships cut across the boundaries of physical geography (see map 3.1).

States are significant political entities, but they are not the only possible form of significant political and geographic consolidation. An **empire** encompasses far more territory under a single political entity than does a state. As the fifth century dawned, the Roman Empire dominated the political geography of Europe and the Mediterranean, consolidating much of the territory from North Africa to Ireland under centralized and organized governance. In a more modern attempt at empire, Adolph Hitler wrote in *Mein Kampf* about his vision of a 1,000-year Reich, in which Germany would create a territorial and political empire through military conquest and then govern much of the world. He came uncomfortably close to his vision.

After six centuries of rule, the Roman Empire fell apart. Germanic tribes threatened, captured, and assimilated Roman settlements in Western Europe, and the centralized political and territorial control fragmented into localized fiefdoms. Charlemagne and his Franks tried to recreate political and territorial empire in Europe around 800, but his efforts were short-lived, as barbarians from the East overran his Frankish empire. By 1000, the political map of Europe reflected a large number of small, localized political entities. Feudal relations between lord and peasant defined social order and authority in these agricultural economies, which remained isolated from other parts of the world in both economic and political terms.

Cross-Cutting Authority: Lords, Popes, and the Holy Roman Emperor

Around this time, the Roman Catholic Church was actively extending its spiritual influence and authority by assimilating Franks, Germanic tribes, barbarians, and others into Christianity. Soon, the reach of the Church began to overarch small and highly localized political entities, and its religious authority began to compete with the secular, nonreligious authority of the local feudal lords. The inhabitants of these feudal entities faced three major, crosscutting authority relationships, each placing separate demands on their resources.

First, a line of political authority existed between the local lord of a feudal domain and his subjects. In many cases, these small feudal fiefdoms were little more than isolated hand-

MAP 3.1   Europe in the Sixteenth Century

- Russian Empire 1500s
- Holy Roman Empire 1500s
- Ottoman Empire 1500s

NORWAY
SWEDEN
LITHUANIA
DENMARK
IRELAND
ENGLAND
POLAND
FRANCE
SPAIN

Russian Empire
Holy Roman Empire
Ottoman Empire
SYRIA
TRIPOLI
EGYPT

Source: Bruce Buena de Mesquita, *Principles of International Politics* (Washington, DC: CQ Press, 2003).

fuls of villages and farms, whose inhabitants—peasants and an emerging class of traders and merchants—owed their obedience to the local feudal lord. Under this hierarchical relationship, the local lord, their king, made demands on their labors and extracted his due in terms of their agricultural production, physical labor, and economic enterprise.

The religious and spiritual power of the pope created a second channel of authority, which also needed support from the lower orders. Local priests extracted resources from their local populations by making demands on local lords, passing collection plates, soliciting alms, tithing, and other forms of taxation, which took the form of labor, commodities, and money. The Church had a novel means to create incentives for donating such resources to its coffers. Whereas the local lords sent their tax collectors into the farms and villages to exact payment, often with the threat and application of force, the Church was able to appeal for donations by promising eternal salvation, threatening eternal damnation or excommunication, or offering some other religious perk or penalty. The local representatives of the Church (friars, abbots, priests, bishops, cardinals, and others) employed the influence of the local lord in their activities, but they also challenged and competed with such secular authority.

A third track of political authority placed the Holy Roman Emperor in a hierarchical relationship with the inhabitants of the lands where the Roman Catholic Church had extended its spiritual reach. The emperor was a secular political authority, already a king who governed a physical territory, but also the figure whom the Church had anointed as defender of the faith. This arrangement, which provided the Church with a means of projecting military force at a time of religious proselytizing and rapid expansion of Christianity, invested the Holy Roman Emperor with an odd mix of secular and nonsecular power and authority. Like the local feudal authorities, the emperor needed resources to govern his local lands, but he also required the means to engage in a wider range of activities at the behest of the Church. To pay for such activities, the Holy Roman Emperor needed to cast his revenue nets beyond his immediate lands, placing him in competition with the local kings for resources.

Amid these three channels of authority, no single one had a clear monopoly of political authority over any given territory. Political and religious authority was thus confounded and in competition over the same pool of scarce resources. This situation might not be problematic when all three channels agreed upon objectives and the means to obtain those objectives, but any disagreement could create a source of tension and a foundation for cleavage and conflict. Disagreements between the Church, the emperor, and local lords over objectives or demands on the resources of the local populations would inevitably put such overlapping authorities at odds in a world of scarcity, and there was no established hierarchy or other mechanism to peacefully resolve such conflicts.

Transformation of Social and Economic Organization

Economic and social activity in Europe was undergoing significant transformation at the same time these three channels of political and religious authority were evolving. The destruction of the Roman Empire by tribes from the East had left a vacuum of large-scale political authority in Europe. Social and economic activity fragmented without the centralized adjudication mechanisms of the Roman governors and the enforcement power of the Roman legions. Brigands and thieves plagued the countryside, inhibiting wide-scale economic and social activity and forcing people to band together in search of protection and shelter from the violence. Eventually, local lords emerged as a means of protection against such threats, but the military forces of these lords were little more than gangs of thugs in the employ of an individual whose power was based on being more successful in the exercise of violence than the leaders of competing gangs. The inhabitants of these communities, ruled by their thuggish leaders, exchanged the fruits of their labors for security, sometimes willingly but often under the threat of force.

As local lords consolidated their authority and provided protection for the societies within their domains, towns started to grow into centers of economic activity, trade, and new forms of social and economic organization. The new forms of economic activity led to the creation of wealth, the development of commercial classes, and eventually the introduction of money systems to replace barter. The economic tentacles of these emerging urban centers reached farther and farther into the countryside as farmers brought their goods to market, but such tentacles were vulnerable and required protection. The expansion of commercial areas and the growth of trade between such areas required security and order to protect merchants, provide contracting mechanisms, adjudicate complaints, and enforce the rulings of the adjudicators. These activities, in turn, required resources such as men, weapons, and money.

Who had such resources? The towns and their commercial areas were becoming locations of surplus resource accumulation, or wealth. In search of security, the emerging commercial classes there were willing to form coalitions with political entrepreneurs, the local feudal lords, who obtained resources from them in exchange for providing protection for their commercial activity. The commercial classes gained security and order, which nurtured continued commercial expansion; the lords gained greater and greater tools of coercion. Such protection arrangements enabled communities to reach farther and farther into the countryside, and exchange increased between communities.

Consolidation of Territory and Authority

The expansion of exchange between communities brought local lords into contact with other local lords. Sometimes these contacts led to competition and conflict over the authority to adjudicate exchange and enforce laws, the distribution of wealth, and the access to resources to pay for the military protections of territory and exchange. The more entrepreneurial lords used the economic surplus from their emerging commercial classes to challenge their competitors. They acquired more advanced weaponry and larger militaries, which enabled them to overcome the resistance of other nobles and to consolidate and expand their territorial influence. As they became rulers of larger and larger territorial spaces, they needed more and more resources to administer that territory, which meant more bureaucracy and larger armies to administer and collect taxes. This expanding spiral— territorial expansion by local nobles, elimination of political rivals within that territory, centralization of the mechanisms of coercion (military), and development of bureaucracy to administer those areas (cumulating taxes and resources)—characterized the formative years of state-building in Europe. Successful thugs became lords, successful lords became kings, successful kings challenged the authority of other kings, and eventually some would challenge the authority of the Holy Roman Emperor and even the pope.

The Instability of Cross-Cutting Lines of Authority

The cross-cutting lines of political and religious authority between the local lords, the pope, and the Holy Roman Emperor eventually proved unstable. Tensions emerged as these authorities competed for resources and allegiances. In 1517 Martin Luther challenged the spiritual authority of the pope by nailing his demands for reform to the door of his church. Seeking peaceful reform and change, Luther's hammer blows instead mobilized the tensions between the cross-cutting lines of authority and unleashed destructive religious wars.

In conflict with the Church, many German princes supported Luther's proposed reforms and tried to impose them within their territories. Whether these renegade princes sincerely supported Luther's ideas or merely saw in them a strategic opportunity to consolidate their authority, their actions nevertheless challenged the religious authority of the Church and caused a split in its ranks. Support for Lutheranism spread throughout central Europe, but not all principalities and kingdoms adopted the reforms; many remained loyal to the Church. This schism produced conflicts between principalities over the issue of religion, between the agents of the pope and those principalities turning away from the dictates of Roman Catholicism, and between the Holy Roman Emperor (as defender of the faith) and those rebellious principalities.

The sixteenth and early seventeenth centuries were dominated by violent wars motivated by this challenge to the power of the Church in Rome to impose its religious authority upon territories governed by local political rulers. These conflicts culminated in the Thirty Years' War, in relative terms among the deadliest wars in European history: one in four males of Germanic heritage died in this conflict over religious and secular dominion. The peace agreement that ended the war established the state as the dominant form of political authority and organization, which continues to this day.

THE TREATY OF WESTPHALIA AND SOVEREIGNTY

The Thirty Years' War ended with the signing of the Treaty of Westphalia in 1648, which redrew the lines of political and religious authority in Europe (see map 3.2). The treaty resolved the debate over who had the authority to determine the religion of a territory—the most important political question of the time—and formally ended the problem of the cross-cutting authorities and multiple loyalties that had characterized Europe before the onset of the religious wars. The Treaty of Westphalia established the principle that the king, or sovereign, of a territory had the sole legitimate authority to determine the religion of the inhabitants of his territory. This principle severely curtailed the authority of the pope and the Holy Roman Emperor, who thus became secondary to kings.

MAP 3.2	Europe in 1648

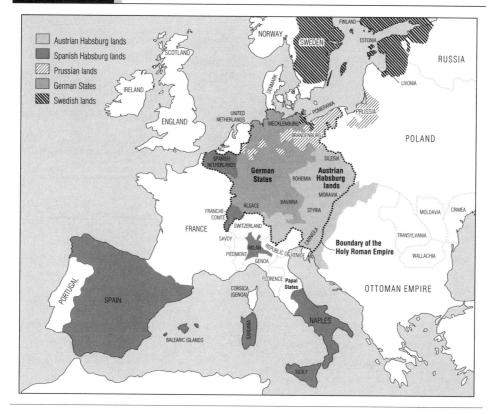

Source: Bruce Buena de Mesquita, *Principles of International Politics* (Washington, DC: CQ Press, 2003). Used by permission.

The Treaty of Westphalia established territoriality as the dominant basis for Europe's political map. Geographical area became the most important criterion for organizing political space under a single dominant authority. A territory and the people living within that territory belonged to the king or sovereign. The Church and the pope could still wield some influence over these inhabitants, particularly in spiritual affairs, but under the Treaty of Westphalia, the authority of the religious establishment was subordinated to that of the crown.

This change in the organization of political authority—the creation of a dominant secular authority attached to a specific geography—gave birth to the modern state system and introduced the principle of each state's sovereignty within its territorial borders. We call this arrangement the **Westphalian state system** in recognition of its origins. **Sovereignty** is the principle that the government of a state, and by definition a territory, is the supreme legitimate authority within its territorial boundaries. This concept has become one of the most common and important organizing principles in modern international relations and law. In theory, it means that no state can exercise legitimate authority within another state's boundaries, which implies that each state is independent in the management of its domestic affairs, that the state's political authority within its geographic boundaries is sacrosanct.

The Principle and the Practice of Sovereignty

In principle, sovereignty supplies a nice, clean organizing principle for international affairs—you stay out of my domestic affairs and I will stay out of yours—but the empirical world is rarely so clean and well-behaved. In practice, sovereignty is frequently infringed upon. At best, sovereignty is a creative and convenient fiction that policymakers embellish when they find it useful and try to ignore when they find it a hindrance. It is a concept that is much more pliant and more often contested than conceded in the abstract discussions of international law. The processes of globalization create particular challenges to the principle of sovereignty, for they bring one state's population into contact with the inhabitants of other states. The gains from international exchange occur because the productive energies of different states are pooled into larger and larger production structures and markets, which encourage specialization across national boundaries. But these globalizing processes also produce costs for societies and can challenge the authority of states, most often inadvertently, when the actions of a government are limited by activities that originate beyond the borders of the state.

To make matters more confusing, governments sign treaties that commit them to follow defined practices and particular behavior. Such restrictions can constrain the latitude of governments to enact the policies they prefer, thus limiting their policy autonomy. For example, a government may commit by international agreement to control the fishing catch of its nationals, to constrain the production of specific pollutants by industries within its territorial boundaries, or to institute specific civil and human liberties to protect their citizens. Do such external agreements, which limit the autonomy of governments within their territorial borders, constitute infringements upon sovereignty?

We resort to two possible explanations to counter this apparent breach of the principle of sovereignty. First, we can declare that some basic principles of human rights trump the principle of sovereignty—that some rights are inalienable and cannot be infringed by sovereign governments. By making this statement, we are accepting the premise that when principles conflict, some principles are more important than others. Yet, if this reasoning applies, it can only apply to a limited number of principles. Moreover, this is not a very satisfying rationale, given the origins of the principle of sovereignty, which emerged originally as a means of subordinating individual religious choice to the state. It is difficult to argue that basic human rights and individual dignities outrank sovereignty on the hierarchy of principles when the concept of sovereignty itself originally empowered the state to manage individual religious choice, which many would claim as a basic human right.

Second, we can argue that governments' decisions to negotiate international agreements or to open their borders to exchange are voluntary choices. In such cases, governments have not lost their sovereignty but have voluntarily ceded their policy autonomy as a sovereign choice. They have assigned or delegated their sovereign responsibilities to others, in an act of self-restraint. In practice, national governments in the global arena, absent a central authority, are regularly engaged in negotiating their sovereign authority. As the political scientist Stephen Krasner noted, in such a system, sovereignty has always been up for grabs. The ongoing tensions between policy autonomy and international interaction, between sovereignty and interdependence, are an inevitable part of the modern nation-state system.

Common Violations of the Principle of Sovereignty

Given the difference between sovereignty in principle and in practice, what does it mean when a government violates the concept of sovereignty by exercising influence in another state's domestic affairs? An infringement upon sovereignty is technically a hostile act, but in practice the meaning of the intrusion depends upon the seriousness of the violation and its consequences. War is the most extreme form of infringement, but much less violent challenges to sovereignty occur regularly. Americans would respond unfavorably to another government's purchasing advertisements supporting one candidate or another in an American election, yet another government's trade or labor policies may help one U.S. political party build support within a specific constituency. Many governments of Arab nations argue that American politicians support Israel because of the influence of the American Jewish lobby, which they claim is manipulated by the Israeli government. Whether this charge is true or not, it is made in order to raise the ire of Americans against Israel by suggesting that U.S. foreign policy (a sovereign choice) is being manipulated by the Israeli government. Ironically, the Arab governments use this strategy in an attempt to influence political debate within the United States—which is technically an infringement upon sovereignty that is very similar to the behavior that they attribute to the Israeli government.

The Federal Open Market Committee (FOMC) of the Federal Reserve, a key policymaking committee of the U.S. central bank, regularly meets to discuss and adopt policies that will affect the supply and cost of money in United States, with the goal of managing the country's macroeconomic conditions. However, due to the central position of the U.S. economy in the global economy, the choices of the FOMC, a part of a U.S. government agency, will also affect economic conditions in many other nations. FOMC choices will influence the cost and supply of capital in the United States, but also in other states. Shifting the cost and supply of capital in the United States will influence the investment and consumption of industries and inhabitants within the United States, which will have the added effect of slowing or accelerating global economic activity. The fact that policy choices by a U.S. government agency can have a large impact on economic activity in other nations could be considered, technically, an infringement upon the principle of sovereignty. But to avoid such infringement upon the sovereignty of others, the Federal Reserve would have to refrain from taking actions that are in the interest of the U.S. economy, which would be an infringement upon the sovereignty of the United States.

These examples highlight the tension between a key organizing principle of modern international relations—policy autonomy, or sovereignty—and the connections across national borders that produce the increasing interdependence that is a characteristic of modern global affairs. The concept of sovereignty underpins the modern state system, but it is a concept that competes and conflicts with other core characteristics of globalization in a state system. Focusing on the concept of sovereignty helps us to understand sources of tension and conflict in the system, as it highlights the different bases for political and economic organization in global relations.

ANARCHY: CONFLICT, COMPETITION, AND COOPERATION

The combination of scarcity, the position of the state as the dominant form of political organization in an international system that lacks a central authority, and the principle of sovereignty creates a global social context that resembles Thomas Hobbes's description of the state of nature, wherein life is "solitary, poor, nasty, brutish, and short." We call this condition a state of **anarchy.** What does anarchy mean, and what is its relevance to how political activity that occurs *between* nation-states differs from the political activity that occurs *within* nation-states, in their domestic arenas? Since the Treaty of Westphalia, the government of a state has been the dominant authority within its domestic arena. There is a hierarchy of legitimate authority within a state: all other authorities are subordinate to the authority of the state. The existence of this hierarchy means that a dominant central authority exists within a state to govern, to help structure social relations, to mediate and adjudicate disputes, to extract and allocate scarce resources, and to enforce laws.

International relations, those interactions in the global arena between states, are characterized by the absence of such a central authority. With the Treaty of Westphalia and the establishment of the dominance of sovereign authority, all states are, in principle, equal in their authority over their domestic arenas. There is no central authority or formal hierarchy in the global arena to perform the functions that the government of a state performs in the domestic arena. No dominant central authority in international relations looms over other authorities to resolve disagreements and disputes between lesser authorities. By definition, any such external authority would impinge upon each state's sovereignty.

We do have bodies of international law and principle, but they are formed by cooperative agreements—international treaties—that are negotiated by sovereign state governments. Technically, these laws are not binding upon states that are not signatories to the international agreements creating them. Moreover, they do not appear to be binding even upon a signatory of the agreement if its government decides to ignore or reject its obligation. In the absence of a central authority to enforce such obligations, reneging on them does not often bear the same costs as violating domestic laws in domestic political arenas. A government that reneges upon its international agreements rarely faces the threat of incarceration; it may be ostracized in the court of public opinion, treated as a pariah by other governments, and sanctioned through a variety of other measures, but these are penalties applied by competing authorities in the international arena. International law does not carry the same weight as domestic law, for its application relies upon the self-constraint of sovereign governments and the willingness of sovereign governments to impose penalties upon other sovereign governments.

Absent a recognized central authority with the legitimacy to coerce and cajole, the activities of functionally equal states often do conflict. Sovereign governments may have conflicting agendas, especially given the assumption of scarce resources. If a sovereign government implements policies that affect others—especially if it does so in a negative way—then it likely violates the sovereignty of those other states. But within the state system of social relations, the lack of an overarching central authority to resolve such disagreements creates a social context that is open to competition and cooperation, dispute and disagreement, negotiation and compromise, and sometimes, violent conflict.

Self-Help Dispute Resolution under Anarchy

How do such disputes between sovereign governments get resolved? Governments must rely on their own capabilities and tools to obtain their preferred ends—a **self-help system** that returns us to Hobbes's notion of the state of nature. Creatures in a state of nature, without an external restraint mechanism to resolve disputes, depend on their own means of survival, not relying on the goodwill of others or on a collection of principles that others might willingly violate. Instead, they develop tools and strategies to increase their chances to survive and prosper. Not all succeed.

Do the demands of self-help in a state of anarchy preclude cooperation and compromise, mandating violence since only the strong will survive? On the contrary, turning to cooperation and compromise, while reserving conflict as a last resort, provides a strategy that has proven successful in such an environment—a victory of brains over brawn, of coalition-building over individual self-reliance. Centuries ago, the banding together of individuals and families into small pastoral communities eventually succeeded in defeating the raids of marauding hunter-gathers. How do we know this? A look at the more successful societies in the world today reveals the heirs of the cooperative pastoral society strategy and no exemplars of the marauding strategy. We can find some descendants of the barbarian marauders among less successful political economies, but not among the advanced industrialized political economies. Strategies of cooperative social behavior appear to have been more conducive to surviving and prospering, than were strategies of noncooperation and conflict.

The state of anarchy helps to account for the fact that states are functionally similar and do not take advantage of specialization of function. Governments are not willing to contract their survival, or their peoples' well-being, to other governments in a world that lacks a dominant central authority to enforce such obligations. Policymakers are willing to sign treaties limiting or outlawing human rights abuses, categories of weapons, slavery, and economic and environmental policies that may impose undue hardships across national borders, but they refrain from placing blind faith in the self-restraint and good intentions of the other signatories when there is no central authority to ensure their compliance. As a measure of insurance against the anarchic state of social relations in the state system, governments insist upon developing their own tools and devices in the attempt to get others in the international arena to behave in accordance with their interests.

Realism

This reliance of governments on their own means, rather than on international treaties and law, is called **realpolitik,** or **realism.** This is a self-help strategy for constructing public policies to address a world of *what is,* not a world of *what ought to be.* Realists make no assumptions about the beneficence of others or about the reliability of international legal obligations in the context of global anarchy. Realists assume that governments will respond to such a context in a world of scarcity by seeking to survive, perhaps at the expense of others and regardless of any normative notions of morality and humanity. This may seem like a pessimistic view of human behavior, but it is a conservative, risk-adverse strategy. Realism does not preclude cooperation, prosperous coexistence, and normatively desirable outcomes. Instead, it argues that obtaining such outcomes requires that governments recognize the proclivities of others and act to constrain activities that can undermine such outcomes. For realists, the ends justify the means.

Realism is a strategy for dealing with the state of anarchy in international affairs. The term *anarchy* may describe a world of disorder within a brutal state of nature, a dog-eat-dog world where conflict and disorder are ever-present, or it may describe a world of order and stability, an arena characterized by cooperation and agreement. The framework of realism suggests that the differential abilities of states can actually produce a hierarchy among states, generating a structure within the state of anarchy. The strategic mechanisms of realism may thus provide a means by which order can exist in such a structure, allowing states to engage in cooperative and peaceful exchange, resolution of disputes without violence, and compromise.

CONCLUSION

The context of international relations differs from that of domestic politics. This fact is an independent variable that we must consider when trying to account for behavior in global affairs, but it is not the only variable, as we shall quickly see. In the modern nation-state system, each government is the supreme legitimate source of authority and coercion within the state's boundaries, but the international arena lacks such a legitimate central authority to prescribe formal rules and laws and to adjudicate and enforce them. Consequently, international affairs have been described as a state of nature or anarchy, wherein behavior is guided by the law of the jungle and the survival of the fittest. Governments must rely upon their own capabilities to advance their objectives, and the development of a collective identity, or nation, can assist them in their quest. This context of anarchy does mean that conflict is constant or that cooperation and peaceful resolution of disputes are unlikely. Instead, from purely a contextual perspective, order can emerge in such an anarchical system from the distribution of capabilities across states and the existence of a hierarchy based upon that distribution. The next chapter explores the concepts of power and hierarchy that can create order in the anarchical context of international affairs.

EXERCISES

1. Describe the main characteristics of a state.

2. The United States and South Africa are two very different countries, but they are functionally equal. Explain how these two countries can be functionally equal and yet so different at the same time.

3. What is common knowledge, and how does it contribute to the concept of nation?

4. What is a nation, and how does it differ from a state?

5. Can a nation exist without a state, or vice versa? Give an example of a state that does not function as a nation as well.

6. What are some of the forces that build common knowledge and help to integrate people into a nation?

7. As students of international relations in general and international political economy specifically, why do we care whether states become nation-states?

8. Before the Thirty Years' War, most Europeans lived in settings where they faced three cross-cutting lines of authority. What were the different authorities, what problems resulted from this cross-cutting of authority, and why?

9. The United States enacts domestic tax and labor policies, but these policies can affect economic activities in Japan. How does this create a problem for the concept of sovereignty?

10. How does the structure of political activity in international politics differ from that in domestic politics? What are the implications of this difference?

11. Hobbes wrote that in a state of nature, life is "solitary, poor, nasty, brutish, and short." Does this apply to international relations? If so, how and why?

12. Many factors can contribute to the formation of a nation, but many of them are not necessary or sufficient contributions. Name some of the factors that can be helpful but are not necessary or sufficient. What is the one quality that does seem to be necessary and sufficient for the development of a nation? Now, thinking about these different factors, what does "necessary and sufficient" mean?

13. Explain the tension between sovereignty and interdependence.

FURTHER READING

Alter, Peter. 1985. *Nationalism.* London: Edward Arnold.

Brubaker, Rogers. 1996. *Nationalism Reframed: Nationhood and the National Question in the New Europe.* Cambridge: Cambridge University Press.

Carr, E. H. 1946. *The Twenty Years' Crisis, 1919–1939.* 2nd. ed. London: Macmillan.

Oye, Kenneth, ed. 1986. *Cooperation under Anarchy.* Princeton, N.J.: Princeton University Press.

Snyder, Jack. 2000. *From Voting to Violence: Democratization and Nationalist Conflict.* New York: Norton.

Waltz, Kenneth. 1959. *Man, the State, and War.* New York: Columbia University Press.

———. 1979. *Theory of International Politics.* New York: Random House.

4 Power and Hierarchy in the International System

International politics, like all politics, is a struggle for power.

Hans J. Morganthau

LOOKING FOR ORDER AND PREDICTABILITY

Describing the international arena as a state of anarchy or a state of nature does not mean that it necessarily lacks order and predictability. Relations between governments can be quite predictable. Implicitly, we know in advance that Ecuador will not resort to military force to resolve a fishing dispute with the United States. Implicitly, we recognize that the preferences of the U.S. government are likely to condition international environmental negotiations more than the policy preferences of the government of Ghana. Implicitly, we assume that European Union (EU) preferences on agricultural policies will have greater influence over the patterns of global agricultural production and trade than the preferences of Kenya. Such predictability suggests that some systematic mechanism, or mechanisms, exist to provide order and stability in international relations. Can we make the mechanisms that generate such order more explicit?

Hierarchies can help create order in social relations and allow some predictability about such relations. Order and predictability are important, for they allow people to plan ahead and to select appropriate strategies given some reliable assumptions about how others will behave. The simplest, and perhaps the most useful, device for examining international relations is a hierarchy based upon differences in the abilities of state and nonstate actors to influence outcomes—what political scientists call differences in *power*. Such a hierarchy differs from the power structure within a domestic political arena, where the dominant authority of the central government is embedded in a legal system and overshadows other forms of authority that may exist in society. Power underpins domestic governance, but it is cloaked within legal frameworks.

POWER DEFINED AS A RELATIVE CONCEPT

Power is an abstract concept that is difficult to precisely define, observe, measure, and quantify. Yet, it is the currency of politics. As many economists focus upon differences and changes in wealth to examine the economic sphere, many political scientists look to differences and changes in power as a key to understanding political behavior and outcomes. In their quest to examine this critical concept, however, political scientists give it a variety of meanings. Power has been defined as a set of attributes or capabilities; the processes of influence; the ability to control resources; the capacity to influence the behavior of others and events; and the ability to manipulate the structure of social interactions. For our purposes, **power** refers to the tools, the means, to achieve one's own ends. Power is the ability to prevail and overcome obstacles, to achieve a desired outcome by influencing the environments and choices of other decision makers.

Power is a relative phenomenon in social affairs. Having more or less power takes on meaning and relevance within the context of social interactions. Evaluation of a political actor's power becomes useful as a method of political analysis in comparison with the power of others and in assessment of its effect upon the behavior of others. Power is an aspect of every relationship, adversarial or friendly, although it is generally more apparent in adversarial than in friendly relations. If both sides to a political interaction agree on an outcome, the application of power may not be obvious; its role becomes more apparent if the parties disagree. Yet, power is at play in both cases.

As power involves a relationship between parties, we should recognize that each party in a relationship has some power over the other. Influence is not unidirectional, flowing from one party to another. Instead, the application of power involves a flow of influence in both directions. My exercise of influence over you, in order to affect how you behave, also means that you exercise influence over me, for you have affected how I behave. This relative power exchange assumes that without the exercise of influence, you and I would both have behaved differently than we have done. So, even when the very strong attempt to exercise influence over the very weak, to change their behavior, the very weak have exerted some influence over the very strong. This reciprocal effect often gets neglected when we try to analyze politics by using differences in power capabilities to think about political behavior, but it becomes more apparent when we consider the idea of costs.

The exercise of power can produce great benefits to those who prevail, but such benefits are rarely, if ever, cost-free. The use of power imposes costs, even upon the winner. For example, to alter another state's behavior through military means imposes human and economic costs upon a state even if it wins the conflict: people die and their talents are lost to the future;

FIGURE 4.1	The Spectrum of Policymakers' Tools for the Exercise of Power

the direction of economic resources and human energy into military preparations means that those resources are not being applied to other endeavors. These are costs. To influence another government's behavior by means of economic sanction and political pressure diverts resources from other activities, and it may deny the benefits of economic interaction to the state applying the sanctions. These are costs. To influence another state's policies through foreign aid and other forms of assistance requires a government to tax its own people to garner the necessary resources, which might have been used otherwise. Again, these are costs. Such costs are important to consider when we analyze political behavior. Politicians consider the expected benefits of exercising power, but they must also weigh the expected costs in light of the likely outcome or benefit. Sometimes what appears to be the best outcome in terms of benefits turns out to be a poor choice, given the costs of obtaining that outcome.

THE TOOLS OF STATECRAFT AND DIPLOMACY

Our discussion of power becomes more concrete if we consider the various kinds of pressure that governments, politicians, and policymakers employ as they seek to influence the behavior of others. In both domestic and international arenas, public or private policymakers can resort to a range of strategies to affect the incentives and calculations of the target actors by shaping their perceptions of the costs and benefits of different courses of action. In international affairs, we think of these options as the tools of statecraft and diplomacy, which can be sorted into a set of categories that range along a spectrum of influence (see figure 4.1) from the most passive (persuasion) to the most violent (force).

Persuasion

Persuasion, the most passive of the tools of statecraft, encompasses the art of discussion, the skillful use of language and logic, argument and debate, entreaty and cajoling, education, and diplomatic negotiation. It is the art of convincing others to see things your way by demonstrating the soundness of your logic and leading them to see your preferred policy as consistent with their best interests. A vast amount of activity in the global arena falls into this category of power relations. Governments routinely exchange diplomatic missions and send messages with the primary intent of persuading other governments to adopt a particular policy or approach. They manipulate the public release of information through the media and other channels in an attempt to change the thinking of others and to alter their behavior. Governments also use these tools of persuasion to influence the activities of nonstate actors such as businesses, charities, foundations, aid groups, and other nongovernmental organizations.

Offer of Rewards

The next category on the spectrum of power and influence involves the offer of rewards. As governments and other actors in global affairs seek to manipulate the behavior of others, they may dangle the temptation of positive benefits if the targets of influence will change their behavior accordingly. These promises may include such rewards as the potential for future lucrative contracts and investment, favorable preferences in future trade negotiations, an increased potential for foreign aid and assistance, a promise of assistance in future interactions with other parties, or even the promise, stated or implied, not to obstruct a choice of action in the future. Some such promises may be viewed as extortion or bribery. For example, during the run-up to the 2003 Iraq war, the U.S. government offered substantial resources to the Turkish government in an attempt to convince it to allow U.S. military forces to use bases in Turkey as staging areas for the planned invasion. This attempt at manipulation proved unsuccessful, but it demonstrates the practical efficacy of the offer of rewards. In another example, developing states often seek election to the rotating openings on the UN Security Council, as governments holding such seats can offer to vote with the United States in exchange for foreign assistance.

Granting of Rewards

The promise or offer of rewards in the future is not the same as the actual delivery of rewards today, which is generally more costly than making a promise. Granting a reward in exchange for a change in behavior, or a particular choice of action, is a common tool of influence. For example, the more advanced economies in the European Union (EU) made substantial capital transfers to less advanced EU economies in order to obtain their cooperation in concluding the Maastricht Treaty, a core agreement in the formation of the EU. The U.S. government supplied significant foreign aid assistance to Israel and Egypt as part of the deal to get those governments to agree to the peace agreement known as the Camp David Accords. The Marshall Plan committed vast resources to the reconstruction of Western European states after World War II in exchange for those Western European governments' cooperation in containing the Soviet Union. Persuasion, the promise of rewards, and the delivery of rewards are the sweet and tempting carrots of the carrot-and-stick metaphor.

Threat of Punishment

The alternative to the carrot as a tool of influence is the harsh and threatening stick, which is represented not by a single category or strategy but by a variety of strategies that continue along the spectrum of influence. Threat of punishment follows the provision of rewards on this spectrum. Much as the promise or offer of reward is not actually the provision of a reward, the threat of punishment is not actually the application of punishment. Threats to impose economic sanctions, to increase tariffs or other barriers to entry to a state's markets, to abrogate treaties of cooperation, to scale back foreign assistance, to withdraw from agreements, or to isolate a state diplomatically constitute potential consequences in the future if the targets of such threats should fail to adjust their behavior. The threat of punishment may be direct and explicit or subtle and implied, but in either case, the target of such a threat is faced with the problem of trying to estimate its credibility, as the possible implementation of the threat lies in the future. If the target of a threat or promised reward estimates that there is no prospect of its being implemented, then it is not credible. Empty promises of threat or reward constitute **cheap talk,** which can be quite damaging to the parties making the empty promises if it undermines the credibility of future threats or promises that may be sincere. In that case, a target may choose to ignore very real threats or promises, resulting in high costs both to the party trying to exercise influence and to the target of that intended influence.

For example, in 2001 the United States imposed steel tariffs on foreign producers to protect its domestic steel industry. After obtaining a positive ruling from the World Trade Organization (WTO), other governments threatened to impose retaliatory tariffs against a variety of U.S. products if the U.S. tariffs were not reversed before a set deadline. U.S. policymakers viewed the threat of retaliatory tariffs as credible, and so, faced with the threat of punishment, they reversed course on the protective steel tariffs before the deadline. A contrary situation developed when U.S. policymakers announced a policy of deterrence and containment against the Soviet Union and its allies in the late 1940s. Although they asserted that the umbrella of deterrence included South Korea, the Soviets and their allies calculated that the United States would not defend South Korea—that the U.S. threat was empty. History tells us that the Soviet interpretation of the U.S. threat as cheap talk proved extremely costly to both sides.

Nonviolent Punishment

Proceeding along the spectrum of influence, the next category that involves the use of the stick is the implementation of nonviolent punishment. This strategy moves beyond the threat of punishment to the actual application of penalties, such as those mentioned earlier as threats. The application of forms of punishment short of the use of military force can still be harmful and disruptive if it imposes hardships upon members of the target government or its society. Recall of an ambassador, closing of a diplomatic consulate or embassy, withdrawal of diplomatic recognition, a negative vote in an international body such as the UN Security Council or the WTO, imposition of economic sanctions, economic boycott, withdrawal from a cooperative economic or political-military agreement, termination of foreign assistance, cancellation of preferential trade arrangements, and public castigation are examples of strategies of nonviolent punishment that are meant to convince another party to alter its behavior or to punish a party for its activities in the hope of ending or discouraging those activities in the future.

For example, the policy of containment of the Soviet Union, begun under President Truman in the late 1940s, formed the backbone of U.S. foreign policy until the collapse of the Eastern Bloc governments in 1989–1991. One component of containment imposed export controls on what could and could not be exported from the United States and its allies to the Soviet Union and its allies. The objective of such controls was to deny the Soviets specific gains from trade with the United States and its allies; they also denied the gains of such trade to the United States and its allies. Containment was intended to degrade Soviet capabilities over time and to impose hardships on Soviet policymakers and their constituents. The designers of containment hoped that imposing hardships upon the average Soviet consumer would eventually create dissension in the Soviet economy. In retrospect, the policy seems to have worked, as frustration within the political economies of the Eastern Bloc boiled over in the late 1980s.

How did containment impose nonviolent punishment? Withholding trade access and limiting the export of particular commodities to the Soviet Union forced the Soviets and its allies to alter their production structures. The Soviets' inability to take advantage of participation in the larger global economy and the resulting specialization it would create in the Soviet production structure generated inefficiencies in the economies of the Soviet Union and its allies, which led to shortages of consumer goods. In another example of nonviolent punishment, President Jimmy Carter instituted a boycott of the Olympic Games that were held in Moscow and imposed new trade sanctions on the Soviets after they invaded Afghanistan in 1979. These sanctions were not meant to reverse Soviet policies in Afghanistan, but to impose penalties upon the Soviets for such policies and to affect their future calculations about military adventurism and expansionism.

Force

The final category on the spectrum of influence involves the use of military force, which holds the potential for the most violent application of power. Not all uses of military force actually turn violent, however. Sometimes the use of force is only threatened or implied; its application depends upon the response of the target of influence. Military blockades (such as the naval quarantine of Cuba during the Missile Crisis of October 1962), port calls by warships in trouble spots (showing the flag), flyovers by warplanes, moving troops into situations that would be in harm's way if hostilities were to break out (such as the basing of American troops in Germany during the cold war and along the demilitarized zone in Korea), and the extension of military assistance to another country in the form of military advisers to help train local troops (such as those the United States sent to Vietnam before 1965 and to the Philippines following September 11, 2001)—all are examples of the use of military force in the hope of influencing outcomes without resorting to violence.

Sometimes the implied use of force fails to convince another actor's policymakers to alter their activities. Then the original policymakers must confront the choice of whether or not to actually initiate violence. The violent use of force in a situation where it has been previously threatened or implied is not straightforward. In economic terms, projecting military force abroad is expensive enough, but putting a state's youth in harm's way is also politically and socially costly, as it disrupts families and communities. These potential costs mean that policymakers will hesitate to turn to such measures unless they believe the situation warrants. Policymakers must weigh the differences in costs between threatened and actual use of violence (following through on the threat); the costs of not using force once it has been threatened (the costs of crying wolf); how important the preferred outcome is, and how likely that outcome is to be attained through the use of force.

As an example, consider the meeting of Germany's Adolf Hitler and British Prime Minister Neville Chamberlain at Munich in 1939. English and French policymakers calculated that by appeasing Hitler at Munich they could forestall a major European conflict, even after they had threatened the use of their military forces to challenge Hitler's territorial grab. Critics of the Munich settlement assert that the British and French accommodation emboldened Hitler by undermining the credibility of their threats to use violence, and, hence, increased the likelihood of the very conflict they were trying to avoid. Now labeled the Munich Appeasement, this abortive settlement has become one of the most potent analogies in diplomatic history, being cited repeatedly to discredit accommodation as a policy choice. Raising the specter of Chamberlain at Munich can end, or at least seriously influence, policy debates over whether to use military force, as it raises the fear of very costly consequences for failing to act (that is, better today than tomorrow).

Obviously, physical force has been used throughout history as an important tool of influence and statecraft. Battlefields testify to its use; families of a war's casualties serve as visible reminders of its costs; academics engage in grand research projects designed to better understand war; historians, political scientists, anthropologists, sociologists, and psychologists publish reams upon reams of research into the use of armed conflict as a tool of influence; and protestors routinely demonstrate against the use of military power as a tool of statecraft. Despite the horror of militarized conflict and most policymakers' desire to avoid it, states and statesmen keep returning to the use of force as a viable tool for exercising power. This situation is probably inevitable, given the social context of a self-help state system, which lacks a legitimate central authority to resolve and adjudicate disputes. Nevertheless, we should recognize that military force is only one tool of influence, and one that is used infrequently relative to the others. A focus upon military conflict alone provides an incomplete examination of the uses of influence and power, neglecting other forms that are more characteristic of day-to-day interactions in the international political economy.

COST CALCULATIONS AND THE TOOLS OF STATECRAFT

Policymakers use the tools of statecraft and diplomacy to create incentives to act one way instead of another by affecting calculations of expected costs and benefits. If persuasion, the promise or imposition of rewards, or the threat or imposition of punishment are to alter the cost-benefit assessments of a target of influence in the global political economy, these strategies of influence must motivate that target's policymakers to compare their proposed course of action against alternative choices. As policymakers seek to affect the behavior of others, they must evaluate what tools might influence the calculations of others, as well as what is the probability of successfully exercising influence with each tool, and at what cost. Remember, the use of power imposes costs upon the loser and also upon the winner. Trying to alter another policymaker's choice requires the use of resources that might have been used for another activity. It is critical to consider such costs, as doing so gives us a powerful tool for analyzing political behavior. When we assume that policymakers consider the benefits and the costs of different applications of power (the likely outcomes and their rewards or penalties), we can weigh the expected benefits of each strategy against its expected costs and try to understand why a policymaker selects a particular strategy. We can use backwards induction to infer how policymakers may have perceived costs and benefits as they weighed their choices.

Generally, the tools of influence impose increasing costs and conflict as we move along the spectrum of influence from persuasion through force (see figure 4.2). These costs can affect prospects for the political survival of policymakers as well as for the well-being of their larger societies. We can reasonably assume that policymakers will try to limit their individual costs and their societies' costs given their policy objectives. They will attempt to select the best form of influence in terms of the cost, efficiency, and efficacy in obtaining a desired outcome. They will seek to avoid overkill, for using a more costly tool of statecraft when a less costly strategy would succeed proves inefficient, undermines the expected gains from a change in behavior by the target of influence, and affects the credibility of their own efforts. For instance, the United States at the turn of the twenty-first century is capable of exercising overwhelming power in terms of military capabilities, but these resources are inappropriate tools for exercising influence in many situations. The 1991 Gulf War and the 2003 Iraq invasion clearly demonstrated the effectiveness of U.S. military power in defeating conventional military forces, but in most situations the use of such military force would be too inefficient and too costly. Governments rarely resort to force as a first option.

FINDING ORDER IN ANARCHY: CAPABILITIES AND ATTRIBUTES

Although the modern international system has been described as a state of anarchy, order can arise in this system based upon differences in power capabilities and the attributes that con-

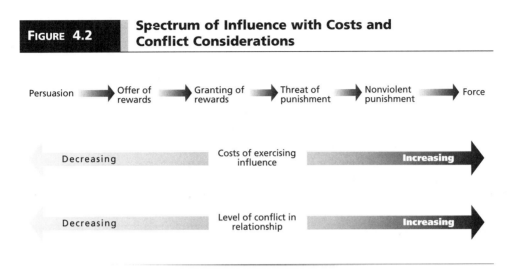

FIGURE 4.2   **Spectrum of Influence with Costs and Conflict Considerations**

tribute to those capabilities. Such a **power hierarchy** reflects the varying capabilities of different states and their policymakers to employ the tools and strategies of influence. Policymakers from different states may not have the same range of options when placed in similar circumstances, even though their states are functionally equal. The U.S. president has a wider range of options than does the president of Mexico when his state is confronted by a national security threat that arises halfway around the world. A German government's offer of preferential trade arrangements is likely to carry more influence than the same offer by the government of Ghana. A threat of economic boycott by the Japanese government will weigh more heavily than a threat of economic boycott by the Peruvian government. Policymakers in Mexico, Ghana, and Peru may want to exercise the same influence over outcomes as the policymakers of the United States, Germany, and Japan, but their ability to do so differs.

Motivation versus Capability

This difference in power, in the hierarchy of influence, highlights the difference between motivations and capabilities. It calls attention to the difference between the range of tools that policymakers can theoretically employ and their actual ability to use such tools. Policymakers from different states may have identical motivations in terms of advancing the welfare of their states and similar preferences over public policy and outcomes, but they have different capabilities for achieving their goals. Surely the leaders of Senegal, Azerbaijan, Poland, or other states would like to occupy the place held by the United States as the dominant state in terms of influencing the framework and practices of the global political economy. In this regard, they are similarly motivated and comparable to U.S. policymakers, but this is a comparison only of motivation and preferences, not of capability. Motivations and the spectrum of influence generalize across governments and policymakers, but the ability to select and implement strategies on this spectrum of influence is state- and case-specific.

Differences in capabilities across states constitute the key to a hierarchy of influence, for such differences can create order in a state of anarchy. So what underpins differences in capabilities of policymakers and governments? Where do we look if we are trying to understand why one state has prevailed over another, or who will prevail in a future test of power and will in the global arena? Policymakers do not simply select a tool of influence without considering the likelihood of its success and the costs of exercising influence. This twofold assessment requires that they consider the ability of the target to resist—which means that they must also try to evaluate the power capabilities of those they wish to influence and compare those capabilities with their own. So we need to move beyond the tools and strategies of influence to consider the capabilities that underpin the ability, or inability, of policymakers to use those tools and strategies.

Because power is a relative phenomenon in social affairs, the analysis of social behavior involving power requires evaluating differences in the power capabilities of those involved in a social and political interaction. Yet, power is much more difficult to quantify and to observe than is wealth or money, the currency of economics. As a shortcut to attain a rough indication of a state's relative power, therefore, political scientists often substitute observable measures of its attributes and capabilities—such as gross domestic product, degree of industrialization, exposure to international trade, age distribution of a state's population, or size of active-duty military personnel—for unobservable power. This substitution is reasonable, since policymakers draw upon a state's attributes and capabilities when they seek to exercise influence, and power should be positively associated with these same attributes. This logic simply means that if all else remains unchanged, increasing a key attribute will correspond to an increase in power and decreasing a key attribute will correspond to a decrease in power.

Tangible and Intangible Attributes

Given that many of a state's attributes are more observable and measurable than the phenomenon of power, let's consider some such features that can contribute to power. Both tangible assets and intangible resources contribute to a state's capabilities. What is the difference between these two components of a state's power potential? **Tangible attributes** are generally naturally occurring phenomena—resources that can be touched, observed, and sometimes counted, as well as employed and manipulated by people to advance their agendas. Minerals, petroleum, arable land, population, climate, forests, rivers, mountains, and other natural physical assets fall into this category. **Intangible attributes,** as the name suggests, are less concrete—they are created and transformed by people. Economic, political, and social organization make up this category. Tangible and intangible resources can contribute to power independently, but their *interaction* can create tremendous shifts in the power capabilities of a state. Many states have comparable levels of tangible resources but differ markedly in their ability to use them to influence the behavior of others. Tangible assets are important, but intangible resources are key to unleashing their potential to produce a significant transformation in a state's power potential.

Tangible Assets

What tangible assets affect a state's power potential? There are many physical features that can contribute to the power potential of a state, but let's focus on four broad categories: geography, climate, population, and natural resources. In general, large is better than small in terms of how these categories affect the power potential. A state's geography—size, topography, and location—can affect its ability to exercise power and prevail. The Russians, and later the Soviets, used the vast reaches of their territory as part of their defensive strategy to absorb and eventually repel attacks by the armies of Napoleon and Hitler. But great physical expanse can also be a hindrance if it inhibits economic exchange, increases the difficulty of defending points of potential attack, presents more obstacles to supply of forces, and creates problems for communication and control.

Some states must deal with a difficult topography that creates barriers to mobility and economic exchange, but other states have natural highways such as rivers that aid in transit and trade. Some states are isolated, while others are surrounded by many neighbors. Some are islands; others have contiguous land borders with their neighbors. Some states' borders and territory present physical barriers to entry and exit that can inhibit the flow of people and commodities, while the physical geography of others is easily passable. Oceans, mountains, rivers, and sheer distance may create potential obstacles to invasion forces, but such barriers can be overcome. European feudal lords and kings believed that the Alps protected their region from invasion, but Hannibal brought his troops and their elephants over that mountainous barrier when he invaded the Roman Empire. During World War II, both the Japanese and, later, the Americans crossed oceans to invade the territory of their enemies. Many attribute the emergence of England and the United States as world powers to their physical isolation from continental Europe, as well as other potential predators and competitors. A state may have weak neighbors that it can influence, or it may be influenced by stronger neighbors. As former Canadian Prime Minister Pierre Trudeau noted, when the United States sneezes, Canada catches a cold. All the members of the European Union have equal voting power within the EU structure, but Germany, as the largest and most central political economy in Europe, seems to weigh more heavily on EU decisions and policies than other member states.

Climate is another tangible feature that can affect the power capabilities of a state, but its influence is not straightforward. Inhospitable climates can slow economic enterprise, but they may also deter invasion and help defeat attackers. The Russian winter and spring were almost as responsible as the Czarist and Soviet armies in slowing and then reversing the attacks of Napoleon's and Hitler's armies. Desert sands can clog modern economic machinery and modern tools of warfare. Dense rain forests hold valuable resources that can be used to influence others, but they are also great resources for guerilla campaigns against invading armies, as has been demonstrated in the Philippines, Burma, and Vietnam. Climate can also affect the progress of industrialization and economic activity. Before the advent of air conditioning, the heat and humidity of tropical and equatorial climates slowed the pace of work and exacted a toll on machinery and human productivity—only "mad dogs and Englishmen" tended to work at midday during the summer in India—while states with more temperate climates faced no such barriers to economic activity. Some climates are more conducive to agricultural production, so that some states have more productive arable land than others solely because of their geographic location. This physical feature affects the ability of a state's population to feed itself and others, and food resources are potential tools of influence in international affairs. Yet, in some cases, modern systems of climate control negate these climatic effects.

Large states usually support larger populations than small states, but not always. All else being equal, human assets are a resource for both military and economic enterprise. States with large populations can generally maintain larger militaries than small states, and larger populations can often support larger economies and create greater economic surpluses than smaller populations. Societies can redistribute such surpluses to other activities, such as the exercise of influence. But population size is not the sole consideration when considering a state's people as a resource. The age distribution of a population is also important, for even if large, an aging population may be a less productive resource than a younger population in a less populated state.

States with a disproportionate number of retirees or workers nearing retirement may encounter difficulties in staffing their militaries, maintaining momentum in their economies, and providing social welfare. An effective military depends on a large pool of youth from which to draw troops. An expanding economy relies on a supply of labor to perform its work. Constraints on the labor supply can slow economic growth. States with aging populations face dilemmas in choosing between financing military programs and infrastructure improvements and funding social welfare provisions, pensions, and retirement systems; between investing in productive enterprise and expending resources on a segment of the population that has retired from economic production. With an increasing share of a state's population in retirement, an increasing tax burden falls on its younger population even to maintain the status quo in government expenditures. This budgetary constraint can limit a state's ability to use its resources to exercise influence in the global arena.

Other characteristics of a population—growth rates, job skills, educational levels, and general health—can affect a state's power capabilities. Expanding populations place demands upon a society's support systems, but a fruitful and capable populace that is growing in size increases the possibilities of making discoveries and developing strategies that can increase a state's power potential. High levels of education are partly responsible for the economic success of the advanced industrialized societies in the past and the present, and for their likely success in the future. Education acts as a multiplier of human talent; it represents an investment of capital in human labor potential, which transforms that potential and increases its productivity. Increased productivity generates greater surplus per capita, which can be reallocated to other activities, such as the exercise of power.

Health and nutrition can affect a state's capacity to exercise influence, its position in the global power hierarchy, and its future prospects. Healthy populations are more economically productive, provide better pools of manpower to staff militaries, and place smaller burdens on government and societal systems, which leaves more resources to be used elsewhere. Something as simple as prenatal health care makes a significant difference in the long-term health and productivity of a state's population. Healthy children with better diets perform better in school than do sick and malnourished children, which translates into differences in productivity and capability later in life. We can look at measures of health care provision, disease and caloric intake to assess a state's current and future capabilities in the global political economy.

For example, Botswana and many other African states currently face a health crisis of immense magnitude: a huge proportion of their people are infected with HIV, whose treatment demands a significant commitment of resources just to maintain life. The cost of antiviral drugs and HIV pharmaceutical cocktails, the demands upon health care workers and medical facilities, and the burdens shouldered by families and their community resources are overwhelming, even in developed countries with far smaller infected populations. For a developing state, such demands are catastrophic in terms of prospects for economic development. Even if adequate drug treatments were affordable and available, the demands on health care workers and family members for home health care and support would limit the numbers of people available for productive economic enterprise or military service. Healthy populations can be expected to be more productive in any activity than unhealthy populations.

Large states often harbor greater natural resources, but not always. States with more arable land are usually better able to feed themselves and others than are states with less arable land (but not always). A state endowed with rich farmland may fail to take advantage of its ability to produce food and other crops if its society is engaged in civil conflict. The economic advances of the nineteenth and twentieth centuries, which led to tremendous shifts in the global power hierarchy, depended upon access to natural resources. Resources, once they are extracted and mobilized, sustain modern economic enterprise: coal and iron fueled the Industrial Revolution of the 1800s, while oil, metallurgy, chemicals, and electronics were essential to the economic growth of the twentieth century. Being self-sufficient in such resources is not a necessary condition for economic development, however. Nor is it even efficient on an economic dimension, for international trade provides a means of importing resources as inputs to economic activity.

In the global political economy, trade, specialization of production, and the import of raw materials make immutable sense economically. Trade and the resulting specialization of productive activities improve the economic welfare of a society, but they reduce self-sufficiency and increase reliance upon the productive activities of those beyond one's borders. The networks of global exchange also offer policymakers levers by which they can attempt to influence the activities of others. This is not an argument for self-sufficiency. First, the economic gains and improvement in welfare from global exchange generally far exceed the costs and risks posed by increased exposure to political manipulation. Second, interdependence goes both ways along such networks. Exercising power across such networks imposes costs as well as potential gains upon the state trying to exert influence.

Having natural resources within a state's boundaries may offer some advantage that affects a state's power potential, but not always. Controlling such resources may insulate a state from the influence of others and may provide tools for use in influencing others, or it may expose the resource-rich state to greater external influence. Since the 1973 Arab-Israeli war, the oil-producing states of the Mid-East, through the mechanism of the Organization of Petroleum Exporting Countries (OPEC), have used the world's dependence on oil as a political tool to exercise influence over policy debates in other states. Their actions produced the oil crises of the 1970s, and the long lines at gas pumps in the United States. Such disruptions caused by the manipulation of energy supplies has prompted ongoing policy debates in many states about how to reduce dependence on Mid-Eastern oil and how to insulate domestic political arenas from the influence of these oil-producing states.

But controlling such resources can also expose the oil-rich states to external pressures. These same political economies that have used oil as a tool to exercise political influence in recent years were themselves invaded, dominated, and manipulated in some form or another over the century preceding the oil crises they precipitated in the 1970s. Would these states have attracted such attention if they did not possess such a valuable resource? Whether it is true or not, many in the Arab world interpret U.S. military activity and interest in the Mid-East as part of a policy to intimidate the oil-producing states so as to ensure stable access to the energy resources of their region. These states' prominence and influence on the world stage flows from their oil production, but this resource also provides incentives to governments of oil-importing states to try to influence the activities of the oil exporters. Their petroleum reserves give them a tool of potential influence over the actions of others, while the same reserves make them a target of influence by others.

Sensitivity and Dependence

The ability to use a natural resource as a tool of influence depends upon a variety factors. First, we need to recognize that natural resources are not all alike. Economies and societies need some resources more than others, which raises issues of **sensitivity** and **dependency**. A state that is not sensitive to, or dependent upon, a particular resource enjoys a condition of autarky, or independence from that resource, which is therefore unlikely to be useful as a tool to influence its activities. But a state that is sensitive to or dependent upon a particular resource is vulnerable to influence because of it. Differences between sensitivity and dependency are matters of degree: states that are only sensitive to the availability of a particular resource are less exposed to potential manipulation and influence than are states that are dependent upon it.

What affects a state's level of sensitivity or dependency? One important factor is the prospect of **substitutability.** Can economic enterprises and societies find new sources of the commodity or substitutes for the commodity at affordable prices? In the 1970s, when the OPEC cartel managed to successfully manipulate both the supply and the price of petroleum, OPEC members transformed their economic leverage into political leverage. Banana and copper producing states then attempted to mimic the success of the OPEC cartel by creating banana and copper cartels that would set production targets for the purpose of manipulating supply and increasing revenues from exports of these resources. But unlike oil, bananas and copper were commodities for which consumers soon found affordable substitutes and alternative supplies. Consumers switched from bananas to other fruits or bought them from other suppliers. Consumers of copper wire substituted aluminum wire or found copper producers who would operate outside the cartel. Discovering and developing new sources of petroleum or other forms of energy, however, takes substantial time and money. Even under the best possible conditions, such alternatives would not be available for decades, and only then after considerable investment. Moreover, the cohesion of the OPEC cartel prevented defections that would have undermined their production agreements, and so they were able to restrict the worldwide supply of oil.

These cartel examples demonstrate differences in the **elasticity of demand and supply** for particular commodities. Changes in world oil production are relatively slow, while demand for oil production is relatively high and inflexible, regardless of price. Demand for oil will not change markedly even with significant increases in the price, and this condition of *inelastic* demand and *inelastic* supply endows oil producers with potential tools of influence in the political arena. In the case of banana consumption, a significant increase in the price of bananas was met by a shift in consumption to other fruits. Consumer demand for bananas was flexible and affected by price—a condition of *elastic* demand. Even if the supply of bananas were inelastic, the willingness of consumers to readily and easily substitute other fruits for bananas undermined the ability of the banana cartel to manipulate the banana market and use their resource for political influence. A similar set of conditions limited the ability of the copper cartel nations to manipulate price in the market so as to use copper as a tool of political influence. Clearly, oil is a special commodity with unusual properties of supply and demand.

The Limits of Tangible Resources as Tools of Influence

The phrases "not always" and "all else being equal" recur in discussion of tangible, physical attributes. Such resources contribute to potential power capabilities, but focusing solely upon tangible assets can obscure key differences that separate states' ability to prevail and to influence others. Although large states that enjoy significant endowments of tangible resources often prevail and are effective at exercising power over smaller states that are less well-endowed, the smaller states with fewer tangible resources sometimes prevail instead. The United Kingdom dominated the global political economy for much of the nineteenth century even though it had a smaller population, less mineral and coal reserves, and less arable land than many other states. For half a century, Israel has prevailed in military conflicts with adversaries that enjoy much larger populations, territories, and resources. The peasant economy of Vietnam persisted and prevailed first in a conflict with the larger and wealthier advanced industrialized state of France and then over the even more impressive political and military power of the United States. In the 1980s, the feudal warlords of Afghanistan battled and prevailed over the forces of the Soviet Union, one of the world's superpowers at the time. By the measure of population, China and India should have surpassed the United States as the dominant state in the global political economy, but the beginning of the twenty-first century finds the United States as the world's sole superpower. Discrepancies in power potential based upon tangible resources do not always predict success in world affairs.

Intangible Resources

The intangible resources that contribute to a state's power are less concrete and physical than its tangible assets. Of the many such intangible resources, we can focus on three broad categories: economic organization, political organization, and social organization. Why do we consider organization as an intangible resource? Can't we observe organizational structures in states? Granted, many states have defined formal organizational structures that can be depicted in flow charts and formal diagrams, but these structures tell us little about the effectiveness of organization or how organization actually works to affect the state's capabilities.

More than in the case of tangible assets, understanding the contributions of intangible resources to a state's power potential is key to understanding what separates more influential from less influential political economies. How do organizational resources affect the ability to prevail and exercise influence in international affairs? Many states enjoy an abundance of tangible resources, but some exploit their naturally occurring resources more effectively than others. Differences in the organizational capabilities of governments, economic actors, and societal actors help account for differences in the ability to exploit, transform, and more efficiently employ the tangible attributes of power. Economic, political, and social organization contributes to power by affecting the mobilization and transformation of tangible resources such as population, physical resources, and geography. People, petroleum, iron ore, arable lands, rivers, and other physical assets are not as useful in their raw forms as they are once they have been transformed by education and socialization, metallurgy and smelting, application of modern fertilizers and irrigation systems, and the construction of cargo vessels and dams. Organization acts as a multiplier of tangible resources by transforming them into something greater than their naturally occurring state.

Political, economic, and social organization are not independent resources, but overlapping and potentially synergistic. Greater economic organization contributes to a more sophisticated, productive, and diverse economy, which provides governments with greater economic resources for influencing the behavior of others. More sophisticated political organizations are better able to contain societal conflicts, manage individual risk and uncertainty, extract and reallocate resources from their societies, and create environments conducive to economic activity. Social organizations help to develop communities and community identities, build social coalitions, manage individual risk and uncertainty, and defuse social conflict. Social organizations become vehicles to articulate preferences and needs in political arenas, and they help to support group interests in economic arenas.

Economic Organization and Development

Even though the organization of political, economic, and social arenas overlap and are synergistic, let's consider each separately. Economic organization focuses upon the ability to incorporate, manage, and transform resources in economic activity. How efficiently does a country's economy employ the tangible resources at its disposal? For economists, one of the great puzzles to decipher is what accounts for growth. All economies are not equal; some are larger than others and some have expanded at more rapid rates than others. Over time, some grew very rapidly—today's developed economies—and some grew much more slowly if at all—today's developing economies. Some of this inequality might be explained by differences in population, differences in the rate of population change, differences in physical resource base, new discoveries of tangible resources, or differences in investment patterns. The classic growth model in economic theory contains two independent variables: capital and labor. In this model, increasing the outcome of the dependent variable of growth requires an increase in either capital or labor.

Empirical evidence suggests that the classic growth model in economic theory is insufficient to account for modern economic growth. From the early 1800s onward, national political economies were increasingly differentiated by their varying outputs from comparable amounts of tangible resources. Some appeared to use their resources more efficiently and productively, as they enjoyed much greater output per worker. The economies of what became the modern industrialized states expanded much more rapidly than could be explained by changes in the supply of capital or labor, and much more rapidly than did the economies we now call developing economies. Returning to their chalkboards, economists revised the classic growth model by adding technology as an independent factor to help explain changes in growth. For many, technology is a phenomenon such as the semiconductor or the chips in their computers and cell phones, or the chemical and biological creation of pharmaceuticals. But technology involves much more than a scientific breakthrough, insight, or outcome. Technological change includes the processes of scientific investigation, the processes of transforming scientific insights into applied products, the processes of transforming labor, and the processes of organizing workplaces and production.

Henry Ford's doubling of the daily wage and introduction of the assembly line transformed the means of producing automobiles. The higher wage attracted better workers and a more stable workforce; the assembly line encouraged efficiencies from economies of scale and learning. His innovations, which became known as Fordism, were technological changes in production structures and the organization of economic activity. Similarly, differences in the organization of national educational systems help to account for differences in economic activity across nations. Changes in educational systems through state-mandated educational requirements and through the development of postsecondary and graduate educational institutions have transformed labor and the processes of invention and innovation. German universities transformed the field of chemistry, which revolutionized the production of dyes and helped turn Germany into an economic and political powerhouse. The advent of the land-grant system in the United States led to tremendous investment in agricultural, mining, and forestry research, with significant spin-offs in our understanding of chemical, biological, and economic processes. The G.I. Bill opened university doors to new populations of students, which led to a significant transformation in the U.S. labor force. The National Defense Education Act encouraged the development of math, science, and engineering skills, which could lead to technological invention and innovation. Such technological changes in the processes and organization of education affect the organization of economic activity. Such changes, and others in the organization of economic activity, have revolutionized industrial production in many industries, transformed the skills of labor and increased its productivity, led to more efficient use of resources, and increased social welfare. These examples demonstrate the importance of organization for transforming inputs to economic activity.

Economic organization increases the overall wealth and welfare of a society. States that stagnate in the organization and transformation of economic activity have less surplus to be invested, taxed, and reallocated to other endeavors. Your parents, society, and government have invested part of their surplus in your education, an investment in future productivity. Governments tax surplus to fund infrastructure investment, social welfare programs, education, research and development, foreign policy, and national security—all activities that contribute to the potential to influence the behavior of others in the global arena. Surplus is not simply a function of overall economic size, for a state with a large population can have a larger gross national income (GNI) than a state with a smaller population, but still have a smaller surplus. Surplus is a function of both overall economic size and the productivity of each worker (GNI per capita). Table 4.1 shows differences in GNI and GNI per capita incomes across a range of political economies. States with a higher GNI per capita can extract more resources from each worker than can states with a lower GNI per capita. In this

TABLE 4.1	**Gross National Income and Gross National Income per Capita by Income Classification, 2000**	
	Gross National Income (GNI) (in $ billions)	**GNI per Capita**
World	31,171	5,150
Low income states	1,030	420
Low middle income states	2,327	1,140
Upper middle income states	2,986	4,620
High income states	24,829	27,510

Source: Data are from the World Development Indicators produced by the World Bank.

Note: Low income is defined as less than or equal to $755 per capita; middle income is $756 to $9,265 per capita; and high income is $9,266 or greater per capita

table, the high-income states are the OECD advanced industrialized economies that dominate activities and the rules of the game in the capitalist global political economy. Even a cursory glance at the table conveys that economic success correlates highly with the capacity of governments to exercise influence in world affairs. The effect of economic organization on the accumulation of wealth and surplus is an important contributor to a state's power potential and ability to prevail in global affairs.

Unlike acres of arable land, population size, petroleum or mineral reserves, or other tangible assets, intangible resources such as economic organization are difficult to measure. The effects of organization may be observable, but organization itself is much more difficult to directly observe and measure. Economists have devised some useful measures of the consequences of economic organization, which can be used as proxy (substitute) measures of economic organization. These substitutions assume that economic organization will affect economic outcomes. Measures such as gross national income, gross national product (GNP), or gross domestic product (GDP), productivity or GNP per capita (GNP/n), level of industrialization, and percentage of the labor force engaged in agricultural production tell us a lot about the organization of economic activity, quality of workforce, societal wealth, and accumulation of surplus.

Political Organization and Development

The success of economic organization relies heavily on the organization and capacity of the political arena. Economic actors operate within political arenas and under rules constructed by politicians and policymakers. Political arenas define property rights and the rights of economic actors to the fruits of their labor, provide tools such as currencies that can facilitate

This May Day parade in Moscow and Boeing assembly plant in Washington state illustrate resources and paths to international influence: guns versus butter and military versus economic. In assessing means to power, many people focus almost instinctively on military tools, such as the missiles being displayed in Red Square. They tend to overlook other sources of influence, as in this case the transformation of productive assets into commercial airliners. Boeing's planes will be sold in global markets, influence global activity, and connect the world through modern transport. Such activity functions as a multiplier in a political economy, promoting economic advances and generating wealth that can be used to influence others.

exchange, establish contracting procedures and adjudication mechanisms such as courts and regulatory agencies to resolve disagreements in the economic arena, back those property rights and dispute adjudication mechanisms with the enforcement mechanisms of the state, and affect the macroeconomic environment through taxes, programs, regulation, and manipulation of money supply. As states are functionally equal, they all attempt to perform such functions. But political arenas vary in how they perform such functions and how well they perform them. Some governments are better than others at stabilizing and managing risk and uncertainty for economic actors from the political arena, which allows economic actors to have more confidence in their forecasts, better manage risks to their activities, and take greater chances on future outcomes. Political arenas that nurture productive economic activity are those that encourage economic actors to lengthen their time horizons and place greater bets on the future by expanding investments that will be repaid, if successful, in the future.

Political development and organization sit at the heart of government capacity to provide an arena conducive to economic activity, investment, and risk-taking on the future. Political organization is the capacity of a political system to carry out tasks imposed upon it domestically and internationally. A government's ability to perform well depends upon its ability to extract, mobilize, and allocate resources; to convince members of society to act in the collective interest; to manage conflicts in society that could create divisions, turn violently divisive, or undermine confidence in the future;

and to engender confidence in a broad swath of society to take risks on the future with their personal resources. These are difficult tasks. No clear blueprint exists for well-intentioned politicians and policymakers who want to create a political and societal arena with such characteristics. If political development were simple and formulaic, then we would observe far more politically and economically developed states in the world today.

To complicate matters, not all politicians and policymakers seek the best possible long-term outcome for their societies. Some politicians are not well-intentioned, but even well-intentioned political leaders face short-term narrow pressures that create hurdles to their political survival and may run counter to long-term societal welfare. We began with an assumption that politicians seek to survive. Political survival may depend more upon policies that appeal to short-term special interests and narrow constituencies than upon policies meant to address broader and more long-term societal interests. All societies have divisions, groups, or individuals with divergent preference orderings that pressure politicians to act in the short term and often at the expense of the long-term welfare of their societies. Societies that succeed at managing such forces through their political organization and the development of constructive political institutions prove far more successful in managing the domestic arena, expanding domestic economic and social opportunities, and increasing the capacity of the state to act in world affairs. But such societies are in the minority on the world stage.

Let's quickly consider the mechanisms of political development, institutions, and organization and how they operate. If success is defined broadly in terms of overall societal welfare and not in terms of narrow segments of society, the successful instances of political development, political institutions, and political organization are those that encourage investment in the future (risk-taking in society), manage societal conflict and disputes constructively, and succeed in advancing the long-term welfare in society. Successful political organization engenders respect for the authority of the state that does not rely solely on state tools of violent coercion, constructs a rule of law that encourages respect and tolerance for the rights of others, encourages notions of fairness that extend beyond dominant societal subgroups, provides protections for minorities, and restrains the inclinations among members of society to resort to violence rather than to peaceful methods of dispute resolution.

All this is easier said than done! Just think how many failed states cannot convince enough members of society to cooperate instead of fighting, to adjudicate disputes peacefully through established legal mechanisms instead of through violence, to contribute resources to the state for reallocation to others (taxation as a contribution to the future), or to send their children off to a distant school (another contribution to the future welfare of society). Skilled and dedicated workers at the World Bank, the U.S. Agency for International Development (AID), and numerous other development organizations have been trying to promote such conditions in developing political economies since the end of World War II. Despite their skill and commitment, they have met with far less success than desired. Newspapers are filled with stories about civil wars, failure to establish civil societies and national identities, breakdowns in civil society, political leaders' abusive use of the tools of coercion against segments of domestic society, and economic failures and policies that discriminate against some portions of society to enrich those who have a special connection to political leadership of the state.

Societies are made up of individuals. Individuals usually have group associations that affect their decision calculus, but they still must make choices about their actions in society. These choices and how they aggregate provide the micro foundations of societal outcomes. So we want to ask how political development, institutions, and organization might influence individual preferences and decision processes, and how they affect the aggregation of individual preferences and choices to produce societal outcomes. For successful political development, political organizations and institutions must affect the individual-level calculations of a broad swath of society and create incentives for individuals to make choices that improve their well-being and at the same time contribute to the general well-being of their broader society. Less successful political development also affects the incentives of individuals in societies, but it promotes individual actions that may be individually rational but are at odds with the greater social welfare.

Political development, institutions, and organization consist of far more than the physical edifice of the state. Buildings, monuments, and governmental infrastructure are physical manifestations of the state, but they are only limited indicators of the development of the political arena. States with high degrees of societal conflict and violence could easily have large government mechanisms, such as militaries and police, to combat that conflict, but the high level of violence tells us that political development, institutions, and organization have failed to constrain individual calculations and actions that work against overall societal welfare. How do political development, institutions, and organization convince individuals to become stakeholders or shareholders in the future of national society, so they will forgo short-term individual rewards to gain long-term benefits for themselves and society? The temptation to garner short-term gains at long-term expense is a social trap, a suboptimal equilibrium like those described in chapter 2. Chapter 3 discussed the importance of national identity and nationalism, based upon a sense of common destiny, for transforming the state into a nation-state. Common destiny means having a similar stake in a future—stakeholding or shareholding. Nationalism and political development evolve hand-in-hand, not as independent processes. Nationalism is a tool that can be used artfully by political entrepreneurs to advance the process of political development, but it can also be mobilized to discriminate against segments of society.

At the heart of political development and the development of shareholding in society are the linkages that connect members of society to the state, the masses of the population to the political elites. Remember that power and influence involve relationships, which work in both directions. So we want to ask what are the channels by which elites penetrate and motivate masses and groups in society? This is a question about elites' ability to act as **agenda-setters** and entrepreneurs, creating demands and preferences in society from the top down. But we also need to ask what are the channels by which masses communicate their preferences and demands to elites? This is a question about **representation** and the ability to convey demands and preferences in society from the bottom up. How sophisticated and encompassing are such channels? This is a question about how much of society they incorporate, and about the reach and depth of the channels of communication and influence.

So what mechanisms can link society to the state's political elites? In the political sphere, elections, public opinion, legislatures, political parties, class-based organizations, narrowly defined special interest groups, bureaucracy, and media are conduits of communication and influence that can be employed to develop identity and stakeholding, create political institutions and incentives to affect individual choice, aggregate and mobilize interests, extract and reallocate resources, extend representation, provide leadership, manage societal conflict, foster the development of civil society, and develop bargains between the state and society such as the modern welfare state. Signals, information, and pressures move in both directions along these channels: from the political elites to the broader society, and from the broader society to the political elites. The breadth and depth of these channels—how much of society they encompass and organize—help political scientists to investigate the nature of participation and representation in the political arena, bottom-up demands and responsiveness of political elites to those demands, and top-down political manipulation in societies.

As with economic organization, effective political organization acts as a multiplier, interacting with other tangible and intangible resources of a state. Governments and societies that have broadened the base of political participation and enhanced the channels of representation connecting political elites and masses have proven more successful at extracting and allocating resources for societal ends. Such societies are far more capable of manipulating the tangible and intangible assets at their disposal, which increases the power potential of the state. In the last chapters of this text, we more extensively examine the influence of such forms of political development and organization upon the calculations and activities of members of society, and their consequent impact upon public policy and the global political economy.

As analysts of political behavior trying to understand why things happen in world affairs, we want to try to evaluate the contribution of intangible resources such as economic, political, and social organization. But intangibles are difficult to observe and measure. For economic organization, we use measures of economic outcomes as substitutes for direct measures of the processes of economic development and organization. Proxy measures and assessments of political development and organization are more difficult to construct than their economic counterparts. The connection between political outcomes and the processes of political development and organization are more tenuous. Nevertheless, some measures have been advanced to try to capture differences across states in political development and organization.

Political scientists have developed tools for assessing the institutional climate of a state. Measures of tax avoidance and tax compliance tell us about the capability of the state to extract resources and the willingness of a society's members to pay their taxes—both proxy assessments of the level and depth of political organization and development. Examinations of government budgets provide information about the ability of governments to allocate resources to various types of programs, which can tell us about the breadth and reach of the channels of political organization. Does government fund a wide range of programs to address the interests of a broad set of constituencies in society or do its programs target a much narrower segment of society, a patronage clientele? Government turnover, electoral participation, competitiveness of elections, stability of the electoral process, regime change, public opinion assessments, connections between local and national political organizations, adjudicatory fairness of the legal system, and candidate recruitment are other tools for assessing political development and organization.

Some economic variables can prove useful in assessing the organizational capacity of the state. Government policies seek to influence specific macroeconomic conditions such as inflation, unemployment, stability of the exchange rate, investment and savings, or liquidity and money supply. As policymakers try to influence such conditions, they encounter pressures from within their domestic political economies that encourage short-term, politically expedient choices that amount to long-term macroeconomic mismanagement. Measurements of such variables can tell us how well governments succeed or fail in managing such target conditions and how well they succeed or fail in constraining short-term political pressures that could be detrimental to long-term social welfare. These performance evaluations, in turn, provide information about government capacity and the level of development and organization of the channels connecting policymakers to society. Governments cannot unilaterally attain their preferred outcomes on such macroeconomic conditions, for the actions of private economic actors are critical to such outcomes. How well governments do in attaining their preferred outcomes on such macroeconomic conditions depends upon their ability to convince private economic actors that those are the appropriate targets. Well-developed channels and connections between policymakers and private economic actors are essential to successful manipulation of such macroeconomic conditions.

Interest rates on government financial instruments can also offer information about the political capacity and development of governments. Interest rates on bonds are the cost of capital for the borrower. If you purchase a government bond as an investment, you are lending money to that government. The interest rate on the bond is the fee the government pays you for your loan. As a lender you will demand higher fees, or payments for your money, as the risk or uncertainty of your investment increases. If we assume that more politically developed and organized societies and governments are better able to manage such risk and uncertainty, this superior capability should be reflected in the cost of capital. Governments that are more capable—have greater political development and organization—should pay less to borrow capital than governments that have less political development and organization. Again, this proxy measurement assumes a strong association between the intangible resources of political development and organization and the ability of the state to overcome problems and prevail.

Other intangible resources such as cultural and social organization can affect the capacities of societies and governments. Social and cultural organization and development also help to build identities, create civil societies, and generate networks within communities and states. Social and cultural identities and networks can be as useful—more useful in many cases—as economic connections in motivating people. Religious, cultural, and social organizations can create dense, active networks that can be transformed into tools to organize and mobilize interests, place demands upon governments, and affect activities within political and economic arenas. Strategic policymakers can mobilize social and cultural networks to advance political agendas. The politics surrounding humanitarian assistance, abortion, stem-cell research, gay rights, terrorism, and ethnic conflict become more powerful as they tap into social and cultural networks and organization.

CONCLUSION

Why do we care about tangible and intangible resources, about power and hierarchy in global affairs? Differences in the distribution of tangible and intangible resources translate into differences in the power capabilities of states in the international arena. They establish a basis for hierarchies among autonomous, sovereign units. Such hierarchies are important in global affairs, given the absence of a central authority and the resulting anarchical state of affairs. They provide order to anarchy. Anarchy is often equated with disorder, sometimes accurately. Differences in power can produce violence, as wars and disputes attest, but differences in power can also provide tools for obtaining cooperative and productive outcomes in international affairs. Differences in capabilities and the hierarchies built on them can restrain governments from acting as if they were in a violent state of nature, convincing them instead to act as part of a community. The violence of conflict in the global system can distract our attention from the extraordinary amount of cooperative behavior in an arena that lacks a rule of law provided by a central authority, its adjudication mechanisms, and its enforcement mechanisms. The vast quantities of goods, services, capital, people, and information flowing daily across national boundaries require a tremendous amount of cooperation and agreement, yet no central authority exists to support those flows, protect contracts, resolve disputes, and punish those who cheat. Hierarchies can replace the formal mechanisms of central authority with an informal mechanism of hierarchy based upon differences in power distribution, but not always. The informal mechanisms of hierarchy can break down and lead to violence and chaos, just as the formal authority mechanisms of domestic political arenas can break down and lead to civil conflict.

Intangible assets make the greatest difference in states' power capabilities, as they organize human activities and act as multipliers of tangible resources. Differences in the organization of political, economic, and social life separate subsistence states that have few surplus resources to expend on influencing the activities of others in the global arena from states with abundant surpluses that can be allocated to support more advanced and expensive strategies of statecraft. Political and industrial revolutions produced changes in power capabilities that enabled Britain to exert disproportionate influence over European and international relations in the nineteenth century, the United States to exercise inordinate influence over world affairs since World War II, and the West to dominate the organization of world affairs from the 1500s until today. Hierarchies affect the "rules of the game," or how international affairs are organized, the nature of conflict, and the form of exchange.

Advances in political, economic, or social organization and development tend to make a state a more effective international actor. If advances in political, economic, or social organization and development interact and produce synergisms, states and societies can undergo amazing increases in their power potential and their ability to affect the behavior of others and to resist pressures from others. Such differences in power and position in hierarchy can provide a good indicator for explaining and understanding why some prevail and some falter, and for predicting what preferences will dominate in global affairs. Hierarchies based on differences in power provide tools for managing the potential disorder of anarchy, which may be necessary to overcome the barriers to cooperation that exist in a system lacking central authority.

EXERCISES

1. Generally, what is the most costly tool of influence for a state or policymaker in international politics?

2. Why do policymakers worry about the costs of exercising power in world affairs?

3. Cite an example to explain how the United States has used its power to influence affairs in the international political economy? Which tools of statecraft were used?

4. Explain how education and health affect a state's power capabilities.

5. On October 22, 1962, after reviewing newly acquired surveillance photographs, President John F. Kennedy informed the world that the Soviet Union was building secret missile bases in Cuba, a mere ninety miles off the shores of Florida. After weighing such options as an armed invasion of Cuba and air strikes against the missiles, Kennedy decided on a less dangerous response. In addition to demanding that Russian Premier Nikita S. Khrushchev remove all the missile bases and their deadly contents, Kennedy ordered a naval quarantine (blockade) of Cuba in order to prevent Russian ships from bringing additional missiles

and construction materials to the island. Name two tools of statecraft relevant to this example and cite which action illustrates each.

6. Governments have a variety of options when it comes to influencing the behavior of others in world affairs. We call these options the tools of statecraft, or tools of influence. Name three broad strategies of influence and give an example of each.

Policymakers usually try to be efficient in their use of such tools of statecraft, choosing the tool that is most likely to bring positive results at the lowest cost. Rank the three broad strategies of influence that you provided in the first part of this question in terms of costs, from least to most costly.

7. Explain how elasticity of demand affects an economy that is sensitive to a particular resource as compared to that economy's condition of autarky (independence) in relation to another resource.

8. Use tables 4.2 and 4.3 below to answer the following questions. When we think about power in international affairs, we often focus on military size. The first table, the number of men in uniform, tells us one story about the distribution of power in international affairs. The next table tells us another story. Using the data from 1880, construct two different hierarchies of power based on the two different tables.

What might account for the differences in the distribution of capabilities from table 4-2 to table 4.3?

TABLE 4.2	**Military and Naval Personnel, 1880–1914 (in thousands)**				
	1880	**1890**	**1900**	**1910**	**1914**
Germany	426	504	524	694	891
France	543	542	715	769	910
Russia	791	677	1,162	1,285	1,352
United States	34	39	96	127	164
Austria-Hungary	246	346	385	425	444
United Kingdom	367	420	624	571	532
Japan	71	84	234	271	306

Source: Adapted from Paul Kennedy, *The Rise and Fall of Great Powers* (New York: Random House, 1987), 203.

TABLE 4.3	Total Industrial Potential in Relative Perspective, 1880–1938 (U.K. in 1890 = 100)				
	1880	**1890**	**1913**	**1928**	**1938**
Germany	27.4	71.2	137.7	158	214
France	25.1	36.8	57.3	82	74
Russia	24.4	47.5	76.6	72	152
United States	46.9	127.8	298.1	533	528
Austria-Hungary	14.0	25.6	40.7	—	—
United Kingdom	73.3	[100]	127.2	135	181
Japan	7.6	13.0	25.1	45	88

Source: Adapted from Paul Kennedy, *The Rise and Fall of Great Powers* (New York: Random House, 1987), 201.

FURTHER READING

Art, Robert J. 1980. "To What Ends Military Power?" *International Security* 4 (spring): 4–35.

Clausewitz, Karl von. 1982. *War, Politics and Power.* New York: Penguin Books.

Machiavelli, Niccolò. Reissued 2003. *The Prince and the Discourses.* New York: Penguin Books.

Morganthau, Hans J. Various editions. *Politics among Nations: The Struggle for Power and Peace,* revised by Kenneth W. Thompson. New York: Knopf.

Nye, Joseph, Jr. 1991. *Bound to Lead: The Changing Nature of American Power.* New York: Basic Books.

Organski, A. F. K., and Jacek Kugler. 1981. *The War Ledger.* Chicago: University of Chicago Press.

Rothgeb, John M., Jr. 1993. *Defining Power: Influence and Force in the Contemporary International System.* New York: St. Martin's.

Schelling, Thomas C. 1967. *Arms and Influence.* New Haven: Yale University Press.

Strange, Susan. 1988. *States and Markets.* London: Pinter Publishers.

Tzu, Sun. 1971. *The Art of War.* New York: Oxford University Press.

5

Economic Liberalism and Market Exchange in the Global Arena

[Every individual] generally, indeed, neither intends to promote the public interest, nor knows how much he is promoting it . . . he intends only his own gain, and he is in this, as in many other cases, led by an invisible hand to promote an end which was not part of his intention. Nor is it always the worse for the society that it was no part of it. By pursuing his own interest he frequently promotes that of the society more effectively than when he really intends to promote it.

Adam Smith (1776)

BASELINE EVALUATION

Increasingly, the global political economy is characterized by economic market exchange and democratization of national political relations. The U.S.–Soviet competition during the cold war represented a battle between different forms of organizing domestic and international political-economic relations, between decentralized market exchange and hierarchical central planning, between broad-based multiparty competition of democratic governance and single-party socialist authoritarianism. It was a conflict over the rules of the game in political and economic affairs. Mikhail Gorbachev, who ascended to the leadership in the Soviet Union in the 1980s, introduced significant policy changes. He initiated economic reforms, labeled **perestroika,** which introduced market mechanisms and pressures to the Soviet economy. These reforms encouraged consumer demands in the Soviet economy, decentralized decision making and industrial management, and supported private economic

This chapter draws upon a rich variety of sources, including Ronald H. Coase, "The Nature of the Firm," *Economica* 4 (1937): 386–405; Gary J. Miller, *Managerial Dilemmas: The Political Economy of Hierarchy* (1992); Douglass North, *Institutions, Institutional Change, and Economic Performance* (1990); and Andrew Schotter, *Free Market Economics* (1984).

initiatives. Gorbachev also adopted political reforms, called **glasnost,** which helped to unleash individual choice and broader citizen participation in political life.

Soviet economic and political reforms spilled over into Eastern Europe. In 1989 the populations in many states there rejected communist rule, and the rest of Eastern Europe soon followed. Growing nationalist and ethnic forces within the Soviet republics pressed for greater political decentralization and fragmentation. By fall 1991, republic after republic announced secession and declared independence. The Soviet Union disintegrated. The events of 1989–1991 ended the cold war competition between the different forms of organizing domestic and global political-economic relations. Market exchange in the economic arenas and democratization in the political arena seem to have prevailed, at least for the foreseeable future.

In theory, market exchange liberates individual economic choice, and **democratization** encourages choice in political arenas. Choices in economic markets are consumption decisions, or votes, on economic commodities. Political arenas, especially democratic political arenas, can likewise be viewed as markets, wherein individual political choice is liberated by representation and electoral mechanisms. Choices in such political markets are consumption decisions, or votes, on political commodities, be they politicians or policies. There are important similarities between economic and political markets—both in how they operate and in how they fail—but also some important differences.

This and the next chapter introduce frameworks for exchange in economic and political markets. These baseline models reflect how the world should theoretically work. Like all models, they parse away many aspects of reality to focus on specific relationships and mechanisms. Exchange in actual economic and political markets rarely looks exactly like the exchange depicted in these theoretical constructions, which returns us to the question, why build and use such models? Because evaluating one state of the world requires comparing that state to some alternative state, a counterfactual. This process of comparison provides a comparative metric. Alternative depictions of the world reflect, implicitly or explicitly, distinct underlying theoretical frameworks as well as differences across those frameworks. Productive criticism of one state of the world requires reference to another state that is based upon an alternative argument about how humans behave and why.

To evaluate, examine, and critique the current global political economy demands a clear understanding of the theoretical frameworks that sit at its core. These frameworks provide baselines, or points of comparison, for evaluating the choices of market and political actors. They help investigators and policymakers to develop expectations about how the global political economy should function—to which they can compare actual outcomes. They illuminate inconsistencies between the theoretical frameworks and empirical behavior. Chapters 7–11 describe four periods of global political economic relations, offering empirical examples that will serve to reveal the strengths and weaknesses of our abstract models. Before we consider those examples, however, we must make explicit the theoretical bases of the frameworks that dominate academic and policy discussions. These ideal types offer base-lines for evaluating how well economic and political markets function, where and why they might fail, and some potential ways to adjust our theoretical frameworks.

LIBERAL ECONOMIC EXCHANGE

The theoretical framework that underpins today's modern global political economy is called **economic liberalism;** it is rooted in the writings of Adam Smith, David Ricardo, John Stuart Mill, Thomas Malthus, and scores of philosophers and economists who followed. At the heart of economic liberalism is exchange within **competitive markets.** Competitive economic markets are decentralized mechanisms that coordinate the allocation, distribution, and use of the raw materials, labor, and capital that go into economic activity. Markets perform these functions by affecting the calculations and incentives of consumers and producers, aggregating and coordinating their behavior and encouraging production and consumption of some commodities while discouraging the production and consumption of other commodities. The choices of consumers and producers are decentralized, nonhierarchical, and not coordinated by some centralized mechanism such as a government or a business firm. Market exchange is relatively symmetric, involving voluntary contractual relationships. Other allocation mechanisms exist: governments, businesses, and other organizational entities may allocate resources by nonmarket means. Many of these mechanisms differ from the market mechanism in that they are hierarchical and often involve nonvoluntary relationships.

How do markets work? In competitive markets, producers of goods and services meet potential consumers of those commodities. Consumers have preferences over what they want to consume, and, in a world of scarce resources, they face budget constraints on their consumption choices. Because they cannot consume everything they desire, they must discriminate in their consumption, as we discussed in chapter 2. In decentralized markets, we assume that consumers base their choices upon hierarchies of preference and budgetary constraints—the size of their wallets. They make trade-offs based upon their **self-interest** and upon their budgets. Producers also face budgetary constraints as they purchase the inputs to their productive activities. This economic framework requires us to make no noble assumptions about human motivations—only that humans are self-interested (or egoistic) and that they behave as if they are rational. Working with these less idealistic assumptions allows us to examine the actions and preferences of human actors to see if they conform to the conditions of completeness and transitivity, which we also considered in chapter 2.

The Price Mechanism

Markets aggregate individual choices by means of a **price mechanism,** which coordinates individual consumption preferences, or **demand,** with producers' activities, or the **supply** of specific goods and services. The price mechanism influences the use of societal resources by changing the behavior of producers and consumers, given the supply of commodities and services and the demand for those commodities and services as conditioned by their costs. The market and its price mechanism discipline producers and their production choices: if they offer commodities or services that consumers do not want, do not want at the price offered, or do not want in the quantity produced, producers face incentives to change either what they produce, the price of what they produce, or the quantity of what they produce. If producers do not adjust to such demands, they will find the survival of their enterprises threatened. Consumers will reward producers who respond to their demands and penalize producers who do not. Similarly, the activities of producers can affect the incentives and demands of consumers, for consumer choices may change as producers change what they offer and the prices at which they offer it.

Adam Smith called this dynamic process the **invisible hand** of the market—an unseen force that guides self-interested individual behavior in competitive markets and promotes the welfare of society without deliberate intent. Noble human motivations are not needed to attain good collective outcomes, for individual self-interested choices aggregated through competitive market mechanisms will produce them automatically. Gordon Gekko, in Oliver Stone's movie *Wall Street,* reveled in this sentiment with the pronouncement, "Greed is good."

In effect, the invisible hand is a giant information mechanism that polls members of a society about all their wants and desires, their cost constraints and the ability of producers to adjust their activities to meet those wants and constraints—an amazing task. Neither today's most sophisticated computers nor those expected in the foreseeable future can offer the computing and storage capacity necessary to replicate the outcomes that are coordinated by price mechanisms in competitive modern markets.

Factors of Production

Markets coordinate the use of different resources in society via the invisible hand of the price mechanism. The production of commodities requires a mix of resources, which fall into three broad categories: land, labor, and capital. Economists call these inputs **factors of production.** Each nation has some mix of land, labor, and capital—a combination referred to as its **factor endowment.** Different allocations and mixes of factors of production across nations are the differences in the factor endowments of those nations. These differences are not static; they can change over time with population change, discoveries, technological shifts, and growth or decline.

Land

The physical resources available in nature—such as arable land, water, and raw materials either animal, vegetable, or mineral—are categorized as **land.** Sometimes such resources are easy to find and use, but more often some combination of labor, intelligence, and capital must be expended to transform them from their natural state into useful form. Man develops tools to hunt and trap animals or to fell trees, invents strategies to harvest fish, digs mines to extract coal and iron, drills holes to find oil, and tames beasts of burden to help in farming.

Labor

The second factor of production, **labor,** consists of the efforts that men and women put into producing a commodity, whether extracting a resource from the ground, planting and harvesting a crop, milling or refining a raw material, inventing, or teaching. This resource category encompasses blue-collar, white-collar, physical, menial, and mental labor. Population size, age distribution, and gender breakdown—as well as societal attitudes and rules about who should work and for how long—affect the amount of labor that is available in an economy. Prohibiting child labor, creating retirement insurance or some other form of social security, requiring schooling up to a specified age, or limiting the length of the workweek and workday shrinks the physical size of a labor pool. Qualitative aspects such as health and education affect the ability of labor to generate outputs. Qualitative improvement of this productive ability requires the interaction of labor with another factor of production.

Capital

The final factor of production, **capital,** differs from the others in one important characteristic: it does not occur naturally. People construct, or invent, capital and then use it to transform the other factors of production to make them more productive. Capital can be invested in the training and education of labor; in the development of tools, technologies, and skills to transform raw materials such as crude oil into plastics and other synthetics; in the invention of fertilizers and crop technologies that increase agricultural output per acre farmed or per worker; in the building of plants and factories to improve the efficiency and manufacturing of commodities; in processes of production innovation; in scientific laboratories and research facilities to further discoveries that may improve the productivity and welfare of society. The schools you attend are examples of the massive application of capital to transform a factor of endowment (you) into a far more productive member of society. The investment of capital in your training via higher education increases your value and capability as an input to production. Would you trust someone without benefit of this investment to perform surgery on you? This application amounts to an increase in human capital, a synergistic interaction of labor and capital.

Capital is the critical ingredient in the mix of the factors of production; the abundance or scarcity of capital separates more advanced and wealthier political economies from those that are less developed and less affluent. A society that enjoys an abundance of capital can usually make more productive use of its labor and land than can societies that are comparably endowed in those factors but have less capital.

The Normative Appeal of Economic Liberalism

Liberal market exchange appeals to many on moral grounds, both for its democratic emphasis on individual choice and for the efficiency with which it can create social gains.

Individual Choice

Much of the normative appeal of ideologies of economic market exchange and democratic governance stems from their foundations in individual choice and free will. These concepts are powerful and seductive because people generally dislike having their actions dictated by others, even if those at the top of a hierarchy harbor the best intentions for members of their group. Even in hierarchies with benign leaders, such as those in many businesses, people find working in a hierarchy unpleasant at times. Some of the unhappiness in nondemocratic states arises from government intrusions upon individual liberty and autonomy, from the lack of broad-based representation. People in such societies rarely claim that their lives would be better if government were less democratic and more authoritarian. When members of nondemocratic societies venture to voice their concerns and suggest alternatives, they generally call for expanding the base of representation and limiting the ability of the few to constrain the actions of the many. Sometimes this produces rebellion and change, as in the French, Mexican, and Russian Revolutions, the battles to extend suffrage to women in the United States and other nations, the civil rights movement in the United States, and the breakdown of the Soviet bloc beginning in 1989.

Members of democratic societies also complain about their governments and demand reforms when politicians and policy fail to produce desired outcomes. In many democratic states, carping over politics seems to be a favorite national pastime, surpassing soccer or baseball. Interestingly, demands for reform in democratic societies often contain the same prescription as reform demands in nondemocratic societies: that representation be improved, not diminished. When democratic governance and representation fail to produce good policy outcomes in societies, members of such societies tend to blame a breakdown in the channels of communication—a breakdown in representation itself—between those elected as representatives and those being represented. In such cases, the demands from society are to fix representation, to improve the channels of communication, and to make government more representative of the people. Chapter 4 discussed such channels as tools of the state for exercising influence and mobilizing the resources of society. Successful democratic societies have a greater density of such channels than nondemocratic societies have, which may help to account for the ability of democracies to extract and mobilize greater resources per capita for the exercise of power at times of national crisis than nondemocratic societies can muster.

Social Efficiency

If markets work well, they enhance social welfare and are socially efficient. What do we mean by efficiency? **Efficiency** has multiple usages in economic activity. In terms of production, it is a comparative gauge of the inputs of land, labor, and capital that go into the production of individual goods or services. How much land, or raw material resources, goes into the production of the commodity? How much labor—often defined by the number of hours of labor required—is needed to produce a unit of the commodity? How much capital is required to produce a unit of the commodity? More efficient production involves less inputs, or costs, than less efficient production does. **Productivity gains,** or improvements in efficiency, occur when a producer discovers a means to reduce the inputs per unit of production. Such gains are made when labor becomes more effective in less time or when a producer discovers a way to reduce the input of raw materials. More often than not, such productivity gains are achieved by transforming labor or resources through the application of capital.

Efficiency has a broader significance in terms of market exchange. Efficient markets facilitate the production and consumption of goods and services, given the mix of individual preferences in society. An efficient market optimizes the use of the resources that go into economic activity to satisfy the aggregated wants and preferences of the members of society. No absolute standard of efficiency can apply to every society and market, for what is efficient differs for each society, depending upon the desires of its members. Markets maximize social welfare when the market mechanism accurately aggregates those preferences and leads to the production of goods and services that best meet those desires—in other words, when no other level of production of goods and services could produce greater overall societal happiness. The production of any other level of goods and services might make some specific members of society better off, but, given the preferences of all members of society, it would make society as a whole worse off. At any given moment, an efficient market reflects an allocation of resources and efforts that is in equilibrium, wherein movement to another allocation could not advantage one member of society without hurting another and thus lowering the overall satisfaction of the mix of preferences in society.

For many, this efficiency in distributing resources and efforts contributes to the moral appeal of markets. Proponents of competitive markets find them morally attractive because they depend upon individual choice, involve relatively symmetric and voluntary contractual relationships among nonhierarchical parties, and *if they work properly* should result in good societal outcomes given the aggregated preferences of members of society. Effective market mechanisms lead to the optimal allocation of a society's scarce resources: they increase productivity, maximize use of the factors of production, and expand the range of consumption possibilities for a society in response to the efforts of its members. Real wages increase, which means that, in the aggregate, members of society can purchase more with their labor. In economic lingo, an efficient and competitive market places a society on the frontier of the **production possibilities curve,** or the outer boundary of what a society could conceivably produce and consume given its resources and the preferences of its members. This is an aggregate statement about the collective condition of the society—the social outcome—and not about the lot of particular individuals in the society.

THEORETICAL PREREQUISITES FOR EFFICIENT COMPETITIVE MARKETS

The empirical world always falls short of the theoretical world. No markets are perfectly efficient, no markets are perfectly competitive, and no markets produce perfect social outcomes. The moral underpinnings of market exchange come from the attractiveness of individual voluntary choice *and* the possibility of market exchange to improve or maximize societal outcomes as compared to other types of allocation mechanisms in society. The core finding in welfare economics is that competitive markets will allocate resources efficiently and will make society better off. But this desirable outcome depends upon markets working as they were theoretically envisioned, or at least not faltering too badly. What conditions are important for markets to work as envisioned and to produce socially desirable outcomes based upon the aggregation of decentralized nonhierarchical and voluntary individual choices? Our answer lies in what constitutes competitive markets and what conditions must be present for such markets to exist.

Clear Property Rights and Low Transaction Costs

Competitive markets require clear definition of **property rights** and the ability for market participants to negotiate, monitor, and enforce contracts at relatively negligible costs. Participants in a competitive market must enjoy a clear understanding of who owns what, as the exchange of goods and services in a market involves the exchange of property rights over those goods and services. The costs of determining such property rights and negotiating, monitoring, and enforcing the terms of an exchange, or contract, are called **transaction costs**—the costs of doing business or engaging in exchange relationships. In competitive markets with clear definition of property rights, these costs can be small or negligible. But **uncertainty** or confusion over property rights can undermine or limit exchange and increase transaction costs. The more uncertain property rights are, the more parties to an exchange must expend effort and resources to protect themselves against uncertain property rights—for example, who wants to buy a car from someone who might not own that car? This uncertainty means that the costs of negotiating, monitoring, and enforcing the terms of an exchange are no longer negligible; it adds costs to an exchange and generates inefficiencies that detract from the overall value of an exchange. If transaction costs become sufficiently large, they undermine the social efficiency of market exchange.

Competition

A variety of factors affect transaction costs, the prospects of competitive exchange, and the efficiency advantage of market exchange as compared to other forms of allocation. Efficient markets require competition, so that no individual buyer or seller, or cartel of buyers or sellers, can manipulate the price mechanism. When a single producer is able to manipulate the price of a commodity by affecting the supply of that commodity in a market, that producer is said to have a **monopoly**; we call the market condition in which sellers are so few that the actions of any one of them will materially affect price and have a measurable impact on competitors and consumers an **oligopoly.** In competitive markets there are enough other producers to supply the commodity that any attempt to manipulate supply would fail. This competition factor also exists on the demand side: there is no single consumer, or cartel of consumers, whose actions can affect the demand for a commodity and hence gain the ability to manipulate the price of that commodity. Participants in efficient and competitive markets are all **price takers,** meaning that no one individually controls the price.

In competitive markets, price is dictated by supply and demand as coordinated by the price mechanism. Producers or consumers who try to manipulate the price of a commodity will fail as long as a sufficient number of other producers or consumers are in the market. If a single seller or buyer, or cartel of sellers or buyers, can manipulate supply or demand, they have gained the ability to manipulate price and have incentives to manipulate the market to increase their individual welfare. Under these circumstances, resources will not be employed efficiently to meet the wants and desires of the members of society. A monopoly or oligopoly of producers will lead to decreased consumption of goods in general. Consumers are harmed by increased costs and decreased consumption, which outweigh possible gains to the monopolist in the form of increased profits. The same is true if a single consumer, or cartel of consumers, can manipulate demand and, consequently, price. Producers will be harmed by decreased profits and lower production, and the costs to society will outweigh the gains to the consumers who have manipulated price. Competitive markets rely upon Adam Smith's invisible hand functioning without manipulation.

Externalities

Another important condition for competitive and efficient markets is that transactions in such markets have no effect—costs or benefits—on third parties. Such influence is called an **externality.** *Third parties* are those people who are not directly involved in an exchange. Externalities can be positive or negative, but both can affect the efficiency of a market by imposing undesirable transaction costs that divert resources from production and consumption. Society will produce and consume less overall as resources are diverted into transaction costs. Let's consider two examples: a positive and a negative externality.

Think of national security as a commodity that is purchased by members of society. Everyone wants some level of national security or defense—for one thing, peaceful conditions allow for easier economic exchange. But such goods are expensive. Some optimal level of defense could be provided if the voluntary mechanism of economic markets were efficient at allocating resources to national security. Yet such commodities have an interesting quality that could lead to their underprovision in a voluntary market. In such a market, we could pass a hat and ask members of society to contribute to the purchase of defense goods. Yet if you and most other members of society pay for defense goods to defend our territory, I will get the benefit of national security regardless of whether or not I pay my share. I cannot be excluded from the provision of this commodity. This quality is called a *positive externality,* for without being partner to the exchange of resources for national security, I get to consume that commodity nonetheless.

The presence of positive externalities encourages **free-riding,** or consumption of a commodity without contribution. If enough people believe that they will get the benefit of national security without contributing, or if enough people believe that the commodity will be underprovided due to the presence of too much free-riding by others in society, society may face a dilemma of insufficient contributions to provide adequate national security. The presence of positive externalities can thus lead to a suboptimal amount of national security. There are, however, devices to limit such shirking. We could organize a community of potential contributors and negotiate a multiparty contract among the members of the group, but people can violate contracts. So ensuring that enough people act in accordance with the multiparty contract requires monitoring the contributions and sanctioning those who do not meet their obligations. This device involves non-negligible transaction costs, for monitoring and enforcing contracts are expensive. Resources that could go into defense are channeled into monitoring and enforcing agreements to contribute to defense. Such transaction costs mean that the amount of national security and other goods purchased by a society is less than what an efficient market would produce, but voluntary market exchange for this type of good generates positive externalities that threaten the very provision of the good.

Environmental pollution offers an example of a *negative externality*. Take the case of coal-fired power generating plants in the midwestern region of the United States. For years those plants spewed a form of pollution into the atmosphere that drifted east and became acid rain, which damaged the ecosystems of lakes in northeastern United States and Canada. Fish stocks in those lakes declined precipitously; many lakes became sterile as a consequence of acid rain. Environmental regulations that required using cleaner coal and adding cleaners and scrubbers to the exhaust stacks of the midwestern power plants eventually led to a dramatic decrease in the level of harmful pollutions that contributed to acid rain.

How was acid rain a negative externality? The production and consumption of energy from midwestern power plants took place almost exclusively between producers and consumers in the Midwest. Due to weather patterns, midwestern lakes were relatively unaffected by acid rain. Those living in the northeastern United States and in eastern Canada did not participate in the production and consumption of energy from the plants in the Midwest. They were third parties to the exchange of that energy—people who are not directly or voluntarily involved in the exchange—but they were affected by the exchange. The activities of those in the Midwest forced significant costs on those in the northeastern United States and eastern Canada: changing their recreational activities, prompting legal suits to constrain midwestern producers from using dirty coal and to force plant upgrades, necessitating large-scale programs to rectify the pH levels of lakes by adding base chemicals, creating diplomatic recriminations and tensions between the United States and Canada, causing health problems, and requiring studies to assess the environmental effects of energy generation by midwestern plants.

These third-party costs were not reflected in the production and consumption decisions of energy producers and consumers in the Midwest, but they imposed costs on those not involved directly in the exchange and led to inefficient allocation of resources. If severe enough, externalities, positive or negative, can undercut the benefits of market exchange and detract from the efficient allocation of resources that advances overall societal welfare, as the costs to third parties exceed the benefits to the parties directly involved in the exchange.

Asymmetric Information

Another important—perhaps the most important—condition for competitive and efficient markets is complete or full information. Parties to an exchange should be equally informed; none should be deprived of information that is important to the exchange. **Asymmetric information,** whereby one party to an exchange knows more about the commodity being exchanged than the other parties, can introduce an unfair advantage that detracts from the efficiency of the exchange. Asymmetric information is one form of **incomplete information.**

Let's think about how asymmetries in information can affect the efficiency of market exchange. Imagine that you want to purchase bananas at the supermarket. You have a choice of bananas that are imported from Africa or from Latin America. Significant differences exist between Latin American and African bananas in terms of variety, quality, and cost of production. Such differences contribute to an ongoing trade war between the European Union, the United States, and Latin American and African states that produce bananas. In a competitive market, where all sellers and buyers are equally well-informed, such differences should map into consumer choice. Let's say that African bananas cost less but Latin American bananas taste better. In a market where consumers and sellers are all fully informed, some people will purchase Latin American bananas and some others will purchase African bananas. Both groups would be guided by their different preferences over taste and cost. Some people would purchase African bananas, even if Latin American bananas are considered better, as they would willingly trade off taste for the lower cost. They are conscious of this trade-off and make their decisions with full information.

In this market, buyers can easily distinguish between the types of bananas, and they will know if a banana is incorrectly priced. Your produce manager cannot charge too much for the cheaper banana by substituting it for the other without changing the price. Nor will she charge too little and cheat herself by underselling the market rate for the more expensive banana. Full information means that voluntary exchange will take place at the real market price, given the wants and desires of society. There will be no inefficiencies created by paying too much or too little, which would lower the ability of buyers of sellers to consume other products.

What if you cannot differentiate between African and Latin American bananas? Like most people, you are probably not an agronomist with a specialty in banana cultivars, and becoming one would require a significant investment in resources, which would not likely be

In July 2005 this Costa Rican banana worker prepares newly harvested bananas for shipping. In August, the World Trade Organization (WTO) ruled that a new European Union (EU) tariff on imported bananas was illegal and discriminated against nine Latin American banana-producing nations. These countries have been involved in a long-running trade dispute with the EU—known as the "banana wars" of the 1990s—in which they accused the EU of erecting preferential trade arrangements that favored former colonies in the African, Caribbean, and Pacific (ACP) group. The WTO ruled that EU practices during the banana wars discriminated against U.S. and Latin American companies and gave the EU until January 2006 to introduce a new set of tariffs for the fruit.

an efficient use of your time and resources just so you could tell the difference between banana types when you are at the supermarket. So, you are at the market and having a problem distinguishing Latin American from African bananas. But the produce manager at the market has no such problem, because she is a banana professional, has been dealing with bananas for years, and can easily differentiate between varieties of bananas. Moreover, she knows that consumers will pay more for Latin American bananas because they believe that Latin American bananas are superior. Yet she pays less for African bananas and knows that most of her customers can barely tell the difference between a banana and a plantain, let alone differences across varieties of bananas. She has asymmetric information—which she decides to use to her advantage. She goes to her importer and purchases African bananas, but she displays them under the label of Latin American bananas. She charges her customers for Latin American bananas even though they are getting African bananas. In this way, she is increasing her profit margin.

This misuse of asymmetric information creates inefficiencies in the market. Banana consumers are paying too much for African bananas, believing they are Latin American bananas; they are being cheated. They might well be happy with African bananas, but they should be paying less for them. Then they would have more resources left over to buy other commodities, such as kiwis, blueberries, cars, cameras, a college education, or any other commodity. The produce manager is both gouging her customers and limiting their other consumption choices. Moreover, Latin American banana producers are harmed, as consumers unknowingly shift their consumption away from that commodity. This means less revenue for Latin American producers, which could affect economic conditions in their countries, perhaps lowering wages, creating unemployment, and feeding political instability. Reputable produce managers—those who do not take advantage of consumer ignorance by selling African bananas as Latin American bananas—are also damaged, because their profit margins are narrower than those of the disreputable produce manager, and this unfair advantage may either drive the reputable stores out of business or force them to adopt dishonest strategies in order to compete.

In this situation, buyers with asymmetric information face difficulties distinguishing good sellers or good products from bad sellers or bad products. This problem, called a **pooling equilibrium,** leads to inefficiencies in the production and consumption of goods and services, as consumers are making their purchasing choices with false or inadequate information. As the likelihood increases that consumers cannot distinguish good from bad products, or good from bad sellers, they may pay too much for products from less reputable sellers and too little for products from good sellers. This outcome damages the consumer and the good seller but advantages the less reputable seller and her products—because people rarely admit they are selling you an inferior product. This problem affects production and consumption in society, creating inefficiencies that are simply the difference between what is produced and consumed under asymmetric information and what is produced and consumed under conditions of full information. Facing a dilemma of sorting out good from bad claims, consumers need to create a **separating equilibrium** from a pooling equilibrium. In a separating equilibrium, buyers can distinguish among products and sellers.

The effectiveness of market exchange in allocating resources efficiently depends upon the extent to which markets work as theoretically envisioned. But models of the world (theories) are simplifications; by definition, they do not really exist. The theoretical conditions necessary for a perfect market do not exist in the empirical world. When the core conditions for efficient competitive markets are violated, there is a **market failure** (see chapter 12, where we consider breakdowns in economic and political market exchange). Market failure means only that societal resources are not allocated as efficiently as theoretically possible—society produces and consumes less than the optimal levels. Market exchange still occurs in most instances of market failure, however, for only in the most extreme cases does exchange break down completely.

MONEY: A FUNCTIONAL APPROACH

Examining modern economic activity reveals the importance of **money** and credit.[1] Before the use of money and credit, exchange was defined by barter, goods or services traded for other goods or services. The bartering process imposed significant transaction costs and

---

[1]This section draws upon Benjamin Cohen, *The Geography of Money* (1998).

created barriers to exchange. The invention of money and credit revolutionized exchange, replacing barter as the primary means of exchange. Exchange by means of money and credit was far more efficient and helped stimulate the growth of exchange over time and space. To understand why requires asking, what is *money*? The answer to that question may appear obvious to anyone who carries bills and coins in a wallet, purse, or pocket, but the idea of what constitutes money is actually much more sophisticated and nuanced. Money can be anything—physical, legal, or conceptual—that performs several key functions: it serves as a tool of exchange, a storehouse of value, and a unit of accounting.

A Tool of Exchange

As a tool of exchange, money serves as a means of payment, a device to meet the contractual obligations of an exchange. This method differs from a traditional barter economy, in which people exchange one commodity for another commodity—a bushel of corn for two chickens, a basket of beans for a pail of paint, a gallon of fuel for a pair of jeans. With barter, each party to an exchange must actually want or need the other's commodity if the trade is to occur. The owner of the corn must want the chickens, and the owner of the chickens must desire the corn. Exchange would not occur without the coincidence of these mutual wants— and both parties must be in the right place at the right time. Consequently, barter is a relatively inefficient form of exchange, as it only occurs if the farmer with chickens happens to want corn and finds a farmer with corn who happens to want chickens.

Money reduces the inefficiencies of barter by removing the need for each party to coincidentally want the other party's commodity. Instead, one party can sell its commodity, and, with no immediate consumption need for another commodity, can wait for another time to make a consumption decision. Money breaks the single barter transaction into multiple transactions, expands the number of parties potentially engaged in such transactions, and extends the immediacy of the single barter transaction into multiple transactions that can extend over time and space.

A Storehouse of Value

In order to serve as a means of payment to replace barter, money must come to be a storehouse of value. Successful money holds wealth over time, maintains its purchasing power over time, and is recognized as having those properties over time by contracting parties. Money takes on value and holds value over time when a social grouping bestows that quality upon it by means of common agreement and understanding among the members of the group. This stockpiling of value in money may involve voluntary agreement among the group members (a market solution), or it may result from nonvoluntary imposition and enforcement of a common understanding (a government solution). For example, in the 1700s and early 1800s, societies were awash in many different monies—private and public. Banks issued their own monies, governments issued monies, and sometimes other organizations created monies (again, the term includes anything that serves as a tool of exchange, a storehouse of value, and a unit of accounting). As governments defined particular monies as legal tender—meaning that they could be used to settle claims and had special standing in courts of law—the number of different monies in societies decreased. Government money was usually empowered by a definition of legal tender, which led to its increasing use and a squeezing out of private monies.

A device that maintains purchasing power over time and is commonly recognized by different parties permits immediate barter transactions to be broken into multiple transactions over time. It also expands the size of the market from trading with mostly those one knows and trusts to being able to trade with those of no acquaintance. With the use of money, the owner of the chickens does not have to trade for bushels of corn to rid herself of her chickens, but she can sell her chickens and then wait to purchase something she prefers to corn. She can exchange her chickens for money and know that the money will be good at some later time because it stores value. This practice limits her risk and uncertainty about the person to whom she sells her chickens. Money as a storehouse of value expands the range of economic activity, improves consumption possibilities by expanding the time horizon of economic transactions, and creates greater efficiencies as people purchase only what they want.

A Unit of Accounting

Finally, if money serves as a tool of exchange and a storehouse of value, it must come to hold some commonly agreed value. This definition imbues it with the ability to serve as a unit of accounting for the valuation of goods, services, and wealth. We can record output, property values, and the cost of labor by means of a common accounting standard even when we are not trading. Such a means of accounting provides a way to compare the economic activity of yesterday with that of today, and then again with that of tomorrow. It allows us to assess differences across economic activities. Measurement and accounting are integral to modern economic activity and advance.

MECHANISMS AT THE CORE OF GLOBAL LIBERALISM

Market exchange within national boundaries can lead to more efficient use of societal resources, but what about market exchange across national borders? International trade can link national markets to create a larger, more efficient global market. As philosopher and economist John Stuart Mill explained in his classic text, *The Principles of Political Economy,* published in 1848:

> The benefit of international exchange, or in other words, foreign commerce (Setting aside its enabling countries to obtain commodities which they could not themselves produce at all) . . . consists in a more efficient employment of the productive forces of the world.

International trade based upon market exchange is a cornerstone of the expansion of globalization, global capitalism, and the development of a modern global political economy.

But extending market exchange across national borders is not simple or straightforward. Even today, after several centuries of the expansion of global capitalism, debates continue about the value and wisdom of international trade based upon market exchange. In such debates, the mechanisms underpinning international market exchange and the effects of trade are often misconstrued. Some believe that the mechanisms of international trade have created greater interdependence across national political economies, enhancing welfare and promoting universal harmony. Others view international trade as a threat to sovereignty and a hindrance to national political economies.

Many have depicted globalization and international trade as a zero-sum relationship between states. (Recall from chapter 1 that zero-sum games are situations wherein one party's gain results in another party's loss.) Critics have rallied to the antiglobalization ranks for fear of the loss of jobs, investment, and economic opportunities. Those seeking to restrict trade and globalization discuss trade as a competition among nations rather than a positive-sum relationship whereby both parties to an exchange benefit from the exchange. The virulence and persistence of such negative attitudes appear with increasing regularity during electoral campaigns, despite the overwhelming recognition among economists that the mechanisms of trade produce welfare gains for society as a whole.

In his presidential bid as an independent in 1992, Ross Perot warned of a "giant sucking sound" to indicate that the U.S. economy would lose jobs to the Mexican economy if the North American Free Trade Agreement (NAFTA) were ratified. Eight years later, another independent candidate, Ralph Nader, warned of similar job losses and the exit of investment capital from the United States as a result of globalization. Unions, manufacturing workers, and owners of semi-skilled manufacturing enterprises have raised similar fears about the flight of jobs and capital from the more advanced political economies to the developing political economies. These claims raise the specter of a one-way highway, on which all capital, job creation, and trade flow in one direction, eventually impoverishing the northern political economies and enriching the southern political economies. These claims amount to zero-sum thinking, whereby one profits only at another's expense. Such claims may be useful in mobilizing political support and obstructing international exchange, but they misrepresent the facts and contradict the logic and empirical evidence of trade.

Such debates and disparagements highlight the importance of understanding international trade, how it works, and how the expansion of market exchange across national borders affects the welfare of societies and the structure of production and consumption in societies. In this section, we examine the mechanisms that make up the process of international exchange, including comparative advantage (which developed from absolute advantage), factor endowments, factor intensities, the balance-of-payments mechanism, and the exchange-rate mechanism.

Absolute Advantage

Before the era of modern international trade took hold in the early 1800s, a principle called **absolute advantage** guided the practice of trade between nations. This principle holds that if one trading partner is more capable and efficient at producing particular commodities than its other trading partners, then it should specialize in the production of such commodities and trade for goods on which others enjoy absolute advantage. Absolute advantage reflects a comparison of production costs for the same commodity across borders—comparing the cost of producing apples to apples, and oranges to oranges. A useful means of comparing production costs is focusing on the labor cost, or amount of labor time needed to produce a commodity. This process of comparison forms the basis of a **labor theory of value.** More efficient producers have lower labor costs, or lesser amounts of labor per unit of production, which constitutes one measure of productivity per unit of production.

Under the concept of absolute advantage, the justification for trade across national boundaries was to obtain commodities that a nation's workers could not produce more efficiently than workers abroad. One nation might be more proficient at producing semiconductors, automobiles, corn, aspirin, or some other product than others. Conceivably, a nation could produce all goods more efficiently than any of its potential trading partners in a commodity-by-commodity comparison; this nation would enjoy an absolute advantage in every form of production. For example, workers in the United States might be more proficient than workers in France at producing cars, semiconductors, software, corn, cheese, wine, and most other products. With absolute advantage as a guide, there would be no justification for Americans to import any of these French commodities, since a commodity-by-commodity comparison demonstrates that French labor is less efficient and hence the French products more costly than if produced in the United States—that is, American labor produces the same products in less time than French labor.

Comparative Advantage

In the early 1800s, economic thinker David Ricardo developed the principle of **comparative advantage,** which has since become the foundation of modern international trade. How does this principle differ from absolute advantage, and what does the difference mean for international trade? When the gaps in efficiency between two trading partners are greater for some products than others, one trading partner has a comparative advantage in the product with the greatest gap in efficiency.

Examples Illustrating Specialization

In the example proposed above, American labor enjoys an absolute advantage over French labor for those products it produces at a lower per unit labor cost. However, this comparison neglects the possibility that American labor might be more efficient at producing software than it is at producing cars or wine. In this example, even though the United States has an absolute advantage over France in the production of software, cars, and wine, American labor might be much more efficient (enjoying a large absolute advantage) than French labor at producing software but only a little more efficient (enjoying a small absolute advantage) in the production of automobiles or wine. Thus, the United States would have a comparative advantage in the production of software.

For an example closer to home, assume that your class valedictorian will be better at most careers than the rest of her cohort. She has an absolute advantage over her colleagues whether she chooses law, business, physics, engineering, medicine, psychology, writing, or political science. But despite having an absolute advantage over her colleagues, she may find her abilities more suited to one career over another. This is her comparative advantage, as she fits all career choices better than her peers (her absolute advantage), but some more than others (her comparative advantage). Given the assumption of scarcity that underpins the approach to political economy in this book, and recognizing that her labor is a scarce resource, the valedictorian must make a choice among careers. She will do well at any career but better in some than in others.

The same scenario is true in the example comparing American and French labor. The American labor force is more productive than French labor, but there are a limited number of work hours in a week and therefore limits to the total number of work hours for a nation's workforce, given the size of the working population. These factors are not easily manipulated—you cannot increase the size of the American or French labor force overnight. So, given these constraints on labor, what should American labor produce if it has an absolute advantage and can produce everything more efficiently than the French? Recall that in this example, American labor is far more efficient at producing software than at producing cars or wine. Such relative differences in efficiency within a nation's production capabilities and across nations for particular goods constitute the underpinnings of comparative advantage. They create the opportunity for trade to enhance economic welfare even for a nation that enjoys absolute advantage in producing every good. How can this be so?

By taking advantage of relative disparities in production costs (differences in the amount of labor needed to produce a unit of each commodity), a nation can enhance its aggregate welfare through **specialization** in the production of those products for which it has a greater comparative advantage and trading for those goods for which it has a lesser comparative advantage, even if there is an absolute advantage in all products. By specializing in those commodities with the greater comparative advantage (or smaller absolute disadvantage) and exporting those products, a nation's population can use the earnings from the exports to purchase products with a smaller comparative advantage and still have more of all commodities to consume. In the language of economics, a society that engages in trade and takes advantage of specialization has expanded its **consumption possibilities.** The next section offers a short hypothetical example that distinguishes between absolute and comparative advantage.

A Hypothetical Example of Absolute and Comparative Advantage

By the mid- to late 1800s, the cost of transport had declined dramatically, increasing the potential appeal of international exchange by significantly reducing the transaction costs. For the purpose of simplicity in our example, we assume that such transaction costs are now negligible. Focusing on the production and exchange of two commodities, grain and textiles, between the United States and the United Kingdom, we use the labor theory of value—meaning that the value of a commodity is determined by its labor content—to price these commodities. This method of valuation simplifies our example and eliminates the need to adjust for multiple currency values and exchange rates, although the same relationships would hold using multiple currencies. Now, before we begin to think about trade, let's examine what one day of a worker's labor produces in each political economy (see table 5.1).

TABLE 5.1   **A Hypothetical Example**

	Grain production per day	Textile production per day
United States	60 bushels	20 yards
United Kingdom	20 bushels	10 yards

Our first conclusion is that the United States enjoys an absolute advantage in the production of both grain and textiles, because its labor force has higher productivity than British workers in both products—60 bushels of grain vs. 20, and 20 yards of textiles vs. 10. According to absolute advantage (the economic logic preceding David Ricardo's insight), the welfare of the United States cannot be improved by importing either of these commodities from the United Kingdom. Conversely, the United Kingdom can improve its social welfare by importing both of these products from the United States, but it must have earnings from exports to pay for these commodities, and our stylized model precludes production and trade in other commodities.

Now, let's consider this same example through the lens of comparative advantage. First, we look for relative differences in the extent of the U.S. advantage in production across the two products. The United States enjoys a 3-to-1 advantage in grain production (60 vs. 20 bushels) and a 2-to-1 advantage in textile production (20 vs. 10 yards). Even though the United States enjoys an absolute advantage in producing both commodities, it has a greater relative advantage in the production of grain. U.S. labor is more efficient at producing grain than textiles (or cloth). The reverse is true for the United Kingdom: even though it has an absolute disadvantage in both products, its relative disadvantage is greater in the production of grain than textiles. Thus, the United States has a comparative advantage in the production of grain; the United Kingdom has a comparative advantage in the production of textiles.

We can illustrate these differences in relative advantage by pricing these commodities in relation to each other without considering trade. In the United States, 60 bushels of grain can purchase 20 yards of cloth—or 3 bushels of grain purchases 1 yard of cloth. In the United Kingdom 20 bushels of grain can purchase 10 yards of cloth, or 2 bushels of grain purchases 1 yard of cloth. This means that textiles are cheaper in the United Kingdom than in the United States. Flipping the example to consider the price of grain in each political economy before trade, 1 yard of textile can purchase 3 bushels of grain in the United States but only 2 bushels in the United Kingdom. Grain is cheaper in the United States.

Here, we begin to observe the potential gains from trade for both the United States and the United Kingdom, even though the United States enjoys an absolute advantage in the production of both commodities. Without international trade, a U.S. grain worker can use her 3 bushels to purchase 1 yard from a U.S. textile producer, but with international trade she can take her 3 bushels of grain and purchase 1.5 yards from a U.K. textile producer. U.S. consumers can still consume the same amount of grain they always consumed, but now they can also consume 50 percent more textiles—a clear improvement in their consumption possibilities and welfare despite the absolute advantage of the United States in the production of both commodities. Without international trade, a British textile worker can use her 1 yard to purchase 2 bushels from a U.K. grain producer, but with international trade she can use that same 1 yard to purchase three bushels from a U.S. grain producer. U.K. consumers can still consume the same amount of textiles they always consumed, but now they can also consume 50 percent more grain—a clear improvement in their consumption possibilities and welfare.

A U.S. grain worker should be willing and excited about the prospect of engaging in international trade with a British textile producer because it expands the amount of commodities she can consume for the same amount of labor, and the same is true of a U.K. textile worker. This means that even with an absolute advantage, the United States can expand its consumption possibilities and welfare if it exports the product for which it enjoys a relatively greater production advantage and imports the product for which it enjoys a relatively smaller production advantage. Of course, this equation does not work to the advantage of grain producers in the United Kingdom or textile producers in the United States, both of whom will discover that their products are at a disadvantage against those of their foreign competitors, even though the U.S. textile producer enjoys an absolute advantage over the U.K. textile producer. The mechanism of international exchange thus creates incentives for U.S. textile producers either to improve their efficiency and lower their prices vis-à-vis grain production or to shift away from textile production and toward grain production or some other form of production that enjoys a comparative advantage. The same is true for British grain producers.

Revisiting Factors of Production

Let's consider another approach to comparative advantage that will contribute to our understanding of the political economy of globalization. Ricardo's principle of comparative advan-

David Ricardo was a financial broker, country gentleman, member of Parliament, journalist, and one of the foremost economic thinkers in history. His 1817 treatise, *Principles of Political Economy and Taxation*, articulated his famous theory of comparative advantage, which transformed thinking about international trade. In this treatise, Ricardo made other extraordinary contributions to economic theory: a labor theory of value and a theory of growth. Together these pieces formed a consistent approach to economics known as the Classical or Ricardian school of economics.

tage, like the principle of absolute advantage it replaced, relied upon a labor theory of value. Comparative advantage was defined as a favorable difference in the relative costs of production, which derived from a comparison of labor costs per unit of production across commodities. This approach does not explicitly consider other potential inputs to production, such as the availability of raw materials, climate, investment in training that might make labor more productive, or investment in research that might lead to discoveries that could transform production. In short, it ignores the other two factors of production, resources (land) and capital. These inputs are implicitly embedded in the labor theory of value, as they can make labor more productive, but they are not considered explicitly. Agricultural labor becomes more productive with good soil and adequate rainfall. Coal miners became more productive with the introduction of the steam engine and power drill. Bankers became more productive with the invention of savings, credit, and investment mechanisms. Textile manufacturers became more productive with the introduction of the water-powered mill and the power loom. They are able to produce more in less time.

Factor Endowments and Heckscher-Ohlin

In the 1920s, two Swedish economists, Eli Heckscher and Bertil Ohlin, made more explicit the role of inputs other than labor. They transformed the principle of comparative advantage based upon a labor theory of value into an economic principle based upon differences across nations in their allocations of productive inputs—or factor endowments. Their approach, which became known as the **Heckscher-Ohlin model,** was later refined by other economists, most notably by Wolfgang Stolper and Paul Samuelson, in the Stolper-Samuelson theorem introduced in 1941. (Chapter 14 expands on Heckscher-Ohlin and Stolper-Samuelson when discussing international sources of potential cleavages in domestic political arenas.)

The Heckscher-Ohlin model emphasizes differences in the distribution of factors of production across national boundaries, building on several propositions. First, commodities differ in the relative quantities of the factors that are necessary to produce them. We refer to these different quantity requirements as **factor intensities**—some use more capital, some more labor, and some more land. Producing airplanes, which requires more capital than producing corn, is a *capital-intensive* industry. Producing cotton, which requires more labor and land than producing an accounting service, is *labor* or *land intensive*. Second, countries differ in their factor endowments. Some have more capital per laborer and some less; some have more capital per usable natural resource (land) and some less. Nations that have more labor relative to land are called *labor abundant*. Nations that are resource-rich relative to their labor resources are called *land* or *resource abundant*. Nations with a lot of capital per laborer or land are called *capital abundant*.

For example, the United States is capital and land abundant, but labor poor. Despite its huge physical geography, China is labor abundant but land poor. China is currently undergoing a transition in its factor endowment, however, as it seems to be moving from being a capital-poor economy to a more capital-abundant economy—time will tell. Mexico looks similar to China because it is labor abundant but capital and land poor. Japan is capital and labor abundant but land poor.

Given the conditions of supply and demand, abundant factors tend to be relatively less expensive inputs to production than are scarce factors. This difference in cost creates relative advantages and disadvantages across types of production, given differences in the factor intensities of products and the factor endowments of states. Differences in factor endowments interact with the differences in factor intensities across commodities to create comparative advantages between countries in producing different products. A country can benefit from international trade by specializing in the production of those commodities whose factor intensities match its factor endowments while trading for those products whose factor intensities fit less well with its factor endowments. This outcome, conditioned by the market, is the fundamental insight of the Heckscher-Ohlin model. With international trade, labor-abundant economies should specialize in production of labor-intensive products and export those products in exchange for land-intensive products. Land-abundant economies should specialize in producing land-intensive products and export those products in exchange for labor-intensive products.

The Stolper-Samuelson Extension

The **Stolper-Samuelson theorem,** an extension of the Heckscher-Ohlin model, recognizes that the liberalization, or greater opening, of trade benefits the abundant factors of production in an economy. Such factors are in greater supply than are scarce factors of production, and, consequently, their prices as inputs to production will be relatively lower. Producers will be encouraged to employ lower-cost inputs to production because those producers who require relatively higher-cost inputs will be penalized. Over time, the shift toward production that employs relatively abundant factors of production due to their lower costs will raise the relative prices of the abundant factors in an economy as demand for those factors increases. With more liberal trade, the price of capital will eventually increase in the capital-abundant economy, the price of labor will increase in the labor-abundant economy, and the cost of resources will increase in the land-abundant economy.

Over time, if there are no trade barriers, this dynamic will cause the prices of factors of production to converge across national boundaries. Conversely, increased barriers to trade will protect scarce factors of production from the competition of their abundant counterparts located in other states, increase the costs of those factors, and reward relatively expensive and inefficient factors of production. The consequences of more or less liberal trade can spill over into political arenas by generating winners and losers from economic activity, influencing the preferences of those winners and losers, creating cleavages in society, and affecting those groups' capabilities to form coalitions along cleavage lines and influence political outcomes (see chapter 14).

Regardless of whether the mechanism of comparative advantage derives from a labor theory of value or from factor endowments, the gains from trade are based upon the efficiency gains produced by specialization. The production possibilities in any state are bounded: a nation cannot produce petroleum by-products without oil, or a nuclear power plant without highly trained (capital-intensive) labor. But with trade and the resulting specialization in production, a nation's factor endowment is applied toward those forms of production in which it is most efficient. The resulting efficient use of resources leads to larger gains in what society can consume for the same amount of labor.

The Balance of Payments

How can the zero-sum claims we discussed at the beginning of this section on trade mechanisms persist and thrive in the face of economic theory and facts? Such claims survive because they are politically useful: helping protect people from change and taking advantage of peoples' fears and distrust of foreigners. Antitrade arguments build and depend upon poor understandings of how international exchange works and the central role of the **balance of payments** in international exchange. The balance-of-payments mechanism sits at the heart of international trade, where it serves as a giant thermostat, regulating and equilibrating trade and capital flows in the international political economy.

The balance of payments reflects a nation's economic interactions with those in other nations. It is an accounting of all the goods, services, and capital exported and imported across national borders. In economic theory, the balance of payments tends toward a long-run equilibrium whereby, over time, a nation's imports will balance out exports, and vice versa. Such an outcome will not be reached in any particular year or over a limited number of years, but over many years, the balance of payments will tend toward equilibrium. The balance-of-payments mechanism is divided into two primary categories: the current account and the capital account.

The Current Account

The **current account** describes the import and export of goods, services, and several ancillary items. It tells us about the effect of a state's domestic demand upon production and employment beyond its national borders and about the influence of foreign consumption upon a country's employment and production within its borders. A surplus in the current account means that a state is exporting more goods and services than it imports, which results in an inflow of capital based upon the net difference between imports and exports. A deficit in the current account means that a state imports more goods and services than it exports, which produces an outflow of capital.

When someone in the United States purchases a German-manufactured BMW, the U.S. current account is debited and Germany's current account is credited; when a U.S. firm purchases the services and banking advice of Deutsche Bank, the U.S. current account is debited and Germany's current account is credited; and when a German travel agency purchases the services of a U.S. tour agency, the U.S. current account is credited and the German current account is debited. Credits constitute foreign obligations and payments to domestic factors of production; debits represent domestic obligations and payments to foreign factors of production. Credits fuel employment in the domestic arena, while debits create jobs abroad.

Credits and debits create demand for currencies. Foreigners who owe U.S. producers an obligation—a credit in the U.S. current account—need to obtain U.S. dollars to pay off that claim, which creates a foreign demand for U.S. dollars. Conversely, U.S. firms or citizens with foreign obligations—debits in the U.S. current account—must obtain foreign currencies to pay those claims, which creates a domestic demand for those foreign currencies. Much of this currency exchange goes unobserved, even by those purchasing the foreign goods or services. The American who purchases the German-made BMW does not actually obtain euros to pay for that purchase, for most transactions take place in the domestic currency where the transaction occurs. However, a behind-the-scenes settlement process for such international transactions places demands for currencies to settle international obligations. We will quickly see the importance of this process as the supply and demand for currencies affects the prices of different nations' goods and services, influencing demand and providing a tremendous equilibrating force in the balance-of-payments mechanism.

The Capital Account

The **capital account** comprises capital inflows and outflows related primarily to investment at home and abroad, not consumption. Such investments fall into several different categories. **Foreign direct investment (FDI)** is investment in the control of productive facilities overseas—whether full control or only partial control. FDI occurs when Ford builds a production facility in Mexico, BMW constructs a factory in the United States, IBM opens a semiconductor plant in Thailand, or the Swiss firm Nestlé purchases the Ralston Purina Company of St. Louis, Missouri.

The other major component in the capital account is **portfolio investment,** which does not create control of an overseas facility, as does FDI. Credits or debits in the portfolio category include the sale or purchase of foreign stocks and bonds (financial instruments and obligations), borrowing from a foreign bank, or lending capital to foreign borrowers. Again, credits and debits reflect obligations of foreign parties to domestic parties or of domestic parties to foreign parties. These obligations translate into foreign demands for the domestic currency, or domestic demands for foreign currencies, when it is time to square accounts.

Long-Term Equilibrium from the Exchange-Rate Mechanism

The **exchange-rate mechanism,** reflecting the value of one currency versus another, provides the means of adjustment in the balance-of-payments mechanism and its equilibrating tendency. How does the changing demand for currencies, needed to settle the obligations reflected in the balance of payments, generate equilibrating pressures on the balance of payments and affect the flow of goods, services, and capital over time? In the mid-1700s, David Hume provided the intellectual underpinnings for explaining why the flow of goods, services, and capital across national boundaries would tend toward a balance in the long run, with some years in deficit and some years in surplus but always returning toward a balance. Hume's writings on "specie flow," the flow of money, provided elegant and powerful insights grounded in a quantity theory of money. Hume viewed money as a commodity that is exposed to the forces of supply and demand—demands such as the need to meet foreign obligations. Simply, if a nation's domestic money supply decreases because of the need to purchase foreign monies to fulfill foreign obligations, as accounted in the balance of payments, there is less domestic money to purchase goods and services or to pay labor in the domestic market. This reduced money supply puts downward pressures on the price of domestic goods, services, and labor, as there is less money to go around. In his 1753 essay, "Of the Balance of Trade," Hume provided a nice mental example:

> Suppose four-fifths of all the money in Great Britain to be annihilated in one night, . . . what would be the consequence? Must not the price of all labour and commodities sink in proportion and everything be sold *cheap[er]*. [emphasis added]

Conversely, if a state's balance of payments is in surplus—exports exceeding imports—foreigners must obtain that country's currency to meet their obligations. This situation results in a repatriation of the national money, which increases the supply of the state's currency in the home market and leaves less abroad. With an increase in the supply of domestic money, prices on domestic commodities, services, and labor can increase. Or, as Hume went on to hypothesize:

Suppose that all the money in Great Britain were multiplied fivefold in a night, must not . . . all labour and commodities rise to such an exorbitant height. . . .

Changes in the quantity of money, and the resulting changes in prices of domestic goods and labor, result in a self-correcting balance-of-payments mechanism. If the shrinkage in domestic money supply produces a decline in a country's prices for domestic goods, services, and labor, its products and services decline in price in overseas markets also. A decrease in these prices, at home and abroad, would then lead to an increase in their attractiveness relative to products produced by overseas producers, all else being equal. But, of course, everything else is not equal.

Contractions in domestic money supplies in states experiencing balance-of-payments deficits are accompanied by increases in money supplies of those states experiencing balance-of-payments surpluses. As expansion of the money supply in those surplus countries produces an increase in the prices of their domestic goods, services, and labor, those products and services increase in price in overseas markets also. This increase in prices, at home and abroad, then leads to a decrease in their attractiveness relative to products produced overseas in nations experiencing balance-of-payments deficits. Put together, prices related to domestic production fall in states experiencing balance-of-payments deficits due to the shrinking quantity of money, but prices related to domestic production rise in nations experiencing balance-of-payments surpluses due to the expanding quantity of money. Prices of domestic goods and services become comparatively cheaper than foreign goods and services in the deficit states but comparatively more expensive in the surplus states. This relative shift in the prices of goods and services produced overseas versus those produced at home enters into the calculations of consumers possessing limited resources. It shifts their consumption choices and puts self-correcting pressures on the balance of payments.

This money flow rests at the heart of the international trading system. States experiencing balance-of-payment deficits or surpluses will incur changes in domestic money supplies that, over time, produce changes in domestic prices in relation to foreign prices, which lead to changes in consumption of domestic versus foreign goods and services. This ongoing process generates a pendulum effect in the balance of payments—deficit to surplus, surplus to deficit, and on and on. Many refinements and discoveries have been appended to Hume's specie flow model since the 1700s, but the basic mechanism still applies.

CONCLUSION: EXPECTATIONS FROM THE BASELINE ECONOMIC FRAMEWORK

David Ricardo's principle of comparative advantage overcame major obstacles to international exchange presented by national boundaries. Ricardo's insight transformed thinking about international exchange and led policymakers to reconsider the gains and losses from international exchange. The concept of comparative advantage showed them that all sides could gain from the expansion of trade and the specialization of production—that trade is a positive-sum, not a zero-sum relationship, regardless of absolute advantage. Ricardo's discovery, combined with Hume's insights about the relationship of prices to monetary flows based on exchange, underpins our understanding about the benefits of international economic exchange and the balancing mechanism that regulates trade. The recognition of the benefits of international exchange advanced by Ricardo and by scores of later economists— a recognition that has been well-supported by empirical research and so has become accepted orthodoxy in economics—leads to predictions and prescriptions about the policies that liberal political economies should pursue.

Our analytic frameworks should allow us to describe the characteristics of a liberal system and to predict what we should observe, given the expectations that arise from our understanding of liberal economic exchange. First, if market exchange leads to maximum economic growth, efficiency, and the greatest advances in aggregate economic welfare, we should expect that policymakers in a liberal political economy will pursue policies that encourage greater market exchange in the domestic arena. Such policies should produce the greatest level of satisfaction in their polities. Therefore, we should expect to see policies in the domestic arena that promote, not obstruct, market exchange. We should expect politics and economics to remain separate arenas except in those areas in which public policy could help to promote market exchange—as in defining property rights, adjudicating and enforcing contracts, promoting disclosure so that buyers and sellers are equally well-informed about the products being exchanged, ensuring competitive markets, and managing other forces that could produce market failure.

Next, if promoting market exchange in the domestic arena is good, then expanding such exchange to take advantage of specialization and discipline in larger and larger markets would be better. If aggregate social welfare is enhanced by market exchange because the invisible hand coordinates the use of factors of production given society's wants and desires, then coordinating larger and larger pools of factors of production should only increase the efficiency of the invisible hand and the satisfaction of society. Policymakers in liberal political economies should seek to promote greater trade and exchange across borders, regardless of the actions of other states' policymakers. They should seek to lower barriers to entry at home and abroad because increased market exchange enhances the social welfare of their populations, and they should enact such policies unilaterally if others do not. From a liberal perspective, if other states' policymakers choose to maintain discriminatory barriers to trade, they are only hurting their own populations—which is no reason for liberal policy makers to adopt similar policy stances and detract from the social welfare of their own polities.

What about conflict in an international political economy based upon liberal market exchange? Chapter 3 notes that conflict may be an inherent component of a global political economy built around nation-states as the dominant form of political organization. Does economic liberalism produce the same expectations? Since the distribution of benefits in a liberal international political economy are mutually beneficial—a positive-sum scenario wherein the absolute gains are positive for those adopting liberal economic policies—should we expect any degree of inherent conflict or persistent cleavage in the international political economy? On a theoretical level, should a rational policymaker adopt nonliberal policies that are detrimental to the social welfare of her society? The answer is no; there is no basis in liberal economic theory for such policies. Greater interdependence leads to increased welfare for societies engaged in more open exchange. This social-welfare argument for interconnectedness provides the foundation for expectations that interdependence increases harmony and reduces tensions between countries, regardless of the nation-state system.

In *The Principles of Political Economy and Taxation* (1817), David Ricardo posed just such a benevolent and harmonious view of trade and globalization:

> Under a system of perfectly free commerce, each country naturally devotes its capital and labour to such employments as are most beneficial to each. The pursuit of individual advantage is admirably connected with the universal good of the whole. By stimulating industry, by rewarding ingenuity, and by using most efficaciously the peculiar powers bestowed by nature, it distributes labour most effectively and most economically: while, by increasing the general mass of productions, it diffuses general benefit, and binds together, by one common tie of interest and intercourse, the universal society of nations throughout the civilized world.

Expectations of enhanced social welfare from increased interdependence lead to expectations about the policies of governments toward trade with other states and about the nature of international politics. In an international arena dominated by market exchange and liberal rules of the game in economic interactions, we should expect politics and economics to remain separate arenas except in those areas in which public policy can help to promote international exchange and interdependence. As a large component of any political arena, economic welfare should encourage cooperative international political relations and public policies to reflect a benign rather than a malevolent interdependence. As in domestic political arenas, we should expect policymakers to enact policies between states that promote greater trade and exchange across borders. Conflict can interrupt such relations, so we should expect policies that reduce rather than exacerbate international tensions.

What is the purpose of international organizations such as the International Monetary Fund, the World Bank, the World Trade Organization, the United Nations, the World Health Organization, and numerous other multilateral development organizations? What types of policies and frameworks should we expect to see such organizations promote? What is their role? From a liberal economic perspective, we should expect to see such organizations encouraging discussions, debates, and policies that would promote interdependence and international exchange. They should be constructive mechanisms for providing infrastructure advantageous to exchange across borders and for helping to reduce barriers to the coordination that would aid such exchange. Certainly, some barriers to exchange across borders are more difficult to circumvent than those within borders, for different states have different rules about private property and the exchange of property, different notions of contracts, different rules of adjudication and enforcement, and different monetary systems. These differences can produce barriers to exchange, even unintentionally. From a liberal economic perspective, international organizations can help by addressing such problems and influencing governments to adopt policies that will enhance their societies' social welfare.

The expectations just described are consistent with a liberal economic framework. To summarize, if markets work as anticipated in economic theory, we should expect to see particular forms of political behavior in domestic and international arenas. From a liberal economic perspective, we should expect the following behaviors:

- Policymakers pursue policies that encourage greater market exchange in their domestic arenas.
- Politics and economics remain separate domestic arenas except in those areas in which public policy could help to promote market exchange.
- Policymakers enact policies that promote greater trade and exchange across borders, regardless of the actions of other states' policymakers.
- Greater interdependence produces increased harmony and reduces international tensions between nations.
- Politics and economics remain separate arenas in international relations except in those areas in which public policy could help to promote international exchange and interdependence.
- International organizations are constructive mechanisms for provision of infrastructure advantageous to economic exchange across national borders and reduction of barriers to coordination that would aid such exchange.

These expectations provide a baseline, or yardstick, for evaluating market exchange and government policies in the global political economy, for considering the strengths and limitations of such theory, and for determining when such theories approximate empirical behavior and when (and why) they do not.

EXERCISES

1. What is the role of preferences in a competitive market? What do they have to do with self-interest?

2. Why must all participants in efficient and competitive markets be price-takers?

3. What is the difference between a positive and a negative externality? Why is free-riding associated with positive externalities? Give examples of a positive and a negative externality in international relations not cited in the book. Explain how they work.

4. Why is information important to efficient market exchange?

5. Explain how the three functions of money are at work when you save your earnings from a part-time job and use them to buy CDs of your favorite music.

6. Why are international monetary arrangements important to international trade?

7. Explain how a deficit in your nation's current account affects workers and producers in another country.

8. What transaction costs may be incurred with the definition and enforcement of property rights, and how does this affect the efficiency of market exchange?

9. Every nation has a different factor endowment, or distribution of the factors of production, which means that they are comparatively rich in some factor or factors, but lacking in other factor(s). From what you know, or using resources in your school's library or on the Internet, describe the factor endowments for Russia and for Denmark. In each case, which factors are relatively abundant and which are relatively scarce?

10. Explain the difference between absolute and comparative advantage.

11. What is the long-term tendency of the balance-of-payment mechanism? Why?

Further Reading

Caves, Richard E., Jeffrey A. Frankel, and Ronald W. Jones. 2002. *World Trade and Payments.* 9th ed. Boston: Little, Brown.

Coase, Ronald H. 1937. "The Nature of the Firm," *Economica* 4:386–405.

Krugman, Paul. 1999. *Pop Internationalism.* Cambridge, Mass.: MIT Press.

Hume, David. 1741. "Of the Balance of Trade," in *Essays, Moral, Political, and Literary.* Reprint, Indianapolis: Liberty Fund, 1987.

———. 1752. *Political Discourses.* Reprint, New York: Walter Scott, 1906.

Kenen, Peter. 2000. *The International Economy.* 4th ed. Cambridge: Cambridge University Press.

Miller, Gary J. 1992. *Managerial Dilemmas: The Political Economy of Hierarchy.* Cambridge: Cambridge University Press.

North, Douglass. 1990. *Institutions, Institutional Change, and Economic Performance.* Cambridge: Cambridge University Press.

Polanyi, Karl. 1957. *The Great Transformation.* Boston: Beacon.

Ricardo, David. 1817. *The Principles of Political Economy and Taxation,* chapter 7. Reprint, Amherst, N.Y: Prometheus Books, 1996.

Roberts, Russell. 2001. *The Choice: A Fable of Free Trade and Protectionism.* Upper Saddle River, N.J.: Prentice Hall.

Schotter, Andrew. 1984. *Free Market Economics: a Critical Appraisal.* New York: Palgrave Macmillan.

6

Political Markets and Exchange

Most of the time we do the right thing if we have enough information and enough time to think about it.

President Bill Clinton, Riverside Church, New York City, August 29, 2004

MARKET EXCHANGE IN THE POLITICAL ARENA

Applying the economic arena's logic of the market mechanism to political arenas provides a powerful analytical tool for examining politics. But let's first ask whether this is a reasonable analytical strategy—can we extend the market analogy to politics? In economics, markets are aggregation and allocation mechanisms, coordinating rational, goal-oriented individual behavior of consumers and producers, which choreographs the use of society's scarce resources. Politics is also a social aggregation and allocation process—it aggregates preferences and choices, coordinates and allocates the use of resources in society, and produces social outcomes. As a famous political scientist wrote, "politics is about who gets what and how." If the market analogy is to apply, we must have the following reasonable expectations: (1) that citizens act as rational consumers of political goods, (2) that politicians, policymakers, and bureaucrats act as rational producers of political goods, and (3) that the exchange between citizens as consumers and politicians as producers of political goods conforms to our expectations of what constitutes market exchange.

Can we assume that citizens, politicians, policymakers, and bureaucrats act as if they are rational consumers and producers in an exchange relationship? Do they act as if they are making trade-offs across political goods based upon their ranking of the alternatives, the costs of the different alternatives, and the expected utility of one choice over another? Is it reasonable to assume that when citizens vote, they are attempting to exercise their preferences about the agendas and actions of political parties, public policies and programs, politicians, government bureaucrats, and their bureaucracies? Is voting an attempt to purchase a political outcome? When people vote, do they exchange their votes for the possibility that a preferred politician and her agenda will ascend to office, a preferred outcome on a referendum will attain, or a preferred party and its policy agenda will prevail? If so, they are participating in an exchange relationship as rational consumers, with policymakers, politicians, bureaucrats, and political parties as the producers of political goods.

On the production side of political exchange, do politicians, policymakers, public bureaucrats, and political parties seek support from voters and the populace by marketing political goods? Do they seek to peddle public policies, sell their agendas, and market candidates? What happens to politicians, political parties, policymakers, and bureaucrats if they succeed in marketing their products and agendas, and what happens if they fail? If they succeed, are they rewarded as successful economic producers are in a market—do they gain market share and influence? If they fail to sell their products and agendas, are they penalized in the way that unsuccessful producers are in economic markets—do they lose market share and influence, or even go out of business? If successful and unsuccessful producers in political arenas experience fates similar to successful and unsuccessful producers in economic markets, the market analogy gains traction and applicability to political behavior. From this perspective, citizens and politicians do seem to fit the analogy of rational consumers and producers of political commodities.

THE MECHANISM OF POLITICAL EXCHANGE

Even if political consumers and producers act as if they were rational, do the means of their exchange approximate those of market exchange? Is the market mechanism an appropriate and useful characterization of political exchange? A variety of market and nonmarket types of exchange occur in societies. In all but the most repressive authoritarian regimes, consumers and producers of political commodities do not unilaterally determine the supply, demand, and price of those political commodities. In most political arenas, the interaction of numerous producers (politicians, parties, and policymakers) and numerous consumers (voters and citizens)—and the aggregation of their choices and actions—create the social outcomes we observe in political arenas. This interaction of political producers and consumers draws our attention to the aggregation processes in political arenas, the mechanisms by which individual choices interact and are compiled to generate social outcomes. Are the aggregation mechanisms in political arenas akin to those in economic markets?

Elections are an appropriate place to begin evaluating whether we can view political exchange as a market relationship between producers and consumers of political commodities. Elections constitute a decentralized mechanism for aggregating societal preferences. They are built around individual choice. If we look around the world, we quickly recognize that elections are only one way to organize political life. Many people live in political arenas where the exercise of political choice at the ballot box is an anomaly. Autocracies, monarchies, and anarchies do not offer meaningful, stable electoral processes. This does not mean there is an absence of political exchange, but that the transfer of political commodities between political producers and consumers takes place through some aggregation mechanism other than individual choice in a decentralized political market—generally a more centralized hierarchical mechanism. Here, the rules of exchange are, generally, more arbitrary, ad hoc, and circumscribed than in arenas with stable electoral processes. Individuals in such systems can still exercise choice by voting with their feet in protest or rebellion, but their ability to obtain political commodities by exchanging their votes at the ballot box are limited or nonexistent.

Democratic and decentralized political arenas seek to provide individuals with voice (influence) over their political circumstances by granting them property rights over their votes, which they can exchange for political commodities such as policies and politicians. An election is an aggregation device that creates the opportunity for individuals to exercise their property rights over their votes. Hopefully, this aggregation device accurately assembles individual choices and preferences into an outcome that generates the greatest amount of social welfare in the political arena. Just as a variety of market mechanisms exist in economic exchange, a range of electoral forms dot the political landscape. For example, members of the U.S. Congress are elected by a plurality rule, whereby the "winner takes all." This rule means that the candidate with the most votes wins the election, and the people who voted for losing candidates do not obtain a share of the representation proportional to the votes their candidates received. In systems such as the European parliamentarian democracies, even those who vote for candidates that do not receive a plurality of the vote (the largest vote share) receive some proportional representation in the legislature, if their candidate's share of the vote exceeds a predefined threshold (for example, 10 percent of the vote).

Voluntary versus Nonvoluntary Exchange

The differences across the examples described here suggest a potentially important difference between economic market exchange and political exchange—the potential for nonvoluntary consumption in political exchange. In economic markets, the parties to an exchange participate voluntarily as they exchange property rights over one commodity for property rights over another. They do not knowingly consume a commodity that they do not wish to consume. We can assess consumers' interpersonal utility for one commodity versus another by what they consume and how much they are willing to spend. This voluntary quality of consumption choices underpins the normative appeal of economic market exchange: it enshrines the rights and liberty of the individual.

Yet, nonvoluntary consumption of political commodities appears to occur with great frequency in political arenas. Nonvoluntary consumption is most evident in states governed by authoritarian regimes, which often redistribute societal resources by hierarchical fiat, denying political consumers any property rights over their votes and political consumption decisions. An exchange takes place in this arena, but we cannot make any assumptions about the voluntary nature of that exchange and we hesitate to claim improved social welfare where most citizens have had no say in the exchange. These regimes are clearly not efficiently functioning political markets, but the market analogy can still provide a useful framework for considering such authoritarian political arrangements as examples of market failure and diagnosing the damage such regimes do to social welfare.

But nonvoluntary consumption also appears to take place in political arenas that enshrine the notion of individual electoral choice, such as the European and U.S. examples cited earlier. In these political arenas, a voter casts her vote for a particular candidate or policy, but those who voted for Al Gore in 2000 or John Kerry in 2004 still had to consume George W. Bush and his administration's policies. In the United States, when a voter's preferred candidate or policy loses in an election or referendum, she still has to consume the specific political commodity she voted against unless she then moves to another state or place that is more to her liking in terms of the production of political commodities. Certainly, throughout history, many people have migrated from one society to another for political reasons. Almost without exception, migrating people have searched for more liberty and choice in their consumption of political commodities, not less. But exit is often difficult: economic means, language, family and social ties, culture, space as a scarce resource, and geographical affinity may all affect the ability of an individual to migrate in order to avoid consumption of a particular political commodity. We could sidestep our dilemma of voluntary versus nonvoluntary political exchange by asserting that individuals consume an assortment of social, political, and economic commodities and must make trade-offs across such commodities because we live in a world of scarce resources. Because we make trade-offs across goods, we can't always have our cake and eat it too, as the saying goes. This is true, but it does not negate the distinction between a voluntary, symmetric exchange in a decentralized market (where parties that are viewed as equal in terms of their choice to participate in the exchange) and an exchange that involves asymmetric authority of one party to direct the actions of others (where one party enjoys more influence over the exchange than the other parties to an exchange).

If our losing voter remains in place, does this decision indicate whether she is subject to voluntary or nonvoluntary consumption of a political commodity? Our answer lies in why our voter votes. If she votes because she values the process more than any specific outcome, then it is voluntary exchange even if she dislikes the specific outcome. Her participation purchases and legitimates the broader democratic process, and not any specific political good. Many people vote because they value the process of democratic politics, peaceful resolution of political differences through electoral processes, and societal compromise even if they disagree with specific outcomes. But, if our voter's candidate or policy loses in the election and she does not find inherent merit in the process that produced that outcome, her subsequent consumption of the political commodity produced by the election is nonvoluntary. Nonvoluntary political exchange may not improve social welfare if people value particular outcomes over processes. In fact, it can detract from individual liberties, depending upon what commodity political consumers must consume.

Inevitably, in political settings with asymmetric authority, even good democratic settings, some political exchange will involve some nonvoluntary consumption. Both authoritarian and democratic regimes employ asymmetric authority and hierarchical imposition, but they do so to significantly different degrees. Unlike voluntary exchange, nonvoluntary transactions pose an analytic dilemma in evaluating the individual benefit, social efficiency, and social welfare that may result. We have no standard for making interpersonal welfare comparisons. With nonvoluntary transactions we cannot assess how much voters actually value a candidate or policy they did not support. We can observe trade-offs, costs, and prices in voluntary exchange, as well as consumption choices that allow us to assess the value of commodities purchased and not purchased by individuals. But with nonvoluntary exchange, such as voting for the losing candidate or policy and then having to consume the winning candidate or policy, we cannot determine how much our losing voter values the winning candidate or policy—she must consume the winning candidate or policy regardless of the costs to her. This nonvoluntary quality undermines our ability to assess the relative gains or costs to society.

Social Choice and Voting Rules

Elections offer a mechanism for aggregating individual preferences in political exchange. In elections, a **voting rule** defines the process by which societies decide upon the political commodities they will consume. As we've discussed earlier, a wide variety of voting systems are employed around the world. Voting rules such as dictatorial rule, majority rule, plurality rules, supermajority rules, unanimity, and other rules are all mechanisms that aggregate the political preferences of a society's members—or some of its members—and coordinate those preferences with the production of political commodities by politicians, governments, and political parties. Each system has its strengths, weaknesses, and trade-offs. Drafters of national constitutions and designers of electoral systems must weigh the strengths and weaknesses of different voting rules and definitions of political property rights as they seek to build the structure for political exchange in their societies.

The fact that a voter must consume the winning candidate or policy regardless of whether that outcome reflects her preferences begs an important question. Are some types of aggregation mechanisms or voting rules more effective than others at accurately and efficiently compiling and protecting individual choices in a political arena and producing outcomes that also improve social welfare? A school of inquiry called **social choice theory** studies aggregation mechanisms in search of voting mechanisms that accurately aggregate the preferences of society's members, optimizing individual liberty and social outcomes. Voting rules such as majority rule, plurality rules, supermajority rules, unanimity, and other rules are designed with the intention of aggregating individual preferences to produce a social outcome. Each voting rule has its strengths, weaknesses, and trade-offs in terms of efficiently aggregating individual preferences, enhancing social welfare, and limiting the problem of nonvoluntary exchange. To date, however, no voting rule in political exchange overcomes all the problems of nonvoluntary consumption, nor is such a voting rule likely to be developed, given the theoretical requirements of such a rule. This dilemma also is true of economic exchange, but it is far less visible to the average observer.

Despite the potential of nonvoluntary exchange, the market analogy offers a powerful and useful tool for examining political behavior, if we guard against naiveté and remain aware of the prospects for nonvoluntary exchange. Just as it does in the economic arena, using the market framework to examine choices and exchange in political arenas offers a baseline to evaluate how well political exchange works in terms of efficiently and accurately connecting individual preferences with social outcomes. Moreover, the framework provides tools for determining when and why exchange in political markets falls short of the idealized case.

REVISITING THEORETICAL CONDITIONS FOR EFFICIENT MARKETS

The normative attractiveness of market exchange comes from its theoretical potential to improve social and individual outcomes as compared to other types of allocation mechanisms in society, while still protecting individual liberty and voluntary choice. As we noted in the previous chapter, the empirical world always falls short of the idealized theoretical world. No markets are perfectly competitive, and no markets perfectly aggregate individual preferences to produce ideal social outcomes. No markets are perfectly efficient. We have also noted that political exchange can involve nonvoluntary relationships among hierarchical parties. But some economic and political markets do better than others, and some do dramatically better! Obtaining desirable outcomes from market exchange depends upon markets working as closely as possible to how they were theoretically envisioned—or at least not failing too badly.

Let's take the core conditions for efficient market exchange in economic arenas, which we examined in chapter 5, and apply those same conditions to political arenas. A socially efficient and competitive political market optimizes the production and consumption of political goods, as well as the use of the resources that go into political and economic activity, given the mix of individual preferences in society. Political market exchange maximizes social welfare if the market mechanism accurately aggregates individuals' preferences and leads to the production of political and economic goods that best meet those desires; in other words, no other level of production of political and economic goods could produce greater overall societal happiness. In this ideal case, the production of such goods lies on what is called the "production-possibility frontier," as seen in figure 6.1. As we move along this particular production-possibility frontier, we get different mixes of two commodities—guns and butter—but each mix uses societal resources efficiently and produces the maximum amount of societal happiness. We call this frontier **Pareto optimal,** meaning that we cannot move off this frontier to improve the welfare of some specific members of society without damaging the welfare of others and of society as a whole, given the preferences of all members of society. This is an equilibrium wherein another distribution of resources and efforts cannot benefit one member of society without hurting another and lowering the overall efficiency of the production and consumption of goods given the mix of preferences in society.

Being on the production-possibility frontier—or being Pareto optimal—in a political market is easier said than done: it is only possible if exchange fulfills the set of essential conditions to efficient exchange in economic markets: (1) that parties to an exchange have clearly defined property rights and can negotiate, monitor, and enforce contracts at relatively negligible costs; (2) that no individual buyer or seller, or cartel of buyers or sellers, can manipulate the price mechanism; (3) that transactions in such markets have no effect on third parties; and (4) that all parties to an exchange enjoy complete or full information. Let's examine each of these conditions in the context of political exchange.

Property Rights and Transaction Costs

Clear definition of property rights and the ability of parties to an exchange to negotiate, monitor, and enforce contracts at relatively negligible costs are critical to efficient and competitive markets. What does this mean in the context of political exchange? In political markets, citizens trade their votes for goods produced by politicians, policymakers, bureaucrats, and political parties. They can also trade their labor and financial resources by working on campaigns, making contributions to campaigns, advocating public causes, or funding efforts in behalf of such causes. Clear definition of property rights means that there is no ambiguity over who can vote or what they can contribute in exchange for political commodities. With clear definition of property rights, citizens own the property rights over their votes, the labor they can donate to political causes, and their financial contributions to political activities. They can freely exchange these forms of support for the promise of political goods, and politicians know whether their supporters can deliver at the ballot box.

Clear definition of property rights in political exchange also means that there is no ambiguity about whether policymakers can or cannot deliver the political commodities that they offer in exchange for voter support. For example, in elections for student council and class officers, candidates often run on platforms that promise greater oversight and input to school policy and performance, better food in the school cafeteria, or improvements in the functioning of the school library or computing systems. Yet, candidates for student council or class office do not have the ability or authority to make such changes. They do not own or control the property rights over such policies—that is, they do not have the ability to exchange improvements in such areas for their colleagues' votes. The property rights for such changes lie in the hands of school administrators, local government, and, ultimately, taxpay-

| FIGURE 6.1 | **The Production-Possibility Frontier of Political and Economic Goods** |

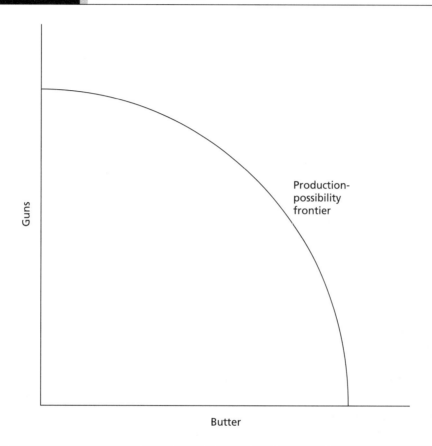

Production-possibility frontier

Guns

Butter

ers and voters. If fellow students vote for candidates based upon such promises, they misunderstand who owns the right to make such changes—they are misinformed.

Clear definition of property rights is insufficient to ensure efficient political exchange, if the transaction costs of such an exchange are prohibitive. If an election, a referendum, a legislative act, or a political promise constitutes an exchange between voters and policymakers, the costs of negotiating, monitoring and enforcing the terms of the exchange must be small or negligible if the exchange is to be efficient. For example, in the American South after Reconstruction, African Americans were systematically discriminated against in political arenas. Barriers such as Jim Crow laws were constructed to prevent them from registering to vote and exercising their political franchise. Even if such citizens could have clearly asserted their property rights over their votes, the transaction costs of doing so were prohibitive.

Southern whites used legal obstructions, psychological and physical harassment, beatings, and lynching to deprive African Americans of their rights in political markets. In another example, the transaction costs of voting against Saddam Hussein and his party in Iraqi elections were prohibitively high for Iraqi citizens, even though there was little ambiguity about who had the right to vote. Election observers from the United Nations, the Carter Center in Atlanta, and other organizations routinely monitor elections and plebiscites in emerging democracies, looking for evidence of voter fraud or tampering (ambiguity over the property rights of a vote) and systematic intimidation or discrimination against a particular segment of society (significant transaction costs). Both can undermine efficient and competitive political exchange.

Voters must also be able to easily assess whether policymakers are fulfilling their commitments, and policymakers must be able to easily evaluate whether voters are voting as promised. Are politicians delivering the policy goods that they promised in exchange for votes and support, and are voters actually casting their votes and throwing their support as promised? The more difficulty or uncertainty voters and policymakers encounter in determining whether the other party to a political exchange is actually fulfilling its part in the terms of the exchange, the more likely that one party or another can cheat. If voters know that policymakers cannot easily monitor their support, voters can more easily assert their support in exchange for a political good, but then not deliver their support at the ballot box. If policymakers know that voters will have a difficult time evaluating whether they have lived up to their commitments, they can more easily claim to have delivered policies that they did not.

Even if it were possible to overcome such uncertainty, citizens and policymakers would have to invest substantial resources in monitoring the actions of each other. Thomas Jefferson viewed an active free press as necessary for democracy, as it would seek out and provide information that could help overcome voters' uncertainty about their policymakers. If successful, a free press can monitor the activities of voters and policymakers and so help to overcome their uncertainty about the political exchange, but this investment of social resources is, nevertheless, inefficient. If the actions of politicians and voters were transparent and easily monitored, a press—free or not—would be unnecessary. With greater and greater uncertainty, political exchange becomes less and less efficient and may even break down. Ambiguities over who can vote, how citizens can participate in political life, and what political commodities are to be exchanged can detract from the value of political exchange and creates inefficiencies in political markets: voters feel disenfranchised and stay home, while politicians ignore constituent needs, become corrupt, and use their positions to redistribute societal resources to special interests, cronies, or family.

Manipulation of the Price Mechanism

As in economic markets, a key condition for competitive and efficient political markets is that no single provider or consumer—or collusive cartel of providers or consumers—of political commodities such as policies or politicians can unilaterally manipulate and determine the terms of political exchange (supply and price in economic markets). Consumers of political commodities must be able to choose among viable alternatives. There must be sufficient competition in political arenas so that producers of political commodities cannot act as monopolists or oligopolists, or consumers as **monopsonists** (single buyers) or **oligopsonists** (one of very few buyers). A monopolist in a political market acts as an authoritarian provider, not providing her citizens with alternatives or allowing citizens to select an alternative. Cleopatra, Caesar, Hitler, Stalin, Saddam Hussein, and other dictators stifled political competition and prevented their citizens from selecting an alternative to their leadership. By eliminating their opponents, they prevented political competition. The citizens of their states had no effective choice among the political commodities they consumed, nor could they easily or comfortably exit those arenas or refuse to contribute to the provision of those commodities. Tax collection in such states is often far more intrusive and violent than in well-functioning democracies. Authoritarian leaders essentially manipulate the supply and price of political commodities in their political arenas.

Effective political competition underpins healthy democracies. Competitive elections and other representative devices provide mechanisms for consumers of political commodities to articulate *meaningful* preferences among alternatives. Under such conditions, the producers of political commodities care about consumer preferences, which conditions the producers' activities. Voters in competitive democracies can decide whether to continue consuming the political products of an incumbent regime or to throw the buggers out and opt for another set of political commodities offered by an alternative regime. Effective political competition enables societies to constrain their policymakers, to accept or reject their policies, and to choose among alternatives. In competitive political markets, elections and other forms of representation such as public opinion, interest group activities, litigation in courts, and debate in the media are aggregation mechanisms comparable to the price mechanism in economic markets. They provide signals to producers of political commodities that can influence their decisions about what political commodities to supply and how much—or what not to provide.

In competitive political markets, producers of political commodities who ignore consumers risk their own political survival, for elections are the ultimate form of term limitations in such markets. Producers of political commodities cannot use the political arena to pursue their narrow individual interests irrespective of the broader societal interests. Political competition pushes politicians to take their public's needs into consideration. The mechanisms of competition in political markets coordinate the individual needs of politicians and the individual needs of political consumers to produce social outcomes that are inherently more socially efficient than those produced by a monopolist. You may not appreciate this outcome if you are the potential monopolist, but you will if you are not the monopolist. Effective political competition coordinates supply and demand in the production of political commodities.

The requirements for producers of political commodities to ensure competitive and efficient political markets also apply to the demand or consumption side of the political exchange. In a competitive and efficient political market, no single consumer, or cartel of consumers, can unilaterally affect the demand for a political commodity, determine an election, or extract special privilege against the will of the broader society. Complaints about special-interest politics, insider access, and worries about the influence of money upon politics are concerns about the ability of narrow swaths of society to manipulate the provision of political commodities and distort the political marketplace. In international trade, agricultural producers in many societies (France, Japan, the United States, Denmark, and many others) have been able to obtain public policies such as tariffs, quotas, and government subsidies for their economic sector even though these protectionist policies damage the majority in each of their societies. Special-interest politics raises the possibility that the votes of specific individuals or groups may count more than others in the political market, and that the provision of political commodities would look different if such special interests did not exist or were constrained from exercising disproportionate influence.

Many societies have attempted to constrain special interests in order to limit the emergence of cartels of consumers of political commodities. Many constitutions seek to protect their societies against influential cartels of political consumers by creating institutions that define and protect specific rights, such as the voting franchise, political speech, religious practice, and access to due process. They prohibit the trading of such rights as political commodities. Many constitutions prohibit voters from selling their votes to other voters, even if it is a voluntary surrendering of the right to vote, in order to limit the ability of any individual or narrow group to garner disproportionate influence over the production of political commodities—an influence that would distort political exchange and generate social inefficiencies. Imagine that Bill Gates, the richest man in the world, could use his wealth to purchase your voting franchise. Would you sell your vote for $10, $100, $1,000, or more? If you could sell your vote, Bill Gates could use his wealth to purchase enough votes to determine the outcome of an election or referendum.

How much competition is enough to create the possibility for socially efficient political exchange? Clearly, a single producer of political commodities is insufficient. Political consumers with no alternatives cannot refuse to consume the monopolist's goods or drive the monopolist out of political business. Of course, people may be able to emigrate or revolt, but this will not help to break the monopolist's stranglehold by creating political competition and alternative producers of political commodities. If one is not enough, are a large number of producers of political commodities required to ensure a competitive and socially efficient political market? Not necessarily: a competitive political market requires only enough producers of political commodities to offer consumers of those commodities a choice of another policy or politician, if one producer ignores their preferences. When political consumers—citizens and voters—can switch their choices and substitute another political commodity, they can discipline producers who fail to respond to their demands.

In the United Kingdom, can citizens who voted for winning Labour Party candidates in one election switch their votes to Liberal-Democratic or Conservative Party candidates in the next election if they become dissatisfied with the performance and policies of the Labour Party? Does such a switch, or threat of a switch, by voters constrain politicians from acting as monopolists in the production of political commodities? Can German voters withdraw their support from a Christian Democrat government to support a Social Democrat government instead? Can U.S. voters shift their support from a Republican politician to support a Democrat? A competitive political market requires only enough alternatives among producers of political commodities so that voters can shift their support in order to discipline politicians. Just as the price mechanism coordinates supply and demand in a competitive and efficient economic market, elections coordinate supply and demand in a competitive and efficient political market. As for the question about how much competition is enough to create the possibility for socially efficient political exchange—it does not take a lot. The necessary number will be a function of the voting rules and electoral institutions of a society. Under some institutional arrangements, two producers of political commodities can be enough to create a competitive political market and enhance social efficiency, while more than two could be inefficient! We explore such an example at the end of this chapter.

Third-Party Externalities

In the previous chapter, we noted that competitive and socially efficient exchange requires a relative absence of third-party externalities. Transactions in competitive markets should have no effect on parties who are not directly or willingly involved in an exchange. Externalities can be positive or negative, but both affect the efficiency of a market by imposing undesirable transaction costs. We used the demand and supply of national security to illustrate the free-riding problem of positive externalities. If national security were a purely voluntary exchange between citizens and their governments, many people might be tempted to free-ride on their fellow citizens' contributions toward the provision of national security, which could lead to insufficient contributions to provide adequate national security. Forced contributions through mandatory taxes, a threat of government penalties, or an ability to create, monitor, and enforce contractual agreements with defined obligations for the parties can limit such shirking, but these measures add transaction costs to an exchange in the political marketplace. Such transaction costs are inefficient compared to the ideal case of provision of political commodities by purely voluntary exchange, but only relatively so if they are needed to overcome the free-rider problem and lead to the provision of a political commodity that society wants.

The potential for nonvoluntary consumption in political markets falls into the realm of negative third-party externalities. For example, policymakers often face requests from domestic economic producers in their societies for protections from foreign economic producers. Agricultural producers in advanced industrialized societies continually seek government protections and assistance against agricultural commodities from developing political

In 1999 French farmers protested against declining agricultural prices, U.S. trade sanctions imposed in response to European Union (EU) agricultural policies and subsidies, and the importation of fresh vegetables and fruits from neighboring countries. Their protests pressured French and EU policymakers to maintain subsidy policies that provide farmers with a reasonable standard of living but can lead to higher food prices for consumers. Such policies follow in the tradition of Europe's Common Agricultural Policy (CAP), created after World War II when food shortages prompted governments to subsidize agricultural production in the interests of self-sufficiency. While CAP funding has decreased, it remains a significant subsidy that boosts the costs of agricultural commodities in the EU and discriminates against non-European agricultural producers.

economies. These producers organize and offer to exchange votes, campaign contributions, and other forms of political support in exchange for government intervention in international trade. In response to such pressures, governments may do nothing, or they may initiate tariffs, subsidies, quotas, or other barriers to trade—thereby exchanging a public policy for political support. In the case of agriculture, policymakers in Europe, the United States, and Japan have extended substantial protection to farmers in their respective countries. Indeed, agricultural subsidies are the largest component of the European Union budget.

If these societies were populated only by policymakers able to provide such policies and economic producers seeking such policies, this would be an efficient exchange in a political market and the government would be highly responsive to constituent needs—a nice representative society. But these societies also include workers in industries other than those seeking protections from foreign producers, and these people like to consume goods in the protected sector of the economy. Few of those who live in an advanced industrialized state are part of the agricultural sector, yet all who live in that state consume agricultural products. Not part of the exchange between the protected sector and the government, these nonagricultural workers must now pay higher prices for the products from this protected sector of the economy, which reduces their ability to consume other things. The political exchange between the government and the sector seeking protections has imposed costs on other people in society who did not take part in the political exchange.

Some survey research suggests that many people appear willing to accept such third-party externalities to protect the jobs and industries of fellow citizens of their state, but would they be willing if they knew that the cost of the third-party externality deprived them of $1,000, $2,000, or more of consumption possibilities? Some degree of third-party externalities may be almost inevitable due to the persistent likelihood of nonvoluntary consumption in political exchange, but we must ask the same question posed in the previous chapter: at what point does a negative or positive third-party externality severely distort political exchange and heavily damage social outcomes? Many third-party externalities are relatively insignificant, and in some situations, the parties being damaged are aware of the externality and willing to bear its costs. In other cases, the parties to a political exchange that generates a third-party externality are willing to provide some compensation to mitigate the costs of the externality. Nevertheless, if severe enough, third-party externalities can undercut efficient and competitive political exchange.

Information

In a perfect world, competitive and socially efficient political exchange requires a situation in which all parties to an exchange enjoy relatively complete or full information. They would have relatively equal access to any information that is important to the exchange, and such access would be relatively easy and affordable, so that no party to the exchange would have an excuse to be ill-informed about the terms of exchange. Voters would be able to accurately distinguish between candidates, parties, and their policies. Producers of political commodities would be able to accurately recognize the preferences and demands of those to whom they want to sell their commodities. In chapter 5, we briefly examined the threats that asymmetric information and incomplete information create for competitive and efficient economic exchange in the imperfect, real world. These unequal conditions pose similar threats to competitive and efficient political exchange.

Some players in political arenas who know more about policy issues or political candidates may use their information advantage to legitimately and sincerely educate the citizenry in quest of reducing informational deficiencies and promoting better-informed public debate about policy issues—often these people are members of the media or the academic experts often interviewed in the media. Here, people enjoying an information advantage may simply be trying to reduce the information asymmetries in an electorate. However, other players in political arenas may strategically use an information advantage to gain added leverage for their own preferences in political exchange. To manipulate the production of policy in exchange for support (a political exchange), politicians and their staffs may selectively pick and choose who to educate and mobilize, what information to publicize and what information to keep private, what information to ignore or bury, and how they interpret or cast information. Shockingly, politicians may be inclined to be less than honest in the portrayal of issues as they pursue political survival and the success of their policy agendas—who would have guessed! But such behavior is completely consistent with our initial assumptions about the goals and incentives of politicians. In search of political survival and support for the political commodities they peddle, politicians and political parties have developed increasingly sophisticated strategies for advertising their issues, building selective lists of which citizens they should call to educate about controversial issues, and determining which potential voters to remind about an upcoming election and which ones not to remind.

The ability of political actors to strategically manipulate an information environment and distort the social efficiency of political exchange depends upon the presence of asymmetric information. Let's examine the Iraq conflict as an example of asymmetric information in political exchange. In 2002–2003, President Bush and members of his administration argued that the presence of weapons of mass destruction (WMDs) in Iraq violated UN resolutions and presented a clear and present danger to the security of the United States. In the midst of the brewing international crisis, UN weapons inspectors reentered Iraq after a hiatus of approximately five years to try to ascertain the state of the country's weapons programs. Unable to obtain full UN support or widespread international cooperation, President Bush rejected the mission of UN weapons inspectors and opted for a military solution, war. The arguments put forth to justify U.S. military operations to the U.S. population and Congress highlighted the threat posed by Iraq's weapons of mass destruction and the dangers of waiting for confirmation of their existence. Critics of the Bush administration decried the rush to war and argued for giving the weapons inspectors more time to complete their mission in Iraq. The public debate between supporters and critics of the administration's policy focused upon whether Iraq did or did not have WMDs—whether or not the Iraqi weapons programs had been dismantled as promised after the first Gulf War. This debate continued after the triumphant invasion, as U.S. weapons inspectors also failed to uncover stockpiles of such weapons. But was this question about the existence of WMDs the right focus for the political exchange between policymakers and the U.S. public that led to the invasion of Iraq by U.S. forces?

Probably not, given the postwar history of U.S. national security policy and strategy. Instead, the debate should have focused upon the security threat to the United States—what threat such weapons would pose to the United States and its allies, what strategies could best manage such a threat if it existed—rather than exclusively on the alleged existence of weapons of mass destruction. After all, the Soviets had possessed WMDs since Stalin. At the height of the cold war, the United States and the Soviet Union had more than 10,000 deliverable nuclear warheads, enough nuclear firepower to destroy life as we know it on earth. Now, these are weapons of mass destruction! And this catalog doesn't even take into consideration the biological and chemical weapons in the U.S. and Soviet arsenals. The People's Republic of China, the United Kingdom, France, Israel, India, Pakistan—and now probably North Korea and perhaps Iran—are members of the "nuclear club," while many other nations have some biological or chemical tools in their arsenals that may qualify as weapons of mass destruction. In terms of brutality and threat, Stalin and the Soviets dwarfed Saddam Hussein and Iraq. In a conventional war in Korea, China and North Korea had fought the United States and its allies to a standstill. Israel sits in violation of numerous UN resolutions. All these facts are problematic, given the terms of the argument leading up to the Iraq war.

In framing of the policy question and subsequent debate, President Bush and his administration made the existence of Iraqi weapons of mass destruction the crucial determinant of U.S. policy—not the threat of such weapons to the United States or whether such a threat could be managed by some action other than war. They succeeded in framing the debate along these lines, as voters, the media, and political opponents alike focused on the existence of WMDs in the hands of Saddam Hussein: Do they exist or don't they? Critics of the administration argued for giving the UN inspectors more time, but what if the inspectors had been given more time and then had found weapons of mass destruction? By the terms of the debate, those same critics would then have been obliged to support U.S. military action. The manipulation of the information environment thus prevented consideration of alternatives if WMDs were actually proven to exist during the run-up to war. The Bush administration used the debate to dramatically restructure U.S. national security policy by incorporating, for the first time, a stated policy of preemption. U.S. presidents had always had the option of military preemption at their disposal, but it had never been an official linchpin of U.S. military strategy. Under this restatement of U.S. national security policy, the very existence of weapons of mass destruction was sufficient to justify—even require—military preemption.

Let's consider this policy choice in the context of a different and more complete information environment. For more than forty years following World War II, U.S. national security strategy had been built around the theory of deterrence and containment: if you smack me, I will smack you back, hard, and perhaps even destroy you. Policymakers and strategists believed that a stable threat of assured retaliation and destruction was the best strategy to prevent an attack in the first place. Why would an enemy attack the United States if such action guaranteed swift and sure destruction? Would rational leaders of adversarial governments willingly commit suicide by inviting the destruction of their societies? In order to maintain the necessary stability, this policy required a clear ability to retaliate, the ability to survive an attack and deliver a devastating counterblow, and a target to retaliate against. Another state would offer such a target because its specific geographic location could be attacked. U.S. military procurements during the cold war sought to ensure the requisite capabilities in armaments for a stable and survivable military response and in intelligence and early-warning systems to make threats of deterrence credible—since retaliatory capabilities are not much of a deterrent if you do not know whom to attack.

Where was the discussion of the Iraqi threat in terms of this tradition in U.S. national security policy? Had U.S. capabilities eroded so much as to preclude consideration of deterrence and containment as a viable alternative, or had Iraqi capabilities increased exponentially since the Gulf War, so as to undermine any logic of continuing such a policy? Quite the contrary: the collapse of the Soviet Union and its sphere of influence had left the United States as the sole military superpower in the world; the relative military capabilities of the United States had only grown more formidable since the 1991 Gulf War; and the advance of smart weaponry had extended the U.S. advantage over potential rivals and provided policymakers with more accurate and flexible options than during the cold war. By contrast, the capabilities of the Iraqi military had substantially decayed since the Gulf War, when U.S.–led coalition forces easily threw Iraqi troops out of Kuwait. More than a decade of trade embargoes and sanctions had limited the ability of the Iraqi army to upgrade its weapons, or even to service and maintain the weapons it retained at the end of the Gulf War. U.S. military jets continued to enforce a no-fly zone in the north and south of Iraq; the Iraqi armed forces could not even conduct military operations by air against rebellious factions within their own territory under the no-fly zones. With or without weapons of mass destruction, any military conflict between the United States and Iraq would clearly have been one-sided.

If containment and deterrence remained credible and effective policies, why was the potential for continuing these policies absent from the debate during the run-up to war? We could simply blame the Bush administration for manipulating the information environment and narrowing the terms of the debate over policy options, but this excuse would be too easy. In our political-economy framework, we expect political actors to attempt to manipulate the terms of political exchange for self-interested ends, but such tampering should prove difficult in a relatively complete information environment where all parties to the political exchange (consumers and producers) have relatively equal access to information with low transaction costs. Under these conditions, an information environment cannot be manipulated to emphasize some aspects of a policy problem and neglect others. Relatively complete information, or transparency, would surely have prompted voters, political opponents, and the media to challenge the Bush administration to engage in a debate over deterrence and containment, rather than too quickly shifting focus to preemption. The absence of such discussion signals, in hindsight, a failure by the media, the political opposition, and the voters to act as informed political consumers, as is necessary for socially efficient political exchange.

As in economic exchange, the underlying dilemma facing consumers of political commodities is to break a pooling equilibrium—distinguishing good sellers or products from bad sellers or products—into a separating equilibrium, which allows them to distinguish accurately and efficiently among political actors and their policy agendas. Consumers of political commodities can counter the advantage of asymmetric information by becoming informed about issues, policies, and politicians or by developing strategies that enable them to participate in political exchange as if they were well-informed. Political consumers can look for shortcuts that allow them to act as if they were well-informed even though they are not. For example, political consumers can mimic the behavior of other voters who are better informed and whose preferences and values they share or admire; they can take the advice of special-interest groups that generally represent their preferences. In these cases, less-informed political consumers piggyback on the efforts of more-informed political consumers.

Effective competition in a political marketplace also helps to constrain the dilemma of asymmetric information if such competition provokes debate and increases the availability of relevant information—both access to that information and the skills needed to evaluate and process that information. Competition in the political marketplace, provided by multiple producers of political commodities, can also constrain the problem of asymmetric information if the strategic use of asymmetric information is relatively evenly distributed across the competing producers—in other words, if they all mislead equally and effectively, counterbalancing each other. Information asymmetries may well be the single largest threat to political and economic market exchange.

AN EXAMPLE: THE MEDIAN VOTER AND POLITICAL EXCHANGE

Let's consider a highly stylized example of exchange in a political market. In order to provide a baseline for comparison, assume that the conditions for a socially efficient political market exchange do exist. This means that consumers and producers of political commodities—voters, politicians, policymakers, and political parties—are well-informed about political issues, public policies, and the preferences of others in the political arena. There is no threat of asymmetric information. Moreover, effective competition exists in the political marketplace to discipline consumers and producers of political commodities. Voters have sufficient choice among competing parties and politicians to restrict the potential of monopolistic manipulation of the political arena. Also assume that the threat of third-party externalities is limited, property rights are clear, and transaction costs are negligible—in other words, producers and consumers of political goods have no incentives to be ill-informed, to avoid participating in political exchange, or to cheat or *strategically* manipulate others in political exchange. The only exchange we anticipate under these conditions is *sincere* exchange between the producers and consumers of political commodities, and we expect the political arena to provide an aggregation mechanism, such as elections, to coordinate production and consumption of political goods. Political consumers choose among competitive political producers by casting their votes in an election.

This brings us to the aggregation mechanism, or voting rule, that acts similarly to the price mechanism in economic markets. We need not worry about nonvoluntary consumption here, as we assume that a voter's participation in an election is a voluntary vote to ratify the process of exchange, even if the voter's own preference loses in the election. We consider a variety of voting rules more closely in chapter 15, when we focus on institutions, or rules of the game. For our example here, we posit a political system that uses a winner-take-all, or first-past-the-post voting rule, one of the simplest voting rules. This is a **plurality rule,** which means that the candidate, referendum, or policy that wins the most votes in an election takes the whole prize—whatever position or facet of government control was at stake in the election. We expect every voter or political consumer in the system to participate in each election. Why? Because with clearly defined property rights, a relative absence of transaction costs, no potential for manipulation of the election by a monopolist or monopsonist, oligopolist, or oligopsonist, and relatively full information, a political consumer has no incentive to avoid participating in a political exchange and every incentive to participate in order to obtain an outcome closer to her preferred outcome.

Returning to one of our original assumptions—that politicians seek to survive—let's further postulate that governments, parties, and politicians seek to win elections, continue in office, and control the distribution of political commodities in society. In democratic systems with our choice of voting rule, a political party, or coalition of parties, is selected by a plurality of voters in a competitive election to form a government and control the levers of governance. Such elections occur at regular intervals, for systematic, regular elections are the formal institutional paths stipulated in a constitution or some other legal framework. Losing parties accept electoral outcomes and do not attempt to seize control of the government by extra-electoral means. And, most critical for political market exchange, the governing party or parties must preserve political freedom, political speech, and open access to political information, for these conditions are essential if consumers of political commodities are to be well-informed and avoid the trap of asymmetric information. Restrictions on political and civil liberties such as speech and association amount to imposing transaction costs and erecting barriers that damage socially efficient political exchange.

In our stylized model, a political party is a group of people who seek by election to accede to control of government. They generally share similar but not necessarily identical preference orderings of individual and societal outcomes, and they view control of the government as an integral component to achieving those outcomes. Control of government will help to promote their objectives even if those goals are purely selfish—such as greed, power, and prestige. In fact, we make no assumptions about the nobility of individual motivations, although we do trust in the ability of competitive political markets to mobilize and constrain such egoistic private interests for public good. Hence, political parties and the policies advanced by political parties are constructed simply to win elections and government control.

A voter in this democratic system looks at the political parties and their policy agendas as statements about the political commodities these parties and their candidates are offering. With two or more parties, the voter as political consumer evaluates the alternatives across the producers, compares her expected utility from different electoral outcomes, and votes for the party (candidate) that generates the greatest expected utility. In a two-party system, she attempts to build a ranking between the alternatives that exhibits the property of completeness; for three or more parties, she attempts to build a ranking that has the property of transitivity, as described in chapter 2. A voter may rationally choose not to vote for a party whose platform and positions promise the greatest expected utility, but whose chance of winning the election seems small. This is a significant problem in a multiparty system, but not in a competitive two-party system, as we will see.

We have assumed that the primary objective of political parties is to win elections and gain control of government. A party that proves continually unsuccessful at winning elections should rationally shift strategies and adopt policy positions that appeal to more voters; otherwise, it risks becoming irrelevant, marginalized, and ultimately defunct as a producer and purveyor of political commodities. Running such a risk is a difficult choice for party members who are motivated by power, status, and greed, so, if rational, they will push the party to change its policy proposals to make them more appealing to political consumers, the voters. The interaction of voters and parties in elections can thus propel changes in party positions and in the political commodities offered by parties.

How does a losing party make such changes? What is a winning strategy for a political party in developing the political commodities it offers to political consumers? Are choices in policy offerings and changes in those offerings random, or can we make systematic statements—predictions—about a party's choice of policy positions? As political parties and their members compete for electoral victory and control of government, they attempt to offer voters a basket of political commodities that will separate them from their competitors, while, at the same time, considering the make-up of the electorate. Differentiating your party from another would be relatively easy if you did not consider electoral prospects; a political party that was unconcerned about electoral victory could select policy positions anywhere in the political spectrum and far away from other political parties. But we have assumed that the purpose of political parties is to win elections and control government. This desire to win constrains both policy choice and the party's ability to differentiate itself from other parties, and thus it provides us, as political analysts, with leverage to make systematic statements about what policy positions a party is more or less likely to adopt.

This process of analysis brings us to consider the make-up of the electorate, the body of political consumers. First, we must ask, are voters' preferences on one policy issue related to their positions on other issues? Do individual voters have some underlying theory, or framework of beliefs, about state/society relations that makes their preferences on different issues more than random? For the sake of simplicity, political scientists often portray this underlying framework, or ideology, as a position on a left-right political spectrum (see figure 6.2). Voters may be distributed along this dimension in a unimodal, single-peaked pattern like the familiar normal distribution, or bell curve (see figure 6.3), or they may be arrayed in a bimodal or polymodal pattern with multiple peaks, or in some other distribution (see figure 6.4).

For analytical ease, let's assume that voters are normally distributed along this left-right spectrum. (We can relax this assumption later.) Remember that political parties seeking electoral success must find policy or ideological positions that appeal to a plurality of the voters.

FIGURE 6.2	**A Left-Right Ideological Spectrum**

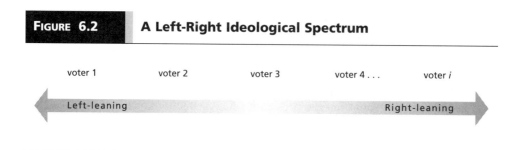

FIGURE 6.3	**A Unimodal Distribution of Voters along an Ideological Spectrum (in this case a normal distribution or bell curve)**

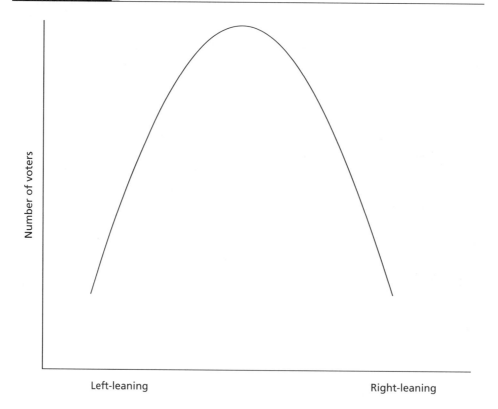

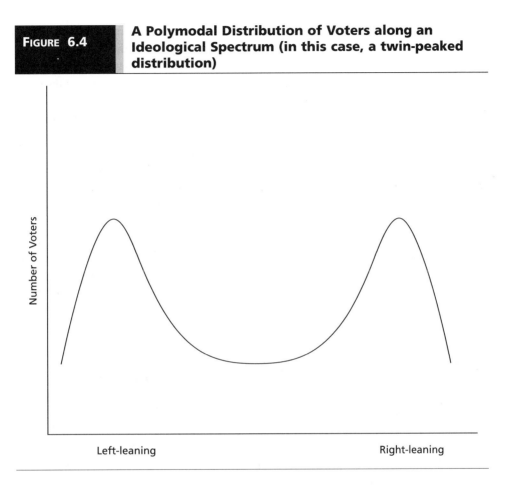

| FIGURE 6.4 | **A Polymodal Distribution of Voters along an Ideological Spectrum (in this case, a twin-peaked distribution)** |

Number of Voters

Left-leaning

Right-leaning

Therefore, in a two-party, winner-take-all system, if N = total number of voters, the winning party must appeal to $N/2 + 1$ of the voters, or 50 percent plus 1, to win an election and control government. But who is the critical voter in this election, and where is she located on the left-right political spectrum? The voter who determines the outcome of the election is located exactly in the middle of all the voters arrayed on this spectrum. We call her the **median voter.** In this system, by voting in an election, you move the position of the median voter toward your policy preferences as you affect the size of N; by not participating, you move the median voter position away from your policy preferences. Hence the importance of participation in elections, for abstaining only contributes to an electoral outcome that is more distant from your own preferences on the left-right spectrum.

Knowing that they need the support of the median voter if they are to win in this electoral system, the two competing parties will move toward the median voter and, consequently, toward each other. (We make no prediction that individual voters will move toward the median voter's position, just parties.) Each party's extremists—by definition those located farthest from the median voter—will prefer their party to the other party even as the parties converge on the median voter, as long as their party remains closer to their end of the spectrum. The two parties cannot completely converge, for if they become exactly alike, or are perceived as being exactly alike, their extremists may opt out of the election—as was the case with the disenchanted voters who claimed that there was no difference between the Republican and Democratic parties in the 2000 U.S. elections.

Convergence upon electoral strategies, platforms, and policy promises in order to attract the median voter does not, however, guarantee either the delivery of such policies or their stability if delivered. In a society with a normally distributed electorate, the pressures of election will drive policy toward the median voter and produce relatively stable outcomes as the forces of society push toward the median voter. In a society with large extremist components—a bimodal distribution with weighting toward the extremes, as in figure 6.4—parties will similarly converge on electoral positions, issues, and promises, but having gained office, the winner will be pulled toward its extremists and pressured to adopt policies that are more radical than those preferred by the median voter, and very radical compared to those preferred by supporters of the opposing party. In such a system, both democracy and policy performance are far less stable.

In a two-party, winner-take-all system, convergence of party strategies and policy promises is almost inevitable, given our assumption that individuals coalesce into parties and then develop policies expressly to win elections. If we push harder on this model of political competition and political exchange, we can deduce that a durable, stable third party will prove unsuccessful and dysfunctional for voters. Two parties constitute an equilibrium in this system. Let's explore why. Based upon our initial assumption that individuals coalesce into parties to seek control of government by election, we have determined that the optimal electoral strategy is to appeal to the median voter. But in a winner-take-all, three-party system, at least one party is likely to fail, fail, and fail again in its attempt at electoral success, because there will always be at least one party between this third party and the median voter. The third party is therefore not viable in the long term, and this situation confronts its members and leadership with a dilemma. In the search for electoral success, this party's repeated failures may drive its voters to a competing party with the most similar views—effectively killing the third party. Or, this perpetually losing party may be inclined to merge with another party, joining forces to improve the chances for electoral success—again effectively killing the third party. This process of consolidation is likely to continue in a three-or-more-party, winner-take-all system until each of the two parties left standing has a good chance of electoral victory.

A third party in this system, however ephemeral, will push the electoral outcomes and the political commodities produced by the winning party away from its preferred position on the left-right spectrum. Assuming that voters cast their ballots for the party closest to their individual positions, a third party is going to take votes away from the party located between the third party and the median voter, and closest to the third party's position. Thus Ross Perot took more votes away from George H.W. Bush than from Bill Clinton in 1992, and Ralph Nader more from Al Gore than from George W. Bush in 2000. Perversely, this process drives the electoral outcome toward the option most distant from the preferences of the third party's voters. This ironic outcome would be less likely to occur in a system with a proportional voting rule, wherein a party can achieve some electoral success and representation in a legislature by winning a vote total that is above a prescribed threshold but less than a plurality. But under this type of multiparty electoral rule, the desire to control the levers of government will encourage the formation of coalitions among parties located near each other on the left-right political spectrum.

Thus, understanding both the relevant voting rule and the distribution of preferences in a society offers insight to the nature of that society's politics. A voting rule, which provides the electoral institutional structure of a polity, will systematically help determine both the number of viable political parties its system can support and the nature of political competition and exchange therein. The distribution of voters will offer systematic leverage to discern the stability and durability of political exchange and policy implementation. Are voters (political consumers) unimodally and normally distributed, or polymodally distributed? A unimodal distribution acts as a magnet, pulling party positions and policies toward the central tendency of the distribution, the peak. In a society with large extremist components, a polymodal distribution with weighting toward the extremes, parties may converge on electoral positions, issues, and promises to attract more moderate voters—particularly with a winner-take-all electoral rule or some version of a proportional rule that drives electoral strategies to the center. Regardless of the electoral rule, however, once it is in office, the attraction of large numbers of extremist voters in a polymodal electorate will push the winning party or coalition of parties to adopt policies that are more radical and more in line with the preferences of their extremists than the policies preferred by the voters near the center of the political distribution.

CONCLUSION

The social efficiency of political exchange depends upon the extent to which voting rules and other aggregation mechanisms produce collective outcomes that sincerely and accurately aggregate the preferences of individuals over political commodities such as policies and politicians. If the key conditions for socially efficient political market exchange hold or are approximated—clear property rights, low transaction costs, competitive exchange, fully informed participants in the political market, and limited third-party externalities—the possibility for strategic manipulation of the political arena by one or more parties declines dramatically, and the likelihood of socially efficient political market exchange increases regardless of all the selfish predilections of the individual members of society. Just as in economic markets, socially efficient exchange in a political market requires not that members of society be noble and altruistic, but that the key conditions hold so that the voting or market mechanism accurately aggregates individual preferences. Fully informed consumers in such a competitive political market will condition the producers of political commodities through the aggregation mechanisms of voting and other forms of political participation.

In a nice, elegant system wherein everything works according to theory, simply observing the voting rules and the distribution of preferences in a society offers a useful framework for understanding the nature of its politics. Unfortunately, the empirical social world is more complex and often deviates from the ideal. In chapter 12 we explore what happens when the core conditions for efficient, competitive political and economic market exchange are violated and so produce market failure. Market failure in political markets means only that political commodities are not produced and consumed as efficiently as theoretically possible. In democracies, political market exchange still occurs in most instances of market failure; only in the most extreme cases does the exchange unravel completely.

The first section of the book ends here, having described some basic tools of political and political-economic analysis. The next section provides some historical background to both the globalization of world affairs and the breakdown in that globalization. We will study in more depth the phenomena of political and economic market success and political and economic market failure. Finally, in the third major section of the book, we will more closely examine why political and economic markets succeed and why they fail.

EXERCISES

1. What are two key differences between political and economic markets?

2. If a monopoly or oligopoly is a manipulation of the price mechanism in economic markets, what are the comparable manipulations in political markets?

3. What role is played by the media in a political market?

4. What constitutes competition in the political sphere?

5. What are the conditions for social efficiency in political exchange?

6. Explain the importance of information for a competitive and efficient political market.

7. Construct a hypothetical distribution of a society's voters and then deduce the nature of politics based upon that distribution.

8. Who and what is the median voter?

9. Describe and explain two voting rules. How will these rules influence political exchange?

FURTHER READING

Coase, Ronald H. 1937. "The Nature of the Firm," *Economica* 4:386–405.

Ordeshook, Peter C. 1992. *A Political Theory Primer*. New York: Routledge.

Riker, William. 1986. *The Art of Political Manipulation*. New Haven: Yale University Press.

Schotter, Andrew. 1981. *The Economic Theory of Social Institutions*. Cambridge: Cambridge University Press.

7 Around the World in Eighty Days: The Advent of Globalization

> Under a system of perfectly free commerce, each country naturally devotes its capital and labour to such employments as are most beneficial to each. This pursuit of individual advantage is admirably connected with the universal good of the whole. By stimulating industry, by rewarding ingenuity, and by using most efficaciously the peculiar powers bestowed by nature, it distributes labour most effectively and most economically: while by increasing the general mass of productions, it diffuses general benefit, and binds together by one common tie of interest and intercourse the universal society of nations throughout the civilized world.
>
> *David Ricardo (1817)*

GLOBALIZATION IS NOTHING NEW

Globalization became a popular topic toward the end of the twentieth century. At that time, much of the commentary approached globalization as a fascinating new phenomenon that would radically transform relations within and between states. This perspective, which still dominates in the early twenty-first century, is naïve, for it neglects the historical record. In fact, the globalization of market relations and the accompanying transformation in political and social relations was underway well before the latter half of the twentieth century. Modern globalization began a century earlier, linking the political economies that made up the Atlantic economy and helping to fuel their economic and political transformations. Nineteenth-century economists, philosophers, and policymakers devised the theoretical underpinnings of today's economic globalization and pushed for the policy reforms that started us down the road of

---

This chapter draws upon Kevin O'Rourke and Jeffrey Williamson, *Globalization and History: The Evolution of a Nineteenth Century Atlantic Economy* (2000); Barry Eichengreen, *Globalizing Capital: A History of the International Monetary System* (1996); and Eric Hobsbawm, *The Age of Capital: 1848–1875* (1996) and *The Age of Empire: 1875–1914* (1989).

increasing interdependence and global capitalism. The changes they unleashed helped to reshape the global hierarchy as well as the social and political contracts within states. Those states that partook of globalization—the movement of goods, capital, services, and people across national boundaries—experienced tremendous surges in economic welfare and in the advance of political rights and liberties.

The United Kingdom played the central role in the evolution, invention, and implementation of ideas, policies, and technologies that provided the scaffolding for the political and economic changes of globalization and democratization in the 1800s. As the dominant political economy for a good part of the nineteenth century, it embarked upon what came to be known as the Industrial Revolution before other political economies did so. British scientists and industrialists invented and funded technologies that brought distant societies closer together, lowered the costs of transport, and reduced the time lapse of distant communication. British economists and philosophers created ideas that set an intellectual agenda for capitalism and market exchange within and across state boundaries. British politicians and policymakers adopted those ideas and turned them into commercial, monetary, and military policies that lowered barriers to international exchange. British financiers developed financial instruments and strategies that helped to manage the risks that had hindered international exchange, turning London into the first truly global financial market of any significant size and establishing the British as the bankers to the expansion of global capitalism.

Intentionally or not, British policymakers and private financiers provided four **collective goods**—commodities or services that any member of group can consume and enjoy—that helped promote economic expansion and international exchange. From the mid-century onward, they supplied the collective goods of convertibility, liquidity, lender of last resort, and market access under duress to those political economies that sought to take part in the expansion of global capitalist relations. Other states also took advantage of such goods, to help manage the risks involved in globalization and lower the potential costs of exchange. These collective goods helped to reduce volatility and crises in the global arena, furnished resources and markets that encouraged growth, stabilized expectations of economic actors, and allowed those actors to overcome their fears about the risk of investment and exchange across state boundaries. Other nations contributed to the first big wave of modern globalization, but the United Kingdom took the lead and set the pace.

This first bout of globalization, which began in the early to mid-1800s, was rooted in an evolution of intellectual thought, public policy change, technological shifts, and the activities of private economic actors in markets for goods and capital. Changes in these arenas led to lower national barriers to international exchange, increasingly integrated commodity markets, convergence in prices across many economies, development of a global capital market based in London, and mass migrations from one state to another. Such changes linked national economies and created winners among those who profited from the tremendous expansion of trade in goods, services, and capital. This chapter considers the activities and changes that fueled globalization in this early period.

INTELLECTUAL CHANGE: COMPARATIVE ADVANTAGE, EFFICIENCY, AND WELFARE

Despite the tendency of pundits, policymakers, businessmen, and others to downplay academics and their ideas in comparison to the activities of those in business and government, academics have played an important role in the progress of civilization. The economist John Maynard Keynes, who developed ideas that helped to transform political economy in the twentieth century, put it bluntly:

> [T]he ideas of economists and political philosophers, both when they are right and when they are wrong, are more powerful than is commonly understood. Indeed the world is ruled by little else. Practical men, who believe themselves to be quite exempt from any intellectual influences, are usually the slave of some defunct economist.

Indeed, the advance of globalization and global capitalism owes a great debt to David Ricardo, an intellectual, economist, stockbroker, and member of the British House of Commons, who created one of the most elegant and influential ideas in economics. In so doing, he supplied the intellectual underpinnings for trade among nations regardless of their productive capabilities and advantages. In 1817 Ricardo published a series of essays called *On the Principles of Political Economy and Taxation.* One essay, "The Political Economy of International Trade," would prove revolutionary, for it introduced the idea of *comparative advantage.*

We discussed the economics of comparative advantage extensively in chapter 5, but we should recognize the historical significance of Ricardo's discovery as well. The principle of comparative advantage represented a revolution in economic thought that challenged and soon replaced absolute advantage as the accepted trade theory of the time. Extending intranational market exchange to the international arena required overcoming intellectual, political, and physical barriers to cross-border exchange that were entrenched in the public policies of the early 1800s. Economists had made arguments for free trade between states before Ricardo's essay, but they had justified it only under conditions of absolute advantage. Ricardo's innovation was in showing that international trade could be advantageous even for a state that enjoyed absolute advantage in every form of production. Comparative advantage demonstrated that gains from trade depend not upon absolute efficiencies and advantage in producing commodities, but upon differences in relative efficiencies and advantage within and across states. Ricardo's insight meant that differences in labor productivity—and, in later versions such as Heckscher-Ohlin, diversity in the distribution of factors of production across nations—created the potential for welfare gains from specialization in production and broader exchange. The combination of specialization and exchange leads to increased benefits, increased welfare, and expanded consumption possibilities for a society—even if it enjoys absolute advantage in the production of every commodity.

Ricardo's arguments about comparative advantage became the center of trade policy debates during the first half of the 1800s, providing powerful leverage for those favoring the expansion of international exchange to use against those opposing the lowering of obstacles to trade. Later, his innovation would become accepted wisdom among economists and policymakers—even when it was ignored. Ricardo's pivotal recognition of the political economy of trade was echoed by John Stuart Mill, who wrote that the "benefit of international trade is a more efficient employment of the productive forces of the world."

SHIFTS IN PUBLIC POLICY

Physical barriers such as mountains and oceans can impose obstacles to the expansion of trade. More important than such physical barriers, however, are the human obstructions that trade can face, in the form of policies that include tariffs, immigration laws, subsidies, taxes, sanctions, differences in standards such as the gauge of railroad tracks or the type of electrical current, blockades, wars, food and health regulations, currency restrictions, boycotts, export restraints, and other man-made devices that can hinder the flow of commodities, capital, information, and people across state boundaries. Sometimes these policies intervene unintentionally in trade, but more often they are created intentionally by governments that shape public policy in response to some preferences in their domestic societies or in exchange for the support of some domestic constituency.

Mercantilism and Protectionism as the Legacy of War

The 1800s began with a man-made legacy of protectionism and **mercantilism.** From a mercantilist perspective, trade and the international flow of capital were good if they disproportionately fed the coffers of the state's sovereign versus those of foreign sovereigns, and consequently contributed to the political-military might and position of the state. Exchange across borders was viewed as a zero-sum interaction, whereby gains for one side in political-military influence were presumed to be balanced by comparable losses on the other side. This presumption made all parties suspicious of exchange, as they often could not be sure whether they were gaining or losing in this framework.

The mercantilist legacy was a function of interstate conflict. During the late eighteenth century and early nineteenth century, costly conflicts between Great Britain and France colored exchange across boundaries in Europe and between Europe and the New World. This rivalry was trade distorting, which means that trading relations would have looked very different absent the British-French conflict. By 1815—the year of Napoleon's defeat at Waterloo by troops under the command of the Duke of Wellington—the flow of goods, capital, technology, and people had been heavily influenced by military events.

This legacy proved durable, carrying over into the peace that followed the sixty years of intermittent conflict. By then, the production structures of the European economies had adapted to limited trade and the distortions in trading patterns, from which many economic interests had profited. British beer production and consumption had expanded as war interrupted French wine imports. Great Britain had been a net food importer before the wars, but the cross-Channel hostilities reduced food imports from the Continent. British rural and agricultural interests profited from the barriers to exchange, as their crops replaced imports even though continental producers were generally more efficient in the production of many agricultural commodities.

The wars' end raised fears of declining competitiveness for such producers, and not only in Great Britain. Absent the threat of blocked sea lanes and trading channels, agricultural producers in other European states began to fear the productive capabilities of the New World and of nations on the European periphery, such as Spain and Portugal. In England, members of Parliament from the ruling Tory party reacted by passing legislation to protect British agricultural interests from more efficient foreign producers. The British Corn Law of 1815 limited the sale of imported grain when the price of domestically produced grain fell below a specified level. This law had the effect of sometimes closing British markets to foreign grain and thus inflating the price of domestic grain by limiting market supply. It allowed inefficient British producers to avoid searching for more efficient production strategies.

As predicted by the Heckscher-Ohlin model of trade, these protections sheltered and rewarded the less abundant factors of production—in the British case, the rural land interests—while the relatively more abundant factors of production, capital and labor, which were located in the cities, lost out as the costs of food increased. This pattern of protection for less abundant factors of production was repeated across Europe. Some nations protected agriculture, while others, such as Sweden, Russia, and France, limited the importation of manufactured products in order to shield less competitive domestic producers. In a sense, these protections were an attempt to maintain the status quo, by locking in the gains created by the French-British wars' massive intervention in trading patterns. Governments enacting such protections sought to resist the dynamic forces that would be unleashed upon production structures by more liberal trading relations.

The Rise of British Protrade Political and Policy Pressures

The British Parliament revised the Corn Law Act in 1828, replacing the prohibitions against grain imports tied to domestic prices with tariffs that varied inversely with the price of grain in the domestic market—higher grain prices in the domestic market meant lower tariffs, while lower prices brought higher tariffs. However, the protections of both the original and revised versions would soon come under attack and be whittled away as a policy competition developed between opposed interests in the society. Rural agricultural interests favored maintenance of the Corn Law protections because they maintained relatively high prices for agricultural commodities and kept their products competitive against those of foreign producers. But these artificially high agricultural prices penalized labor and capital, which made up the manufacturing sector, thus feeding a growing rural-urban divide in British politics. Rural interests dominated the Tory party, while the urban interests sought representation through the Whig party. Under the leadership of Richard Cobden, opponents to the Corn Law formed the Anti–Corn Law League, which drew its strength from the manufacturing centers of Manchester and other cities.

Political Reform and Expansion of Suffrage

Pressures for political institutional reforms, which would change the nature of representation and elections in the United Kingdom, coincided with the growing divide over trade and boosted the momentum for a shift to more liberal trade policies. Demographic changes had led to a growing disconnect between British society and the House of Commons, supposedly the representative institution in the British political system. Never very representative of the broader British society, the House of Commons had become even less representative as the weight of the English population shifted northward and into the industrial urban centers. Because the voting franchise was extremely limited—predominantly major landowners—a small number of men, mostly members of the House of Lords, elected most of the House of Commons. A significant portion of these powerful lords reflected the interests of the southern and rural regions even as the United Kingdom was becoming more urban.

As revolutionary disturbances on the Continent echoed across the English Channel, reformers sought to transform the electoral rules for selecting members of the House of Commons to make it more representative of British society. A Whig reform proposal was rejected in 1830 by the Tory government, led by the Duke of Wellington (of Waterloo fame), who served as prime minister. His unwillingness to compromise led to a loss of confidence in the Tory government, however, and the Whigs took over control of the government. After several failed attempts, the Whigs succeeded in passing a reform bill in the House of Commons. It passed the Tory-dominated House of Lords and became law in 1832, but only after rioting threatened the foundations of British government.

The Reform Bill of 1832 expanded the suffrage, increased the size of the electorate, began to redistribute electoral power by class and geography, and injected increasingly active two-party competition into British politics. The size of the electorate grew by over 50 percent, although still only about one-eighth of the total British adult male population had the right to vote after this reform. This political institutional shift increased the representation of those who benefited from increased international exchange. The middle classes gained political power, particularly in the industrial towns and among the business interests. Ironically, after the changes wrought by the Reform Bill, the conservative Tories became the advocates for industrialized labor, promoting child-labor restrictions and a ten-hour workday. Despite these reforms and the political advances of the industrialized middle classes, however, labor

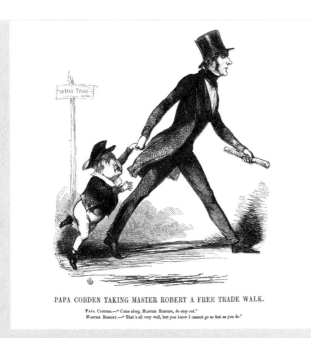

PAPA COBDEN TAKING MASTER ROBERT A FREE TRADE WALK.

PAPA COBDEN.—"Come along, MASTER ROBERT, do step out."
MASTER ROBERT.—"That 's all very well, but you know I cannot go so fast as you do."

In an 1845 political cartoon in *Punch*, Richard Cobden, founder of the Anti-Corn League, leads British prime minister Robert Peel to free trade. To rally opposition to a protectionist corn law, Cobden and other free trade advocates appealed to the preference of consumer, urban, and industry interests for low-priced imported corn and other grains. Peel rejected the protectionist interests of his Conservative Party and embraced the concept of free trade. The adoption of free trade as a policy principle helped the United Kingdom expand its trading empire, position itself at the heart of the emerging liberal global economy, and build its hegemonic leadership.

still suffered, and its continued exclusion from elections and government fed a rising interest in socialism and Chartism, both anti-capitalist movements that advocated the formation of labor unions and working-class representation in elections.

Repeal of the Corn Laws

By the mid-1830s, British Prime Minister Robert Peel, a Tory and son of a cotton manufacturer, began to reverse course on the Corn Law protections and to decry the government barriers to trade. In opposition to the majority of their party, Prime Minister Peel and the Duke of Wellington joined forces with Cobden and his Anti–Corn Law League to seek the repeal of the Corn Laws. Peel was reacting to a changing political landscape: the shifting of economic power in England as the nascent Industrial Revolution gathered momentum, transferring economic importance away from rural agricultural landlords and toward the capital and labor of manufacturing; a growing intellectual awareness—due to the work of Ricardo and other economists—of the gains from trade; and the realization that expensive food damaged the living standards of working people. His recognition of these circumstances helped to transform Peel from a protectionist to a free-trader; in 1846 he succeeded in repealing the Corn Laws.

Peel's conversion to free trade took considerable political courage, even with the shifting economic landscape, because it flew in the face of his political party and its most influential constituents' immediate interests. The strife his actions created within the ranks of the Tory party effectively destroyed his political career. Perhaps the repeal was inevitable, given the growing importance of British manufacturing and the Industrial Revolution, but Peel's courage provided a key step in the liberalization of trade barriers and helped to unleash a new chapter in world history.

Further Expansion of Suffrage in Britain and the Continent

Most of the British male population still lacked the right to vote, despite the significant advance in political liberties brought by the Reform Bill of 1832. However, the forces of economic change, increased labor movement activity, and the promotion of socialism and Chartism fueled demands for greater enfranchisement. In 1867 a Conservative government passed the Second Reform Bill, which extended suffrage to more than one-third of the adult male population. Enlarging the electoral base expanded the range of interests to which elected officials must appeal and thus transformed representation. Protrade interests in society gained more and more electoral clout, reducing the influence of the more protectionist agricultural and rural sectors of society.

Hoping to avoid revolution and rebellion, other European nations began to follow the British lead in peaceful transition to wider enfranchisement. Democratic initiatives of differing degrees, from the adoption of constitutional monarchies to broadly extending suffrage, arose across the Atlantic economy, altering the political landscapes and reshaping attitudes toward protection and trade.

Initially, the expansion of suffrage tended to politically empower those who gained from international exchange, especially given the United Kingdom's central role in the liberalization of trade policy. But expansion of suffrage is a double-edged sword: those who were disadvantaged by trade—the holders of scarce factors of production—could also be empowered through the pathways of representation and a more accessible political arena. Wider enfranchisement initially supported greater liberalization, but extended suffrage does not inevitably equate to the promotion of protrade policies. With the expansion of representation, all policies become more vulnerable to mass pressures, as politicians must appeal to a broader constituency to survive, and much less is left to the whims of elites. With greater mass participation, those who could successfully organize for political action to advance their preferences would increasingly influence the outcomes of policy debates over the openness of an economy.

Bilateral Trade Treaties and Most-Favored-Nation Status

With the British move to embrace more open trading relations, freer trade was aided by **bilateral** (nation-to-nation) **trade negotiations** with other nations. Perhaps even more influential than the repeal of the Corn Laws, the Cobden-Chevalier Treaty of 1860 removed or reduced many of the trade barriers between the United Kingdom and France—the two largest European economies at the time. A host of trade agreements followed Cobden-Chevalier, as Prussia, Belgium, Spain, and other nations signed treaties reducing barriers to international exchange.

Cobden-Chevalier introduced a novel and productive mechanism called **most-favored-nation status (MFN)** to international trade agreements. MFN automatically extended any trade concession, such as a lower tariff barrier, to the British or French that either might

TABLE 7.1	Average Tariff Rates on Manufactured Products, 1820–1913 (in percentages)		
	1820	**1875**	**1913**
United Kingdom	45–50	0	0
France	*	23–15	20
Germany	8–12	4–6	13
United States	35–45	40–50	44
Italy	*	8–10	18
Russia	*	15–20	84
Japan	*	5	30

Source: Data extracted from Paul Bairoch, Economics and World History (Chicago: University of Chicago Press, 1993).

Note: Asterisks indicate that restrictions in importation of manufactured products make calculations of tariff rates insignificant.

grant to a third nation. This reciprocal arrangement helped to create a principle of nondiscrimination, which seeks to inhibit governments from using trade policy to extend privilege to one country but not to others. Many of the bilateral trade agreements that followed Cobden-Chevalier included a MFN clause, creating a network of bilateral agreements in which a concession to one trading partner would cascade to other trading partners. This automatic extension of market concessions created a potential for more and more liberal trade arrangements systemwide, even though negotiations took place nation-by-nation via bilateral trade agreements. Little steps could produce large changes. Table 7.1 shows a general decline for many states in tariffs and relative lowering of barriers to trade from the early to mid-1800s.

Other Liberalizing Policy Shifts and a Caveat

Other British policy shifts around this same time helped promote globalization. Loosening of the Navigation Acts, which for years had limited British colonies to trade only with the mother country, and only on British ships, allowed those colonies to begin trading with other nations. A Tory government also lowered emigration barriers that had hindered the emigration of skilled British workers. Both reforms enhanced the international mobility of important economic assets.

Such policy reforms certainly contributed to increased globalization. But, we should keep this history—the repeal of the Corn Laws, the advent of liberalizing bilateral trade agreements, and other policy reforms—in perspective. They may have been *necessary conditions*, but they were not *sufficient conditions* to account for the expansion of global exchange. Even after the lowering of formal barriers to international exchange, those willing to engage in the processes of globalization still faced significant obstacles. Risk, uncertainty, physical difficulties, and other barriers still created impediments to the cross-border mobility of goods, services, people, and information. Let's now consider these other obstacles that needed to be overcome.

RISK AND UNCERTAINTY

Today, as in the nineteenth century, those engaged in international trade face uncertainties that may affect their willingness to engage in international exchange. They worry about risk arising from contractual commitments across national boundaries and legal jurisdictions. Is a contract in one state considered a binding contract by another government? What are the prospects for one party or another to default on cross-border contractual obligations? Parties to exchange have to assess the stability of exchange rates between different national currencies, as trade across borders involves contracts in a variety of currencies. Will an exchange made today be worth the same tomorrow, next week, or in a month? And the parties have to worry about trade financing and liquidity in the international arena. Will there be sufficient resources available to ensure continued economic expansion and access to capital so that parties to trade can pay their bills?

With the lowering of trade barriers, private economic actors must be willing to take advantage of the new more open environment if exchange across borders is to succeed and contribute to the expansion of economic welfare. But other factors may affect their willingness to play in the international arena if they generate risk or uncertainty that threatens to outweigh the returns on their activities. If risk, or perceived risk, becomes too large, economic actors may decide to refrain from engaging in cross-border economic activity altogether, or demand higher compensation for such activities in order to offset the additional risk. Either way, the elements of risk and uncertainty can limit global exchange even if formal barriers such as tariffs are lowered.

At the heart of these issues of risk and uncertainty are key differences between international exchange and exchange within domestic arenas. Unlike trade conducted within a domestic context, international exchange takes place across multiple legal jurisdictions and legal frameworks, as well as across multiple currency areas. The sheer multiplicity of these structural conditions creates some degree of uncertainty for those engaged in international exchange. If the associated risk factor becomes sufficiently daunting, the prospects for international exchange can break down or be damaged.

Incomplete Contracting, Default Risk, and Banker's Acceptances

International trade requires entering into contractual relationships across borders. An exporter or producer in one nation contracts with an importer in another nation to deliver a particular commodity. Large-scale and efficient exchange rarely involves "cash on the barrelhead." Instead, such exchange almost always uses some form of *credit*—one of the more significant economic inventions in history. Credit is a commitment to pay for today's exchange at some future time, which means that an importer can obtain commodities from an exporter with a promise to pay for those goods by a set time in the future. This arrangement gives the importer time to sell her goods and so obtain the capital necessary for payment. It also allows her to import more goods than she would be able to afford if constrained by her cash on hand. Her inventory can therefore be larger and more diverse, providing her customers a greater range of choice. The terms and value of such exchange are specified in a contract. Most often, the terms are formally spelled out in legal documents, but sometimes the contracts are less formal, as in the diamond trade, where much of the trading takes place over a handshake.

What if one party attempts to change the terms of a contract by delivering something or some amount other than what is expected, or an importer delays or reneges on payment? A buyer or borrower reneging on payment, partially or wholly, constitutes a **default risk** to the seller. Who adjudicates such a dispute? If the exchange takes place within one legal jurisdiction, this problem is fairly straightforward, although it can still prove problematic. German law governs exchange that takes place between contracting parties within German borders, and German courts adjudicate in the case of a dispute; likewise, U.S. law governs exchange within U.S. borders, and U.S. courts adjudicate disputes. But what about an exchange between a German party and an American party that takes place across national boundaries? Who adjudicates a dispute in such a case, when there is no overarching international authority, international court, or international trade police to assert and enforce a binding resolution?

Short-term incentives almost always exist for one party to renege on an agreement—this is why contracts exist. If there were no incentive for attempting to unilaterally change the terms of a deal, there would be no need for contracts, lawyers, and judges to adjudicate disputes, for they would be nonexistent. Consequently, those who specialize in writing contracts (generally members of the legal profession) try to specify the terms and obligations of a deal so as to limit the possibility of one party or another unilaterally changing the terms. Unfortunately, all contracts are incomplete, since even the specialists cannot foresee all the contingencies that may threaten the deal. Moreover, a good contract alone may not be sufficient if one party can later simply claim, "I lied," without fear of significant penalty. International trade raises concern about the ability to fairly adjudicate and enforce the terms of a contract across borders. If one party to an exchange is uncertain about the other party's commitment to abide by the contractual terms of the deal, and the mechanisms of adjudication and enforcement are ambiguous due to multiple national jurisdictions, trade may simply not occur.

Fortunately for international exchange, shrewd British bankers in the mid-1800s solved the problem by expanding and extending ingenious financial instruments called **banker's**

acceptances and **letters of credit** to international trade. These devices are financial guarantees that a party to an exchange can obtain from her bank to lower the risk and uncertainty of nonpayment of a contractual obligation across national boundaries. How? They replace the individual importer's commitment to pay for an international transaction with the commitment of her bank to pay for that transaction. A trader purchases this service from her bank, which guarantees payment to the other party's bank. A banker's acceptance or letter of credit replaces individual credit with institutional credit (the credit of her bank), thus substituting a bank's reputation for an individual's reputation as a guarantee of payment.

Banks do business with other banks frequently and repeatedly, within and across borders, which increases the costs to a bank for reneging on a contract—a banker would not want to develop a reputation for unreliability among other bankers, as she would then encounter increasing difficulty in conducting business. Meanwhile, the importer must agree to pay her bank for the banker's acceptance or letter of credit, thus incurring a legal obligation to her bank. Because this credit contract usually takes place within one nation's boundaries, any contractual dispute that occurs between the importer and her bank, which issued the banker's acceptance or letter of credit, gets adjudicated within the importer's national courts, which pose a more credible and binding threat of adjudication and enforcement upon the importer than would be the case if the dispute were to involve some form of cross-border adjudication. Banker's acceptances and letters of credit thus serve to limit uncertainty and risk about payment obligations across national boundaries.

Currency Risk and Monetary Regimes

Multiple currencies also create risk and uncertainty for those engaged in international exchange. Unlike trade between Connecticut and New Hampshire, in which the inhabitants of both states use the dollar, trade between the United States and Germany involves two different currencies, the dollar and the euro. These currencies fluctuate in relation to each other, and, at any given time, one may be more stable or valued as money (a tool of exchange, a storehouse of value, and a unit of account, as defined in chapter 5). This situation of flux is called a foreign exchange or **currency risk.** If, in a trade contract, the importer or the importer's bank promises to pay a specified amount in a particular currency at some point in the future, any relative decline in the value of that currency before that time means that the exporter or the exporter's bank receives less than anticipated for the exchange. Over the course of the contract period, the exchange has declined in value for the exporter and increased in value for the importer. Conversely, if the currency in which the trade is denominated appreciates in value, the reverse happens. Some currency fluctuation is a risk that is accepted as part of the cost of doing business, especially if the movements in currency values are relatively predictable. Indeed, large markets in currency futures have emerged since the early 1970s to help manage such risks by allowing those engaged in international exchange to "lock in" a future price for a currency. But what if great uncertainty exists over the valuation of national currencies? Then traders who cannot comfortably anticipate the future value of their exchanges may become reluctant to engage in exchange priced in those currencies, or they may simply demand immediate payment, which also reduces trade.

The problem of pricing one currency vis-à-vis another is a function of what we call an **international monetary regime** or system. Such a regime is a set of formal and informal rules, conventions, and norms that govern international financial transactions—the monetary and financial relations between states. A monetary regime specifies what policy instruments governments may use, what those instruments can legitimately target as policy, and when they can be used. In the early 1800s, a variety of monetary systems existed across national economies. Some countries used gold as the standard of value for their currency, others used gold and silver (called bimetallism), and a few found other standards. These differences in state preferences and choices spilled across borders to create uncertainties in the valuation of currencies internationally and so posed obstacles to international exchange. In *Globalizing Capital: A History of the International Monetary System* (1996), economic historian Barry Eichengreen notes:

> The international monetary system is the glue that binds national economies together. Its role is to lend order and stability to foreign exchange markets. . . . Nations find it difficult to efficiently exploit the gains from trade and foreign lending in the absence of an adequately functioning international monetary mechanism.

Beliefs about currency risk can either undermine or facilitate trade. Too much risk and uncertainty about a currency or currencies can drive exchange away from those currencies by triggering **Gresham's Law,** which states that bad money drives out good money. Centuries ago, a coin's value was determined by its precise weight—the amount of gold or silver it contained. Some people would shave the edges off their coins, harvesting small amounts of gold or silver each time; when they had enough metal, they would mint a new coin. But this process left the shaved coins no longer worth their specified value. If enough uncertainty existed over whether coins were shaved or not, merchants might decide not to accept any of the coins in question, whether good or bad. Hence, bad money (the shaved coins) would drive out, or devalue, good money (the unshaved coins). Many coins today have ridges on their edges to discourage shaving, or at least to allow the parties to an exchange to recognize that a coin has been shaved. Gresham's Law is specifically about commodities that serve the function of money, but its logic generalizes to any market or exchange where people encounter difficulties distinguishing between good and bad versions of a commodity. Overcoming currency risk and uncertainty requires convincing parties to international exchange either that fluctuations in a currency's value are unlikely to occur or that they are predictable and manageable. Parties to an exchange must be reasonably confident that the exchange will not lose its expected value due to currency risk.

THE GOLD STANDARD

In the mid- to late 1800s, currency risk and uncertainty were reduced, and stability of expectations enhanced, by convergence upon a particular international monetary regime called the **gold standard.** The governments of the Atlantic economy enhanced beliefs in the stability and value of their currencies by making real commitments to maintaining the value of their currencies vis-à-vis gold.

By setting their currencies to gold, governments established the exchange rates of their currencies in relation to other currencies that were also fixed to gold. Gold became the mediation mechanism, stabilizing the number of French francs that an economic actor would exchange for a British pound, the number of American dollars for a British pound, the amount of American dollars for a German mark, and so on. Table 7.2 displays the values of national currencies in gold—their exchange rates—during the gold standard era of the latter 1800s.

TABLE 7.2	**Currency Values in Terms of Gold during the Late 1800s**		
Country	Currency	Value of 1 unit of national currency in USD ($)	Value of 1 ounce of gold in national currency
Australia	Pound	4.86	4.2
Austria-Hungary	Corona	.202	102.32
Belgium	Franc	.193	107.09
Denmark	Krone	.268	77.13
Finland	Markka	.193	107.09
France	Franc	.193	107.09
Germany	Mark	.238	86.85
Great Britain	Pound	4.86	4.25
Greece	Drachma	.193	107.09
India (British)	Rupee	.444	46.55
Italy	Lira	.193	107.09
Romania	Leu	.193	107.09
Russia	Ruble	.514	40.21
Spain	Peseta	.193	107.09
Sweden	Krona	.268	77.13
United States	Dollar	1	20.67

Source: Adapted from www.cyberussr.com/hcunn/gold-std.html.

At the beginning of the nineteenth century, prior to the convergence on the gold standard, a mix of different national monetary arrangements coexisted. Great Britain was on a de facto gold standard, while the Scandinavian states, Russia, the German states, and others used a silver standard for their currency and international payments. France, the United States, and most others, meanwhile, employed a bimetallic standard based on gold and silver. A range of systems based upon different mixtures of gold, silver, or copper served as the basis for settling international obligations—the deficits and surpluses in the balance of payments.

The convergence toward gold as the official reserve asset began by accident in the eighteenth century. In the 1700s, the British mint, the maker of coin, set too low a price for silver. Speculators then exchanged other assets for British silver and moved their silver holdings abroad to where they would be worth more, thus draining silver from circulation in the United Kingdom. Absent silver coin, gold coin in effect became the standard. As the result of a poor decision by the British mint and without any official declaration, the United Kingdom thus informally adopted a gold standard.

Portugal, which enjoyed significant trade with the United Kingdom partly as a result of the British-French wars of the latter 1700s, shifted solely to gold in 1854. France and other European states moved away from bimetallism to gold in the 1870s. Germany's adoption of the mark, based upon gold, in 1871 moved another large political economy into the gold column and added momentum to the convergence upon gold. By 1879, the United States also was on the gold standard for all intents and purposes, albeit unofficially. At the end of the century, most European nations had officially switched to gold, and those that had not officially switched did so informally by **pegging,** or fixing, the value of their currencies to those of nations using a gold standard.

Alternatives to the Gold Standard

Although some believe that the gold standard is unique in reducing risk and uncertainty, other international monetary arrangements can provide stability and limit currency risk just as well. Governments could have supported some standard other than gold. Why not converge on some other standard, as long as it meets the three functional conditions of money—tool of exchange, unit of accounting, and storehouse of value? Any commodity or item that meets these conditions and is accepted by enough parties could serve as the core of an international monetary regime. In fact, gold had some troubling shortcomings that would eventually threaten its role as the monetary standard.

For many, a monetary system based upon something other than gold was preferable. In the early 1800s, prospects existed for other monetary systems, such as a silver standard or a bimetallic standard based on gold and silver. At mid-century, gold was in much more limited supply than silver. This uneven distribution shifted temporarily after an influx of gold from discoveries in California and Australia, which led to a decline in the price of gold in relation to silver and effectively changed exchange rates. In 1859, however, large silver discoveries in Nevada reversed that trend and brought a flood of silver into the international markets. Maintaining a bimetallic standard become more difficult for governments as large swings in the quantity and value of gold against silver played havoc with nations on a bimetallic standard, alternately causing large gold inflows and large silver outflows, followed by large gold outflows and large silver inflows.

In particular, France and the United States found the resulting swings in exchange rates troubling. The intense variability in capital flows placed pressures on national mints and treasuries, and on prices in international exchange. Those on silver or bimetallic standards faced threats of **inflation** as the abundance of silver worked to drive up prices in those economies—remember Hume's arguments about the positive relationship between the size of the money supply and prices, discussed in chapter 5. Despite the resulting variability in prices, the threat of inflation from the growing supply of silver, and the apparent stabilizing benefits of a shift to an international gold standard, some governments on bimetallic or silver standards resisted converting to a more stable gold standard. Why?

Political opposition, dissension, and policy debates over bimetallism versus gold affected many national political arenas. Silver-mining interests and agricultural interests resisted convergence on a gold standard. The silver-mining interests—those who owned and worked in silver mines—obviously benefited from the demand for silver, which would shrink if it ceased to be a key component of national monetary regimes. Agricultural producers preferred silver for another reason: its abundance relative to gold after the silver discoveries in Nevada could promote increases in agricultural and other commodity prices, while a standard based on a scarcer resource such as gold threatened to cause a decline in the price of those commodities.

This dilemma was compounded by the advance of the Industrial Revolution, which increased the production of goods available for consumption and generated more downward pressure on the price of commodities and services—again, Hume's arguments about the relationship between the size of the money supply and prices is instructive. This effect, called price **deflation,** hit the agricultural sector particularly hard, and prices fell dramatically in the late 1800s (see table 7.3), causing severe recessions and hardships among agricultural producers. Wheat prices, for example, fell over 69 percent from 1867 to 1900. Workers and producers in sectors that were particularly hard-hit by deflation preferred a currency regime based on a commodity or metal in greater supply, such as silver.

The unofficial move by the United States to the gold standard in 1879 failed to end the virulent debate among policymakers and others in American society. The policy competition persisted, finally culminating in the presidential election of 1896 between William Jennings Bryan and William McKinley—an election that demarcated a major turning point in the U.S. outlook on world affairs. Bryan, a Democratic Populist, attracted strong support among

TABLE 7.3   **Price Deflation of Agricultural Commodities, 1867–1900**

Commodity	1867	1870	1873	1876	1879	1882	1885	1888	1891	1894	1897	1900	% decrease over this period
						PRICES							
Barley	1.22	0.853	0.963	0.685	0.599	0.631	0.557	0.591	0.522	0.437	0.343	0.407	66.6
Corn	0.781	0.521	0.483	0.361	0.364	0.481	0.322	0.331	0.398	0.451	0.26	0.35	55.2
Cotton				9.71	10.28	9.12	8.39	8.5	7.24	4.59	6.68	9.2	5.3
Hay	14.3	14.45	14.4	9.8	9.63	9.99	10.07	9.24	8.65	8.98	7.21	9.78	31.6
Oats	0.587	0.426	0.374	0.349	0.326	0.371	0.279	0.27	0.306	0.32	0.21	0.253	56.9
Wheat	2.01	1.04	1.17	1.04	1.11	0.888	0.772	0.927	0.831	0.489	0.809	0.621	69.1
Potatoes	1.51	1.18	1.16	1.1	0.72	0.91	0.73	0.65	0.6	0.89	0.92	0.72	52.3
Sweet potatoes	1.93	1.61	1.42		1	1.02	0.93	0.86	0.9		0.88	0.92	52.3

Source: USDA, National Agricultural Statistics Service, www.usda.gov/nass/pubs/trackrec/track03a.htm.

THE SACRILEGIOUS CANDIDATE.

While advocating populist causes and during a run for the presidency in 1896, William Jennings Bryan warned against crucifying U.S. agricultural producers on "a cross of gold." The adoption of a gold standard ensured price stability. However, the government's inability to increase money supply during a period of great productivity increases and rapid economic expansion contributed to severe price deflation in primary products, resulting in a recession in the agricultural sector that devastated its producers. Appealing to banking and industrial interests, William McKinley prevailed in the election, and the United States continued to adhere to the gold standard.

agricultural and mining interests located in the South, the Midwest, and parts of the West, by campaigning for bimetallism and warning that the gold standard would crucify American farmers "on a cross of gold." McKinley, a Republican, drew strong support from the banking and manufacturing sectors, and his victory in this pivotal election confirmed the U.S. commitment to the gold standard. It also represented a victory for those anticipating a growing U.S. role and responsibility in the global arena over those favoring more insular and inward-looking policies.

The 1896 election provided the contemporary context for journalist L. Frank Baum's *The Wonderful Wizard of Oz,* which was considered by many to be a children's story but actually offered a biting social and political commentary on the contemporary divisions in U.S. society and politics. Baum's story captures the tension between eastern banking and industrial interests—the Wicked Witches of the East and West—and agrarian-labor interests—the Good Witches of the North and South. The Wizard is President McKinley, Oz is the abbreviation for *ounce* (the common measure of gold's weight), Emerald City represents Washington, D.C., and Dorothy and her admirable companions on the Yellow Brick Road are those opposed to the "cross of gold" policies that favored banking and industrial interests. In the book, Dorothy's silver slippers click on the yellow bricks, thus suggesting the bimetal mix of gold and silver. The Cowardly Lion symbolizes William Jennings Bryan, the witless Scarecrow represents farmers, and the rusty Tin Man typifies industrial workers. The American spirit is celebrated in their bravery, their wisdom, and their heart, and by Dorothy's wholesome goodness. You'll never see Judy Garland's character in the same light again!

Why Converge on a Gold Standard?

So, why did gold prevail as the standard, rather than bimetallism or some other reserve asset? Why did enough governments converge on gold to make it the heart of an international monetary system? Once again, Great Britain played a pivotal role, as British trade and monetary policies generated pressures on others to converge on the gold standard. With a rapidly expanding economy due to the Industrial Revolution, British consumers had more disposable income to lavish on commodities. As lower barriers to trade made it possible for them to decide to spend part of this new prosperity on foreign goods, British markets became increasingly attractive outlets for foreign producers and soon emerged as the center of the globalizing economy.

The United Kingdom led the drift toward a gold standard with its early and de facto, albeit accidental, adoption in the eighteenth century. The rise of British prowess in international finance and trade gave British preferences disproportionate weight over international monetary policies. The British choice of a gold standard influenced foreign parties that sought to borrow money in London's capital markets or to trade with British merchants. As the international financial center and a source of capital for economic expansion and nation-building, London drew borrowers and savers from other nations, who accessed capital and invested in capital markets that were located in a nation adhering to a gold standard. On the trade side, because British markets were the dominant international outlet for foreign producers, the concerns of British importers over exchange-rate risk influenced policy debates in other political economies that wanted to export to British markets—good business requires that producers address their best customers' needs. The attractiveness of Britain's markets, its market power, endowed the British with influence over international monetary matters that was effective whether intentionally manipulated by British policymakers or not. A similar pattern is repeated today in the global economy, as many governments adjust their exchange-rate policies to match those of their dominant trading partners, with the intention of stabilizing currency risk in their most important international economic relationships.

By the early 1870s, the incentives to reduce currency risk in major trading relationships accelerated the convergence on a gold standard. When France and Germany joined the United Kingdom on a gold standard, pressures increased on other nations to demonetize silver—to move away from silver and bimetallism—and the expansion of trade made it increasingly difficult to resist the impetus to converge on a gold standard. The pressure increased further with the de facto move to gold by the United States, which was rapidly expanding and moving toward becoming the largest economy in the world. By the late 1800s, with the four largest commercial and trading nations (the United Kingdom, United States, Germany, and France) on the gold standard, most other nations adopted gold as well.

Even with the problems presented by price deflation and the political resistance to gold in some nations, it was extremely difficult and costly for any single nation to unilaterally maintain a bimetallic standard. A nation's unilateral rejection of the gold standard while others switched to gold would result in the draining of that nation's gold reserves. Speculators would have economic incentives to purchase that nation's gold with silver and then move it abroad. The resistant nation would be left holding only silver reserves, but then would need gold to settle its international payments; this outcome would only make trade more expensive. Once the major nations and markets moved to gold, it became costly for other nations to resist the gold standard without incurring economic costs to their national economies even if specific sectors might benefit from such resistance. This effect has been called a **network externality,** wherein the globalization of trade and finances created benefits for switching to gold and costs for retaining silver or bimetallism. Silver did not disappear as money, but it no longer served as a major reserve asset. Many nations continued to employ silver coin as well as gold, and many supplemented their gold reserves with reserves of foreign currencies.

The gold standard of the late 1800s and early 1900s enjoyed some success in stabilizing the expectations of those engaged in international economic activities and reducing the currency risk that hampered international trade and lending. To the extent that it worked, it succeeded for several key reasons. First, governments converged upon a common standard and cooperated to support that standard. Second, governments committed to **convertibility** of their currencies upon demand, each agreeing to exchange its currency for gold or for another currency at the established rate of exchange upon request. Committing to convertibility and living up to that commitment, especially when challenged, helped to build the reputations of the governments and contributed to the stability of the gold standard.

Early on, the British government committed to exchanging gold for British pounds sterling upon demand. Its position as the center of global finance and the largest economy helped to make this commitment to convertibility credible—worthy of confidence or believable. If any government and economy could maintain that commitment, it was that of the United Kingdom. Over time, the British guarantee of convertibility gained increasing credibility as the British Treasury continued to live up to its commitment.

British Commitment to Convertibility as a Collective Good

As the United Kingdom was the largest, most influential economy and global capital market, a credible British commitment to convertibility provided the global economy with an important **collective good.** What is a collective good? Sometimes called a "public good" or a "common good," in its simplest form, a collective good is a commodity that, if consumed by one member of a group, cannot be withheld from others in the group. Any such commodity that is available to one member of a group must be available to all members of that group—this is a principle of nonexclusion. There are other characteristics of a collective good, but let's focus on the impossibility of excluding members of a group from consuming the commodity in question.

Well-kept public parks, pristine and plentiful oceans, clean air, and functional public roads all share this nonexclusive quality. However, a collective good can also consist of a bad commodity to be shared among a group—a collective bad, if you will—which shares the quality of nonexclusion. Global warming, air and water pollution, noise pollution, and parks littered with dog droppings are collective bads. The difference between a collective good and a collective bad is often a subjective question related to the collective's preferences, which leads in turn to the definition of the collective itself: what defines the group, or what are the boundaries of the group? A group may be narrowly defined, such as a college fraternity or sorority, where the cleanliness of a function room or an excellent cook is a collective good, and a filthy bathroom or kitchen is a collective bad. In the case of nineteenth-century Great Britain, which provided convertibility of the pound to gold, the collective was defined much more broadly, to include those engaged in the global economy.

A credible commitment to convertibility reduced the risks of holding the British pound sterling, which therefore became "as good as gold." People and governments grew more willing to hold the pound sterling for long periods of time and to use it as the currency of choice to settle transactions. Other governments and economic actors increasingly held British pounds as a reserve currency in addition to gold, while more and more contracts and payments in international exchange took place in pounds. Both of these practices lowered currency risk, reduced transaction costs associated with the exchange of gold as part of the international payment process, and further elevated the importance of British capital markets and policy preferences. The rise of the pound sterling as an international, extraterritorial money gave the British a tool of substantial influence in world affairs, as the pound's reach extended well beyond the borders of the United Kingdom and the British Empire. As a consequence, the British gained even more influence over the rules and direction of the global economy.

Why Would a Government Renege on a Commitment to Its Currency Price?

Commitment to convertibility and maintenance of a stable exchange rate are not simple tasks for a government. If an exchange-rate system is to stabilize currency prices and reduce the currency risks in international exchange, however, each government's commitment to the prices of its currency and to the rules of the monetary system must be credible. In the case of the gold standard, this meant that a government's commitment to the price of its currency in gold must prove convincing, as well as its commitment to convertibility. If a government could renege on such commitments by simply stating that it had lied about the value of its currency or its willingness to convert its currency upon demand—or if private traders believed that such a scenario were probable—any claims about commitment to such a standard would be viewed as insincere, cheap talk.

Let's think about why a government would lie, mislead, or change its policy toward the commitment to a specific price for its currency or its willingness to convert that currency to some other asset. What might induce a government to undermine its own credibility in this way? Political economy provides some insights; let's consider two dynamics that might pressure a government to defect from its commitments: the effect of the exchange-rate mechanism upon the competitive stature of a state's economy and the potential for draining a state's monetary reserves.

First, as we have seen, exchange rates influence pricing in international markets and play a central role in the adjustment of the balance of payments. A nation's exchange rate affects the price and competitiveness of its commodities and services both in international markets and in the **tradable sector** more generally. The tradable sector is that arena where domestic producers of goods and services compete with overseas producers, whether in overseas markets or at home. Since a currency's value affects the competitiveness of a nation's commodities and services, a government may encounter difficulties in committing credibly to a standard whereby its currency is overvalued vis-à-vis other currencies. Domestic producers and labor in the tradable sector, recognizing the ability of the exchange rate to influence the global competitiveness of their industries, may pressure their government to manipulate the price of its currency against others in the global trading arena. The more such pressures threaten politicians' ability to persevere in office, the more they are likely to respond with policies that are designed to enhance the competitive stature of their domestic producers. Policymakers can address these pressures by adopting trade policies such as tariffs, subsidies, or quotas, or they can use monetary policies that manipulate their currency's value.

A less expensive or undervalued currency will make a nation's commodities and services less expensive in comparison to other nations' commodities and services in overseas markets, while making overseas commodities and services more expensive in its domestic markets. Conversely, a more expensive or overvalued currency will make a nation's commodities and services more expensive in overseas markets in relation to other nations' products and services, and overseas goods and services less expensive in its domestic markets. Such relative differences in prices can affect consumption decisions by individuals and businesses both in the domestic economy and abroad. A less expensive currency will help to swing the current account of the balance of payments toward a surplus, and a more expensive currency will push the current account toward a deficit.

Consequently, a state's tradable sector can be made more competitive by the manipulation of a single policy instrument. A government facing a persistent balance-of-payments deficit, as well as pressures from domestic producers, might be tempted to address both situations by manipulating the value of its currency. A unilateral shift in the exchange rate by a nation affects the prices of all its goods and services in the tradable sector. (Using the framework introduced in chapter 1, the exchange rate is the dependent variable, and the pressures arising from domestic producers and labor are independent variables.)

Under the second dynamic that might lead a government to renege on its commitments, the issue of convertibility can pose another dilemma. The convertibility commitment exposes a nation's monetary reserves (gold, foreign currencies, or some other reserve asset depending upon the international monetary system) to potential depletion if some individual, company, or government perceives an opportunity to convert that nation's currency into a reserve asset and then move it overseas in order to purchase another currency or commodity that is relatively undervalued (that is, yielding more for the money). This dynamic can lead to a draining of the target nation's monetary reserves. The conditions for such speculative activities—which are known as **arbitrage opportunities**—exist when people believe that a currency is systematically overvalued or undervalued, or when they believe that a government may not be committed to defending its currency at the stated price. A government can act to defend its currency in such situations, but if enough distrust undermines the valuation of its currency, the pressures of convertibility may lead to the draining of the nation's reserve assets and force the government to revalue its currency.

MORE COLLECTIVE GOODS AND GLOBALIZATION

Other factors contributed to the central role of the United Kingdom in promoting globalization in the late nineteenth and early twentieth centuries. In addition to their commitment to freer trade, gold, and convertibility, the British provided three other collective goods to the global arena that helped to significantly reduce risk and advance globalization and economic expansion: liquidity, lender of last resort, and market access under duress. British capital markets provided the liquidity, or supply of capital and asset mobility, that fostered economic expansion and political development. The British markets and government acted as the lender of last resort, or central bank, for the system in managing financial crises and economic downturns in the international arena. And, even during periods of economic stagnation or decline, the British retained their commitment to free trade and kept the entry barriers to their markets low, thus maintaining market access under duress.

Liquidity

National unification, governance, and economic development required capital to finance armies, ports, railroads, roads, communication infrastructure, and economic enterprise. Much of this capital was raised locally, within the states where the capital was to be applied to projects. But British bankers had created highly efficient capital markets that attracted capital looking for investment opportunities, as well as opportunities looking for capital. London's capital markets provided much of the **liquidity**—a measure of how much capital is available, how mobile an asset is, or how easily it can be exchanged (cash has high liquidity)—that helped to fund state formation and economic development across Europe, the Americas, Australia, and other nations. The British willingness to pump the pound sterling into the global economy turned that currency into a reserve asset that was used to settle accounts between states and private economic actors across boundaries. But it also served to expand the supply of good money in the global economy, which fueled investment in eco-

TABLE 7.4	**Index of per Capita Levels of Industrialization, 1750–1900**					
	1750	1800	1830	1860	1880	1900
United Kingdom	10	16	25	64	87	100
Belgium	9	10	14	28	43	56
United States	4	9	14	21	38	69
France	9	9	12	20	28	39
Germany	8	8	9	15	25	52
Austria	7	7	8	11	15	23
Italy	8	8	8	10	12	17
Russia	6	6	7	8	10	15
China	8	6	6	4	4	3
India	7	6	6	3	2	1

Source: Paul Bairoch, "International Industrialization Levels from 1750–1890," *Journal of European Economic History* 11 (fall 1982): 294.

Note: The index is scaled to the United Kingdom; 1900 = 100.

nomic enterprise, helped to maintain or increase prices (the opposite of price deflation), and contributed to improvements in social welfare.

London's capital markets helped to finance unification of the German and Italian regional states into single nation-states. Latin American governments borrowed in London to finance a variety of public infrastructure projects. U.S. railroad developers sought and obtained financing in London for systemic improvements that would link regions, advance westward expansion, create more efficient intranational trade, and spur the economic development that was rapidly transforming the United States from a developing economy into the world's largest and most advanced economy (see table 7.4). Table 7.5 gives some indication of the changes and magnitude of global borrowing in London's markets.

The importance of London's capital markets for growth, development, and state-building gave British policymakers, public and private, valuable leverage over the choices and actions of others wanting capital for economic and government enterprise. Using the emerging global financial network and the ability to obtain financial assistance or impose financial sanctions, British policymakers extended their sphere of influence and leveraged policies in support of an increasingly global economy.

TABLE 7.5	The Shift in British Capital Markets toward Increased Overseas Lending, 1850–1913

Foreign Investment as Percentage of Domestic Savings (at current prices)

1850–1854	12.3*	1885–1889	46.5
1855–1859	30.2*	1890–1894	35.3
1860–1864	21.5*	1895–1899	20.7
1865–1869	32.2*	1900–1904	11.2
1870–1874	38.0	1905–1909	42.7
1875–1879	16.2	1910–1913	53.3
1880–1884	33.2		

Source: Kevin H. O'Rourke and Jeffrey G. Williamson, *Globalization and History* (London: MIT Press, 1999), 209.

Note: Asterisks indicate numbers that are calculated from original current-account data, rather than gold-adjusted data.

Globalization's costs as well as its benefits soon became apparent. The exposure of London's markets to overseas economic activities brought rewards but also carried new risks. The prospect of lucrative returns on investments in the New World attracted financial speculation, some of which paid off handsomely, while other ventures collapsed and left creditors exposed when some borrowers failed to meet their debt obligations. In these latter cases, the markets were roiled by financial crisis, which exposed major British and European financial institutions to extreme risks and threatened the global economy. Argentina, the fifth largest economy in the world by the end of the 1800s, borrowed so much capital that its economic crises threatened to unhinge the European financial system and collapse British capital markets.

The financial crises created by defaults of U.S. borrowers in the mid-1800s and by Argentinian borrowers later in the century are comparable to such recent events as the Third World Debt Crisis of the 1980s, the Peso Crisis of 1994, the Asian Financial Crisis of 1997, and the Russian Ruble Crisis of 1997—and they elicited comparably overblown rhetoric. When London's investors were outraged and severely damaged by the U.S. defaults, the pre-eminent European banker of his time, Baron Rothschild, emphatically asserted that U.S. borrowers would find no access to new loans and that the "United States could not borrow a dollar, not a dollar." Sydney Smith, a clergyman, wrote as follows in a London newspaper:

> There really should be lunatic asylums for nations as well as individuals. America is a nation with whom no contract can be made, because none will be kept; unstable in the very foundations of social life, deficient in the elements of good faith, men who prefer any load of infamy, however great, to any pressure of taxation however light.

Lender of Last Resort

The emerging network of global finance—the central nervous system of the global economy—provided Great Britain with disproportionate influence over the direction of the global economy, but it also exposed Britain and the global economy to new risks and challenges. British capital markets provided the collective good of liquidity, which helped to generate economic expansion during good economic times, but bad economic times or financial crises threatened the provision of this collective good. The British government, led by the Bank of England and the British Treasury, helped to coordinate the activities of private European financial institutions and multiple governments to ensure an adequate supply of capital during such crises. The British thus took on the function known as **lender of last resort,** another collective good.

A lender of last resort acts to ensure the supply of capital to a financial system at a time when other financial institutions face a liquidity shortage that can threaten the solvency of those institutions and even of the system. Such liquidity shortages may occur as a consequence of excessive demands during an economic cycle or as a result of a crisis that unnerves the holders of capital. At some points during economic cycles, banks and other financial institutions may find themselves lacking the capital to meet the demands of their depositors and clients—a liquidity shortage that can constrain economic activity.

For example, planting seasons create economic cycles in agricultural areas, producing large fluctuations in demand upon bank resources. At the beginning of planting season, farmers need capital to purchase seeds, to pay labor, and to buy or fix equipment. But they cannot bring their crops to market for months, so they must either draw upon their savings or borrow from their banks. This need generates a major seasonal demand upon their banks' resources—usually far more than a bank has on hand. At the other end of the farming cycle, farmers sell their crops and then either deposit their earnings in the banks or pay down their loans. The banks are now faced with too many deposits on hand. As they have to pay interest on those deposits, they must use them to earn money, so the banks loan some of those deposits to borrowers. These loans, in turn, limit the banks' resources on hand when the farming cycle begins anew. When banks in agricultural areas face such a liquidity shortage because of seasonal demand, they reach up the banking food chain to borrow funds from banks in urban areas, which are subject to a different economic cycle and so are not facing the same liquidity problem. The demand for capital to meet the seasonal needs of the agricultural cycle can thus cascade up the banking chain. Hopefully, this upward reach will address the liquidity problem of the rural banks, for if not, they—and perhaps other banks as well—may face a solvency dilemma that can turn into a larger economic crisis.

Similar liquidity problems can occur as a consequence of some unexpected crisis, not simply as an effect of seasonal fluctuations in an economy. Nonetheless, the problem remains a shortage of capital that threatens the solvency of financial and economic organizations. Capital supply can shrink dramatically during an economic crisis, as holders of capital become risk-averse and reluctant to invest, preferring to sit on their surplus capital in order to protect it—figuratively or literally hiding money in the mattress or in a coffee can. A decline in the supply of capital due to the reluctance of investors to lend their surplus increases capital costs for borrowers, who must then pay more to comfort the fears of investors and entice them to lend. Because capital is an important factor of production, such changes in its price and supply affect the costs of economic enterprises as well as the range of enterprises that can obtain capital. This effect influences the prices of commodities produced by those enterprises, as well as consumption choices and choices about economic activities. Shrinkage in capital supply following a downturn can lead to decline in economic activity and turn a temporary crisis into a more serious, long-term problem.

A lender of last resort is the final safeguard against a liquidity crisis. The party that fulfills this function attempts to keep banks and financial institutions solvent by ensuring the availability of sufficient capital to prevent a liquidity crisis. A lender of last resort enacts **countercyclical policies,** or policies against the trend. (Going along with a trend is **procyclical policy** behavior.) Pursuing a countercyclical policy strategy, a lender of last resort attempts to interrupt the trend of a downward cycle by injecting capital into a system at the very time that capital is being drained from the system as others become risk-averse and withhold their capital. This strategy is an attempt to mitigate recessionary downturns, to make them shorter and less painful, by providing capital to promote the economic activity necessary to grow out of a downturn. A lender of last resort can use the same countercyclical approach to constrain a too rapid economic expansion, by withdrawing money from the system. By raising interest rates or using other policy instruments to reduce the supply of money and increase its costs, the lender can slow an expansionary trend in an economy.

We can easily understand why a lender of last resort would act countercyclically to promote growth at time of economic contraction, but why would it work countercyclically to slow an expansionary economy? After all, growth is good! It generates jobs, income, and consumption, and it improves welfare. When a lender of last resort acts to shrink the money supply, the expressed objective is usually to constrain economic expansion that threatens to bring on inflation, which undermines the value of money and thus can be dysfunctional for an economy. If the money supply grows too fast, that money loses value and purchases less and less. As people lose confidence in the value of that money, they are less willing to hold it over extended periods. Long-term investments decline in value, and this decline generates incentives for individuals and firms to consume for today rather than investing for the future.

Most often, governments have performed the lender-of-last-resort function for their domestic economies, although there are instances of private entities undertaking it. For example, the large money-center banks in New York cobbled together an arrangement to perform such a function for the United States during the period from 1837 to 1913, when the United States lacked a public central bank. But such examples are far less frequent than governments' attempts to act as lenders of last resort for their economies. Private providers have also had a more problematic history in providing this service, as their natural incentives are to become risk-averse and protect their enterprises at the very time that the lender-of-last-resort function is most needed by a political economy.

Governments, their central banks, and their treasuries can attempt to act as lenders of last resort for their domestic economies, but only a very wealthy economy, or handful of economies, with significant financial reserves, can perform this function in the larger global arena. Whether or not it was the original intention of the British Treasury and Bank of England, the prominence of London's capital markets, banks, and financiers meant that, for most of the late 1800s, only the British enjoyed such capabilities and position in the global arena. If other states attempted to act as lender of last resort for the system at large but without British participation, those governments would discover that their capabilities were insufficient to stem a global liquidity crisis. Their gold and currency reserves would be drained without resolving the international predicament.

Market Access under Duress

The British commitment to free trade, regardless of the actions of other nations and in the face of domestic protectionist pressures, constituted another collective good during the late 1800s. Economic recessions and dislocations during this period increased domestic pressures for protectionism against imports and prompted some states to temper and even reverse their movement toward freer trade (see table 7.1). These pressures were strongest in agricultural sectors, which were experiencing severe price deflation related to the gold standard and to surplus production. If the United Kingdom, the largest consumer economy and the hub of the global trading system, had raised barriers along with these other nations during a time of global economic slowdown and duress, the growth of trade would have been further curtailed. Economic activity would have faced more severe challenges, and recessionary trends would have been amplified.

Instead, the United Kingdom's resolve to maintain relatively open markets for international goods at this time of economic duress, even as other governments moved to restrict access to their domestic markets, provided an outlet for foreign economic enterprises to sell their products in the British market and an opportunity to temper and counter the recessionary trend in other economies. Although it was a countercyclical policy, this action was not selfless or altruistic. As the largest trading country, the United Kingdom stood to gain if other economies grew and their consumers increased their consumption, some of which would inevitably involve increased purchases of British goods. But this strategy required a long-term perspective on the part of British policymakers and an ability to resist short-term demands from domestic interests as British producers and labor were being damaged in the short run by economic downturns and increasing barriers to entry in some foreign markets.

This collective good has become known as **market access under duress.** Again, only a wealthy and dominant (or near-dominant) nation can provide this collective good to the global system and have the desired countercyclical effect. A small political economy, even if it kept its barriers to trade low, could not possibly consume enough goods to turn around the global economy.

TECHNOLOGY

Any accounting of nineteenth-century political economy that neglects technology ignores some pivotal changes that empowered globalization and transformed social relations. Certainly, new economic ideas, political reforms, the absence of international conflict, and the stable monetary regime anchored by the United Kingdom fueled the growth of a global economy in the 1800s. These conditions may have been necessary to account for the extent and depth of globalization, but they were not sufficient.

Barriers such as great distance, seemingly impassable deserts or mountain ranges, vast oceans, pandemic disease, and other forces of nature can obstruct and hinder international exchange even when political economies are open to such exchange. Such obstacles make transit difficult perhaps, but they are not insurmountable, given the will and creativity displayed by such determined human adventurers as Hannibal, who crossed the Alps to invade Rome in 218 B.C.; the Portuguese mariner Vasco da Gama, who navigated the Horn of Africa in 1498, searching for rewards from exploration and trade in eastern goods; and Christopher Columbus, who crossed the Atlantic in 1492 in search of an easier and faster route to the lucrative spice trade of the Orient, only to discover the New World. These conquerors and explorers benefited from technological change and discovery. Hannibal harnessed the technology of animal husbandry, as his armies employed war elephants to battle the Romans. Breakthroughs in navigational technology empowered the efforts of Columbus, da Gama, and other explorers.

Technological and industrial revolutions transformed production in the Atlantic economies. These revolutions generated economic pressures that pushed people to move from rural to urban areas; dramatically increased wealth while decreasing the number of people subsisting on day-to-day earnings; lowered the cost of transport; reduced the time of communication across great distances from days and weeks to near-real-time messaging; and inspired a search for raw materials to feed industrial engines. The Industrial Revolution diffused wealth across more and more of the population, creating middle and working classes with disposable income and growing consumption appetites, which in turn fed the demand for more goods and services. Technological inventions and innovations in transport—railroads, steam engines, screw propellers, and steel hulls—introduced greater efficiencies that allowed larger quantities to be transported and at far smaller cost. The advent of refrigeration meant that perishable goods could be shipped over great distance and time to arrive in distant markets as fresh as many local goods.

Transportation

Technological advances in transport revolutionized the movement of goods and people, lowered costs, rapidly increased shipping capacity, and reduced the time of getting goods from producers to consumers in distant markets. Such improvements in transportation capabilities contributed as much as any other factor to the integration of markets and national political economies. These changes also empowered the specialization and comparative advantages produced by differences in national factor endowments; production structures shifted as global market exchange rewarded some producers and penalized others.

Construction of canals, harbors, and navigable inner waterways produced the first breakthroughs in transport. Water transport was dramatically more efficient and cheaper than shipping by road—especially the dirt roads that dominated the internal transportation networks of many political economies. The Atlantic economies invested heavily in canal construction and the installation of locks on existing waterways to create and expand transport capabilities. British investments produced a huge increase in navigable waterways in the United Kingdom: shipping costs on such waterways undercut those on roads by 50 percent or more in the early 1800s. In the United States, the Erie Canal, constructed between 1817 and 1825, decreased shipping time between Buffalo and New York City by almost two-thirds and reduced shipping costs by over 80 percent. Other canals and waterways, such as the Baltimore and Ohio Canal, created comparable productivity gains, and Europeans garnered similar gains as international cooperation harnessed the Rhine River system. The opening of the Suez Canal in 1869, in tandem with the steamship (needed because the still air of the Suez was not friendly to sailing ships), generated similar cost and time improvements for trade between the Far East and Europe, and restored the Near East to a position in world trade that it had not enjoyed for centuries.

The railroad, another major innovation in transport, also brought markets together. At an 1869 ceremony in Utah, dignitaries gathered to drive the last spike that completed the first transcontinental railroad in the Americas. Motivated partly by the desire of the U.S. government to link the East and West for national security reasons during the Civil War, this development in transportation foreshadowed the emergence of a national market in the United States, in which prices in California converged with prices in Chicago, St. Louis, New York, and Boston. A rapid expansion of rail lines across the Atlantic economies (shown in table 7.6) linked disparate markets and led to an increase in the frequency and density of economic interactions within and across national borders. Commodity prices converged in markets linked by rail networks.

Railways, canals, and the improvement of national navigable waterways led to large productivity gains as domestic shipping costs fell and more and more tonnage could be shipped efficiently. Goods produced at a distance became increasingly competitive with goods produced nearby. The benefits of railways and newly navigable fresh-water passages reached across national boundaries when nations were contiguous, but the economic gains and pressures for

TABLE 7.6	The Expansion of Railway Mileage, 1850–1910			
	1850	1870	1890	1910
Austria-Hungary	954	5,949	16,489	26,834
Australia	—	953	9,524	17,429
Argentina	—	637	5,434	17,381
Canada	66	2,617	13,368	26,462
China	—	—	80	5,092
France	1,714	11,142	22,911	30,643
Germany	3,637	11,729	25,411	36,152
India	—	4,771	16,411	32,099
Italy	265	3,825	8,163	10,573
Japan	—	—	1,139	5,130
Mexico	—	215	6,037	15,350
Russia (in Europe)	310	7,098	18,059	34,990
United Kingdom	6,621	15,537	20,073	23,387
United States	9,021	52,922	116,703	249,902

Source: J. Hurd, "Railways and the Expansion of Markets in India, 1861–1921," *Explorations in Economic History* 12 (1975).

market integration they produced could not be extended to those separated by seas without technological gains in ocean transport. It was fortunate, therefore, that underpinning the railroad revolution was the development of the steam engine, which also found its way into the design of merchant shipping.

Steam engines and other technological inventions such as the screw propeller, steel hulls, and subsequent advances in engine design led to rapid increases in the size of ocean-going ships, the weight they could transport, their speed, and the reliability of shipping schedules no longer at the mercy of wind and weather. British steamships began to regularly traverse the English Channel by the second decade of the 1800s, and transatlantic steamer service began in 1838. By 1870, the tonnage of ships powered by mechanical engines exceeded the tonnage of shipping powered by wind and sail.

Larger, faster, and more predictable ocean shipping reduced delivery times and lowered the costs of transport. Domestic producers now faced price competition from abroad: consumers in Liverpool could choose between British domestic grain and lower-cost grain from the United States, Argentina, or Canada. Ironically, Indians found that cotton shirts made in the United Kingdom were cheaper than shirts made in Bombay, even though the raw cotton often had come from India. Consumers enjoyed expanded consumption possibilities—a greater range of choice and value—as the transport revolution reduced costs, increased productivity, linked markets, and expanded opportunities for efficient producers.

By the mid-1800s, journeys that decades earlier had taken weeks and months, now took only a week. New Orleans and New York were highly separated markets in 1800, but by 1850 they had become highly integrated, as, increasingly, were London and New York, Paris and London, and Rotterdam and Boston. Differences in commodity prices declined with the advances in navigation; technological change interacted with political change, and world trade expanded rapidly—as can be seen in figure 7.1 and table 7.7. Improvements in overall social welfare corresponded to increases in international exchange and the resulting specialization of national production structures.

Still, not everyone benefited from these changes. Inefficient producers and labor, once protected by great distance and expensive shipping, now faced competition from more distant and efficient producers and labor. Grain and other agricultural exports from the New World challenged agricultural producers in Europe. At first, only agricultural goods that did not easily spoil made the long journey, and the New World producers of such commodities quickly demonstrated their competitive advantage over European producers. Farmers in Europe responded to this initial loss of competitive advantage by shifting production away from grain production toward animal husbandry, supplying perishable goods such as fresh beef, dairy products, and other fresh animal products. Even with the advances in transportation technology that reduced shipping times and lowered shipping costs, these goods still faced the prospect of spoilage during transit.

The advantage and security of animal husbandry was short-lived, however, as the development of refrigeration technology in mid-century soon overcame the problem of spoilage. By the 1870s and 1880s, agricultural producers in the United States, Argentina, Canada, Australia, New Zealand, and other New World economies were shipping meats, butter, and other perishables under refrigeration to European markets. Soon the European agricultural producers, hurt by these innovations in transport, responded to their loss of comparative advantage by pressuring their governments to raise tariffs and other protections. Inefficient producers thus sought government intervention to delay or avoid their costs of adjusting to the new global economy and to force the costs of adjusting on others. Despite the mid-century trend toward lower and lower barriers to entry, tariff rates ceased their decline after 1870. Consumers and foreign producers were penalized by the advent of tariffs, paying higher prices and selling fewer goods.

FIGURE 7.1	**Change in the Tradable Sector, 1800–1910: The Expansion in Trade, as an Aggregate of Imports and Exports, for Each State**

7.1a Fast and Significant Change

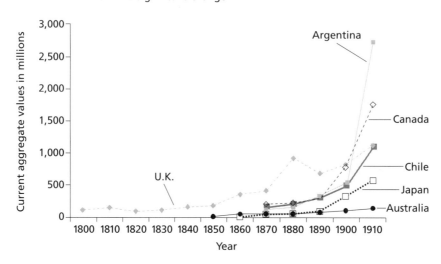

7.1b Extraordinary Change

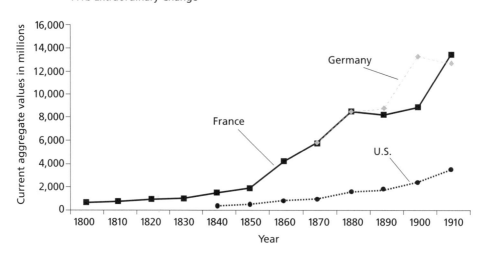

Source: Data from B. R. Mitchell, *International Historical Statistics* (New York: Palgrave Macmillan, 2003).

TABLE 7.7	World Trade, 1720–1913	
	Volume Index	**Annual Growth (in percentages)**
1720	1.13	
1750	1.9	1.75
1780	2.18	0.46
1800	2.3	0.27
1820	3.1	1.5
1830	4.3	3.33
1840	5.4	2.3
1850	10.1	6.46
1860	13.9	3.25
1870	23.8	5.53
1880	30	2.94
1890	44	2.97
1900	57	3.5
1910	81	3.87
1913	96	4.34

Source: W.W. Rostow, *The World Economy: History and Prospect* (Austin: University of Texas Press, 1978).

The Industrial Revolution and Migration

Technological invention and innovation transformed far more than transport. The Industrial Revolution involved the application of new ideas and technology to economic processes and organization that led to a shift from agrarian to industrial production. In some states, people were willing to invest their surplus in economic activities that would pay off in the future as opposed to consuming in the present. Such investment generally required a government and society that limited the risks of violence, excessive corruption, and damage to property rights, which could scare people away from investing in activities that would pay-off in the future. Governments and societies that successfully managed such threats created incentives for individuals to extend their time horizons in making economic choices, thus leading to longer-term investments in people, resources, and enterprise. The resulting transformation in economic and industrial activity was reflected earlier, in table 7.4.

Such economic transformations created a need for workers in the emerging industrial centers. As industrial production tended to concentrate in urban areas near transportation arteries, people moved from the rural areas to urban centers to find employment. The Atlantic economies in particular experienced a rapid shift in their rural-urban population distribution, which tore at the social and familial networks based in agricultural communities and resulted in populations that were more mobile and amenable to relocation. The safety nets of rural life provided less support for those who moved to the urban centers.

The industrialization of economic activity also changed the relationship between workers and their economic activities. Prior to the Industrial Revolution, both agricultural and nonagricultural production tended to involve workers who owned their means of production. Working as craftsmen and apprentices, they owned their own labor and sold the fruits of their labor. With industrialization, however, workers increasingly worked for wages—becoming commodities themselves as they sold their labor to the owners of the factories—and they no longer owned what they produced. This economic revolution transformed the workers' relationships to what they produced and to the emerging power of capital, which in turn led to a shift in their political outlook. Labor, Chartist, and socialist movements arose to voice their demands within political economies, and by mid-century, such movements were threatening the foundations of monarchist political authority in Europe. These pressures culminated, in 1848, in short-lived revolutions and governments' swing to the left, only to give way to a quick retrenchment as conservative, but increasingly democratic, governments reasserted dominance.

The economic draw of urban areas, the weakening of the rural social fabric by the movement to the cities, and agricultural distress at mid-century weakened the incentives of individuals to remain in rural regions. These factors, combined with increases in disposable income and the declining costs of transit, encouraged migration, as individuals who had previously been constrained by social ties and limited finances discovered that they had sufficient resources and incentives to purchase passage. Migration increased dramatically by the mid-1800s. Some left their homes to seek dreams and opportunity, many fled economic hardships such as the Irish famine, and others migrated to escape political and religious persecution. At first, much of this movement was from rural to urban areas within nations, then from one European nation to another, but soon, the leading destinations were in the New World of the Americas and Australia. Table 7.8 shows the growth and magnitude of international emigration by origin. The British Isles, for example, lost approximately 50–60 people per thousand of its population through emigration for almost every decade of the mid- to late 1800s. Political, economic, and religious opportunities existed abroad long before the great migratory movements of the nineteenth century, but people did not emigrate much in those earlier times. Economic and technological transformations of the 1800s are pivotal to accounting for why major migrations occurred in the latter half of that century and not earlier.

Communication

Trade, migration, and the flow of capital linked societies as part of the process called globalization, but the communication of ideas and the development of more and more sophisticated communication networks also connected societies, economies, and financial markets. The invention of the telegraph, for instance, increased the availability of timely information that might affect economic choices in such markets and sped capital market integration domestically and internationally. Time and information are key factors in the calculus of investment: delays in the transmission of information relevant to economic activity or in the ability to purchase or sell a financial investment increases risk, which can affect investors'

TABLE 7.8	Emigration Rates by Decade, 1851–1910 (per 1,000 mean population)					
Country	1851–1860	1861–1870	1871–1880	1881–1890	1891–1900	1901–1910
Austria-Hungary			2.9	10.6	16.1	47.6
Belgium				8.6	3.5	6.1
United Kingdom	58.0	51.8	50.4	70.2	43.8	65.3
Denmark			20.6	39.4	22.3	28.2
Finland				13.2	23.2	54.5
France	1.1	1.2	1.5	3.1	1.3	1.4
Germany			14.7	28.7	10.1	4.5
Ireland			66.1	141.7	88.5	69.8
Italy			10.5	33.6	50.2	107.7
Netherlands	5.0	5.9	4.6	12.3	5.0	5.1
Norway	24.2	57.6	47.3	95.2	44.9	83.3
Portugal		19.0	28.9	38.0	50.8	56.9
Spain				36.2	43.8	56.6
Sweden	4.6	30.5	23.5	70.1	41.2	42.0
Switzerland			13.0	32.0	14.1	13.9

Source: Kevin H. O'Rourke and Jeffrey G. Williamson, *Globalization and History* (London: MIT Press, 1999), 122.

willingness to invest or loan capital and the costs they charge for that capital. Any such increase in risk can constrain economic activity and reduce investment.

Prior to the invention and widespread application of the telegraph, investors located far from their investments faced long delays in their access to price information and other data that might be relevant to their investments. During the Napoleonic Wars, some financiers used carrier pigeons to obtain the latest news from the battlefield so they could base their financial decisions on the most current information—giving them an information advantage over investors who waited for news by horseback. Even more time-challenged were investors in New York or Boston, who had to anticipate the price of a financial instrument in the London markets weeks in the future. Two weeks was the average time required for a transatlantic voyage, and, since each transaction required one transit to bring the news from London and another to deliver the investor's instructions back to an agent there, these Americans were making their investment decisions in the only global capital market, London, on the basis of a minimum four-week lag in information at the time of the actual trade.

This time delay was longer for investors in Australia, and shorter for investors on the European continent. Regardless, foreign investors were basing their financial activities on old information, and even those investors situated in London were trading on old information if the loans and investments they were funding were located overseas. Imagine that you were a British investor with a financial stake in an American economic enterprise at mid-century, and you were at least two weeks behind in information as you contemplated increasing or decreasing your investment. What would happen if during that time the southern states seceded from the United States, or the battles of Bull Run, Antietam, or Gettysburg took place? Any such event could influence the expected value of your investment, but as an investor in London you would be acting with no knowledge of it.

The introduction of the telegraph meant that investors were suddenly able to trade with at most a day's delay in current information about the price of an investment and other news that could affect its prospects. The United Kingdom and continental Europe were linked by telegraph in 1851, with the laying of an underwater cable from Dover to Calais. In the United States, the major centers of New York, Philadelphia, Boston, Washington, D.C., Hartford, and Baltimore were quickly connected by telegraph, and a transcontinental connection linking the East and West coasts opened in 1861. A transatlantic cable was first put into operation in that same year, but more permanent service lagged until the laying of sturdier cables in 1865 and 1866.

The telegraph radically transformed the transmission of information, making people in one part of the world aware of activities in other parts of the global arena with increasing speed (as shown in table 7.9) and at rapidly increasing levels of traffic (as shown in table 7.10). The telegraph helped to integrate financial relations and activities across national boundaries, advancing London's position as the center of global finance, in particular. It encouraged more investment and created more opportunities for investors and borrowers alike. It also increased the transmission of financial shocks, as well as benefits, from one market to another. This technological change made the greatest difference in nations with large territories, such as the United States, as the telegraph shrank those distances to no more than a day in terms of trading time and information lag.

THE DARK SIDE OF GLOBALIZATION AND COLONIALISM

So far, our discussion may have suggested that the process of globalization in the nineteenth century produced a win-win situation for all those involved—as if economic growth, polit-

TABLE 7.9   **The Speed of Travel of Information to London, 1798–1914**

Event	Date	Place	First Times of London Report	Miles per Hour
Battle of the Nile	8/1/1798	Egypt	10/2/1798	1.4
Trafalgar	10/21/1805	Portugal	11/7/1805	2.7
Earthquake, Kutch, India	6/16/1819	India	11/16/1819	1.1
Treaty of Nanking	8/29/1842	China	11/21/1842	2.8
Charge of the Light Brigade	10/25/1854	Crimea	11/11/1854	4.0
Indian Mutiny, Delhi Massacre	5/12/1857	India	6/27/1857	3.8
Treaty of Tien-Sin	6/26/1858	Tianjin, China	9/16/1858	2.6
President Abraham Lincoln Assassinated	4/14/1865	Washington, DC, USA	4/27/1865	11.7
Assassination of Archduke Maximilian	6/19/1867	Queretaro, Mexico	7/1/1867	19.2
Assassination of Tzar Alexander II	3/13/1881	St Petersburg, Russia	3/14/1881	118.7
Nobi Earthquake	10/28/1891	Nobi, Japan	10/29/1891	245.8
Messina Strait Earthquake	12/28/1908	Italy	12/29/1908	398.0
Assassination of Franz Ferdinand	6/28/1914	Sarajevo	6/28/1914	118.6

Source: Adapted from Gregory Clark, *The Conquest of Nature: A Brief Economic History of the World, 10,000 BC–2000 AD,* chap. 12, "The Great Divergence: World Economic Growth since 1800," p. 20 (www.econ.ucdavis.edu/faculty/gclark/GlobalHistory/Global History-12.pdf); www.wcrl.org.usda.gov/cec/java/int-long.htm; www.getty.edu/research/conducting_research/vocabularies/tgn/index.html.

TABLE 7.10	**Telegraph Traffic, 1850–1920 (in millions of telegraphs)**							
	1850	1860	1870	1880	1890	1900	1910	1920
United Kingdom			8.60	29.90	66.50	89.60	86.70	88.00
France		0.70	5.70	17.00	27.00	40.00	50.00	51.00
Germany	0.04	0.73	8.66	13.50	22.20	39.70	48.20	79.60
Italy		0.10	2.00	5.90	8.30	9.40	15.20	20.70
United States			9.20	29.00	56.00	63.00	75.00	156.00
Canada							10.00	17.00
India			0.58	1.66	3.41	6.50	13.09	19.05
Japan			0.01	2.03	4.21	16.23	28.64	70.93
Argentina						3.90	8.80	10.00
Australia			0.86	3.68	9.25	8.38	12.49	18.41
New Zealand			0.24	1.31	1.96	3.90	8.36	14.00

Source: Data from B. R. Mitchell, *International Historical Statistics* (New York: Palgrave Macmillan, 2003).

ical liberalization, and improved social welfare accrued to all those who participated in globalization. This would be a mistaken conclusion, however, as might be seen in the case of those European agricultural producers faced with competition from more efficient New World producers of the same goods. Nineteenth-century globalization generated substantial improvements in the lot of many, but it also produced dislocation, discomfort, trauma, and outright disaster for some of those touched by the phenomenon. Inevitably, market exchange leads to some temporary dislocations as a result of economic change and transformation, but these effects should fade as people adjust to the discipline of the market mechanism. But in the nineteenth century, the processes accompanying globalization also created a more enduring and troubling legacy in the form of colonialism.

Creative Destruction and Dislocation

With expansion of market exchange and the integration of national markets into a larger global market, producers and labor were exposed to the forces of comparative advantage and market discipline. Some discovered that they were less competitive than producers and labor located in other political economies. Competitive markets push producers and workers to adjust in order to regain their competitiveness, learn new skills, or discover another form of production in which they do enjoy a comparative advantage. A competitive market forces such transformation upon producers and labor, generates waves of structural change, and creates economic advance in society. In 1942 Joseph Schumpeter, an economist at Harvard College, coined the term **creative destruction** for this process. Theoretically and in the long run, if markets work as anticipated, creative destruction produces more socially efficient outcomes and increases collective welfare.

Unfortunately, this transition can be painful in the real world. The adjustments brought on by creative destruction create transaction costs that are absent from the world of neoclassical economic theory—the costs of finding a new job, learning new skills, and adapting to a more competitive environment can range from negligible to overwhelming. Such costs can be quite high in the short term for many and in the long term for some, particularly for older people or those with dependents. It is not easy to shift to a new type of employment, which may require different skills or even relocation to a new setting. The compulsion to change practices, seek new jobs, learn new skills, and adapt to a newly competitive environment can be a harsh experience for individuals, for their families, and for their communities.

The rapid pace of globalization in the nineteenth century left some individuals, families, and communities damaged even as their larger societies benefited. Poorhouses, charities, community organizations, and nascent governmental social welfare programs provided threadbare safety nets that provided only subsistence-level support and most certainly afforded no dignity. The shift of populations to urban areas made such dislocations more visible than before, when the poor in rural areas could still farm their fields and raise animals for sustenance. Charles Dickens exposed the cruelty of this state of affairs in *A Christmas Carol,* when the character Scrooge replies to a request for a charitable donation for the indigent by asking indignantly, "Are there no workhouses, are there no poorhouses?"

Focusing on the improvement in *overall* social welfare and efficiency overlooks the costs that befall *individuals* and their immediate communities. But such localized and individual costs are inevitable products of a globalization process based upon competitive market exchange—a part of the process of creative destruction. These costs persist in twentieth-century globalization as well, but the manifestations of such dislocation are often masked by the modern social welfare state, which affords a better safety net. The expansion of market exchange and global capitalism presents societies and governments with the policy dilemma of capturing the collective gains of globalization while managing the individual costs. This tension plagues all political economies as they become more integrated into a global economy. Failure to manage the individual costs humanely can lead to attacks on the process of market exchange itself, which may damage collective outcomes.

Colonialism and Imperialism

A far more disquieting phenomenon further tainted nineteenth-century globalization. Colonialism, the expansion of imperial control, appeared as one of the more unfortunate outgrowths of globalization. Centuries earlier, European traders and explorers had connected societies that were highly differentiated by religion and social practices. Their travels and activities foreshadowed not only the development of modern trade relations, but also that of European colonial empires. Early in this period of expanding trade and economic exchange, the tentacles of European territorial ambition were limited to protecting the market centers and fueling stations that were critical to the flow of commodities across great distances. With the stark exception of the struggle for conquest of the Americas, early European commercial exploits built upon trade with indigenous populations. As the European merchants traded for local goods, they generally avoided explicit or heavy-handed interference in local forms of production and social organization. They generally recognized local governance structures, worked with those structures, and did not try to impose their own governing institutions. Only occasionally were troops or naval vessels dispatched to resolve disputes between the European traders and local elites. These ventures were basically trading regimes rather than political-military empires.

Napoleon's defeat in 1815 left the British as the only significant colonial empire for almost sixty years. By 1870, however, the colonial ambitions of many powerful political economies—at first the French, Spanish, Dutch, and Germans, who were later joined by the Americans and Japanese—had emerged as a significant aspect of international political and economic affairs. In the rush to build their colonial empires, these emerging world powers partitioned much of the earth, dramatically altering the geopolitical face of the globe. Maps 7.1a and 7.1b show the expansion and consolidation of this new and different form of colonial empire.

The new colonialism, **imperialism,** involved far more intrusive political and economic domination. Market forces no longer tempered the activities of producers and labor in the colonies. Under imperialism, the disciplining mechanism that altered production structures had little to do with global forces of supply and demand, which would reveal weaknesses and reward strengths based on comparative advantage and specialization. Instead, heavy-handed political dictates by an invasive colonial administration determined production strategies and the goods produced. Imperial powers employed the tools of hierarchy, not markets, to manage and change the production structures of the colonized, and they developed large bureaucracies devoted to managing their colonial possessions. And, thanks to the Industrial Revolution, the military capabilities of the colonial powers now dwarfed any local resistance by those being colonized. For the colonial powers, the military resources needed to maintain control were actually relatively small.

Native industries languished as colonial powers invested only in the production of commodities for export and in the infrastructure to assist those exports. Production shifted to extractive industries and cash crops such as rubber, cotton, jute, gold, diamonds, tin, cocoa, and coffee. Investments in roads, railways, ports, plantations, factories, and other infrastructure were designed to address the needs of the colonial power, not those of the colonized.

MAP 7.1a U.S., British, and Japanese Colonialism, c. 1900

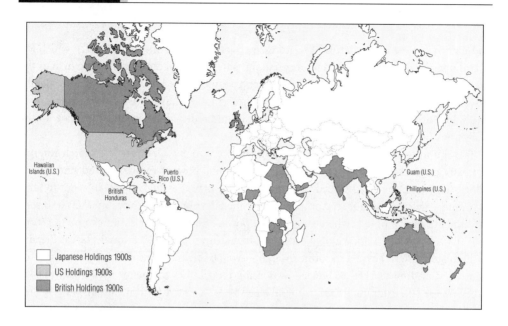

Hawaiian Islands (U.S.)
Puerto Rico (U.S.)
British Honduras
Guam (U.S.)
Philippines (U.S.)

☐ Japanese Holdings 1900s
▨ US Holdings 1900s
▨ British Holdings 1900s

MAP 7.1b European Imperialism in Africa, c. 1914

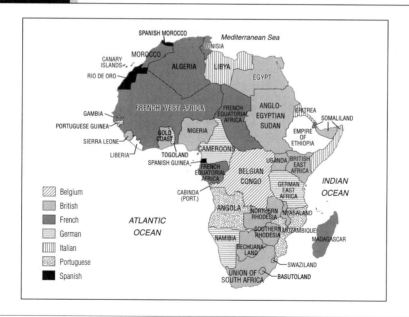

SPANISH MOROCCO   Mediterranean Sea
TUNISIA
MOROCCO
CANARY ISLANDS
ALGERIA   LIBYA
RIO DE ORO   EGYPT
FRENCH WEST AFRICA   FRENCH EQUATORIAL AFRICA   ANGLO-EGYPTIAN SUDAN   ERITREA
GAMBIA   SOMALILAND
PORTUGUESE GUINEA   EMPIRE OF ETHIOPIA
SIERRA LEONE   GOLD COAST   NIGERIA
LIBERIA   TOGOLAND   CAMEROONS
SPANISH GUINEA   FRENCH EQUATORIAL AFRICA   UGANDA   BRITISH EAST AFRICA
CABINDA (PORT.)   BELGIAN CONGO   GERMAN EAST AFRICA   INDIAN OCEAN
ANGOLA   NORTHERN RHODESIA   NYASALAND
ATLANTIC OCEAN   SOUTHERN RHODESIA   MOZAMBIQUE
NAMIBIA   MADAGASCAR
BECHUANALAND   SWAZILAND
UNION OF SOUTH AFRICA   BASUTOLAND

▨ Belgium
▨ British
▨ French
▨ German
▨ Italian
▨ Portuguese
▨ Spanish

Sources: Map 7.1a, Bruce Buena de Mesquita, *Principles of International Politics* (Washington, D.C.: CQ Press, 2003). Used by permission. Map 7.1b, from exploringafrica.matrix.msu.edu and information supplied by the author.

The shift in production structures toward cash crops reduced economic diversity, which left the colonies increasingly exposed to perverse shifts in the global economy. By the turn of the twentieth century, societies that had once been capable of feeding themselves were debilitated, at the mercy of the global economy and their colonial masters. Declines in prices elsewhere decreased the gains from trade in the colony and reduced the purchasing power of the indigenous population.

The rationales offered for colonial expansion were many. One was the search for raw materials and inexpensive inputs to sustain the colonial powers' industries and standard of living. Another rationale advanced the need to invest surplus capital abroad in order to limit inflationary increases at home. Another argued the advantages of captive markets and self-contained trading empires, where the colonial power's commodities could escape the competitive pressures of an open global economy. Ironically, under this rationale, Great Britain, the home to modern liberal economic thought—which celebrates the efficient collective outcome produced by market exchange—was using its colonies to shelter itself from market forces. Yet another argument for colonialism was formulated by Rudyard Kipling, in his poem, *White Man's Burden:*

> *Take up the White Man's burden—*
> *Send forth the best ye breed—*
> *Go bind your sons to exile*
> *To serve your captives' need;*
> *To wait in heavy harness,*
> *On fluttered folk and wild—*
> *Your new-caught, sullen peoples,*
> *Half-devil and half-child.*

Kipling thus romanticized the white man's burden as a crusade to bring modern civilization, European rationality, to those of non-European origin.

Whatever the rationale, the reality was that of political, military, and economic domination. Although the European and American governments advanced notions of political liberty and rational constitutionalism—and were themselves experiencing a golden era of political and economic enlightenment—those same nations denied those very concepts to the peoples they colonized. In the Spanish American War of 1898, U.S. troops marched off purportedly to liberate Cuba and the Philippines from Spanish colonial domination, only to replace Spanish colonial domination with U.S. colonial administration. The imperialism and colonialism that emerged in the latter 1800s besmirched both rational constitutional governance and the reputations of the European powers, Japan, and the United States. Extending their political and economic spheres by military means and imposing governance structures on indigenous populations, these colonial imperialists sullied the record of nineteenth century globalization, contravened the market forces propelling that globalization, and tainted the international relations of the twentieth century.

CONCLUSION

A combination of public and private inventions and policy shifts promoted the processes of globalization during the nineteenth century. The principle of comparative advantage, policy shifts that lowered man-made barriers to trade, the invention of MFN in bilateral trade treaties, and transportation revolutions promoted the expansion of cross-border exchange. Public and private innovations helped to manage the currency and default risks of international exchange. Banks intermediated cross-border default risk through the issuance of financial instruments, while governments stabilized expectations about currency values and exchange-rate risk through convergence on the gold standard and the commitment to convertibility. These measures promoted international trade by making the risks more predictable and acceptable to the individuals and firms engaged in such trade. The primacy of London's capital markets—dominated by those holding firmly to liberal economic beliefs— and the nurturing role of such British governmental institutions as the Treasury and the Bank of England helped to reduce procyclical pressures during economic downturns by supplying capital liquidity that could stimulate economic investment and activity. These mechanisms worked well enough that British financiers and public officials found themselves at the core of the expanding global economy. Some observers attribute the long peace of the nineteenth century—the relative absence of international conflict that colored the 1700s and 1900s—to the influence of British finance.

EXERCISES

1. What was the purpose of the Corn Laws and the Navigation Acts? Who benefited and who lost?

2. What makes a collective good? What collective goods did the United Kingdom provide in the late 1800s, and how did they affect globalization?

3. The collective goods that Britain provided in the late 1800s seem intricately connected to the maintenance of a cooperative environment conducive to the international exchange of goods, services, and capital. Are these factors independent or dependent variables in relation to globalization? Explain.

4. Explain why the United Kingdom was able to provide such collective goods but other governments could not, even if they so desired.

5. Name another collective good (not one of those already mentioned), and tell why is it a collective good.

6. Explain MFN and its significance to international affairs.

7. In the late 1800s, the United Kingdom and the United States adhered to the gold standard. If a creditor in Great Britain loaned money to someone in the United States, and then the United States were to switch to a bimetallic standard, what implications would this have for the British creditor?

8. Explain the principle of creative destruction and how it served to increase the collective welfare of society.

9. Explain the difference between absolute and comparative advantage as they relate to the agricultural producers of the late 1800s who were affected by advancing transportation technology.

10. Technological change played a key role in the globalization of the 1800s. Provide several examples of technological change that helped to increase economic exchange across borders, and explain how they worked to promote globalization.

11. Some of the collective goods provided by the United Kingdom during the 1800s were countercyclical public policies. What is a countercyclical policy and why is it important?

12. The expansion of suffrage in the late 1800s is said to be a two-edged sword in respect to free trade. Explain.

13. What made governments' commitments to the gold standard credible, rather than cheap talk?

FURTHER READING

Cohen, Benjamin. 1998. *The Geography of Money*. Ithaca, N.Y.: Cornell University Press.

Eichengreen, Barry. 1996. *Globalizing Capital: A History of the International Monetary System*. Princeton, N.J.: Princeton University Press.

Hobsbawm, Eric. 1996. *The Age of Capital: 1848–1875*. New York: Vintage Books.

———. 1989. *The Age of Empire: 1875–1914*. New York: Vintage Books.

Kennedy, Paul. 1989. *The Rise and Fall of Great Powers*. New York: Vintage Books.

O'Rourke, Kevin, and Jeffrey Williamson. 2000. *Globalization and History: The Evolution of a Nineteenth Century Atlantic Economy*. Boston: MIT Press.

8

The World between the Wars: A Breakdown in Globalization

By 1914, there was hardly a village or town anywhere on the globe whose prices were not influenced by distant foreign markets, whose infrastructure was not financed by foreign capital, whose engineering, manufacturing, and even business skills were not influenced by the absence of those who had emigrated or by the presence of strangers who had immigrated.... Not everyone was happy with the new global economy.... Rich landowners demanded protection from cheap farm products. Workers pointed to unfair competition from imports made with cheap foreign labor and claimed their jobs were being robbed by immigrants. Capitalists in declining import-competing industries argued that it was only fair that they get compensation for the losses they suffered on sunk investments. And domestic policymakers began to feel they were losing their ability to manage prices, interest rates, and markets; they felt increasingly vulnerable to financial panic, industrial crisis, and unfavorable price shocks generated in distant corners of the globe.

Kevin O'Rourke and Jeffrey Williamson, Globalization and History: The Evolution of a Nineteenth Century Atlantic Economy *(2000)*

WHY THE SHIFT?

The long peace and stability and the growing prosperity of the 1800s proved too good to last. These conditions were fragile, and the seeds of their breakdown were sown in the successes of globalization. Increasing trade and the Industrial Revolution produced significant gains in wealth, which funded the expansion of the state into new areas of social welfare, but these factors also underwrote an enlargement of states' military capabilities. Public education advanced the development of national identity through the teaching of citizenship and improved the quality of the labor available for economic activities and

This chapter draws upon E.H. Carr, *The Twenty Years' Crisis, 1919–1939* (1946); Barry Eichengreen, *Globalizing Capital: A History of the International Monetary System* (1996); John Keegan, *The Second World War* (1989); David Kennedy, *Freedom from Fear* (1999); Charles P. Kindleberger, *Manias, Panics, and Crashes: A History of Financial Crises* (1978); and Charles P. Kindleberger, *The World in Depression, 1929–1939* (1986).

to the military. Improvements in government bureaucracies and the increased use of the census led to better accounting of populations, which improved the ability of the state to conscript soldiers and also enhanced its ability to extract taxes to pay for the training and materials for a military.

World War I, the Great Depression, and World War II interrupted and then reversed the trend toward globalization. The depression, which began in 1929 and lasted until the beginning of World War II, imposed great hardships upon the peoples of the world. The gains of the 1800s made a U-turn during this period, as economies that had been growing by leaps and bounds slowed to a halt and then shrank. Statistics can describe the declines in gross domestic product and international trade, as well as the increases in unemployment and the food lines, but they cannot convey the full harshness of the suffering, of the loss of dignity and life that overwhelmed the populations of many states. Traditional family structures broke down as parents found themselves unable to feed their children: fathers deserted their families in humiliation and embarrassment, while mothers were known to have boiled shoelaces to add some nutrition and flavor to the water that served as a meal. Indeed, the effects of the depression proved as violent an assault on people and communities as the world wars that were its bookends. The worldwide suffering served as a breeding ground not only for noble attempts at political reform and experimentation, but also for extremist politics, as societies and communities sought solutions to the burdens of their people.

What precipitated the Great Depression? Why did the market system falter and fail so dramatically instead of redressing its inefficiencies through market corrections? Why did the mechanisms of supply and demand fail to regulate the system and restore equilibrium? Why did monetary and fiscal policies fail to halt the downward spiral of economic activity? Why did these shocks spill across national borders to create an international economic crisis of stunning magnitude and pain, producing violent political dislocations?

Various explanations have been offered to account for the breakdown in globalization that coincided with the two major world wars and the Great Depression. Some focus upon the years between the wars, highlighting the collapse of national economies and the failure of governments to manage divisive forces in their political economies. Others emphasize the role of the 1929 market crash, or the failure of U.S. monetary policies to address the building crisis, or shifts in trade policies and rising protectionism. This chapter focuses on several major factors contributing to the breakdown of the global and national economies during the interwar years.

First, the legacy of the 1800s began to pose difficult decisions for policymakers, as they sought to limit, manage, and allocate the adverse effects of globalization that were threatening some of their constituents. Second, World War I devastated national political economies, presenting them and the global economy with severe challenges, including catastrophic losses in labor; instability and pressures in the exchange-rate mechanism; debt and reparation demands; shortages of liquidity and vulnerability of credit mechanisms; growing obstructions to international trade; a growing willingness of governments to intervene in their economies to shift the costs of globalization abroad and so damage their neighbors; and an absence of international leadership. National policymakers faced key questions about who would carry the burden of adjusting to economic dislocations at the same time that their resources and capacity for action were sorely diminished by the ravages of war. These problems led to a breakdown in the provision of key collective goods that had helped to promote globalization in the 1800s, and this breakdown created conditions conducive to the rise of political extremism.

ALLOCATING COSTS OF ADJUSTMENT

This book began with several core assumptions. One was that policymakers act as if they are rational. So we must try to understand the twentieth-century reassertion of government obstructions to international trade and labor mobility and other policy choices as rational, goal-oriented choices regardless of their outcomes. Another assumption was that politicians want to survive, which involves being responsive to those they represent, whether that constituency entails a broad swath of society, as in democracies, or a smaller segment of society, as in less democratic regimes. Varying degrees of constituent satisfaction or dissatisfaction with politicians are registered in elections, coups, assassinations, and other forms of regime change or regime validation.

With the expansion of suffrage and democratic governance in the 1800s, politicians in the Atlantic economies faced increasingly difficult tests of survival in elections. Wider enfranchisement broadened the diversity of interests demanding representation by these democratically elected officials and provided pathways for those damaged by economic change to lobby their elected officials for barriers to globalization, if they could organize successfully for political action. Growing political participation increased the prospect of policymakers encountering a **time inconsistency problem,** in which their political survival could be affected by constituent groups whose short-term goals were at odds with the long-term welfare of society. Many of these short-term pressures demanded redistribution of the costs and benefits of economic progress through the policy and regulatory mechanisms of the state.

Societies and governments choose how to allocate the **costs of adjustment** that inevitably accompany the creative destruction caused by competitive markets, or any other significant process of change. Costs of adjustment are the challenges and dislocations that people and societies confront as they adapt to economic and social change. Such costs are unavoidable in dynamic economies—good or bad. Unwillingness to accept such costs represents a resistance to change and an unwillingness to take a chance to obtain new gains. Costs of adjustment may include the costs of unemployment, lost income, and the dilemma of making ends meet; the costs of searching for new employment and, possibly, moving to find new opportunities; the costs of retraining and education; the costs of lost opportunities in the future; and social costs such as divorce, alcoholism, family violence, or breakdown in community.

Governments and societies have three choices in the face of these costs of adjustment: (1) to let those personally experiencing the negative effects of economic change bear the full costs of adjustment; (2) to redistribute those costs more broadly to the domestic society at large via the safety net mechanisms of the social welfare state; or (3) to export those costs abroad via the linkages of globalization, placing them upon other nations' workers, producers, and voters. If those experiencing a dislocation are successful at organizing for political action and placing their concerns on the political agenda, they may succeed in avoiding the full costs of adjustment and shifting some of those costs to others in their society, abroad, or both. Despite the rapid advance of globalization during the late nineteenth century—and the many gains that accrued to societies from exchange of goods, services, capital, people, and information across national boundaries—groups and segments of society that were being affected negatively by global pressures began to criticize the processes of globalization and to pressure their governments to redistribute the costs of adjustment. Politicians, worried about their chances of political survival, could not afford to ignore these societal pressures if they were well-organized and politically influential.

THE LEGACY OF RAPID CHANGE IN THE 1800S

By the late 1800s, trouble was brewing in national economies that could spill over into international affairs. Price deflation in key economic sectors had created dislocations in national economies that led to pressures upon politicians to resist further trade liberalization and, in some cases, to reverse the trend toward lower tariffs and greater openness. Policymakers in several nations had begun to restrict immigration, which was one of the central processes driving globalization and factor price convergence across national political economies. New World economies such as the United States, Canada, Australia, and some Latin American states—where labor was a relatively scarce factor of production—had fueled their economic expansions with the labor of Irish, Italian, German, Norwegian, and Russian immigrants, along with those of other nationalities. Despite a need for more labor, however, California passed a series of initiatives in the 1880s designed to limit the immigration of Asians, and other governments also began to impose more restrictive barriers to entry for immigrants.

Governments had been proactive in the mid-1800s in creating conditions favorable to globalization and economic progress, but increasingly they implemented restrictive trade and immigration policies that threatened to interrupt the gains from globalization and undermine their societies' welfare. These policy changes limited potential gains from specialization of production and mobile labor markets. Policy interventions to slow and restrict globalization constrained the consumption possibilities for societies overall, but they improved the lot of a few at the expense of many. Why would politicians adopt policies that interrupted processes so beneficial to their societies?

Agriculture and Costs of Adjustment

The recessions of the late 1800s affected every economic sector, but especially agriculture and the producers and labor in the primary product sector, which included agriculture, minerals, metals, and other primary commodities. They were hard-hit by price deflation, which led to declines in farm incomes. (Table 7.3, in the previous chapter, shows the deflation in prices of agricultural commodities.) At the crux of the farmers' dilemma were too much production and the tight money supply policies associated with the gold standard: more and more commodities were being produced with only marginal increases in the labor force due to natural processes (births and increased longevity) and only marginal increases in the money supply due to its ties to gold. The limit on money supply interacted with the increase in supply of goods and services to generate downward pressures on price. This linkage returns us to Hume's recognition of the relationship between the size of money supply and prices—if downward pressures are severe enough, price deflation results.

Farm income would increase if the supply of agricultural commodities were to decline. In a laissez-faire global political economy, this contingency would require that farmers limit their production, either voluntarily or through some form of coordination, or that a sufficient number of agricultural producers go out of business as a part of the process of creative destruction. But voluntary constraints upon production require an amazing amount of coordination across vast geographic space and, in many cases, across national boundaries. Such coordination is unlikely without some coercive mechanism, because individual farmers would have incentives to defect on such voluntary constraints, particularly if other farmers did limit their production. Defecting would increase their incomes at the expense of others—in other words, they would be free riders.

Consequently, if a farmer believed that other farmers were going to defect—free-ride—by overproducing, it would be foolish for her not to overproduce as well. Even though such actions would contribute to an oversupply of farm commodities and aggravate price deflation, why should she let other farmers reap all the incremental gains of overproducing? This situation offers another example of a social trap, in which individual rationality undermines collective welfare. The individual incentives in this dynamic led to more and more overproduction as each farmer planted more cropland in an attempt to make ends meet, but this individual rationale just added fuel to the problem of price deflation and oversupply in agriculture. Moreover, the process of creative destruction, the weeding out of inefficient farm producers through business failures, proved uncertain, for farmers could live off the land even as their economic enterprises faltered. The farmers were resistant to weeding out! This peculiarity made agricultural producers slower to adapt to the discipline of global capitalism—a legacy that persists today.

Agricultural producers were threatened with bearing the full costs of adjustment to price deflation, which could lead to a drastic increase in farm failures and bankruptcies. Unable to resolve their problems through concerted, voluntary coordination of production targets, producers and laborers in agriculture and other sectors turned to government to redistribute their costs of adjustment. Farmers were particularly well-placed to appeal to government for policies to address their dilemma because in many societies they had substantial ties to political representatives due to history and geography. Historically, landowning was a prerequisite for political enfranchisement, so rural areas and farmers had been overrepresented in legislatures before the expansion of suffrage, and this legacy persisted. Geographically, farmers were distributed across broad areas and, consequently, could often appeal to a large number of elected representatives.

Two alternative mechanisms were available to address this problem of dwindling farm income: (1) an increase in the money supply, which could reverse price deflation, or (2) limiting the supply of a commodity and increasing its price through some government intervention. Global convergence on the gold standard limited the possibilities of dramatically increasing the money supply. Even if an alternative to the gold standard were adopted at a national level, the ability of capital to migrate would undermine this alternative unless the alternative standard were to be adopted across many political economies. Unilateral adoption of an alternative monetary system would lead to a drain on national gold reserves, as people would convert their currency holdings to gold. Because increasing the money supply was therefore not a viable option, agricultural producers' only viable strategy was to limit supply, but the difficulties of exercising voluntary constraints across the entire community remained formidable.

Retrenchment and Tariffs

Unable to coordinate an effort of self-restraint, agricultural and other commodity producers sought to limit the supply of commodities from abroad. These communities succeeded in overcoming the barriers to political action by mobilizing to exercise their political voice in favor of shifting the costs of adjustment to others. They lobbied government to halt the decline of trade barriers, and in many states they succeeded not only in halting the decline but even in reinstating higher barriers to entry. As table 7.1 in the previous chapter shows, tariff rates initially declined in the mid-1800s but started to climb again in many nations by the late 1800s. The United Kingdom maintained its open border policy, providing the collective good of market access under duress, but other major economies and markets raised tariffs and other barriers to entry.

While not affecting supply, a tariff or import tax on a foreign product artificially increases the price for that supply. Because a tariff on foreign commodities increased their prices relative to their domestic counterparts, domestic producers hoped that consumers faced with a change in the price of foreign commodities would alter their consumption choices, given their wallet or **budgetary constraints.** When such barriers did change domestic consumption decisions and shift consumption from foreign-produced products to domestic-produced products, the tariffs forced the costs of adjustment onto the backs of foreign producers and labor, whose products lost market share, and upon the broader domestic society, where prices for those commodities (domestic and foreign) increased.

This process of retrenchment did not necessarily mean an absolute rejection of globalization, but it did moderate the processes and mechanisms promoting globalization. Such actions were harbingers of the embedded tensions between globalization and distinct national identities. The processes of globalization operated within a social context of separate nation-states, where global economic processes interacted with national political and social processes, and those disadvantaged by global processes could appeal to national mechanisms for redress. These inevitable tensions contributed to the dilemmas facing governments during the years leading up to World War I.

THE UNSETTLING LEGACY OF WORLD WAR I IN THE INTERWAR YEARS

Political scientists and historians continue to debate about why World War I occurred. Some base their explanations upon the technological imperatives of particular military force structures and the dynamics of military mobilizations. Others suggest that the cognitive frameworks of the different national leaders contributed to misperception, miscommunication, and missed opportunities for peaceful settlement and diffusion of the looming military crisis in 1914. Others argue that the dynamics of domestic political economies contributed to the onset of the conflict. Some claim that the development of national identity and expansion of the notion of citizenship enhanced the likelihood of conflict by promoting jingoism, which only ensured a greater level of violence than in previous wars. Others point to the structure of balance-of-power politics and the inflexibility of alliance structures in dealing with power shifts in international relations. Yet others highlight the importance of critical events such as the assassination of Archduke Franz Ferdinand and his wife in Sarajevo in June 1914.

Regardless of its definitive cause or causes, many agree that World War I was a war few really wanted. Sadly, the world stumbled into a conflict of tragic proportions. Here, however, we are less interested in the war's causes than in its consequences for the global political economy. Called "the war to end all wars," World War I produced a ghastly amount of death and destruction in a four-year period. It also left a troubling legacy of great dislocation and uncertainty in the global political economy—traumas that inhibited postwar recovery, unsettled the global political economy, contributed to the slide into the Great Depression, fanned the fires of political extremism, and fueled animosities leading to the eventual resumption of global hostilities in World War II. Indeed, the two world wars were less separate conflicts than a single war with an intermission.

World War I interrupted globalization, and after it ended, the nations of the Atlantic economy sought to rebuild their political economies. The aftermath of any war challenges policymakers as they try to regain the economic and political stability that is critical to advancing prosperity and welfare during peacetime. After this war, they faced particularly difficult obstacles as they sought to recapture the economic and political hopes of the late 1800s, for the legacies of the war hindered economic recovery and left a residue of political animosity within and between nations. In this environment, a combination of poor policy choices by some leaders and the sheer inability of some nations' policymakers to implement good policies even when they tried handicapped the rebuilding of national political economies. Let's consider several important legacies of World War I that presented major obstacles to the restoration of stable political-economic life.

Population Loss

The war to end all wars revolutionized the technology of warfare, producing a quantum leap in the violence of war. World War I debilitated the material, human, and social resources of the European combatants, leaving only the United States relatively unscathed, due largely to its late entry into the war and its geographic separation from the main fields of battle. As the major combatants turned away from war and took up the task of peacetime rebuilding, they encountered sluggish economies and barriers to reconstruction. Economies that had been supplying the materials of war now had to be retooled to produce goods for consumer consumption. Such retooling required the key inputs of labor and capital for economic activity, but both of these factors were lacking in postwar Europe due to the high material and human costs of the conflict.

Growing economies need labor to work the factories, harvest the soil, teach in schools, and provide productive energy and creativity, but the war's toll of death and disability severely constrained the supply of labor. Approximately 10 percent of the population (20 million men) of the European combatant states joined the fight in the first months of the conflict; far more soon followed as grist for their national war machines. The proud soldiers who marched off to war in 1914 bore little resemblance to the armies at the turn of the previous century, for these modern warriors had been strengthened by significant gains in economic welfare, improvements in health care and diet, and the expansion of education. These men, their fathers, and their grandfathers had provided the labor, energy, and creativity that had transformed the economies of Europe in the mid- to late 1800s. This cream of European progress, however, was soon devastated by four years of brutal trench warfare. Graveyards along the Western Front, "cities of the dead," serve as grim reminders of the horrors of World War I, in which entire generations were killed, crippled, or traumatized. Table 8.1 details the numbers of men who went to war and of those who were killed or wounded, and the proportion of their national militaries that were casualties. Even those who stayed home did not escape the suffering: spouses, parents, and siblings were victimized as well as they awaited

TABLE 8.1	World War I Mobilization and Casualty Rates				
Country	Mobilized	Killed	Wounded	Missing/ POW	Casualties (as % of mobilized)
Germany	11,000,000	1,773,700	4,216,058	1,152,800	65
Russia	12,000,000	1,700,000	4,950,000	2,500,000	76
France	8,410,000	1,375,800	4,266,000	537,000	73
Austria-Hungary	7,800,000	1,200,000	3,620,000	2,200,000	90
United Kingdom	8,904,467	908,371	2,090,012	191,652	36
Italy	5,615,000	650,000	947,000	600,000	39
Romania	750,000	335,706	120,000	80,000	71
Turkey	2,850,000	325,000	400,000	250,000	34
United States	4,355,000	126,000	234,300	4,526	8
Bulgaria	1,200,000	87,500	152,390	27,029	22
Serbia	707,343	45,000	133,148	152,958	47
Belgium	267,000	13,716	44,686	34,659	35
Portugal	100,000	7,222	13,751	12,318	33
Greece	230,000	5,000	21,000	1,000	12
Montenegro	50,000	3,000	10,000	7,000	40
Japan	800,000	300	907	3	0.1
Totals	65,038,810	8,556,315	21,219,252	7,750,945	58

Source: Susan Everett, *The Two World Wars,* vol. I, *World War I* (Lincoln, Neb.: Bison Books, 1980).

word of their loved ones. Such waiting imposes mental and physical traumas that wear on the human spirit and thereafter reduce the ability of individuals to contribute productively to societal outcomes.

Clearly the breadth and depth of the losses incurred in World War I denied the major combatant nations the fruit of their most economically valuable citizenry, as several generations of men who were in the prime years of productivity and creativity were snuffed out in the trenches of Europe. Evaluating the human costs of war goes far beyond considering the numbers of killed and wounded, for costs are, by definition, the paths not taken when a course of action is chosen. The costs of World War I were what Europe might have become politically, economically, and socially if the war had not occurred. Of course, this counterfactual is impossible to assess accurately. We can only speculate, but we do know that ideas and creativity died with those casualties. Who can say what processes and inventions were not created, what talents were not brought to bear on public and private dilemmas, what leaders never entered politics or industry, or what students never went to universities to become teachers and investigators? We cannot predict what those people would have created or contributed; but we can be fairly sure that their contributions would have made for a different world.

The Exchange-Rate Mechanism: Currency Instability and Convertibility

Chapter 7 discussed the importance of an effective exchange-rate mechanism as a collective good to overcome obstacles to international exchange. Instabilities in exchange rates create currency risk and uncertainty, which affects the expected value of exchange. In the prewar years, a fixed exchange-rate system that was based upon gold produced stability, which limited the currency risk that could hinder international exchange. The Bank of England and London's private capital markets helped to manage the system and maintain stability in the price of currencies, and this stability was abetted by the British commitment to convertibility. World War I, however, introduced several major problems for stability in the exchange-rate mechanism.

The financial demands of war led governments to disassociate their currency values from the prewar gold standard and created imbalances in the value of currencies in relation to each other. During the war, governments suspended both convertibility and their commitment to maintain the prewar par value of their currencies vis-à-vis gold. Currencies were allowed to float, which meant that market forces determined their prices. Imbalances in this floating-currency mechanism could hurt those in the tradable sector in one country and help those in the tradable sector in another country if one state's currency became overvalued relative to the other's. Imbalances in exchange rates threatened to hinder the rebuilding of trade relations, as governments faced pressure from their domestic constituencies to address the imbalances—to manipulate the value of a state's currency to the advantage of its domestic producers. In this environment, policymakers sought to restabilize currency values, and many—the British in particular—argued for a return to the par value of currencies that had existed before the war. As nations tried to return to the gold standard by the mid-1920s, the continuing problem of imbalances in exchange rates were compounded by price deflation in commodity sectors.

Remember that prices in a fixed-exchange-rate system should eventually adjust through changes in the money supply, which result from capital flows to pay for trade. But a rigid system with fundamental imbalances in exchange rates puts pressure on governments to deal more rapidly with such problems by changing the value of the currency or resorting to other policies that can affect trade. If governments respond to such pressures by devaluing their currencies in order to make their goods more competitive in the global arena, they can threaten the stability of currency prices, as well as the stability of the exchange-rate mechanism itself.

The British commitment to the collective good of convertibility, which had helped to generate confidence in the prewar gold standard, was also in question. A credible commitment to convertibility requires that a government maintain sufficient gold reserves to exchange for its currency upon demand. If other governments and people believe that a commitment to convertibility is credible—that a government does have sufficient reserves to meet demands to convert and will meet those demands—then demands to convert should be manageable and not threatening to monetary stability. But several factors challenging the relationship between gold reserves and currencies in the postwar period threatened the credibility of any commitment to convertibility and the exchange-rate mechanism.

Even before the war, the costs of mining and the limited discovery of new gold veins had constrained growth in gold reserves. This slow growth limited expansion of the money supply even as production of many commodities increased, which led to deflationary pressures in some commodities, particularly agricultural products. Economic sectors that were feeling the strains of deflation pressured their governments to increase the money supply to inflate prices—even if this increase would lead to a shift in the ratio of gold reserves to currency. As some governments acquiesced, the amount of currency in circulation grew faster than the world's supply of gold. The resulting discontinuity between additions to official gold reserves and growth in the money supply threatened the credibility of a commitment to convertibility.

Regardless of the limitations of world gold production, World War I placed such demands upon governments that convertibility would have been very difficult to maintain as official policy. The need to finance the war—which represented a huge leap in the size and degree of conflict, and hence in its costs—taxed the capital resources of the European combatants. The war effort demanded a tremendous amount of very expensive materials, for which the United Kingdom and her allies turned to the United States. Initially, as they paid for such materials with their gold reserves, these governments limited convertibility and imposed controls on gold exports so that they could afford to pay for these war materials. In times of such dire need, governments were no longer willing to exchange their gold for currency.

Even with such drastic changes in policy, the Allied governments quickly spent their reserves paying for war materials. And, although they taxed their publics heavily to raise funds to pay these expenses, increasing tax revenues could not make up the budget shortfalls. As in past wars, the governments had to borrow to pay for their continued war efforts. The United States extended credit in the form of loans that conferred obligations to tax the supply of capital that would be available in the future. By the end of the conflict, the United Kingdom, France, and other war-torn economies faced massive debts (see table 8.2).

TABLE 8.2	War Debts of Major Combatants
Country	**Debt Total (in $ millions)**
United Kingdom	4,277
France	3,405
Italy	1,648
Belgium	379
Russia	192
Poland	159
Czechoslovakia	92
Yugoslavia	52
Romania	38
Greece	27
Austria	24
Estonia	14
Armenia	12
Finland	8
Latvia	5

Source: Thomas A. Bailey, *Diplomatic History of the American People,* 10th edition (Englewood Cliffs, N.J.: Prentice Hall, 1980).

Governments were able to incur debt to pay for their purchases of war materials abroad, but they still needed to find a means to meet their domestic economic obligations. They began to issue money that was not backed by gold, further divorcing money supply from gold reserves. This money, called *fiat money,* was used for domestic purposes. The creation of fiat money created inflationary pressures. Differences in the rate of fiat money creation across countries led to differences in their inflation rates, and because these differences affected domestic prices, they prompted significant variations in exchange rates. Inflation and exchange-rate instabilities persisted in the aftermath of the war. In this context, changes in the supply of currency, fiat money, and limited gold reserves created uncertainties over the price of currencies.

With the end of the war, why not return immediately to the stability of the prewar gold standard and convertibility? Because they were already facing serious gold reserve shortages, an immediate return to the gold standard would have led to a further gold exodus from **weak currency countries**— those states with the greatest differences between their gold reserves and their expanded supplies of currency. Much smaller discrepancies existed between money supply and gold reserves in **strong currency countries.** A return to convertibility would have prompted an exchange of weak currencies for gold as people worried about the prospects of such currencies holding their value or declining in value through further inflation. Once weak currencies were exchanged for gold, people would either purchase a strong currency that was more likely to maintain its value or hold their assets in gold. This exchange would have led to an exodus of gold from weak currency states to strong currency states, exacerbating the economic problems of those states most damaged by the war. Only the United States, a strong currency country, maintained the convertibility of its currency in this environment. Given the vast amount of U.S. gold reserves and the strength of its currency, there was little likelihood of a gold exodus from the United States.

Despite the barriers to returning to the gold standard and convertibility immediately following the war, governments hoped to do so sometime in the future. By the mid-1920s, government attempts at stabilization and return to the gold standard appeared near success. Many governments began to restore stability to their exchange rates by constraining inflation. But this effort involved limiting the money supply, which ran the risk of reviving deflationary pressures in national economies, so most governments sought to stabilize and fix their exchange rates at current levels rather than at prewar levels.

The United Kingdom, in its quest to support stability in the exchange-rate system and to recover its prestige and central role in managing the global economy, sought to return to the prewar gold standard and the prewar value of the pound (its par value). Restoring the pound to its prewar par value meant that the British needed to increase its value in relation to other currencies, such as the French franc, even though it was already overvalued. By the mid-1920s, the United Kingdom had returned to the prewar par value of its currency, but this exchange-rate imbalance proved perverse for British producers and labor. British commodities that had already been relatively expensive in global markets became more so, and the British balance of trade suffered in relation to nations with relatively undervalued currencies. This situation led to capital outflows from the United Kingdom and other countries with fixed, overvalued currencies.

The war and war debts severely wounded the United Kingdom's ability to continue playing the dominant role it had played in the promotion of globalization before World War I. It could no longer credibly support convertibility or manage problems in the exchange-rate system. The credibility of any nation to perform such functions relies upon having access to sufficient financial resources, or at least the belief by others in the system that it has sufficient financial resources. Such belief can be enough to prevent a rush to convert currencies into gold and thus to motivate private economic activity and investment.

Unfortunately for the British, the financial resources that had been so integral to their success in promoting the expansion of the global economy in the late 1800s were now in New York. The United Kingdom's gold reserves had declined tremendously. If people now believed that the British Treasury and the Bank of England could not access sufficient gold reserves to be able to exchange currencies for gold upon demand, adherence to the prewar gold standard and the policy of convertibility would run the risk of increasing the incentives for others to exchange their currencies for British gold before there was no gold left in the British Treasury. No one wanted to be at the end of the line if the British ran out of gold, so the individual incentives of firms and governments to get there before no gold was left could produce a run on the British Treasury. Without sufficient official gold reserves, the pound was no longer perceived as "good as gold." The British were caught in a dilemma.

Even if they could marshal enough official gold reserves and capital resources at home through London's financial markets, trying to support the prewar price of the pound in gold imposed large costs on the British people in terms of unemployment, tighter money at home, and slower domestic recovery. Maintaining the prewar value of the pound in gold would damage British producers and workers if the value of other currencies declined in relation to gold or the pound. The wartime inflation had led to changes in the relative prices of national currencies—almost all fell in value, but some became undervalued and others overvalued in relation to each other. The price of commodities from nations with overvalued currencies became less competitive, while the price of commodities from nations with undervalued currencies became more competitive.

The return to the gold standard and convertibility in the mid-1920s, even at markedly devalued exchange rates for many states, failed to restore the stability and prosperity of the prewar years in the global political economy. Severe constraints on money supplies resulted from limited gold supplies in weak currency states, increasing balance-of-payment deficits in such states as a consequence of gold outflows due to the return to convertibility and worsening imbalances in trade. Currency crises related to gold and capital outflows from the weak currency states occurred with greater and greater frequency.

Many central banks raised interest rates to counteract gold and capital flight, attract capital inflows, and maintain confidence in their currencies. The pressure of gold outflows on money supply and higher interest rates—even though designed to work at counterpurposes—fed deflationary pressures on prices. There was less money chasing the same amount of commodities and services. Higher interest rates failed to restore confidence, strengthen currencies, and attract sufficient capital inflows to counteract capital flight. Meanwhile, the higher interest rates imposed by a state's central bank worked to slow domestic economic activity and increase unemployment. These results led to greater pressures for currency devaluation. Policymakers were caught in a horrible bind, in which strategies to fix one problem exacerbated another problem, and all the problems were serious.

To counteract deflationary pressures arising from the linkage between gold reserves and money supply, many governments again began to limit convertibility in order to prevent further decline in their gold reserves. Many also adopted currency-exchange controls to try to maintain and increase domestic money supply and protect against deflationary pressures. When these policies failed, many states moved to further sever the connections between gold and currency values by letting their currencies float. By the 1930s, many nations formally moved away from the gold standard to a **floating-exchange-rate** mechanism. The return to the Holy Grail of the gold standard had lasted only about five years, 1926–1931.

Beggar-Thy-Neighbor and Currency Devaluation

Economic distress, price deflation, and imbalances in the exchange-rate mechanism led to increased pressure upon national policymakers to strategically devalue their currencies in order to assist their domestic producers and labor. Currency devaluation might address a dislocation within a national political economy, but a policy of currency devaluation shifts the costs of the economic dislocation overseas and imposes economic burdens on other nations' producers and labor. Policies that shift the costs of adjustment from one political economy to another are called **beggar-thy-neighbor policies.** These efforts are designed to promote the welfare of one nation's producers and labor at the expense and relative impoverishment of other nations' producers and labor.

Absent international cooperation and agreement upon exchange-rate adjustment, such unilateral currency devaluations can lead to a round of retaliatory and potentially destabilizing competitive devaluations. Why should any nation's producers and labor willingly and quietly accept burdens imposed by unilateral changes in another nation's policies? Why should British producers and workers, for example, be expected to accept a greater likelihood of unemployment and family economic hardship so that U.S. producers and workers can benefit? Unilateral changes in policies that impose burdens abroad run the risk of encouraging **tit-for-tat policy reactions,** or retaliation in kind.

Imbalances in the exchange-rate mechanism and unilateral attempts to manipulate exchange rates in the postwar era generated a recipe for severely stressing the global political economy: an absence of multilateral cooperation to coordinate national policies, the United Kingdom's inability to manage pressures on the exchange-rate mechanism as it had done before the war, and the inexperience and unwillingness of the United States to play a constructive leadership role. Beggar-thy-neighbor policy pressures spilled over into other policy arenas, particularly trade policy and other monetary policies. Governments confronted by growing distress in their national political economies increasingly turned to macroeconomic and trade policies that shifted costs of adjustment abroad and invited retaliation. The problems in the exchange-rate mechanism would convince later policymakers that monetary disorder, currency devaluations, and floating exchange rates contributed to the economic disaster of the Great Depression and the political-military catastrophe of World War II. Right or wrong, these lessons would color the design of the post–World War II system.

Breakdown in the Liquidity and Lender-of-Last-Resort Collective Goods

The shortage of capital resources in London created another significant barrier to economic revitalization during the interwar years. Modern economies need mobile capital—liquidity—for growth. A shortage of labor can be overcome through the adoption of capital-intensive strategies such as substituting capital for labor and increasing the productivity of relatively scarce labor. In fact, increasing productivity through the use of technology and the application of capital has been the primary reason for the development of modern economies. With the devastation imposed upon Europe's human resources by the war, the need for capital became even more important for reconstruction. Capital was necessary to invest in labor, to rebuild and retool industrial plants, to educate, and to enable consumers to spend. Without sufficient capital, businesses and individuals quickly confronted limitations on their ability to rebuild and to take chances on the future.

Prior to the war, London's financial markets sat at the heart of a rapidly expanding global economy, providing liquidity for public and private enterprise, domestically and internationally. These markets became amazingly efficient at transferring capital from savers to borrowers. Investors found that they could move in and out of investment positions more quickly in British markets than in other financial markets, thus limiting their risk exposure. This discovery created an increasing returns dynamic—more and more borrowers sought out British merchant banks to help raise funds for their endeavors as the size, depth, and liquidity of these markets increased. The position of London's capital markets and the connections between British financiers and the Bank of England placed the British at the center of the global economy and endowed them with capabilities for crisis management during economic downturns. Their capital resources were critical not only for providing procyclical stimulus, but also for injecting countercyclical stimulus during periods of distress. The former was important to continuing a cycle of economic expansion, while the latter helped to constrain economic downturns that might otherwise provoke politicians to respond to short-term domestic political pressures with policies that could be counterproductive to the global economy.

Unfortunately, the war diminished the capital resources available in London and other European capital markets. Some investors in Europe still enjoyed a capital surplus despite the flows of capital to the United States, but those investors faced uncertain macroeconomic conditions in Europe, such as the postwar inflation, then deflation, and instabilities in the exchange-rate mechanism. These conditions tended to make investors risk-averse with their capital and restricted their investments in European reconstruction. Governments could have provided more economic stimulus by increasing the money supply, lowering central bank interest rates, or purchasing government securities. But in the immediate postwar period, many governments were also trying to contain inflation and restore stability to the price of their currencies; increasing the money supply would have counteracted these efforts. Thus the reduction in capital due to the war and the need to fight inflation and restore stability limited the availability of capital resources passing through the London markets. New York's capital markets faced no such constraints on capital availability, but New York financiers were relative newcomers to the world of global finance. Their inexperience limited their ability to recognize and play the role British financiers and markets had played during the expansion of economic globalization of the later 1800s.

The Effect of War Debts and Reparations on Liquidity

The Treaty of Versailles in 1919 formally ended World War I. The European allies of the United States emerged victorious but also suffused with great hostility toward the losers and burdened with staggering debt obligations to the United States. Their animosity and frustration was reflected in the terms of the treaty, which imposed stringent conditions upon Germany, including limitations on German military forces, as well as vast reparations to be paid by Germany. Reparations—payments by the losers to cover the winners' costs from a conflict—were not new in the history of warfare. The United Kingdom had exacted payments from France following the defeat of Napoleon, and France had paid reparations to Bismarck's Germany following the Franco-Prussian War of 1871. Northern carpetbaggers extracted resources from the South during the Reconstruction period following the U.S. Civil War. But World War I had far outstripped previous conflicts in size and costs, and so the pressures of war debt facing the European allies, the need for capital to rebuild, and lingering bitterness over the conflict materialized in unusually severe reparation expectations. The French, whose territory was left scarred by trench warfare, were particularly resolute in their demands for reparation. Both the Allies' debt to the United States and Germany's reparations debt to the Allies added significantly to the liquidity dilemma in world markets.

Officially, the Treaty of Versailles established a principle of reparation, which led to a commission that was to determine amounts. In the spring of 1921, the commission determined that Germany owed 132 billion gold marks, or US$33 billion, in reparations to the Allies. Germany faced approximately fifty years of reparations payments, during which time a significant portion of any gains from German economic activity would have to go to the French and British instead of being channeled into improvements in the German standard of living or per capita income. But Paris and London each also owed billions of dollars to Washington, and the United States expected repayment. Germany immediately encountered difficulties in making reparations payments. Unlike France, German territory was unscathed by the horrors of trench warfare, but the German population and economy were as devastated as those of the Allies by the years of conflict. The reparations demanded were well beyond the ability of even an economically healthy Germany—and postwar Germany was far from economically healthy.

In his treatise, *The Economic Consequences of the Peace,* John Maynard Keynes warned that the terms of the peace were dangerous for Europe and for the global economy. An economist and consultant to the British and German governments, Keynes argued for suspension of the reparations and forgiveness of the Allied war debts, which, he worried, would constrain liquidity and create formidable obstacles to global growth and recovery. Fearing that the treaty undermined German economic prospects and insulted German national pride, Keynes anticipated that Germans would turn increasingly bitter toward the imposed reparations and that this bitterness would lead to a renewal of German nationalism based upon feelings of persecution and unfairness. Such resentments, he warned, could eventually lead to a resumption of hostilities.

Keynes's entreaties fell on deaf ears. The victors, owing huge war debts to the United States and facing a liquidity crunch, put tremendous pressure on Germany to keep up with its reparations payments. When the Germans threatened to default on the reparations, the British were willing to revise the payment schedule—even to forgo reparations—but they tied their position to the war debts they owed to the United States. If the United States were to forgive

Allied war debts, the British would be willing to forgo reparations. Such an accommodation might have provided breathing room to reduce tensions between the former combatants, liquidity to prime the growth pump in Europe, and room for more moderate political forces to prevail over extreme nationalist parties. Unfortunately, U.S. policymakers rejected their allies' appeal to rescind their war debts. President Coolidge responded at different times, "They hired the money, didn't they?" and "They borrowed the money, yes or no?"

Even if the United States had agreed to forgive the Allied war debts, the French might have refused to reconsider reparations, which they considered their due. As the Germans fell behind in their payments, in 1923 French troops occupied the Ruhr region, a coal and steel area that was key to German economic recovery. Seizure of the region exacerbated Germany's difficulties in rebuilding, injected greater stress and rancor to Franco-German relations, and further scarred the German national psyche. German workers in the Ruhr factories and mines responded to the French occupation with passive resistance, sabotage, and even violence, while Adolf Hitler used the occupation to mobilize support for his emerging national socialist (Nazi) movement. Hitler's movement played on national pride, claiming that Germany had been defeated in World War I by forces within Germany and not by the military strength of its adversaries. The German government's acquiescence to the French occupation therefore provided fodder for those who rationalized Germany's defeat in the war by blaming domestic factors.

U.S. loans to Germany might have relieved some of the pressures of German reparations payments, but U.S. policymakers and financiers were reluctant to loan funds without revision of the reparations schedule, and the Allies were unwilling to alter their reparations expectations without war debt forgiveness—thus constructing a vicious social trap with the United States as the key obstruction to escaping the trap. Reparations and war debts affected both the prospect of obtaining commercial loans for economic expansion and the costs of such loans. Lenders in capital markets considered the risk of default in their calculations about whether or not to make a loan, and at what price—deriving information about the risks to their capital from delays in making payments or threatened defaults. Governments that delayed or reneged on their payments could thus affect the ability of enterprises in their societies to obtain commercial loans. Policy preferences and the linkages between war debts, reparations, and new loans left little room for constructive compromise. Table 8.3 summarizes the four major nations' policy preferences on the issues of debt and reparations.

The Absence of Hegemonic Leadership

During the 1800s, the British provided leadership and collective goods to overcome barriers to cooperation in the global arena and promote the expansion of a liberal global economy. They acted as a **hegemon**—a leader helping to manage seemingly incompatible policy preferences across governments, establishing the rules of the game, and assuming a disproportionate share of the costs of maintaining those rules. Unlike the United Kingdom before World War I, no system leader emerged in the postwar period capable of resolving the dilem-

TABLE 8.3	Policy Preferences on War Debt, Commercial Debt, and Reparations
Country	**Preferences**
United Kingdom	Is willing to cancel German reparations, but only if its war debts are forgiven.
France	Refuses to forgive German reparations, but wants its war debts forgiven.
Germany	Wants reparations canceled, but wants to meet commercial debt obligations to maintain credit worthiness.
United States	Refuses to connect war debts to reparations; will not forgive war debts, but will accept a moratorium on both.

mas produced by incompatible policy preferences or willing to assume the costs of leadership and provision of the collective goods needed to promote liberal exchange and economic expansion. The United States was the potential linchpin of any positive resolution of the liquidity dilemma produced by the countervailing obligations of war debts and reparations. The debts owed to the United States provided U.S. policymakers with a tool that might have been used to break the stalemate—by promising to forgive the Allies' war debts as a lever to pressure the British and French to forgo German reparations. The British were already willing to accept such a compromise, although lasting French bitterness toward Germany and the prospect that capital inflows from reparations might exceed outflows for payment of war debts made the French more reluctant to forgive reparations. Unfortunately, American policymakers chose not to exercise their leverage.

The issues of war debt and reparations dominated much of the international agenda of the early 1920s, feeding the liquidity problems that confronted political economies seeking to rebuild and expand. Disagreements over these intersecting issues created tensions that spilled over into other international discussions and created barriers to the kinds of cooperation that would have been useful in managing the economic crises that would erupt in the late 1920s and 1930s. There were some international attempts to address the problems caused by reparations, war debts, and currency instability. Most notable among these efforts were the Dawes Commission in 1923 and the Young Commission in 1928. The Dawes Commission (chaired by Charles Dawes, a U.S. banker) sought to stabilize the German budget and currency by rescheduling reparations payments and arranging for a substantial loans from the United States to Germany. The Young Commission (chaired by Charles Young, the chairman of General Electric) led to another rescheduling of German reparations in 1929. Both produced false hopes.

German Hyperinflation

In the period preceding the Dawes Plan, fearing the political consequences of reparation demands, increasing unemployment, and poor domestic economic conditions, the German government and central bank started to increase its money supply, with the short-term goal of meeting payrolls and constraining unemployment. Unfortunately, such policies, absent real economic growth, can prove inflationary to prices. Recall that price inflation occurs when money supply increases at a faster pace than the supply of goods and services—more and more money chases a relatively stable supply of goods and service. This process can lead to a rapid increase in the nominal price of goods and services and a decline in the purchasing power of a currency. German government policies aimed at maintaining payrolls and limiting unemployment thus turned perverse and unleashed strong inflationary pressures on the German economy. The monetary stimulus quickly got out of hand, generating extraordinary **hyperinflation,** which destroyed the value and purchasing power of the German Reichsmark.

From May 1921 to July 1922, nominal prices increased by over 600 percent. Prices jumped another 18,000 percent from July 1922 to June 1923, and then registered a whopping 850 billion percent increase from July 1923 to November 1923. To place this situation in comparative perspective, before World War I the German mark, the British shilling, the French franc, and the Italian lira all had about equal value, and all exchanged at the rate of four or five to the dollar. By the end of November 1923, the exchange rate between the dollar and the mark was 4.2 trillion marks to one dollar (see table 8.4). The printing presses at the Reichsbank ran twenty-four hours a day to try and keep up with this hyperinflation of prices, only adding to the crisis.

What did this mean for Germans?

> A student at Freiburg University ordered a cup of coffee at a cafe. The price on the menu was 5,000 Marks. He had two cups. When the bill came, it was for 14,000 Marks. "If you want to save money," he was told, "and you want two cups of coffee, you should order them both at the same time." [1]

On a trip through Germany during the hyperinflation period, Pearl Buck described the situation as follows:

> The cities were still there, the houses not yet bombed and in ruins, but the victims were millions of people. They had lost their fortunes, their savings; they were dazed and inflation-shocked and did not understand how it had happened to them and who the foe was who had defeated them. Yet they had lost their self-assurance, their feeling that they themselves could be the masters of their own lives if only they worked hard enough; and lost, too, were the old values of morals, of ethics, of decency.[2]

---

[1] Excerpted from Adam Smith (George J. W. Goodman), *Paper Money*, (New York: Summit Books, 1981), 57–62.
[2] Excerpted from Adam Smith, *Paper Money*.

TABLE 8.4	The Exchange Rate of the Dollar to the Mark, 1914–1923
Period	**Rate**
Prior to 1914	US$1 = 4.20 Mk
End of 1914	4.60
1915	5.00
1916	5.50
1917	6.40
1918	7.00
1919	42
1920	70
1921	185
1922	7,350
January 1923	4,000
February 1923	27,300
March 1923	20,975
April 1923	29,800
May 1923	69,500
June 1923	154,500
July 1923	1,000,000
August 1923	10,000,000
September 1923	160,000,000
1 Oct 1923	242,000,000
10 Oct 1923	3,000,000,000
20 Oct 1923	12,000,000,000
31 Oct 1923	73,000,000,000
1 Nov 1923	130,000,000,000
10 Nov 1923	630,000,000,000
15 Nov 1923	2,000,000,000,000
End of November 1923	4,200,000,000,000

Source: Baltimore Philatelic Society, www.balpex.org/philatelist.html.

Shoppers showed up at bakeries, butcher shops, and groceries needing wheelbarrows to carry the necessary quantity of marks to purchase foodstuffs. Within a very short period of time, notes of 20 million marks attained common usage. This period of hyperinflation, with its crushing impact on German welfare and its pernicious effect on German politics, left a strong memory. In the years since, that memory has played a significant role in the monetary politics of Germany and what is now the European Union (EU): for fear of stimulating inflation, the Bundesbank, and now the European Central Bank of the EU, have been dominated by a focus on monetary stability at the expense of promoting growth.

The Rise of Political Extremism

Many investigators blame hyperinflation for the rise of political extremism in Germany, the success of the German National Socialist Party (the Nazi Party), and the ascension of Adolf Hitler to power. Certainly its pressures did damage confidence in the nascent democratic government and helped to fuel the rise of more extreme political movements in postwar Germany. The Nazis and the Communists, at opposite ends of the political spectrum, both grew rapidly in this environment. Hitler garnered confidence as his Nazi Party

After World War I, excessive monetary stimulus in Germany led to hyperinflation that quickly eroded the value of the German reichsmark. German economic activity declined as the reichsmark dramatically lost purchasing power. With hyperinflation, Germans soon needed baskets of currency to make daily purchases. In this environment, Hitler and other political extremists sought to build a political base.

won thirty-two seats in the first postwar election. But the hyperinflation of prices provided only one motivation for the drift toward political extremism in Germany and other European states. For Hitler and the Nazi Party, rancor over the government's management of the domestic economy only added fuel to an already burning fire of political unrest. Political dissent was rooted in a broader national dissatisfaction with the way the war had ended— a widespread belief that the Treaty of Versailles was too harsh and inequitable, producing economic ills, and that the Germany military had been abandoned on the field of battle by politicians and undermined by enemies within the German state.

Strategically, Hitler paired the economic dislocations arising from hyperinflation with the disagreements over the harsh peace treaty to boost his political movement from a small band of disaffected military veterans into a significant political party. The Nazi Party grew rapidly in this environment, but it remained a minority party even with the economic distress of the people. In the midst of the hyperinflation crisis, Hitler overestimated both the extent of public animosity toward the democratic government, the Weimar Republic, and the degree of support for his movement within the military. In November 1923 he gambled that his coup in Munich—the so-called Beer Hall Putsch—would mobilize public dissatisfaction over hyperinflation and the military's discontent over its emasculation as a result of the Treaty of Versailles, leading to the overthrow of the current regime and the establishment of a new regime under Hitler's control. But he had miscalculated: the coup failed, as the military remained neutral and the police quelled his attempt. Imprisoned for nine months, Hitler redirected his efforts to gain control of the government by focusing upon a constitutional ascension to power through the ballot box.

The economic crisis eased, the German economy recovered, and political extremism faltered in the mid-1920s. Supported by the assistance provided under the Dawes Plan, the German government implemented stringent measures that conquered hyperinflation, stabilized the value of the currency, and restored the credit mechanisms necessary for economic growth. German industry revived, and unemployment fell. Therefore, the hyperinflation in the German economy of the early 1920s was not alone sufficient to account for Hitler's rise to power. That difficult period provided the opportunity to lay a foundation for the Nazi Party early in the decade, but Hitler's support stagnated with economic recovery.

The world economy soon encountered another economic crisis, however. The onset of the Great Depression undermined the provision of liquidity that was so critical to the continued expansion of the German economy and other economies recovering from World War I. The German economy staggered, slumped, and then retreated. In September 1929, a month before the New York stock market crash, German unemployment stood at 1,320,000 people in a nation of approximately 60 million. As the new economic crisis took hold, that number grew to approximately 3 million people by September 1930, around 4.5 million by September 1931, and over 6 million by early 1932.

In this stressful economic environment, dissatisfaction with the government grew, and political movements of the far right (the Nazis) and left (the Communists) found greater traction. Hitler exploited the tremendous economic distress and dislocation that arose in Germany after 1929 to expand the base that he had built earlier, enabling his rise to power through the ballot box and legitimate constitutional means. After garnering the levers of power through a series of legitimate democratic elections and government formation, however, he turned sharply authoritarian, suspending parliamentary powers and consolidating his authority as both the head of state (the presidency) and the head of government (the chancellorship) into a single position (the Führer), thus destroying the democratic Weimar Republic.

U.S. Financial Market Speculation and the Crash

The liquidity crunch that had hampered postwar economic recovery and expansion improved significantly in the mid-1920s, but a new liquidity shortage hit the global economy by the end of the decade that would undo these hard-won economic gains. Let's look at this new crisis, which undermined the economic recovery and led to world into depression.

Many popular accounts single out the October 1929 New York Stock Exchange (NYSE) crash as the primary cause of the liquidity crunch that contributed to the Great Depression. Clearly, the market crash was a significant factor. Before World War I, the British had provided liquidity to the international system, acted as lender of last resort, and supported a stable international monetary system, but the war drained their capital reserves and undermined their ability to continue credibly playing such a role. Postwar attempts by British policymakers and financiers to provide these collective goods imposed unsustainable costs upon British workers and producers—unemployment, lack of investment capital at home, and threats to the competitiveness of British products in global markets—which led the policymakers to suspend such efforts.

The United States, and New York specifically, replaced London as the center of capital and global financial holdings. The purchase of war materials during World War I, the resulting war debts, and reparations payments generated massive capital flows into the New York markets, fueling growth in stock prices and trading, and further enhancing the attractiveness of these markets to holders of capital in the United States and abroad. From the beginning of 1928 to just before the crash, the Dow Jones Industrial Average (DJIA), a financial index based on core industrial companies' performance, grew twofold, as did the number of market transactions. With increases in market valuations, New York markets acted as a magnet for surplus capital from around the world—which made these markets key to international capital liquidity. However, financial panic set in on Black Thursday, October 24, 1929, and a still bigger shock hit on Black Tuesday, October 29, when 16.4 million shares were traded—a record trading volume that stood for almost the next half-century. The October 1929 collapse in New York followed significant declines in markets elsewhere: the German markets had encountered rough sailing by early 1928, London markets fell in mid-1928, and Paris dropped in February 1929. Confidence in financial market mechanisms was already being tested before October 1929.

The 1929 market crash was important, but it was not sufficient by itself to precipitate a decade-long global depression. The stock market expansion of the 1920s was not disconnected from changes in the underlying economy. Despite rapid price and market expansion, stock prices were not terribly out of line with earnings for firms listed on the NYSE. The U.S. industrial base had emerged healthy from the war, and it expanded significantly in the years preceding the crash. For example, increase in U.S. automobile ownership generated growth in a core industrial sector that spilled over to those industries that supplied automakers. Steel and oil producers, upholsterers, electronics manufacturers, and builders of the expanding network of roads and infrastructure related to modern transport all gained from the expansion of automotive production. Jobs were created as cars were built and bought and roads constructed. Modern transport also improved agriculture and shipping.

Moreover, comparable stock market crashes have occurred that did not lead to depressions, or even significant recessions. Not all market crashes precipitate liquidity shortages, and no other significant market crash during the twentieth century was accompanied by a liquidity crisis comparable to that leading to the Great Depression. Nevertheless, the 1929 stock market crash, the resulting decrease in wealth, and a decline in confidence in modern capital markets were all connected to a crisis in capital liquidity that undermined economic activity.

Crisis in the Credit Mechanism

A greater dilemma than the actual 1929 crash lay in the mechanisms that provided credit in the United States and the fact that those mechanisms had become increasingly intertwined with the stock market. People, firms, and governments borrow capital through credit mechanisms to finance a host of activities—home mortgages, plant expansion, school construction, and other projects. In the 1920s, banks, as credit institutions, obtained much of the capital they loaned from the deposits of their account holders and the earnings on those funds. Individuals and businesses deposit money in banks, and banks pay their depositors interest on that money. Deposits are essentially loans by those with surplus capital to banking institutions, and the interest rate that banks pay to their depositors is the cost of capital to the banks. Banks must find a way to make those deposited assets earn money, so that they can pay interest to the depositors, make enough money to pay for their own operation, and have some left over as profit. In order to do so, a bank takes those deposits and loans them to individuals and enterprises experiencing a shortage of capital.

In the rapid stock market expansion of the 1920s, greed overtook reason and common sense, as speculators began to borrow, and borrow heavily, to purchase equities in the stock market. Stockbrokers borrowed funds from domestic and foreign credit institutions (banks) and then loaned those funds to their clients to purchase stocks. An investor could thus purchase a large position in stocks with only a small amount of her own money up front. Credit from her broker financed the rest of her purchase, which she anticipated paying off with the gains made from the sale of her stock.

More and more stock positions were supported with borrowed capital. This trend was sustainable as long as stock prices were stable or continued to rise, people were willing to purchase stocks at such price levels, and credit institutions could continue to provide additional credit at attractive prices. Under such conditions, those who had borrowed to purchase their stocks could sell some stocks to pay off their loan obligations, and the credit institutions could then afford to make new loans. At the very least, a borrower could turn over the asset, the stock, to the credit institution that had loaned the capital used in the stock purchase. The merry-go-round would keep spinning.

So far so good, but what if the stock's value were to fall substantially below the value of the loan obligation? What if a lot of stocks should fall substantially below the value of the loan obligations—so that the loans became significantly more expensive than the stock asset? In fact, this was the situation that confronted investors, speculators, brokers, credit institutions, and central bankers during and after the 1929 market crash. As the value of their loans now exceeded the value of the underlying asset, the bankers began to worry about their ability to recover their funds and about the viability of the brokers to whom they had loaned capital. Moreover, with brokers owing funds to multiple banks, each banker feared being last in line to demand payment of such loan obligations. This fear generated a first-come, first-served pressure on banks to beat the others to the punch. These foreign and domestic credit institutions, worried about their exposure, began calling in their loans to brokers.

The rush by credit institutions to redeem their loans threatened to reduce capital liquidity in the market—to shrink the amount of money available. This effect, in turn, could lead to further collapse in stock prices, as there would be less money chasing the same amount of stock, and, potentially, to a full-scale reduction in capital liquidity that would extend beyond the immediate setting of stock prices. Recognizing this potential, New York banks and the Federal Reserve attempted to check the panic and restore stability by taking over loans from outside credit institutions and injecting their own capital to shore up the faltering market. The Federal Reserve continued to maintain the money supply through manipulation of the discount rate (at which it loans capital to banks) and through its open-market operations (by which the Fed can inject money into the economy by purchasing government securities).

Central banks attempted to quell the emerging liquidity crisis by lowering their discount rates and increasing money supply. Many actually succeeded in increasing money supply over the next year, but economic expectations are heavily influenced by psychology and perceptions, particularly in the short term. Central banking policies only succeed if they convince private holders of capital to act consistently with those policies. These actions by the central banks proved insufficient to stem the fears of private credit institutions or those providing capital to those institutions. Perhaps the central banks could have averted the crisis by adding more to the money supply, but, by late 1930, the reluctance of private actors to expand credit began to shrink the money supply in spite of the banks' efforts to the contrary.

Brokers, confronted with demands by credit institutions to repay their loans, called in the loans that they had extended to investors to finance their stock purchases. Investors then rushed to liquidate their stock positions in the hope of meeting their loan obligations and limiting their losses. This frenzied liquidation had an effect like throwing gasoline on a fire—it increased the supply of stock for sale, which produced even greater downward pressure on stock prices. The social dynamic, the interaction of individual choices, thus exacerbated a downturn and turned a market correction into a market collapse. Individuals made rational and prudent decisions, but those decisions aggregated to create a destructive social trap—a **fallacy of composition.**

When the market collapsed, the large amount of market speculation funded by credit spilled over to threaten the viability of the credit institutions themselves. Banks depend upon revenues from their loan portfolios to pay off their depositors and fund new loans. Providing credit in the form of new loans is critical to ensuring liquidity for economic expansion and activity. But if enough outstanding loans cease to provide the necessary revenues, the banks can neither pay their depositors nor extend new loans. If depositors cannot withdraw their capital from the bank, they will stop depositing funds there, or perhaps even panic, as many depositors need those funds to pay bills and purchase necessities. The credit institution itself may fail, and certainly the amount of capital in the system will decline.

For example, imagine you have $5,000 and you borrow $95,000 to purchase an asset, a house, for $100,000. Then the real estate market in your community collapses and your house declines in value to $60,000. You have been making your monthly mortgage payments, but you still owe $90,000. Are you going to continue meeting your loan obligations and so pay the credit institution $30,000 more than your property is worth? Rationally, you may decide instead to default on your loan. The bank will likely foreclose and own your house; it will then turn around and sell the house, but for only $60,000, which is its new market value. The bank has lost $30,000 on this set of transactions—not a good business deal, for it now has $30,000 less to fund new loans and meet depositor demands.

Now remember, the real estate market in your community has collapsed, which means that you are not the only homeowner in this position. The collapse in real estate prices is a **structural condition**—it affects everyone in the entire community. All credit institutions anticipate some defaults as a course of normal business, because people occasionally mismanage their affairs. But a structural downturn generates conditions under which many borrowers default on their loan obligations, even if they have managed their affairs wisely. The cumulative amount of defaults may begin to exceed the expectations of the lenders and their capacity to manage their losses. The banks are destabilized, becoming unviable— unable to extend new loans or to make good on obligations to their depositors—as their balance sheets run damaging deficits. Such insolvency is more likely to occur if the downturn is structural.

Essentially, this was the problem facing credit institutions and societies after the 1929 stock market crash. In the aftermath of the crash, many banks were excessively exposed as a consequence of the speculative use of credit in the stock market. Many became either fully or nearly insolvent, lacking the funds to extend new credit or to meet their depositors' requests for withdrawals. With time, banks can sometimes weather such solvency problems by attracting new deposits and increasing their earnings. But in the aftermath of the crash, depositors began to fret over the security of their deposits in banks that were beginning to look vulnerable, while those with a capital surplus became increasingly reluctant to deposit their capital in banks. Worried depositors began to withdraw their funds in anticipation that the banks might not have sufficient funds to meet all depositor demands——another instance of the "first come, first served" pressures of a social trap. Many banks actually did not have sufficient funds to meet depositor demands and suspended operations (see table 8.5), which only confirmed public fears and so escalated the credit crisis. The public lost confidence in the intermediary mechanisms—the banks and credit markets—that sat between those with a surplus of capital and those needing capital for their economic endeavors.

To make matters worse, the credit that speculators had borrowed to invest in the stock market came from a much broader range of institutions than U.S. commercial banks located in New York City. If only New York commercial banks had faced the threat of numerous defaults from such speculation, the crisis might have been contained by their coordination with the U.S. Federal Reserve Bank. But stockbrokers had borrowed capital not only from banks in New York City to loan to speculators but also from banks located elsewhere in the United States, from nonfinancial U.S. firms, from foreign credit institutions and firms, and from other sources. This extensive borrowing created a broader network, a global financial web, along which the credit crisis could spread. The market crash had long-term negative

TABLE 8.5	Number of U.S. Banks and Bank Suspensions, 1929–1934	
	Number as of December 31	
Year	**Total Banks**	**Banks with Suspended Operations**
1929	24,633	659
1930	22,773	1,350
1931	19,970	2,293
1932	18,397	1,453
1933	15,015	4,000
1934	16,096	57

Source: Historical Statistics of the United States: Colonial Times to 1970 (1975), vol. 20–30, p. 912.

effects due to the widespread breakdown in the credit mechanisms—which created the most severe wave of liquidity problems to befall nations during the interwar years and paved the way for a decade of economic misery and political extremism.

The Breakdown in Trade

The market crash, the liquidity crunch, and the insolvency crisis in banking and credit institutions led to reduced consumption and placed pressures on production structures in national economies. With less money and less access to credit—and fearing worse things to come—people reduced their consumption of domestic- and foreign-produced commodities. Prices declined as less money and credit chased the same amount of commodities (remember Hume). Producers faced increasing difficulty in meeting their obligations and in employing their workers. Unemployment jumped as conditions worsened.

Scared and angry, producers and workers pressured their governments for relief. Policymakers, fearing a threat to their political survival, responded with policies that sought to protect domestic markets for domestically produced goods. Hoping to redistribute the costs of the economic downturn away from their workers and producers and onto the backs of workers and producers abroad, governments intervened in international trade by increasing tariffs and other barriers to trade. Such beggar-thy-neighbor policies rejected the gains from comparative advantage, specialization, and the discipline of exchange in a larger market. They also imposed costs on nontradable sectors of political economies and consumers, as they influenced the prices of the goods and services they consumed. Seeking to protect specific segments of a political economy, these policies damaged the broader political economy at home and abroad.

Trade slowed and then began to decline. In the first four years of the Great Depression, international exchange fell by 60 percent, as shown in Figure 8.1. Sometimes such protective policies work as intended to successfully redistribute costs abroad and shelter specific segments of national political economies, but even when successful, they impose costs on the broader economic welfare—a protected sector benefits at the expense of the broader national society and to the detriment of economic welfare in other national political economies. In this case, furthermore, the initial imposition of higher trade barriers turned into a sustained policy of economic warfare, as governments resorted to more and more strategies to protect their domestic markets and advantage their domestic producers in international exchange. Rather than bringing the anticipated relief, this economic warfare by means of beggar-thy-neighbor policies damaged the very sectors those policies were designed to protect. The breakdown in trade imposed large costs upon the tradable sectors of economies, as the trends toward lower revenues, lower wages, and increased unemployment accelerated. These costs then spilled over into other parts of national economies, as the breakdown in trade eroded consumption choices and gains from specialization. Trade could have been a pathway to the expansion of economic activity and welfare, a means to grow out of the economic downturn, but government policies in response to constituent pressures closed this road. This breakdown in international exchange contributed significantly to the severity and duration of the Great Depression.

Let's take a closer look at this breakdown in trade, whose lessons remain critical today, as public debates over trade and outsourcing raise many of the same issues and appeal to the same fears. Threats to international trade had begun to emerge before World War I. After lowering tariffs and negotiating bilateral trade agreements that contributed to the expansion of trade in the mid- to late 1800s, many governments found themselves facing pressures in their political economies to slow or reverse these trends toward trade liberalization. Expanding democratization in the 1800s pulled more and more of the national populations into the electorate, thus changing the representative demands upon politicians. The increasing connections between political elites and their masses translated into new temptations to manipulate trade policy to shift costs away from one's own vocal and politically mobilized constituents to other governments' constituents. This response can be an appealing electoral strategy, even if overall society would benefit more from free trade—it all depends upon who votes and why.

In this environment, many governments started to increase tariffs and to adopt other protectionist measures for specific economic sectors, particularly agriculture. Such policies sought to protect against price deflation and maintain aggregate demand for the output of their domestic businesses and labor—to protect jobs and revenues. Government interventions in trade attempted to redistribute the costs of adjustment and to shelter those parts of the economy threatened by the dynamics of comparative advantage, specialization of production, and creative destruction. Protections for a specific sector's goods imposed higher

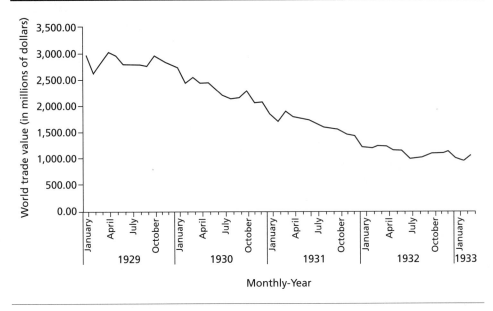

Source: Charles P. Kindleberger, *The World Depression, 1929–1939* (Berkeley: University of California Press, 1986), 170.

costs for those goods upon a broader domestic base, affecting their consumption choices and economic welfare, although consumers often did not notice, or did not mind, the impact of a nickel here and a dime there on their personal budgets. The willingness of the broader society to bear such costs in order to protect the economic activities of a narrow segment of their society might seem noble, but protections also imposed costs on other nations' labor, producers, and societies. Protections beggared (impoverished) neighbors who had no representation in the nation raising barriers to trade.

The prewar pressures for trade protections continued to grow in the years following the war. As currency instability, slow economic recovery and growth, and other economic stresses posed threats to workers and enterprises in the tradable sector, policymakers tried a variety of strategies and policy tools to manage these pressures on their domestic producers. Production subsidies, tariffs, price controls, international attempts to arrive at production targets to control supply, development of **imperial preferences** (whereby a colonial power and its colonies enjoyed privileged access to each other's markets), and government purchase and storage of surplus production in order to reduce supply in the marketplace were some of the tools employed in attempts to manage the political and economic difficulties in tradable sectors.

National policymakers were surely aware of the threat posed by protectionism. During the 1920s several international conferences—some held under the auspices of the League of Nations—attempted to address these trade issues and to contain governments' inclination to protect their domestic sectors from the price pressures of the global market. These efforts failed to stem the increasing protectionist pressures, however, and national policymakers continued to enact intrusive tariff legislation that nibbled away at trade openness. The British adopted the Safeguarding of Industries Act of 1921. The U.S. Congress passed the Fordney-McCumber Tariff Act of 1922, which raised tariffs upon a range of imports in the United States and allowed the president to raise or lower tariffs on any product by up to 50 percent after advisement by the U.S. Tariff Commission. Other countries followed suit: in 1925 France and Italy increased duties on cars, India on piece goods, and Australia on a variety of commodities. Italy raised duties on wheat in 1925, which led to an escalation of protections on this commodity as other nations reciprocated with similar protections. Germany returned to tariffs on wheat after 1926.

Despite such protections, trade expanded during the 1920s. This upsurge should not be too surprising, given the drastic break that had been imposed on international trade by the hostilities of World War I—war is not good for trade, and world war is especially harmful. So the end of hostilities offered an artificially low baseline for international trade, setting the stage for an increase despite the adoption of trade protections by many governments. But by the end of the 1920s, the growing liquidity crunch, ensuing price deflation, and economic fear threatened more and more producers and labor. As tradable sectors faced increasing hardships, politicians faced increasing pressures from their constituents to adopt protectionist strategies.

In 1930 the largest and most significant political economy—that of the United States—enacted the Smoot-Hawley Act, one of the worst pieces of legislation ever crafted by Congress (recall the discussion of Smoot-Hawley at the beginning of chapter 1). In spite of its noxious potential, the act passed overwhelmingly. More than 1,000 economists signed a letter to President Hoover, decrying the irresponsibility of the legislation and beseeching him to veto the bill. Many other governments also warned U.S. policymakers about the damage that Smoot-Hawley would do to international trade. Nevertheless, Hoover signed the bill into law.

Even with its history as a protectionist political economy, the United States had not previously attempted any measure comparable in size and range to Smoot-Hawley, which imposed the largest tariff increases ever across 20,000 commodities. Its provisions raised tariffs above the already high rates that had been established under Fordney-McCumber eight years earlier. Not content to sit by and let their citizens be beggared by U.S. policy, other governments, predictably, responded by raising their tariffs. Smoot-Hawley thus unleashed tit-for-tat retaliation by Switzerland, Canada, Italy, Spain, France, Cuba, New Zealand, Australia, and many others states.

It is unlikely that Rep. Willis Hawley, R-Ore., and Sen. Reed Smoot, R-Utah, are congratulating each other on severely damaging the global economy and driving the world into a severe depression—which is what they did in 1930 with the passage of the Smoot-Hawley Act on tariffs. The act led to a dramatic increase in U.S. tariffs at a time when the U.S. was running a balance of payments surplus and had emerged as a creditor nation. Because of the economic strength of the United States and the difficulties facing other nations, the attempt by the act to divert U.S. demand away from foreign goods added to a growing crisis in the global economy and invited other governments to retaliate.

Tit-for-Tat Retaliation

Such tit-for-tat retaliation, while rational and understandable from a politician's perspective, only made matters worse. Although many governments engaged in beggar-thy-neighbor policies, Smoot-Hawley was perhaps the most damaging, given the size of the U.S. economy and market, and its potential for stimulating a countercyclical market for distressed goods. As the largest economy by far, the United States possessed policy capabilities that were critical to interrupting the downward economic trend. If its policymakers had adopted a countercyclical strategy of maintaining market access under duress and promoting exchange, the depression might well have been shortened or contained. But the actual U.S. policy was, instead, procyclical—adding fuel to the forces threatening globalization and peace in the global political economy. It made little economic sense for policymakers in other states to persevere with countercyclical, protrade policies when the largest market had adopted procyclical, antitrade policies in this environment. The U.S. policy simply precipitated a stampede to the fire exits.

Governments started with tit-for-tat increases in trade protections, and, when those tools failed to improve the conditions of producers and labor in the tradable sector, policymakers shifted to other beggar-thy-neighbor policy instruments to promote domestic interests at expense of foreign interests. They resorted to currency devaluation as a means to affect their producers' prices in domestic and overseas markets. Devaluation is a centralized, broad-range strategy that affects the prices of *all* goods produced in a nation vis-à-vis other nations' commodities. But, like the tit-for-tat retaliation in tariffs, devaluation engendered tit-for-tat devaluations that undermined currency stability

| FIGURE 8.2 | **The Gold Standard: Its Initial Breakdown, Resurgence, and Demise, 1870–1939** |

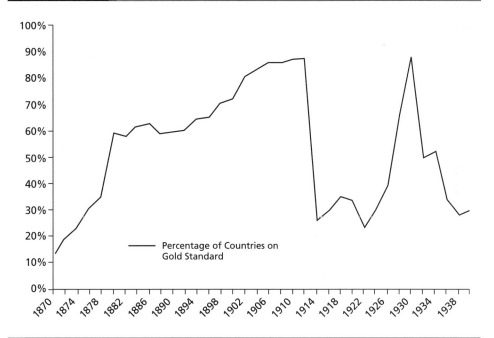

Source: Antoni Estevadeordal, Brian Frant, and Alan M. Taylor, "The Rise and Fall of World Trade, 1870–1939," National Bureau of Economic Research, Working Paper 9318, November 2002.

and created further barriers to international exchange. The devaluations also sabotaged any efforts to maintain the reconstructed gold standard—figure 8.2 shows the dramatic decline in the percentage of the world's nations adhering to the gold standard during the 1930s as a result of pressures to devalue.

The rapid tit-for-tat rise in trade barriers in 1929–1930 and the ensuing tit-for-tat currency devaluations led to dramatic declines in exports. As mentioned earlier, the value of world trade fell precipitously after 1929, contracting by over 60 percent between 1929 and 1933 (see figure 8.1). The decline in trade exacerbated economic contraction, increased liquidity shortages, limited efficiencies from specialization, decreased consumption possibilities, increased unemployment, and fed the growing depression. A decline in social welfare was the perverse consequence of behavior intended to protect domestic economies. Instead of protecting domestic industry and labor, tit-for-tat responses to beggar-thy-neighbor policies wreaked even more damage. This paradoxical outcome demonstrates, again, the fallacy of composition dilemma raised earlier in the discussion of the growing liquidity crunch, whereby individually rational actions interact to damage individual interests and the larger political economy.

Capability and Willingness: British Inability and U.S. Failure

Chapter 4, on power, distinguished between capability and willingness—a difference that is critical to understanding the breakdown in the global economy during the interwar years. In the immediate aftermath of World War I, a reviving global economy faced significant challenges. Even if they had the will, the British no longer enjoyed the capacity to provide the collective goods that had greased the wheels of the global economy in the mid- to late 1800s. Other major combatants were similarly strained, except one: the United States, which emerged from the war with the world's largest and healthiest economy. Indeed, the United States had actually profited from the war. Expansion of the U.S. military, in anticipation of the conflict, meant that more troops needed to be clothed, fed, quartered, and armed, and so the military mobilization had helped to expand the U.S. industrial base. Training also proved a boon to the education and health care of poorer U.S. citizens, improving their future capabilities as labor, should they survive the conflict.

As a late entrant to the war, the United States avoided the horrible devastation of its draft-age population that other states suffered. Therefore, the economic gains from the mobilization of its population and industrial base were not lost to death and injury on the battlefield. As U.S. industry sold war materials to the combatants, European capital reserves flowed to the United States to pay for those materials. And later, when those reserves had been exhausted, the extension of credit to Allied governments to fund more purchases produced war debts that were really obligations of future transfers of liquidity from Europe to the United States. Such transfers would help fund U.S. economic expansion, but they would hinder European recovery following the war.

In the aftermath of the conflict, the United States had the capacity to take up the role that the British had played in the expansion of globalization in the second half of the nineteenth century. The U.S. economy harbored tremendous wealth relative to others. A huge percentage of the world's gold reserves had become U.S. assets (see table 8.6), and, as the largest and healthiest economy in the world, the U.S. had sufficient economic resources to provide the collective goods of liquidity and convertibility that had been a cornerstone of the prewar monetary system. The United States also had the capacity, if its policymakers desired, to provide countercyclical lending and market access during times of economic downturn. But U.S. policymakers failed to take up the mantle of responsibility from the British.

U.S. policymakers' prewar beliefs and practices heavily influenced their postwar thinking about the global arena: they resisted shifting from the traditional U.S. isolationist, reactive stance to a more proactive and liberal engagement with the world. Early in its history, the United States had adopted protectionist trade policies to promote the growth of its nascent industries; generations of American policymakers had heeded Washington and Jefferson's

TABLE 8.6 Gold Reserves of Central Banks and Governments, 1913–1935 (as percent of total reserves)

Country	1913	1918	1923	1924	1925	1926	1927	1928	1929	1930	1931	1932	1933	1934	1935
United States	26.6	39.0	44.4	45.7	44.4	44.3	41.6	37.4	37.8	38.7	35.9	34.0	33.6	37.8	45.1
Russia/USSR	16.2	—	0.5	0.8	1.0	0.9	1.0	0.9	1.4	2.3	2.9	3.1	3.5	3.4	3.7
France	14.0	9.8	8.2	7.9	7.9	7.7	10.0	12.5	15.8	19.2	23.9	27.3	25.3	25.0	19.6
Germany	5.7	7.9	1.3	2.0	3.2	4.7	4.7	6.5	5.3	4.8	2.1	1.6	0.8	0.1	0.1
Italy	5.5	3.0	2.5	2.5	2.5	2.4	2.5	2.7	2.7	2.6	2.6	2.6	3.1	2.4	1.6
Argentina	5.3	4.5	5.4	4.9	5.0	4.9	5.5	6.0	4.2	3.8	2.2	2.1	2.0	1.9	2.0
United Kingdom	3.4	7.7	8.6	8.3	7.8	7.9	7.7	7.5	6.9	6.6	5.2	4.9	7.8	7.3	7.3
India	2.5	0.9	1.3	1.2	1.2	1.2	1.2	1.2	1.2	1.2	1.4	1.4	1.4	1.3	1.2
Canada	2.4	1.9	1.5	1.7	1.7	1.6	1.1	0.8	1.0	0.7	0.7	0.7	0.6	0.6	0.8
Brazil	1.9	0.4	0.6	0.6	0.6	0.6	1.1	1.5	1.5	0.1	—	—	0.1	0.1	0.1
Spain	1.9	6.3	5.6	5.5	5.5	5.4	5.2	4.9	4.8	4.3	3.8	3.6	3.6	3.4	3.3
Japan	1.3	3.3	7.0	6.5	6.4	6.1	5.7	5.4	5.3	3.8	2.1	1.8	1.8	1.8	1.9
Netherlands	1.2	4.2	2.7	2.3	2.0	1.8	1.7	1.7	1.7	1.6	3.2	3.5	3.1	2.6	2.0
Belgium	1.0	0.7	0.6	0.6	0.6	0.9	1.0	1.3	1.6	1.7	3.1	3.0	3.2	2.7	2.7
Switzerland	0.7	1.2	1.2	1.1	1.0	1.0	1.0	1.0	1.1	1.3	4.0	4.0	3.2	2.9	2.0
Australia	0.5	1.5	1.5	1.5	1.8	1.2	1.1	1.1	0.9	0.7	0.5	0.4	—	—	—
All other	9.9	7.8	7.1	6.9	7.4	7.3	7.4	7.3	7.0	6.3	6.4	6.0	6.9	6.7	6.6

Source: Barry Eichengreen, Globalizing Capital: A History of the International Monetary System (Princeton, N.J.: Princeton University Press, 1996).

admonitions against binding political engagement with Europe. Nothing in the experience of World War I forced American policymakers to dramatically alter these received attitudes opposing more open trade or more proactive internationalist policies. President Wilson tried to drag the United States toward such an engagement, but he failed.

Even with the world's largest economy and greatest capital reserves, U.S. institutional mechanisms were probably not up to the task of providing the collective goods that would be needed to promote stable and productive international economic relations. In the United States, Main Street's distrust of banks and of Wall Street had produced a financial system that created obstacles to the sound financial management and coordination necessary for acting as the world's financial center and lender of last resort. Whereas the British Treasury, the Bank of England, and private financiers in London had been able to cooperate to manage and contain many global financial and economic crises during the 1800s, the U.S. system did not yet have the organizational capacity to replace the British. Regional skepticism and distrust had prevented U.S. policymakers from even developing a central banking system until 1923, when Congress passed the Federal Reserve Act. Providing financial collective goods to the global political economy would have been extremely difficult, if not impossible, absent a strong, well-established, and respected central bank to coordinate the activities of private financiers during times of crisis.

The U.S. retreat to prewar isolationist policies, its institutional limitations, and other constraints on U.S. policy proved problematic for rebuilding the postwar global economy. Instead of sending capital abroad in a countercyclical effort to forestall economic downturns and promote economic expansion, the United States continued to receive capital from Europe. Doubts surfaced about the wisdom of enforcing German reparations payments, but U.S. refusal to forgive the war debts of its allies prevented them from reducing the German reparations burden. Slow growth in Europe made New York's financial markets attractive for holders of scarce European capital, but the United States failed to provide other collective goods such as market access under duress. Even in the absence of the financial distress that was plaguing the rest of the Atlantic economy, U.S. trade policy did not embrace a move toward the free-trade stance that could have helped to promote growth in other national economies by providing open markets for their goods.

CONCLUSION

The troubles and travails of the interwar years contributed to the breakdown in the global political economy and, eventually, to World War II. The unwillingness of U.S. policymakers to assume hegemonic leadership and provide the collective goods that would promote liberal economic activity and expansion, the United Kingdom's inability to provide liquidity and act as lender of last resort, instability in the exchange-rate mechanism, German reparations and Allied war debts, the stock market crash, and the undermining of credit institutions severely damaged growth prospects in the global arena. Perhaps, if the victors had been more generous to the vanquished at Versailles, if credit mechanisms had been better regulated to prevent excessive speculation and the risk of insolvency, or if central banks had created more liquidity by lowering their interest rates and pumping capital into the system, the Great Depression and the rise of tyrannical political leaders could have been avoided. But this is pure speculation.

Policymakers learned some critical lessons from their mistakes in the interwar period; in their deliberations over the design of the post–World War II global political economy, they would seek to avoid committing the same mistakes. In that later case, deliberations over the make-up of the postwar global political economy—over the rules of the game—began well before the fighting ended. Allied policymakers began their discussions at summits and conferences midway during the war. The next chapter considers these important lessons, examining their effect upon the design of postwar international economic organizations, the rules of the game for the global economy, domestic safety nets, state and society bargains, and the global order.

EXERCISES

1. World War I demanded a tremendous amount of resources from the nations involved. The United States provided loans to help its allies pay for their war efforts. What implications did these loans have for the future of the debt-ridden Allies? How did the loans contribute to the Great Depression?

2. Describe a political method a government might use to allocate unemployment costs due to competitive foreign market prices, and give an example. Who bears the costs of adjustment? How?

3. The United Kingdom was at the center of the first modern international financial system. How did World War I affect its performance in this capacity?

4. What negative effects did increased tariffs and immigration restrictions have on globalization? Why would nations adopt such policies, which would undermine their society's welfare?

5. What key shift occurred in the relationship between individuals and their governments in the late 1800s that put pressure on governments and politicians to reconcile increasing international trade with domestic welfare concerns? Explain.

6. In the late 1800s and early 1900s, more and more commodities were being produced with only marginal increases in the labor force and only marginal increases in the money supply due to its ties to gold. What result did this trend have?

7. Societies and their governments have choices about how to allocate the costs of adjustment that inevitably accompany economic transformation. Name and explain one of them.

8. Most of the time, we normatively view expanded suffrage, which endows greater political and civil rights on a wider population, as a positive development. But such changes may have made World War I more violent and deadly. How?

10. An absence of liquidity due to war reparations and debts, instability in international monetary affairs, and the loss of a productive generation fed domestic distress and created problems for governments and their economies. Break down this statement and identify the independent and dependent variables.

11. Identify each of the following terms and explain its significance to the study of world politics:

    Time inconsistency
    Smoot-Hawley
    Beggar-thy-neighbor
    Hyperinflation
    Structural condition

12. Debilitated by World War I, the European nations struggled to rebuild their economies. What factor deprived Germany of the capital it sorely needed to stimulate its economy and to fund rebuilding?

13. In the late 1800s, the United Kingdom had a smaller population and fewer natural resources than such other major European powers as France, Germany, and Russia. Yet it assumed a hegemonic role in that period. What does it mean to be the hegemon in a liberal global political economy—what does a hegemon do to provide stability in this situation?

14. What is the difference between a fixed- and a floating-exchange-rate mechanism?

FURTHER READING

Carr, E.H. 1946. *The Twenty Years' Crisis, 1919–1939*. 2nd ed. London: Macmillan.

Eichengreen, Barry. 1996. *Globalizing Capital: A History of the International Monetary System*. Princeton, N.J.: Princeton University Press.

Keegan, John. 1989. *The Second World War*. New York: Penguin.

Kennedy, David. 1999. *Freedom from Fear*. New York: Oxford University Press.

Kindleberger, Charles P. 1978. *Manias, Panics, and Crashes: A History of Financial Crises*. New York: Basic Books.

———. 1986. *The World in Depression, 1929–1939*. Berkeley: University of California Press.

Polyani, Karl. 1944. *The Great Transformation*. New York: Rinehart.

Temin, Peter. 1989. *Lessons from the Great Depression*. Cambridge, Mass.: MIT Press.

9 The Bretton Woods System: The Rebuilding of Globalization

In the long sweep of time, America's half-century-long ideological, political, and military face-off with the Soviet Union may appear far less consequential than America's leadership in inaugurating an era of global economic interdependence.... Who could have foretold that the nation that had flintily refused to cancel the European's war debts in the 1920s would establish the World Bank in 1945? That the country that had embraced the Fordney-McCumber and Smoot-Hawley tariffs would take the lead in establishing the General Agreement on Tariffs and Trade ... and would create the International Monetary Fund? And who could deny that globalization—the explosion in world trade, investment, and cultural mingling—was the signature and lasting international achievement of the postwar era, one likely to overshadow the Cold War in its long-term historical consequences?

David M. Kennedy, Freedom from Fear *(1999)*

PAST MISTAKES

World War II grew out of an acrimonious and unworkable peace; a deep and widespread depression in the global economy; a failure by states to overcome barriers to international cooperation and economic exchange; an inability of politicians to resist pressures from their domestic political economies to shift costs of adjustment overseas and across borders; and a lack of mechanisms and strategies within states to insulate their politicians from such pressures. This chain of policy choices and defaults produced the most horrific conflict in human history, as the supposedly civilized states of the industrialized world outdid the violence of any past human conflict. World War II demonstrated the brutality of modern technological warfare on a global scale. Again, the statistics are numbing, as reflected in one military historian's catalog of the breadth of the tragedy:

> Some 50 million people are estimated to have died as a result of the Second World War.
> ... By far the most grievous suffering among the combatant states was borne by the
> Soviet Union, which lost as least 7 million men in battle and a further 7 million citi-

zens; most of the latter, Ukrainians and White Russians in the majority, died as a result of deprivation, reprisal and forced labour. In relative terms, Poland suffered the worst among the combatant countries; about 20 per cent of her prewar population, some 6 million, did not survive. About half of the war's Polish victims were Jewish, and Jews also figured large in the death tolls of other eastern European countries, including the Baltic States, Hungary and Romania. Civil and guerrilla war accounted for the deaths of a quarter of a million Greeks and a million Yugoslavs. The number of casualties, military and civilian, were far higher in eastern than in western Europe. . . . In three European countries, however, France, Italy and the Netherlands, casualties were heavy. Before June 1940 and after November 1942 the French army lost 200,000 dead; 400,000 civilians were killed in raids or concentration camps. Italy lost over 330,000 of whom half were civilians, and 200,000 Dutch citizens, all but 10,000 of them civilians, died as a result of bombing or deportation. . . . The Western victors suffered proportionately and absolutely much less than any of the major allies. The British armed forces lost 244,000 men. Their Commonwealth and imperial comrades-in-arms suffered another 100,000 fatal casualties (Australia 23,000, Canada 37,000, India 24,000, New Zealand 10,000, South Africa 6,000). About 60,000 British civilians were killed by bombing. . . . The Americans suffered no direct civilian casualties; their military casualties, which contrast with 1.2 million Japanese battle deaths, were 292,000. . . . Germany, which had begun the war and fought it almost to Hitler's "five minutes past midnight," paid a terrible price for war guilt. . . . Over 4 million German servicemen died at the hands of the enemy, and 593,000 civilians under air attack. . . . It seems possible that a million Germans died in the flight from the east (to escape the advancing Soviet forces) in the early months of 1945. . . . In the winter of 1945 most of the remaining Germans of eastern Europe were systematically collected and transported westward . . . it is calculated that 250,000 died in the course of the expulsion from Czechoslovakia, 1.25 million from Poland and 600,000 from elsewhere in eastern Europe.[1]

Even before the war ended, Allied policymakers began to discuss how to construct a new peace. They sought to avoid the missteps of the past and build the foundations for a healthy global political economy that would constrain the anarchy of the global arena and the temptations to resort to political, economic, and military violence. Both the distribution of power and a basic conflict of ideologies presented challenges. World War II left two states with disproportionate influence at the top of the power hierarchy in the international system: the United States and the Soviet Union. These states had competing views about the organization of economic and political society. But Operation Barbarossa, the German attack on the Soviet Union in 1941, had made strategic allies out of these ideological enemies.

The industrial machinery of the United States, still stagnating from the Great Depression, shifted into high gear for the production of war materials and served as a bulwark against fascism. Sheltered by oceans from the ravages of war, the renewed industrial capabilities of

---

[1]John Keegan, *The Second World War* (New York: Penguin, 1989), 590–593.

the United States provided material assistance to the British and Soviets as they manned the front lines against the German aggressors. American trucks, tanks, aircraft, food, and other materials flowed into the United Kingdom and the Soviet Union to help stem and then reverse the German onslaught. American trucks provided Soviet forces with greater mobility and transport capacity than their foes could match, while felt boots made in America protected their feet against the brutally cold Soviet winters.

Unlikely partners, Josef Stalin, Winston Churchill, and Franklin Roosevelt (and later Harry Truman) met at conferences in Tehran and Potsdam to discuss the conduct of the war and to initiate postwar planning. The end of the war brought high hopes for peace and prosperity, but history, suspicion, competition, and ideological differences between the communist Soviet regime and the democratic capitalist systems of the United States and the United Kingdom made the wartime alliance a fragile structure, which would unravel quickly. Almost immediately after the war's end, tensions arose over Allied responsibilities in an occupied Germany and the rules of the postwar global political economy. The United States and Britain favored a system of decentralized market exchange, while the Soviets preferred a system based upon state-directed allocation. These incompatible preferences would divide the global political economy into two hostile spheres of influence, lead to a cold war, and color international affairs for most of the next fifty years.

In this environment, U.S. and British policymakers began to design a framework that would avoid past mistakes, promote international economic cooperation, resolve disputes, and embed liberal economic relations in a nation-state system. Recognizing that laissez-faire market exchange in a nation-state system had contributed to the downward spiral of the global economy, they faced a dilemma of how to embed liberal economic relations in a self-help nation-state system. Their answers involved the construction of cooperative international arrangements that would restrict beggar-thy-neighbor inclinations, rebuild trade, and create an international monetary order based upon a system of stable exchange rates. U.S. military and economic capabilities would be crucial to establishing a politically and militarily secure arena conducive to trade, obtaining cooperation from partners who might disagree on specifics, financing the provision of important collective goods, and supporting institutional arrangements to restrict damaging choices by governments that could unravel economic exchange and cooperation.

LESSONS FROM THE INTERWAR YEARS AND THE POSTWAR DILEMMA

Numerous mistakes of the interwar years had damaged the global economy and led to the renewal of tensions and then war. We will focus on a handful of critical lessons policymakers learned from the experiences of the interwar years. To avoid making the same mistakes in the future, policymakers after the war needed to come to terms with the pathologies of the interwar years that had undermined rational constitutional governance, fed the rise of political extremism, promoted unbridled economic nationalism, led to the unraveling of the global economy, and ultimately brought on the most devastating conflict in human history.

Conducting their historical autopsy, policymakers learned several vital lessons from the descent into global chaos. First, *market exchange is not necessarily self-correcting and self-sustaining.* Laissez-faire economics taught that markets were, indeed, self-correcting and self-sustaining, and this approach had seemed to do pretty well for a period at the end of the nineteenth century and beginning of the twentieth century. Market economies experienced sustained growth as exchange within and across borders expanded. This early success, however, generated false confidence in the ability of markets to discipline unproductive behavior, reward productive activities, and produce inexorable economic growth; governments in market economies grew hesitant to intervene to regulate economic activity. But the experiences of the 1920s and 1930s starkly demonstrated that markets can become dysfunctional.

Market exchange requires government support to ensure that societies can reap the welfare gains from functioning markets. Governments must provide the domestic and international scaffolding that protects efficient market exchange and limits market failure. Domestically, this need suggested a greater role for government regulation of market exchange to constrain economic actors when their choices could seriously damage confidence in markets. Internationally, protecting market exchange would require developing mechanisms for promoting cooperation between governments in order to overcome barriers to exchange across borders and to ensure the provision of the collective goods that reduce obstructions to international exchange. As we have seen, the British had provided many of these collective goods during the 1800s and early 1900s.

This necessity led postwar policymakers to the second major lesson: *Economic nationalism and international economic instability can be devastating if carried to extremes.* Governments had resorted to beggar-thy-neighbor policies to shift the costs of economic adjustment overseas and across borders, and they had used protectionist policies and currency devaluations to protect their domestic producers and labor at the expense of those in other states. These policies of economic nationalism explicitly sought to advance the interests of one state's constituents over another, the health of one state over another. Although the history of trade protection shows that governments sometimes get away with such intervention in market exchange, the experience of the interwar years demonstrated that this strategy can be dangerous, if it invites retaliation that substantially obstructs cross-border exchange. The beggar-thy-neighbor policies of the interwar years provoked tit-for-tat retaliation and construction of formidable barriers to international exchange. These factors undermined the exchange necessary to promote growth, which contributed to worsening international economic instability.

This lesson highlights the tension between sovereignty and interdependence. Domestically, policymakers react to constituent pressures, but with growing interdependence they must become more cognizant of the cross-border influences and consequences of their policy choices. Movement from relatively closed to more open economies means that policymakers cannot select policies in a vacuum. But a puzzle remains: why would tension exist between sovereignty and interdependence if international exchange improves the economic welfare of society? Why would governments adopt policies that are adverse to their society's welfare?

At the core of this puzzle is the time inconsistency dilemma discussed in chapter 8. Ideally, we want our policymakers to develop policies that are time-consistent—good today and good tomorrow—so that they will not face pressures to change these policies from period to period. But creating time-consistent policies can prove difficult, given that politicians want to remain in office—a difficulty that is particularly acute in democratic societies where elections pose regular threats to political survival. Politicians worried about short-term political survival in more representative environments may have to respond to the demands of organized groups by creating policies that can damage the long-term welfare of the larger community. Failure to pass such penny-wise, pound-foolish policies can be political suicide for politicians in these political economies. Ironically, expanded suffrage and interdependence, both considered normatively good objectives, can interact to increase the time inconsistency problem and the provision of policies that damage social welfare. This perverse situation cropped up across the Atlantic economy in the interwar years, creating a democratic trap for policymakers who might have hoped instead to encourage international cooperation and exchange.

This perception of political vulnerability led the postwar policy analysts to a third critical lesson: *The interaction of rational choices by policymakers in a self-help system can produce unexpected and destructive outcomes.* If only one government in the Atlantic economy had faced a time inconsistency problem, perhaps only that society's long-term social welfare would have been damaged, as other governments could select policies that promoted long-term gains. But, in fact, many governments faced such short-term pressures, and so the desire of politicians to remain in office across many states led to the implementation of tit-for-tat, beggar-thy-neighbor policies that severely damaged the global economy. The interaction of rational choices by policymakers of many states in a self-help system produced the interwar crisis.

Recognizing and addressing these harsh lessons from the interwar years posed daunting challenges for the statesmen who met to design a system that would promote growth and exchange in a self-help nation-state system. In order to avoid the traps that had mired their counterparts during the interwar years—and still lurked in the background of any such system—the makers of policy sought the following arrangements:

- To constrain economic nationalism
- To embed liberal economic interactions into the system

- To insulate politicians from pressures for short-term electoral gain that could damage trade and undermine long-term gains
- To ensure the provision of key collective goods and limit social traps

The challenge confronting policymakers was to construct domestic and international mechanisms that could manage the time inconsistency problem, restrain governments from adopting policies that could undermine a liberal economic system, and promote cooperation between governments so market exchange could function. They needed to create both intragovernmental mechanisms to lessen the pressures on democratic governments to respond to constituent pressures and intergovernmental scaffolding to reduce international obstructions to market exchange. Because international trade was not only an important engine of growth, but also a means to translate dislocations across borders, it was essential to design mechanisms that would protect politicians from the temptation to manipulate trade and exchange-rate policies for short-term gains, and, ideally, would enable them to risk promoting policies that invested in the future even if other polices would be more popular in the near term.

The leadership capabilities of the United States were essential to any arrangements that would reflect those lessons and avoid falling into past traps. The inability of the British and the unwillingness of the United States to provide key collective goods during the interwar years had contributed to the beggar-thy-neighbor momentum, but the United States now was far more capable than it had been after World War I, and far more willing to play such a role. Because the U.S. economy dwarfed all others in the aftermath of World War II, attempts by other nation-states to address the lessons of the interwar years would be meaningless and futile if the United States again refused to play the central role of underwriting collective goods and promoting cooperation.

POSTWAR DOMESTIC STRATEGY AND MECHANISM DESIGN

John Maynard Keynes and Franklin Roosevelt were major figures in redesigning the relationship between governments and the economy. Upon taking office in 1933, President Roosevelt tried one policy experiment after another in a determined effort to restart economic growth in the United States and battle the dislocations of the Great Depression. Successful or not, his experiments were effective at redefining state-society relations and the role of government in the economy. These experiments were certainly controversial, provoking debate and some virulent opposition, but voters rewarded Roosevelt for his efforts by reelecting him again and again.

Roosevelt improvised and moved from one policy experiment to another, searching for strategies that would reduce economic hardship and improve the economy. Meanwhile, John

Maynard Keynes, a British economist, advanced a comprehensive framework that challenged prewar economic thinking. The ideas presented in his seminal work, *The General Theory of Employment, Interest, and Money*, made Keynes perhaps the most influential economist of the twentieth century. Keynesian economics dominated the postwar design of capitalist political economies and postwar government economic policy until the 1980s, when it was challenged by the ideas of another economist, Friedrich Hayek.

Before the Great Depression, economic policy in the democratic capitalist economies was dominated by a monetarist approach, which advocated using **monetary policy** to manipulate the supply of money—expanding it to promote growth during an economic downturn or contracting it to restrain inflation during rapid economic expansion. Keynes accepted these strategies as good in the long term, but he argued that the consequences of monetary manip-ulation would kick in too slowly during harsh times. Significant segments of an economy could be exposed to continued severe dislocations while waiting for the alteration in money supply to work its way through an economy. Keynes also worried that these lags exposed politicians to societal demands for redress that could lead to economic nationalism or other detrimental policies over time. The history of the interwar years backed his assertions.

Keynes believed that the design of government institutions and policies could counteract such pressures, protect society from the extremes of such downturns, and insulate politicians from demands that would prove perverse in the long term. This approach would involve a restructuring of state-society bargains (the social contract), as it transformed the role and responsibilities of the state versus those of society. Keynes proposed that governments add other policy tools to their arsenal to complement monetary policy. During particularly dif-ficult times of economic downturn, governments should be more proactive in stimulating economic activity and cushioning those who fell on hard times. Keynes suggested that a countercyclical use of **fiscal policy** (tax and expenditure measures) would kick in faster and supplement monetary policy in priming the economic pump of a society. Countercyclical fiscal policy involves expanding government expenditures and/or reducing taxes during eco-nomic downturns. Keynes also thought that governments should be willing to engage in deficit spending to stimulate their economies during periods of decline. A careful use of fis-cal and monetary policy would allow governments to better manage their economies and would act as a safety valve by moderating economic downturns and preventing them from running their course.

Keynes also advocated the creation of government programs to provide temporary relief for those suffering dislocations, which otherwise could feed discontent and produce de-mands for detrimental economic nationalist policies. Keynesian fiscal and monetary policies sought full employment, but recognizing the impossibility of attaining such a goal and the need for some mobility in labor markets, Keynes advocated safety nets to cushion workers from the costs of adjustment caused by economic change, whether from globalization or some other transformation in productive relations. This approach led to the rise of unemployment assistance and social insurance programs to protect workers and their families from economic changes beyond their control. These programs shifted some of the costs of adjustment due to economic change from the individual to the broader society. Instead of leaving individuals to bear the full brunt of economic dislocation, governments could redistribute part of the burden by taxing their societies to provide some form of temporary social insurance. In their programs of experimentation, Roosevelt and leaders of other governments had already adopted some social insurance policies, but Keynes provided a systematic argument that linked monetary, fiscal, and social welfare policy.

The transformation of government's role in the economy from simply manipulating money supply to the far more activist and interventionist use of fiscal and social welfare policy to manage individual risk represented a tremendous shift in governance and state-society relations. The social contract was redefined. Both a government's obligations to its citizens and the citizens' expectations of their government were radically reshaped.

POSTWAR INTERNATIONAL STRATEGY AND MECHANISM DESIGN

Policymakers recognized a need for international governmental organizations (IGOs) to ensure the provision of collective goods beneficial to growth and international exchange, limit the social traps of the self-help nation-state system, and embed liberalism within this system. These organizations would complement the domestic strategies of Keynesian economic management and social safety nets, working as safeguards in case domestic strategies to protect liberal economic relations failed to insulate politicians from pressures to adopt beggar-thy-neighbor policies. By building IGOs to promote cooperation, policymakers sought to avert these dangerous choices by governments. But would sovereign governments delegate enough of their authority to make such international organizations useful? Constructing IGOs could help by creating specialized networks of communication between governments, promoting greater familiarity between policymakers of different states, offering formal complaint and adjudication mechanisms, and developing professional bureaucracies within governments that had a stake in the objectives of the international organization.

Again, leadership by the United States was critical to the construction of postwar IGOs. While the rest of world emerged from World War II physically and economically devastated, the United States left the battlefield with incomparable military, technological, and economic superiority. In 1945 the United States produced 40 percent of the world's total output of goods and services, and it held 574 million out of the total 965 million ounces of gold in all nations' official reserves. This huge gap in capabilities, and the need of many nations for U.S. economic and security assistance, endowed the United States with unparalleled and disproportionate influence in the global arena.

The period after World War I had demonstrated that capabilities alone were not sufficient to ensure leadership, willingness and interest were needed as well. Unlike their reluctance in the interwar years, U.S. policymakers now embraced the challenge of designing a framework for the global political economy. This new willingness to exercise leadership was not based on altruistic good nature, but on a self-interested desire to promote a system of global capitalism and liberal economic relations that would best mesh with U.S. domestic economic activity and U.S. security interests. The experiences of the interwar years had educated U.S. policymakers about the need for such leadership to protect liberal economic exchange. So they threw their resources aggressively into the construction of a postwar system that would avoid the mishaps that had followed World War I. Moreover, U.S. and British policymakers recognized the military prowess of the Soviet Union, and they wanted to design postwar global economic arrangements to counter the growing communist threat on the horizon. They sought to promote global economic arrangements that were conducive to democratic capitalist political-economic systems.

The United States emerged from World War II as a major creditor nation, just as it had done in the aftermath of World War I. Because the wealth and productive capabilities of the United States had bankrolled the fight against the Axis powers, the Allied nations once again owed substantial war debts to the United States. But U.S. policymakers had learned an important lesson about the need for liquidity to rebuild economies and the negative consequences of excessive debt and reparations for reconstruction and economic activity. President Truman moved quickly to forgive the war debts and reject reparations, and he would soon support massive capital lending and rebuilding grants to many war-torn nations.

Displaying leadership early on, the United States hosted international negotiations in the midst of World War II to discuss the design of the postwar global economic system. Bretton Woods, New Hampshire, played host to some of these meetings, where negotiations and agreements led to the framework for what became known as the Bretton Woods system. The United States and the United Kingdom dominated the negotiations, as policymakers discussed how to construct a market-oriented, nondiscriminatory trading system that would reduce barriers to trade and restrain governments from resorting to protectionist tactics; how to build a monetary system that would manage pressures on trading mechanisms and balance of payments; and how to promote reconstruction and development.

Active leadership and commitment of resources by the United States was essential to any agreement that hoped to survive the stresses of a self-help nation-state system and the pressures that could arise within domestic political economies. The design of the postwar system, begun at Bretton Woods, is best reflected in the three IGOs that became the foundation of the postwar global political economy. The General Agreement on Tariffs and Trade (GATT), the International Monetary Fund (IMF), and the World Bank constituted the three organizational and institutional cornerstones that would embed liberalism in a global political economy comprised of nation-states.

Trade and the GATT

Discussions at Bretton Woods recognized the importance of trade for economic expansion and a healthy postwar system that could avoid the pitfalls of the interwar years. Negotiations focused upon reducing barriers to trade and promoting its expansion. After some disagreements and debates, negotiators compromised and built a rule-driven system that promoted nondiscriminatory trading arrangements and initially emphasized the reduction of tariffs. Because it is more robust in the face of changes, a system based upon rules that guide government policymaking differs from a system that targets quantities in trading relations.

Tariffs affect the prices of imported goods by adding a tax on top of the price. If tariffs on imported goods become sufficiently large, they can influence consumer choices in favor of domestic goods. Ironically, economic theory suggests that the focus on tariff reduction and the neglect of other obstructions to trade—such as quotas, subsidies, and discriminatory trade blocs—target the least offensive government intervention and leave the other, more troublesome interventions alone. Tariffs give domestic producers an advantage in the domestic market, but those producers do not usually retain the proceeds of the tariff. Tariffs are taxes that governments collect and usually redistribute in the form of government programs; at least part of the penalty that domestic consumers pay as a tariff is returned to the broader society. Other trade interventions, such as quotas, allow domestic producers to keep the consumers' cost of the trade intervention; economists call such interventions a complete **dead-weight loss** to the economy.

In the past, governments employed trade policy to discriminate among potential trading partners—to exclude some and include others. Trade policy was a foreign policy tool to strengthen alliances and extend special privileges, but it also created distortions that limited the gains from trade and the growth of interdependence. **Nondiscriminatory trading arrangements,** in contrast, seek to inhibit governments from using trade to extend a privilege to one country but not to others. They seek to protect the tools of trade policy from political manipulation, which can create economic distortions in international exchange that can translate into structural inefficiencies in productive endeavors and detract from the economic gains from trade.

The willingness of U.S. policymakers to promote freer trade represented a significant shift from the past, in which U.S. trade policy had built on a history of protectionism to shelter U.S. markets and promote the growth of U.S. manufactures. By 1900, the United States had become an economy with significant concentrations in manufacturing and service, which looked to export markets, yet policy change lagged behind. Only after the onset of the Great Depression did U.S. policymakers recognize the pitfalls of this beggar-thy-neighbor protectionism and the importance of more open trade for domestic economic welfare. Still, protectionist forces remained strong in the United States and hampered the ability of Congress to reduce tariffs. In 1934, as a roundabout strategy, Congress passed the Reciprocal Trade Agreements Act (RTAA), which delegated to the executive branch authority to reduce tariffs by up to 50 percent through bilateral negotiations that extracted similar concessions from other states. Since this authority did not require the president to submit a bilateral agreement to Congress for approval, the delegation of authority provided congressional members with some insulation from protectionist pressures.

Negotiations begun at Bretton Woods produced an agreement to form the International Trade Organization (ITO), but the ITO proved unacceptable to Congress because it reached far beyond the narrow bounds of trade policy to include mandates for full employment and economic development. A temporary agreement in 1947 produced a substitute for the ITO called the General Agreement on Tariffs and Trade (GATT). Twenty-three states initially signed the agreement. The GATT provided a multilateral framework of rules to promote the nondiscriminatory expansion of trade and to govern what governments did to affect trade.

Lower tariffs on manufactured goods dominated GATT negotiations from the beginning. This priority reflected the economic and political strengths of the early GATT signatories, the industrialized states, which enjoyed advantages in the production and export of manufactured goods but were less competitive in the production and export of agricultural goods. However, since farmers in many industrialized nations enjoyed significant political power, negotiators were persuaded to develop a system that lowered barriers to manufactured goods while allowing protectionist assistance to remain for agricultural sectors. The Common Agricultural Policy (CAP) of what is today the European Union is a prime example of such a policy; it is a legacy of the political power of farmers in European states. With CAP, a significant portion of EU resources subsidizes inefficient European agricultural production. Other industrialized nations, including the United States, also subsidize agricultural production, albeit to a lesser degree. The exclusion of agriculture in GATT's early years thus discriminated against farmers in developing states—and this bias continues today.

The GATT was built around three core strategies: the use of multilateralism and most favored nation status (MFN) to reduce tariffs, recurring rounds of negotiations to address barriers to trade, and dispute resolution. These strategies seem to have paid off, as tariff levels fell dramatically, trade expanded, and governments began to bring their disputes to the adjudication processes of the international organization rather than resorting to unilateral response. In 1995 the GATT was replaced by the World Trade Organization (WTO), which had 148 members as of February 2005. Today, the WTO and the world trading system face renewed challenges, as states retain their sovereign ability to act unilaterally and to defect from the principles established under the GATT.

Multilateralism and MFN

The adoption of multilateralism was a significant departure from the bilateralism that had dominated trade policy in the 1800s and early 1900s. Bilateral trade agreements (those between two nations) tend to decrease the transparency of negotiations and to increase the chance for discrimination. The ability to use bilateral trade policy to discriminate across states—to include some and exclude others—encouraged the use of trade as a tool of alliance. But bilateralism was an inefficient strategy for expanding trade even when used in a nondiscriminatory manner. If the objective was to expand trade by extending identical privileges to many nations, a multilateral agreement could accomplish more than many bilateral agreements linked by sequential bargaining, one bilateral negotiation after another. With many parties participating, a multilateral negotiation offered greater transparency, less vulnerability to secretive manipulations, and lower likelihood of special targeted provisions that could discriminate among states.

The mechanism of most favored nation (MFN), discussed in chapter 8, sat at the heart of the multilateral GATT. Very simply, a trade concession to one signatory of the GATT became a trade concession to all the signatories who enjoyed MFN status. MFN transformed bilateral agreements between GATT members into multilateral concessions that diffused across all GATT signatories with MFN status. For example, the United States and the United Kingdom were signatories of GATT. If, in a bilateral negotiation, the United States reduced tariffs on British steel in exchange for a British tariff reduction on U.S. autos, the United States then had to apply that tariff rate to the steel of all other members of GATT that enjoyed MFN status and the United Kingdom was obliged to apply the same tariff rate to autos from other GATT signatories with MFN status. Multilateralism and MFN limited the use of trade concessions as discriminatory tools of foreign policy and constrained the prospects for reemergence of the discriminatory trade blocs that had damaged trade during the interwar years.

Recurring Rounds of Negotiations

Policymakers hoped that multiple rounds of trade negotiations would create an inertia that built upon and reinforced the success of the original GATT. Some label this the bicycle approach: if you stop pedaling, you fall off, but if you continue to pedal, you gain speed and ability. Multiple rounds of negotiations target a series of gradual changes instead of a single large shift. Creating a coalition among a large number of negotiating parties to support a single dramatic shift generally proves more difficult—perhaps impossible—than obtaining agreement for smaller incremental shifts. Over time, however, a series of incremental changes can produce dramatic shifts. Frequent rounds of negotiations can also improve relations across borders by building reputation, trust, and familiarity. GATT and its demands for frequent negotiations led to the development of professional domestic and international bureaucracies with personal and professional commitments to GATT's success. Policymakers from different states could use their personal and professional ties to help sidetrack protectionist pressures by promoting discussions and compromise at times when protectionist pressures arose.

Multiple rounds of negotiations produced significant tariff reductions. Eight rounds of negotiations occurred under GATT, beginning with the Geneva Round in 1947 and ending with the Uruguay Round, which concluded in 1994 (see table 9.1). Another, the Doha Round of the WTO, began recently. The first five rounds of GATT negotiations were restricted to reducing tariffs, while other barriers to trade remained untouched. The average tariff at the end of the Uruguay Round stood at 4 percent, which represents a huge decline in tariff barriers since the beginning of GATT. Meanwhile, the scope of negotiations has expanded to include nontariff barriers (NTBs) as well.

Dispute Resolution

The GATT and WTO have established mechanisms to highlight disagreements and adjudicate disputes among members—public processes created by international agreement. Formal dispute mechanisms shine the light of day upon disagreements. If a government concludes that its producers are being slighted, having a dispute process in place provides an alternative to immediately resorting to retaliatory policies that could further damage trade. The GATT/WTO adjudication process may find no damage or inappropriate activity, but if the process discovers a violation of the GATT/WTO agreements, it can recommend reme-

TABLE 9.1	GATT and WTO Rounds of Negotiations	
Year	**Round**	**Subject covered**
1947	Geneva	Tariffs
1949	Annecy	Tariffs
1951	Torquay	Tariffs
1956	Geneva	Tariffs
1960–1961	Dillon	Tariffs
1964–1967	Kennedy	Tariffs, antidumping measures, development
1973–1979	Tokyo	Tariffs, nontariff barriers
1986–1994	Uruguay	Tariffs, nontariff measures, rules, services, intellectual property, agriculture, textiles, dispute settlement, WTO creation
2001	Doha (WTO)	Agriculture, services, intellectual property, nontariff barriers, investment, technology transfer, regional trade agreements, transparency

dies. Participation in the dispute process endows such penalties with legitimacy and inhibits the offending party from then engaging in tit-for-tat retaliation. More often than not, however, states found by the dispute process to be in violation of the GATT/WTO rules remove the offending policies before the imposition of penalties.

Dispute adjudication mechanisms can help to establish reputation in the international community. If a formal adjudication process finds a state in violation of the GATT/WTO rules, this finding generates reputation costs. Governments generally resist being defined as pariah states, or scofflaws, in an adjudication process they have supported by signing an international agreement. Finally, a formal dispute resolution process allows time for disagreements to cool and be negotiated rather than escalating to beggar-thy-neighbor policy contests in the heat of anger.

NTBs, Escape Clauses, and Regional Trade Agreements

Despite the focus on tariffs, many NTBs such as quotas, voluntary export restraints (VERs), and structural impediments present significant obstacles to trade. A quota caps the amount of a particular commodity that can be imported. VERs are bilateral agreements wherein one state and its producers voluntarily promise to limit exports to another state. Of course, the term *voluntary* is open to interpretation: when the Japanese government and its automobile manufacturers first agreed to limit their exports to the United States at the urging of the Reagan administration, the implicit understanding was that if the Japanese refused, the U.S. Congress was likely to impose far harsher, nonvoluntary restrictions. Assuming there is consumer demand, thus artificially limiting the supply of a commodity increases its price. Domestic producers benefit from such limits on foreign imports, as unmet consumer demand will turn to domestic products even if consumers prefer the foreign product. Structural impediments are aspects of an economy that may limit the supply of goods available to consumers. Distribution networks, cultural practices, warehouse availability, exclusive contracting arrangements, and special financing arrangements that favor domestic producers over foreign producers can all influence the supply of foreign goods.

In a shift to broaden its reach, the last three rounds of GATT negotiations included discussions about NTBs. The Tokyo Round created rules to guide governments' use of tools such as countervailing duties and antidumping restrictions. The Uruguay Round broached issues of intellectual property protection, trade in services, financial liberalization, structural impediments to trade, and agricultural and textile trade. The Doha Round of the WTO continues this trend, reflecting awareness that significant barriers to trade persist and recognizing the changing role of developing countries.

Governments use other tools to intervene in trade, sometimes aiding a politically influential economic sector by means of **subsidies,** which are government financial assistance to producers. In many cases, absent the subsidy, producers would be forced to sell their products at above-market prices in order to earn a profit; but then consumers would not purchase those products, and the producers would lose, or perhaps go out of business.

Alternatively, these producers could sell their products at market prices, but if their costs of production exceeded the market price, again they would lose. A subsidy allows such producers to remain in production. In other cases, competitive industries may receive subsidies simply because they are politically effective. In both situations, taxpayers foot the bill—the many subsidize a few.

Policymakers have also resorted to the threat of antidumping investigations to discriminate against foreign producers. **Dumping,** which occurs when a producer sells its products below its production costs, is predatory behavior designed to drive competitors out of business and grab market share; after dumping has damaged or eliminated the competition, the dumping producer raises its prices. Dumping is defined under GATT and WTO rules as an unfair trade practice, which governments can penalize. A government must first begin an antidumping investigation to determine whether dumping has occurred. This process involves determining what the real costs of production are for the foreign producer and what constitutes fair value—which is problematic because labor costs, production techniques, and other inputs to production vary significantly from one state to another. Since the process includes such ambiguities, however, policymakers can manipulate antidumping investigations so as to favor domestic producers regardless of whether or not dumping has actually occurred. Domestic producers who recognize this systematic bias increasingly use the threat of antidumping investigations to deter foreign competitors or to force them to raise their prices. If a foreign producer receives notification of an antidumping investigation and realizes that it is likely to lose the investigation after paying significant legal costs, it may simply withdraw from the market or change its pricing structure to avoid the process.

Quotas, subsidies, and other NTBs can provoke retaliation by governments in the form of **countervailing duties (CVDs),** which, under GATT and WTO rules, impose legitimate tariffs to penalize foreign producers who have received unfair government assistance and, as a consequence, are damaging domestic producers who would otherwise be legitimately competitive. Because they assess punitive damages, CVDs are a legitimate response to protect domestic industries from such damaging foreign intervention, but they can also be used strategically to create barriers to trade. Policymakers have found that applying a loose definition of a subsidy allows them to claim the existence of a subsidy where one may not actually exist, and then to apply a CVD to protect their own producers.

GATT (and now the WTO) have allowed governments to protect their domestic industries under special circumstances by means of **escape clauses** that permit temporary protection of an industry to provide time for adjustment and to ease dislocations. The need for inclusion of an escape clause demonstrates again the tension between interdependence and sovereignty. Without such loopholes, would states want to risk becoming parties to agreements like GATT? Unfortunately, however, governments sometimes abuse these escape-clause mechanisms in order to circumvent the spirit of more open trade.

More recently, **regional trading agreements** and **free-trade areas** are affecting trade by creating blocs of states that agree to lower or eliminate barriers to trade between members.

Such agreements combine multiple smaller markets into larger unified markets. Although this practice discriminates between members of the agreement and nonmembers, which is seemingly antithetical to the MFN principle, GATT provided, and the WTO continues to provide, exclusions for such agreements if they conform to certain requirements—for example, no increase in the tariffs imposed against nonmembers. GATT's sanction of what appears to be discrimination in these cases reflects some legitimate confusion about what free-trade areas and regional trading agreements are likely to produce in the long term. They may expand aggregate world trade as trade increases between members of the agreement. If they create significant new trade between members while only marginally diverting trade between members and nonmembers, they may increase consumption possibilities for consumers without seriously damaging specialization of production and social efficiency. But they may instead damage long-term social welfare if they significantly divert trade between members and nonmembers, distort production structures, and embed structural inefficiencies in the system. These potential dangers lie at the heart of controversies over such agreements.

The European Union (EU) is the largest example of a regional trading agreement, with twenty-five member states. The North American Free Trade Agreement (NAFTA) between Canada, Mexico, and the United States is another example of a free-trade area. In 2005 the Central American Free Trade Area, or CAFTA, expanded free-trade arrangements in Latin America, and ongoing discussions hold the promise of enlarging NAFTA by bringing in new members from Latin America. The United States also partners with Israel in a free-trade agreement. The Andean Pact creates a regional trading agreement between Colombia and Venezuela. MERCOSUR eliminated barriers between Argentina, Brazil, Paraguay, and Uruguay. Agreements between states to create regional markets are appearing in Asia and Africa as well. This ongoing expansion of regional trade agreements magnifies the importance of determining whether such agreements are trade-creating and liberalizing, or trade-diverting and protectionist.

Monetary Arrangements and the IMF

At Bretton Woods, Harry Dexter White led the U.S. mission and John Maynard Keynes headed the British mission. White and Keynes sought to balance their respective states' priorities in constructing a system of stable monetary relations, which they viewed as an essential handmaiden to trade and economic expansion. Such a system needed to manage balance-of-payments problems, insulate the exchange-rate mechanism from short-term political manipulations, provide an orderly means to adjust exchange rates when currencies were fundamentally over- or undervalued, limit currency risk, and constrain the international transmission of financial shocks.

Many systems were plausible, but White and Keynes faced the task of producing an agreement that balanced a set of objectives that were not fully compatible. Keynes and the British sought, first and foremost, a system that promoted full employment. The British worried that unemployment could become the adjustment mechanism for balance-of-payments problems, and they feared that idle workers were a source of political instability. Keynes argued for a system that allowed governments the latitude to restrict capital mobility, erect trade restrictions, and change their exchange rates if necessary to promote full employment.

U.S. negotiators sought instead to promote capital mobility, limit the ability of states to shift their exchange rates, create an international oversight mechanism to oversee changes in exchange rates, and link the construction of an international monetary system to the **principle of nondiscrimination** in trade. The latter objective was a direct blow to the British imperial preference system, which provided Commonwealth states and colonies preferred access to each other's markets—a discriminatory trade restriction, from the U.S. perspective.

Demands upon Monetary System Design

Let's stop and ask, what is a monetary system? A set of arrangements, rules, and conventions that govern monetary and financial relations between states, a monetary system specifies what policy instruments governments may use, what those instruments can target, and when they can be used. Policymakers generally prefer a monetary regime with rules and conventions to chaos, but, as the interwar years demonstrated, policymakers can rationally produce chaos. The breakdown in monetary relations during the interwar years produced a system with only one rule: governments can use any instrument or policy to intervene in monetary relations, and at any time. This was the worst form of monetary system—one that designers of the new system sought to avoid.

The U.S. and British negotiators considered three key questions in the design of a monetary regime: (1) what role would exchange rates play in the balance-of-payments adjustment process? (2) what would be the reserve asset? and (3) how much capital mobility should be allowed or encouraged? Let's first consider the role of exchange rates in the balance-of-payments adjustment process. Recall that the balance of payments reflects a state's economic interactions with other states; it is an accounting of all the goods, services, and capital exported and imported across national borders. At any moment, a state's balance of payments is likely to be in surplus or in deficit, but a balance-of-payments position cannot be permanently in surplus or in deficit—it adjusts over time, tending toward a long-run equilibrium. Often, such adjustments are gradual and relatively seamless, but occasionally a persistent balance-of-payments deficit or surplus signals a fundamental imbalance in an economy and demands more drastic adjustment, manipulation, and intervention to restore balance.

A variety of mechanisms can produce an adjustment in the balance of payments. These mechanisms include changes in domestic prices, in employment, or in exchange rates. In an adjustable-exchange-rate system, movements in the exchange rate alter relative prices in the system, which changes the prices of one state's goods and services vis-à-vis those of other states, thus influencing consumption choices and moving the system toward equilibrium. A fixed-exchange-rate system forecloses this adjustment mechanism, forcing the balance-of-payments adjustment on either domestic prices or employment.

For example, a balance-of-payments deficit signals a relatively expensive currency in a fixed-exchange-rate system, but the price of the currency cannot shift to effect the balance-of-payments adjustment. This situation puts downward pressures on domestic prices in the economy with the relatively expensive currency (Hume's reduced money supply chasing the same quantity of domestic goods). If domestic prices quickly adjust downward, domestic price deflation generates the balance-of-payments adjustment as the cost of domestic goods and services becomes relatively cheaper in domestic and global markets, which prompts a shift in consumption and helps to adjust the balance of payments. If domestic prices adjust downward too slowly, however, the price of domestic commodities remains relatively expensive compared to foreign commodities. Sales of domestic commodities suffer, and domestic producers must lay off employees or reduce wages—either of which actions reduces consumption and leads to the balance-of-payments adjustment.

The second question for design of a monetary regime asked, what would be the reserve asset in the system? Obviously, gold was the reserve asset under the gold standard, but in the early to mid-1800s, some governments had opted for bimetallism, wherein gold and silver served as reserve assets. Postwar policymakers were wary of a return to the pre–World War I gold standard, because economic expansion had outpaced the growth in the supply of gold in the late 1800s and led to price deflation, which produced excessive hardship in economic sectors such as agricultural commodities.

Third, how much capital mobility should be allowed? Should capital flow freely across borders, or should states erect barriers to capital mobility, such as capital controls, exchange restrictions, export and import licensing, or other regulatory restrictions? What should be the connection between national financial markets? Few state barriers to capital mobility had existed during the globalization of the late 1800s, when global capital sought out investment opportunities across borders, financed development in emerging states such as the United States and Argentina, enabled investors to diversify their portfolios, and imposed penalties upon states and their economic enterprises that disappointed global capital. This flow of global capital promoted rapid economic change and development. But the interwar years had also demonstrated the downside to high capital mobility and dense connectivity of national capital markets. The New York markets attracted capital from around the world that could have rebuilt economies after World War I, but, instead, this flow of capital fed a financial bubble that eventually burst and shocked capital markets worldwide.

As Keynes, White, and their delegations met, they recognized that a robust exchange-rate system needed the following qualities: (1) the ability to effect relative price adjustments to address fundamental disturbances; (2) compatibility with the pursuit of robust monetary policies; and (3) the capacity to contain market pressures. Inevitably, a state will suffer economic disturbances—such as inflation, chronic unemployment, stagnation, and so on—many of which can adversely affect its balance-of-payments position. The most troubling of such disturbances is one that persists over time; it is called a **fundamental disequilibrium,** as the balance-of-payments mechanism fails to adjust. A fundamental disequilibrium signals that for some reason the prices of a large number of domestically produced goods and services in a state's tradable sector are overvalued, which means that changes in a large number of domestic prices will be required to address the underlying problem.

States and societies can effect such relative price adjustments with a variety of instruments. They can erect protectionist barriers to increase the relative costs of foreign commodities. They can reduce wages or lay off workers, which changes consumption. They can increase efficiency and productivity, producing more for the same labor and effectively cutting prices on those goods. Or, they can adjust their currency's exchange rate and devalue, which effects a relative price adjustment across all prices. But pushing governments toward trade protections to address fundamental disturbances would be dysfunctional if trade was to sit at the heart of the postwar global economy. The British commitment to full employment limited the use of labor markets to address fundamental disturbances, which left exchange-rate adjustment as the policy instrument of choice to address a fundamental disequilibrium—but how much change should be anticipated, when, and how often? Too frequent changes can create currency risk and threaten expectations in trade. Legitimizing exchange-rate manipulation to address a fundamental imbalance also creates greater opportunities for policymakers to use the exchange rate as a beggar-thy-neighbor policy tool.

To create a robust adjustable-exchange-rate mechanism means balancing the tension between the gains from stability and the gains from flexibility. How do policymakers commit to monetary policies and restrain the temptation to realign their exchange rates to address problems other than fundamental imbalances? If a state can too easily realign its currency's value, it is always tempted to force adjustment costs overseas through the exchange-rate mechanism, whether the underlying problems are fundamental or temporary. Robust monetary policies are those that withstand such pressures and commit to effecting shifts in relative prices via the exchange-rate mechanism only under severe dislocations. This commitment requires developing an ability to resist pressures to manipulate the exchange rate. But resisting those pressures can disappoint constituents and threaten political survival—a time consistency problem. Policymakers have therefore developed a variety of strategies to tie their hands and signal commitment to robust monetary policy, including central bank independence, currency control boards, development of a reputation for changing rates only when faced with a fundamental disequilibrium, and transparency.

Financial markets and societal pressures will eventually challenge even the most robust monetary and exchange-rate policies, however. It is then that we can discover how robust a government's commitment is to those policies and whether it can resist or contain the market and societal pressures that challenge its monetary and exchange-rate policies. Today, policymakers hope that traders in currency markets will remain indifferent to the value of their currencies. But if currency traders think that a fundamental imbalance may exist—signaled by persistent balance-of-payments problems, high unemployment, inflation, or some other macroeconomic indicator—they may shed their indifference and bet against the government's commitment to the price of its currency. With such challenges, traders are betting that the currency is over- or undervalued. They sell a currency if they believe it is overvalued, going to depreciate and lose value; they buy a currency if they think it is undervalued, going to appreciate and gain value. If traders sell or buy enough of a currency, they can change the supply of that currency in currency markets and effect a real change in its price. Then the question becomes whether a government will attempt to defend the value of its currency, and whether it has the capacity to do so.

The Bretton Woods Monetary System

The Keynes and White missions wanted to limit the incentives and abilities of governments to export negative domestic economic conditions to other states through monetary instruments. They produced two plans for postwar monetary arrangements—a British plan and a U.S. plan—both of which sought to use institutional design to insulate monetary relations from domestic political pressures. The plans overlapped, but they also differed significantly. The eventual reconciliation of the differences across the Keynes and White plans laid the foundation for the Articles of Agreement of the International Monetary Fund (IMF) and the postwar system. The U.S.-British compromise produced a system that differed from the gold standard in three critical characteristics: (1) a central coordinating organization, the IMF, with an ability to extend credit to finance balance-of-payments shortfalls and a charge to exercise oversight of national economies; (2) an adjustable-pegged exchange rate; and (3) accepted limitations on capital mobility.

First, the gold standard had been constructed from the bottom-up. States opted into the gold standard through decentralized policy choices, government by government, and not as a result of a compromise formulated by negotiators at an international conference and coordinated by an international organization. No international organization oversaw the gold standard to smooth out differences between states. No international organization existed for use by policymakers to try to prevent anarchy in monetary relations. Policymakers met instead at ad hoc international conferences or in the back rooms of the Bank of England when crises loomed, but there was no established organizational framework or expertise to help governments avoid such crises or provide crisis management. The IMF was created to avert some of the problems of too much decentralization, to provide an established framework and staff to supply national policymakers with expertise and knowledge, to offer a forum with rules and procedures that could help member states discuss threats and coordinate their actions, and to try to limit the economic nationalist proclivities of policymakers in an anarchical nation-state system.

The IMF's Articles of Agreement directed the organization to reduce monetary obstacles to trade, exercise surveillance over member states' economic policies, and extend financing to cover temporary balance-of-payments shortfalls. Providing a mechanism to finance temporary balance-of-payments deficits helped to insulate governments from the pressures to manipulate currency values and domestic economic policies. Temporary shortfalls were assumed to be self-correcting, but some time might be required for the pendulum to swing back and restore balance. The short-term financing facility sought to offer governments some breathing space and so constrain them from resorting to actions such as tariffs, impediments to trade, and predatory devaluation to redress their balance-of-payments deficits.

Temporary financing was extended to a state based upon a formula tied to its state quota, which was determined by economic size. States faced limits upon their ability to draw upon their IMF quotas; access to the IMF financing facility became progressively more difficult as account deficits grew larger. This limiting factor gave the IMF a lever to discipline states with persistent balance-of-payments deficits. As a condition to access this financing, the IMF could ask a state to address specific national economic problems that the IMF thought were contributing to the state's persistent balance-of-payments problems. This factor is called **conditionality,** as it imposes conditions upon the extension of further credit. To impose the right conditions required expertise and information about the member economies and their economic policies, which required the IMF to exercise surveillance over its members.

The second difference from the gold standard's fixed exchange rate was an adjustable-pegged exchange rate, established by the IMF's Articles of Agreement. Many adjustable-rate systems are possible, from freely floating rates to more rigid adjustable pegs. Seeking to limit instability, the IMF's Articles of Agreement created an adjustable peg, which allowed adjustments in a currency's exchange rate but only under unusual circumstances. The Bretton Woods system permitted exchange-rate adjustment when a state faced a fundamental disequilibrium in its economy and balance of payments, but only after notifying the IMF for changes up to a 10 percent devaluation; larger changes required IMF approval. Providing an orderly and legitimate process for a government encountering a fundamental disequilibrium to adjust exchange rates recognized that governments needed to sustain growth and promote employment. Devaluation was preferable to chronic unemployment or economic ills that could prompt unilateral beggar-thy-neighbor policies. Orderly devaluation with international oversight was an escape mechanism for governments that also restrained the tendency of national policymakers to view monetary shifts as an easy way out of domestic economic ills. Notifying the IMF prior to devaluation created costs for governments and encouraged states to resort to devaluation only after trying other policies. For the most part, this strategy seemed to work, as states hesitated to devalue under the Bretton Woods arrangements.

The IMF's Articles of Agreement provided for an adjustable peg but also sought to limit exchange-rate volatility and keep currencies within a narrow trading range. The Articles of Agreement directed the United States to declare a **par value** of the dollar, to fix the dollar's value to gold (one ounce gold = $35). Other countries then declared their currencies' par values in terms of gold or of a currency convertible to gold, such as the dollar. The Articles of Agreement required governments to maintain their exchange rates within ±1 percent of their par values. The United States committed to supplying the collective good of convertibility, convincing others to willingly hold dollars as a reserve asset as long as they believed in the U.S. commitment to convertibility. This arrangement, and the commitment by the United States to convert dollars into gold upon demand, made the dollar the leading currency and reserve asset in the system.

The dollar's prominent role gave the United States advantages in the postwar system, but it also constrained U.S. policymakers. The United States could run balance-of-payments deficits as long as others were willing to hold dollars in place of gold. Other governments and the IMF ignored U.S. balance-of-payments deficits, as the dollars flowing from the United States created reserves and liquidity abroad; the system depended upon dollars for liquidity. The desire of others to build dollar reserves allowed U.S. policymakers to escape the discipline of the balance-of-payments mechanism and enabled the United States to finance its deficits at relatively low interest rates and without much exchange-rate risk. On the downside, the latitude of U.S. policymakers to change their currency's par value was far more limited than that of policymakers in other states. All other states set their currencies' par values in dollars, so any change in the dollar's price would change prices throughout the system, potentially creating price instability internationally and threatening economic activity. As the leading reserve currency, the U.S. could turn to the exchange-rate mechanism only as a last resort to address domestic economic dislocation. Power and privilege have their reward, but also their price.

The third difference from the gold standard was the new monetary system's willingness to limit capital mobility. White favored full capital mobility, but Keynes argued for the ability of governments to restrict capital flows that could create destabilizing volatility and threaten balance-of-payments positions and full employment. The preferences of the British prevailed. They pointed to the 1929 New York financial shocks, which had quickly spread across the globe, to emphasize the destabilizing potential of volatile capital flows. They also worried that capital outflows in the aftermath of the war could drain an economy of the liquidity necessary to rebuild and generate employment. To promote reconstruction, governments were likely to adopt inflationary policies that could provoke capital outflows if holders of capital lost confidence in a currency's value. But governments that needed to stimulate growth and promote employment had little choice, as opting for more fiscally conservative policies would risk deflation. With governments unwilling to constrain government expenditures and with barriers to changing exchange rates, unrestrained capital flows would operate as the adjustment mechanism in the balance of payments. This situation would threaten employment. The Bretton Woods agreement therefore accepted, even encouraged, constraints on capital mobility to avoid losses in the capital account, regulate the unsettling downside of financial markets, encourage growth, and promote the full-employment goal of the postwar social contract in many nations.

Development and the World Bank

The World Bank supplied the third pillar of intergovernmental cooperation in the postwar global economy. The World Bank is an intergovernmental financial organization like the IMF, but with a different role in the postwar system. The IMF was created to manage international monetary arrangements and promote stability in the exchange-rate mechanism, while the World Bank was to provide economic aid and technical expertise in rebuilding war-damaged economies and promoting the development and expansion of economic infrastructure in developing economies. Economic expansion, while offering the prospect of being better able to work and feed families over time, hides a lot of ills that can push politicians to adopt policies that safeguard their short-term political survival but damage society in the long run. Initially, the Bank focused primarily on the reconstruction of the European and Japanese economies damaged by war, and only secondarily on promoting economic growth in the developing nations. This priority was due partly to the geopolitical importance of the European and Japanese political economies in the emerging tensions between the U.S. and Soviet spheres of influence, and partly to the relative absence of developing nations on the scene due to the persistence of colonial empires after the war. Despite fighting a war to make the world safe for democracy, U.S. policymakers looked the other way as the European powers reasserted their prewar colonial claims and authority.

The World Bank was built around three financing facilities, or windows, each designed to extend loans to promote development. The main lending window is the International Bank for Reconstruction and Development (IBRD), which targets middle-income economies and was designed primarily to aid in postwar reconstruction by supplying assistance to stimulate economic development. Today, the IBRD borrows in capital markets and loans capital to developing states at a small markup that is needed to help cover the World Bank's operating expenses. Because investors view the World Bank as an excellent risk, the IBRD can borrow at the best rates and then make loans to developing nations at rates far below what they could expect if borrowing on their own. A second and smaller window, the International Finance Corporation (IFC) also borrows in markets and then loans to emerging economies. A third window, the International Development Assistance (IDA), extends loans or grants to states facing the most difficult barriers to growth. Today, approximately 70 percent of IDA funds are awarded as grants.

The multilateral resources of the World Bank proved too limited to meet the reconstruction needs of the European and Japanese political economies, given the immediate problems of countering economic dissension in their polities and the prospects of domestic communist parties succeeding at the ballot box. Under President Truman, the United States therefore bypassed the multilateral mechanism of the World Bank and filled the gap in these regions with a tremendous infusion of bilateral economic and technical assistance called the **Marshall Plan.** This targeted U.S. effort left the multilateral World Bank to shift its emphasis from reconstruction to development. With the explosion of independence movements, the dismantling of colonial empires, and the emergence of newly sovereign states in the developing regions of the world, the difficulties of the task facing the World Bank multiplied. For approximately sixty years, the World Bank has been the key institution in funneling financial assistance and expertise to developing nations.

Challenges of Development

The World Bank faced the most daunting task of all the postwar liberal economic IGOs. Unlike the GATT and IMF, which have managed economic tensions and relations between states, the World Bank targets the micro foundations of economic activity within states. It seeks to transform those foundations into healthy, developed economies so that their governments can more easily cooperate to create harmonious relations across states. The implicit assumptions in undertaking this task were that greater disparities across states placed greater strains and demands upon cooperation, and that promoting growth would reduce such disparities and improve the conditions for cooperation. Unfortunately, the problems addressed by the GATT and by IMF look like child's play given the problems of development that the World Bank faces. Economists and policymakers quickly discover that development is the stickiest and most impenetrable economic problem. Despite the efforts of generations of smart economists and the lessons learned about economic activity in relatively developed economies, the lack of success in developing economies signals the paucity of knowledge about transforming developing economies into developed economies.

To date, economics proves better at understanding established economic behavior than at analyzing dynamic transformations. Economic historians describe such transformations, but the causal explanations that inform good policy prescriptions fall short. Theories have led to policy experimentation, but the evidence suggests that those theories remain incomplete and insufficient to the task of generating growth and transforming economies. In retrospect, this is not surprising: the industrialized states of Europe, North America, and northeastern Asia did not emerge fully developed, nor did they follow the same development paths, nor were their paths linear and continuous. The economic histories of developed nations are full of meandering experimentation and failure—one step forward, two steps back, and then two steps forward, one step back. Some call economics the "dismal science," not because of poor science and lack of effort, but because of the difficulty and complexity of identifying causal economic mechanisms.

Despite the earnest efforts of organizations like the World Bank, the problems of poverty, nutritional deficiency, illiteracy, gender discrimination, ethnic and racial violence, disease, and idleness abound. In some developing states, the daily wage remains below one dollar. The infant mortality rate in the richest quintile of states is four deaths per thousand, but in the poorest quintile, it is two hundred deaths per thousand. In developing states, millions of children die annually from dehydration, millions more from pneumonia, tetanus, polio, measles, and other diseases that can be easily and cheaply treated by vaccines and antibiotics. Deficient diets lead to caloric, vitamin, and nutritional shortfalls that cause blindness, thyroid problems, anemia, mental impairment, and death. The desperation that grows from such suffering drains societies by taxing the resources of caregivers, diverting labor that could be used for more economically productive activities, and promoting slavery and debt bondage. Children in desperate societies turn to prostitution or war, unenviable professions for adults but even more obscene and immoral for children. Gender inequality and discrimination are greatest in poor societies, where spousal abuse of women is often simply a matter of happenstance and expectation. Money may not buy happiness, but poor and desperate societies do terrible things to their people.

Yet literacy, economic welfare, and gender equality have been improving decade by decade in many regions, albeit not nearly fast or far enough. Latin American states have made some progress since World War II, while Japan, South Korea, Taiwan, and Singapore have achieved stunning successes, becoming the poster children for development. The rapid expansion of the Chinese economy since the thawing of its political-economic relations with the West and the adoption of economic reforms at home continues apace. But many African states have fallen behind where they were a decade ago, two decades ago, or three decades ago; and even where conditions have improved, significant problems remain and the potential for backsliding is very real. Lagging development is more than a burden for the people living in

These freshly dug graves in Gaborone attest to the devastation of the HIV/AIDs epidemic on Botswanan society. Developing countries face many barriers to development. Approximately 20,000 children die every day from problems associated with extreme poverty. Many countries in Africa and elsewhere struggle with a high rate of HIV infection, which, in decimating populations and turning workers into caregivers at home, drains labor pools and increases the number of parentless children, who become vulnerable to violence, prostitution, and other forms of exploitation. Botswana is unusual in that it has the highest per capita HIV infection rate in Africa, but also one of the fastest economic growth rates—a miracle by some standards given HIV's effect on local economies and social well-being.

poverty in those nations, for its related problems can spill across borders to damage international security and economic affairs. Failed economies are failed polities that nurture the seeds of violence, discrimination, and international terrorism. The track record of the World Bank and other development organizations is unsatisfying in addressing the root causes that fuel such problems—but not for a lack of trying. Frustration with the relative lack of success so far makes it tempting to turn a blind eye to development problems, but ignoring them will only risk greater dislocations and violence.

Strategies to Promote Development

The World Bank has tried a variety of strategies to overcome barriers to growth. Abstractly, economic theory posits that change in growth is a function of changes in three factors: *capital,* *labor,* and *technology.* Increases or improvements in the supply of labor; increases or improvements in physical and human capital; and, most important, technological changes that transform the inputs of labor and capital should affect economic activity, increase output per capita, and improve economic welfare. The economic history of the West supports this elegant framework, which informs the World Bank's development activities. World Bank programs have attempted to improve a state's labor pool, increase its human and physical capital investment, and provide technology to improve the productivity of its labor and capital.

Initially, World Bank programs targeted a perceived **financing gap** in developing states—the difference between the level of domestic investment considered necessary to promote economic growth and the level of domestic savings. Believing that an inadequate level of investment stymied the economic activity that could transform developing states into developed states, policymakers at the World Bank and other development organizations started programs to close this financing gap by extending financial assistance to developing states (the focus of the 1950s and early 1960s). When this assistance failed to spark development, however, the World Bank shifted strategies to improving the quality and supply of physical capital. While continuing to provide funds to address a perceived financing gap, World Bank programs shifted to increasingly help fund the physical infrastructure of development—providing industrial and agricultural machinery and assistance in the development of infrastructure such as roads, buildings, and communication networks. Unfortunately, poverty proved remarkably resistant. In many countries, such efforts even seemed to lead to less economic activity, more income inequality, more poverty, and more violence, as this well-intentioned international assistance was captured by small segments of society who used it to advance their narrow interests at the expense of their larger societies.

Discovering that the manipulation of financial and physical capital was insufficient to stimulate growth, the World Bank turned to strategies to influence the quality and supply of labor. It funded efforts to increase literacy and improve the skills of workers—a capital improvement in the quality of labor. Today, many developing states have basic literacy rates that are comparable to the developed states, but they still have not achieved stable growth.

Contrary to expectations, there appeared to be little correlation between education and growth in many developing states. Conjecturing that perhaps quantity, not quality, of people was the problem, the World Bank and other development organizations next turned to population planning, assuming that high birth rates acted as a brake on growth. But, like previous strategies, this tactic failed to overcome the barriers to growth. In retrospect, the evidence suggests that wealth does lead to lower birth rates, but little evidence supports the contrary proposition that lower birth rates lead to development. In the developed states, birth rates declined after growth took hold, not before.

Beginning in the 1980s, the World Bank and other development organizations started to tie developmental assistance to regulatory reforms in a state's political economy. This strategy, known as the **Washington Consensus,** recognized that governments could help or hurt economic activity, and so it pushed for reforms of government policies and institutions that conceivably were handicapping market exchange. The Washington Consensus promoted stable and clear property rights, a rule of law with transparent adjudication and enforcement mechanisms, independent central banks, attacks on corruption and cronyism, and responsible macroeconomic policies. This approach emphasized the role of governments in creating a context conducive to growth so that investments in labor, capital, and technology might work as expected. Unfortunately, this strategy also appears to have fallen short.

Many celebrities from the movies, music, and pop culture have been drawn to these problems of the human condition and have tried to use their stature and influence to mobilize development initiatives. Currently, Bono of the music group U2 uses his public notoriety to garner attention for **debt forgiveness** as a development strategy. Proponents of this strategy argue that the debt burden of developing states acts as a ball and chain, slowing or retarding investment in economic activity because states must send their capital abroad to pay off loans instead of investing in the domestic economy. This reasoning returns to the financing gap logic, but debt forgiveness has been tried in the past as a means of addressing this problem, with little success. Worse, much of the evidence shows that debt forgiveness has led states with clean slates to run up new debt burdens without stimulating economic development, thus further damaging their credit reputations. Perhaps a problem here is that the debt of the wrong states is forgiven: in the past the states with the worst records have enjoyed the greatest amount of debt forgiveness.

Despite the commitment of substantial financial, human, and physical capital, and emotional resources, no panacea or silver bullet has yet been uncovered that provides a clear means for overcoming the obstacles to development. The problems associated with economic stagnation, the handful of unambiguous successes in Asia, and some partial successes in other parts of the world motivate continued efforts to discover and unleash the mechanisms of growth. But the history of development efforts and the stubbornness of poverty should make us wary of quick fixes and overblown claims about building healthy political economies, especially in places such as Afghanistan and Iraq that are double-burdened with political conflict.

Economic history strongly suggests that we do not yet know how to unlock the economic growth model so that changes in capital, labor, and technology will produce the expected growth—or else we would have a world filled with modern, developed political economies.

ACTIVE ENGAGEMENT AND THE TRUMAN DOCTRINE

The reconstruction of the European political economies proceeded slowly despite U.S. willingness to forgive war debts, the Bretton Woods arrangements to promote trade and stability in the exchange-rate mechanism, and assistance from the World Bank. The citizens of these damaged states suffered through several harsh winters, drought and agricultural failures, recession and high unemployment, and hunger. With the Eastern European political economies already under Soviet influence, President Truman became increasingly concerned that the inability of the Western European political economies to rebuild after the war was promoting internal dissension and threatened to bring national communist parties to power by the electoral process in Greece, Turkey, Italy, and other places. If national communist parties were to succeed at the ballot box, Truman feared that the Soviets could extend their sphere of influence over Western Europe through legitimate electoral means. The major European allies of the United States, the United Kingdom and France, were hardly better off economically than the states where national communist parties were knocking on the electoral door, so they were incapable of extending economic assistance to the others.

Truman faced a difficult task in convincing Americans of the emerging communist threat in Europe. After the war, many Americans turned their focus inward and adopted an increasingly isolationist posture. In particular, the Republican members of Congress from the Midwest and West opposed foreign engagement and extended overseas commitments. However, a U.S.-Soviet confrontation over Berlin in 1948–1949 and the Soviet detonation of an atomic bomb in August 1949 helped Truman and his secretary of state, General George Marshall, convince Americans and their congressional representatives to abandon their isolationism and confront the communist threat, including the growing electoral prospects of domestic communist political parties in Western Europe.

President Truman's restatement of U.S. foreign policy strategy, the **Truman Doctrine,** was the most important shift in U.S. foreign policy since the American Revolution. Unveiling this new policy in a speech to Congress in 1947, Truman asserted, "I believe that it must be the policy of the U.S. to support free peoples who are resisting subjugation by armed minorities or by outside pressures." The Truman Doctrine thereby inserted U.S. policymakers proactively into world affairs to support states oriented toward democratic governance mechanisms and market-based economic mechanisms. He claimed the authority to challenge nondemocratic, nonmarket political economies that threatened the political-economic order he believed was most conducive to U.S. well-being. Rather than the passive and reactive stance maintained by previous generations, the Truman Doctrine advanced a strategy of active engagement to use the tools of power to challenge communist influence and expansion and to mold world affairs. The two pillars on which the Truman Doctrine was built were containment and the Marshall Plan.

Containment

Containment involved the use of military and economic capabilities to encircle and challenge the Soviet Union and its sphere of influence. This strategy involved constructing collective security pacts among states. In Europe, it became the motivation for forming the North Atlantic Treaty Organization (NATO). Since the European allies of the United States lacked the capabilities to contain the Soviets militarily if they should move west, Truman recognized that credible military containment required the redeployment of U.S. troops and support capabilities to Europe. This military presence was intended to signal to the Soviets the U.S. commitment to the defense of the Western European democracies. Several hundred thousand U.S. troops could not stop an invasion of Soviet forces by conventional means, but their physical presence committed U.S. nuclear weapons to the defense and safety of Western Europe. Successive U.S. presidents extended this policy of containment by deploying U.S. military and covert capabilities to challenge threats, real or not, of communist expansion in Asia, Latin America, and Africa.

Containment also involved policies that were designed to constrain economic advance and create economic dislocations within the Eastern bloc economies, and to promote economic activity within the Western alliance and friendly nonaligned nations. By means of systematic economic sanctions, containment sought to deny to the Eastern bloc nations gains from trade and exchange with the larger global economy. The long-term objectives of economic containment were to undermine Soviet capabilities in the competition between communism and capitalism, to create economic hardships within the Eastern bloc political economies, and to breed dissatisfaction among the publics of the Eastern bloc nations. This basic strategy is the logic underpinning the use of any form of economic sanctions.

How did economic containment work? First, Western governments limited Eastern bloc access to Western markets, goods, capital, technology, and ideas that could contribute to postwar rebuilding, construction of healthy competitive economies, or the development of military technologies. Limiting such exchange denied the gains from specialization due to trade, investment, and transfer of technology and production strategies. This limitation imposed inefficiencies on the production structures of the Eastern bloc states and detracted from their economic capacities. The important counterfactual question is this: what would the Eastern bloc economies have looked like without containment? Viewing military and economic containment as security threats from the West, the Eastern bloc governments exacerbated the inefficiencies and distortions in their production structures by shifting assets toward production of national security goods and away from consumables. The designers of containment hoped that this excessive allocation of Eastern bloc productive capabilities to national security needs would strain the Soviet bloc in terms of unmet consumer demand and breed consumer dissatisfaction, which could grow into political discontent and pressures for reform of communist governments—or even a rollback of communism.

The policies of constraint, denial, and sanction extended to the IGOs created at Bretton Woods. These organizations were dominated by the United States and United Kingdom, which exercised their disproportionate voting power to ensure that these organizations would refuse to extend assistance to political economies in the Soviet sphere. Many of the restrictions were relaxed during the period of East-West détente that began in the late 1960s, but many—such as technological export restrictions—remained active until after the breakup of the Eastern bloc and demise of the Soviet Union in 1991.

Excluding the Eastern bloc from the larger global economic exchange also denied the Western nations gains from trade with the Eastern bloc. Western policymakers, however, calculated that the costs to the West would be far smaller than the costs to the East from this loss of trade. Larger arenas of economic exchange, such as that of the Western bloc, tend to produce greater gains from exchange than do smaller arenas, like that of the Eastern bloc; consequently, the denial of gains from trade between the East and West would be proportionally more damaging to the Eastern bloc economies. So even if the economic sanctions imposed under the policy of containment were damaging to Western economic interests, the potential long-term political strategic gains were considered worth the cost.

The Marshall Plan

For Truman, "supporting free peoples who are resisting subjugation by armed minorities or by outside pressures" involved not only constraining the threat to free peoples, but also promoting their economic, political, and military well-being. Truman therefore asserted that the United States must help to strengthen the political, social, and economic arenas in friendly states that appeared vulnerable to Soviet pressure or to domestic communist movements. If successful, the strategy of promoting growth in political economies tied to the Western markets while limiting economic gains in the Eastern bloc economies would expand the relative disparities between the Western and Eastern blocs and highlight the superiorities of democracy and market exchange. The Soviet threat thus provided the United States with additional leverage to exert leadership over the postwar political economy. U.S. policymakers used U.S. aid to push for more liberal trade within Western Europe, while granting Western European producers greater access to U.S. markets than U.S. producers found in Europe. They hoped that this encouragement would help to strengthen the Western European states, produce a healthy economic bloc, and create a bulwark against Soviet influence. This U.S. policy served as a step toward formation of the European Economic Community (EEC).

At the Harvard College commencement in 1947, General George C. Marshall, Truman's secretary of state, announced another policy initiative designed to promote postwar reconstruction and to provide a bulwark against the rise of domestic communist movements in the Western European states. The Marshall Plan asked Congress to support a massive infusion of U.S. aid to states trying to rebuild their war-torn economies. Seeking to avoid a liquidity crunch like the one that had hindered rebuilding after World War I, Truman sought to use the wealth of the United States to ensure a sufficient supply of capital for rebuilding. Arguing that such a program would not only promote U.S. economic health by creating economies that would purchase U.S. goods, but would also advance U.S. security interests by creating healthy economies tied to the U.S. economy and undermining the success of communist parties—which relied upon economic dislocation to build support in those nations—U.S. policymakers hoped to form a strategic bond of economic cooperation between the U.S. and recipient nations.

Truman invited governments to submit plans for their economic recovery. The Soviets and states within their sphere of influence were invited to participate, but this gesture was mere public relations, as these states could not accede to the conditions attached to the promised assistance. The Marshall Plan proved extremely successful, as massive amounts of U.S. aid flowed abroad, creating liquidity for growth and providing materials for revamping production. U.S. manufacturers benefited, as this financial largesse was cycled back to the United States to purchase industrial machinery, farm equipment, and other inputs to economic activity. During the period from 1947 to 1952, U.S. financial assistance, including Marshall grants and private loans, rose at times to nearly 2 percent of U.S. GNP—an astounding commitment of resources in comparison to the diminutive size of Western foreign aid budgets today.

The Marshall Plan worked as a catalyst for economic recovery. By 1952, Western Europe was surpassing prewar industrial and agricultural production levels, and the benefits of this phenomenal economic revival extended beyond Western Europe. More than two-thirds of European imports during this period came from the United States, which created opportunities for U.S. workers and producers. As U.S. manufacturers and labor profited from the renewed economic vitality in Europe through trade, their support for expanded international trade and greater integration into the global economy increased—not a trivial matter, considering the damage done by U.S. protectionist policies during the interwar years.

The Marshall Plan complemented military containment by creating healthy and connected market-oriented economies. The greater economic integration wrought by the extension of assistance and the growth of trade provided an economic bulwark against communist expansion, which helped to improve political-military relations and solidify opposition to the Soviet Union. The initial fear of significant electoral success by indigenous communist parties disappeared with the revival of domestic economies in Western European states.

The Truman Doctrine was an important volley in the conflict between competing ideological views and blocs in the global power hierarchy. With both sides seeking to avoid a catastrophic military confrontation, the conflict between the Soviet Union and the United States morphed into a cold war—which occasionally threatened to turn hot with potential confrontations in Europe, Korea, Cuba, Vietnam, and the mid-East, in which one side confronted the clients of the other. But U.S. and Soviet leaders averted any direct shooting confrontations between their own forces, and so an uneasy peace continued into the 1960s and 1970s, when tensions thawed and the doors opened to détente and more constructive East-West engagement.

BREAKDOWN IN THE BRETTON WOODS MONETARY ARRANGEMENTS

Policymakers designed the Bretton Woods monetary system as a handmaiden to trade, meaning it to ensure the expansion of trade and interdependence of markets for goods and services. But this system of monetary arrangements carried seeds of its own destruction. Problems began almost as soon as the ink dried on the Articles of Agreement that had created the International Monetary Fund and the Bretton Woods monetary system. Many of these problems were manageable in the short run, but eventually cracks appeared in the system that would undermine the foundations of the adjustable-peg arrangement. The Bretton Woods monetary system lasted until August 15, 1971, when President Richard Nixon unilaterally suspended convertibility of the dollar and demanded renegotiation of the dollar's value. During the twenty-five years of the Bretton Woods era, economic trade and growth had expanded at a fairly remarkable rate. U.S. growth averaged about 3 percent, the Western Europeans experienced even stronger growth as they recovered from the devastation of war, and Japan rebuilt and became a major industrial power with a compounded growth rate of approximately 12 percent during the 1950s. Most industrialized nations experienced good price performance with low inflation.

Suspension of Convertibility and Imposition of Capital Controls

Initially, the Bretton Woods signatories committed to openness to capital flows and convertibility of their currencies into gold or another currency, but these promises fell by the wayside immediately as most governments created barriers to **capital mobility** and suspended convertibility. Policymakers worried that balance-of-payments positions, convertibility, and capital flight could prevent access to the capital needed to stimulate domestic economic activity, and they feared that capital mobility could also be destabilizing and limit policymakers' ability to regulate financial markets. Policymakers in war-torn economies faced persistent balance-of-payments deficits, as their enterprises and governments borrowed capital abroad and imported goods and services to rebuild their industrial and agricultural enterprises. Under the gold standard system, deflation and David Hume's specie flow would address this balance-of-payments adjustment problem, but the need to restore employment levels made deflationary policies politically unacceptable. Technically, a change in the adjustable peg would provide an adjustment mechanism, but it would also signal a fundamental disequilibrium or crisis in an economy. Policymakers refrained from taking this course because signaling an economic crisis would likely cause more problems for capital flows than an adjustment in exchange rates could fix.

Governments suspended convertibility and imposed capital controls (restrictions on who could acquire foreign currencies and when) in order to manage the balance-of-payments problem and limit the outflow of capital. Suspending convertibility protected currency and gold reserves in a state's treasury. Capital controls to restrict the outflow, and sometimes the inflow, of capital were permitted under the Bretton Woods arrangements, although the long-term goal was mobility. Governments used import licenses and exchange restrictions to help limit capital outflows. These measures helped governments to manage their balance-of-payments positions by limiting the demand for exports and constraining potentially destabilizing currency flows. In 1959 many governments restored current-account convertibility. Some relaxed their capital controls and allowed importers to acquire foreign currencies to buy goods abroad without special licenses. As the return to convertibility placed greater strain on the adjustable peg, many policymakers confronted increasing pressures to adjust their currency's peg.

The Leading Currency Problem and the Triffin Dilemma

A greater threat appeared at the end of the 1950s and beginning of the 1960s, when currency and gold traders began to question the connection between the dollar and gold. The dollar acted as the reserve currency for the system, a substitute for gold—governments and other investors were willing to hold dollars as a reserve asset as long as the dollar was perceived as good as gold. The U.S. commitment to convertibility, to exchange dollars for gold or some other currency on demand, underpinned the willingness of others to hold dollars as a reserve asset, but it also exposed the system to two dilemmas, which presented fundamental and eventually unsurpassable challenges to the Bretton Woods system: the leading currency problem and the Triffin Dilemma.

First, to avoid chronic price instability in the Bretton Woods system, at least one currency had to restrain itself from exchange-rate changes vis-à-vis other currencies. This guardian of stability was the dollar. The United States declared a par value of the dollar—fixed its value in relation to gold. Other countries then declared the par values of their currencies in terms of dollars. As the dollar's role as the leading currency and reserve asset increased under the Bretton Woods system, the system depended more and more upon the success of the United States in maintaining the dollar's par value. If any other state declared a fundamental disequilibrium and adjusted its exchange rate, all the prices in that state's tradable sector would be affected, but if the leading currency country were to announce a fundamental disequilibrium and adjust its exchange rate, prices throughout the system would be affected. This situation is known as a **leading currency problem.** Every other economy's preference for a stable and passive leading currency limited the ability and willingness of U.S. policymakers to change the dollar's par value, but it also gave them enormous leverage to escape the constraints faced by policymakers in other governments. Other states had to give the United States latitude in its balance-of-payments and macroeconomic management as they sought to avoid price instability. President Charles de Gaulle of France, however, believed that this situation allowed U.S. policymakers to pursue irresponsible economic policies and shift some of the costs of those polices abroad.

Second, Robert Triffin, a Yale economist, noted a logical inconsistency—the **Triffin Dilemma**—in the Bretton Woods dependency upon the dollar as the reserve currency. As trade and economic activity expanded, a fixed-rate system would require an increase in usable reserves—an increase in the supply of acceptable money to finance trade and investment. As a reserve asset, however, gold was available in very limited quantities, and new supplies were increasing very slowly. At its established price and supply, gold would be insufficient to meet the liquidity needs of the system. This was the same problem that had burdened the gold standard of the pre–World War I era. The Bretton Woods arrangements addressed the shortcoming of gold as a reserve asset by encouraging the use of the dollar as a reserve asset. But this use meant that the only mechanism to pump liquidity into the system—expand the number of dollars in the system—were U.S. balance-of-payments deficits. Initially, these deficits resulted from an imbalance between the capital and current accounts: the United States enjoyed a substantial surplus in its current account, but a significant deficit in its capital account. More dollars flowed in than out to pay for goods and services, but even more flowed out than in as investments and loans. Triffin saw a long-term inconsistency between persistent U.S. balance-of-payments deficits, which created liquidity for the system and led to a growing number of dollars held outside the United States, and the size of U.S. gold reserves, convertibility, and the value of the dollar.

With the notable exception of Charles de Gaulle, most non-U.S. policymakers ignored the persistent balance-of-payments deficit of the leading currency country. As the banker to the system, lender of last resort, and provider of collective goods, the United States provided an outward flow of dollars that stimulated the economic activity essential to postwar reconstruction and the building of a liberal global political economy. Expanding political economies needed the liquidity provided by U.S. balance-of-payments deficits. Foreign governments and banks rebuilt their economic foundations with dollars. By adding dollars to their reserves, other states were able to restore convertibility by the late 1950s. The vitality of the U.S. economy masked the threat posed by the Triffin Dilemma for many years. As long as they perceived the U.S. economy as fundamentally healthy and dominant—and the dollar therefore as good as gold—other governments could ignore the deficits. This perception underpinned the willingness to hold dollars as a reserve asset rather than converting them into gold. But if the number of dollars held abroad continued to increase, the total would eventually exceed the U.S. official gold reserves. This situation could provoke questions about whether the dollar was, in fact, as good as gold, and so threaten confidence in convertibility.

By 1960, the amount of dollars held overseas did exceed U.S. official gold reserves, and this dollar overhang (dollar holdings outside the United States) did lead to questions about whether the dollar was as good as gold. The growing imbalance between U.S. gold reserves and dollars held abroad placed increasing pressure on the decision to convert dollars to gold at the U.S. Gold Window (a metaphor for the exchange process at the U.S. Treasury). No one wanted to undermine confidence in the dollar, but neither did anyone want to show up at the U.S. Gold Window with her dollars after U.S. gold reserves had been exhausted. This dynamic created the potential for a rush to exchange dollars for gold—an unsustainable dilemma that injected new risk into the system. If governments were to start exchanging dollars for gold, the United States would have to either suspend convertibility or change the par value of the dollar. This destabilizing outcome was the ultimate threat posed by the Triffin Dilemma.

Growing Pressures on the Dollar-Gold Relationship

Other changes at the end of the 1950s and during the 1960s eroded confidence in the health of the U.S. economy, raised questions about the relationship of the dollar to gold, and threatened the Bretton Woods monetary system. In the late 1950s, the U.S. economy went through a temporary but sharp recession. The Federal Reserve lowered U.S. interest rates to promote growth, but this reduced the incentives to hold dollars or dollar-denominated financial instruments and increased the incentives to convert dollars into gold or other currencies in order to pursue higher rates of return. As a consequence, the United States lost about 10 percent of its official gold reserves in 1958. Then, as the recession eased, interest rates rose and the incentives to exchange dollars for gold or other currencies diminished, but the loss of gold reserves and the run on the dollar had impressed traders in financial markets, who began to worry about the connection between dollars and gold. Was the dollar as good as gold? Could the United States sustain its commitment to convertibility and maintain the dollar's par value, despite the increasing imbalance between official gold reserves and dollars in the system?

The United States continued to lose gold reserves over the next several years, but at a slower rate than in 1958. However, in October 1960, just before the tightly contested presidential election between Kennedy and Nixon, a shock hit the gold markets. The price of gold in private markets shot up to $40/ounce, although its official par value remained at $35/ounce. Such a disparity between the public and private values of gold—which had never happened before under the Bretton Woods system—suggested uncertainty over the relationship between the dollar and gold, and uncertainty about the policies a Democratic president might adopt in regard to the exchange rate and convertibility. Perhaps the dollar was overvalued at $35/ounce of gold—was there a fundamental disequilibrium? If so, an overvalued dollar made U.S. commodities in the tradable sector relatively expensive vis-à-vis foreign commodities and acted as a drag on U.S. growth. A Democratic president would be more likely to represent economic interests that favored growth over price stability (e.g., labor) whereas a Republican president would be more likely to represent economic interests that favored price stability over growth (e.g., bankers and owners of financial assets). In his campaign, in fact, Kennedy had advocated more aggressive growth policies.

If this disparity were to persist, it could lead to a run on official reserves, as financial traders could buy gold for $35/ounce from governments committed to convertibility and then sell it for $40/ounce in the private markets—an arbitrage opportunity with an extremely attractive rate of return. Realizing that concerns about the relationship between the dollar and gold could affect his electoral prospects, Kennedy reacted immediately, stating his unwavering support for the current par value of the dollar. Gold returned to $35/ounce in private markets and the market perturbation ended, but the seeds of doubt sown in 1958 had been reinforced. Financial traders began looking closer at the U.S. economy for signs of vulnerability that could foreshadow a looming crisis of the Triffin Dilemma. They did not have far to look.

U.S. Financial Constraints and International Reactions

For the first time since World War II, the United States began to experience the external financial constraints that other nations had faced all along. President Kennedy entered office promising to end a recession and expand the economy. His administration had a variety of monetary and fiscal tools available to stimulate the economy, but the exchange-rate problem constrained his choices. Governments use monetary policies to affect the supply and cost of capital as they attempt to prod or restrain their economies. Kennedy's government could increase money supply or lower interest rates to stimulate investment and economic activity, but the Federal Reserve had already eased interest rates at the end the Eisenhower presidency. Lowering the rates further or increasing the supply of dollars could raise questions about U.S. commitment to the dollar's value and produce destabilizing speculative market pressures on the dollar. Alternatively, the Kennedy administration could reinforce the U.S. commitment to the dollar's value by pushing more restrictive monetary policies, but this would risk another recession, violate his campaign promises to expand the economy, and threaten his reelection prospects. Kennedy turned to fiscal policy. He reduced taxes in an effort to stimulate investment and also increased government expenditures—for defense and domestic programs. Tax cuts plus rising expenditures ran the risk of enlarging public deficits and debt if the economy did not grow fast enough to offset the change in tax rates. Kennedy might have avoided this gamble by using monetary policy to stimulate the economy, if not for the constraint of the exchange-rate mechanism.

Perversely, the success of U.S. postwar efforts provided another damaging signal. U.S. postwar leadership had proven remarkably successful in rebuilding a liberal global economy. The revitalization of Japanese and European political economies was a good outcome, but the growing economic strength of these trading partners made them more assertive in international economic discussions. Some observers pointed to the growing assertiveness of others in international forums as evidence of U.S. hegemonic decline, which could undermine its willingness and ability to provide collective goods to maintain the postwar arrangements. In the early 1960s, new international cooperation and institution-building indicated potential instability in the Bretton Woods system.

In 1962, ten states (Belgium, Canada, France, Germany, Italy, Japan, the Netherlands, Sweden, the United Kingdom, and the United States) agreed to provide additional credit lines to the IMF in case its resources were to become insufficient to support one of the system's key currencies. This arrangement, the General Agreements to Borrow, meant that substantial funds ($6 billion) would be made available to defend against speculative attacks on key currencies. Hidden between the lines, the arrangement's veiled intent was to ensure that the IMF and the United States had the resources to defend the dollar without forcing U.S. policymakers to sell U.S. gold reserves. Because a loss of U.S. gold reserves might signal weakness to markets, which could encourage speculation and undermine confidence in the dollar, the signatories agreed to intervene in gold markets to ensure stability in the monetary system by maintaining gold's price at close to $35/ounce. These ten states became known as the Group of 10 (G-10), an elite club (Switzerland later became a member) that would meet regularly to coordinate actions in defense of stable international monetary and financial relations. The formation of the G-10 led to the creation of other intergovernmental groups (G-7, G-5, etc.) to promote cooperation and manage threats to global economic relations. But the advent of all these new groups begged the question: If the Bretton Woods system was not at risk, why construct new international scaffolding to defend it?

Despite the willingness of other governments to engage in such concerted market interventions to protect the dollar's value, growing capital account deficits continued to worry U.S. officials. The growth of multinational corporations (MNCs), predominantly U.S.-based, was increasing the dollar overhang outside the United States, as U.S. MNCs borrowed in U.S. capital markets to fund their overseas activities. Hoping to escape the Triffin Dilemma and threats to dollar convertibility, the Kennedy and Johnson administrations searched for strategies to restrict dollar outflows. They could have used monetary policies to raise the rate of return on dollar-denominated financial instruments in the hope of attracting foreign capital to the United States and reducing—or maybe even reversing—the net outflow of dollars, but such policies would, at the same time, increase the costs of borrowing in U.S. capital markets. This effect could have decreased the outflow of dollars if borrowers moved to overseas markets to borrow capital, but use of these policies was politically difficult because they would increase the costs of capital for all borrowers, whether for domestic or overseas use, and likely damage an economy that was recovering from a recession. Pushing for monetary policies that slowed U.S. economic activity would also have violated Kennedy's campaign promise to revitalize the economy—potential political suicide.

Policymakers in the Kennedy and Johnson administrations looked elsewhere to slow the outflow of dollars. They recognized that the relative efficiency of U.S. capital markets, which were far more flexible and attractive than overseas markets, contributed to dollar outflows, as borrowing in the New York capital markets by U.S. MNCs and other states' firms and governments financed their non-U.S. operations. Policymakers therefore pondered how to reduce the attractiveness of U.S. capital markets, making them more costly and less efficient sources of capital for overseas activities without raising interest rates, which could slow the U.S. economy. They could enact capital controls, but this would signal a sharp philosophical break with postwar U.S. preferences for liberal trade and capital movement. Such a dramatic reversal of course by the system leader would likely create more, rather than less, of a crisis. A less disruptive alternative was taxing capital borrowed for overseas use, which U.S. Treasury experts thought might produce the same effects on capital outflows as capital controls or higher interest rates, but without the unsettling stigma of capital controls or the risk of slowing economic activity within the United States.

In this vein, the Kennedy administration adopted the Interest Equalization Tax (IET) of 1963, which was expanded two years later; it lasted until 1974, when it was repealed by the Nixon administration. The IET taxed borrowing in U.S. bond markets that was to be used abroad. The tax sought to push borrowers away from U.S. markets by artificially raising the cost of capital and constraining the efficiency of U.S. markets—to make borrowers indifferent between borrowing their capital in the United States or abroad. When the IET failed to stem dollar outflows, in 1965 the Johnson administration adopted the Voluntary Foreign Credit Restraint Act (VFCR) in another attempt to limit outflows. The VFCR established voluntary quotas on U.S. bank lending to U.S. MNCs for their foreign direct investments. The quotas became mandatory in 1968.

In response to the IET and the VFCR, U.S. MNCs and others did shift some borrowing overseas. This shift encouraged the development of markets in dollar deposits and dollar securities abroad, a very significant development in the global financial infrastructure. Despite the fact that they are not specific to Europe or the euro currency, these new venues are called **euro markets;** they trade financial instruments denominated in currencies outside the national boundaries of those currencies. Nevertheless, the IET and the VFCR failed to reduce dollar outflows enough to reverse the brewing threat to the Bretton Woods arrangements.

About the same time as the U.S. adopted the IET and the VFCR, French president Charles de Gaulle recognized the vulnerable linkage between the dollar and gold and began a campaign to unsettle the dollar's role as the dominant reserve asset in the system. De Gaulle believed that the dollar's position in the system afforded the United States enormous privilege in global affairs; allowed U.S. policymakers to escape the discipline faced by other states as the liquidity needs of the system benefited from persistent U.S. balance-of-payments deficits; and permitted U.S. policymakers to export the effects of its policies rather than implementing politically difficult policy changes at home. His position had merit, but his solution was problematic: he called for a return to the gold standard, which would create a slew of other problems. De Gaulle's call for return to the gold standard likely was not sincere, but a strategic ploy to call attention to the increasingly vulnerable link between the dollar and gold. The French pressured U.S. policymakers by slowly exchanging dollars for gold, highlighting the imbalance between dollars in the system and U.S. official gold reserves.

Pressures on the dollar-gold relationship grew. In 1968 the G-10 nations decided to stop transferring public gold into the private gold market—refusing to sell official gold reserves to private citizens. This decision, which removed the possibility for arbitrage, amounted to a confession by governments that they could no longer be confident of maintaining a market price of $35/ounce and essentially shifted the terms of convertibility. The rate for official exchanges between nations remained $35/ounce, but the value of gold in private markets was now divorced from its public price. Going forward, two different prices for gold—a private price and a public price—became the norm. Discrepancies between public and private prices suggested what traders in private gold markets believed was the real value of the dollar. They signaled that they believed the dollar was significantly overvalued.

Meanwhile, the Vietnam War became a political, military, and economic quagmire for U.S. policymakers. Aside from the tensions that Vietnam imposed on U.S. political relationships with its allies who disagreed with the war, many governments believed that U.S. economic policies related to the war were exporting inflation into the global system. U.S. defense expenditures exploded during the Vietnam War, but U.S. policymakers, worried about public dissent, refrained from raising taxes to pay for them. Instead, they financed the war through public borrowing and increases in the money supply. During the same period, the Federal Reserve resisted raising interest rates. Together, these U.S. policies led to inflationary growth, and, because the United States was the largest and most influential member in an increasingly global political economy, its economic policies spilled over into other economies. Other nations' policymakers, thinking that the United States was exporting its inflation through the outflow of dollars and unsettling price stability in other nations, expressed increased interest in system reform.

Suspension of Dollar-Gold Convertibility

In the late 1960s, with confidence waning in the dollar-gold relationship, the ability of the U.S. to maintain convertibility at $35/ounce, and the soundness of the U.S. economy, the United States reported its first balance-of-trade deficit since World War II. The U.S. balance-of-payments deficit since the war had been due to the capital account, not the current account, for the United States had enjoyed a trade surplus over that same time. Running both a capital-account deficit and a current-account deficit threatened confidence in the U.S. economy and the belief that the dollar was as good as gold. Countries cannot run balance-of-payments deficits without the pendulum swinging back toward surpluses, except in cases of a fundamental disequilibrium that signals structural problems in an economy. The United States had run such deficits since World War II, in spite of the logic of the economic mechanism, only because of its special position as the leading currency country, the dollar's role as the primary reserve asset, and the need for dollars to provide liquidity to fund reconstruction and postwar expansion. As a provider of system liquidity and a lender of last resort, the United States had been encouraged to increase its money supply and run balance-of-payments deficits. U.S. policymakers thus could adopt polices that in other states would signal poor economic management and a fundamental disequilibrium.

Other states' policymakers and the IMF willingly looked away, as the system needed dollar outflows and they believed in the fundamental health of the U.S. economy. Policymakers took the continued success of U.S. producers in the global economy, its balance-of-trade surplus, as a signal of U.S. economic vibrancy and health. Even though the current and capital accounts did not balance, they both pointed in the right direction to undercut fears about balance-of-payments adjustment pressures on the U.S. But the U.S. current-account deficit beginning in the late 1960s raised fears about pressures on U.S. leaders to address a fundamental disequilibrium, either by affecting the dollar exchange rate or adopting some other policies such as protectionism. This possibility threatened to throw the system into disarray and increased the pressures to convert dollars into gold before U.S. policymakers changed the rules. Like a snowball rolling down a hill, momentum was building for change.

The balance-of-trade deficit signaled a brewing domestic dilemma for U.S. policymakers. Current-account deficits suggested that a fundamental imbalance in the dollar's value was penalizing U.S. producers and labor in the tradable sector. With postwar rebuilding and economic expansion, foreign producers had grown increasingly competitive vis-à-vis U.S. producers, and their gains were assisted by an overvalued dollar. This situation was less problematic when the U.S. producers dominated trade by wide margins, since a buffer existed to cushion the blows of creative destruction. But the trade deficit signaled the end of this buffer and rising problems for U.S. politicians as the effects of the overvalued dollar were felt in U.S. labor markets. As the leading currency country, the United States wanted to avoid changing the value of the dollar in order to preserve price stability in the system. Devaluation would generate a large shock that could undermine confidence in the dollar and in U.S. leadership. U.S. politicians faced quite a dilemma: they could maintain the dollar's value and face discontent among U.S. labor and producers that could lead to protectionist pressures and electoral losses; or they could devalue the dollar to redress a fundamental disequilibrium, thus assisting the competitiveness of U.S. producers and labor and promoting their electoral chances at home, but potentially creating a systemic economic crisis.

The trap was inescapable. By 1971, U.S. policymakers could no longer resist the dynamics and continue to defend the Bretton Woods monetary system. The dollar was fundamentally overvalued by at least 10 percent. Worried that Congress might adopt trade policies that undermined the embedded liberalism of the global political economy, President Nixon unilaterally changed the system on August 15, 1971, by suspending convertibility and demanding renegotiation of the value of the dollar. Convertibility would only be restored under a reformed monetary system and a realignment of exchange rates that would address the fundamental disequilibrium and make U.S. companies more competitive. Nixon sought to have the major trading partners of the United States revalue their currencies, rather than devaluing the dollar. The economic effects of such a move would be similar for the United States, but the political consequences would differ, as the responsibility for the system dysfunction would fall more heavily on others. Obviously, policymakers in other states preferred devaluation of the dollar to revaluation of their currencies. The negotiations were extremely contentious, threatening to disrupt international cooperation. But thirty years of postwar cooperation had built a robust foundation, and the discussions culminated in the Smithsonian Agreement in December 1971. This agreement retained the adjustable-peg system, but with several key changes: the dollar was devalued and bands of the peg were expanded to ± 2.25 percent from par value. When he signed it, an exuberant President Nixon declared the Smithsonian Agreement the greatest monetary agreement of all time. Yet it would last less than two years!

CONCLUSION

The planners at Bretton Woods laid the foundation for a liberal global political economy. Having learned from the missteps of the interwar years, they constructed a framework of national agreements, domestic governance mechanisms and safety nets, and international governmental organizations that sheltered politicians from domestic political pressures to shift the costs of economic dislocations abroad. Not trusting the ability of policymakers to unilaterally resist beggar-thy-neighbor pressures from their domestic constituencies, the Bretton Woods designers devised international governmental organizations in the form of the World Bank, GATT, and the IMF to limit the policy mobility of national policymakers and to provide resources and pathways for safeguarding and reinforcing liberal economic exchange in a self-help nation-state system. With the United States providing key collective goods and bankrolling the system at a time when other governments found themselves devastated and impoverished by war, a liberal global political economy emerged and strengthened in the years following the war. This growing economy combined with political-military policies to form a bulwark against the communist political economies of the Soviet sphere. Despite the eventual, and inevitable, breakdown in the Bretton Woods monetary system, the efforts of the planners succeeded well beyond anything they could have imagined when they first met in the mountains of New Hampshire.

EXERCISES

1. What critical lessons did policymakers learn from the interwar years that they needed to confront as they discussed arrangements for the post–World War II global political economy?

2. Why did the failures of the interwar years require both domestic and international policy reforms?

3. How did delegating some authority to the executive branch in the Reciprocal Trade Agreements Act (1934) affect U.S. trade policy and why?

4. Name three nontariff barriers. How do they work to influence the pattern of trade?

5. How does Keynesian economic policy differ from monetarism?

6. What is a fundamental disequilibrium? What does it signal?

7. How did the dollar's role as leading currency and reserve asset hinder/help the United States?

8. Explain the logic behind the policy of economic and military containment. How did the Marshall Plan contribute to containment? What did U.S. policymakers hope to accomplish with containment and the Marshall Plan?

9. Explain the dynamic underpinning the Triffin Dilemma.

10. Explain why President Nixon suspended convertibility in 1971.

FURTHER READING

Bhagwati, Jagdish. 1988. *Protectionism*. Cambridge, Mass.: MIT Press.

Easterly, William. 2002. *The Elusive Quest for Growth: Economists' Adventures and Misadventures in the Tropics*. Cambridge, Mass.: MIT Press.

Eichengreen, Barry. 1996. *Globalizing Capital: A History of the International Monetary System*. Princeton, N.J.: Princeton University Press.

Gardner, Richard N. 1980. *Sterling-Dollar Diplomacy in Current Perspective: The Origins and Prospects of Our International Economic Order*. New York: Columbia University Press.

Keylor, William R. Various editions. *The Twentieth-Century World: An International History*. New York: Oxford University Press.

Triffin, Robert. 1960. *Gold and the Dollar Crisis: The Future of Convertibility*. New Haven, Conn.: Yale University Press.

10

The World Post–Bretton Woods: Globalization Advances

Of all the changes of the world economy of recent decades, few have been nearly so dramatic as the resurrection of global finance. A half century ago, after the ravages of the Great Depression and World War II, financial markets everywhere—with the notable exception of the United States—were generally weak, insular, and strictly controlled, reduced from their previously central role in international economic relations to offer little more than a negligible amount of trade financing. Starting in the late 1950s, however, private lending and investment once again began to gather momentum, generating a phenomenal growth of cross-border capital flows and an increasingly close integration of domestic financial markets.

Benjamin J. Cohen, The Geography of Money *(1998)*

FUNDAMENTAL SHIFTS IN GLOBAL FINANCE

The end of the Bretton Woods system and its successor, the Smithsonian Agreement, marked a fundamental shift in global political economic relations, especially in global financial relations. The years following 1973 brought increasing rejection of narrow-pegged-exchange-rate mechanisms, the adoption of floating-rate mechanisms with potential for much greater exchange-rate volatility, attempts at resurrecting collective-currency pegs through cooperative action such as the European Monetary System and the European Monetary Union, a shift in the role of monetary policy in national arenas, a rebalancing of the role of state and market mechanisms, increasing global capital mobility, and greater financial liberalization. Altogether, these shifts marked a distinctive transformation in global financial relations—a reawakening of financial globalization that would lead to greater integration of national political economies into a larger global political economy and thereby challenge the policy autonomy of governments.

Under Bretton Woods and the Smithsonian Agreement, policymakers had used monetary policy—the manipulation of money supply—extensively to maintain the stability of a currency's value. With the end of the Smithsonian, the adoption of floating exchange rates by many states represented a dramatic shift in international monetary arrangements and in the use of monetary policy. Monetary policy became liberated from the stability of the exchange rate and freer to address domestic economic pressures.

Keynesian beliefs had colored postwar planning at Bretton Woods, rebalancing the role of markets and governments in managing international economic relations. The demise of Bretton Woods brought a shift away from such Keynesian strategies as heavy reliance on fiscal policies, domestic social protections, controls on capital movements, and collective international management, instead placing greater emphasis on markets to reward or penalize economic activity. This shift toward market forces and away from state allocation mechanisms, which is known as **neoliberalism,** led to greater capital mobility across borders, increased global integration of national economies, and constituted a potential sea change in state-society relations.

Changes in the activities of the International Monetary Fund and other IGOs and governmental bodies would reinforce this neoliberal shift. The IMF had managed the Bretton Woods monetary system, coordinated defense of its narrow-pegged system, alleviated short-term balance-of-payments pressures, and provided a systematic procedure for addressing fundamental balance-of-payments disequilibrium due to the exchange-rate mechanism. Losing its raison d'être with the demise of the Bretton Woods system, the organization recreated itself by building upon the skills of its economists to become a source of expertise for managing national economies. IMF prescriptions and assistance increasingly constrained government intervention in national economies and promoted market reforms. The IMF inserted itself into state policy arenas by attaching policy prescriptions and conditions to its financial assistance, most often at times of economic crisis when governments had little ability to refuse its directives. This shift reached beyond the IMF, to involve the participation of other important organizations such as the World Bank and departments of the U.S. government. Together, they formed what has become known as the **Washington Consensus,** a policy framework that relies more upon the notion of self-correcting markets to discipline governments and economic enterprises. We return to the Washington Consensus later in this chapter.

POST–BRETTON WOODS MONETARY ARRANGEMENTS

Even though Bretton Woods ended in 1971, its basic framework persisted via the Smithsonian Agreement until its failure in February 1973, and the two pacts' influence continued to linger in global monetary affairs until 1978, when the Second Amendment to the IMF Articles of Agreement (the IMF's charter) eliminated the role of gold as a reserve asset and legalized floating exchange rates. A patchwork of monetary arrangements emerged post–Bretton Woods and Smithsonian that included the following features:

- Floating rates
- Collective-currency pegs, such as the European Monetary System (EMS)
- Monetary unions, such as the European Monetary Union (EMU)
- Loose, adjustable pegs of a state's currency to the currency of its major trading partner
- Currency control boards that tightly pegged a state's currency to the currency of its major trading partner

These arrangements run the gamut from a float, whereby supply and demand in currency markets determine a currency's value, to a tight peg, whereby a government commits to its currency's value and defends that value through intervention in currency markets, managing its money supply, international cooperation, and the use of other policy instruments.

Both Bretton Woods and the Smithsonian pegged exchange rates either to gold or to another reserve asset, such as the dollar. Both systems aimed to tightly constrain changes in the prices of currencies in order to limit uncertainty and instability in the exchange-rate mechanism, which could hinder international exchange. The designers of these systems hoped to protect politicians from constituent demands for beggar-thy-neighbor policies such as using the exchange rate to force the costs of adjustment to trade and growth abroad, onto other nations' producers and labor.

Unlike the inflexibility of the gold standard, the Bretton Woods and Smithsonian arrangements had offered a means by which state policymakers could adjust their exchange rates. Policymakers could ask the IMF to adjust the par value of their currency if their state faced persistent trade deficits that constituted a fundamental balance-of-payments disequilibrium, reflecting structural problems in the nation's economy or a seriously misaligned exchange rate. Such adjustments were politically expensive, for they required a state's politicians to appeal to the IMF for approval. This action suggested a surrender of sovereignty and involved admitting partial mismanagement of their domestic economies. Such adjustments in the par value of a currency did occur during the postwar period, but they were relatively limited given the potential appeal for politicians to manipulate a nation's exchange rate to improve a nation's competitiveness in the tradable sector of the economy.

The imposition of capital controls by many governments at the beginning of the Bretton Woods system provided their policymakers with leeway in responding to serious balance-of-payments pressures that signaled fundamental misalignment of their currencies. The perception that a currency was seriously misaligned (over- or undervalued)—and therefore likely to prompt the sponsoring government to seek an adjustment in its par value—could lead to massive outflows of capital, absent capital controls. Such outflows could force rapid and destabilizing shifts in the value of a currency, or worse, exit from the Bretton Woods system. Successful limits on the ability of capital to exit allowed policymakers to resist adjustment of their currency's par value and so support the narrow-peg system. Even if they proved unsuccessful at addressing the balance-of-payments pressures and maintaining a currency's par value, capital controls afforded policymakers the opportunity to seek a stable adjustment in the currency's par value.

The gradual liberalization of capital controls and the reawakening of global financial markets beginning in the 1960s led to increases in international capital mobility. And with greater capital mobility, many policymakers found themselves under greater and greater pressure to adjust their currencies due to changes in their balance-of-payments positions. It became increasingly difficult to maintain their commitment to the narrow pegs of the Bretton Woods and Smithsonian monetary systems. They could defend parity within the bands of the system, but this arrangement would not remove balance-of-payments pressures that signaled a fundamental misalignment in the currency. Such pressures would continue to build.

As capital controls were relaxed, policymakers realized that the mere suggestion that a state was going to adjust its currency's par value could lead to outflows of capital and potential crisis. The situation was increasingly troubling for policymakers across many states, and, by 1973, the system was in crisis. President Nixon's "greatest monetary agreement of all time" tottered and began to collapse. As some currencies moved beyond the ±2.25 percent bands established by the Smithsonian system, that system became too costly, economically and politically, for the United States. An overvalued dollar helped European and Japanese exporters, as their nations ran surpluses in their trade accounts with the United States, but American producers and labor in the tradable sector suffered. The United States experienced persistent balance-of-payments pressures and repeated attacks on the dollar. These attacks required U.S. and other states' monetary authorities to intervene to actively support the dollar's par value.

The Float

U.S. policymakers were inclined to let the dollar float. As the dominant currency in international transactions, a floating dollar would put tremendous corrective pressures upon the currencies of states running surpluses. Because they benefited from the dollar's plight, however, the Europeans and Japanese preferred a system of adjustable-pegged rates, intended to maintain the par values of an adjustable peg. This arrangement would place the burden on the United States to adjust. Negotiations to address the frailties of the system attempted to save the adjustable peg, but they failed to produce a resolution. Finally, finance ministers from the United States, the United Kingdom, France, Germany and Japan—known as the Group of 5 (G-5) and also as the Interim Committee—became the locus of negotiations.

In the G-5 deliberations, the Europeans and Japanese continued to push for an adjustable peg, but U.S. policymakers resisted. As holder of the key reserve currency, the U.S. position was central to the final outcome. Instead of adopting a system of pegged but adjustable rates, as preferred by the Europeans and the Japanese, the G-5 advocated a stable system of exchange rates. Let's consider the difference: instead of stable rates (pegged rates) the G-5 proposed a stable system based upon expectations that members would support stable exchange-rate policies by implementing sound macroeconomic and monetary policies. It did not advocate a specific exchange rate for each currency, but a stable system of exchange rates. Conceivably, a variety of different exchange-rate mechanisms could coexist, as long as governments worked to maintain a relatively stable relationship among those different mechanisms and to limit shocks that could transmit instability across the system.

The G-5 proposal led to the Second Amendment to the IMF Articles of Agreement in 1978, which formally legalized floating exchange rates and eliminated the role of gold as a reserve asset. Under the new system, governments were responsible for managing their domestic economies so as to reduce economic and exchange-rate instability. The IMF thus gained a responsibility to oversee economic activities by its members that could affect the stability of the exchange-rate system.

The new system brought a variety of exchange-rate arrangements. The United States and some other states moved to a float, whereby currency prices were determined primarily by supply and demand in currency markets. Both the persistent U.S. current-account deficit, which had provided the liquidity essential to rebuilding and economic expansion since World War II, and the inflationary policies adopted by the United States during the Vietnam conflict created a vast supply of dollars in the international system and downward pressures on the dollar's value. After adoption of a float, the dollar depreciated dramatically against many currencies, while the deutschmark, the yen, and the pound sterling appreciated quickly. Many feared that a floating-rate system would generate wild and recurring swings in the value of currencies, which would create currency risk damaging to international exchange. Others predicted that market forces would quickly push rates to their equilibrium levels with little volatility after the initial change in values. Neither prediction was accurate: floating exchange rates proved more volatile than the pegged systems, but the volatility did not approach the instability feared by supporters of an adjustable peg. After the initial exchange-rate perturbations, any further extreme shifts in currency values tended to reflect the effect of currency markets disciplining governments for mismanagement of their economies.

Floating exchange rates did not mean that all governments refrained from intervening to manage the price of their currencies. Many actively intervened in currency markets to adjust the supply of their currencies through monetary and fiscal policies, becoming buyers and sellers of currencies, using capital controls to limit capital inflows or outflows, changing reserve and deposit requirements for foreigners in their banking systems, placing limitations on foreign purchases of domestic securities, and engaging international cooperation. Other governments were more flexible, more willing to allow market forces to determine the values of their currencies and less willing to intervene in currency markets.

The decline in the value of the dollar reversed by the late 1970s, as U.S. policies and inflows of foreign capital to the United States strengthened the dollar and increased demand for dollar-denominated financial instruments. In 1979 Paul Volcker, newly appointed as chairman of the Federal Reserve Board by President Carter, moved to throttle the inflation in the United States that was feeding stagnation in the global economy. He used Federal Reserve policies to raise interest rates and reduce money supply, which pushed up the value of the dollar. As gaps between foreign and U.S. interest rates grew, foreign capital discovered that U.S. interest rates provided a greater rate of return on their financial investments. Demand for dollar-denominated assets increased, the demand for dollars increased, and the value of the dollar appreciated.

President Reagan's policies during the 1980s reinforced the inflow of foreign capital into the United States and the appreciation of the dollar. When his administration cut taxes even as it was undertaking a dramatic expansion in national security outlays, government revenues fell further behind government outlays. To pay for this expanding public deficit, the U.S. government sold government bonds—debt obligations. As its deficit increased, the government had to sell more and more bonds and offer more and more attractive rates of return to draw in investors. This policy pushed interest rates (the rate of return) on U.S. government bonds up, which made U.S. government debt even more attractive to investors. U.S. government debt was regarded as relatively risk free, but it offered rates of return better than many investment opportunities in the global market that carried substantially greater risk. As these financial instruments were denominated in dollars, investors needed dollars to buy them, so the demand for dollars increased and the value of the dollar appreciated further. Adding even more fuel to the upward pressures on the value of the dollar was the fact that private industries had to increase the rates of return on their debt offerings in the United States in order to compete with the U.S. government for capital. Interest rates rose in both U.S. public and private debt markets.

The dollar's rise continued until 1985, as the Reagan administration refrained from manipulating the exchange rate. The Europeans and Japanese were slow to push the United States to manage the dollar's value because their tradable sectors benefited from the dollar's appreciation. But by the mid-1980s, U.S. producers and labor were pressuring Congress for relief, demanding the adoption of protectionist trade measures. The rise of these protectionist pressures worried the Europeans and the Japanese—who feared that erection of U.S. trade barriers would limit their ability to sell in U.S. markets and damage their producers and labor—as well as the Reagan administration—which believed that such protectionist measures could undermine its neoliberal agenda of promoting market forces over government management of economic affairs.

Faced with a choice between more active management of the exchange rate and protectionism, the policymakers in the Reagan administration decided to promote a stable and orderly depreciation in the value of the dollar vis-á-vis other currencies. But this gradual adjustment process required substantial cooperation between the monetary authorities of the major states. By now, the size of currency markets precluded unilateral intervention to significantly shift a currency's value. Producing an orderly shift in a currency's value required a sustained commitment of resources, and, even then, currency traders might not have confidence in a state's willingness or ability to pay such costs. If currency traders were not *indifferent* to a state's commitment, they might bet against the government's position in the currency markets. Only a joint commitment by the major nations to a currency's value could convince traders to be indifferent to that value. Such commitment was essential to an orderly realignment of a currency like the dollar. In 1985 the G-5 met at the Plaza Hotel in New York and adopted a joint policy to reverse the appreciation of the dollar. The dollar fell rapidly after the so-called Plaza Accord—within a year it had declined between 30 and 40 percent against its major trading partners.

This substantial depreciation in the dollar affected the competitiveness of non–U.S. producers in the tradable sector and led to pressures on other governments to stem the appreciation in their currencies. In 1987 the G-5 met at the Louvre in Paris to discuss whether to stabilize the dollar's value or to continue letting it depreciate, and, if they were to agree upon stabilization, what policies should be adopted in support of stabilization. The ministers agreed to stop the dollar's decline, stabilizing it at current levels. Central banks, acting together, then intervened in currency markets to prop up the dollar

After the Louvre Agreement halted its decline, the dollar rose in value for the next several years. But by 1989, it began to decline again to the benefit of U.S. producers and labor and the competitiveness of their products in the tradable sector. Within a few years, the fall in the value of the dollar was again creating problems for non–U.S. producers and labor abroad. Japanese producers and labor faced the most serious problems. In the early 1990s a real estate bubble burst in Japan, threatening the stability of financial credit institutions, slowing domestic consumption and investment, and leading to stagnation in the Japanese economy. A declining dollar added to Japanese economic woes, and it also hindered economic expansion in the European economies.

Despite these foreign concerns, Presidents George H.W. Bush and Bill Clinton allowed the dollar to continue to decline through benign neglect. No strong interests in U.S. society argued for strengthening the dollar, as compared to the mid-1980s when U.S. producers and labor had pushed for the dollar's depreciation. Why was domestic pressure forthcoming in one instance and not the other? Overvalued currencies create significant problems for their nations' producers in the tradable sector, as the prices of their goods increase relative to those of other nations' producers; undervalued currencies have the opposite effect, lowering the prices of their producers' goods in the tradable sector. In nations with undervalued currencies, consumers may be hurt, as they encounter higher-priced imports and an increased likelihood of inflation. But, compared to producers, consumers are a diffuse and unorganized interest, and so they encounter difficulties in presenting a united front, agreeing upon common objectives, voicing those objectives, and acting in a concerted manner to demand government policy change. Producers in the tradable sector are a more concentrated interest, and, as a consequence, they are more likely to overcome barriers to collective action and to appeal to governments for redress.

Currency Pegs

Many governments feared the potential volatility of a floating exchange rate—memories of the last systematic experience with floating exchange rates, during the interwar years, did not inspire confidence. Policymakers in small, developing political economies were particularly fearful of exchange-rate instability, because exports often constituted a relatively large portion of their overall economies. Moreover, they looked to foreign assistance and investment inflows to promote economic expansion, and they worried that excessive exchange-rate volatility could create currency risk, damage their domestic producers in the tradable sector, deter foreign investment, and promote capital flight. Hoping to reassure foreign investors and create stable expectations, therefore, many of these states pegged their currencies to the currency of their major trading partner. Many of the Latin American states pegged their currencies to the dollar, many former British colonies pegged their currencies to the pound, and many former French colonies pegged their currencies to the franc.

Most governments that took this step chose to adopt a peg with some flexibility in its band, which meant that their currencies could trade within a reasonable range of the dominant currency to which it was pegged and still remain within the peg. But some states adopted an extremely narrow version of a peg called a **currency control board,** which tightens the trading band of a currency. The statutory provisions that created a currency control board generally dictated the ability of a government to affect money supply. These provisions tied government monetary policies to **hard currency** reserves in the national treasury—those currencies that can readily be used and accepted in international transactions because they will hold their value over time and present relatively little currency risk to the parties of a transaction. Today, most international transactions are conducted in the hard currencies of the dollar, the pound, the euro, the yen, and a few others. As hard currency reserves increased, the government increased money supply, and as reserves decreased, it was mandated to decrease money supply. Generally, the connection between hard currency reserves and money supply was transparent and tied to a specific formula, which limited the ability of policymakers to change money supply independent of the changes in hard currency reserves. Effectively, a government tied control of its currency and money supply to its success in trade and the monetary policies of its major trading partner. Adoption of a currency control board was an extreme policy with the aim of constraining national policymakers, limiting inflation, and importing the stability and discipline of a major currency.

Governments often maintained capital controls to support their pegs. They hoped that controls could limit the outflow of capital during speculative attacks on their currencies, provide them with added resources to combat such attacks, and consequently limit such attacks that could damage their economies and place the governments at risk from their societies. But with growing financial globalization (the increasing openness and integration of national financial markets), the ability of governments to maintain capital controls and currency pegs became more difficult. Governments needed to intervene in currency markets to maintain their currencies' value within a prescribed trading range, but the amount of hard currency reserves necessary for such active intervention steadily increased. By pegging the value of a currency to its major trading partner, a small state exposed itself to the demands of the macroeconomic and monetary policies of its larger trading partner.

For example, monetary policy choices by the Federal Reserve or U.S. budgetary choices that affected the value of the dollar would require governments and central banks in states pegged to the dollar to adjust their policies. This meant that small governments with very limited resources would be exposed to policy choices by big governments with vastly greater resources. To compound this problem, the governments of the larger states would usually make their policy decisions based upon their domestic political economies, with little concern for the influence of their choices upon their smaller trading partners.

Well-intentioned policies to limit exchange-rate volatility, such as capital controls or a narrow peg, often backfired. They could create opportunities for currency traders to bet against a government and could raise barriers to investment. If enough traders in currency markets believed that a government's currency was fundamentally misaligned and doubted its ability to maintain its pegs and capital controls, this belief increased the likelihood of a speculative attack. Moreover, the ability to get in and out of an investment—mobility—is a means to limit risk. Controls limiting the mobility of capital could stymie investment if investors preferred arenas that allowed easier entrance and exit. Many of the financial crises of the 1990s, including the Mexican peso crisis, the Russian ruble crisis, the Asian financial crisis, and the Argentinean crisis, resulted from pegs that came under attack in currency markets by traders who viewed those pegs as fundamentally misaligned. Attacking the governments' commitments to maintain their pegs, the currency traders overwhelmed the ability of these governments to defend their currencies and led to massive devaluation—in some cases almost 30 percent—in the prices of their currencies. This devaluation degraded the purchasing power of people in those countries and imposed significant economic hardships, particularly on the lower income groups.

The European Snake

The potential volatility of a floating-rate system concerned policymakers in some of the advanced industrialized nations. The tradable sectors in many Western European states constituted a larger portion of their economies than was the case in the United States and Japan. By design, the Western European economies had grown increasingly connected by trade. The European Coal and Steel Community (ECSC) and its successor, the European Economic Community (EEC), were created to increase European economic interdependence, control

German aggressiveness by integrating Germany's economic fortunes with those of its neighbors, and limit beggar-thy-neighbor policies by creating a network of cooperative agreements. As a result, intra-European trade and the exposure of their national economies to the global arena increased, which meant that they were more sensitive to shifts in exchange rates.

Seeking to constrain exchange-rate instability, many European states cooperated to create a collective-currency peg, which came to be called the **European Snake.** The parties to the Snake specified a fluctuation band that would limit the trading range of their currencies vis-á-vis each other, define the responsibilities of the members to intervene and support their currencies and those of other members, and create financing facilities to help states with weak currencies remain within the trading band. The parties to the Snake agreed to retain the ± 2.25 percent bands of the Smithsonian Agreement.

The Snake quickly came under pressure as the global economy was hit by oil shocks in the 1970s. Energy costs reduced the competitiveness of the European economies at the same time that the dollar began to depreciate. This combined effect put divergent pressures on the Snake, as some currencies grew weaker and others remained relatively strong. Weak currency countries pushed the bottom boundaries of the Snake, while strong currency countries pushed at its upper boundary. Differences in domestic monetary and fiscal policies added to the pressures, as currencies threatened to move outside the band of the Snake. Facing economic slowdown and increased unemployment, the French enacted expansionary policies to promote growth, but these actions weakened its currency. The German central bank, the Bundesbank, fearing inflation more than slow growth, reacted against the inflationary pressures of increasing oil prices, thus limiting the adoption of expansionary policies in Germany and keeping the German currency strong. Such differences in macroeconomic policies sent mixed messages to traders in the currency markets, which increased the potential for speculative attacks.

The Snake was being pulled in different directions by its two major currencies. Each government wanted the other to intervene and realign its currency, but neither wanted to realign its own currency. Other members faced the same tension, and the debate focused on whether the weak or strong currencies should be the currencies to realign. The size of the German economy and the strength of the deutsche mark had made it the core currency of the Snake, but the weaker currency countries had no means to affect the policies of the Bundesbank. Unable to influence German monetary policy or to coordinate the policies of member states, weak currency states faced the choice of surrendering control over their monetary policies (adopting Germany's anti-inflationary price stability stance) or withdrawing from the European Snake when they could no longer defend their currencies. Arguments continued throughout the 1970s, and, after numerous attempts at realignment, France, the United Kingdom, Italy, Denmark, Sweden, and Norway were forced to withdraw from the Snake at one time or another.

The European Monetary System (EMS)

By the late 1970s, the inability of many states to stay within the 4.5 percent band of the European Snake led to discussions, particularly between the Germans and French, over the formation of a **European Monetary System (EMS).** At the heart of the negotiations sat a tension between strong currency states and weak currency states over who would adjust to protect the collective-currency peg if national currencies threatened to move beyond the boundaries of the peg. The commitment of the German Bundesbank and other central banks to price and currency stability made their currencies strong. But in other states such as France, policymakers faced electoral pressures, constituent demands, labor unrest, and other societal pressures that prompted pro-growth policies even at the risk of inflation. Elevating growth over price stability as a policy objective led to increases in money supply that could depreciate the value of a currency. States implementing such policies drifted toward the bottom of the band of the currency peg. The Snake had no agreement over who was to adjust if some currencies became too weak relative to the strong currencies, or if some currencies became too strong relative to the weak currencies.

Bilateral discussions between France and Germany paved the path to the EMS. French-German agreement was critical. The French wanted strong-currency states to adopt expansionary policies and weak-currency states to implement contractionary policies in defense of the peg. They also sought to have strong-currency states intervene in currency markets in defense of the collective peg to strengthen weak currencies by using the strong currency to buy the weak currency. German policymakers also recognized the need to intervene to help weak-currency nations, but they feared that a commitment to intervene and purchase weak currencies could flood the currency markets with too much of the strong currency, undermining its strength as a strong currency and damaging the anti-inflationary commitment to price stability in the strong-currency nation.

The French-German negotiations finessed this divide by linking Bundesbank intervention to the ability of weak-currency states to reestablish their rates within the peg or to their willingness to realign (devalue) their currencies. If a weak-currency state could not adjust its policies to remain within the peg even with the intervention of strong-currency countries, or if a weak-currency state was unwilling to devalue, the Bundesbank could decide not to intervene in support of a weak currency. Intervention by Germany or other strong-currency states thus depended upon the willingness of weak-currency states to either adjust their policies or devalue. Each side had an out, but both made the necessary gestures to promote cooperation.

The French-German agreement provided a basis for the European Community (EC) member states to form the EMS in 1979. EMS targeted a collective peg with ± 2.25 percent bands, but allowed some weaker-currency states (such as Italy) a wider, transitional band of 6 percent. Governments could implement capital controls in defense of their currencies to provide some policy autonomy. All but one EC nation, the United Kingdom, joined this **Exchange Rate Mechanism (ERM)** at the start. This collective peg worked remarkably well during the 1980s, as none of the original parties to the ERM moved beyond the band. Pressures did arise that threatened the system, but orderly devaluations of weak currencies helped to manage the stresses. By the early 1990s, the EC had expanded, and almost all its members were operating within the ERM. Stability in the EMS encouraged European leaders to broach greater European integration. Encouraged by success in the exchange-rate regime, policymakers thought greater integration was possible and predicted that it would help European economic producers compete better with U.S. and Japanese economic enterprise.

In the early 1990s, a global economic slowdown, declining European competitiveness, increasing European unemployment, and the desire to assist Eastern European political economies after the breakdown of communist rule in 1989 increased pressures on the EMS, which limited the ability of the EMS states to manage tensions within the ERM. As the strong-currency anchor of the ERM, Germany faced a special problem. West Germany's financing of the political and economic unification of the two Germanys transformed Germany from one of the largest creditor states into one of the largest debtor states overnight. Germany borrowed heavily to finance unification, which led to increases in European interest rates because of Germany's dominant position in Europe. The EMS was being taxed by global events.

By the last quarter of 1992, the EMS came under attack as currency traders began to speculate over the future of European monetary cooperation. Currency traders bet against the willingness and ability of EMS governments to defend currencies that contributed to European unemployment and economic stagnation. Weak currencies fell to the lower boundary of the band, and then below the band. The British pound, Italian lira, Portuguese escudo, Spanish peseta, Swedish krona, Irish punt, Danish krone, and French franc faced increasing pressures as currency traders challenged governments to keep their currencies within the bands of the EMS. Governments defended these currencies with a mixture of tools, including raising interest rates, currency market interventions by central banks and finance ministries, tightening capital controls, and finally devaluations. Both strong- and weak-currency governments dipped deeply into their hard currency reserves to defend the EMS.

By mid-September 1992, the United Kingdom and Italy had withdrawn from the ERM and allowed their currencies to float. But the crisis did not subside, as currency traders kept the pressure on other weak EMS currencies. More devaluations followed. By the end of July 1993, the EMS appeared ready to completely collapse—the financial reserves of a group of advanced industrialized governments could no longer withstand the currency market pressures. The EMS governments capitulated by expanding the ERM bands to 15 percent—not quite a float, but still quite a large change in the band.

The European Monetary Union (EMU)

The European Coal and Steel Community, the predecessor of the EEC, had hoped to reduce the prospect of European conflict by linking German and French economic fortunes. The EEC built upon this foundation with cooperative agreements that aimed to increase European economic interdependence. The level and robustness of monetary cooperation in the EMS, even if only partly successful, was quite remarkable, given the willingness of the United States and Japan to let their currencies float and the declining competitiveness of European economic enterprises vis-á-vis U.S. and Japanese industries. The prospect of defecting from the collective-peg system offered the temptation of a more competitive exchange rate, but the relationships created by a framework of cooperative agreements during the postwar years withstood the temptation to defect. Members withdrew from the ERM only after a period of concerted and severe crisis in 1992.

During the mid-1980s, discussions advanced over greater monetary integration in Europe. Such unification had been envisioned as early as the late 1960s, but governments had been unwilling to surrender monetary sovereignty and accept the elimination of national monies. On the trade front, meanwhile, declining competitiveness and increasing unemployment pushed the agenda of integration and monetary union. In 1986 the Single European Act targeted the creation of a unified European market in order to take advantage of economies of scale and scope, to increase the competitiveness of European producers, and to reduce unemployment. As this goal would require removing obstructions to exchange within the EC, the Single European Act promoted the harmonization of regulatory arrangements across the EC states and the dismantling of other barriers to the flow of goods, services, and inputs to production within the EC.

Nonetheless, national monies were viewed as obstacles to greater integration. They gave governments tools to escape the costs of adjustment from greater market integration, or to shift those costs onto EC neighbors. EC members could still be pressured by protectionist constituents to use monetary policies, the exchange rate, capital controls, and other policy tools that would hinder trade and limit long-term gains from economies of scale and scope. This persistent vulnerability to protectionist pressures placed monetary unification at the center of discussions about greater integration.

In 1988–1989 the Delors Commission (named after the president of the European Commission, Jacques Delors) advocated monetary union and the adoption of a common currency, the removal of capital controls, and the elimination of autonomous national monetary authorities, which were to be replaced by creation of a European Central Bank (ECB) that centralized monetary authority. National central banks would become agents of the ECB. Some hoped for greater political unification, but the Delors Commission resisted explicit recommendations to promote political unification and avoided centralization of fiscal policies, protecting national policy autonomy in this area. It did advocate constraints on deficits, a government debt ceiling, and other macroeconomic targets, which in effect would limit some fiscal policy autonomy. It envisioned that monetary union would be easier to attain if member economies were more alike than different—that greater macroeconomic alignment across members was necessary to reduce the stress on monetary union.

The Delors Report led to formal intergovernmental negotiations, which in 1991 produced the Maastricht Treaty, creating a three-stage timetable for monetary unification (see table 10.1). Stage I, which began in 1990, sought the end of capital controls, which would remove barriers to the formation of a unified financial market. Borrowers from across the EU, public and private, would compete in a unified market that would discipline governments and industries seeking to borrow capital if they implemented policies that investors considered uncompetitive. Investors could essentially reward good performance with lower capital costs (interest rates) and penalize what they perceived as poor activity with higher capital costs. The end of capital controls, which had provided some insulation from such pressures, reduced the ability of governments to adopt macroeconomic policies that were inconsistent with the policies of other member states.

TABLE 10.1   **The Maastricht Treaty**

Stage	Components
I	An end to capital controls
	• Removed barriers to forming a unified financial market
	• Reduced governments' ability to adopt macroeconomic policies inconsistent with those of other member states
II	Harmonizing macroeconomic policies through convergence goals
	• The Maastricht criteria
	• European Monetary Institute: helped to coordinate policies
	• Reduced divergent pressures that threaten monetary union
III	Monetary union
	• Retained distinct national currencies at first, with fixed exchange rates
	• Phased in the euro to replace national currencies
	• National central banks ceded authority to manipulate monetary policy (money supply and interest rates)

Stage II targeted the harmonization of macroeconomic policies by establishing convergence goals—the **Maastricht criteria**—which governments had to meet by 1997 as they moved to Stage III. As part of Stage II, Maastricht created the European Monetary Institute (EMI) to aid EC members in coordinating their policies as they worked to meet the convergence criteria. EU policymakers believed that these convergence goals were central to reducing divergent pressures that could threaten the success of monetary union. The underlying assumption was that if political economies were more alike than different in their policy beliefs, expectations, and practice, they would respond similarly to stress. EU governments were expected to achieve certain targets by 1997 if they wanted to qualify for the European Monetary Union (EMU) and a common currency; if states met the following criteria, it was believed that they shared similar approaches to long-term government borrowing, deficits, inflation, and exchange-rate stability:

- Government deficits below 3 percent of GDP
- Government debt below 60 percent of GDP
- Inflation rate not to exceed by more than 1.5 percent the average of the three best performing members of the EU
- Long-term government bond yields (interest rates) not to exceed by more than 2 percent the average of the three best performing members of the EU
- Maintenance of its currency within the ERM bands for two years

Stage III, monetary union, was set to begin on January 1, 1999, even if only a minority of the EU members met the convergence criteria. The beginning date could shift if EU members agreed to another date. Initially, those states qualifying for EMU would retain their national currencies, but these currencies would fix exchange rates vis-á-vis each other. Functionally, fixing exchange rates creates a single currency with conversion rates between different denominations of cash, much like the relationship between pennies, nickels, dimes, quarters, and dollars. A new currency, the *euro,* would phase in over a multiple-year period and eventually replace national currencies. In Stage III, national central banks would cede their ability to manipulate monetary policy to the ECB: They would no longer control money supply or interest rates. EU members remaining outside the EMU could join an ERM anchored by the euro and with bands up to 15 percent.

In late 1991 the EU appeared fully committed to implementing the three stages. But economic conditions and a crisis in the ERM in 1992 began to hollow out support for monetary union. A growing proportion of the publics in member states began to question the wisdom of surrendering monetary policy to the EU. Monetary unification had been easier to promote during the good economic times of the late 1980s; it became much more difficult as member economies stagnated in the early 1990s, and public opinion polls in the EU revealed a growing indifference, even dislike, for the EU agenda. By June 1992, a Eurobarometer poll showed support for the single-market program at 44 percent—a decline of 13 percent from its highest level of public support in 1987. Enthusiasm for the EU had fallen least in less economically advanced states such as Greece, Portugal, Spain, and Ireland, and most in the original EEC member states of Luxembourg, Belgium, France, and Germany.

The Danish referendum to ratify the Maastricht Treaty in June 1992 reflected the growing shift in public sentiment. After the Danes voted against ratification, all of a sudden the Maastricht Treaty, monetary union, and the EU were seen to be in danger. Currency traders viewed the Danish referendum and growing public resistance to the Maastricht Treaty as a lack of credible commitment by EU members, and they began to challenge the ERM in currency markets, thus contributing to the 1992 ERM crisis. The crisis was eventually resolved in the second half of 1993 and the bands of the ERM expanded to 15 percent. A French referendum on Maastricht passed in September by a narrow margin as the pro-monetary union forces prevailed.

Despite threats, the EMU stayed on schedule, and Stage III went into effect in January 1999. Eleven EU members joined EMU, placed their monetary policies under the ECB, and for all intents and purposes adopted a single currency. The central banks of Austria, Belgium, Finland, France, Germany, Ireland, Italy, Luxembourg, Netherlands, Portugal, and Spain thus transferred their ability to manipulate monetary and exchange-rate policies to the ECB. Financial institutions, financial markets, and governments immediately began using the euro as a unit of account and settlement. Although it would be three years before people on the street started using euro notes and coins, conversion rates between EMU members' currencies became fixed, essentially creating a single currency. Greece met the convergence criteria and joined EMU in January 2000. Then, on January 1, 2002, euro notes and coins entered everyday circulation, and by the end of February 2002, the Austrian schilling, Belgian franc, Dutch guilder, Finish markka, French franc, German mark, Greek drachma, Irish punt, Italian lire, Luxembourg franc, Portuguese escudo, and Spanish peseta were all removed from circulation.

To the degree that EMU lowered real and cognitive barriers to cross-border exchange and capital mobility within the EMU area, it increased competitive pressures upon producers and fueled greater integration of the single market. EMU also promoted the integration of fragmented financial markets into larger and deeper markets with greater liquidity. Governments and industries would have to compete for capital in increasingly unified financial markets, which would help investors and borrowers by creating more opportunities to lend and borrow capital, to manage risk through portfolio diversification, and to obtain more efficient pricing of capital. Moreover, the run-up to Stage III led to greater policy discipline, EU cooperation, and coordination of national macroeconomic policies, including fiscal and labor market policies as well as monetary policies. Even EU members that did not join EMU used the Maastricht criteria to limit government intervention in economies that supported uncompetitive practices. With greater financial market integration, such markets could penalize those that adopted policies contrary to EMU guidelines, thus placing anti-inflationary and price stability pressures on all EU members.

Monetary union has helped to reassert Europe's position in the global political economy. The economic, demographic, and physical size of the EMU, the growing international use of the euro and its price stability, and the increasing size of integrated European financial markets have reinforced the role of Europe in international affairs. A large, integrated market with a single currency tends to be more influential than many smaller markets with many currencies. The use of the euro as a reserve currency and means of denominating international trade has expanded—it is a tool of exchange, a unit of account, and a storehouse of value. Monetary union can add fuel to the pressures for political unification if greater alignment of economic interests helps to create shared values and identities that lead to greater pressures for convergence on domestic and foreign policies.

EMU is an extraordinary and remarkable experiment in governance. Monetary union has transferred governance of an important policy tool of sovereign governments—monetary policy—from national central banks to a supranational institution, the ECB, by means of an international treaty between sovereign states. Nevertheless, EU members have maintained their identities as distinct states in the international system, indicating that theirs is a hybrid experiment that muddies the very basis of the Westphalian state system.

FINANCIAL GLOBALIZATION AND LIBERALIZATION

The post–Bretton Woods period witnessed three distinct trends that transformed global finance and altered state-market relationships: (1) a reawakening of *financial globalization,* whereby national financial systems became increasingly connected to one another; (2) *financial liberalization,* as the market forces of supply, demand, and price competition were unleashed in financial markets; and (3) dramatic changes in *international capital mobility,* the ease or difficulty of moving capital across borders or transforming one financial asset into another. The changes in financial globalization, financial liberalization, and international capital mobility are some of the most significant changes in social relations during the latter part of the twentieth century—affecting how governments and industries borrow, their cost of capital, public and corporate governance, the connections across political economies, and the influence of financial markets on global economic relations.

Financial globalization involves the lowering of barriers to cross-border capital flows. This practice has led to an expansion in **global capital,** or capital that can move from one nation to another. Financial globalization includes **foreign direct investments (FDI)**—cross-border capital flows that result in significant ownership and management control of overseas economic enterprises—as well as all cross-border portfolio financial transactions, such as lending and borrowing, trading in currencies or in some other form of financial instrument (bonds, equities, or some financial derivative), or the provision of any financial service. These cross-border flows fall into two categories: **money market** flows and **capital market** flows. Money markets involve the trading of financial instruments that have a maturity of less than one year; capital markets issue and trade financial obligations with maturities longer than a year. Traders in money markets exchange currencies, currency futures and options, and other short-term obligations. Capital markets involve the exchange of capital for longer-term economic activities such as investment in plant and people. On average, money market flows are more volatile and liquid. This mobility across state boundaries affords holders of capital an ability to reward or penalize economic and governmental activity—to impose discipline.

The late 1800s saw the mechanisms of capital accumulation and allocation reach across national boundaries to connect lenders and borrowers of diverse nationalities. Active global capital markets based primarily in London played a major role in the economic development of the Atlantic economies before the stock market crash of 1929 and the Great Depression. But, the breakdown in financial globalization in the early twentieth century and the postwar design to limit financial globalization meant that the mechanisms of capital accumulation and allocation were predominantly national for much of the twentieth century.

Financial globalization reemerged after decades of stagnation, when international borrowing accelerated in the 1960s. A trickle of cross-border interactions turned into a deluge as global capital flows expanded to levels unseen since before the depression (see figure 10.1). Global capital markets now play essential roles in promoting economic activity. They influence who can get capital and at what price. They affect prospects for economic advancement and improvements in social welfare, create networks of interdependence that link societies across national boundaries, obstruct regulatory oversight and control, and produce pathways for transmission of economic improvements as well as dislocating shocks from one nation to another. Financial globalization feeds interdependence and alters conceptions of ownership, risk, investment, geography, and the state.

Financial globalization constitutes only one component of this late-century shift in capital relations. Financial liberalization, another component, refers to market liberalization in the financial sector, or the unleashing of market forces of supply, demand, and price competition for capital. It prompted innovation in financial services and strategies, as well as creative destruction in the financial arena. Regulatory liberalization in the major markets encouraged competitive pricing of capital and greater **disintermediation** and **securitization** of borrowing. Disintermediation involved shifting large-scale borrowing by economic enterprises away from commercial banks, where the banking institution guaranteed a specific rate of return to savers and intermediated their risks, and toward securitized financial instruments such as bonds and equities. Securitization took financial liabilities and transformed or packaged them into financial instruments such as bonds and stocks that could be sold in financial markets. Together, disintermediation and securitization meant that the saver (investor) accepted the full risk of the loan to a borrower but also reaped the full reward. With liberalization, those seeking to borrow capital increasingly preferred issuing securitized financial instruments (bonds and equities) in disintermediated markets instead of commercial loans in intermediated markets. Figure 10.2 displays the activities of borrowers in OECD

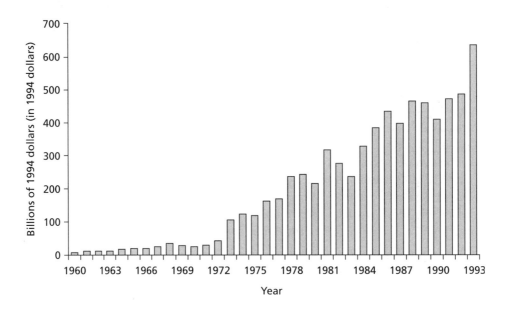

| FIGURE 10.1 | International Borrowing, 1960–1993: Mid- and Long-Term International and Foreign bond and Loan Instruments |

Source: OECD Financial Statistics Monthly.

states (the advanced industrialized political economies), developing states, and the Eastern European states of the former Soviet sphere of influence in intermediated and disintermediated global financial markets. Borrowers in the advanced industrialized economies accessed these markets far more heavily than did borrowers from other political economies, enjoyed a disproportionate rate of increase, and increasingly favored disintermediated instruments. Borrowers from non-OECD political economies found potentially greater access to global financial resources than they had in the past, but more often they were limited to less flexible and more costly intermediated financial instruments. Liberalization generated increasing complexity and linkages within and across markets. Financial infrastructures within nations deepened, even as financial interactions between nations expanded.

Financial globalization and liberalization afford tremendous opportunities and corresponding challenges for public and private policymakers, offering new opportunities and strategies for individuals, firms, and governments to acquire capital, lower capital costs, and manage risk. Borrowers can increasingly access capital at home and abroad, seeking lower-cost capital in more efficient and liquid markets. But these trends can also strain national political

FIGURE 10.2 Intermediated and Disintermediated Borrowing by Borrower, 1973–1993: Mid- and Long-Term International and Foreign Instruments

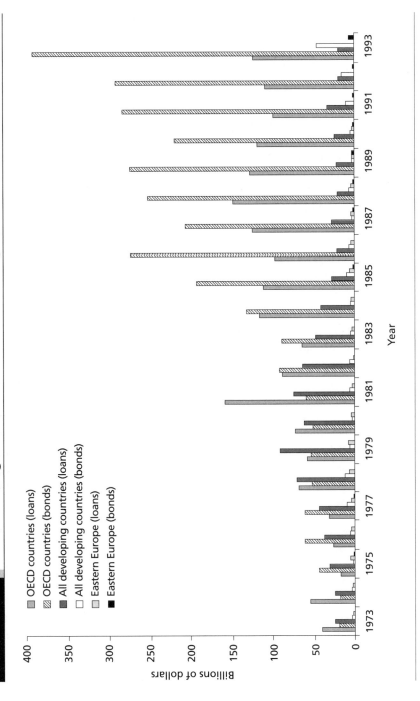

Source: OECD Financial Statistics Monthly.

economies, pose dilemmas for policymakers, and constrain national policy autonomy. Even though globalization and liberalization generally help many borrowers in terms of improved access and lower capital costs, the transformation in global financial relations systematically helps some more than others. Financial globalization divides those who can borrow in global capital markets from those who cannot (see figure 10.3). This effect raises tremendous normative implications for the distribution of wealth, opportunities, and influence in the international political economy. Systematic variations in access to capital separate the haves from the have-nots, creating or exacerbating tensions and divisions in and across societies. Nations with poor economic growth and opportunity are economic disasters for their populations, but they also can spawn political discontent and serve as breeding grounds for political violence and terror, which can damage national polities and spill across national boundaries.

The relative paucity of access to global capital markets for borrowers from developing nations does not mean that such disparities in capital flows exist across all forms of investment capital. One area of investment capital in which borrowers from developing nations have gained some footing is **foreign direct investments (FDI),** cross-border capital flows that result in significant ownership and management control of overseas economic enterprises. In developing nations, FDI has grown at a much faster rate than the ability to borrow in global capital markets (see table 10.2). Of course, this form of international capital mobility, which produces foreign ownership of economic activity in domestic spheres, raises questions of domestic control and management of the economy, and it sometimes sparks nationalist discontent and protectionist policies even as it creates economic opportunity.

Decision makers must now consider the reaction of global capital to their decisions. Some believe that financial globalization and liberalization provide public and private policymakers with new resources, but many fear that this increased cross-border capital mobility may diminish the autonomy and capabilities of national policymakers. Regardless, the role of financial globalization and liberalization will be an increasingly important consideration in international affairs. Policymakers are growing more attentive to movements in financial markets and cross-border mobility of capital. James Carville, President Bill Clinton's 1992 campaign manager, noted the growing influence:

> I used to think that if there was reincarnation, I wanted to come back as the president or the pope. But now I want to be the bond market: you can intimidate everybody.[1]

Explanations for Globalization

Recall our discussion in chapter 1 about looking for causality in global affairs. In our systematic investigation of the phenomenon of globalization, we should be able to identify how independent variables may cause the dependent variables. Could such factors as technology and competition or changes in politics and policy cause globalization?

---

[1] *The Economist*, October 7, 1995, Survey pg. 3.

FIGURE 10.3 International Borrowing by Category of Borrower, 1960–1993: Mid- and Long-Term International and Foreign Bonds and Loans

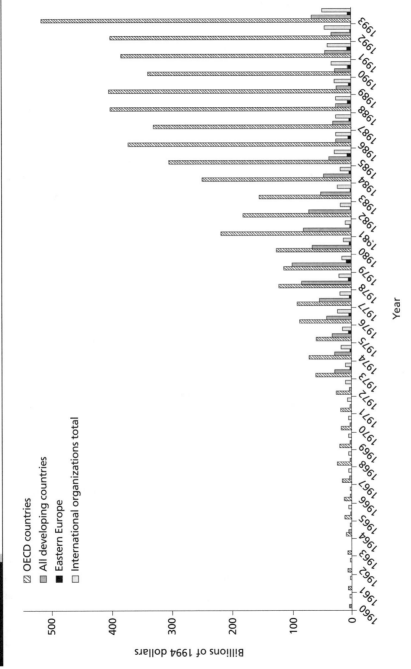

Source: OECD Financial Statistics Monthly.

TABLE 10.2	**Foreign Direct Investment in Developing Nations (annual averages)**
1982–1986	$19 billion
1983–1988	$19 billion
1987–1991	$31 billion

Source: United Nations Conference on Trade and Development, *1995 World Investment Report: Transnational Corporations and Competitiveness*, Annex table 1, pp. 391–396.

Technology and Competition

Many accounts of the transformation to global financial markets highlight either the importance of technological changes in communication and financial instruments or the pressures of international competition, emphasizing **systemic factors** that work across borders. Rightly or wrongly, technological change and competitiveness receive both the blame and the accolades for much of globalization. These accounts offer systemic perspectives, as the forces driving change reside outside the domain of any specific national arena and operate across all national arenas. Competitiveness and technological change are the independent variables in this framework, and financial globalization and liberalization are the dependent variables. Clearly, such factors are important components of any explanation for financial globalization and liberalization, but are they sufficient?

History poses tough analytical problems for such explanations, which may prove to have identified necessary conditions, but not sufficient conditions. First, what startling changes occurred in technology or international competition during the 1960s and 1970s that correspond to the equally dramatic takeoff in financial globalization and liberalization? Does examination of that time period reveal breakthroughs in communications and information technologies that sweep across nations as a systemic shift? Can we observe a dramatic shift in competition across nations and markets? Changes in satellite communications and computer processing and the invention of new financial instruments did occur during this period, but did these developments fuel revolutionary advances in terms of their influence upon economic interactions? An increasing density of economic interactions across borders did feed cross-national competitive pressures, but these changes had been taking place since World War II.

Second, financial globalization and liberalization were well underway in the late 1800s and early 1900s, when London was a sophisticated financial center that supplied capital for economic activities and nation-building around the world. But financial globalization and liberalization slowed in the early 1900s and then actually regressed with the Great Depression, after which global capital markets disappeared as major factors in the global political economy for almost forty years. Assuming the causality of technological change or competitiveness, backward induction would lead us to conclude either that technological change had reversed itself or that the pressures of competitiveness had declined from World War I to the 1960s.

Yet history shows that technology did not reverse directions in 1929 and again in the 1960s. Transformations in communications, advances in computing and information processing, and financial developments within national markets provide abundant evidence of ongoing technological development throughout the twentieth century, even as global capital markets stagnated. Nor did participants in the global economy lose their competitive zeal in the 1920s, only to regain their competitive instincts in the 1960s. Technological change and competitiveness may have been necessary conditions, but given the movements of our independent and dependent variables, they cannot have been sufficient conditions.

Politics and Policy

Giving primacy to government choices and domestic policy competition over those choices offers another causal path to understanding globalization, liberalization, and changes in world affairs. According to these explanations, decisions by key governments to lower their barriers to capital mobility, adopt a floating exchange-rate mechanism, and enact financial regulatory reforms within their domestic financial markets spilled across national borders. Here, government policy change is a critical independent variable for understanding financial globalization and liberalization. Unlike technology or competitiveness, governments can reverse policy course.

In the 1920 and 1930s, government actions reversed the movement toward financial globalization. Instability in their exchange-rate mechanisms, strategic manipulation of exchange rates to beggar-thy-neighbor and transfer costs of adjustment abroad, and policies that detracted from liquidity in the system added to economic instability and created barriers to recovery after World War I. After World War II, as policymakers sought to avoid the same mistakes, many governments adopted capital controls to limit capital outflows. They were concerned that unrestrained capital mobility might encourage capital flight and create liquidity problems in rebuilding economies, expose political economies to destabilizing movements, and limit governments' ability to regulate financial markets. Policies such as foreign-exchange restrictions, licensing special agents to engage in foreign-exchange markets, limits on amounts of money that travelers could take in and out of a country, and regulation of institutional transactions across national borders were obstacles to the export of capital. Meanwhile, some states, worried about destabilizing short-term capital inflows, imposed controls to limit such inflows. For years, such limits on capital mobility inhibited the expansion of global finance, except in the United States.

Post–World War II, the United States was noteworthy for its lack of capital controls. Along with the availability of capital, this feature placed U.S. capital markets at the center of the global economy. A persistent U.S. capital-account deficit provided liquidity and helped to fund the rebuilding of national and global economies, but the expanding size of this deficit began to concern U.S. policymakers. Over the course of twenty years, a massive dollar overhang emerged (the Triffin Dilemma), whereby overseas dollar holdings exceeded U.S.

official gold reserves. This disparity threatened convertibility and confidence in the dollar. But the growing pool of overseas dollars also created prospects for a significant—albeit underdeveloped—capital market in dollar-denominated assets outside of the United States.

The Kennedy and Johnson administrations' efforts to limit the dollar outflow and reduce the threat to Bretton Woods—the Interest Equalization Tax (IET) of 1963 and the Voluntary Foreign Credit Restraint Act (VFCR) of 1965—created incentives for borrowers to access the overseas pool of dollars, despite its inefficiencies. The IET and VFCR failed to protect the dollar and Bretton Woods monetary arrangements, but they did spur the development of the euro markets. Recall from Chapter 9 that euro markets trade financial instruments that are denominated in a nation's currency outside the boundaries of that nation. So *dollar*-denominated instruments that trade in Europe or Japan are euro markets, *yen*-denominated instruments that trade in the United States are euro markets, and *euro*-denominated instruments that trade in Tokyo are euro markets. By the time President Nixon suspended dollar convertibility in 1971, the euro markets had expanded dramatically and become far more efficient.

The expansion of the euro markets was an important step toward financial globalization. Suspension of convertibility and the U.S. movement to a floating exchange rate after the demise of Bretton Woods and the Smithsonian Agreement removed the rationale for the IET and VFCR. They were repealed in 1973 and 1974, lowering barriers to U.S. capital markets. Moreover, many other advanced industrialized economies began to drop their capital controls in the 1970s, as the success of postwar reconstruction eliminated the rationale for them. The end of such controls in the advanced industrialized nations dismantled barriers to global capital mobility. The removal of controls in the United Kingdom and Japan in 1979 and 1980, respectively, proved especially significant, as they were the two most sophisticated financial centers outside New York. International borrowing and capital flows expanded dramatically in the wake of such policy shifts.

Several other important governmental actions contributed to globalization and liberalization of finance from the late 1960s onward. First, government expenditures in the industrialized nations expanded during this period. When faced with a financing dilemma, governments avoided politically unpopular avenues such as limiting programs, increasing taxes, or resorting to **seignorage** (an overexpansion of money supply by issuing more currency so a government can pay its bills and finance its programs, which creates an inflation tax) by borrowing in disintermediated and securitized markets. Such borrowing helped increase the size of these markets. In many cases, such borrowing reached far beyond domestic capital markets, as governments of successful economies, or governments of economies that looked like they were going to overcome barriers to growth and development, were able to access capital in global markets. Since the 1980s, as much as a third of U.S. government debt has been financed by overseas capital.

Second, many governments privatized much of their public sectors. In many nations, governments owned railroads, airlines, banks, telecommunications enterprises, defense firms, and other companies. With privatization, governments transferred ownership of many of these state-owned enterprises (SOEs) to private shareholders by selling off assets in private financial markets. In Europe, these issues led to large increases in financial market capitalization, liquidity, and efficiency.

Third, after the collapse of the Bretton Woods and Smithsonian monetary arrangements, the dollar, the yen, and some other currencies began to float. Floating exchange rates can add currency risk to trade and affect people's willingness to engage in international exchange. With greater variability in exchange rates, currency markets (short-term money markets) and financial futures markets became extremely important for managing such risk. In particular, **financial futures markets** in currencies—betting on the future value of currencies—allow hedging against exchange-rate risk and supply insurance mechanisms to manage currency risk. In such markets, traders purchase a currency future and lock in the price of that currency at some future date. Commodities markets already traded futures in tangible goods such as pork bellies, rice, grains, cattle, oil, corn, and coffee, but intangibles such as financial instruments had not traded as commodities in any substantial way before the 1970s.

Financial instruments began trading as commodities in futures markets in the early 1970s, after the U.S. Congress redefined what constituted a commodity. Defining intangibles as commodities allowed the construction of financial futures and derivatives and meshed with the need to manage currency risk in a floating-exchange-rate system. Trading in currencies and currency futures exploded. Growth in this type of trading increased international mobility in short-term money markets, enhanced the prospects for short-term financial movements in the international system, and led to a more tightly interconnected financial infrastructure across markets.

Markets in financial futures can lower currency risk, but they also connect financial markets, enable currency traders to speculate against a government's commitment to its macroeconomic policies and exchange rate, and may transmit shocks during a crisis. Currency traders can reward governments for adopting and maintaining policies they perceive as good and sustainable, or they can pressure governments and destabilize a currency, and maybe even an economy, if they believe that a government cannot sustain its commitment to the price of its currency or its commitment to macroeconomic policies. As we noted earlier, traders challenging governments in currency markets set off crises involving the European monetary system, the Mexican peso, the Russian ruble, and a handful of Asian currencies during the 1990s.

Petrodollars and a Debt Crisis

Beginning in the 1960s, regulatory changes, the demise of capital controls in the industrialized nations, and other public policy shifts helped to liberalize financial markets and opened international avenues for those with surpluses of capital to trade with those needing capital. In this changing regulatory environment, bankers, institutional investors, financiers, and market entrepreneurs harnessed technologies to unleash financial innovation and competitive market pressures, open national doorways to capital flows, and awaken global financial markets. Financial globalization and liberalization promise a more efficient allocation of capital as they expand the capital pool that borrowers can access. Changes in technology and competitive pressures act as intermediate factors, but are insufficient by themselves to account for the shifts in financial globalization and liberalization.

The increasing density and volume of global financial relations and their ability to link national political economies can produce tremendous economic opportunities and gains. Despite their promise, these connections across financial markets and national borders are not well understood, however, because of their growing complexity. As sophisticated as practitioners of global finance appear to be, they are continually learning about the linkages across boundaries and financial markets. Often these discoveries arise out of crises that damage societies and people. The increasingly complex web of global finance transmits opportunities, but it can also serve as a **contagion network** that communicates dislocations and risks across societies.

For example, no sooner had the Smithsonian Agreement failed and the world embarked on a new system of global financial relations, a series of events and processes began that would challenge the stability of this newly emerging infrastructure. By 1973, the Organization of Petroleum Exporting Countries (OPEC) had already begun pushing for increases in the price of oil. For years, Western oil companies had owned the production of oil—they paid a price to the local government for each barrel produced, but the companies owned the drilling rigs and the oil extracted. Now, however, the OPEC states sought to increase their share of oil revenues. Libya, a key member of OPEC, had garnered limited success in raising the price of oil when Muammar al-Qaddafi seized power and demanded a price increase. For leverage, he threatened to nationalize oil production—to seize ownership of Western-owned production facilities and transform them into an SOE. In 1970 the Western oil companies agreed to Qaddafi's demands. The other OPEC states took note, as the Libyan initiative succeeded without provoking intervention or retaliation by Western governments.

Over the next several years, OPEC pushed for more price increases. In 1971 OPEC and the oil-production companies agreed to a five-year pact that increased oil's price from $1.80 to $2.29/barrel over the period. An agreement in 1972 between several of the Arab OPEC members and the oil companies provided for the gradual transfer of control over production to the governments in those states. Learning to flex its muscles, OPEC had obtained increases in price and a gradual nationalization of production.

Then, in October 1973, the outbreak of a new Arab-Israeli war galvanized the Arab OPEC membership. Overcoming barriers to collective action in response to the military situation, the Arab members of OPEC colluded to use oil as a political-economic tool for applying pressure on other governments to withdraw their support for Israel and change the global geopolitical landscape. By mid-October of that year, the Arab oil-producing states unilaterally raised the price of their oil to $5.12/barrel. By the year's end, the price sat at $11.65, and OPEC, not the Western oil companies, now controlled the price of oil. Taking advantage of this opportunity, the OPEC states pressured the oil companies to transfer either majority or total ownership of their facilities to the governments of the states in which they were located—a revolutionary change in the ownership and production of oil. The large Arab oil-producing states—Saudi Arabia, Iran, and Kuwait—could use their significant production capacity to manage the global oil supply system. This situation provided the OPEC states with tremendous political-economic leverage, which they began to exercise on the world stage.

The Arab OPEC states partly succeeded in their agenda of isolating Israel. Many governments shifted their policies toward Israel, and some states, particularly developing political economies, severed diplomatic relations with the country. Israeli aid and agricultural development teams were sent home from states where they had been providing expert assistance. Post-1973, Israel found itself increasingly isolated in the United Nations, relying more and more upon the willingness of the United States to use its veto power in the UN Security Council to protect Israeli interests.

Ministers of the Organization of the Petroleum Exporting Countries discuss production targets, pricing policy, and the use of oil as an instrument of political leverage at a December 1973 meeting in Kuwait. The outbreak of the October Arab-Israeli war and failed negotiations with oil companies to revise prices led OPEC, dominated by Arab states, to overcome barriers to collective action. Members raised prices, cut production, and most joined in limiting oil shipments to Western industrialized supporters of Israel. The quadrupling of oil prices sparked a worldwide recession in 1974–75.

By 1974–1975, the price of crude oil floated around $30/barrel. It peaked near $50/barrel during the Iranian Revolution in 1978, when Iranian oil exports ceased—Iran contributed between 15 and 20 percent of OPEC's total oil exports. At this point, the rising price of oil only marginally affected the demand, for consumers still needed oil to heat their houses and to power their cars, and industries still needed energy to operate their plants. So, the price increases translated into tremendous oil revenues for the OPEC states.

The OPEC states recycled these revenues, **petrodollars,** into the global economy by two paths: increased consumption and bank deposits. Because the increase in oil revenues was so dramatic that no conceivable level of consumption could recycle all the petrodollars, OPEC governments deposited vast sums into private banks, mostly Western banks located in the large financial centers. The banks owed interest on these deposits, and, consequently, they faced the task of making these deposits perform by lending them to borrowers who were able to pay interest.

The banks found that potential borrowers in oil-consuming countries—particularly developing states—faced with significantly larger energy bills due to the increase in oil prices, were happy to borrow petrodollars to pay for their current-account deficits. This created a cycle. Oil-producing states raised oil prices and earned large revenues, which they deposited in banks. Unable to reduce oil consumption significantly, oil-consuming states ran large deficits and borrowed the deposited petrodollars to finance their deficits; they owed the bank interest on these loans. Unfortunately, the increased costs of oil crowded out other consumption and slowed economic activity. Exports of nonoil commodities then slowed, limiting earnings of the hard currency reserves necessary to pay loan obligations. This looming shortfall of hard currency reserves in developing nations should have provided a cautionary note, but the banks had so many petrodollars to recycle that they just floated more and more loans, thereby connecting the well-being of financial institutions in the large Western money centers (New York, London, Paris, Tokyo) to the economic well-being of developing countries. The stability of the entire banking system was increasingly connected to the cycling of these petrodollars.

Many of these loans to borrowers in developing countries were adjustable-rate loans, which meant that the cost of capital (the interest rate on the loan) was tied to some interest rate such as the U.S. Federal Funds rate or a U.S. Treasury Bill rate. If those rates decreased or increased, the interest rate on the loan would decrease or increase in response. During the mid-1970s, these rates were relatively low. So even though developing countries were borrowing heavily to finance economic development and to shore up their current-account deficits due to higher energy costs, while their hard currency earnings were declining due to the crowding out of nonoil commodity consumption, the relatively low interest rates enabled them to still meet their loan obligations.

But in 1979 the cost of capital began to rise, and rise quickly. The U.S. economy had been burdened by inflation and stagnation since the end of the Vietnam War, but when President

Jimmy Carter appointed Paul Volcker as chairman of the U.S. Federal Reserve, he committed to reduce inflation by rapidly increasing the cost of capital in the United States. Chairman Volcker used the tools of the Federal Reserve to raise interest rates and reduce the supply of capital in the global economy. This action slowed the global economy, reducing production and consumption. For the developing political economies, this effect proved disastrous. Already faced with trade deficits due to higher energy prices, which limited their hard currency earnings and forced them to borrow to finance their deficits, they now confronted an even greater shortfall in export earnings as consumption in the Western economies declined due to the rise in interest rates and the economic slowdown.

Moreover, the cost of the capital borrowed by the developing political economies was rising quickly. They had borrowed much of the capital under adjustable-rate agreements, and those rates were now climbing fast as international interest rates soared. Under Volcker, the U.S. prime rates—the interest rate available to the lowest-risk borrowers—climbed from around 7 percent to over 20 percent in one year. The interest rates on mortgages, car loans, business loans, and other loans doubled and tripled in many cases. Borrowers in developing countries were in a quandary. They owed money from borrowing to finance their trade deficits, but now those loans were dramatically more expensive. At the same time, their revenues from exports were falling quickly. Their political economies would have to work harder to pay the interest on their loans, but the decline in consumption in the advanced industrialized states precluded this option. Faced with economic dislocations at home that could destabilize their polities, many political leaders in developing nations increased government expenditures to promote growth and provide some safety net. But these desperate measures only exacerbated the fiscal problems and deficits of these states.

Developing countries were caught in a debt trap, and, by connection, so were the banks that had recycled the petrodollars in loans to these countries. By 1982, the debt exposure of the most indebted countries had increased by more than 300 percent over their levels of indebtedness in the mid-1970s. Argentina was the first to be overwhelmed—it suspended payments on $37 billion in debt obligations following the Falklands War in 1982. But other countries faced similar, if not worse, problems. In August 1982 the Mexican government announced that it could not meet its payments on obligations of $85 billion. By December, Brazil, with $91 billion in loan obligations, followed the lead of Argentina and Mexico. By the end of 1983, almost all Latin American and many African states were in trouble and had threatened to suspend the servicing of their debts. This debt trap has been labeled the Third World Debt Crisis.

There is an old adage: if you owe the bank $100, it's your problem, but if you owe the bank a billion dollars, it's the bank's problem. As the connections across markets and across state boundaries tied together the fortunes of developing political economies and the western banking infrastructure, the major banks of the world faced a potential default of over $200 billion in obligations. The IMF, the U.S. government, other Western governments, and the Bank for International Settlements (an international organization based in Switzerland that oversees accounting and settlements of international transactions) moved quickly to stem the crisis. They provided short-term credits and bridging loans to help the governments of developing states meet their short-term obligations. They cajoled the creditor banks to delay the collection of debt-servicing fees for several months. Finally, they arranged debt rescheduling in exchange for austerity programs on the part of developing states and additional financing from the creditor banks.

IMPLICATIONS OF FINANCIAL GLOBALIZATION

Increasing interdependence has prompted debates between advocates and critics of globalization: some praise globalization for its potential to enhance social welfare, promote universal harmony and common interests, and constrain governments from adopting policies damaging to their publics; others warn that globalization undermines sovereignty and state autonomy, erodes the ability of governments to provide social welfare goods, promotes the growth of inequity and injustice, and dismantles distinct identity. Globalization generates substantial social welfare gains through specialization and comparative advantage, but not without posing significant costs and risks to individuals and groups that find themselves less competitive in the face of global market forces. Postwar planners feared that if such risks were not contained, they could turn into demands upon politicians to interfere in liberal economic exchange. The postwar social welfare state helped to manage such risks by redistributing costs away from those dislocated by change to the broader society.

Today, both critics and supporters of globalization worry that the winners from globalization will use their resources to influence public policy, escape tax burdens, and limit the redistribution that underpins the social welfare state. They worry that these advantages might exacerbate disparities, mobilize disaffected groups, and produce backlashes that could ultimately damage both globalization and social welfare. In particular, the increasing mobility of capital has become a lightning rod in these debates. What are the implications of increasingly mobile capital for state-society bargains and for the ability of governments to adopt and implement policies? Could financial globalization affect the ability of governments to produce public policies, enact and implement economic regulation, and generate social welfare goods that manage the risks to individuals, groups, and communities? In order to address these concerns, we need to consider two frameworks: the "capital mobility hypothesis," which applies to all societal and governmental bargains involving mobile capital, and the "unholy trinity," a more specific framework that explores the relationship between exchange-rate policy, monetary policy, and capital mobility.

The Capital Mobility Hypothesis

The **capital mobility hypothesis** posits an inverse relationship between the mobility of capital and the policy autonomy of government or less mobile assets of production. This hypothesis speculates that more mobile economic actors gain disproportionate bargaining power in political and societal arenas, as increased openness enables those with mobility to exit or threaten to exit. This threat of exit empowers highly mobile economic enterprises with bargaining leverage to constrain government policies, avoid taxation, limit regulation, or reduce the redistributive demands of the social welfare state. This situation could expose less mobile assets of production to added risk, shift the burdens to fund state programs to those actors, or alter the balance in negotiations between management of more mobile industries and their labor. True or not, increasingly the *fear* of capital mobility is used strategically as a lever to extract concessions in labor negotiations and discussions with policymakers. The dynamic of the capital mobility hypothesis underpins debates over the outsourcing of jobs, the relocation of industry, and the offering of tax abatements and incentives to attract and retain industry.

Using the logic of the capital mobility hypothesis, we can produce testable expectations about a rollback in state autonomy, a tit-for-tat race to the bottom of minimal provision of government services and regulation, and an increasing shift of globalization's costs of adjustment to those put at risk by openness. For example, if capital with greater openness gains bargaining leverage, the following effects may be expected:

- Capital should be able to find greater escape from redistributive tax burdens in more open societies than in less open societies.
- Capital should be able to create larger barriers to redistribution and social welfare programs in more open societies than in less open societies.
- The growth of state sectors should be smaller in more open societies than in less open societies.
- Tax burdens should increasingly fall on less mobile factors.

Despite attempts by holders of capital to threaten exit, the effects of capital mobility on state autonomy, on state-society bargains, and on the distribution of the costs of adjustment remain ambiguous. The empirical world offers conflicting evidence. Contrary to the expectations of the capital mobility hypothesis, state sectors have grown with globalization. More open economies generally have bigger governments than less open economies. The advanced industrialized nations with the larger tradable (that is, more open) sectors maintain larger social welfare states, impose more regulatory demands on business, and operate with more rigid labor market agreements. Today, most cross-border flows of capital go from one advanced social welfare state to another, from one regulated economic arena to another, and not to smaller social welfare states or relatively unregulated economic arenas. In the late 1800s, the growth of global capital coincided with the origins of the modern social welfare state. As governments added social welfare functions to their national security functions, it was states with greater openness and mobility that led this shift in state responsibilities.

This ambiguity suggests that perhaps we need to examine the capital mobility hypothesis more closely. Exit, outsourcing, and relocation of production facilities constitute one set of strategies for maintaining and improving competitiveness. Improving productivity through human and physical capital investment, innovation and invention, and restructuring of industrial organization are other strategies that can help companies maintain their competitiveness and undercut a need to relocate to other nations. Governments still fund social welfare goods, but in many cases they have shifted away from demand-side social welfare goods, such as unemployment insurance and other safety net policies, and toward provision of supply-side goods, such as education, health care, and infrastructure, which improve the efficiency of productive factors.

The capital mobility hypothesis also assumes that policymakers will respond to the demands of mobile capital because they fear the effects of its departure upon social welfare, as well as its threat to their political survival. If, as we assumed at the beginning of this book, policymakers value political survival, they will formulate their policies in response to the preferences of those who can credibly commit to participating in the domestic political arena. Therefore, the ability to exit easily may actually undermine the impact of capital's demands, since politicians may also be concerned about less mobile assets that have no alternative but to remain in their communities and participate in political life.

The Unholy Trinity

The **unholy trinity,** based on a model developed by economists J. Marcus Fleming and Robert Mundell, examines the relationship between exchange-rate policy, monetary policy, and capital mobility. The **Fleming-Mundell model** predicts an inherent tension between currency stability—which derives from a condition of relatively fixed exchange rates, whether the narrow peg of the Bretton Woods system or a broader but stable peg—capital mobility, and monetary policy autonomy. Governments can obtain two of the three components of the trinity, but not all three at the same time, unless by fluke. Indeed, the tension between the components of the unholy trinity was at the root of the major currency crises of the 1990s, as governments sought to have all three. During these crises, traders in currency markets saw what they considered to be an incompatibility between a state's stated exchange rate and its government's monetary policy. The absence of capital controls, a relatively new phenomenon in many of these states, allowed traders to use the mobility of capital to challenge government policies, which forced the government to either surrender its goal of exchange-rate stability or monetary policy, or to attempt to reassert capital controls.

Let's list the different permutations of the unholy trinity (see figure 10.4). First, a government can preserve exchange-rate stability and monetary policy autonomy by limiting capital mobility. Second, a government can maintain exchange-rate stability and openness to capital flows, if it surrenders monetary policy autonomy to markets. Third, if a government wants to preserve openness to capital flows and the possibility of enacting monetary policy, it can escape exchange-rate pressures by forgoing a peg and letting its currency float. When a government floats its currency, it is no longer imperative for the government to defend the value of that currency if it comes under attack; rather than fending off a speculative attack, a float allows market pressures to determine a currency's value.

FIGURE 10.4	The Unholy Trinity: Exchange-Rate Policy, Monetary Policy, and Capital Mobility

If governments . . .	they can preserve . . .
Limit capital mobility	Exchange-rate stability + monetary policy autonomy
Surrender monetary policy autonomy to markets	Exchange-rate stability + openness to capital flows
Allow currency to float (escaping exchange-rate pressures)	Openness to capital flows + monetary policy autonomy

Capital openness, an increasingly common characteristic of post–Bretton Woods monetary arrangements, is key to the unholy trinity. Capital controls limit the mobility of capital across state boundaries, as well as the ability of currency traders to attack a government's management of its monetary policies or a pegged exchange rate. Without capital controls, currency markets can challenge a state's monetary and pegged-exchange-rate policies that appear inconsistent.

How do such challenges occur? If a government with a pegged currency adopts monetary policies that are inconsistent with its balance-of-payments position, it creates a significant balance-of-payments disequilibrium. Such a disequilibrium, produced by the tension between a government's stated value for its money and its attempt to influence the amount of money in circulation, prompts currency traders to question the government's commitment to its monetary policies or to its pegged exchange rate. Since they do not believe it will hold its value, traders will reduce their holdings of that nation's currency, by using it to purchase more stable currencies. This process can lead to capital flight from the offending state, an increased supply of its currency in currency markets, and downward pressure on the price of the currency. In defense of their currency, a central bank and finance ministry must then use their hard currency reserves to purchase their currency in order to reduce its supply in currency markets. A reduction in their hard currency reserves, however, will exacerbate the balance-of-payments problem, as the hard currency reserves necessary for paying off their international obligations have disappeared.

If the government persists in trying to maintain a stable peg and implement an independent monetary policy in the face of such pressures caused by the mobility of capital, a currency crisis is likely. Confronted by such pressures and constraints, a government's alternatives are to accept market discipline and forgo independent monetary policies, to obstruct capital movements by imposing some form of capital controls, or to surrender its defense of the pegged rate. Increased capital mobility and the resulting integration of financial markets has unleashed the force of speculative capital, which can punish inconsistencies in government macroeconomic policies with destabilizing flows of speculative capital. Not even the strongest central banks can unilaterally withstand such pressure if it becomes intense enough.

GOING FORWARD: THE IMF AND THE WASHINGTON CONSENSUS

Under Bretton Woods, the IMF focused upon maintaining stable pegged rates, addressing balance-of-payments pressures that threatened the peg, and, if necessary, overseeing an orderly process of adjustment in currencies from one par value to another. The end of the peg, along with growth in global capital markets and capital mobility, posed dilemmas for the IMF. The Bretton Woods arrangements had legitimated an intergovernmental structure that monitored, coordinated, and supported a system of stable exchange rates. The breakdown in that system left governments without an intergovernmental agreement about what constituted legitimate exchange-rate policies. This lack of coordination increased the risk that governments might manipulate their exchange rates to gain competitive advantage. Recalling the disaster of unilateral, beggar-thy-neighbor monetary affairs during the 1920s and 1930s, policymakers feared that such actions could produce monetary disorder, thereby threatening trade, investment, and interdependence.

The growth of global financial markets and capital mobility could discipline a government that was strategically manipulating its currency to affect its balance of payments or competitiveness, but what if many governments went down this path? Would it lead to a social trap? In the absence of a legitimate intergovernmental authority to coordinate, monitor, and negotiate differences in monetary arrangements, policymakers feared that market discipline would prove insufficient to contain monetary disorder. They recognized the need to build a new framework for international monetary arrangements that would act as a rule of law, accommodate new exchange-rate strategies ranging from floating to pegged, complement the discipline of international financial markets, and contain the prospects of monetary anarchy. Such concerns led to negotiations that transformed the IMF's responsibilities and expanded its reach beyond managing monetary arrangements to advising governments on their macroeconomic policies.

Earlier we discussed the disagreements between U.S. and French policymakers over monetary relations after Bretton Woods and the Smithsonian. The French sought to retain pegged rates and the use of capital controls, and they wanted to constrain the role of the dollar as the central currency in the international system, since they believed that it gave U.S. policymakers the ability to export their economic ills. In contrast, U.S. policymakers favored the free mobility of capital, as well as governments' ability to let their currencies float.

The resolution of this French–U.S. disagreement sits at the heart of the Second Amendment to the IMF's Articles of Agreement, adopted in 1978. The Second Amendment eliminated the role of gold as a reserve asset, legitimated floating exchange rates, assigned to the IMF the responsibility for overseeing an effective international monetary system, and, most important, restored a legal basis for the management of international monetary arrangements that would help to guide IMF activities and government policies, and to restrain monetary anarchy. Instead of a system designed to promote stable par values, the revision of the Articles of Agreement directed the IMF to promote a stable system of exchange rates by reducing any undue volatility that could spread from one nation to another.

To help the IMF in carrying out this mission, the Second Amendment to the Articles of Agreement expanded the IMF's surveillance of its members' economic affairs. Members were expected to provide the IMF with economic information and to consult with the IMF if requested. IMF data gathering and surveillance thus moved beyond monitoring exchange-rate policies and current-account balances to overseeing other aspects of economic activity that could affect exchange rates. The expansion of surveillance recognized that macroeconomic policies could have substantial influence on exchange rates. Labor markets, inflation, deficit spending and debt, tax policy, corruption, financial regulatory arrangements, trade policies, and other economic policy areas became legitimate targets of IMF interest in the pursuit of stability in the exchange-rate system.

As a function of their sovereignty, governments naturally resent outside interference in their domestic arenas. The revision to the Articles of Agreement addressed this potential threat to sovereignty by including a general proposition that required the IMF to respect members' domestic political and social policies. Still, its charge to exercise surveillance and to promote an effective monetary system allows the IMF to move beyond technical consultation—to use its financial reserves, and its ability to borrow more, as a carrot in exchange for commitments from governments to implement IMF-recommended policy reforms.

No advanced industrialized state has accessed the IMF's financial reserves since the 1970s to address balance-of-payments problems, structural economic difficulties, or macroeconomic dilemmas that could threaten international monetary affairs. These states have been able instead to access global financial markets, which allows them to avoid IMF intervention. But developing and transitional political economies have neither sufficient hard currency reserves nor the ability to borrow in global financial markets to defend their currencies or monetary policies against a concerted attack. In such difficult situations, they may turn to the IMF for financial assistance to stem the crisis. Such crises provide the IMF with opportunities to use its capital reserves to leverage commitments from governments to reform their economic policies.

The IMF initially limited its assistance to addressing short-term liquidity problems that contributed to currency instability, but soon such assistance expanded to include medium-term loans targeted at more stubborn structural problems in an economy. This change of focus recognized that short-term liquidity problems, which threaten a currency's stability, might be symptomatic of deeper structural problems. If so, providing short-term liquidity during a currency crisis could address a symptom and offer a government some respite, but this action would be unlikely to repair the structural macroeconomic conditions that had produced the short-term crisis. Without addressing these deeper structural problems, the government could face a likelihood of recurring short-term crises.

The IMF extends assistance, but usually only after a government signs a **letter of conditionality,** which includes a commitment to address problems that purportedly brought on the crisis in the state's currency and may require domestic reforms that the IMF believes address more fundamental problems in the nation's economy. In a letter of conditionality, the IMF trades financial assistance for policy reforms. The ability to offer financial assistance to governments needing such resources thus gives the IMF leverage over government economic policies, inserts the IMF into the management of domestic macroeconomic arenas, and makes it a central player in the management of crises that threaten international monetary stability.

The IMF's increasing focus on the macroeconomic conditions of its members is part of a broader shift in the relationship of states and markets that is known as the Washington Consensus. The postwar Bretton Woods system had built upon Keynesian foundations, which rejected the laissez-faire notion that markets were self-sustaining and self-correcting. Bretton Woods had sought to ensure liberal economic exchange by encouraging governments to employ countercyclical fiscal and monetary policies to mitigate destabilizing economic swings, social welfare policies to limit dislocations that could lead to pressures upon politicians to adopt policies that damaged market exchange, and international cooperative mechanisms to constrain beggar-thy-neighbor policies. The Bretton Woods era saw a shift toward greater government regulation of the economy with the objectives of limiting the harsher aspects of market discipline, constraining market failure, and protecting market exchange.

The Washington Consensus shifts course by placing greater emphasis upon the corrective pressures of market discipline and seeking to reduce government regulation and intervention in the economy. Thus, with a swing of the intellectual pendulum, the Washington Consensus and what have been labeled neoliberal policy prescriptions supplanted the Keynesian framework of the Bretton Woods era. The name of this new approach reflects the prominence of Washington, D.C., and the organizations located there, in international economic affairs.

The Washington Consensus promotes economic openness in trade and capital movements, liberalization of financial markets that are open and transparent, fiscal policies that lead to balanced budgets, anti-inflationary monetary policies, stability in exchange-rate relations, expansion of private enterprise, and a reduction in SOEs. Financial openness, market liberalization, and transparency are its central values. Financial markets provide the discipline that rewards or penalizes political economies, but governments are critical to creating the macroeconomic conditions that these markets mediate—too much or too little intervention gets penalized, while the right amount attracts investment and exchange.

The need for economic assistance for development or for managing economic crises has empowered the Washington Consensus and prompted dramatic reforms in domestic political economies. IMF and U.S. Treasury assistance often comes with conditions attached that push the agenda of the Washington Consensus. In many states, this leverage has led to the privatization of SOEs, increased fiscal constraint by governments, restructuring of labor bargains and markets, financial liberalization, removal or reduction of capital controls, and increased trade openness. In some nations, the pressure to constrain the public sector and meet proscribed macroeconomic targets has produced constraints on social welfare provisions and led to recommendations to privatize aspects of national social welfare systems.

The emphasis upon openness, capital mobility, and market pressures has increased the density of linkages that connect national political economies and expanded the sensitivity of workers, producers, companies, and markets in one country to those in another. Doubts about the Washington Consensus provoke vibrant debates about which framework is most likely to be conducive to stable monetary relations, to promote growth, to improve social welfare, and to manage volatility. The intellectual pendulum could swing back as economic crises and disparities produce complaints and challenges to the Washington Consensus. The conditionality imposed by the IMF and the Washington Consensus in response to financial crises has occasionally produced hardships in domestic political economies, failed to generate expected economic rewards, rattled politicians as they seek to survive in their political arenas, and created opportunities for speculation about alternatives.

For example, the Washington Consensus pushes fiscal restraint upon developing nations at the very time that increasing globalization exposes their citizens to greater risk. By requiring constraints on government deficits and debt, conditionality limits the ability of developing states to fund safety nets when they are most needed to insulate politicians from constituent demands that could damage globalization. Without adequate safety nets, constituents may press for less globalization rather than more. In the wake of the 1997 Asian financial crisis, which led to significant devaluations in many states' currencies in that region, the IMF and other organizations making up the Washington Consensus offered financial assistance that was tied to stringent conditions. These conditions required adoption of neoliberal policies—fiscal and monetary constraint, greater trade openness, and no capital controls—whose underlying idea was that the discipline of the global market would correct the ills that were presumed to have created the financial crisis. Instead, these policies slowed economic activity, imposed hardships on low- and middle-income workers, and created domestic political unrest for governments. Rejecting such policy demands and assistance, the president of Malaysia instead instituted capital controls and reimposed state management of globalization. Ironically, the historical experience of the developed nations themselves had also followed a different path than the policy prescriptions of the Washington Consensus: in the 1800s, the industrializing nations had paced the globalization of that era, but they had also led the way in the development of fiscal expenditures and social safety nets that cushioned their citizens from the increased risks that accompanied globalization.

The harsh aftermath of the Asian financial crisis of 1997 has produced some soul-searching within many of the organizations that make up the Washington Consensus. Whichever way the pendulum swings next—toward greater reliance upon market discipline or toward increased government regulation—events on the world stage, economic crises, the temptations of beggar-thy-neighbor tactics, and the need to find means to cooperate will continue to provoke debates, policy experimentation, and new insights and reforms.

CONCLUSION

The breakdown in the Bretton Woods and Smithsonian adjustable-peg monetary systems and the movement to a range of monetary arrangements worried many policymakers who remembered the floating-exchange-rate system of the interwar years, as well as the resulting monetary anarchy and breakdown in globalization. Instead of these results, however, the post–Bretton Woods era witnessed a tremendous explosion in global capital mobility, global lending, and financial innovation that challenged state boundaries and encouraged greater globalization, not less. Trade continued to expand as it had during the Bretton Woods era, but the developments in global finance have helped to rearrange state-society relations and complemented a shift away from Keynesian economic management toward neoliberal policies.

In this brave new world of global finance, markets enjoy greater ability to reward or punish government policy choices. In this environment, the prospects for governments and their societies that get policies right are favorable, but those governments and societies that manage their political economies poorly can face harsh discipline in this environment. The shifts in the international political-economic system increase the likelihood of greater disparities between those who can play in the game of global finance and those who cannot. These changes also add to the uncertainty about how national political economies are connected. The innovations of the post–Bretton Woods era increase the complexity and density of linkages across national political economies. Both good and bad effects can be conveyed across linkages that are not yet well understood and are consequently difficult to manage and mitigate, in the case of bad effects.

In the language of causality introduced in chapter 1, the changes in global finance, by creating great complexity, have muddied our understanding of how the global economy operates and how events in one state influence activities in other states. Much of the time, better outcomes result from these changes in globalization, but sometimes our ambiguous understanding of this new, more complex environment limits our ability to recognize and avoid potential crises. The challenge for policymakers, public and private, is to develop better understanding of a system of economic and political interactions that is undergoing tremendous change at the same time.

EXERCISES

1. What is EMS?

2. In the post–Bretton Woods era, international organizations such as the IMF shifted away from their emphasis upon Keynesian policies in their recommendations to governments. What do we call the set of policy prescriptions that replaced those of the Bretton Woods era, and what principles does it emphasize?

3. What is the Washington Consensus? What types of public policies does it promote? Give two examples.

4. What are the three policy components of the "unholy trinity"? Explain the tension between them.

5. Explain the difference between a system of stable exchange rates and a stable system of exchange rates.

6. You work in the finance ministry of a Latin American nation. For the past several years, your nation's currency has demonstrated unusually high levels of inflation and volatility. In addition to the price and welfare effects they create in your domestic markets, persistent inflation and volatility affect the willingness of international investors to invest in your nation. Your nation is also being pressured by the IMF to address these problems. One of your Latin American neighbors has adopted a currency control board to address such policy concerns. What is a currency control board and what are its strengths and weaknesses? Should your nation also adopt a currency control board?

7. Technological change has helped to lower obstacles to the international flow of capital. Many attribute primary responsibility for financial globalization to such changes. Did technological innovation cause financial globalization? What other factors contribute to it? How?

8. How does financial globalization differ from financial liberalization?

9. Summarize the three stages created in the Maastricht Treaty. What are the convergence criteria of the Maastricht Treaty? What is the logic underpinning the need for the convergence criteria?

10. Generally, financial globalization improved access to capital resources for many, but some have gained disproportionately. Who has gained disproportionately and why? Who has suffered from the disparity?

11. According to the capital mobility hypothesis, what is the relation between capital and political bargaining power? How does this work?

FURTHER READING

Cohen, Benjamin. 1998. *The Geography of Money.* Ithaca, N.Y.: Cornell University Press.

Eichengreen, Barry. 1996. *Globalizing Capital: A History of the International Monetary System.* Princeton, N.J.: Princeton University Press.

Goldstein, Morris. 1998. *The Asian Financial Crisis: Causes, Cures, and Systemic Implications.* Washington, D.C.: Institute for International Economics.

Helleiner, Eric. 1994. *States and the Reemergence of Global Finance: From Bretton Woods to the 1990s.* Ithaca, N.Y.: Cornell University Press.

Keylor, William R. Various editions. *The Twentieth-Century World: An International History.* New York: Oxford University Press.

Maxfield, Sylvia. 1997. *Gatekeepers of Growth.* Princeton, N.J.: Princeton University Press.

Pauly, Louis W. 1997. *Who Elected the Bankers? Surveillance and Control in the World Economy.* Ithaca, N.Y.: Cornell University Press.

Rodrik, Dani. 1997. *Has Globalization Gone Too Far?* Washington, D.C.: Institute for International Economics.

_____. 1999. *The New Global Economy and Developing Countries.* Washington, D.C.: Overseas Development Council.

Sobel, Andrew C. 1994. *Domestic Choices, International Markets: Dismantling National Barriers and Liberalizing Securities Markets.* Ann Arbor: University of Michigan Press.

_____. 1999. *State Institutions, Private Incentives, Global Capital.* Ann Arbor: University of Michigan Press.

Détente and the End of the Cold War: Globalization during Transition

> There are many people in the world who really don't understand, or say they don't, what is the great issue between the free world and the Communist world. Let them come to Berlin. . . . All free men, wherever they may live, are citizens of Berlin, and, therefore, as a free man, I take pride in the words "Ich bin ein Berliner."
>
> *President John F. Kennedy, Berlin, June 26, 1963*

> General Secretary Gorbachev, if you seek peace, if you seek prosperity for the Soviet Union and Eastern Europe, if you seek liberalization: Come here to this gate! Mr. Gorbachev, open this gate! Mr. Gorbachev, tear down this wall!
>
> *President Ronald Reagan, Berlin, June 12, 1987*

COLD WAR TO POST–COLD WAR TRANSFORMATION

Any discussion of world affairs in the late twentieth century must consider the superpower tensions between the United States and the Soviet Union, the cold war between Eastern and Western blocs, the thawing and renewal of East-West economic relations that began with détente, and the dismantling and disintegration of communist regimes from 1989 to 1991. Following a long period of hostile, sometimes violent, confrontation between competing forms of political-economic relations, tensions began to ease. Trade, migration, capital flows, and the exchange of information and culture improved across the East-West divide, creating connections that brought the communist Eastern bloc into active engagement with the larger global capitalist political-economy.

East-West economic linkages improved in fits and starts, and by the end of the century, the communist governments of the Eastern bloc nations had fallen and their successor regimes had started down the path of economic and democratic liberalization. The Soviet

Union and its domination of the Eastern bloc sphere became an artifact of historical memory. Aside from a dramatic change in political-military relations, the end of the Soviet empire removed the twentieth century's most significant threat to a global political economy built upon market transactions. With greater integration and continued political-economic transformation, these nations will become significant contributors to the global economy and important actors in global affairs. Many have large educated populations and potentially large domestic markets, and some are rich in raw materials.

THE COMMAND ECONOMIES GRADUALLY JOIN THE GLOBAL ECONOMY

The increasing integration of the Soviet, East European, and Chinese economies into the global economy began in the 1960s, but the most dramatic changes took place in the post–Bretton Woods era, and they deserve special attention. When these states were under communist rule, from the end of World War II through 1989–1991, we called them **command economies** due to the hierarchical organization of economic activity. In a command economy, economic activity is centrally directed via the hierarchical mechanisms of the state, unlike the decentralized organization of economic activity in a market economy (recall the discussion in chapter 1 of centralized and decentralized economies). After 1989 and the breakdown in Communist Party control in these states, we began labeling them **transitional political-economies**, since they are trying to change the organization of their political, economic, and social relations to allow greater political competition and decentralized economic exchange—a shift from hierarchical communist political economies to more democratic, market-oriented political economies.

For years following World War II, the command economies of the Soviet Union and its Eastern bloc remained largely separate from the larger global economy. This isolation was partly a matter of policy choice by the Soviet leadership, which sought to consolidate its authority within its sphere of influence, and partly a function of the policy of **containment** adopted by the United States and the Western bloc in the late 1940s as the cornerstone of their cold war strategy. Eastern bloc participation in market-oriented global finance and trade remained relatively limited for many years as domestic economic policy preferences and international tensions hampered East-West economic interactions. Eastern bloc nations traded heavily with each other, although Soviet bureaucrats and policymakers directed much of this trade from their positions in the power hierarchy. The bulk of economic activity in the Soviet Union and Eastern bloc centered on a series of five-year plans that established production targets. Such economic activity and trade faced no market discipline; specialization occurred as a matter of bureaucratic fiat, rather than market-driven creative destruction. Eastern bloc nations participated in an organization called the Council for Mutual

Economic Assistance (Comecon), which was the economic equivalent of the Warsaw Pact (the Soviet-led political-military alliance).

A gradual thawing of East-West political-economic relations from the mid-1960s onward led to an influx of ideas, advice, goods, technology, assistance, and investment from the Western bloc into the Eastern bloc economies. The pace of such inflows quickened following the dismantling of the Eastern bloc and the disintegration of the Soviet Union between 1989 and 1991. The expanding participation and increasing integration of the Eastern bloc nations into the global economy required significant changes in the foreign policies of East and West, as well as major shifts in the domestic political-economic policies in the East. The changes advanced in two stages: first, a thawing of political-military relations in the late 1960s and early 1970s promoted the initial integration of these economies into the global political economy; and second, domestic economic and political liberalization in the late 1980s and early 1990s fueled further integration. Shifts in the domestic political economies of the Eastern bloc nations, changes in the perspectives of policymakers in the Western bloc, and events and lessons in global affairs combined to promote greater cooperation and integration, but the changes and lessons took time, and many were painful and costly. The remainder of this chapter covers these two aspects of integration between East and West, between command economies and market economies.

DÉTENTE AND SHIFTS IN THE INTERNATIONAL POLITICAL-MILITARY CONTEXT

The end of World War II left Europe divided into two camps—a Soviet-led Eastern bloc and a U.S.-led Western bloc—that were separated by distinct ideologies and approaches to the organization of political-economic life that made them inherently hostile to each other. Although these two leading states had been allies during the war, relations between the Soviet Union and the United States soured quickly after the defeat and division of Germany. A series of confrontations over the status of Berlin, a nuclear weapons race, the Korean War, the construction of the Berlin Wall, and other crises punctuated the cold war, in which U.S. and Soviet combat troops faced each other in central Europe and U.S. and Soviet military advisers aided opposing sides in many regional conflicts around the globe, but the superpowers themselves never engaged directly in physical combat—at least not admittedly.

The cold war continued into the 1960s, but the East-West showdown peaked and then relaxed during that decade. This easing up led to **détente**, a reduction of political-military tensions and improved economic relations. Several political-military factors helped to promote more constructive engagement. First, the peaceful resolution of the Cuban missile crisis and the narrowing of the U.S.–U.S.S.R. strategic gap led to greater East-West cooperation to reduce the possibility of catastrophic military conflict. Second, the ascension of Willy

Brandt and his political agenda in West Germany promoted the resolution of issues that had persisted since the end of World War II and obstructed a political settlement in Europe. Third, the conclusion of the U.S. intervention in Vietnam removed important obstacles to more amicable relations between East and West. Fourth, discontent within the Communist bloc created opportunities for the West to seek rapprochement with both the Chinese and the Soviets.

The Cuban Crisis and a U.S.–Soviet Strategic Gap

In 1962 the Cuban missile crisis brought the world to the precipice of nuclear confrontation, terrifying policymakers and their publics. Premier Nikita Khrushchev's attempt to base Soviet intermediate-range missiles in Cuba revealed weaknesses in the Soviet's strategic weapons capabilities and proved its inability to challenge U.S. supremacy as a global power beyond the Eurasian land mass. The Soviet retreat in the face of U.S. ultimatums then embarrassed Khrushchev and caused many in the Soviet leadership to lose confidence in him, which fueled his downfall and the ascendancy of Leonid Brezhnev to power. The face-off uncovered strategic shortcomings and diplomatic limitations that could generate miscommunications, foster misunderstandings, and impose dangerous time pressures upon decision makers, whose potential missteps could lead to dangerous policy choices, including an otherwise avoidable use of nuclear weapons.

The lessons of the Cuban crisis prompted changes in U.S. and Soviet diplomatic and military policies that would help to improve East-West relations within a decade. Soviet policymakers shifted away from the confrontational approach that had led to the Berlin and Cuba crises, while those on both sides sought to change the dynamics of the nuclear relationship in order to reduce the likelihood of unintended nuclear confrontation. Soviet and U.S. policymakers engaged in a series of arms control discussions to limit destabilizing weapons, reduce uncertainty, and promote dialogue in the superpowers' relationship. The Nuclear Test Ban Treaty, the Hot-Line Agreement, the Outer Space Treaty, the Nuclear Non-Proliferation Treaty, the Strategic Arms Limitation Treaty (SALT I), SALT II, the Mutual and Balanced Force Reduction talks that led to the Conventional Armed Forces in Europe Treaty, and other agreements arose from this diplomatic engagement that started in the aftermath of the Cuban crisis. These negotiations restructured the international political-military landscape, eased East-West tensions, and created precedents for interbloc cooperation.

Concurrent with these political initiatives to reduce potentially catastrophic mishaps in the nuclear relationship, the Soviets sought to achieve strategic parity with the United States. They increased the pace of their long-range weapons programs, built up their strategic intercontinental missile forces, improved their intermediate-range nuclear weapons for the European theater, enlarged their submarine-based nuclear missile capabilities, and created an ocean-going surface fleet capable of projecting Soviet power beyond the Eurasian land mass. The Soviets achieved the goal of nuclear parity with the United States by the time of the

Nixon administration, ensuring that both sides had the ability to inflict horrifying and unacceptable losses upon the other side, even after suffering an initial attack by the other side. This situation of **mutually assured destruction (MAD)** became the status quo.

It may seem paradoxical that the improvements in Soviet strategic capabilities that led to nuclear parity actually contributed to improving interbloc relations and the integration of the Eastern bloc economies into the global economy. Yet the shifts in Soviet military strategy and weapons development empowered Soviet policymakers to undertake a diplomatic shift toward more constructive engagement with the West. The emergence of strategic equivalence between the superpowers removed the possibility of one-sided nuclear intimidation and extortion, punctuated the threat of mutual destruction, illuminated the dysfunctional nature of an uncontrolled arms race, and created a foundation for negotiation among equals. Both sides became increasingly interested in limiting the expensive nuclear arms race and the destabilizing competition between them. The Cuban missile crisis revealed the dangers of previous policies and force structures. Recognizing the threat pushed the United States and the Soviet Union toward arms control negotiations, changes in force structures, more constructive engagement, and improving channels of communication.

The Two Germanys and Political Settlement in Europe

Even with improvements in East-West diplomatic relations, unresolved issues regarding the status of East and West Germany hampered rapprochement between the two sides. The fate of the two German states and of Berlin, along with West German territorial disputes with Poland and Czechoslovakia over the redrawing of national boundaries in 1945 remained serious obstacles to normalization of relations (see Map 11.1). Following the division of Germany into two states in 1949, West German Chancellor Konrad Adenauer rejected East German sovereignty and announced the objective of a unified German state. The Hallstein Doctrine enshrined this position in 1955, claiming for the West German government the sole right to represent all Germans.

The Hallstein Doctrine denied the authority of the East German state and declared that the West German government would regard diplomatic recognition of East Germany as an unfriendly act. West Germany severed diplomatic relations with East European governments that recognized East Germany, with the exception of the Soviet Union. Over the same period, the West German government refused to renounce its claims upon territory awarded to Poland and Czechoslovakia following World War II. West German hopes for unification and a redrawing of postwar boundaries, its refusal to accept the political and territorial status quo, kept alive Soviet and East European fears of a resurgent Germany and restrained its allies from seeking normalization of relations. This implicit threat posed a major obstacle to a thawing of the cold war and a normalization of economic relations.

West German intransigence softened in 1966 with the election of a new governing coalition, which elevated Willy Brandt (a Social Democrat) to the position of foreign minister,

MAP 11.1   Europe at the End of the Cold War

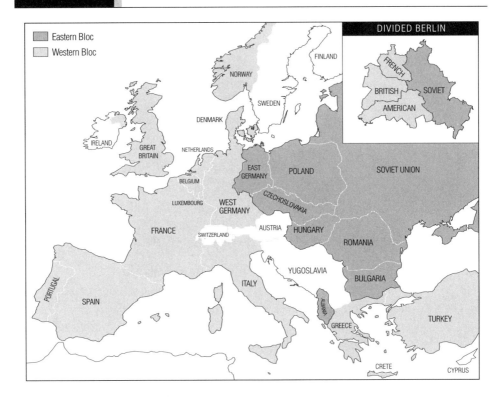

where he signaled a significant shift in the West German position with his policy of **Ostpolitik**, or Eastern policy. *Ostpolitik* sought the normalization of relations with East European states, even if it meant forgoing both unification and claims on the territories ceded to Poland and Czechoslovakia at the end of World War II. Brandt did not reject unification as a goal, but *Ostpolitik* dropped it as a precondition for the normalization of relations. West Germany established formal diplomatic ties with Hungary in 1967 and continued work toward the normalization of political and economic relations with other East European states. Prospects for political settlement of German issues improved further with the West German elections in 1969, in which Brandt's Social Democrats dominated the coalition government that emerged and Brandt ascended to the chancellorship.

As chancellor, Brandt continued his efforts to normalize relations with Eastern Europe. He reduced Soviet fears of a reawakened, aggressive Germany by signing the Nuclear Non-Proliferation Treaty and negotiating a nonaggression agreement with the Soviets, which recognized the territorial status quo in Europe. Next, West Germany entered into a nonaggression treaty with Poland that accepted the German-Polish boundaries imposed at the end of

World War II. In 1973 West Germany recognized the existing German and Czechoslovak borders and renounced the Munich Pact of 1938, abandoning any claims on the Sudetenland. The West German territorial claims that had posed obstructions to a political settlement in Europe no longer existed.

East German sovereignty and the question of Berlin were the major remaining barriers to improved European political relations. The demise of the East German leader Walter Ulbricht in 1971 and the rise of Erich Honecker as his successor opened the door for a resolution of these remaining stumbling blocks. The four occupying powers in Berlin (the United States, the United Kingdom, France, and the Soviet Union) formally recognized the "special relationship" between West Berlin and West Germany and rejected East Germany's demand that it control access to the entire city. In December 1972 the Soviets pressured East Germany to sign the Basic Treaty with West Germany, which called for greater commercial ties between the two Germanys and the exchange of diplomatic missions. In 1973 East and West Germany gained membership in the United Nations as individual sovereign states. The successful resolution of all these matters—German territorial demands, the Berlin dilemma, and sovereignty issues—underpinned the political settlement in Europe, transformed the global context, and substantially lowered barriers to improved East-West commercial relations.

Vietnam

U.S. military involvement in Vietnam imposed another obstacle to improved East-West relations. The United States became engaged in Indochina in the 1950s, providing support for French colonial and neocolonial activities. The United States recognized the French puppet government of Emperor Bao Dai and subsidized a significant portion of French military costs during the French-Vietminh conflict. However, the Vietnamese nationalists under Ho Chi Minh persevered, clinching victory with a stunning defeat of the French forces at Dien Bien Phu. In 1954, after eight years of conflict, the French signed a peace treaty in Geneva and withdrew from Indochina, but the United States remained involved. The Geneva Agreement divided Vietnam temporarily, leaving Ho Chi Minh and the Vietminh as rulers north of the 17th Parallel, while Ngo Dinh Diem, an anticommunist and U.S.-educated Catholic, led the government south of the line (see Map 11.2).

The treaty called for a national plebiscite to be held under United Nations auspices within two years, in order to unify the country and determine its sole government. But U.S. President Dwight Eisenhower, anticipating that such an election would produce a united Vietnam governed by Ho Chi Minh and his supporters, blocked the national vote. Instead, in 1954 policymakers from the United States and other countries agreed to form a regional security pact called the South East Asia Treaty Organization (SEATO), which committed the member states to defend South Vietnam and other regional governments against communist aggression. Under the guise of SEATO obligations, U.S. military and economic support flowed in to assist Diem and the South Vietnamese government. U.S. assistance expanded over time, as a guerilla war broke out in the South following the cancellation of the

MAP 11.2 **Divided Vietnam**

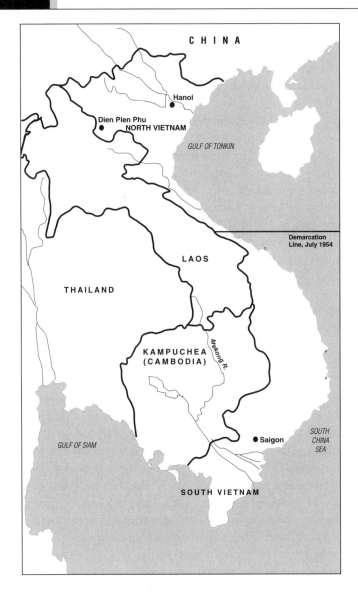

plebiscite. Meanwhile, the Soviet Union and the People's Republic of China provided Ho Chi Minh's government with military and economic aid.

Diem's government proved incredibly corrupt and oppressive, stimulating noncommunist opposition, which formed a coalition with the communist Viet Minh to oppose Diem.

The number of U.S. military advisers to the South Vietnamese government continued to grow. Only about 300 U.S. military advisers had been assigned to the South Vietnamese government after the Geneva Agreement in 1954, but this number had more than doubled before the end of the decade. When President Kennedy took office in 1961, there were almost 900 U.S. advisers helping to train the South Vietnamese forces. This number then tripled before the end of the year, and it exceeded 16,000 advisers by the time of Kennedy's assassination in 1963.

By 1965, the United States had moved beyond its advisory role to become an active combatant on the ground. At first, President Lyndon Johnson sent in two battalions of U.S. marines, but the number quickly increased to over 184,000 ground troops by year's end. The number of U.S. troops involved in military operations in Vietnam swelled to almost 550,000 at the height of U.S. engagement. The Soviets, Chinese, and other members of the Eastern bloc could go only so far down the road of normalization of relations with the West as long as U.S. troops were actively engaged in military conflict with a nation in the communist sphere.

Resistance by North Vietnamese regular army troops and Viet Cong guerillas frustrated U.S. and South Vietnamese efforts. As casualties mounted and time wore on, domestic disagreements over U.S. involvement created significant cleavage and dissension within the U.S. polity, coloring American electoral politics. Under President Nixon and Secretary of State Henry Kissinger, the United States and North Vietnam finally negotiated a settlement that led to U.S. military withdrawal from Vietnam in 1973. Without U.S. military backing, it was only a matter of time before the government and military of South Vietnam faced defeat by the North. In 1975 North Vietnamese troops triumphed over the South Vietnamese, occupying Saigon and the South, and the two Vietnams became a single state.

Resolution of the conflict in Vietnam and the resulting decrease in U.S. adventurism created an opening for improved East-West political and economic relations. The U.S. experience in Vietnam revived the nation's isolationist leanings, increasing American wariness of foreign entanglements. Vietnam educated U.S. policymakers both about the limitations of U.S. power and about the need for domestic consensus in foreign policy, and it led to U.S. political-military retrenchment in the global arena. As U.S. policymakers became more cautious about U.S. military commitments overseas, questions arose in Europe about U.S. commitment to its West European partners. The European allies of the United States faced the possibility of a reduced U.S. military commitment to Europe, which could force politically unpopular increases in their own defense expenditures. Reduction of East-West political-military tensions in Europe offered a more appealing alternative to such defense expenditures.

As the American public grew disillusioned with the cold war and U.S. foreign policy became more cautious, Western European governments, fearing a U.S. retrenchment in Europe, sought to improve relations with the Eastern bloc. In Europe, all the major parties recognized the advantages of normalizing East-West relations, pursuing détente, and stabilizing military relations. The Mutual and Balanced Force Reduction negotiations in Vienna and the European Security Conference in Helsinki in 1973 grew out of this recognition. American withdrawal from Vietnam also removed a major obstacle to Soviet-American and Sino-American rapprochement. With the U.S. withdrawal from Vietnam, the Soviets and Chinese lost an important motivation for a common front, and longstanding Sino-Soviet tensions reemerged.

Discord within the Communist Bloc

From its onset, the Sino-Soviet alliance had proved to be an uneasy coalition. Prior to the victory of Mao Zedong's Communists over Chiang Kai-shek's nationalists in 1949, the Soviets had recognized the nationalists as the official government of China. Although some U.S. policymakers advocated exploiting the potential division in the Communist bloc by recognizing the triumphant Chinese Communist regime on the mainland, the Korean War destroyed any prospects for Sino-American rapprochement during the 1950s and pushed the Soviets and Chinese closer together. Despite earlier Soviet recognition of the nationalist government, the Chinese Communists looked to the Soviets for assistance. Responding with military assistance during the Korean War and committing to long-term development loans, the Soviet Union became China's primary trading partner in the 1950s.

But Soviet assistance came at a price that was sometimes distressingly high for the Chinese. The Soviets required repayment for the military assistance extended during the Korean War. Moreover, the level of Soviet economic assistance proved disappointing—economic development aid extended to India and other noncommunist states by the Soviets actually exceeded their aid to China. And much of the aid to China came tied to Soviet access to Chinese resources. In 1957 the Soviets offered technical assistance to China's nascent nuclear program, but only if China agreed to Soviet control of Chinese nuclear weapons and greater coordination of the two nations' foreign policies. When the Chinese rejected this demand as an infringement upon their sovereignty, the Soviets responded by withholding assistance to China's nuclear program.

Significant territorial disputes fueled Sino-Soviet tensions. Officially, the Soviet Union remained neutral during the 1959 Sino-Indian territorial dispute over Tibet and the Himalayan frontier and also when bloody border clashes again broke out between China and India in 1962. But India, a noncommunist state, was receiving substantial economic and military assistance from the Soviet Union before, during, and after the Sino-Indian conflicts. The Soviets remained silent during the Quemoy and Matsu crisis between the mainland Chinese Communists and the nationalists on Taiwan. Border disputes between China and the Soviet Union itself provided more dramatic and prophetic signs of tense Sino-Soviet relations. When the Chinese disputed Soviet claims to territory that Russia had obtained by treaties during the 1800s, the disagreement turned violent as Chinese and Soviet troops clashed along the border. As such military confrontations escalated, the Soviets redeployed troops, aircraft, and nuclear weapons from Eastern Europe to the Chinese frontier.

Sino-Soviet disagreements grew after the Soviet embarrassment in the Cuban missile crisis, and the Sino-Soviet rift spilled over to other nations in the Communist sphere. By the mid-1960s, the West sensed an opportunity to exploit the growing divisions in the Communist bloc, but Vietnam continued to overshadow Sino-Soviet divisions. However, Vietnam began to fade as an obstruction by the end of the decade, as the Nixon administration took office in 1969 and pursued settlement with North Vietnam. Hoping to take advantage of Sino-Soviet tensions, the United States also embarked on a diplomatic strategy to normalize relations with China and exploit the split in the Communist bloc.

U.S. policymakers began playing the so-called **China card,** by implementing such policies as relaxation of American trade and travel restrictions, ping-pong diplomacy, shuttle diplomacy by Secretary of State Henry Kissinger, support of Pakistan against China's enemy India, and significant changes in U.S. policy toward Taiwan. These measures paved the way for President Nixon's groundbreaking visit to the Peoples' Republic of China in 1972. Sino-American rapprochement allowed China to balance the Soviet military buildup on its borders by redeploying troops to the northwestern Chinese frontier. Détente, the end of U.S. involvement in Vietnam, and the growing divisions in the Communist bloc thus transformed the international political-military context and created opportunities for improvements in East-West relations.

DOMESTIC SHIFTS IN THE EASTERN BLOC AND CHINA

At the same time that the global political-military context was becoming more conducive to improved East-West relations, domestic conditions in the Eastern bloc fed growing interest among Eastern bloc policymakers in greater interaction with the global economy. Comecon's inability to keep pace with West European economic growth, Polish food riots in 1970, and increasing tensions over Soviet economic exploitation of its

President Richard Nixon and Chinese premier Chou En-lai enjoy a stroll in Hangchow, China, in February 1972 during a historic visit that resulted when Nixon took advantage of dissension in the communist bloc to play the "China card." Secretary of State Henry Kissinger had laid the groundwork for improved U.S.-Sino relations during secret trips to the People's Republic. Nixon's opening to China represented a dramatic move toward the normalization of U.S.-Sino relations and the integration of China into the global political economy.

East European allies roused significant concerns and dissatisfaction over Eastern bloc economic policies. Unmet domestic consumer demands led to increasing frustration among the Eastern bloc polities and produced domestic pressures for increased economic openings to the West. These pressures led Eastern bloc policymakers to seek greater exchange with the West in search of materials, capital, skills, and information that could promote faster economic expansion and address the unmet needs of Eastern bloc consumers. In the end, a series of policy changes led to economic and political liberalization that undermined Communist Party control in many Eastern bloc states.

Access to Western Markets, Technology, and Capital

In 1964 a faction led by Leonid Brezhnev and Alexei Kosygin pushed Nikita Khrushchev from power following the Cuban missile crisis. Brezhnev, who by 1969 had outmaneuvered Kosygin for the Soviet premiership, viewed improved economic and diplomatic ties with the West as a pathway to stimulate Soviet economic growth. The East-West arms race had led to swollen military budgets, tying up capital that could be invested in economic growth if it were not being spent on an arms race that no one could win. Greater economic integration with the Western bloc economies would promote economic specialization and improve access to materials, information, skills, and capital that could promote economic advancement. What a nation imports is more critical to development than what it exports. The Eastern bloc states turned to the West for capital, technology, and other assistance to develop their raw materials and modernize their industrial base.

Despite the trend toward improving relations, political and economic détente stalled in the late 1970s. The direction of trade quickly turned disturbingly one-sided, as Eastern bloc exports to the West slumped. Large increases in energy costs produced by the OPEC crises squeezed non–energy export markets and led to further reduction of Eastern exports to the West. This increasing gap between imports and exports hindered the Eastern bloc states' ability to finance development through hard currency earnings from exports, but it also signaled a potential balance-of-payments crisis if the shortfall in earnings should prevent them from meeting their international payment obligations. As noted in chapter 10, hard currencies are those that can readily be used and accepted in international transactions because they will hold their value over time and present relatively little currency risk to the parties of such transactions.

Eastern bloc policymakers could limit Western imports—goods, technology, and expertise—in order to reduce the balance-of-payments pressures, but doing so would delay the development of the East's resources, slow the construction and conversion of industrial plants, and add to the dissatisfaction among Eastern bloc consumers. Rather than thus limiting imports, delaying modernization, and risking more disaffection in their polities, Eastern bloc policymakers turned to the global capital markets as an alternative. Borrowing in global capital markets offered an avenue to cover their chronic balance-of-payments deficits and to finance continued economic expansion. Global borrowing by Comecon states more than doubled from 1974 to 1975, as these states accessed approximately $2.1 billion in commercial loans and $140 million in bond issues in the global capital markets.

Seconds Thoughts and Over-Leveraged Political Economies

By the late 1970s, Western governments and financiers began to pull back from extending such liberal credit to the Eastern bloc states as worries grew about the size of the trade deficits of most Comecon nations and their growing debt obligations in relation to hard currency earnings from exports. Questions arose about the ability of Eastern bloc borrowers to service their growing debt obligations, about the potential consequences for the stability of the global economy if they should fail to meet those obligations, about the risks to Western political economies from this threat, and about the wisdom of greater integration under these circumstances. Western public and private decision makers had assumed, mistakenly or not, that the centralized management of the Eastern bloc economies could protect against a possible failure to service their external debt obligations and that the Soviet Union would stand behind the debt obligations of its allies. But the lack of information about their indebtedness, creditworthiness, and economic projects began to feed uncertainty and to affect the willingness of Western financial institutions to extend credit to Eastern bloc borrowers. Senator Henry Jackson expressed these worries openly before a congressional investigating committee in April 1977:

> By all accounts, Soviet and East European indebtedness to the West has reached major proportions. And yet, estimates of that debt vary widely—from about $27 billion to about $45 billion overall. By any measure, these sums are substantial—and they are growing. It is all the more disturbing that official and private estimates of that debt diverge so greatly. An apparent inability to gain consistent and reliable information about the extent of Soviet and East European borrowing is, itself, a significant part of the problem.

> Large-scale loans to the Soviet Union and the East European countries were once thought of as a way to gain "leverage" over these governments. What may be happening instead is that the debtors are on the verge of obtaining leverage over Western governments by the substantial interest in repayment that the Western banking system may be acquiring. . . .

> Are we on sound ground if we assume that the Soviet Union and the states of Eastern Europe will be able to earn enough hard currency to repay their mounting obligations?

Renewal of Political-Military Tensions

On the political front, East-West rapprochement also stalled despite the achievement of the 1975 Helsinki conference, which marked the formal end of the cold war in Europe and resolved territorial and sovereignty issues that had plagued East-West relations since World

War II. cold war tensions and the nuclear arms race reemerged as U.S.–Soviet arms control negotiations stumbled over technological advances in Soviet weaponry. Theater nuclear weapons—those limited by range to a particular area of operations—in Europe became problematic as the Soviets replaced old intermediate-range missiles with more capable systems. Seeking to reinforce the credibility of the U.S. deterrent umbrella over Western Europe, President Carter committed a new generation of intermediate-range nuclear weapons to deployment in Europe.

Then, in late 1979, Soviet troops entered Afghanistan to support the pro-Soviet government in Kabul against militant opposition. This action marked the first time since World War II that Soviet troops had formally intervened outside Eastern Europe. Earlier that year, the overthrow of the shah of Iran by Muslim fundamentalists had severely damaged U.S. strategic capabilities in the oil-rich region and produced a significant cutback in Iranian oil production, which caused long lines at gas pumps and contributed to a global economic slowdown. In the context of this shift in the regional geopolitical landscape, President Carter viewed Soviet military adventurism in Afghanistan as a threat to vital U.S. interests —specifically, access to oil resources.

Carter announced that the United States would use all resources necessary to protect vital U.S. national interests in the region—a commitment that became known as the Carter Doctrine. In response to Soviet intervention in Afghanistan, U.S. policymakers repaired damaged relations with the military regime in Pakistan, sought military facilities in the region to replace those lost in the downfall of the shah, provided assistance to the Afghan rebels fighting the Soviet-supported Kabul government, created a rapid deployment force for the Persian Gulf region, and increased U.S. military capabilities throughout the region. Ironically, the U.S. assistance to Afghan resistance forces included aid to a young Saudi named Osama bin Laden, thus helping his rise to influence.

The Reagan administration continued and accelerated these initiatives. At the beginning of his first administration, President Reagan dramatically increased U.S. defense expenditures, thereby exploding government deficits and debt but reaffirming the U.S. policy of containment that had been the cornerstone of U.S. foreign policy since the Truman administration. These additional U.S. defense expenditures also raised the costs and stakes of the U.S.–Soviet arms race. The renewal of cold war tensions, uncertainty about the ability of Eastern bloc nations to service their growing debt burdens, and the Third World Debt Crisis all coincided to interrupt the integration of Eastern bloc into the global economy. But this interruption would prove temporary, and China offered a hint of the future.

Chinese Steps toward Liberalization

Under the leadership of Deng Xiaoping, China rejected lingering inclinations toward the self-reliant and centralized development strategies of Mao Zedong, moving instead to embrace export-oriented production, a limited free market, and an increasing amount of private ownership. The Chinese actively sought overseas development assistance and direct loans by requesting United Nations Development Program (UNDP) assistance in 1978; China soon became the largest recipient of UNDP funds.

China joined the World Bank, the IMF, and the Asian Development Bank, and in 1980 it began receiving IMF and World Bank assistance. The country had obtained over $5.5 billion in World Bank funds by mid-decade. Chinese policymakers moved cautiously, trying to constrain China's level of external indebtedness even as they sought overseas capital, but they abandoned their restraint by the mid-1980s. Over $7 billion of foreign direct investment flowed into China between 1979 and 1987. This flow of capital and investment to China reflected not only the appeal of China's potentially huge domestic market, but also the success of Sino-American rapprochement and mutual apprehensions over Soviet military adventurism in Afghanistan. The invasion of Cambodia by Vietnam, a Soviet client, reinforced Chinese and U.S. concerns. Political-military events, which exacerbated Soviet-American tensions, thus strengthened Sino-American relations.

Gorbachev: Arms Control, Perestroika, and Glasnost

During this period, the Soviet Union had been burdened with unstable leadership, experiencing four changes in leaders in a little over three years: Brezhnev died in 1982, his successor, Yuri Andropov, in early 1984, and Konstantin Chernenko, Andropov's successor, in 1985. When Mikhail Gorbachev ascended to the leadership of the Soviet Communist party in 1985, he began moving to halt and reverse the deterioration of the Soviet economy, to limit the costly political-military competition with the United States that was detracting resources from the expansion of economic welfare at home, and to reduce U.S.–Soviet tensions. He also introduced important policy changes, which ultimately led to the dismantling of the Eastern bloc and the breakup of the Soviet Union.

Internationally, Gorbachev sought to curtail the arms race with the United States that sapped resources from productive enterprises in the Soviet economy. After nearly a decade of stalled arms-control negotiations, the United States and Soviet Union reached several agreements. In 1987 the two parties signed an Intermediate-Range Nuclear Forces agreement (INF Treaty), which led to removal of intermediate-range nuclear missiles from the European Theater. The Conventional Armed Forces in Europe (CFE) talks in 1990 produced a treaty that provided for a balance of conventional forces in Europe, while the Strategic Arms Reduction Talks (START) in 1991 led to a treaty limiting the numbers of long-range missiles and nuclear warheads. Gorbachev's diplomacy and these successful arms-control negotiations led to improvements in East-West relations.

Domestically, Gorbachev moved daringly to restructure the Soviet political economy. Economic reforms, **perestroika**, introduced limited market mechanisms that encouraged consumer demand, decentralized decision making and industrial management, and supported private economic initiatives. The political reforms of **glasnost** accompanied these economic reforms. Whereas perestroika encouraged consumer choice and individual initiative in the economic arena, glasnost promoted greater choice and participation in the political sphere.

East European supporters of reform gained strength from the introduction of glasnost and perestroika in the Soviet Union, and they too pressed hard for changes in their domestic arenas. East European governments came under even more severe pressures from their polities, however, as demands for reform outpaced those in the Soviet Union. In 1989 the populations in many East European states rejected Communist Party rule, and the rest of Eastern Europe soon followed. Unlike Hungary in 1956 or Czechoslovakia in 1968, this time the Soviets refrained from intervening to halt the sweeping changes unleashed in their satellite nations. By late 1990, the two Germanys had reunited, the Warsaw Pact had disappeared, and Comecon had disbanded. Popular pressures and uprisings led to the demise of Communist leadership throughout Eastern Europe and the transfer of political leadership into new hands.

The political transformations achieved within the Soviet satellites pale in comparison to changes in the Soviet Union itself. Glasnost and perestroika raised expectations, but economic conditions barely improved—for many Soviets, conditions even deteriorated, as agriculture and oil production declined and GNP fell. Economic stagnation and a shortage of basic goods plagued Soviet leadership and fed pressures for greater political decentralization. Nationalist and ethnic pressures grew in the Soviet republics. The Baltic republics pushed for autonomy and secession, and the legislatures in other Soviet republics voiced preferences for greater autonomy. Conflict between Christians and Muslims arose in the Caucasus. In the fall of 1991, the Soviet Union disintegrated as republic after republic announced its succession and independence. Privatization and democratization had led to perhaps the most stunning transformation of the European political-economic landscape in the twentieth century.

CONCLUSION

Global integration by the Eastern bloc economies increased following détente in the late 1960s and early 1970s, decelerated with the resumption of East-West tensions at the end of the Carter administration and during the early years of the Reagan administration, and then accelerated again with the increased Chinese integration into the global economy and a new easing of East-West tensions. Integration again slowed temporarily amidst the revolutionary changes of the late 1980s. These trends can be seen in the data on international borrowing by these political economies that is reported in figure 11.1.

Examination of more data suggests significant differences in how the former Eastern bloc political-economies and China are faring in terms of their transitions and integration into the larger global economy. Ironically, China, the state with the least amount of political liberalization, has emerged as the most integrated in terms of trade volume, becoming an attractive destination for development assistance and foreign direct investment (FDI). As a group, the former Eastern bloc political economies lag behind China, despite their greater movement on political liberalization and transition. Figure 11.2 displays the changes in trade

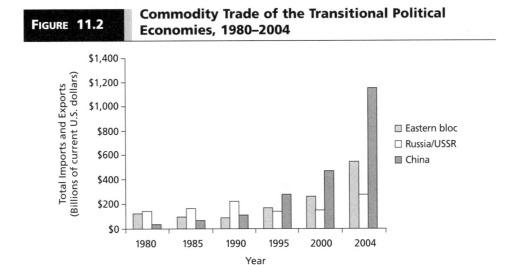

| FIGURE 11.1 | Soviet/Russian and Eastern European Borrowing in Global Capital Markets, 1971–1993 |

Source: OECD Financial Statistics Monthly.

| FIGURE 11.2 | Commodity Trade of the Transitional Political Economies, 1980–2004 |

Source: World Trade Organization Statistics Database, www.stat.wto.org.

Note: The Eastern bloc consists of Albania, Bulgaria, Czechoslovakia (the Czech Republic and the Slovak Republic), Hungary, Poland, and Romania.

exposure for these political economies; figure 11.3 shows the changes in official development assistance extended to these transitional economies; and figure 11.4 displays the shifts in foreign direct investment.

All the transitional political economies of the Eastern bloc and China have enjoyed some success at becoming more involved in the global economy. Many hurdles remain as these governments attempt to liberalize further in order to expand their economies and develop productive civil societies, undergoing difficult political reforms and transitions in the process. Some are farther along on the political spectrum, while others are advancing more rapidly on the economic dimension. These societies are attempting radical transformations in a relatively short period of time. There are no historical precedents, and reversals are possible.

FIGURE 11.3   **Official Development Assistance (ODA) and Official Aid to the Transitional Economies, 1985–2000**

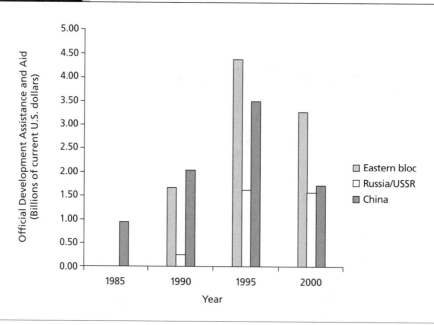

Source: World Bank World Development Indicators, www.worldbank.org/data.

Note: The Eastern bloc consists of Albania, Bulgaria, Czechoslovakia (the Czech Republic and the Slovak Republic), Hungary, Poland, and Romania.

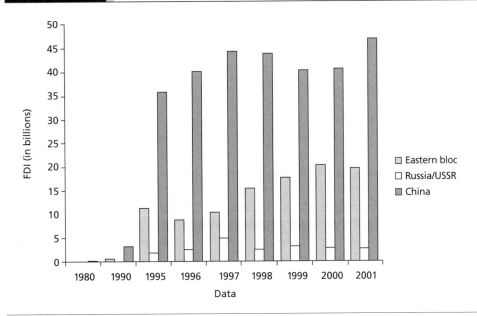

| FIGURE 11.4 | **Foreign Direct Investment (FDI) Inflows to the Transitional Economies, 1980–2001** |

Source: United Nations Conference on Trade and Development, www.unctad.org.

Note: The Eastern bloc consists of Albania, Bulgaria, Czechoslovakia (the Czech Republic and the Slovak Republic), Hungary, Poland, and Romania.

EXERCISES

1. What was the U.S. government's motivation for reestablishing diplomatic relations with China during the Nixon administration?

2. What was the Carter Doctrine, and what was its political context and motivation?

3. What are glasnost and perestroika? How did they change the political and economic arenas in the Soviet Union?

4. Explain the meaning and significance of détente to world affairs.

5. Explain the meaning and significance of *Ostpolitik*.

6. The Cuban missile crisis demonstrated the depth of distrust and hostility between the East and West, but it also contributed to a thawing in those relations. Explain.

7. Construct a causal model/explanation with independent variables in which the dependent variable is the thawing in East-West relations. Justify your inclusion of each independent variable and explain how it is causally related to the dependent variable.

8. Assume that the year is 1949 and you are a top foreign policy and defense adviser in either the United States or the Soviet Union. Both nations have now exploded atomic bombs. You are being asked whether to proceed with research and development into a bomb that is far more deadly than the atomic bomb—a super weapon called the hydrogen bomb. The preferences of each side are as follows: each seeks security and survival, greater strength than the other, and the ability to set the rules of the game. Neither wants to be left behind or dominated. Each has two available strategies: to build or not to build the H-bomb. There are costs involved. If one side builds and the other doesn't, one gets left behind and will be exploited in global affairs. If both build, little if any geopolitical advantage accrues to one or the other. Arsenals cancel one another out, but at very substantial costs—there will be fewer dollars and rubles for education, health care, economic investment. Moreover, any war waged with such weapons would lead to massive devastation (immense costs). We can put the choice of strategies and their outcomes into a game matrix as in chapter 2.

	USSR	
U.S.	Build	Don't Build
Build	Arms race	U.S. dominance
Don't Build	Soviet dominance	Arms limitations

Build a preference ordering for each player independent of the other. What outcome is the intersection of these two preference orderings likely to produce? Is this the best social outcome? Why or why not? If it is not the best collective outcome, what is? Is it a stable outcome?

FURTHER READING

Ambrose, Stephen E., and Douglas G. Brinkley. Various editions. *Rise to Globalism*. New York: Penguin Books.

Kaplan, Fred. 1991. *The Wizards of Armageddon*. Palo Alto, Calif.: Stanford University Press.

Keylor, William R. Various editions. *The Twentieth-Century World: An International History.* New York: Oxford University Press.

Lafeber, Walter. 2002. *America, Russia, and the Cold War, 1945–2002*. 9th ed. New York: McGraw-Hill.

FitzGerald, Frances. 2002. *Fire in the Lake: The Vietnamese and the Americans in Vietnam*. Boston: Back Bay Books.

Sheehan, Neil, Fox Butterfield, Hedrick Smith, and E.W. Kenworthy. 1971. *The Pentagon Papers as Published by the New York Times: The Secret History of the Vietnam War.* New York: Times Books.

12 Political and Economic Market Failure and Social Traps

There are known knowns. These are the things we know. There are known unknowns. That is to say, there are things that we know we don't know. But there are also unknown unknowns. These are things we don't know we don't know.

U.S. Secretary of Defense Donald Rumsfeld, on the war on terrorism, 2003

REVISITING THEORETICAL MARKET FRAMEWORKS

Earlier in this book, we examined theoretical frameworks for the efficient functioning of economic and political markets based upon the aggregation of individual choices. The theoretical frameworks presented in chapters 5 and 6 generate expectations about how individual choices in liberal economic markets and democracies will combine to produce individual and societal benefits—*if* they work according to their theoretical constructions, *if* some critical assumptions are met, and *if* the context of social interaction in which an individual's choices interact with those of others is as expected. In these frameworks, there is no conflict between the self-interested actions of individuals and a good collective outcome that optimizes social welfare. We do not have to make any assumptions about the nobility of individual motivations or whether individuals act in the best interests of society despite their individual interests. These frameworks reflect the "invisible hand" game discussed in chapter 2, wherein we expect individuals to act only in their self-interest—a minimal assumption that does not infer any lofty intentions. The invisible hand structure of social interactions, the context of those interactive choices, coordinates choices to produce an equilibrium that optimizes individual and collective welfare. In an ideal world, this process maximizes production and consumption possibilities of economic and political goods, given the wants and desires of a society's members.

Ideally, the aggregation mechanism of the invisible hand in economic markets, or a similar voting rule in political markets, should ensure that no conflict exists between individual choice and collective welfare in the structure of individual interactions. In theory, at least, the aggregation mechanisms of economic and political markets take self-interested individual behavior and produce nice social outcomes. These frameworks provide theoretical baselines to consider how well economic and political markets actually function in the empirical world.

REVIEWING EXPECTATIONS OF BASELINE MODELS

The application of liberal economic theory to international affairs anticipates that if economic and political markets work as predicted and we operate in a context as described by the structure of the invisible hand game, we should expect the following outcomes:

- Policymakers pursue policies that encourage greater market exchange.
- Politics and economics remain separate except in those areas in which public policy could help to promote market exchange or improve inputs to production, and where economic resources could promote more informed political participation.
- Policymakers in liberal political economies enact policies promoting greater trade and exchange across borders.
- International organizations are constructive mechanisms that provide infrastructure advantageous to economic exchange across national borders and help to reduce barriers to coordination that would aid such exchange.
- Greater interdependence produces increased harmony and reduces international tensions between nations.
- Global economic relations expand and flourish.
- Interdependence, the growth in linkages across borders, becomes self-sustaining.

In theory, the predictions of economic liberalism and political democracy are normatively appealing, but their appeal must be more than theoretical. How well do such theories account for behavior in the social world? Does the empirical world live up to theoretical expectations, or does it fall short? If it falls short, by how much and why? This comparison of theory to the empirical world is critical for trying to understand individual choices, the interaction of such choices to produce social behavior, and the effect of structure and context upon outcomes. Rarely does any form of social behavior comport perfectly with social science theory, so investigators must consider the extent to which empirical behavior deviates from a theory's expectations. From a positivist perspective, we must ask whether some other theory might be more productive and powerful in examining social behavior or more useful in guiding public policy.

Market Failure and Suboptimal Social Outcomes

The pragmatic appeal of economic and political relations based upon individual choice depends upon the aggregation of such choices producing good social outcomes as well as good individual outcomes. But what if the aggregation of individual actions produces only so-so, or even poor, collective outcomes? Two major categories of problems potentially threaten the appeal of economic liberalism and political democracy based upon individual choice: market failure and social traps. First, assuming that the structure of interactions generally conforms to the invisible hand game, what happens when the restrictive assumptions detailed in chapter 5 and 6 do not hold? We claimed there that these assumptions are important to efficient exchange in economic and political markets—but what happens in these markets when such assumptions are not met? This possibility raises the specter of **market failure.** Second, even if the assumptions outlined in chapters 5 and 6 do hold, what if the structure of social interactions turns out not to be an invisible hand situation wherein individual choices interact and aggregate to produce optimal social and individual outcomes, but instead a social context wherein individual choices interact and aggregate to produce suboptimal social and individual outcomes despite the rationality of the decision makers? This situation is called a **social trap.**

Empirical Challenges to the Baseline Models

The preceding historical chapters offer some puzzles and evidence that challenge the baseline frameworks. First and foremost, the experiences of the 1800s, the interwar years, and the post–World War II period suggest that individuals acting in their self-interest do not necessarily produce good social outcomes, or even good individual outcomes. For example, the intellectual breakthroughs of Ricardo and others did not immediately prompt policymakers to adopt policies that would unleash liberal economic exchange in order to obtain maximum individual and collective gains. Instead, barriers to such exchange persisted for years and never completely faded, even during the height of nineteenth-century liberal reform. The same kind of failure occurred in political markets: monarchies persisted and voting rights were only gradually extended—and then often without enthusiasm. Even after reform, the gains from expanding international trade relied upon British policies and actions, which provided collective goods to help in overcoming the barriers to liberal economic exchange.

The years leading up to World War I and the interwar years saw a retrenchment in political liberties, in liberal international economic exchange, and in the provision of key collective goods. The beggar-thy-neighbor policies of the 1920s and 1930s and the attacks on rational constitutionalism provide extreme examples of the retreat to economic nationalism and of the curtailment of democratization. The Fordney-McCumber and Smoot-Hawley Acts in the United States, reconstruction of trade barriers in many nations, manipulation of currency values through devaluations, tit-for-tat antiliberal policies, building of barriers to migration, rise of ethnic discrimination, and revitalization of authoritarian rule and political extremism—all these outcomes suggest inconsistencies between the empirical and theoretical worlds. After World War II, policymakers worked hard to ensure the provision of key collective goods and to build institutional barriers to economic nationalism. But such collective goods and public policies would not be necessary to promote liberal economic exchange and democracy if the structure of individual interactions actually mirrored the invisible hand game or if economic and political markets worked as described in chapters 5 and 6.

In the invisible hand game and in the ideal world of political and economic markets, the dominant strategies of self-interested individuals interact to enhance social welfare. Liberal economic exchange and democratic market exchange should produce good social outcomes, and they should become self-sustaining. If liberal exchange in political and economic markets enhances individual and collective welfare, expectations from the baseline models suggest that such behavior would indeed become self-sustaining. Yet, the late 1800s and early 1900s and, most dramatically, the interwar years demonstrate that liberal economic markets and democratic political markets are not self-sustaining or in the stable equilibrium that the invisible hand game predicts. Instead, in those years, self-interested actions led to policies and actions that detracted from social welfare, and also from individual welfare—a socially and individually pernicious equilibrium. The actions of seemingly rational decision makers produced perverse and destructive outcomes for themselves, their constituents, and their nations.

Revisiting Historical Lessons

How can we account either for the apparent dependence upon collective goods to promote exchange or for the reconstruction of trade barriers in many nations in the late 1800s and early 1900s after a period of liberalization and increasing openness? How can we account for the reversal in the extension of political rights and liberties? Why do so many of the activities in international affairs in that era seem to fall short of the expectations generated in chapters 5 and 6? Is the rationality assumption flawed, or is there a flaw in the assumptions about the structure of interactions among rational individuals? Does the failure to attain efficient political and economic markets point to a problem in our assumptions about individual behavior, in our assumptions about context, or in both?

Let's revisit some of the specific lessons about economic and political market exchange arising from the historical chapters to see if those lessons begin to provide some insight to the discrepancies between theory and the empirical world. First, severe depressions in the late 1800s and the economic and political collapse of the 1920s and 1930s challenge laissez-faire capitalism's belief in the self-correcting behavior of markets. These breakdowns in national and international political economies suggest that markets are not always self-sustaining and correcting. The disciplinary mechanism of global market exchange may work fairly well much or some of the time to produce a *virtuous* cycle of activity, in which individual actions are self-reinforcing and lead to improvements in individual and collective welfare. But history shows that a *vicious* cycle can also occur, wherein the aggregation of individual choices damages individual and collective welfare. The retrenchment of globalization and the rollback of political and civil liberties in many nations during the 1920s and 1930s provide a harsh and violent example of a vicious cycle, suggesting that the structure of individual interactions and the aggregation mechanism of those individual actions may differ from the invisible hand structure.

Second, the history of the expansion of globalization and global capitalism in the 1800s, their breakdown in the early 1900s, and their revitalization in the post–World War II period suggest that economic and political market exchange occurs in an arena fraught with individual and societal risks, and that some scaffolding may be required to limit such risks and to encourage exchange. Laissez-faire capitalism, however, assumed that such risks would be managed by the market mechanism, which would penalize those who did not play by the rules of a competitive market and reward those who did. For example, if laissez-faire capitalism worked as anticipated, those who cheated or reneged on their obligations would be penalized by market forces, which would force them to change their behavior and abide by the terms of an exchange. If laissez-faire capitalism worked as anticipated, currency risk would eventually disappear, as weak, volatile currencies would fall out of use and only strong, stable currencies would be used in exchange. Global markets would penalize holders of weak currencies, which would generate pressures for governments to better manage their affairs.

In contrast, history demonstrates that markets may not always be capable of limiting such risks and protecting exchange. In the late nineteenth and early twentieth centuries, groups and individuals employed political arenas to avoid the costs of responding to the corrective mechanisms of economic markets, which helped to undermine individual and collective welfare. In an invisible hand structure, or in the well-functioning markets depicted in chapters 5 and 6, such evasive maneuvers would be unnecessary and unlikely. But history shows that good economic markets may depend upon good public policies to manage risks that can lead to demands that may damage political and economic markets. This dependence begs the broader question of how political markets affect economic markets, and vice versa, and it also highlights potential problems with the structure of relations in economic and political markets.

CONDITIONS FOR EFFICIENT MARKETS

Let's quickly revisit the theoretical requirements for efficient market exchange that were introduced in chapter 5 and applied again in chapter 6. *Competitive markets require clear definition of property rights and the ability of market participants to negotiate, monitor, and enforce contracts at relatively negligible costs.* In competitive markets, participants to exchange must have a clear understanding of who owns what, as the exchange of goods and services in a market involves the exchange of property rights over those goods and services. In a political market, this understanding requires clarity about who has the right to vote (the property right over the vote) and about the ability of the seller of political goods (politicians and policymakers) to deliver such goods in exchange for votes or political support. An election is a contract between those elected and those doing the electing. Are the terms of such contracts clear, capable of being monitored, and enforceable at relatively low costs? The costs of negotiating, monitoring, and enforcing the terms of an exchange (a contract) are transaction costs. In competitive markets with clear definition of property rights, these costs should be small or negligible.

A variety of factors affect transaction costs, the prospects of competitive exchange, and the efficiency advantage of market exchange as compared to other forms of allocation. Competitive and efficient markets require that no individual buyer or seller, or cartel of buyers or sellers, can manipulate the price mechanism in order to extract what are called extra-market **rents**—gains above what an efficient market would produce that accrue to specific buyers or sellers. This requirement means that no monopoly producer or oligopoly of producers can manipulate the price of a commodity by affecting its supply in a market—that there are enough other producers to supply the commodity so any attempt to manipulate supply would fail. This requirement also holds true on the demand side, where no single consumer (a **monopsony**) or cartel of consumers (an **oligopsony**) can affect the demand for a commodity and hence gain the ability to manipulate the price of that commodity. In competitive markets, producers or consumers who try to manipulate the price of a commodity will fail as long as a sufficient number of other producers or consumers are in the market. Participants in efficient and competitive markets are all price-takers—that is, they respond to price incentives but cannot individually manipulate prices as in the case of price-givers. Competitive markets rely upon Adam Smith's invisible hand functioning without manipulation, for such competition is essential if political and economic markets are to optimize social welfare.

Another important condition for competitive and efficient markets is that transactions in such markets have no effect on third parties—those people who are not involved either as a seller or a consumer of an economic or political commodity. When this condition is not met, the effect on a third party is called an "externality" of the exchange. Third parties do not intentionally reap the rewards or costs of an exchange, but these effects, whether positive or negative, befall them anyway. Negative externalities affect the efficiency of a market by imposing undesirable transaction costs upon parties not involved in the exchange. This effect is particularly apparent in political markets—where members of a society may have to consume political goods produced by politicians they did not support in an election—and it highlights one of the important distinctions between political and economic markets: the greater potential for nonvoluntary consumption in political markets. Although negative externalities may be less apparent in economic markets, they can be seen to be quite frequent if we start looking closely at such third-party costs as pollution, noise, and so on, which divert resources and introduce inefficiencies into exchange, detracting from overall societal welfare even if the immediate parties to the exchange benefit.

Another important condition for competitive and efficient markets is complete or full information. Parties to exchange should be equally informed and not deprived of information that is important to the exchange. *Asymmetric information,* whereby one party to an exchange knows more about the commodity being exchanged than do the other parties, can introduce unfair advantages that detract from the efficiency of the exchange. Asymmetric information is one form of incomplete information, but it specifically means that one party to an exchange knows more than the other parties do, not that all parties are equally uninformed or well-informed.

UNDERSTANDING MARKET FAILURE

Clear definition of property rights, negligible transaction costs, no possibility for producers or consumers to unilaterally manipulate supply or demand, no third-party externalities, and full information are demanding requirements that are rarely met in exchange situations, economic or political, outside the theoretical world. What happens when we fall short of meeting such requirements in our exchange relationships? Failure to meet any of these conditions undermines the gains of efficient market exchange and, by definition, leads to market failure—the failure to most effectively employ the resources of society, given the distribution of preferences in society. Such imperfection does not mean we should abandon economic and political markets as a form of social, economic, and political organization. Exchange in imperfect markets may still produce better individual and social outcomes than can be gained from alternative forms of social organization that address the distribution of economic and political goods. We should avoid hiding our heads in the polemic sand and, instead, seriously consider the flaws of market exchange in the real world by considering the following circumstances: how seriously such requirements are violated; what damages are done to social welfare by imperfections in political and economic market exchange; how those damages are produced and exacerbated; and how such shortfalls can be mitigated by corrective measures.

In order to understand how imperfections in economic and political markets can damage social welfare, we need to examine how the threats to market exchange operate, what are the mechanisms that add costs to the exchange and detract from the efficiency of exchange based upon individual choice, and how these mechanisms hurt individual and social welfare. In effect, we need to act as social forensic pathologists, conducting autopsies of imperfect exchange in political and economic markets to determine how and why things can go wrong when the requirements for efficient market exchange are loosened. Let's consider more closely the contributors to market failure.

Property Rights and Transaction Costs

Confusion over property rights can limit exchange and increase transaction costs. The more uncertainty there is on this issue, the more parties to an exchange must expend efforts and resources to protect themselves against ambiguous property rights. Such efforts may include hiring lawyers and drafting extensive contracts in an attempt to anticipate ambiguities and loopholes in property rights and the expectations of exchange, as well as arranging for auditors to closely monitor exchanges or to mediate discrepancies and disagreements in exchange.

In political markets, ambiguity about the property rights over votes distorts the one-person, one-vote principle in elections. Jim Crow laws embedded this failure in law by limiting African Americans' access to the voting booth in many American states following Reconstruction. Reports of voter fraud, lost ballots, and dead people voting (and voting, and voting) are more examples of political market failure related to uncertainty over the property rights of voting and the transaction costs of clarifying those rights. Treaties between nations are exchange agreements—for example, we will limit the production of greenhouse gases in exchange for *w*, we will limit the number of long-range nuclear weapons in exchange for *x*, we will lower our tariff rates in exchange for *y*, we will come to your defense as an ally in exchange for *z*. Many treaties, however, are drafted in intentionally ambiguous language that confuses a nation's obligations under the treaty. For example, many military alliances require their members to come to the aid of an ally that has been attacked, but not one that has initiated hostilities. The U.S. Senate failed to ratify the League of Nations Charter following World War I because its terms did not permit the U.S. government to exercise discretion about committing American troops to collective security operations. The United Nations Charter provided greater discretion to governments on the choice of providing troops for UN-sanctioned collective-security operations (as when Soviet troops did not join the United Nations effort in the Korean War).

The international trade agreements of the post–World War II era allow nations to impose import barriers if their producers and workers are damaged by unfair competition, but the term *unfair* is intentionally left undefined, open to interpretation and adjudication. Without such loopholes, many, if not all, nations would have refrained from signing the GATT and WTO agreements. Ambiguity may be necessary to obtain sufficient consensus to arrive at a treaty, but the gray areas that are open to interpretation produce uncertainty over property rights and obligations in the exchange that forms the basis of the treaty. Such uncertainty over property rights means that the costs of negotiating, monitoring, and enforcing the terms of the exchange agreement are no longer negligible—they add costs and generate inefficiencies that detract from the overall value of the treaty. If these transaction costs become sufficiently large, they can significantly damage the efficiency of the exchange, and consequently harm the social welfare of the parties to the treaty.

Again, the failure to meet the stringent requirement of well-defined property rights does not necessarily undermine the argument for market exchange and suggest that another form of exchange could perform better in terms of social welfare, but it does open the door to such considerations. Debates over the social welfare effectiveness of market exchange versus some other form of exchange depends upon the degree of market failure and whether mechanisms can be devised to limit the extent of market failure. For example, effective rule of law with fair adjudication and enforcement mechanisms can provide strategies for managing ambiguities over property rights and obligations in exchange. Even though such tools impose transaction costs on market exchange, they can help reduce other costs and reduce the overall inefficiency of imperfect market exchange.

Manipulation of Supply and Demand

What happens to efficient exchange if individual producers or consumers (monopolists or monopsonists), or a cartel of producers or consumers (oligopolists or oligopsonists), can manipulate the supply or demand for a particular commodity in an economic or political market? If a single seller or buyer, or a cartel of sellers or buyers, can control supply or demand, they have the ability to manipulate price, as well as incentives to manipulate the market to increase their individual welfare, even if at the expense of collective welfare. The Organization of Petroleum Exporting Countries (OPEC) has garnered such influence in the production and supply of oil, because its small number of member nations control a disproportionately large share of the world's oil production. By colluding to set production targets (numbers of barrels of oil produced), OPEC can manipulate the price per barrel and increase the individual gains of its members, even if the price per barrel does not reflect what an efficient market would charge. Consumers of oil pay more for oil than they would if the OPEC cartel could not control supply.

The success of OPEC depends upon several key characteristics of oil. First, there is a relatively inelastic demand for oil, and substitution of new supplies or alternative fuels is not easy or cost-efficient in the short term. Inelastic demand means that regardless of price, the demand for oil will remain relatively constant (see figure 12.1). Consumption choices concerning oil products will be relatively uninfluenced by the price of oil, for energy and oil are at the heart of any modern political economy, or any political economy that hopes to be modern. We live in a world powered and heated primarily by petroleum by-products. Moreover, the lack of substitutability means that alternative sources of oil or energy, other than those controlled by OPEC, are either not readily available at a reasonable price in the short term or, if cost effective, not capable of being developed in the short term.

Inelasticity of demand and lack of substitutability for oil provide OPEC members with the ability to manipulate supply and therefore price, if they can successfully collude. Supply manipulation by OPEC helps its members to reap greater profits from their production of oil—far greater than what they would garner in an efficient market. Consumers of petroleum-based products thus pay more for those products than they would in an efficient market and consequently have fewer resources with which to consume other commodities. This higher price is the inefficiency, or cost, of imperfect market exchange in oil.

Such collusion to manipulate supply or demand also occurs in imperfect political markets. Political parties work to limit the number of viable candidates in elections, to constrain voters' consumption choices. Interest groups that form to advance concerns and place policy demands upon politicians may be advantaged in obtaining their policy preferences ver-

FIGURE 12.1   **A Relatively Inelastic Demand Curve**

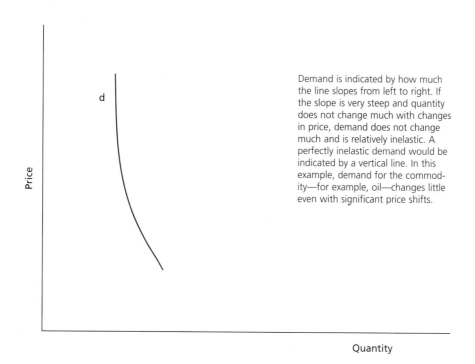

d

Price

Demand is indicated by how much the line slopes from left to right. If the slope is very steep and quantity does not change much with changes in price, demand does not change much and is relatively inelastic. A perfectly inelastic demand would be indicated by a vertical line. In this example, demand for the commodity—for example, oil—changes little even with significant price shifts.

Quantity

sus individuals with similar interests who never succeed in forming a group. Political parties and interest groups pool individual resources and voices to create potentially more powerful and manipulative forces in political markets than that of the lone voter. Citizens have little choice in the purchase of government services, since governments are by definition monopolists in the use of the legitimate forces of coercion in society and in the provision of other governmental services. As citizens, we do not get to purchase our national security from a market of national security providers, our social services from a market of social service providers, or our tax collection from a market of tax collectors. Political markets are constrained in their range of choices, and many of the exchanges they offer are nonvoluntary. A citizen must pay for and receive government services regardless of her desire for those services because the purchase of them is a collective decision. She cannot decide to purchase the national security offerings of the United States, the health care of Sweden, the tax collection of France, the road infrastructure of Germany, the legislative representation of Italy, and the courts of the Netherlands.

In general, collusion by producers or consumers generates inefficiencies that are damaging to collective welfare, but important exceptions exist—natural monopolies such as utilities with high and expensive barriers to entry or too little political collusion that contributes to political fragmentation and conflict. Monopolies or oligopolies do usually lead to an overall decrease in consumption and provision of goods; consumers are harmed by increased costs and decreased consumption. These negative consequences outweigh possible gains to the monopolist by her increased profits. The same is usually true if a single consumer, a monopsonist, or cartel of consumers, oligopsonists, can manipulate demand and, consequently, price. Producers will be harmed by decreased profits and lower production, and the costs to society outweigh the gains to the consumers who have manipulated price. Again, the failure to meet the requirement that neither buyers nor sellers can manipulate the supply or demand for a particular commodity does not necessarily undermine the argument for market exchange and suggest that another form of exchange could perform better in terms of social welfare. But, as in the case of poorly defined property rights, it does open the door to such considerations.

Third-Party Externalities

Another important consideration is that some goods that a society wants may be underprovided, or not provided at all, even in situations where the market mechanism works well. Perversely, an effective market mechanism can actually prevent some socially desirable goods from being provided, or lead to their serious underprovision due to the incentives for rational individuals to free-ride on the activities of others. Free-riding can produce a social trap wherein rational individual choices interact and aggregate to produce suboptimal social and individual outcomes. In such cases, which are often characteristic of political markets, some commodities that society desires may not be provided by voluntary consumption choices. To understand how free-riding contributes to social traps, we have to focus again on third-party externalities.

Third-party externalities, another contributor to market failure, are the costs (a negative externality) or benefits (a positive externality) imposed on individuals who are not directly involved in an exchange, thereby diminishing or enhancing the individual's welfare. If severe enough, third-party externalities can significantly undercut market exchange and detract from the efficient allocation of resources, given the aggregate wants of members of society. Negative externalities damage overall societal welfare, as the costs to the third parties exceed the benefits to the parties directly involved in the exchange. But how do positive externalities damage social welfare by generating benefits to individuals not directly involved in an exchange?

Positive externalities encourage free-riding, or consumption of an exchange without contribution. If enough people believe that they will receive a positive externality from an exchange without contributing to the provision of the good or commodity involved, they have an incentive to free-ride on those who are willing to pay for the exchange. Free-riders, if successful, will enjoy the commodity being exchanged without having to pay it—like having your cake and eating it too! But if enough members of a community calculate that they can free-ride on such exchanges, society may face the dilemma of insufficient contributions to provide a particular good that the members of society actually desire. Perversely, the incentive to free-ride to enjoy a positive externality can winnow away the provision of the commodity that offers positive externalities to others, leading to an underprovision of a commodity or good that many desire. This problem is exacerbated if those who are willing to pay for such goods resent the free-riding by others in society, feel like suckers, and decide not to pay for the goods after all. This reversal generates a vicious cycle leading to market failure.

The dynamics of positive externalities thus create a social trap. Chapter 5 raised this dilemma in the context of national security, but it is prevalent in the provision of any goods that contribute to the infrastructure of a polity or economy. We all want to live in a society of educated people, we all want to drive on nice roads, we all want good power transmission facilities, we all want clean public parks and forests, we all want voters to make well-informed decisions in the voting booth. Trouble arises, however, when many hope that others in society will bear the burden and subsidize the provision of such societal goods while hoping to receive the benefits of such provision for themselves without incurring the costs. In chapter 13, we return to this free-rider problem in the context of collective action, to unpack the structure of this problem and better understand why individuals free-ride even when it damages their self-interest.

The presence of positive externalities leads to a suboptimal amount of such goods. There are mechanisms to limit free-riding and shirking of contribution. We could, for instance, organize a community of potential contributors and negotiate a multiparty contract among the members of the group. Contracting is a part of everyday life in societies. Private individuals and entities enter into formal and informal contracts committing them to specific actions and obligations, and governments and their societies enter into public contracts—reflected in our laws and regulations—specifying the obligations of government to their societies and of members of society to their government and to other members of society. But people can violate contracts. To ensure that they act in accordance with their contractual commitments requires monitoring the terms of the contract and the actions of the parties to the contract, and sanctioning those who do not meet their obligations. This process involves non-negligible transaction costs, which generally increase with the number of parties to a contract and its complexity. Monitoring and enforcing contracts is expensive, as these activities detract from the production and consumption of the goods that the parties

Two volunteers at a Cape Touri beach in Spain work to clean up an oil spill resulting from a contract between two private parties. Environmental disasters are among the most visible examples of a third-party externality. Taxpayers had such an externality imposed on them in the form of an environmental disruption and the millions of dollars required for the clean up. The cost to the social welfare function is how that money would have been used absent the spill.

to the contract desire. In terms of the defense example, resources that could go into production of defense goods are instead channeled into monitoring and enforcing agreements regarding contributions to defense. Such transaction costs mean that the amount of national security purchased by a society is less than what an efficient market would produce, but probably more than voluntary market exchange would generate under the influence of positive externalities.

The existence of externalities and the resulting market failure does not necessarily disqualify market exchange as a distribution mechanism. The fact that markets fail does not mean that we should abandon market exchange for some other form of exchange relations, such as authoritarianism in political affairs or centralized allocation and planning in economic affairs. The normative appeal of market exchange depends upon the extent of market failure, the size of the externalities, and the ability to construct affordable mechanisms that limit the production of such externalities or compel the parties who produce such externalities to compensate those who incur their costs.

The latter approach asks parties to the exchange to internalize the costs of producing the externality, adding those costs to the exchange and limiting the externality. Parties to the exchange might be required to compensate third parties for the burden of the externality or to correct the production of the externality. Consider this example: Ocean pollution resulting from oil spills damages fishing stocks, and hence damages the livelihoods of fishermen who are not directly part of the exchange in the energy sector. The polluters could either compensate the fishermen for their loss of livelihood or pay for cleanup and for technologies that limit spills and their damage. Either way, the cost of pollution would be part of the (internalized) costs of the exchange and not imposed on third parties, the fishermen. We oil consumers might pay more for energy, but that effect would reflect the real costs of the exchange between contracting parties, absent the presence of third-party externalities.

Asymmetric Information

Now let's turn to another threat to efficient market exchange: asymmetries in information. Selecting commodities, whether in economic markets or in political markets, requires consumers or voters to differentiate across a range of options when they make their consumption decisions. There are often significant differences between commodities. In a competitive market where all sellers and buyers are equally well-informed, such differences should map into consumer choices that accurately reflect their preferences. Some people will purchase one commodity over others, vote for one candidate over others, or choose one public policy over others. Such choices will be efficient, as consumers will be opting for the commodity, candidate, or policy that best meets their tastes, given the constraints of cost. A seller of a commodity, whether a political commodity or an economic commodity, cannot substitute one commodity for another without the consumer's awareness. A consumer cannot be misled about her choice, and it will be priced accurately.

What if consumers are not sufficiently well-informed to accurately differentiate between products, politicians, or policies that they might choose to consume? In a complicated world wherein individuals consume across a vast array of alternatives in political and economic markets, consumers cannot possibly be experts in all their consumption decisions. Even if they wanted to be fully informed about all their choices, trying to obtain such expertise would be inefficient, even paralyzing, as their resources and time for such research are limited. Due to consumers' limited time, energy, and capabilities to acquire and process information, they inevitably will make some choices with incomplete and asymmetrical information, whereby the seller of a commodity knows more about the commodity than the consumer does.

People may have problems distinguishing one politician from another ("They're all alike"), one political party from another, one policy from another, or one product from another. But experts or the sellers of a commodity do not face the same dilemma. They have asymmetric information, which they can use to their advantage. Sellers of less desired products can advertise in an attempt to mislead consumers about the true nature of their products and so inflate the desirability of their products. This practice pressures other sellers of more desirable products to advertise in order to try to inform consumers about the true quality of their products. Both cases impose costs on exchange, reduce its efficiency, and detract from overall social welfare. Consumers may purchase the wrong goods or pay too much for a commodity, and sellers of good commodities may gain less than they would if everyone were equally well-informed.

The very presence of political campaigns and commercial advertisements and the extraordinary size of economic activity involved in these endeavors serve as stark evidence of the extent of asymmetric information affecting our consumption choices. If we were really well-informed, political or economic advertising would be useless. Rational companies and politicians would not pay so much for advertising if it did not affect consumer or voter behavior, and it can only do so if consumers and voters operate with incomplete or asymmetric information. Ironically, advertising may serve to exacerbate the dilemma produced by asymmetric information. Why? The advertisement meant to accurately inform looks the same as the advertisement meant to mislead. How is a consumer or voter to decide?

With asymmetric information, consumers or voters face difficulties distinguishing good sellers, good products, good politicians, or good policies from bad sellers, bad products, bad politicians, or bad policies—good or bad is a function of the normative preference of the consumer or voter. Recall from chapter 5 that this dilemma, called a "pooling equilibrium," leads to inefficiencies in the production and consumption of goods and services, or in the production and consumption of political commodities, as consumers or voters are purchasing goods and services or casting their votes and supporting public policies with false or inadequate information. Consumers and voters can be misled, cheated, and manipulated so that they may not be purchasing the goods they think they are purchasing, or voting for the political outcomes they think they want. This result is partly the responsibility of the consumers or voters who expose themselves to the possibility of being misled and manipulated by not expending the time and energy necessary to become informed consumers or voters. Pooling equilibriums, misinformation, and misleading advertising depend upon consumers' and voters' not acquiring the information and skills to know better, when such skills and information can be obtained by consumers and voters who make the effort.

If not for the social consequences of misinformed consumption choices in political and economic markets, one might simply say, "Let the buyer beware," and assume that the voters or consumers should become sufficiently informed to make intelligent decisions that reflect their true preferences. Easier said than done—to be well-informed about every consumption choice we make demands an amazing amount of information and the ability to process that information. Protecting oneself against being misled and manipulated by all sellers of products in economic markets, or by all politicians in political markets, would require an impossible investment of resources by consumers and voters. Each of us would have to have a mind with processing power far exceeding a supercomputer of a capacity yet to be invented. Imagine how much time and effort would be required to make every consumption decision in political and economic markets a well-informed decision.

First, we would have to be able to clearly differentiate across products, politicians, and policies. Second, we would have to be able to evaluate the prospects of the different products, politicians, and policies to produce our desired outcomes. Third, we would have to be able to distinguish sincere policymakers or sellers who mean what they say from the strategic policymakers or sellers who say what is necessary to achieve their desired outcome, regardless of whether their statements are accurate or not. Furthermore, many transactions in modern economies and polities involve exchange over time and space. For example, we select politicians and policymakers for a period of time, and they deliver political goods over that period. Essentially, we buy a basket of political goods at one point with the expectation that they will be delivered at some time in the future. This is a contract, but an incomplete contract with plenty of opportunities to create and exploit loopholes. Fourth, all of this evaluation happens in a social setting, so even if one consumer or voter develops such a capacity, the social outcome depends upon the choices of many voters and consumers. None of these are trivial impositions—the transaction costs, information costs, and contracting problems are not negligible.

Dilemmas of asymmetric information, non-negligible transaction costs, and incomplete contracts increase the likelihood that consumers cannot distinguish good products from bad products, good sellers from bad sellers, good politicians from bad politicians, or good public policies from bad public policies. They may pay too much for bad products from less reputable sellers and too little for good products from good sellers. They may cast their votes for politicians who do not reflect their true preferences and vote against politicians who better represent their preferences. They may support policies that do not reflect their true preferences at the expense of policies that better represent their preferences. Such confusion damages the consumer, the voter, the good seller, the good politician, the good policy, and society. It advantages the less reputable seller and her products, and the less representative politician and her policies. In the end, this problem of poor or asymmetric information affects production and consumption of economic and political goods in society by distorting the ideal of efficient economic exchange and political representation. The inefficiencies produced are simply the difference between what is produced and consumed under asymmetric information and what is produced and consumed under conditions of full information. This effect applies to both political and economic markets.

Essentially, consumers and voters face a challenge of sorting out good from bad claims. They need to transform the pooling equilibrium into a "separating equilibrium." Recall that in a separating equilibrium, buyers and voters can accurately distinguish among products, sellers, policies, and politicians. If the core conditions for efficient competitive markets are violated and voters and consumers fail to accurately distinguish among alternative products, politicians, or policies, market failure takes place. And if such market failure becomes severe enough, we observe near-complete breakdowns in economic markets and political systems.

This scenario paints a potentially dismaying picture for market exchange and democratic governance based upon an assumption of informed consumers and voters. Yet, our assumption of rationality provides tools to help limit such threats. Recognizing the limitations in our ability to acquire, process, and understand information that would limit market failures, we can construct formal and informal devices to limit such threats. In successful market economies and democratic polities, much of the government regulation concerning market exchange, appropriate behavior in the political arena, and the responsibilities of economic and political actors exists to constrain the asymmetric information problem. Disclosure, transparency, contracting provisions, lemon laws, and campaign finance laws are attempts to reduce the problems of asymmetric information and level the playing field between producers and consumers, between politicians and voters.

Individuals and businesses also develop strategies to manage the dilemma of asymmetric information. They ask for advice from friends and neighbors who are better-informed. They hire consultants who have developed special expertise in an area—lawyers, real estate agents, accountants, tax planners, business consultants, and so forth. Such strategies will be imperfect by definition, and they will impose significant transaction costs that reduce social efficiency. But even so, they can improve upon the market failure produced by asymmetric information. The existence of relatively well-functioning democratic market economies demonstrates the capacity of formal and informal mechanisms to limit, though not eliminate, market failure in economic and political arenas. President Abraham Lincoln captured this sentiment when he supposedly remarked, "You can fool all the people some of the time, some of the people all of the time, but not all of the people all of the time."

SOCIAL TRAPS

Let's turn to the second category of problems that can hinder efficient market exchange and lead to the suboptimal provision of individual and social welfare. Social traps may lead to outcomes that are consistent with market failure even when the conditions of a clear definition of property rights, negligible transaction costs, no ability for producers or consumers to unilaterally manipulate supply or demand, no third-party externalities, and full information have been met. Even if the assumptions detailed in chapters 5 and 6 for efficient political and economic markets hold, the structure of interactions of individual choices can lead to an aggregation of those choices that produces suboptimal individual and social outcomes.

Context

Collective and individual outcomes are sensitive to context and to the interaction of one actor's choices with the choices of others. The same rational individual's choices can produce different individual and collective outcomes if we change the context or aggregation mechanism of her choices and those of others. Context—the structure of interaction of individuals' choices—can produce social traps that cause what appear to be maximizing, self-interested choices by individuals seeking to obtain their preferred outcomes to result in subpar outcomes for the individuals and for the larger group or society.

For example, the decisions by policymakers in the 1920s and 1930s to adopt more and more protectionist measures in retaliation for similar policies enacted by other governments appear to be individually rational decisions, given the context of choice and the alternatives available to any individual government. If a government had resisted implementing such barriers to international exchange, even as most other nations did so, the noble government would have likely imposed even higher costs on its population. The interaction of protectionist policies by a large number of governments made opting for protectionist measures a rational, maximizing choice for other governments considering their options. Like a snowball rolling down a hill, the context produced a vicious cycle of individually rational policy choices that extended and deepened the Great Depression. But the possibility of a single government's resisting the downhill momentum would have looked even more foolhardy. Seemingly good choices, given the context and alternatives, produced bad outcomes.

The dilemma posed by social traps is in the aggregation mechanism—how individual choices interact and aggregate to produce social and individual outcomes. Chapters 5 and 6 generate expectations about how individual choices in liberal economic markets and democracies will aggregate to produce individual and societal benefits *if* they work according to their theoretical constructions; *if* some critical assumptions are met; and *if* the context of social interaction wherein an individual's choices interact with those of others is as expected. It is that last condition that concerns us now. In chapters 5 and 6, these contexts are assumed to engender no conflict between the self-interested actions of individuals and a good collective outcome that optimizes social welfare. The beauty of such contexts is that they render it unnecessary to make any noble assumptions about individual motivations or whether individuals act in the best interests of society despite their individual interests. These contexts reflect the invisible hand phenomenon discussed in chapter 2, whereby we expect that individuals will act in their self-interest and that the aggregation mechanism of the invisible hand will combine their choices to produce optimal social and individual outcomes. The aggregation mechanism of the invisible hand in economic markets, or a similar voting rule in political markets, ensures that no conflict exists between individual choice and collective welfare in the structure of individual interactions.

Recreating the invisible hand game from chapter 2 in figure 12.2, we remember that this is a stable Nash equilibrium: a dominant strategy exists for each player. Each player will select a particular strategy (Strategy A) regardless of what the other player does. Moreover, in this case, the intersection of the dominant strategies also produces the best collective outcome. All

FIGURE 12.2　The Invisible Hand Game

	Player 2's Choice	
Player 1's Choice	Strategy *A*	Strategy *B*
Strategy *A*	20, 10	5, −1
Strategy *B*	−1, 5	0, 0

parties are satisfied, and no improvement could be gained for either party by unilaterally selecting another strategy—nor would either party want to select another strategy in this case.

Cycling and Coordination Problems

But what if we operate in a context that differs markedly from the invisible hand context? For example, let's examine the games in figures 12.3 and 12.4, which differ from the invisible hand game in structure (context) and in how they aggregate individual choices. Representing a category of social dilemmas called **cycling problems,** these games capture aggregation dilemmas and mechanisms that are similar to many real-world interactions in domestic and international affairs.

Cycling games constitute coordination dilemmas, which are typical of many social contexts and interactions. Multiple equilibria exist in the example depicted in figure 12.3—the upper-left and lower-right quadrants. Given the payoffs in this scenario, neither individual has a preference for one equilibrium or the other; no dominant strategy exists for either player. The dilemma is in coordinating strategies. If Player 1 selects Strategy A and Player 2 chooses Strategy B, or Player 1 picks Strategy B and Player 2 opts for Strategy A, the interaction of their choices produces suboptimal individual and social outcomes (0, 0). This context creates a cycling problem when the game is played again, as both players will likely shift strategies to try to obtain the better outcome. If the initial choice of strategies has produced a suboptimal outcome and both players then shift strategies, a suboptimal outcome will result again. They will cycle, or chase each other around the quadrants in search of improving individual and collective welfare. Only when one player does not change strategy, or discovers a means to signal her choice beforehand, will the intersection of choices arrive at one of the two equilibria. Once arriving at one of the equilibria, neither player has an incentive to shift strategy—this is a stable equilibrium.

FIGURE 12.3   **A Cycling Game with No Distributional Advantage**

	Player 2's Choice	
Player 1's Choice	Strategy A	Strategy B
Strategy A	1, 1	0, 0
Strategy B	0, 0	1, 1

FIGURE 12.4   A Cycling Game with Distributional Consequences

	Player 2's Choice	
Player 1's Choice	Strategy *A*	Strategy *B*
Strategy *A*	2, 1	0, 0
Strategy *B*	0, 0	1, 2

We call this game a coordination problem because neither actor has a preference for one or the other equilibrium—just a preference for arriving at one of the equilibria. Either equilibrium produces a better payoff than cycling, and once the players are at one of the equilibria, neither has an incentive to change strategies. In this case, no distributional differences separate the equilibria, so both players are indifferent over the choice of equilibrium. But different distributional outcomes across multiple equilibria can still create a cycling problem, as depicted in figure 12.4. Here, two equilibria exist as in the previous figure, but now the two players prefer different equilibria. A cycling problem exists until they arrive at one of the two equilibria, which will become stable even though one player preferred a different equilibrium. Once the cycling stops at one of the equilibria, neither player can unilaterally shift strategies in order to move the outcome to another equilibrium. Each player will prefer *any* equilibrium to cycling, even if the players prefer different equilibria. This cycling problem will prove stickier to resolve in situations with distributional differences across multiple equilibria and different preferences for those equilibria among the players, but it remains a cycling problem nevertheless.

In international affairs, sea and air transit involve coordination problems that could hinder trade, travel, and transport. What color running lights should we use on our ships and planes? Do we put the red running lights on the port or starboard side of ships, on the left or right side of planes? Do we bear to the left or right in shipping channels? Do planes flying east adopt a different altitude or flight path than planes flying west? Do small or large ships enjoy the right-of-way? Do the answers to these questions vary from country to country? All involve safety and commerce issues characterized by multiple equilibria and a potential to cycle. Not settling upon a particular equilibrium can produce hazards at sea and dangers in flight. Resolving such problems generally requires only coordinating choices so that all parties play by the same rules. An international conference, or a unilateral choice by a nation with a large maritime or air transit sector, would likely be sufficient to resolve such a cycling or coordination dilemma, as no parties would strongly prefer one equilibrium to another.

Coordination problems such as territorial disputes after long and expensive conflicts might prove stickier to resolve, but they remain a cycling problem. Imagine that two nations have disagreed for years over a boundary dispute. Because the dispute is expensive, sometimes breaking into armed conflict, both governments and societies are tired of the dispute and wish for resolution, but the dispute can be resolved by drawing a variety of boundaries—which represent multiple equilibria. Both parties will prefer any equilibrium that resolves the dispute rather than continuing the dispute, but each party prefers a different equilibrium. Once a resolution is negotiated, it will be a stable equilibrium, for the only alternative will be a return to tensions, as neither party will be able to unilaterally move the resolution to another equilibrium. This cycling problem is stickier to resolve than the simple adoption of transit rules, as both governments to the boundary dispute will be hesitant to commit to a strategy that ensures the other government's preferred equilibrium outcome. The continuation of cycling, however, will only translate into a continuation of tensions until the boundary dispute is resolved.

Cooperation Dilemmas

Figure 12.5 depicts a type of social trap called a **prisoner's dilemma.** This game also reflects aggregation dilemmas and mechanisms that are inherent to many interactions in domestic and international affairs, but it represents a more difficult social trap than the coordination problem of the cycling game. The prisoner's dilemma is a cooperation problem because it requires the actors to cooperate and to resist playing their dominant strategies in order to achieve a better collective outcome, but the structure of the interaction pushes each player toward her dominant strategy of defecting (noncooperation). Let's consider why.

FIGURE 12.5 **A Prisoner's Dilemma Game**

| | Player 2's Choice | |
Player 1's Choice	Cooperate	Defect
Cooperate	−2, −2	−11, 0
Defect	0, −11	−5, −5

The strategy of defecting is dominant for both players, because the payoffs for defecting trump the payoffs for cooperating. But, if each player selects her dominant strategy, both will receive suboptimal individual payoffs $(-5, -5)$ and the collective outcome will be suboptimal (-10). If both players choose to cooperate and commit to playing that strategy, they can improve their individual outcomes $(-2, -2)$ and the collective outcome (-4). Unfortunately, the structure of the situation contains a social trap: if one player chooses to cooperate, the other player can improve her individual outcome dramatically by not cooperating and choosing to defect. This strategy will deliver the best possible outcome for the noncooperative player (0), the worst possible outcome for the cooperative player (-11), and a worse collective outcome than if both players had selected their dominant strategies (-11). The tension in this structure therefore promotes noncooperation—defecting—in order to minimize risk.

Aspects of social interaction that alter individual incentives and expand the importance of the future for players—such as reputation, or the prospect of frequent and repeated interactions—may help to overcome barriers to cooperation in such circumstances. This effect depends upon how much social actors care about future interactions and about whether their choices today will affect their interactions tomorrow. The more we value future interactions, the more we expand the **shadow of the future** over our current choices. In economics, this influence inversely corresponds to a **discount rate** for the future. A higher discount rate means that we place less value on the future than we do with a lower discount rate—we discount the future at a higher rate. Rarely do we value any future as much as we value the present, but the more we value the future, the more the future influences our current choices. This consideration puts the phrase "Live for today" ("Carpe diem") in another light.

Even when a relatively high value is placed on the future, cooperation in such social situations is difficult to obtain and hard to maintain. But the world is filled with examples of cooperation in overcoming this form of social trap. Tools and mechanisms external to the structure of the social trap can influence individual incentives, promote cooperation, and limit the temptation to defect. Trust, reputation, social norms of cooperation such as the Golden Rule, moral suasion, community pressures and ostracism, social networks, binding contracts, side payments and bribes, hierarchy and enforceable rules, or other tools of compulsion can help to constrain this form of social trap and thus promote better individual and collective outcomes.

Cooperation dilemmas appear frequently in international affairs. Let's return to an earlier example that we've touched on throughout this book. The beggar-thy-neighbor strategies of the interwar years and the tit-for-tat retaliation fall into this category of a social trap generally, and they fit the prisoner's dilemma specifically. Tariff policies such as 1930's Smoot-Hawley sought to obtain improved economic outcomes for domestic producers and labor at the expense of foreign producers and labor. In the case of Smoot-Hawley, if foreign governments had not retaliated against the increase in U.S. tariff barriers, U.S. producers and workers would have gained significantly while foreign producers and workers would have lost significantly—a good outcome for U.S. producers and workers, the worst of all worlds for foreign producers and workers, and a suboptimal outcome for the global economy.

But the dynamics of the context, a social trap, led foreign governments to retaliate. The intersection of mutual beggar-thy-neighbor policies was a stable equilibrium, but it produced suboptimal outcomes for U.S. producers and workers, for foreign producers and workers, and for the global economy. Severe unemployment, decline of international trade, and national and global depressions were not good for anyone. If enough governments had restrained their actions and committed to cooperation, the problems of the depression era would not have been as severe and durable. Individuals, companies, nations, and the global economy would have been better off. But the dilemma lay in the individual incentives to opt for uncooperative strategies, and these incentives were not altered or constrained. If governments could have chosen to cooperate by not raising tariffs, not engaging in currency devaluations, and maintaining more open access to trade, the Great Depression would have been shortened and the collective outcome improved. But all the critical parties defected, adopted beggar-thy-neighbor policies in order to shift the costs of adjustment abroad, and, consequently, deepened and extended the economic downturn.

Fortunately, the same dynamic is at work in the formation of collusive, noncompetitive cartels that wish to manipulate the supply of a commodity and its price in markets. In the earlier example of OPEC, the oil cartel members meet regularly to determine production targets (number of barrels of oil produced) for each member. Yet the incentive for individual members is to overproduce and sell more barrels than their production targets, in the hope that they can reap extra revenues if other members adhere to their stated targets. If one OPEC nation has an incentive to overproduce, others do as well—which can result in more oil at lower prices in the market. If OPEC or other cartels fail to overcome the cooperation dilemma that is intrinsic to their interactions, the outcome will be suboptimal for OPEC and for OPEC members, but it will be good for the larger global economy of consumers and producers. Resolving such cooperation dilemmas proves difficult. Otherwise we would see more cartels such as OPEC manipulating supplies and prices of commodities. Resolving some cooperation problems, such as beggar-thy-neighbor policies in the international arena, can be good for individuals and for societies, but resolving the cooperative problems of market collusion can produce poor social outcomes on a broader scale. Ironically, both situations have similar underlying dynamics and constitute the same social trap.

CONCLUSION: OPPORTUNITIES FOR STRATEGIC BEHAVIOR

Market failures and social traps are common in day-to-day life, in domestic affairs, and in international affairs. Sometimes these problems are relatively trivial, detracting from overall social and individual welfare but not undermining generally constructive social, political, and economic interactions. But sometimes such problems severely damage the well-being of individuals, businesses, and societies. Chapter 8, describing the breakdown in globalization during the interwar years, provides an extreme case of market failure and social traps. The design of the post–World War II system that emerged from the Bretton Woods negotiations and other policy deliberations sought to limit such damaging market failures and to avoid such perverse social traps in the international arena. Such efforts can never be completely successful, but we can hope they will constrain the most perverse and damaging activities that can lead to a complete breakdown in market exchange and political rights.

The presence of social traps and the factors contributing to market failure create opportunities and incentives for strategic behavior, which means taking advantage of a social situation in which your actions interact with the actions of others. This behavior can involve manipulating an asymmetric information environment for personal gain; negotiating loopholes in contacts; avoiding compensating third parties damaged by negative externalities; acting collusively with other producers or consumers in economic and political markets to manipulate supply and price of economic and political commodities; manipulating agendas toward specific ends; and structuring situations to increase the likelihood of one outcome over another. Advertising, the legal profession, any enterprise engaged in structuring information environments, and private and government regulations exist only because of the opportunities to strategically manipulate a social context for individual gain even if such action damages others and the larger social welfare. Advertisers, lawyers, auditors, regulators, and others managing the disclosure of information and its accuracy may attempt to limit the gains from strategic behavior by improving the information environment, creating contractual obligations, penalizing fraud, and restraining other individual activities that can damage societal welfare and the welfare of other individuals. But the same people and mechanisms may also attempt to confuse the information environment, create contractual loopholes, escape penalties for fraud, extract special privileges, or pander to special interests at the expense of other individuals and the broader social welfare.

The dilemmas produced by social traps and market failures are not easily resolved. No easy or ironclad fix exists for such social dilemmas. It is impossible to always constrain strategic behavior that can advantage some but damage others and the larger social welfare. The tools, strategies, and mechanisms used to limit strategic behavior can also be employed in the interest of strategic actors. Some societies manage such dilemmas and failures better than others, and these societies generally enjoy better economic welfare, greater political liberties and civil rights, and more civil societies.

EXERCISES

1. Identify three factors that contribute to inefficiency in political markets.

2. We have noted the importance of social traps to account for what appear to be nonrational social outcomes produced by rational choices. Provide an example in international affairs and explain why it is a social trap.

3. Political and economic markets are susceptible to market failure. What does that mean?

4. What do we call the situation in which no actor in a social interaction can improve her outcome by unilaterally choosing another strategy?

5. What is the difference between coordination and cooperation problems? Which kind is easier to resolve?

6. How does the structure of the Westphalian state system create the potential for a social trap?

7. Below is a game of a social interaction. Does either player have a dominant strategy in this game? Is there a social trap in this interaction? Provide a real or hypothetical example of this interaction in international affairs.

	Player 2's Choice	
Player 1's Choice	Strategy A	Strategy B
Strategy A	5, 5	−10, 20
Strategy B	20, −10	−50, −50

FURTHER READING

Akerlof, George. 1970. "The Market for Lemons: Quality Uncertainty and the Market Mechanism." *Quarterly Journal of Economics* 89: 488–500.

Axelrod, Robert. 1984. *The Evolution of Cooperation.* New York: Basic Books.

Coase, Ronald H. 1937. "The Nature of the Firm," *Economica* 4: 386–405.

Dixit, Avinash, and Barry Nalebuff. 1991. *Thinking Strategically: The Competitive Edge in Business, Politics, and Everyday Life.* New York: Norton.

Downs, Anthony. 1957. *An Economic Theory of Democracy.* New York: Harper & Row.

Hirschman, Albert O. 1970. *Exit, Voice, and Loyalty.* Cambridge, Mass.: Harvard University Press.

Kindleberger, Charles P. 1978. *Manias, Panics, and Crashes: A History of Financial Crises.* New York: Basic Books.

_____. 1986. *The World in Depression, 1929–1939.* Berkeley: University of California Press.

Miller, Gary J. 1992. *Managerial Dilemmas: The Political Economy of Hierarchy.* Cambridge: Cambridge University Press.

North, Douglass. 1990. *Institutions, Institutional Change, and Economic Performance.* Cambridge: Cambridge University Press.

Okun, Arthur. 1975. *Equality and Efficiency: The Big Tradeoff.* Washington, D.C.: Brookings Institution Press.

Polanyi, Karl. 1957. *The Great Transformation.* Boston: Beacon Press.

Riker, William. 1986. *The Art of Political Manipulation.* New Haven, Conn.: Yale University Press.

Shepsle, Kenneth A., and Mark S. Bonchek. 1997. *Analyzing Politics: Rationality, Behavior, and Institutions.* New York: Norton.

13

The Dilemma of Collective Goods, Solutions, and Hegemonic Stability

THE INDIVIDUAL AND THE GROUP

Politics is the interaction of diverse interests to produce social outcomes with distributional consequences in a world of scarcity. Such interactions range from cooperative to conflictual,

The High Contracting Parties, in order to promote international cooperation and to achieve international peace and security by the acceptance of obligations not to resort to war, by the prescription of open, just and honorable relations between nations by the firm establishment of the understandings of international law as the actual rule of conduct among governments, and by the maintenance of justice and a scrupulous respect for all treaty obligations in the dealings of organized peoples with one another, agree to this Covenant of the League of Nations.

Preamble to the Covenant of the League of Nations (1919)

from peaceful to violent; some produce good social outcomes, and others damage social welfare. In order to understand past outcomes and anticipate future social interactions, we need to consider how interests aggregate to produce a collective outcome. We need to think about why some interests successfully aggregate to advance their collective interests and others do not, why some interests in society become actively engaged in the political arena even as other interests remain dormant.

We have already begun to examine the question of collective action and collective outcomes. In chapters 7 and 9, we examined the provision of key collective goods that underpinned liberal economic expansion and globalization during the 1800s and the post–World

---

This chapter draws heavily upon Mancur Olson, *The Logic of Collective Action* (1965) and *The Rise and Decline of Nations* (1982); and Russell Hardin, *Collective Action* (1982).

War II period, when the United Kingdom and then the United States underwrote such goods in the international system. Chapter 8 notes the negative consequences of the underprovision of such collective goods when the United Kingdom no longer could afford to provide such goods and the United States was capable of doing so, but unwilling. The unwillingness of the United States to fill the void left by British incapacity contributed to the economic decline and retrenchment of globalization of the 1920s and 1930s.

But a troubling puzzle remains: if every economy and society benefits from such collective goods, shouldn't all governments and societies willingly contribute to their voluntary provision? Why were the United States and the United Kingdom key to the provision of collective goods that promoted international exchange? Why would nations opt for beggar-thy-neighbor policies instead of making a contribution to the collective good? This theoretical dilemma was raised in the discussion about market failure and social traps in chapter 12. What happens at the individual level to undermine productive social outcomes? Why do decision makers knowingly choose poorly? Why do individuals with mutually compatible interests fail to contribute to group outcomes that would be good for those individuals and their societies?

Trying to answer these questions requires analyzing how individuals interact in groups. We need a theory of group behavior that helps us to understand when individuals will join groups and contribute to group ends and, conversely, when individuals will not contribute to group ends even if they are members of the group and would benefit from obtaining the group's preferred outcome. Arriving at such an understanding will provide some insight to collective action and the provision of collective goods (or bads). This chapter examines these questions, explores some of the strategies used to overcome barriers to collective action, and concludes with discussion of a strategy that is particularly relevant to international political economy.

A PARADOX

Initially, many social scientists believed that individuals with similar preferences in society would coalesce into a group to press their jointly held preferences as an interest group. This approach assumed that individuals would willingly contribute to a group's activities that could further their individual interests. Pushing this assumption to its logical conclusion suggested that all individuals with similar preferences would voluntarily form groups and readily contribute to collective action—that the many interest groups we observe in relatively open societies should constitute all the potential group interests in society. Yet we are immediately confronted by an empirical paradox: many individuals with similar preferences fail to form groups to promote their collective interests, and, therefore, many collective interests remain latent in society. We observe potent trade associations, strong labor unions, intimidating associations of manufacturers, but consumer associations that are weak at best.

The example of national security offered earlier in the book provides another example of this paradox. As individuals we all prefer some reasonable level of national security, but as individuals we fail to voluntarily contribute our share of the resources necessary to obtain this level of national security—we do not spontaneously form an interest group to contribute to the provision of national security.

This problem recurs again and again. We favor conservation and clean air, but we purchase inefficient cars, waste energy, and avoid clean-energy technologies. We like clean and plentiful water, but we grow grass instead of other plants, use chemical fertilizers that damage groundwater, rivers, and lakes, and opt for energy production that produces acid rain. We worry about the viability of ocean fisheries, but we happily consume Chilean sea bass at our favorite restaurants. We fret over emissions of greenhouse gases that contribute to global warming, but we fail to cooperate to limit those emissions in order to improve environmental conditions for ourselves, our children, and our grandchildren. Again and again, public opinion surveys show that we prefer nice social outcomes and policies such as peace, growth, education, foreign aid, health care, clean environments, and collective security. Yet individuals fail to voluntarily contribute sufficient resources to try to achieve such outcomes. Moreover, individuals resist nonvoluntary contributions (e.g., taxes) to fund initiatives to obtain those outcomes.

Ironically, many interest groups coalesce and overcome barriers to collective action in order to resist policies that would improve social welfare. Producers form cartels to manipulate supplies and prices of goods; industrial polluters form coalitions to resist green legislation and environmental reforms. Some groups appear schizophrenic: pharmaceutical companies construct coalitions to lobby for increased governmental contributions to medical research (a help to social welfare) but resist attempts to impose competitive pressures on the prices of their drugs (a hindrance to social welfare).

DISMANTLING THE SOCIAL TRAP

At the heart of collective action, explaining why some interests succeed and others fail to overcome the barriers to cooperation, is a tension between individual rationality and the context of choice. A social trap exists. Returning to our initial assumption that individuals act as if they are self-interested, we must consider how self-interested actors interact to attain—or not attain—collective outcomes, and what is the effect of social context on such interactions. If rational individuals fail to contribute to group activities that promote gains in individual and social welfare, we must surmise either that they do not recognize their self-interest (an information dilemma) or that they are well-informed but believe refraining from contributing to the collective action offers them a greater cost/benefit outcome regardless of the desirability of the collective outcome. The first problem reflects the asymmetric information dilemma discussed in chapters 5, 6, and 12, but let's focus on the second problem here. This situation is a social trap whereby individual rationality conflicts with collective rationality, as self-interested individuals select actions that undermine collective interests, even though those individuals would prefer the collective outcome. Let's unbundle this social trap to understand the dilemma of collective action.

What Is a Collective Good?

When speaking of collective interests, many use the term *public good*, but this concept carries a more restrictive definition that is unnecessary for our purposes, so here we use *collective good* instead. A **collective good** has two defining qualities: nonexcludability and jointness of supply. The first, **nonexcludability,** means that if you are a member of a group for which a collective good exists, you can consume that good regardless of your contribution to the collective effort—you cannot be excluded. The impossibility of exclusion allows shirkers, or noncontributors, in the collective to consume the collective good despite their noncontribution. For example, if you shirk on paying your taxes—your public obligations—but enough other people contribute sufficient resources to the government to produce the collective good of national security, you can still enjoy national security. The group cannot say that everyone in Connecticut receives national security except you (and other shirkers). Clean air, national security, clean water, the Internet, and highways are such collective goods. Not all nonexcludable goods are "good," however, for pollution is also a collective good by this definition—or, if you prefer, a collective bad.

The second defining characteristic, **jointness of supply,** means simply that one person's consumption of a good does not restrict its consumption by other members of the collective (or group). Your consumption of those goods does not constrain my ability to consume those goods if we are members of the same group. If the United States is the collective, and national security is the collective good, people in Utah can consume security even as people in Connecticut consume the same good. The consumption of national security by the citizens of Connecticut does not limit Utah residents from consuming the same security.

These two defining conditions of a collective good are also the keys to the social trap that creates barriers to collective action and the provision of collective goods. Jointness of supply and nonexcludability of a good constitute externalities that create barriers to the provision of public goods, even if all people prefer to live in a world with such public goods. They create opportunities for individuals to free-ride on the actions of other members of the group and still consume the collective good.

Initial Expectations about Provision of Collective Goods

Let's examine the dynamic of collective good provision. When should a self-interested individual contribute to the provision of a collective good? Rational individuals weigh costs against expected benefits, the expected rate of return against the costs of contribution. So, if

$$C_i = \text{costs for individual } i,$$
$$GB_i = \text{gross benefits for individual } i, \text{ and}$$
$$NB_i = \text{net benefits for individual } i,$$

then the cost/benefit calculation for individual i is:

$$NB_i = GB_i - C_i.$$

Following the cost/benefit logic, we would expect individual i to contribute to the collective activity if

$$NB_i > 0,$$

and to refrain from contributing to the collective activity if

$$NB_i < 0.$$

The basic equation merely states that we expect individuals to contribute to the provision of collective goods if their gains from the provision of such collective goods outweigh their costs. Given the logic in this equation, we should anticipate groups forming and contributing to collective action whenever individual expected net gains are positive. This logic seems irrefutable, yet we are constantly confronted by the underprovision of collective goods and the failure of latent groups to coalesce and become active. Let's return to the equation to try to make sense of this paradox.

Positive Externalities and Incentives to Free-Ride

If individual i believes that other members of her group will contribute to the provision of the collective good, and individual i believes that their contributions will be sufficient to ensure the provision of the collective good, then individual i will have an incentive to free-ride and not contribute. She may decide to act as a third party, treating the collective good as a positive externality of an exchange between others. If the collective good will be provided when

$$NB_i = GB_i - C_i \text{ and } NB_i > 0,$$

and individual i anticipates that the collective good will be provided even without her contribution and that, because of jointness of supply and nonexcludability, she will still be able to consume the collective good due to her membership in the group, she can calculate that if she shirks her contribution, her payoff will be

$$NB_i + C_i = GB_i.$$

As $NB_i + C_i > NB_i$, she recognizes that she does better by free-riding than by contributing. She can enjoy the collective good and save her cost of contributing to its provision for some other consumption choice. She can have her cake and eat it too!

The Unraveling of Collective Good Provision

There is, however, a significant problem with this logic. We assume that all decision makers are rational and capable of making the same calculations as individual i, who decided to free-ride. This means that other members of the group should also rationally decide to free-ride and attempt to have their cake and eat it too. And it is this individual calculation among many members of the group that can unravel the provision of the collective good. If enough members of the group decide to free-ride by failing to contribute to the provision of the collective good, that good will be underprovided or not provided at all—rational individual calculations threaten a collective outcome that is desired by those very individuals. Returning to the defense example given in chapter 12, if we pass a hat for voluntary contributions to national security, we are unlikely to obtain enough to fund even a fraction of our defense establishment, yet we all want national security.

To make matters worse, the presence of numerous free-riders can upset members of a group who do contribute to the collective good, even if the condition $NB_i = GB_i - C_i$ and $NB_i > 0$ is still met for those contributors. Rational or not, individuals who underwrite the provision of collective goods may believe that they are being played for suckers if too many members of their group free-ride. Being disgruntled over bearing a disproportional share of a burden may not be rational if the collective good is desirable and the cost-benefit calculation remains positive, but it is, nonetheless, a human emotion that can erect barriers to collective action.

Even if some group members will still contribute to the provision of a collective good in the presence of free-riders, another problem looms that could affect the provision of the collective good. With fewer members contributing, there is no reason to assume that the cost of providing the good will decline. Assuming a fixed cost for the collective good, the prospect of more free-riders and fewer contributors produces an obvious problem: the cost to each contributor will increase. Returning to the basic equation, this means that the calculation may change for contributors who made an initial decision to contribute when they believed that

$$NB_i = GB_i - C_i \text{ and } NB_i > 0.$$

With fewer contributors, the size of C_i increases. At some point, as fewer members contribute and C_i increases for each contributor, the cost-benefit calculation for those willing to contribute will shift, so that

$$NB_i < 0.$$

When this happens, no one will voluntarily contribute to the collective good, even if all members of society would prefer that outcome. The provision of a socially beneficial collective good, desired by many individuals, unravels.

A NEW PARADOX: COLLECTIVE GOOD PROVISION DESPITE THE SOCIAL TRAP

This social trap of free-riding, which threatens the provision of collective goods, turns the original question on its head. We began by assuming that a collective good would be provided if the benefit to society and to individuals outweighed the cost of provision. This assumption led to a conclusion that all affordable collective goods desired by society (or the group) would be provided. But this conclusion is empirically false. Now we have a theoretical mechanism for understanding why rational individuals free-ride by failing to contribute to a collective outcome they prefer, and consequently undermine the collective good. Pushing this mechanism to its logical but socially perverse conclusion, we should observe the provision of collective goods infrequently. Here we meet with another paradox: empirically, we do see an underprovision of collective goods given the original traditional logic, but we also observe the provision of too many collective goods given the logic of the social trap of free-riding. Many collective goods are provided despite this social trap. People cooperate far more in providing collective goods than we should expect, given the dynamic of the social trap, the tension between individual rationality, and desired social outcomes. Explaining the provision of collective goods despite the social trap requires uncovering the existence of mechanisms that help latent groups to overcome barriers to collective action, including the incentives for individuals to free-ride on other members of their group.

MECHANISMS FOR OVERCOMING BARRIERS TO COLLECTIVE ACTION

What explains the difference between situations in which collective action succeeds and those in which it fails? Specifically, we need to examine what mechanisms can limit individuals' incentives to free-ride and convince them to contribute to a collective good. In this section, we consider five categories of devices that can influence the incentives of individuals: compulsion, selective incentives, group size, entrepreneurship, and piggybacking. These mechanisms affect individual calculations by changing their evaluations of the costs (C_i) and, consequently, the net benefits (NB_i).

Compulsion

Compulsion is the exercise of influence to shift the incentives of individuals to contribute to the group effort. It involves the use of power and hierarchy in social relations. Compulsion threatens punishment (perhaps by force), exclusion, or some other penalty for defection from contributing to the collective good. Compulsion transforms a voluntary exchange of resources to obtain a collective outcome into a nonvoluntary exchange of resources to obtain a collective good. It uses hierarchy to impose individual costs or penalties for noncontribution and transforms an exchange from the relatively symmetrical exchange that is characteristic of economic markets to an asymmetrical exchange that more often typifies political markets. For compulsion to be successful, it must be credible.

For example, the forced extraction of contributions through national tax structures tempers an individual's inclinations to free-ride on the provision of public parks, education, highways, clean air, clean water, and stable adjudication of property rights and disputes. The presence of tax structures is not sufficient to ensure contribution, however; tax avoidance troubles many societies. A credible threat of compulsion behind a tax structure can help to overcome this barrier to contribution. If members of a group would elect to free-ride absent the threats of adjudication and sanction, these tax structures must compel contributions by means of underlying threats that change the cost calculation of noncontribution and shift the incentives of individuals. Hierarchies, through the threat and use of sanctions, can transform the incentives of individuals to contribute to a collective good.

The mechanism of compulsion works to overcome barriers to collective action in domestic and international arenas. For example, governments may lower trade barriers, refrain from practices that damage international exchange, or contribute to collective security arrangements, if more powerful nations press for compliance. Members of the Warsaw Pact, the Eastern bloc collective security alliance during the cold war, contributed to the provision of the collective good of security partly because of the hierarchical influence of the U.S.S.R. and its ability to extort contributions through implicit threat of compulsion and, ultimately, explicit punishment.

The governments participating in the Bretton Woods negotiations agreed to a set of international economic practices that required substantial and expensive resources to promote liberal economic exchange and stability. These cooperative agreements amounted to commitments to the provision of collective goods that would help to restore the health of the global economy. The United States shouldered much of the burden. Policymakers in many states faced frequent temptations to free-ride and defect from the Bretton Woods system. Sometimes policymakers succumbed to such temptations, yet they rarely did so in any significant manner that threatened the system. Why? One plausible reason is the potential penalties that the international hierarchy might have imposed on problematic governments or pariah states. In particular, the unambiguous position of the United States at the top of this hierarchy and the network of relations built around U.S. leadership could have created significant problems and penalties for a state defecting from the collective action provisions. Defectors could have incurred penalties from the United States specifically, or from others in the system more generally.

U.S. policymakers used the U.S. position as an occupying power in Germany and as the dominant political economy in the immediate aftermath of World War II to dominate discussions over the design of NATO, its command and control structure, the nature of the weapon systems adopted by NATO nations, its force structure, battlefield tactics, and overall strategy. Again, due to its position and capabilities in the international hierarchy, the United

States dominated the design of other international governmental organizations such as ASEAN, the IMF, the World Bank, and the GATT. One nation did not equal one vote in the creation of the postwar international organizations that were designed to limit collective action problems.

Certainly, many nations received great benefit and assistance from the U.S. contributions to intergovernmental organizations, yet they did not free-ride as one might anticipate. They contributed bases, troops, and other resources to the collective good. One potential explanation for this willingness to contribute is the ability of the U.S. to compel cooperation by threatening to exclude nations that failed to do so. Not that governments had to contribute at a level proportional to the U.S. effort, but the contributions had to be significantly larger than free-riding.

U.S. policymakers used a variety of strategies to extract contributions from the members of the collective. In the cases of Germany, Japan, and South Korea, the presence of large numbers of U.S. forces providing security for those countries enabled U.S. compulsion. In other cases, a fear or implicit threat of a U.S. retreat to isolationism or protectionism helped to induce cooperation on the part of other governments. U.S. policymakers could argue that U.S. taxpayers would not foot the bill if others chose to free-ride. The special position of the United States, like that of the United Kingdom in the late 1800s, empowered this implicit threat. Given the size and position of the U.S. economy throughout the post–World War II period, if U.S. policymakers had chosen to free-ride on the rest of the collective, any provision of collective goods would have been seriously damaged even if all other governments contributed far more than their fair shares. This situation highlights the special case of the U.S. as a hegemon, or dominant power, in the post–World War II period. (We examine hegemony as a special category of collective goods provision at the end of this chapter.)

The Soviet Union also employed compulsion in its sphere of influence in the post–World War II period. Soviet policymakers compelled participation and contribution to the collective security arrangement called the Warsaw Pact and to the economic arrangement called Comecon. These organizations did for the Eastern bloc what NATO, GATT, the IMF, the World Bank, and others did for the Western bloc and many nonaligned nations. Poland, Hungary, Czechoslovakia, Bulgaria, and others could not simply free-ride, even if they so desired. Soviet compulsion was particularly visible during the 1956 Hungarian revolution and the 1965 Czech Spring, when Soviet tanks and troops put down uprisings antithetical to Soviet purposes.

Selective Incentives

Another strategy to help secure contributions to collective actions, a **selective incentive,** involves the transfer of additional benefits above and beyond the collective good in order to induce cooperation in the provision of the collective good. A selective incentive provides an exclusive benefit that may help to change the cost-benefit assessment of latent group members. Targeting specific group members, it shifts the calculation of net benefits (NB_i) by providing an additional payoff. If the incentive targeted all group members, it would no longer be a selective incentive, but a good more similar to a collective good.

Selected incentives can be tangible physical rewards or less tangible rewards such as reputation, pride, or community identification. Tangible rewards, or side payments, take many forms in global affairs. The developed political economies offered a program called Generalized System of Preference (GSP) to obtain support from governments of developing states for the agenda of the GATT, and later the WTO. To exporters from qualifying developing nations, the GSP offered reduced tariff barriers to developed states' markets—a benefit that could potentially provide a comparative market advantage. Only developing states qualified for GSP status, and developed states were excluded, which made GSP a targeted selective incentive that was designed to obtain support from developing nations for the collective good of liberal economic exchange in the global economy.

Selective incentives hold many military alliances together. The collective good of military alliances is security, but many obtain more than national security for their contributions to the alliance. In the NATO alliance, some governments and communities receive selective incentives in the form of rents for military bases for U.S. troops stationed in Europe. Governments have obtained special deals on weapons and training, and many local economies have enjoyed positive externalities as the location of military facilities has led to the expansion of housing and local economic enterprise.

Governments of major states fill their foreign aid budgets with side payments and selective incentives. For example, in 2004 three of the largest recipients of U.S. foreign development assistance were Israel, Egypt, and Pakistan. Foreign aid is a very small part of the U.S. government's budget—about nine-tenths of one percent—but the lion's share of that assistance targets these three nations. Why? The transfers to Israel and Egypt are part of the side payments that President Jimmy Carter used to convince the Israelis and Egyptians to compromise and agree to the historic Camp David Accords. Each nation received selective goods that were exclusionary and specifically targeted to support the collective good of Israeli-Egyptian peace and a decrease in regional instability. U.S. foreign assistance to Pakistan grew dramatically after the terrorist attacks on the World Trade Center and the Pentagon on September 11, 2001. The subsequent War on Terror is a collective good, but obtaining Pakistan's contribution to this collective good has required extensive side payments. The U.S. assistance to Pakistan is a targeted selective incentive that excludes other nations from consuming these side payments. Selective incentives are strategies of reward and sanction targeted at specific members of a group to elicit their cooperation for a broader collective objective.

Such selective incentives are readily apparent in everyday life. Membership requests from the Sierra Club, National Public Radio (NPR), the Public Broadcasting System (PBS), or a local museum or zoo routinely offer a canvas tote bag or umbrella emblazoned with the organization's logo to anyone who agrees to contribute to its activities. That contribution involves both a collective good and a selective incentive. The success the Sierra Club achieves in working for the protection of the environment, the special programming provided by NPR or PBS, or the exhibits at the museum or zoo are the collective goods. Tote bags or umbrellas are the selective incentives, or side payments in return for a contribution, but they are more than merely material rewards—they are symbols that advertise the contributor's commitment to the provision of a collective good, and consequently, help to establish her reputation, status, and identity in the community. Such intangibles can be extremely powerful selective incentives; anyone can purchase a tote bag or umbrella without any advertising more easily and far more cheaply than by making a sizable contribution to a collective good and receiving a tote bag or umbrella that does not carry books or shed rain any better. Yet a simple stroll down any busy city street demonstrates the appeal of such selective incentives.

Even as a member of a university community, you will eventually be approached to contribute to the collective good of higher education: soon after you graduate, you will begin receiving calls and letters asking that you contribute to your alma mater. If you decide to do so, your alumni donation will involve both a contribution to the collective good of higher education and a selective incentive to you, as the university publicly acknowledges your gift. Aside from the warm, cuddly feeling of personal satisfaction you enjoy when making your contribution to such a noble endeavor, your side payment is the reward of public recognition for your contribution.

Entrepreneurship

Entrepreneurship offers another strategy for overcoming barriers to collective action. **Entrepreneurs** are people who help to generate collective goods when they act in their private interest. Although their actions may produce a noble societal outcome, their motivations to act as entrepreneurs may be less than noble, for the mobilization of collective action is instrumental to their private objectives. Seeking to advance their narrowly defined career interests, such as gaining election, politicians seek to transform latent interests in society, which fail to provide collective goods, into active, privileged groups that do produce collective goods for their members. In such cases, the politicians function as entrepreneurs because their private agendas coincide with the promotion of the collective agenda. This process has been called "the public use of private interests."

Entrepreneurs reduce costs to the individual (C_i) by providing energy, organizational skill, and inertia to the provision of collective goods. Relatively latent, unorganized constituencies such as women and environmentalists became more active and engaged in politics when political entrepreneurs created active organizations and movements that focused on children's issues, women's rights, equity in the workplace, clean air, clean water, protection of endangered species, and other relevant issues. By creating the organizations and movements, entrepreneurs mobilized members of these latent groups and transformed them into active groups that contributed to the provision of collective goods. At the same time, the political entrepreneur also increased the likelihood that those who cared about such issues would turn out to vote, and, consequently, advanced the electoral interest of the political entrepreneur herself.

Neighborhood Watch programs that provide the collective benefits of greater security and community are often the consequence of an active entrepreneur in a neighborhood. These programs do not appear spontaneously. Most people care about their neighbors, but their watchful energies and concern often remain unorganized and latent. Overcoming the barriers to the active cooperation that is needed for such a program usually requires the organizational energy and impetus provided by a dedicated individual, or individuals, whose efforts produce collective benefits in terms of neighbors watching out for their neighbors and greater communal interaction. The entrepreneur gains the same collective benefits as the rest of her neighborhood, but she also receives private benefits in terms of reputation, ego, and community leadership.

Similar to Neighborhood Watch programs are many military alliances, such as NATO and the Warsaw Pact, that rely on the entrepreneurship of a leader—the United States and the Soviet Union, respectively in these cases. Another example is the leadership of the AARP (formerly known as the American Association of Retired People), who gain influence and stature if they can expand the organization's membership base by educating older Americans about issues relevant to their later years of life. The efforts of the AARP have helped to transform older U.S. voters into a powerful political constituency that is concerned with health care for the elderly, retirement, and social insurance issues—all collective goods for the membership of the AARP. The AARP has been so successful in its political capacity that U.S. policymakers are more motivated to promote programs to benefit the elderly and retired than programs related to children and the active workforce—a potentially perverse policy outcome if we are interested in economic expansion and growth as a collective good. Meanwhile, the leadership of the AARP, the entrepreneurs, gain personal stature and power in the political arena, becoming power brokers that politicians ignore only at their electoral peril.

Piggybacking

Another mechanism that helps to account for the provision of collective goods despite individual incentives to free-ride is **piggybacking,** which occurs when already established organizations add new concerns and interests to their agenda. The civil rights movements in the United States, for instance, used religious organizations to gain footing, organize support, and promote activities to challenge segregation and discrimination. Social justice is not inconsistent with the objectives of churches, mosques, and synagogues, but these institutions were founded to take care of religious needs and feed the soul, not to publicly and politically advance such social issues. Congressman John Lewis, Reverend Martin Luther King Jr., Reverend Jesse Jackson, Reverend Ralph Abernathy, and many other African-American

Created early in the twentieth century to represent workers and advocate on their behalf against management, unions are now mobilized to promote policies on a much wider range of issues in a phenomenon known as "piggybacking." These union members rallied on Capitol Hill in 2005 in opposition to the Central American Free Trade Agreement (CAFTA), a regional trade arrangement between Costa Rica, the Dominican Republic, El Salvador, Guatemala, Honduras, Nicaragua, and the United States.

religious leaders piggybacked civil rights onto their religious organizations. Churches played a similar role in organizing support for women's suffrage early in the 1900s.

In another example, labor unions were originally established to overcome barriers to collective action by workers, to promote the collective interests of union members in bargaining with management, and to protect their members against arbitrary choices by management. But over the years, union leaders have transformed their organizations into significant political forces on a wide range of issues. Today, union leaders use their organizations, which were established to advance collective bargaining and arbitration, for the articulation and advancement of a much wider range of policy issues, such as pensions, trade protections, pharmaceutical benefits, and environmental issues. It seems unlikely that unions would have initially emerged to advance any of these issues, but once they existed, union leaders could piggyback new issues onto the organizational backs of their unions. The established unions have large offices and staffs located in Washington, D.C., and other capitals, supplying organizational capabilities that can be directed to new issues and the pursuit of new collective goods. Their established organization thus provides unions with disproportionate leverage and staying power in U.S. politics, despite the shrinking proportion of the U.S. labor force they now represent.

In international affairs, many U.S. labor unions have piggybacked international trade issues onto the organizational structures they developed to advance other issues. In the 1940s, 1950s, and 1960s, these unions either looked benignly on free trade or even favored lower barriers to trade. Since the 1970s, however, many union organizations have taken a more active interest in trade policy and have grown increasingly protectionist. The unions have been so successful in piggybacking trade onto their membership representation structures that they have placed debates over fair trade, outsourcing of jobs, environmental regulation, and child labor standards on the agenda of U.S. electoral politics. In Poland in the mid-1980s, a trade union called Solidarity took the lead in pushing for political reforms that led to the downfall of the Communist government. Again, political reform and rebellion were piggybacked onto an established union organization.

Group Size

Group size is another important consideration when trying to understand why individuals with common interests in a collective good may or may not overcome barriers to collective action and the temptation to free-ride. Small groups generally have an advantage over large groups in overcoming barriers to collective action. First, in small groups, individuals are much more likely to know many, if not all, of the other group members, and this familiarity increases the usefulness of ostracism, friendship, companionship, isolation, moral persuasion, respect, admiration, blackballing, censure, and other tools of social pressure in motivating behavior. These tools can be used to impose social rewards and penalties upon individuals for contributing or failing to contribute to the group outcome. Such social pressure, which acts as an incentive for individuals by affecting NB_i and C_i, is more likely to work successfully in small group settings, where the bonds of friendship and familiarity serve to increase the personal costs of noncontribution. In large groups, conversely, anonymity works against these social incentives to collective action. Individuals in large groups are less likely to be known to or familiar with other group members. The bonds of friendship cannot be used to promote behavior where no friendship exists, and it would be equally difficult to ostracize an anonymous target or to employ respect as an incentive when little likelihood exists for repeated social interactions.

Second, in a small group, each individual's contribution may be more critical to the provision of a collective good. A small number of free-riders can undermine the collective effort in a small group, whereas in a large group a significant number of free-riders may be less critical. Awareness of this group size sensitivity is more likely to alter the calculations of individuals in the small group than in the larger group, and to increase their likelihood of contributing to group action.

Relaxing the jointness of supply assumption enables us to consider how the **divisibility** of a collective good interacts with group size to affect the willingness of individuals to contribute to its provision. If a collective good is in fixed supply, the size of the group can influence the size of each group member's share of that good. In such cases, each group member's share will diminish in larger groups, which affects NB_i for each individual. If you are someone who enjoys consuming the collective good of a tranquil and unspoiled public park, are you more likely to contribute to its provision if only a small number of other people consume the same good or if a huge number of people use the park daily? Finite divisible collective goods can make contributions to the good more attractive in smaller rather than larger groups because the individual's consumption of the collective good will be greater in the small group than in the large group. The divisibility factor is

In June 2005, (left to right) presidents Ricardo Lagos of Chile, Luiz Inacio Lula da Silva of Brazil, Nicanor Duarte Frutos of Paraguay, Nestor Kirchner of Argentina, Tabare Vazquez of Uruguay, and Alvaro Uribe of Columbia attended a state dinner at the biannual summit of Mercosur nations. Mercosur—a regional trading bloc created in 1991 and comprised of Argentina, Brazil, Paraguay, and Uruguay—aims to develop a common market in the southern cone by gradually reducing tariffs on trade between member states. The small-group-size dynamics of the organization helped overcome barriers to developing the common market. Bolivia, Chile, Columbia, Ecuador, Panama, and Venezuela are associate members.

thus a problem of crowding, whereby the benefit of a collective good decreases with its consumption by an increasing number of group members.

For example, international fishing treaties limit tonnage of catch to ensure the health and survivability of a fishery, which is a collective good. Such international treaties usually limit catch by nationality, so if the number of fishing vessels increases in Canada, but the catch limits remain fixed, the individual Canadian fisherman's benefit from the collective good declines. This problem may encourage some fishermen to cheat by catching more than their limit or, worse, it may lead to revocation of the fishing treaty.

Contrary to the problem of finite and divisible collective goods, some collective goods have an increasing returns quality: the benefits from the collective good increase with more contributors; net benefits to the individual and net benefits to society increase with more participation. International trade is one such good, as more and more participation rewards specialization, produces greater consumption possibilities for individuals, and increases social welfare. Agreements to limit emissions of greenhouse gases are another collective good that provides increasing benefits to individuals and their societies as participation in the provision of the good increases. Some collective goods may require larger groups simply because of their costs of provision.

Cartels and oligopolies that manipulate supplies and prices of a commodity are also examples of the effect of size. Such cartel behavior undermines the greater public good, as it distorts efficient market prices and reduces overall consumption possibilities, but pricefixing is a collective good to a cartel's members. An economic sector with a small number of producers may more easily surmount barriers to collusion on supply and price than can a sector with a large number of producers. For example, the Organization of Petroleum Exporting Countries (OPEC) benefits from its relatively small number of members, who are relatively homogenous as most are closely tied by geography and political-religious interests.

Because of its small membership and relatively high homogeneity, OPEC can more easily coordinate production targets, determine if a member state produces more than its negotiated quota, and exert pressures on a member that cheats. Compare OPEC to a potential cartel of rice producers: the larger number of rice producers, their geographic dispersion, and their heterogeneity would create more difficult barriers to successful coordination. Whereas the key OPEC producers are geographically proximate, the major rice producers are more widely dispersed. This distance factor would present obstacles to having meetings to fix the supply and price of their rice, affecting who will attend and where, as well as obstacles to monitoring whether members are adhering to their negotiated quotas and to pressuring members to comply.

Some Other Considerations

Compulsion, selective incentives, entrepreneurship, piggybacking, and group size are important to understanding when and why collective action will be successful, but other characteristics of groups and societies can also play a role. The discussion of nationalism in chapter 3 raised the potential of shared values and characteristics in motivating a particular form of group called a nation. All groups by definition have some shared characteristics that separate those in the group from those outside, and the nature of those shared characteristics can affect the willingness of group members to contribute to collective outcomes. Conceivably, more homogenous groups may have lower barriers to collective action than more heterogeneous groups, for people tend to interact more closely with people like themselves than with people different from themselves. People in neighborhoods, religious institutions, schools, political parties, and social clubs tend to have more in common with others in their setting than across such settings. This homogeneity can increase the social pressures and incentives that help to induce contributions to a collective endeavor in the presence of temptations to free-ride.

But we need to be careful here, as earlier we noted that some states are incredibly diverse and yet successful at developing a common identity and acting in the collective interest. As we consider the role of homogeneity versus diversity in group dynamics, we need to ask about the nature and intensity of the shared characteristics that define a group's boundaries. Do the foundations of group organization rest on social, economic, or political footings? Social foundations can provide extra-rational motivations for individual choices that do not exist in groups based on economic foundations. Social networks, religious teachings, cultural identification and influences, social group norms and conventions, and other intangible social pressures can promote collective action in groups based on such qualities, whereas groups based upon economic foundations may have more difficulty relying upon extra-rational motivations for collective action, as their members have joined the group because of an initial economic calculation that focused primarily on tangible costs and benefits. Groups with political foundations are more difficult to pigeonhole, because their members may be heavily influenced either by extra-rational considerations about their community or by narrower individual considerations of benefits.

A SPECIAL CASE OF HEGEMONIC STABILITY

Let's consider one more mechanism that can influence collective action problems in the international political economy: **hegemonic stability.** In this chapter and in earlier chapters we have recognized that troubling social traps burden international market exchange in our decentralized state system. Problems of property rights risk, contract risk, default risk, and currency risk create barriers to cross-border exchange as well as free-rider problems and the temptation of governments to adopt beggar-thy-neighbor policies. How well such risks and threats have been addressed coincides with the ebb and flow of globalization since the early 1800s. The prevalence of such traps suggests that obtaining the benefits of specialization and market exchange across national borders should have been difficult, if not rare, yet liberal economic exchange has occurred, and with great frequency, especially before World War I and after World War II. Only during the interwar years do we observe a retrenchment and a fall into the social trap of rampant beggar-thy-neighbor behavior. We concluded that the market mechanisms of laissez-faire liberalism are insufficient to ensure good economic outcomes and protect against beggar-thy-neighbor policies and other risks to exchange. Other extra-market scaffolding and political cooperation are important to promote market exchange, manage the risks to such exchange across borders, and limit the beggar-thy-neighbor policies that can undermine individual and social welfare.

Earlier, we began to consider the role of a dominant power in promoting cross-border market exchange by providing collective goods that manage the risks and uncertainty of such exchange and stabilize the expectations of economic actors. The chapters on the emergence of globalization in the 1800s, the breakdown in globalization during the interwar years, and its reemergence during the post–World War II era drew attention to the provision of such collective goods, first, by the United Kingdom and, later, by the United States. In turn, these two world leaders supplied liquidity to the system, maintained market access under duress, acted as lender of last resort, and underpinned a stable international monetary system. These actions promoted liberal economic exchange across national borders. The breakdown in the provision of these collective goods that characterized the interwar years was partly responsible for the depth and duration of the Great Depression and for the disintegration of political and economic relations leading to World War II.

These lessons from history suggest that hegemonic leadership, or guidance by a dominant political economy that ensures the provision of collective goods, can stabilize the global economic arena and avoid some of the pitfalls that can handicap liberal economic exchange. The concept of hegemonic stability explicitly recognizes the dilemma that hinders the cooperation requisite to overcoming barriers to cross-border market exchange, and it argues that a *capable* and *willing* hegemonic state can *unilaterally* and *rationally* provide collective goods that help to overcome such obstacles. Hegemonic provision of collective goods builds on the mechanisms of group size and compulsion to offer a specific solution that addresses the questions of how and why collective goods might be more easily provided in the presence of a dominant power or a coalition of a small number of disproportionately influential political economies.

A theory of hegemonic stability in support of a liberal economic political economy has several key components. First, hegemonic stability requires the presence of a dominant state in the international system. The potential for this situation exists when the distribution of capabilities, of power and influence, is extremely unequal across states. The distribution of capabilities in the global arena can vary from relative parity to great inequality, but in the case of hegemonic stability, it is the distribution of capabilities near the top of the international hierarchy that concerns us. A dominant state with a disproportionate share of capabilities can use its capabilities to influence the political, military, and economic rules of the game in global affairs.

Second, a state with hegemonic capabilities must be interested in building a system of liberal economic exchange. Such interest is not a forgone conclusion, but a *choice* among forms of economic exchange. During the interwar years, the United States enjoyed the wealth and capabilities to act as a liberal hegemonic state, but it had neither the will nor the interest. Perversely, in that situation, the United States instead implemented beggar-thy-neighbor policies that, given its disproportionate capabilities, constituted a much more significant attack on market exchange than if another nation had adopted such policies. If a hegemonic state adopts beggar-thy-neighbor policies, other governments have little incentive to resist implementing similar policies, for even if they wanted to maintain policies conducive to liberal exchange, they probably could not unilaterally or collectively overcome the consequences of choices by the dominant nation in a system with highly unequal distribution of capabilities.

The Soviet bloc during the cold war provides another example of a hegemonic state not promoting a system of liberal economic exchange. The Soviet sphere was organized around centralized exchange determined by Soviet policymakers and bureaucrats, not decentralized market exchange. How would international exchange look today if in 1989–1991 the United States and the Western bloc, and not the Soviet bloc, had disintegrated? It is unlikely that Soviet hegemony would have produced the same rules of the game as U.S. leadership has done.

Assuming that a capable and willing government and society exists in the global arena, what are the dynamics that prompt such a state to assume a hegemonic role and provide the collective goods that support market exchange regardless of the choices of other states in the system? Let's return to the original cost/benefit calculation for an individual ($NB_i = GB_i - C_i$) to understand why a hegemonic actor would rationally and willingly provide collective goods that help to overcome the risks and uncertainty of international market exchange, the social trap of free-riding, and the inclination to beggar-thy-neighbor, independent of the policies of other states.

Many collective goods require contributions by only some members of the group. Regardless of the size of a group, a collective good will be provided if enough of its members contribute to its provision, even if other members of the group free-ride. But what constitutes *enough* contributors to ensure the provision of a collective good? How many contributors are enough to cross the threshold between provision of a collective good and nonprovision or underprovision? The number of contributors necessary for the provision of a collective good varies by the cost of the collective good, the capabilities of the contributors, and the net benefits to those contributors. Technically, this quantity can vary from one contributing member of the group to all the members of the group. As the number is a variable, let's call this variable K.

If $NB_i > 0$ for only one actor in a group, the group is small and privileged regardless of overall group size. The group has an effective subgroup of $K = 1$. The collective good should be provided to the group. Why? When $K = 1$ and $NB_i > 0$, then that member will find providing the collective good worthwhile independent of the actions of others. This is the key condition underpinning hegemonic leadership. Under such conditions, collective action will likely succeed, given the efficacious subgroup of $K = 1$. The hegemon, $K = 1$, provides the collective good because she is rational, not altruistic. Extra-rational considerations such as resentment toward free-riders become irrelevant.

During the 1800s, public and private policymakers in the United Kingdom understood that their provision of key collective goods would likely produce $NB_{UK} > 0$ regardless of others' actions in the international arena. British policymakers rationally decided to adopt policies that amounted to providing collective goods for the system because such policies produced a net positive return to the United Kingdom, given the alternative of nonprovision. The United Kingdom was both disproportionately capable and more than willing to establish the foundations for a relatively liberal global political economy during the half century before World War I. During most of this period, the United Kingdom was the effective subgroup, or hegemon, for the international system: $K = 1$. No other nation could unilaterally attempt to provide the collective good and still discover that its $NB_i > 0$ if others failed to contribute, nor was it likely that any combination of nations that excluded the United Kingdom could overcome the barriers to collective action, attempt to provide such goods, and find their $NB_i > 0$. The policy choices of British policymakers were essential. Following World War II, U.S. policymakers faced a similar situation, and, again, with $K = 1$ and $NB_{US} > 0$, barriers to the provision of collective goods were overcome by unilateral action regardless of free-riding by other members of the collective.

What if the size of the efficacious subgroup necessary for successful collective action is greater than one member of the group—if $K > 1$? What if no clear-cut hegemon exists? Does this mean that collective goods will not be provided? Not necessarily! The provision of collective goods is then less likely than when $K = 1$, but significant opportunities for collective action still exist. If $K > 1$ but still relatively small, and $NB_i > 0$ for each member of the subgroup, if the other members of the subgroup contribute, a good potential exists for successful collective action. The size of the subgroup (regardless of the larger group size) plays into the group-size dynamic, for a small K can activate the dynamics that promote cooperation and hinder free-riding. The possibility of collective action is less than in the $K = 1$ case, but it still exists.

If K, the size of the effective subgroup, is large, collective action becomes less likely without other devices such as selective incentives, compulsion, entrepreneurialism, or piggy-backing to induce cooperation. With a large K, the size of the efficacious subgroup converges functionally on the size of its larger latent group. This means that as K increases, the efficacious subgroup also encounters greater and greater barriers to collective action and cooperation, as each member of the subgroup faces temptations to free-ride similar to those in the larger group. During the interwar years, without hegemonic leadership or a small efficacious subgroup where K was small but greater than one, governments had little incentive to contribute to collective action if most other governments elected to free-ride or adopt beggar-thy-neighbor policies. That would be a sucker strategy, as contributing to a collective good in the absence of others' contributions would lead to $NB_i < 0$ for the contributor—not a rational decision. This is a worst-case scenario for liberal economic exchange, in which governments rationally adopt policies that damage collective action, beggar their neighbors, damage social welfare, and, ironically, harm the very individual welfare of their constituents that such policy choices were meant to protect.

The case for hegemonic stability implicitly assumes that the hegemonic state ($K = 1$) will unilaterally pay the costs of providing collective goods that promote cooperative outcomes in a liberal economic political economy. This ideal involves a *benevolent* or *benign* hegemon, but hegemons do not have to be benevolent or benign, not even in a liberal global political economy. Hegemonic stability depends upon the circumstance that one member of the group enjoys both disproportionate capabilities and resources and a willingness to advance a specific form of economic exchange. This inequality in capabilities is benevolent if used only to unilaterally provide collective goods.

But a hegemonic state can also use its tools of influence to pressure others to contribute to the costs of collective action and limit beggar-thy-neighbor policies. In this scenario, a *coercive* hegemon uses its disproportionate capabilities to redistribute the costs of the collective good among a larger group. This strategy reduces the costs to the hegemon, but the provision of the collective good and the resulting social welfare remains essentially equivalent. The case of NATO or the 1991 Gulf War may fit this characterization. However, the same disproportionate capabilities that can lead to unilateral provision of collective goods might also tempt a hegemonic actor to extort extra contributions and extract special privilege. In this scenario, a coercive hegemon redistributes the burdens of collective action but also extracts contributions above the costs of the collective good. In the context of organized crime, we call such excess contributions "protection money." Whether the hegemon then keeps these extra contributions, called "rents," or redistributes them to cronies, the practice creates inefficiencies that detract from overall social welfare. The resulting situation falls short of the social welfare gains that a more benevolent hegemon would produce. Despite Rudyard Kipling's noble interpretation of European imperial rule as the white man's burden, bringing modern civilization to savage settings, modern colonialism is a good example of a hegemonic state (the colonial power) extracting excessive rents from its group in the name of the collective good, but actually damaging the overall social welfare.

CONCLUSION

Reducing collective action to its core components reveals the social trap that hinders cooperation, but it also highlights some strategies to overcome this trap. The problem of the provision of collective goods rests at the heart of many cooperation dilemmas in domestic and international affairs. In large groups, the temptations to free-ride are individually rational, even if free-riding detracts from social and individual welfare. Changing or constraining the nature of interactions within groups offers opportunities to overcome this threat to cooperation and collective action. Reducing the size of the efficacious group, providing selective incentives, compelling cooperation and contribution to collective activities, using political entrepreneurs whose public actions advance their private interests, employing homogeneity and social pressures, and piggybacking on top of established organizational activities offer general strategies to promote collective action. Hegemonic stability theory offers a special situation wherein a single state, or group member, can unilaterally provide a collective good and finds such provision rational.

EXERCISES

1. For years, political scientists believed that collective goods would be provided if $NB_i = GB_i - C_i$ and $NB_i > 0$. What are NB_i, GB_i, and C_i?

   The logic embedded in this formula suggests that any actor for which $NB_i > 0$ would contribute to the provision of the collective good that leads to NB_i, and that, consequently, the collective good would be provided. Yet history is replete with examples of situations where $NB_i = GB_i - C_i$ and $NB_i > 0$, but collective goods are underprovided. Explain why and use the equation to demonstrate your logic. Provide and explain an example of this problem in world affairs.

2. Several strategies can circumvent the underprovision of collective goods. Name two possible solutions to collective goods provision and give a description of how each works. Provide and explain examples from world affairs of these strategies at work overcoming collective action problems.

3. What factors limit individuals' incentives to free-ride and motivate them to contribute to a collective good?

4. Labor unions have employed piggybacking to advance issues beyond labor issues. What are some examples of labor union piggybacking?

5. How does cartel behavior simultaneously undermine and create a collective good? Earlier in the book, we discussed the ability of the members of OPEC to overcome collective action problems in order to manipulate the supply of oil. Take another commodity, such as bananas or copper, and use the formula $NB_i = GB_i - C_i$ and $NB_i > 0$ to construct an explanation for the failure of producers of that commodity to overcome barriers to collective action.

6. Many governments in the world signed and ratified the Kyoto Accord's limitations on emissions of greenhouse gases in order to retard the depletion of ozone in the atmosphere—a collective good. The United States has refused to accept and ratify the accord. What does this refusal by the hegemonic power and by far the leading producer of greenhouse gas emissions mean for the provision of the collective good of less ozone depletion? Use the formula, $NB_i = GB_i - C_i$ and $NB_i > 0$, to explain your reasoning. Given the dynamic in the formula, how should other governments react? How would you advise the members of an international environmental organization to obtain U.S. cooperation?

FURTHER READING

Hardin, Russell. 1982. *Collective Action*. Baltimore: Johns Hopkins University Press.

Olson, Mancur. 1965. *The Logic of Collective Action*. Cambridge, Mass.: Harvard University Press.

___. 1982. *The Rise and Decline of Nations*. New Haven, Conn.: Yale University Press.

14

Interest Groups and International Economic Foundations of Political Cleavage

> The great task in the study of any form of social life is the analysis of [these] groups. . . . When the groups are adequately stated, everything is stated. When I say everything, I mean everything.
>
> *Arthur F. Bentley,* The Process of Government *(1949)*

A MACRO PUZZLE

Liberalism and hegemonic stability theory, two macro approaches to international political economy, offer insufficient leverage for understanding variations in national policies toward international cooperation, trade, capital openness, and globalization. Why does a state lower trade barriers to some goods but raise barriers for other goods? Why does a government discriminate against some goods from another state but not others? Why does a government cooperate with other governments on one occasion but not another? For governments that profess to adhere to the liberal economic tenets of the "Washington Consensus," any barrier to international exchange is problematic within the boundaries of the macro theory. At the macro level, unilateral free trade is unambiguously good for a nation's collective welfare, regardless of its trading partners' policies.

Yet the empirical world persistently contradicts the macro theoretical world of liberal trade theory, sometimes only marginally but at other times violently. As a macro theory, liberalism fails to provide a theoretical mechanism within its own boundaries to account for such variations and seemingly nonrational behavior. After all, from this macro perspective, governments that impose such barriers to entry are reducing the collective welfare and

---

This chapter draws heavily upon Ronald Rogowski, *Commerce and Coalitions* (1989).

wealth of society. Such governments appear be nonrational. But we started with the assumption of rationality. Is this a poor assumption, or can we find a rational explanation for such seemingly nonrational behavior?

How do investigators examine such variations in the policies adopted by governments and societies and interpret them as rational strategies within the boundaries of a macro liberal economic explanation? Often, they create atheoretical stories to account for why particular commodities encounter higher barriers to entry than other commodities, why some capital finds more limited mobility than other capital, and why seemingly nonrational variations exist across products, capital, and states. These stories are attempts to preserve the liberal economic explanation, but, at the macro level, such accounts amount to ad hoc constructions on the part of investigators—they are not grounded in the theoretical framework of liberalism, but are appended to a liberal explanation. No mechanisms within the macro liberal economic framework offer a means for systematically understanding the deviations from liberal economic relations. This means that *ex ante* (before the act), we could not use a macro liberal account to anticipate variations in national openness to global transactions.

Hegemonic stability performs a little better as a macro approach in anticipating and accounting for these variations, since it expects a hegemonic state to provide market access as a countercyclical good for the international system and recognizes that nonhegemonic governments will free-ride on the hegemonic power. The expectation of free-riding means that those governments can, will, and should adopt nonliberal policies, especially during times of economic duress. Yet hegemonic stability also falters as an explanatory tool, as it cannot explain variations in the policies of the hegemonic state or in the policies of those states that choose not to free-ride, although free-riding appears to be a rational policy.

Hegemonic stability expects that the United States, as a hegemonic power at the heart of a liberal global economy, will provide a handful of specific collective goods to the international system, and that these goods will reduce uncertainty and promote liberal economic exchange. One of these goods is market access under duress. But how, then, does hegemonic stability account for enduring U.S. agricultural subsidies or other barriers to entry that disadvantage foreign agricultural producers regardless of duress in the system, the imposition of steel tariffs during a time of global economic slowdown, or countless other examples that run counter to hegemonic stability expectations? Moreover, hegemonic stability anticipates that nonhegemonic powers will free-ride and defect from liberal exchange arrangements by erecting barriers to trade and attempting to intervene through nonmarket mechanisms in the flow of capital. Sometimes they do so, but often they do not, and—more problematically—the variations cannot be systematically explained within the logical framework of hegemonic stability except by ad hoc accounts.

Of course, the social world is complex, and so we should not expect our theories to work perfectly and account for every variation, but we can search for theories and approaches that may perform better. These macro approaches implicitly assume monolithic nation-states wherein only a collective interest and welfare exists. This assumption implies that individuals in societies share a similar preference ordering and make decisions based upon a collective rationality—they evaluate outcomes only on how they affect the collective interest. But this schema neglects methodological individualism, an important focus of this book as explored in chapter 1, and the prospect for divergent individual preferences in society.

Explanations that account for deviations from the macro approaches often appeal to subnational-level devices such as organized special interests, but within the boundaries of macro theories, these explanations are ad hoc: they lack a theoretical mechanism that offers systematic tools for understanding why and when such variations occur. Even if such ad hoc accounts appear to be correct on a case-by-case basis, they are nontheoretical constructions that fail to provide systematic mechanisms for anticipating and understanding future deviations. Successfully explaining deviations in theory means that they are not deviations but variations that are systematically accountable by mechanisms that are explicitly part of that theory. If it is robust, a theory ties these seeming deviations into an account that operates systematically and consistently across cases and contributes to the construction of a social science explanation that is cumulative, works in many settings, and is not unique to a particular setting.

ALTERNATIVE EXPLANATIONS GROUNDED IN MICRO POLITICAL ECONOMY

Looking inside states and building explanations based upon methodological individualism explicitly recognizes the potential for diversity of interests, preferences, strategies, and capabilities at the subnational level. Chapters 8 and 12 examined the concept of market failure, which helps to account for the breakdown in liberal and hegemonic stability explanations. But market failure also anticipates divisions in society that can strategically compete to manipulate outcomes for individual or narrowly defined group objectives regardless of a larger collective good. Many latent divisions exist within societies that can affect policymakers' choices, and these divisions may account for the variations that are unexplained by the mechanisms of the macro approaches. Unfortunately, this recognition of diversity does not simplify the problem of understanding behavior. There are a variety of means of constructing divisions in society.

Starting with the assumption that political and economic markets fail (a foundational assumption), this chapter combines models of international economic exchange with frameworks from micro political economy (how groups and individuals behave and interact as rational social actors) to construct a systematic framework for understanding the sources of political cleavage and coalition in society. The likelihood of some political and economic market failure provides an opportunity to reconcile governments' profession of liberal economic beliefs with their adoption of protectionist measures, erection of barriers to entry, and intervention in the functioning of market mechanisms. Hopefully, we can create theoretical connections between the processes of globalization and the political bargaining within national political arenas that produces policies.

Let's begin by shifting the focus of analysis to the level of individuals, businesses, and groups. Repeated interventions by governments to protect agricultural sectors or specific manufacturing producers and their labor—and to discriminate against foreign producers and labor—do not appear rational under a liberal economic framework. These actions hinder the functioning of market exchange and constrain the expansion of their societies' consumption possibilities and collective welfare. Yet we have assumed that policymakers are rational, which leads to the recognition of potential weaknesses in the macro explanations. If we shift our focus away from societal and state levels of analysis to the individual decision maker, we may find that what appears to be nonrational in the context of a macro-level explanation can be seen as rational within a micro political economic explanation.

Political and economic market failure are problematic for the collective welfare of society, serving as a potential boon to groups and individuals that can manage the failures to their advantage and a cost to those that fail to manipulate the failures to their advantage. Perversely, this phenomenon is also a boon for political scientists, for, without political and economic market failures, political scientists would have little to study, explain, or teach. Using micro political-economic tools, which recognize that strategic action by individuals and groups can manipulate political and economic market outcomes to redistribute the gains and costs of exchange, it can be demonstrated that such suboptimal collective outcomes occur as consequences of individual rational actions. Actions that seem nonsensical at the macro level make sense at the micro level of strategic behavior. The manipulation of government and market mechanisms for individual gain can be rational, regardless of the consequences for social welfare.

INTEREST GROUPS

Opening up the box of the nation-state, we shift our attention to civil society. This perspective will help us to recognize that divergent opinions and preferences over policy exist within a society, and in the abilities of its members to make demands upon government. We consider the ability of individuals with similar preferences to overcome barriers to collective action and act as concentrated and organized groups. These aggregations of individual preference into concentrated and organized coalitions are called interest groups. Overcoming barriers to group action, forming an interest group, is a key step in communicating preferences to public policymakers and influencing their choices. This process involves transforming a latent, unorganized group of individuals into an organized, efficacious group that can represent the collective preferences of the group's members and try to exert influence over public policy choices. Such organization transforms the potential of diffuse and

Democratic presidential candidate John Kerry greets attendees in 2004 at a convention of the AARP, one of the most powerful organized interest groups in the United States. AARP lobbies on issues especially relevant to Americans over the age of 50. Politicians are more likely to address the concerns of older Americans than those of younger Americans because, being better organized, seniors carry more political clout. For instance, AARP lobbied successfully for a pharmaceutical drug benefit for seniors that will add to the U.S. government's increasing debt with little likelihood of promoting economic growth as most of the program's recipients have left the labor force. Comparable government expenditures on education, prenatal health care, day care, or school lunches could improve the quality of the workforce and lead to productivity gains.

disconnected individuals into a group that has much greater capabilities in the political arena than its individual members do.

Latent interests that overcome barriers to collective action to form an active and successful interest group have some general similarities. First, enough individuals in a society must share some common characteristic or common interest in obtaining a specific collective benefit. But shared interest is not sufficient—even if enough individuals in a society are interested in a specific objective, an interest group may not form. Chapter 12 discusses the difficult barriers to collective action, which account for the fact that many potential groups remain latent. Latent groups must exist as foundations for active and effective interest groups, but those that remain latent are the ones that have failed to overcome barriers to group action.

Second, interest groups are often built around a relatively narrow definition of an issue area. This issue domain can expand over time as the group takes advantage of its established group organization to piggyback new issues on old issues. But interest groups generally begin with a narrow definition of an interest area, which helps to overcome barriers to collective actions and limits identity problems (heterogeneity) that can hamper the effectiveness of groups with broadly defined interests.

Third, the success of an interest group is partly explained by its ability to garner access to relevant policymakers. What channels of access exist for any particular interest group? Are those channels of access appropriate to furthering the agenda of the interest group? For example, the American Banking Association (ABA) will be far more successful representing the interests of bankers if its channels of access include policymakers at the Federal Reserve and the Securities Exchange Commission, the Comptroller of the Currency, members and staff of the House and Senate Banking Committees, and other relevant regulators. The ABA will be less successful if it cannot access those regulators, but instead develops access to the Environmental Protection Agency or the Department of Transportation. Developing channels of access is partly a strategic choice of what government actors to cultivate, but it is also a function of the organizational structure of government and statutory restrictions. When considering the demands of civil society upon government, we want to examine what groups organize, how their efforts are concentrated, and whether they have pathways that allow them to communicate their preferences to relevant policymakers.

Fourth, successful interest groups often form coalitions with other interest groups. How and why does this happen? Any particular interest group may be too narrow to mobilize sufficient public pressure to attract the attention of policymakers; forming coalitions across interest groups links the interests and resources of one group with others. Exchanging support across interest groups can produce greater pressure upon policymakers, as such alliances take advantage of specialization and the gains from trade in political markets.

CLEAVAGE: BIOLOGICAL AND SOCIAL FOUNDATIONS

The framework of market failure recognizes the potential for divisions in society. It begins with an assumption of competing interests, offers a lever to demonstrate weaknesses in the macro explanations, and challenges us to look beyond those explanations for more satisfying and useful theoretical frameworks. But it does not provide tools for anticipating the lines along which a society may divide. This is problematic if the boundaries and divisions in domestic society can affect preferences, strategies, capabilities, policy choices, and outcomes in the global political economy. Are such cleavages ad hoc? Or can we provide a systematic basis for anticipating cleavages in domestic society and their public policy interests? The previous discussion of interest groups in society does not offer any systematic leverage for understanding what cleavages and interest groups will appear in society. Why some divisions and not others? To move past ad hoc accounts and create a useful framework for explanation, description, and prediction, we will need tools that help us to recognize the sources of potential divisions in society.

Many sources of potential division exist in societies. Investigators in comparative and American politics spend much time analyzing such divisions. As cleavages separate one group from another, they divide the large national community depicted in the macro explanation into smaller subcommunities. The very notion of community is one of erecting boundaries that separate one group of individuals from another, but often these boundaries are not clean or mutually exclusive, as individuals can belong to a variety of communities. For example, an individual may identify herself as an American but also as a woman, an adherent of a particular religion, a part of a minority group or a particular economic category, an inhabitant of a geographical region smaller than the nation, as well as a member of a professional trade association, of multiple social organizations, or of a political party. These subcommunities can overlap, but not completely. Some such cleavages in society get mobilized for political and social activities, while other divisions remain latent, never organizing or acting strategically as a group toward specific goals.

Cleavages can occur along lines generated by biological or social characteristics of individuals in society. Regardless of our normative preferences to the contrary, individuals often create groups and boundaries based upon biological or social characteristics such as gender, race, ethnicity, or religion. Many biological or social characteristics are easily identifiable, which may contribute to their usefulness in creating a we/them mentality and erecting the boundaries necessary for group identity—even if the key distinguishing characteristic is superfluous or unrelated to real differences in preferences and objectives. Unfortunately, history demonstrates that many cleavages and conflicts within societies occur across lines drawn by race, religion, ethnicity, and gender.

Another characteristic that has been observed to generate social cleavages is national heritage, despite the current citizenship of the people involved. The mass migrations of the 1800s, which were stimulated by globalization, provide a strong example of this characteristic at work, for those who migrated to the United States and became Americans also retained identities linked to their places of origin. Describing the U.S. population as a mix of Irish Americans, German Americans, Chinese Americans, Polish Americans, Norwegian Americans, Jewish Americans, African Americans, and so on, recognizes that current identities can be tempered by heritage. These identities, which are grounded in heritage, can be mobilized for political purposes that reflect different preferences and interests even though all are part of a larger community called Americans. The same holds true for other societies, as every nation has been socially constructed through the amalgamation of groups of differing identities.

Such social differences sometimes, but not always, provide a foundation for political cleavage. For example, the bloody and brutal hostilities in Kosovo during the 1990s are often portrayed as a conflict between Christian Serbs and Muslim Serbs that harkens back to a battle that took place in the region in 1389. In that major battle, Christian Serbs fought and lost to the Ottoman Turks, but the defeat became celebrated in Serbian folklore and is often used to remind Christian Serbs of their separate identity. Yet for years, even centuries, Christian Serbs and Muslim Serbs lived side-by-side in communities, intermarrying, trading, socializing, and celebrating together. If heritage is so powerful in constructing group identity and producing societal cleavage, how could the members of these two ethnic communities get together for so many years; and why did social relations deteriorate along this particular characteristic of identity in the mid-1990s but not in the 1970s?

The variations observable in the historical experience in Kosovo suggest that there is something more at work in generating political cleavage than simply religious identity. Despite recent violence, the apparent absence of cleavage and conflict for many years could mean that religious identity alone was not a necessary or sufficient condition for political cleavage in Serbia—that some other division is masked by the appeal to religion. Biological and social differences are not necessarily divisive, unless they are mobilized to create divisions in a society. For such social and biological characteristics to become sources of political cleavage, people must use them to construct distinct identities with wants and preferences that can be juxtaposed against those lacking the same characteristics.

INTERNATIONAL ECONOMIC SOURCES OF CLEAVAGE

Chapter 5 introduced a mechanism grounded in international exchange that provides a starting point to build a systematic foundation for understanding the international economic underpinnings of divisions in national political economies. The Heckscher-Ohlin framework of trade is built upon the notion that economies differ in the distribution of factors of production—their factor endowments. This insight offers a strategy to begin connecting economic activity with political activity. Every nation has a particular distribution of land, labor, and capital. Variations in these distributions across states produce comparative advantages and disadvantages. The integration of national markets into a larger global market rewards some producers and laborers but penalizes others. The dynamics of exchange between states create interests, cleavages, and impetus for political action within the domestic polities. Building on the Heckscher-Ohlin model, we can focus on factor endowments to understand the resulting distribution of advantages and disadvantages and, consequently, to systematically anticipate and explain potential political cleavages and coalitions in societies.

After building a framework for political competition based upon Heckscher-Ohlin and factors of production, we will consider its weaknesses. Then we will briefly explore two alternative approaches for examining the economic sources of cleavage and coalition in the international arena: economic sector and **asset mobility.** The first approach suggests that economies are divided into industrial sectors that may be more important sources of cleavage and coalition than are factors of production. The second focuses on the particular nature of economic assets and their mobility, asking whether a particular production asset (people, resources, or capital) can be easily reapplied to some other form of production or is relatively immobile and confined to a limited range of applications in producing commodities and services.

The Factor Endowment Framework

The Heckscher-Ohlin model of trade asserts that, with freer trade, a nation will export commodities that are produced by relatively abundant factors of production in society and will import commodities that are produced by relatively scarce factors of production in that society. The Stolper-Samuelson theorem extends Heckscher-Ohlin to demonstrate that increased trade rewards abundant factors of production in a society and penalizes a nation's scarcer factors of production. Drawing on the logic of Heckscher-Ohlin and Stolper-Samuelson, we can predict that abundant factors of production should prefer more open trading arrangements and scarce factors of production should favor more protectionist relations.

More open or more closed trading relations will channel to different groups resources that can be applied to political activities, such as lobbying, campaigning for elections, and public education. As abundant factors of production gain under open trading relations, they will discover that as trade expands they enjoy an increase in the capabilities they can apply to political action. In this situation, scarce factors of production will face a decline in the resources that they can apply to political activities. Turning this logic around, slowdowns and interventions in trade will enrich scarce factors of production. If we assume that the willingness to engage in political action is equal across winners and losers from trade, we can predict that winners from trade, either expansionary or contractionary, will gain political leverage. This assumption will be fragile if either the winners or the losers are more willing to devote disproportionate resources to political activities. Recognizing the fragility of the assumption of equal willingness, however, we can still observe that more open trade economically enriches and politically empowers abundant factors of production but penalizes scarce factors of production, while less open trade economically enriches and politically empowers scarce factors of production but penalizes abundant factors of production.

Now we have a plausible model that systematically links economic activity to political divisions and debates within national political arenas. This *factor endowment framework* defines the most basic cleavage lines in society, potential coalition partners, the nature of political conflict, and the likely winners of such conflict, if we assume that the change in political capabilities involves a simple extrapolation from changing exposure to trade. We can thus use the expansion or contraction of trade as a key independent variable for understanding shifts in capabilities, divisions, and coalitions in domestic political economies. This highly stylized framework—the argument reduced to its basic components—enables the construction of expectations about politics within states from knowledge only about factor endowments and whether trade is expanding or contracting. This can be a very powerful and elegant framework, if it works.

Some Stylized Examples

Imagine a state in a world of expanding trade. This state—let's call it State *A*—enjoys an abundance of capital and labor but suffers from a shortage of land or resources. Capital and labor will benefit, growing richer and having more disposable resources for potential application to political activities. In this society, capital attains a higher return and more productive investment by transforming labor, the other abundant factor of production. State *A*'s land resources, in contrast, will find themselves at a comparative disadvantage in the global political economy—they will lose market share to the land resources of states in which land is a relatively abundant factor of production. Given the factor endowments ascribed to this hypothetical state, we can predict the dominant form of production in this state and where such production would be located geographically. Because of its abundance of capital and labor, we can deduce that State *A*'s economy would specialize in the manufacture of goods and services rather than in agricultural production, which would require an abundance of the land resource that is lacking here. With expanding trade, this economy would be conditioned by the global market to shift production toward the manufacture of goods and services. Such economic activity generally migrates to urban centers.

In State *A*, if labor and capital can translate their economic gains into political action, they will gain leverage in the political arena, not simply on trade-related issues, but on any issue. Holders of land, meanwhile, can use their diminishing economic gains to resist such changes. In this state, labor and capital have overlapping interests in promoting economic openness and are likely to have overlapping interests on other issues, such as social and educational policies, due to the connections of their economic interests. This overlap creates a potential for a political coalition between holders of labor and holders of capital against the interests of land. If these holders of abundant resources are able to form a political coalition and trade continues to expand, their coalition should gain even more capabilities and influence over time. This political cleavage (labor and capital on one side, land on the other) translates into a geographic cleavage between urban and rural areas. As long as trade continues to expand, the urban areas in State *A* should continue to gain disposable resources that can be used to exert political influence.

Now, consider a second state (State *B*) with a different factor endowment, but still in a world of expanding international exchange. In this example, the country enjoys abundant capital and land but scarce labor. Again, due to the abundance of capital, this will be a relatively advanced economy. Unlike the previous example, however, State *B*'s particular set of factor endowments makes it more productive for capital to transform land. The global market will reward capital applied to production and transformation that emphasizes land-intensive activities such as mining, capital-intensive agriculture, and the production and refinement of metals or petroleum products. If trade continues to expand, capital and land will benefit and gain more disposable resources that they can potentially employ for political activities. In this state, land and capital have overlapping interests in promoting economic openness and are likely to have overlapping interests on other issues such as social and educational policies due to the connections of their economic interests.

This factor endowment divide creates a potential for a political coalition between holders of land and capital against the interests of labor. If the abundant factors of production in State *B* are able to form a political coalition and trade continues to expand, this coalition should gain further capabilities over time. Labor can use its diminishing economic gains to resist the policy changes preferred by the potential coalition partners of land and capital. This particular divide does not translate into the urban-rural geographic cleavage of the previous case, but into a cleavage based on wealth and land versus labor—a class cleavage. Political debate and competition should fall along class lines.

In an environment of expanding international exchange, what does the factor endowment framework suggest for politics in capital-poor societies—societies that are less economically advanced than those considered in the previous cases? Their lack of capital means that their land and labor resources remain relatively untransformed in comparison to those of their counterparts in capital-rich societies. Let's begin with a state (State *C*) that is abundant in labor but scarce in capital and land. Since increasing trade rewards labor-intensive forms of production, land and capital will discover that they face a comparative disadvantage in the global economy. At first glance, the dynamics here appear similar to those in State *B*: society faces a potential divide between a coalition of capital and land on one side and labor on the other. Again, this cleavage anticipates class conflict.

Despite similar cleavages, however, who gains and who wins in State *C* under expanding trade differs from the example of State *B*, and this difference should eventually produce different political outcomes, even though the cleavage lines are identical. In State *B*, capital and land gain from expanding trade, but in State *C* labor gains from the expansion of trade. Labor will be gaining relatively more disposable resources that can be applied to political activity in this case, not diminishing resources as before. In State *C*, labor will become a more powerful political force as trade continues to expand. If this capital-poor society accumulates capital with trade and the resulting economic expansion (which increases savings and investment), it eventually will transform to become a capital-abundant state. This is a goal of development. If this happens, we would anticipate a shift in coalition partners and a change in the political cleavages and coalitions of society.

Now, let's consider a capital-poor state (State *D*) that enjoys a relative abundance of land and relatively scarce labor. Trade is still expanding. At first glance, using the factor endowment framework, we anticipate the same divisions—the same lines of political cleavage and likely coalition partners—as in State *A*. We expect labor and capital, as relatively scarce factors, to be potential coalition partners, with the interests of land falling on the other side of the potential divide in society. This division predicts an urban-rural cleavage. Yet, State *D*'s prospects differ from State *A*'s situation of urban-rural conflict. In State *A*, the urban coalition gained and the rural area lost capabilities as trade expanded. In State *D*, however, the rural area expands and the urban area loses capabilities as trade increases. With continued expansion of trade—and everything else remaining equal—we can extrapolate growth in the relative capabilities of land over those of the labor-capital coalition in State D and forecast that, over time, land will become increasingly successful in the political arena in obtaining its policy preferences. The divisions in society here mirror those in State A, but the political outcomes are likely to differ along with the differences in who wins and who loses in the arena of international exchange. Again, if this capital-poor society accumulates capital with trade and the resulting economic expansion, it eventually will transform to become a capital-abundant state. If this happens, we would anticipate a shift in coalition partners and a change in the political cleavages and coalitions of society.

The expansion of trade is not inevitable, as was clearly demonstrated in the interwar years discussed in chapter 8. International trade and globalization of economic relations can shrink as a consequence of economic crisis, war, natural disasters, or the erection of political barriers to cross-border exchange. With trade contraction, political competition should fall along the same divisions as depicted in our stylized examples, as those states' factor endowments remain the same. But who gains and who loses economic resources as a result of the shrinkage will differ, as contractions in international exchange will reward scarce factors of production and penalize abundant factors of production. Changing a nation's relationship to the international arena from one of expanding trade to one of contracting trade reverses who gains and who loses capabilities in our examples. Again, assuming that these gains and losses in capabilities translate into potential gains and losses in political influence, a situation of contracting trade anticipates very different political outcomes from an environment of expanding trade, even though political cleavages can remain the same.

The capabilities that factors of production can potentially expend in the political arena will change with the expansion or contraction of trade. What policies emerge from the divisions in society that are anticipated by the factor endowment framework will also depend upon the ability of likely coalition partners to actually form coalitions and their willingness to expend their capabilities upon political activities.

An Empirical Example

The factor endowment framework offers an elegant theoretical specification about plausible connections between international economic relations and political activity in domestic political economies. The model may be elegant and internally consistent, but it remains a hypothetical story about the causal connections of one set of activities to another set of activities. Empirical testing is needed to evaluate its merit as a useful depiction of behavior. Happily, as the stylized examples above demonstrate, the model allows systematic derivation of testable proposals about political behavior—specifically, about winners and losers, cleavages and coalitions in national political economies. These testable proposals anticipate the nature and content of policy conflict in political economies, given knowledge of two key variables: a state's factor endowment and comparative advantage, and whether trade is expanding or contracting. Our initial assumption of rationality expects that players in the political arena can rank their preferences, evaluate strategies and their relative costs, and form coalitions with those that have compatible interests against those with less similar interests as a strategy to obtain their best outcome. History provides ample opportunities to test this elegant theoretical framework against the empirical world.

Let's use U.S. history to evaluate the factor endowment framework in action. The transformation of the U.S. economy over the past two hundred years allows us to consider different factor endowments at different times, all within a single national context. If the factor endowment framework is analytically useful, changes in factor endowment that occur as a consequence of economic growth and the interaction of the U.S. economy with the global economy should lead to predictable changes in domestic political cleavages, coalitions, and policy competition.

At birth and for almost a century thereafter, the United States was land-rich but capital- and labor-poor. How do we know it was capital- and labor-poor during this period? In chapter 7 we noted that the expansion of U.S. economic enterprises and infrastructure, such as railroads, relied heavily upon financing from London's capital markets. New York's youthful capital markets provided some financing, but they could not meet the needs of the developing economy because there was insufficient capital accumulation in the United States. The U.S. banking house of Morgan established itself by selling bonds and engaging in dealings in London's financial markets for the promotion of U.S. enterprise. Meanwhile, the migration of people from the Old World to Australia, Canada, the United States, and other regions of the New World tells us about the labor scarcity in those areas.

By the late 1800s and early 1900s, the United States had transformed itself into an economy that enjoyed abundance in land and capital, but still sustained a relative scarcity in labor. New York had become a major financial market, rivaling London in terms of capitalization and resources. This transformation in capital accumulation appears in a significant increase in per capita levels of industrial production from 1800 to 1913 (depicted in table 7.4), which indicates a greater role for capital in the production of goods and services. Such a change can only occur with increasing access to affordable capital. So we can conclude that the supply of capital in the United States increased over the course of the century, and with this change, the U.S. economy went from being economically backward to being economically advanced. Labor remained relatively scarce, but immigration continued at a high rate. People tend to move to places where they find economic opportunity; the U.S. economy needed workers and paid a relatively high wage, given the shortage of labor.

What does the factor endowment framework predict for U.S. economic activity, political division and coalition, and public policy competition during these different periods? During the earlier period, it expects that abundant land interests would gain economically with expanded trade, but scarce capital and labor would lose economically as they encountered competition from more competitive labor and capital in nations where those factors were abundant. During this period, the United Kingdom, one of the major trading partners of the United States, enjoyed a relative abundance of labor and capital but a shortage of land. With the repeal of British protections exacted by the Corn Laws and increasing British openness to trade, U.S. and other New World agricultural producers competed successfully in British markets due to their comparative advantage, which enabled them to undercut their British competitors. In this case, expansion of trade led to a dramatic decline in British agriculture. But during this period, British capital and labor-intensive commodities enjoyed a comparative advantage over similar U.S. products, as British manufacturers led the way during the Industrial Revolution. Only with government-erected barriers to entry—protectionism—could U.S. manufacturers compete against British manufacturers in U.S. markets during this period.

Conversely, with contractions in trade during this period, U.S. land resources should have suffered economic penalties, while the relatively scarce factors of labor and capital would have reaped economic gains. A variety of circumstances, including war, natural disasters, and economic distress, may prompt a contraction in trade, and the United States faced two such shocks during the nineteenth century: the Civil War and the depression of the later 1800s. But trade contraction can also be imposed by public policy interventions in the form of protectionist measures such as tariffs, quotas, and other barriers to entry, which can shelter all or part of an economy from the competitive forces of a larger global marketplace by ensuring domestic producers favored access to domestic markets.

The U.S. case initially anticipates an urban-rural cleavage. U.S. farmers should pursue freer trade, because their products are competitive in global markets. As the abundant factor of production in the U.S. economy, they should resist government obstructions to international exchange, for greater economic globalization rewards their efforts. In contrast, the urban coalition of capital and labor, the relatively scarce factors of production, should favor protectionism. With protections, U.S. farmers and consumers would pay more for labor- and capital-intensive commodities than they would without protections to bring the world market price for these commodities up to, or above, the price for similarly produced U.S. commodities. Moreover, in a protectionist environment that sheltered American labor and capital, American agriculture could face retaliatory measures by other governments, which could damage their comparative advantage.

The factor endowment story fits early American history quite well. Alexander Hamilton argued in a famous report to Congress that insulating U.S. manufacturing from the pressure of foreign competition by protecting the domestic market for U.S. manufacturers was essential to enable nascent U.S. industries to emerge and survive. (This strategy, known as **import substitution,** was intensively used as a development strategy by Latin American governments during the twentieth century.) Open competition in manufacturing would have revealed the lack of U.S. comparative advantage in these forms of economic activity versus producers from the Old World. The growth of U.S. manufacturing would have been constrained without protectionism, and Thomas Jefferson's vision of an agricultural United

States dominated by a rural republican elite might have survived and prospered. Slavery might have prospered and been extended to all the new territories, and the Civil War might not have come to pass.

Hamilton recognized the dilemma that free trade posed for U.S. capital and labor interests. Why did he favor protection of labor and capital instead of the interests of land (agriculture)? He may have had a grand vision of the United States as a manufacturing power, but it is also likely that his preferences were shaped by his regional attachment and professional expertise. His state of residence was New York and his expertise was in finance. Farming was more difficult in the Northeast than in the South and the emerging West; fieldstone fences all over New England and New York testify to the difficulty of plowing the soil and managing crops in that region. The Northeast was emerging, instead, as a center of nascent industry and the banking center of the young United States, but it faced more competitive finance and manufacturing from the United Kingdom and the Old World. Hamilton's vision of the United States differed from Jefferson's because his regional concerns were bound up in the interests of labor and capital—even though these factors were lacking in comparative advantage—and not in those of land. This regional bias put him at odds with the farm states of the South and, if he had lived long enough, with the new territories of the West.

The urban-rural division that was based upon economic interests expanded beyond the issue of trade. Rural interests, which resented capital's potential influence, formed farmer cooperatives and alliances that became part of the foundation of populist and progressive movements in the United States. A deep and recurring theme in American history—the division between Main Street and Wall Street, and the distrust of New York bankers and financiers—reflects this cleavage. Andrew Jackson's election and the success of the early Democratic Party mobilized forces along this division, and by the mid- to late 1800s, the cleavage along production-factor lines was captured in the division between the Republican and Democratic parties. At this time, the workers and industrialists of the Northeast, representing the production factors of labor and capital, combined with the more capital-intensive interests of the upper Midwest to elect Abraham Lincoln over the objections of the Democratic Party, which enjoyed electoral success mostly in the Far West and the South. As we saw in chapter 7 (remember the *Wizard of Oz* parable), this cleavage recurred in debates over issues such as the gold standard, price deflation, the formation of a national bank, farm indebtedness, and ownership and regulation of transport facilities—all issues that spilled over into the international arena.

But economies are dynamic. They change, often dramatically, as a result of capital accumulation and investment. The United States was an economically backward, capital-scarce nation during its early years, but with economic growth it accumulated more and more capital through earnings and savings that could be applied to investment in activities to transform and increase the productivity of land and labor. By the beginning of the twentieth century, the United States had shifted from a capital-scarce to a capital-abundant state.

It was still labor-poor, as evidenced by the great waves of immigration that continued through the gates of Ellis Island and other immigration centers, bringing Italians, Irish, Germans, Jews, and others seeking economic opportunity and political refuge. These immigrants filled New York tenements and found employment, albeit often poorly paid and in dreadful working conditions, that greatly exceeded the dismal prospects they had left behind in the Old World.

Such a shift in the relative abundance of capital should lead to changes in the preferences of capital regarding trade restrictions and in coalition politics. The factor endowment framework predicts that the cleavage should shift to land and capital against labor, and that it should create tensions between more capital-intensive labor and less-capital intensive labor. The shift in the abundance of capital should have generated pressures for change in the Republican Party's policy preferences for tariffs and other barriers to entry while increasing conflict between the old coalition partners of labor and capital. Over time, we should anticipate a shift in the lines of political battle from the urban-rural cleavage of land against labor and capital to a cleavage reflecting class conflict, with land and capital allied against labor, and capital-intensive labor against capital-scarce labor.

Historically, the cost of capital declined with its transformation into a relatively abundant factor. Trade was expanding, which increased the gains to abundant factors. Consequently, capital-intensive commodities fell in price, becoming more competitive in global markets. As Democrats, who represented the interests of the abundant land factor, continued to press for reduction of trade barriers, the rewards to capital from expanded trade put pressure on the capital-labor coalition and placed the Republican Party in the difficult position of trying to manage a conflict between its two core constituencies. In effect, Republican politicians had to choose between policies that favored one coalition partner over another, and their choices could vary by political-economic geography, depending upon which coalition partner dominated in specific electoral districts. But over time, even though labor continued to find its greatest access to representation through Republican Party channels, that party's support for labor preferences was becoming weaker compared to its positions on issues relevant to capital.

Republican politicians, who had long represented a capital-labor coalition that was urban and protectionist, began moderating their position on tariffs, moving away from the protectionist preferences of less-capital-intensive labor. When President Theodore Roosevelt, a Republican, advocated tariff reform and increased exposure to the competitive pressures of the larger global market, his actions helped produce a growing divide in the Republican Party. This divide left labor, as the scarce factor of production, which had been allied with the Republicans since Lincoln, in an increasingly exposed position politically. As the gains from trade translated into political influence, expanding trade meant that capital was gaining strength while labor was weakening. Farsighted Republican politicians could envision the growing strength of capital if this trend were to continue, and they feared that if they ignored the trend, holders of capital would begin to defect from the Republican Party, taking with them their growing pool of politically influential resources.

Some of those engaged in capital-intensive industries and farms in the Midwest and East did indeed defect from the Republican Party and gradually shifted to the Democratic Party—the more free-trade party. The election of 1912 reflects this trend and illustrates the Republican coalition split. In that year, President William Howard Taft, a Republican, ran as the incumbent. However, Theodore Roosevelt, a Republican who had served two terms as president and had stepped down in 1908 to support Taft, his hand-picked successor, had since become dissatisfied with Taft and now challenged him for the Republican nomination. When Taft prevailed in this intraparty contest, Roosevelt decided to run as the candidate of a third party, the Bull Moose Party—and he took the progressive/populist wing of the Republican Party with him. With the Republican Party split, Woodrow Wilson and the more progressive/populist Democrats won the White House.

As a first cut, the factor endowment framework does fairly well in providing a connection between international economic activity and U.S. domestic political alignments and policies. But the transformation in American politics raises some additional dilemmas for which the factor endowment framework does not provide a ready explanation, such as the division of a specific factor of production into opposing interests. As some capital began to favor more open trading relations, some holders of capital resisted this change. Moreover, labor began to split, with some factions favoring more open trading relations and others favoring more restrictive trade arrangements. One plausible explanation for the divisions within capital is that the late 1800s was a transitional period; it took time for the holders of capital to recognize their new situation and to realign politically. Perhaps so, but how do we account for the divisions in labor? In terms of the factor endowment framework, there was no change in the scarcity of labor—labor was not going through a transition from being a scarce to an abundant factor of production.

We can adapt the factor endowment framework to address this problem and answer how a specific factor might divide into opposing interests, but this adaptation will also open the door to several alternative explanations. Remember, labor and land are naturally occurring assets, but capital is a human construction. Capital transforms other factors of production through investment, as we see in the application of capital to education, development of skills, shifts in social organization, improvements in plant and tools, and advances in technology and industrial organization. Capital invested in land makes land more productive than in its native state, and capital invested in labor makes labor more productive than in its native state. This transformative potential suggests that considering all land as alike or all labor as alike is problematic, and, indeed, we do observe differences in the capital intensity of some labor versus other labor. Perhaps in the U.S. example from the later 1800s onward, capital-intensive labor—the combination of a scarce and an abundant factor of production in an economic activity—would prefer different policies than those favored by less capital-intensive forms of labor?

If so, treating land, labor, and capital as monolithic factors of endowment can mislead us in our efforts to connect international economic activities with domestic political strategies. The factor endowment approach may be useful—as the analysis of the 1800s in the United States demonstrates—but it has weaknesses also. It initially fails to explain why labor in highly productive and capital-intensive industries (such as the manufacture of electrical equipment, cars, and communication technologies) began to advocate reduction in trade barriers while labor in less capital-intensive businesses resisted such change. We can adapt the framework to account for the transformation of a scarce factor of production by abundant capital, but other explanations may also offer analytical leverage here.

A Critique of the Factor Endowment Framework

As noted earlier, the factor endowment framework does fairly well as a first cut to connect international economic activity with political activity within nations and between nations. But several significant problems can handicap the factor endowment framework and prompt us to pursue other explanatory tools. Let's consider three specific categories of problems:

1. The assumption that gains and losses from trade translate directly and proportionately into gains and losses in political influence
2. Failure to consider the possible impact of different governmental organizational arrangements upon the exertion of influence by societal factors such as land, labor, and capital
3. Uncertainty as to whether factor of production is the appropriate level of aggregation for analysis

The foundations of the first two problems are explored extensively in the discussion of interest groups earlier in this chapter, in chapter 13 on collective action, and in the next chapter on institutions. We will now focus on the third category, offering in the remainder of the chapter two refinements that shift the focus from factors of production to another means of aggregation.

Briefly, the first category of problems suggests that the factor endowment framework neglects the barriers, incentives, and disincentives to organizing for political action. The framework, as presented in this chapter, simply assumes that gains and losses will translate directly and proportionately into changes in political influence. But what if people elect not to use their gains for political activities? Political activity is a possible consumption choice, but those gaining additional disposable resources from the expansion of trade may decide instead to spend their gains on a new car, a hot tub, cases of wine, a new house, or new clothes rather than on political influence. Gains from trade expansion do not necessarily translate dollar-for-dollar into expanded political influence; there must be a conscious choice to spend those gains upon political activity. Additionally, those losing from changes in trade exposure may decide to expend a disproportionate amount of their resources to protect the old status quo, wherein they profited. This unpredictability of consumption choices suggests that a dollar gained is not necessarily equivalent to a dollar lost in terms of the motivational effect of changing trade patterns on political activity.

Even if those losing or gaining from trade do decide to contribute their resources to political activities, substantial barriers to successful political organization remain. In politics, there is strength in numbers and in resources that can be brought to bear upon a policy problem. This potential strength requires the coordination of numerous individuals, often unknown to each other, in a collective activity. Even assuming that factor of production is an appropriate level of aggregation, problems still hinder labor, capital, or land in functioning as blocs in the political arena. Deciding on appropriate policies in response to exposure to trade, communicating responsibilities and activities, sharing costs, and forming coalitions demands a tremendous amount of collective action among dispersed individuals. And, as was thoroughly explored in the previous chapter, there are problematic barriers to collective action.

The second category of problems, the failure to consider the influence of different governmental organizational arrangements upon the exertion of influence by societal factors, reveals a significant weakness in the factor endowment framework as presented in this chapter. Since it essentially treats all governmental arrangements alike by neglecting the causal effect of different governmental forms—that is, governmental arrangements as an independent variable—the factor endowment framework is implicitly assumed to work identically in authoritarian states as in democratic states; the same in winner-take-all electoral systems as in proportional electoral systems; the same in decentralized federal systems as in more centralized systems; and the same in a system with lots of checks and balances as in a system with few checks and balances.

If we simply assume that government style, structure, and operation make no difference in outcomes, we are implying that all governments are essentially alike and unimportant for understanding why some societal interests obtain better representation than others. For a political scientist, this proposition would be equivalent to saying that government has no independent causal influence on the observed outcome; nor does it interact at all with the purported hypothesized dominant mechanism, which here is factor endowment plus changing exposure to trade. Yet political science generates a tremendous amount of research investigating and demonstrating the independent influence of governmental structure and operation upon outcome. So, although this problem is not fatal to the factor endowment framework, it does mean that the factor endowment framework—or any other framework for understanding political behavior and outcomes—should be considered within the context of different governmental arrangements. We consider these "institutional arrangements" and their differing effects more extensively in chapter 15.

The third category of problems concerns the determination of what level of aggregation awards the greatest and most efficient leverage for investigating the causal connections between changing exposure to international exchange and political competition within nations. At the end of the previous section, we raised the prospect that another level of aggregation might prove more useful, as empirical dilemmas arise from the treatment of factors of production as monolithic. At that point, we circumvented this problem by suggesting that a monolithic factor of production such as land or labor might be divided into subcategories by level of capital intensity. But a variety of other alternatives—different types of aggregation devices—are available to systematically connect expansion and contraction of international economic activity with domestic political cleavages, coalitions, and policy competition. Here, we briefly consider two promising but different refinements on the factor endowment framework. These alternative aggregation devices bypass factors of production and instead divide economies by focusing on two different aspects: industrial sector and the nature of the productive asset. The causal chain and logic remain similar to those of the factor endowment framework, but we substitute industrial sector for factors in one refinement and asset of production for factors in the other refinement.

Industry Sector

Recognizing that factors of productions are not monolithic is the same as asserting that some labor may have different preferences than other labor in society, that some capital may have different preferences than other capital in society, and that not all land resources in a society view the world through the same lens. Labor may disagree with labor over policy, land may disagree with land, and capital may disagree with capital. Identifying likely cleavages within a factor of production is thus problematic for a framework based upon divisions between factors of production. We have suggested that we can circumvent this problem by determining whether a monolithic factor is fragmented by differences in the application of capital, and then distinguishing between the preferences of more and less capital-intensive land, and more and less capital-intensive labor.

Alternatively, fragmenting an economy into some divisions other than factors of production makes sense if, with expanding or contracting trade, some labor gains and some labor loses, some land gains and some land loses, and some capital gains and some capital loses. The basic structure and causal mechanism of the factor endowment framework work remarkably well. Perhaps we can improve upon this framework, however, with modifications that shift the level of aggregation of the affected domestic groups. One alternative unit of aggregation is industrial sector. Replacing factors of production with industries as the unit of analysis recognizes that two different factors engaged in the same industry may share more common interests than a single factor that is spread across a wide variety of economic endeavors. This modification hypothesizes that labor and capital in a specific industry share more common interests than the labor in that sector shares with labor in other industrial sectors. For example, capital and labor in the U.S. automotive industry have more in common than does labor across the automotive and semiconductor industries. This hypothesis builds upon a simple recognition that people within an industry share a common interest in their industry's future success, as their livelihood stems from the same industry.

The basic argument from the factor endowment framework remains the same despite substituting industrial sector. Expansion of trade benefits those in industrial sectors that enjoy comparative advantage in relation to their global competitors, and it damages industrial sectors that are relatively less competitive in the larger global market. The reverse pattern holds true for the contraction of trade. But changing the focus of analysis to industrial sector makes it more difficult to describe policy conflict in a state as class or urban-rural cleavages. The foundations of political coalitions will originate instead across industrial sectors, which is a more decentralized basis for political division and coalition than factor of production for two reasons: (1) there are more industrial sectors than factors, and (2) factors span an entire economy, but an industrial sector is usually a compartment of an economy.

Switching from factor of production to industrial sector as the basic unit of aggregation places greater informational demands upon investigators, but it may provide significantly more analytical leverage than the more elegant factor endowment framework. This tradeoff between elegance and complexity is worthwhile if we gain important explanatory power over what appears to be incongruent behavior within the factor endowment or modified factor endowment framework. Making this switch does not mean that we should discard the factor endowment framework, but that we should work to recognize and define its limitations— under what conditions it will prove useful and under what circumstances problematic. By better specifying the conditions that are conducive or problematic to the factor endowment framework, we have gained at least one alternative in the industrial-sector refinement. We can identify more than one refinement if we recognize the level of aggregation as a variable that we can manipulate, and then feel free to choose another unit of analysis—plausibly spanning the range from factor to the individual—when appropriate. Let's move on to consider one other such unit of analysis, the individual as an asset of production.

Asset Characteristics

It should come as no surprise to recognize that individuals participate in politics. So perhaps we should consider individual characteristics as a means for understanding political cleavage in society. The previous sections have clumped individuals into some type of group—as members of a factor of production or an industrial sector. The factor endowment framework divided individuals into three categories based upon their common characteristic as a production factor, and then used this characteristic to anticipate their political activities. The industry-sector refinement clumped individuals into a particular industry sector, hypothesizing that all individuals within that sector share a common motivating interest, and then used this characteristic to anticipate their political activities.

But individuals remain individuals despite their group affiliations. Individuals within a particular grouping, be it a production factor or industry sector, may behave differently in politics than do other individuals of that same grouping. Within a given factor, some individuals may be less motivated to act in their factor's interests than others. Within an industrial sector, some individuals may be less motivated to act in that sector's interests than others. Other individuals may act as if their interests are more tightly bound, more congruent, with their sector or factor's interests.

Yet other individual-level characteristics may motivate people to resist or promote trade openness, or to behave differently in politics than do other members of their group as defined in the previous two models. What other individual characteristics might help to account for this variation? Do individuals vary in some key manner that motivates them to engage more or less in political activity, or makes them more or less likely to form coalitions with other people in similar circumstances?

Let's start by considering individuals and their capabilities as assets of production. Some individuals bring labor to their productive activities, others bring capital, and others supply land resources. This division fits with the factor endowment framework, but in the critique of that framework we recognized the potential for these assets to differ from individual to individual even if they are members of the same factor. Moreover, an individual may actually be a product of the interaction of several factors, especially in more economically advanced societies where capital has interacted with other factors of production and transformed those factors. Training and education turn labor into a capital-intensive labor. The application of technology such as chemical fertilizers and biotechnology turns uncompetitive land into a fertile agricultural asset. If individuals are actually an amalgam of factors of production, can a particular characteristic be identified that cuts across such interactions to provide insight into the question of who will be motivated to expend resources on political action?

Mobility of the asset of production is one such characteristic. *Mobility* means that the individual has the capacity to stop what she is doing and start doing something else in terms of economic production. Some labor is more mobile than other labor, can more easily switch jobs or careers than other labor. Some capital is more mobile than other capital. This quality is described as *liquidity*. For example, capital assets such as a house or a factory are more difficult to sell for reinvestment in other activities than is a portfolio of stocks on the New York Stock Exchange. Some land resources are more mobile than other land resources: a farmer may be able to change crops and use her land to produce another agricultural commodity, but a coal miner may not be able to find another use for her coal mine.

All transitions involve some dislocations to the individual. An economic shock such as changing exposure to international trade that forces an individual to seek other employment and opportunities clearly creates dislocation. But some individuals may be better prepared than others to manage that shock—their skills may make them more capable of finding another job. These people, who are more mobile due to their training, will be less concerned about the shock than are individuals who are less mobile, and consequently they are less committed to resisting the changes that cause dislocation. This logic anticipates that those individuals with the greatest mobility are more likely to move on and participate in an alternative economic activity and less likely to engage in collaborative political activities to defend the status quo. They are less likely to define political cleavages or build political coalitions.

Here, asset mobility becomes an important independent variable as we try to understand the international contribution to national political cleavage, coalition, and competition. An asset's mobility or lack of mobility—the ability to exit and find other opportunities—intermediates the causal relationship between shifts in international economic activity and political outcomes. In this framework, the more restrictive the alternatives become for an asset, the less mobile the asset and the greater the incentives for that asset to work to protect its current economic activity. Consequently, this perception anticipates that less mobile assets are generally more motivated to engage in political action than are more mobile assets.

CONCLUSION

This chapter provides us with a framework, and several alternative approaches consistent with the basic logic of that framework, for anticipating where the lines of political cleavage and competition will be drawn in a society, and for understanding that some coalitions are more likely than others. As noted earlier, several problems burden the factor endowment framework. But the refinements developed here face similar handicaps. Most important, none of these frameworks provides a mechanism for overcoming the barriers to collective action. All these frameworks implicitly assume that if a factor, industry sector, or asset has disposable resources, it will engage in political activity. But the empirical world is rife with examples of interests not coalescing into coalitions for political activity.

These frameworks are elegant and powerful, but their predictive utility is only part of the puzzle. The cleavage lines and likely coalitions identified by these frameworks are latent cleavages and coalitions, which need to organize and overcome barriers to collective action in order to exercise political influence. In chapter 13, we dealt explicitly with this problem of collective action. Now, by combining the lessons from that chapter with the frameworks concerning political cleavage that we have described in this chapter, we can develop a substantial understanding of political competition in national arenas over international and domestic policy issues. In the next (and final) chapter, we will add to our understanding of how domestic political arenas can influence political competition and outcomes by examining how different political institutional arrangements can affect the ability of interests to form coalitions and exercise their political voice.

EXERCISES

1. Consider India today. If you are not familiar with its resources, do a little research to determine its factor endowment. What factors of production are abundant, and which are scarce? What are the political coalitions that the factor endowment predicts? What is the nature of political conflict and competition anticipated by this framework?

2. China is undergoing rapid economic change: twenty years ago, it was clearly a developing political economy; today, its economy is in transition; twenty years from now, it may well be a developed political economy. What was China's factor endowment twenty years ago? Today? And if China succeeds in becoming a developed political economy in the next twenty years, what will its factor endowment likely be then?

   What might such changes mean for political coalitions and the nature of political conflict in China over this span?

   Use this framework to hypothesize about the nature of Chinese trade policy in twenty years, the nature of Chinese educational policy, the nature of Chinese central banking policy.

3. Discuss briefly the problems with the factor endowments framework. Do these problems mean we should discount the whole framework?

4. Explain why we might prefer to use the automotive industry rather than factors of production as a level of aggregation to study political divisions and competition.

5. An alternative to focusing upon factors of production to understand political competition in domestic political arenas is to consider the mobility of the asset of production. Explain asset mobility in the context of individuals. Hypothesize how asset mobility affects an individual's motivation to engage in political action.

6. Different factor endowments across nations can condition economic activity, affect level and type of economic development, and systematically shape political debate and conflict over public policies. If a nation is abundant in land and capital but scarce in labor, what type of economy does the nation have and what is likely to be the nature of political conflict and cleavage in that society?

   What types of trade policy should each factor of production in this economy prefer?

   In this scenario and with expanding trade, what factors gain and what factors lose in relative power capabilities?

7. If a nation is abundant in land but scarce in labor and capital, what type of economy does the nation have and what is likely to be the nature of political conflict and cleavage in that society?

What types of trade policy should each factor of production in this economy prefer?

In this scenario and with contracting trade, what factors gain and what factors lose in terms of relative power capabilities?

FURTHER READING

Frieden, Jeffrey. 1991. "Invested Interests: The Politics of National Economic Policies in a World of Global Finance." *International Organization* 45 (4).

Gourevitch, Peter. 1986. *Politics in Hard Times: Comparative Responses to International Economic Crises.* Ithaca, N.Y.: Cornell University Press.

Milner, Helen. 1988. *Resisting Protectionism: Global Industries and the Politics of International Trade.* Princeton, N.J.: Princeton University Press.

Rogowski, Ronald. 1989. *Commerce and Coalition: How Trade Affects Domestic Political Alignments.* Princeton, N.J.: Princeton University Press.

15 Institutions

What is the market? It is the law of the jungle, the law of nature. And what is civilization? It is the struggle against nature.

Edouard Balladur, Financial Times *(December 31, 1993)*

FURTHER EXPLORATION OF CONSTRAINING SOCIAL TRAPS AND MARKET FAILURE

In theory, Adam Smith's invisible hand in decentralized market exchange produces a nice social outcome wherein self-interested, rational, individual choices aggregate to produce an optimal social result in terms of the efficient use of resources. In this ideal world, we ask individuals to act only in their self-interest to produce a constructive social outcome. But the bulk of this book demonstrates that, time and again, our real world falls far short of such an ideal—the invisible hand mechanism fails, and we do not reach Eden. All too frequently, the rational actions of individuals aggregate to produce suboptimal social outcomes instead. Sometimes these outcomes represent only inefficient use of societal resources without serious social trauma, but at other times, they generate tremendous social, economic, and political disruption.

The dilemma lies not in our assumption of human rationality, but in the context of human interaction, which plays a major role in aggregating individual rational choices. Sometimes the aggregation process produces good and relatively efficient collective outcomes, as in the case of Adam Smith's theoretical invisible hand, but at other times the structure of human interactions and the mechanism that aggregates human choices lead to suboptimal collective outcomes. Worse, those outcomes often constitute strong and stable equilibria. They are no fluke, but are slated to recur again and again. Rational individuals seem trapped by the structure of a situation that leads them to make choices that appear to be individually rational but lead to perverse social consequences. Worse yet, in many of these situations, an individual cannot unilaterally improve her situation independent of other's choices, even if she recognizes the problem. Obtaining a better individual and collective outcome requires coordination and cooperation by many decision makers, and often the situation works against such cooperation.

A variety of factors contribute to these situations, which are called social traps or market failures. The structure of human interaction may contribute to a social trap or market failure even if all those involved completely understand others' beliefs and preferences, their assessments of utility, and the structure of choice and interaction. Ironically, due to the strategic interaction of choices, in many of these cases individuals and policymakers can do better for themselves and their societies by opting for what appear to be suboptimal individual choices. In these situations, individuals often make choices that they know will lead to suboptimal outcomes because they are unable to secure a binding agreement among all the concerned parties to cooperate in order to obtain a better outcome. Each individual's fear that another may defect from such an agreement to cooperate leads her to defect. This is the most stark and disturbing case of a social trap or market failure, as all participants are fully informed and aware of how to obtain a better outcome, yet they fail because the necessary cooperation and coordination is missing. The suboptimal outcome then becomes a stable equilibrium, as confirmed expectations about the behavior of others lead to the same choices again and again.

More often, other factors intervene to create a social trap or market failure. Incomplete and asymmetric information about the structure of a social situation and about the processes by which choices aggregate, misperception of others' beliefs and preferences, and uncertainty over utility can confound rational choice. Here expectations about the likely choices of others are unstable: we are unsure what to think, or we have a false consciousness about what to think, which leads to potentially poor decisions even though the process is systematic and rational. The very presence of incomplete and asymmetric information opens the door to the possibility of strategically manipulating the information environment to influence others' choices in an attempt to advance one's interests at the expense of others and of society as a whole. We cannot ask rational individuals to refrain from attempting such manipulation if they believe that others will not be so constrained.

Differences in capabilities and in the willingness to use those capabilities can transform a decentralized process into a hierarchical process in which those at the top of the hierarchy benefit at the expense of the larger society and of those beneath them in the hierarchy. If individuals attain disproportionate access to resources and capabilities that allow them to manipulate the distribution of goods in society, should we expect them to act in the best interests of society if it means that they will receive less? In the case of politicians and policymakers, should we expect them to act in the best long-term interests of society if it increases the prospects of their political demise?

Societies face a number of dilemmas: how to constrain uncertainty and promote productive stable expectations versus destructive stable expectations; how to limit the manipulation of information for individual gain at the expense of others and of the broader society; how to constrain individual temptations to defect from cooperative contractual obligations; and how to transform the context of human interaction and the mechanisms that aggregate individual choices in order to produce good versus bad social and individual outcomes. These are not easy tasks, or else we would see a world full of economically productive and politically healthy states. In the past several chapters, we have looked at a variety of mechanisms that can exacerbate or constrain social traps and market failures. In this chapter, we focus on the role of institutions—what they are and how they can help to constrain uncertainty and instability, promote stable expectations, structure the incentives of individual decision makers, overcome barriers to cooperation and coordination, contain the time inconsistency problem, and produce a more socially efficient equilibrium.

INSTITUTIONS AS RULES OF THE GAME

First, what do we mean by *institutions*? What are they and what do they do? Douglass North, winner of the Nobel Prize in Economics for his work on institutions and institutional change, defines institutions as "the rules of the game in society, or more formally, the humanly devised constraints that shape human interaction." By this definition, institutions are not organizations, but rules, laws, customs, common practices, norms, and conventions. Often, we resort to factors such as greed, nature, self-preservation, genetic fitness and fecundity, compassion, or the quest for power to explain human behavior. These are motivational primitives. In a state of nature without any rules of interaction save survival of the fittest, such primitives are given primacy in explaining behavior. But institutions stand distinct from such factors as we try to account for why people do what they do, helping to distance our actions and choices from the primal state of nature. Socially constructed institutions attempt to intermediate between such primitive motivations and human actions.

If effective, institutions transform human activity and lead toward social outcomes different from those we would anticipate if only the laws of the jungle or nature applied. Socially effective institutions transform a decision maker's information environment, reduce uncertainty in that environment, create stable expectations, extend time horizons, and, consequently, structure incentives to make collectively productive choices rather than others. Ineffective or socially dysfunctional institutions can feed uncertainty, contribute to unstable expectations, decrease the shadow of the future, and motivate individuals to engage in socially destructive activity.

As such, institutions impose important independent causal influence on social interaction. We can insert them as independent, or explanatory, variables in our models of human behavior. Variations in institutional frameworks, differences in rules of the game from one society to another, can help us to understand and anticipate differences in human activity from one social setting to another. Why do some societies experience economic growth and improvements in social welfare, while other societies prove dysfunctional, as their members repeatedly cheat, steal, and kill? Why can some nations engage in peaceful democratic transitions from one government to another, whereas others fall into the trap of coups, civil wars, and rebellions?

In chapter 2, we used several different games to demonstrate that there is no reason to believe that human physiology, psychology, or biology explains the differences between successful and failed states, productive and dysfunctional economies, or healthy and diseased societies. An educated individual (well-trained as an asset of production) may cooperate with others and act productively in one society, but if we place her in another society, she may lie, cheat, steal, or worse—same individual, but different institutional settings and rules of the game. This means that any attempt to explain social activity with reference only to characteristics of the individual will fall short. Individual characteristics may be important and necessary to any account of social activity, but they are not sufficient once we move beyond the raw state of nature. Institutional settings become important variables as we try to fathom, anticipate, and change social activity.

Formal versus Informal Institutions

Consonant with his idea that institutions are the rules of the game, Douglass North notes that "political rules broadly define the hierarchical structure of the polity, its basic decision structure, and the explicit characteristics of agenda control. Economic rules define property rights, that is, the bundle of rights over the use and the income to be derived from property and the ability to alienate an asset or a resource. Contracts contain the provisions specific to a particular agreement in exchange."[1] But must institutions be codified in formal legal systems, as bodies of law and jurisprudence? Can institutions exist outside of formal laws and regulations? If so, how do such institutions differ from those we find embodied in formal legal statutes? We can distinguish between formal and informal institutions. More than formal codification of the rules of the game, a presence of a third-party adjudication and enforcement mechanism separates formal from informal institutional arrangements.

Formal institutional arrangements involve third-party enforcement mechanisms with the authority and power to adjudicate disputes. Parties to an exchange or human interaction can appeal to this third party to referee, adjudicate, and enforce a resolution to a dispute. Moreover, individuals, whether they win or lose in the adjudication process, recognize the authority of the third party to intervene and mediate disputes. Such mediation is not random, but guided by bodies of rules that get established and codified over time—a legal sys-

---

[1]Douglass North, *Institutions, Institutional Change and Economic Performance* (Cambridge: Cambridge University Press, 1990), 47.

tem. Such legal systems and rules guide expectations about the likely resolution of disputes, and, consequently, preempt and deter many disagreements or activity contrary to the rules of the game.

Constitutions, statutes, regulations, common laws, by-laws, contracts, and other rules and agreements create a hierarchy of formal rules of the game to guide political, economic, and social activity. Constitutions and laws amount to contracts between governments and the governed. The government is also the third-party enforcement mechanism. Idealistically, we like to think that good governments stand outside disputes, do not have a stake in the resolution of a dispute one way or another but only in its resolution, and can fairly adjudicate disputes as an independent dispassionate party. This is the image represented by the statue Scales of Justice, holding the balance scales and blindfolded so not to be swayed unfairly. But no government is independent of its society. Dispute resolution creates winners and losers and affects distributional outcomes in society. As a consequence, the design and construction of formal institutions and laws are targets of organized interests, who may use their capabilities to attempt to embed their preferences in the design of institutions and laws.

Informal institutions complement formal institutions. But, unlike formal institutions, they lack a third-party enforcement mechanism; they are self-enforcing. Parties to an economic, political, or social interaction adhere to the rules of the game because they want to play by such rules or because they fear that other parties to the interactions may impose sanctions or penalties if they do not follow the rules. Similar to the realists' depiction of the nation-state system (discussed in chapter 3), informal institutions rely on self-help and on the parties to the exchange using their capabilities to enforce the rules and impose costs on those who renege on the rules. Parties engaged in social interaction must resort to their own devices to ensure that others cooperate, follow the rules, and meet their obligations. Moreover, if informal institutions are to have traction and causal influence, they must be more than simply differences in capabilities or power. If we can explain parties adhering to the informal rules of the game solely by appealing to differences in power, we do not need institutions to explain social outcomes, only assessments of power.

Norms, customs, conventions, common practices, and rules of the road communicate information and develop expectations about what is acceptable or anticipated behavior. Recognizing such patterns can reduce the costs of some choices and increase the costs of others. This set of informal rules affects the incentives and calculations of rational decision makers independent of differences in capabilities. For example, policymakers of a more powerful government often refrain from the sheer exercise of power over other governments to get their way in world affairs. These policymakers may have the capacity to force their will on others, but they do not do so because such intimidation would be outside the informal rules of the game, beyond the lines of acceptable behavior or convention in world affairs. They may resort to other tools of statecraft, even if it means they will be less successful, because an excessive use of power would be viewed as an inappropriate violation of acceptable practices and would

The World Bank routinely advises governments to develop a rule of law, or formal institutions, to protect property rights within the system of exchange. Stores such as this one in South Korea that sell black-market goods are common worldwide and these operate beyond the boundaries of formal institutions. Informal institutions—which operate without a third-party enforcement mechanism—allow traders to overcome barriers to exchange, thus enabling black markets to flourish and promote economic activity.

induce significant costs. Certainly, U.S. policymakers had the capability to prevail during the Vietnam War if they had exerted the full military capacity of the United States to destroy the country, but such an exercise of power would have violated international norms of acceptable behavior in warfare, placed U.S. decision makers on a par with Adolf Hitler and other mass murderers, and imposed significant future costs on the United States. Informal conventions of the global arena prohibited such an excessive use of force by a superpower against a far weaker nation. In other words, winning is everything if we consider only power capabilities, but winning is not everything if informal institutions impose standards that are independent of power. Then, how one wins, loses, or socially interacts may well matter as much, if not more than, simply prevailing in a contest of power.

Institutions as Social Bargains and Ex Ante Agreements

Institutions constitute *ex ante* agreements, which are contracts about current and future cooperation and interactions. Imagine a world full of social traps and strategic actors, but without institutions. Each day, decision makers would have to delve for information to reduce uncertainty, try to understand the preferences and capabilities of others, analyze different scenarios (potentially an unlimited number of scenarios), and then try to make a rational choice for every single decision they confront. Without some shortcuts or devices to organize the mass of information and reduce uncertainty, many—if not most—individuals would be paralyzed. Absent a clear dominant strategy, the simplest choices would exhaust our resources.

Ever since early humans crossed paths in the grasslands during their wanderings, migratory travels, and hunting and gathering, we have created devices to simplify our decision processes and save our energies for the most complicated and difficult choices. Without such tools, we would spend too much time on each individual choice and might never get to the important and difficult situations. Moreover, without means for resolving the cooperation and coordination difficulties that occur frequently in social interactions, we would be more likely to select poor strategies and produce outcomes that were desired by none of the parties engaged in the interaction.

Therefore, sometimes intentionally and sometimes unintentionally, we have developed rules of the road, not only for the management of current problems, but also to contain similar problems in the future. We develop such rules of the road, or institutions, to help in constraining social traps and problems that we are likely to encounter again. The very existence of cooperation to manage one social trap can help to build foundations for cooperation to manage other social traps, as people develop familiarity, trust, and expectations about those with whom they interact frequently. Before the problematic situation recurs, an informal, perhaps implicit, social bargain emerges among the parties to a prospective social interaction about how to handle such situations. This advance bargain is an ex ante contract or agreement, which serves to reduce uncertainty, limit the need for information gathering and evaluation, and make the decision process far more manageable.

Formal institutions embed such ex ante agreements in legal systems, whereby the parties to a social interaction understand the expected course of action and, if one party should wander off the expected path, know how to appeal and adjudicate the outcome. Aside from the added layer of third-party adjudication and enforcement mechanisms, a formal institution thus has the same ex ante implication as an informal institution. Given the anarchical nature of the modern Westphalian nation-state system, the absence of formal institutions in the international arena may differentiate social, political, and economic interaction within states from such interactions across state boundaries. If so, our focus upon institutions in international affairs should be on how formal and informal institutions in the domestic arena constrain and motivate activity across borders and how informal institutions in the international arena influence that activity.

Institutions as Equilibria

Thinking about institutions as the structuring of incentives and ex ante agreements reduces uncertainty, but only if those involved in a problematic social exchange recognize the problem and the relevant institution for dealing with it. Rather than wondering about an extensive range of alternatives and analyzing different possible outcomes and their likelihood, individuals can converge on an ex ante agreement—if an appropriate one exists—to manage a particular type of situation. This predetermined set of expectations makes the decision process more efficient, as decision makers rely upon choices that were structured in the past and embedded in an agreement, formal or informal. Instead of searching among a wide range of choices, individuals converge upon a particular choice or limited set of choices. The institution structures and limits their set of potential choices.

This mechanism can limit problems of multiple or suboptimal equilibria, and so contribute to cooperation and coordination. We have seen that in many social interactions multiple equilibria exist, and some produce social traps. Some of these equilibria are better than others, but all are stable. In other social traps, a single equilibrium exists, but it is a suboptimal stable equilibrium that is produced by a dominant strategy. In the former situation, institutions can alter the incentives and push individuals to select strategies that lead to a particular equilibrium and not others. In the latter situation, institutions can structure incentives and costs to help decision makers avoid the stable but suboptimal equilibrium by cooperating to produce better collective and individual outcomes that are stable, even if they do not constitute a stable equilibrium by definition. If such institutionally assisted outcomes are stable, we can consider them jointly as an equilibrium because we do not anticipate movement away from the collective outcome. This situation is called a **structurally induced equilibrium.** Absent the institutional structures, individuals would make different choices, which would lead to different individual and collective outcomes, but the institutional arrangement has intervened to push human activity toward a particular outcome among the range of possible outcomes.

Institutions as Incentives and Path Dependency

Institutions can alter the costs of decisions and the costs of the process of decision making. If they reduce uncertainty in a decision-making environment by limiting the range of possible choices, they lower the costs incurred by selecting one of those strategies versus expending resources to evaluate more uncertain alternatives. We say that institutions lower the transaction costs of an exchange, or the cost of transacting the interaction. Since we assume that decision makers are rational and are trying to balance costs and benefits, lowering decision-making costs should create incentives to select among the range of alternatives structured by the institutional environment.

If institutions influence expected costs and benefits among a range of possible choices, they are creating incentives to make one choice over another. By doing so, they shape the direction of change and condition future choices, making those future choices somewhat dependent upon previous choices. We call this phenomenon **path dependence** or **path contingency.** It simply means that knowing what people did in the past to resolve coordination and cooperation traps gives us a pretty good idea about what they will do in the future when they encounter similar situations. Consequently, limiting uncertainty by changing incentives and prompting one choice over another in a current interaction becomes embedded in institutional frameworks, which then make future choices contingent upon past experience and choice.

For example, the GATT framework used rounds of negotiations to lower barriers to trade and expand liberal exchange. Each round incrementally extended and expanded upon institutions constructed in previous rounds. Negotiators did not toss out the old framework and begin anew—instead, they kept what had worked in previous rounds of negotiations, tinkered with what had failed, and attempted to expand the trade agenda into new areas. The agenda for each new round of negotiation thus arose from the previous round, and that round of negotiations from the round before it. Even the extension of negotiations to new areas built upon past lessons and practices institutionalized in the process of negotiation. The precedents and institutional advances of previous rounds of trade negotiations have heavily influenced the path for the current Doha Round of WTO negotiations. If we look closely, we can find commonalities that tie the negotiations of the first GATT agreement to those of the present day.

A Normative Caveat

We like to think that institutions are, necessarily, normatively good human constructions that lead to better social outcomes. This is often the case, but not always. Reducing uncertainty and making the decision process more efficient for individuals does not necessarily mean that such a process produces an optimal social outcome. Institutions reduce uncertainty and make the process of choice more efficient, but this is an effect that can lead to bad as well as good social outcomes. As they shape expected costs and benefits, institutions can just as easily create incentives to engage in activities that damage society as those that lead to activities that improve social outcomes.

For example, an authoritarian regime may construct an institutional framework that creates incentives for people to spy upon their neighbors and report information about their neighbors to the authorities. This practice can lead to tremendous distrust among neighbors, an unwillingness to share information for fear that it might be misused, and a breakdown in social goodwill—all conditions that are ripe for contentious and socially damaging activity rather than cooperation that could advance overall social welfare. Why would a government construct such institutions and create such incentives? Perhaps the members of the governing elite benefit from a divisive society. Seeking to extract wealth and resources from their countrymen for private gain, such a governing elite may support institutions that weaken potential social opposition.

In another example, institutions that assist members of one particular group in overcoming barriers to collective action can lead to a better social outcome, if the interests of the group that coalesces in this way overlap with the interests of the broader society. But groups such as cartels and criminal gangs also seek to overcome barriers to collective action, often to further their group and individual interests at the expense of the broader social welfare. A cartel may want to manipulate the price of a commodity; a criminal gang may want to ensure that its members refrain from divulging information to the authorities in the face of prosecution. Yet, absent some device to promote cooperation, the individual incentives of the cartel members are to defect from the group objective and so reap extra rewards, and the incentive for the criminal is to squeal on her compatriots in order to receive a lesser prison sentence. In the case of successful cartels and gangs, the group develops rules that promote cooperation and limit defection for individual gains. For example, if you cheat on the cartel, the other members will ostracize you; if you testify against the gang, your family will be killed.

Institutional Effectiveness and Durability

If an institution is to be effective in reducing uncertainty, stabilizing expectations, and creating individual incentives for preferred choices, first, it must influence behavior and, second, it must be durable. Durability means that an institution and its effects persist over time and over multiple social interactions. The institution sticks; it influences behavior again and again. Absent stickiness and persistence, a cooperative effort to overcome a social trap may be little more than an isolated incident and momentary success—not an institution. Such success may say little about expectations of future interactions. So what makes an institution durable? Why not simply renege on the rules of the game that constrain a social trap, if it promotes one's individual well-being and benefit at the expense of others? Many times people do so, which indicates the absence or ineffectiveness of institutional arrangements to overcome social traps. But we also observe many examples of people and their governments cooperating, playing by the rules of the game, and limiting the pitfalls of social traps. A variety of pressures promote such institutional effectiveness and durability. Let's focus on five general types of pressures: cost efficiency, third-party enforcement, reputation, status quo, and the shadow of the future. These types are not independent, but they can overlap to create mutually reinforcing pressures.

Cost Efficiency

As an ex ante agreement about interactions, an institution can produce cost efficiencies for decision makers. In a social interaction, an institution can reduce the time and resources spent on overcoming asymmetric information dilemmas, evaluating alternatives, monitoring the activities of others, and policing contracts. These effects limit the costs of interaction and constrain uncertainty over the appropriate course of action if all the parties in the interaction know and understand the rules of the game, which generate efficiencies in the process of the interaction—in the costs of doing business—regardless of whether it produces an optimal social outcome.

Institutions that create such efficiencies can be appealing in a world of uncertainty and limited resources, for they allow decision makers to conserve their time and resources for spending elsewhere. Routines, customs, and patterns of behavior enable people to interact in specific circumstances without expending too much energy evaluating and strategizing. As suggested, this mechanism may not produce optimal social outcomes, but it can lead to results that are good enough that people choose to adhere to the institutions in order to save their scarce resources for more difficult or important interactions. This process of finding an outcome above a set threshold to be acceptable is called **satisficing.**

Third-Party Enforcement

Formal institutions—those with third-party enforcement mechanisms—are the easiest to observe in society. Public and private governments act as third-party enforcement mechanisms for established rules that are intended to govern the relationships of members of their groups.

A fraternity's by-laws assign to its governing body responsibility for adjudicating categories of disputes between fraternity members. By their rules, formation, and organization, the governing authorities of a church, synagogue, mosque, or other religious group act as a third party to mediate disputes among their members. Public governments (states) are buttressed by extensive bodies of law that confer upon those in official positions the responsibility for mediating conflicts between the state and its members, as well as between members of the state.

The authority of such governing bodies comes from a variety of possible sources, which influence the effectiveness of the formal institutions they are supposed to support. The capabilities and the willingness of the third party to use those capabilities can determine the efficacy of a formal institution by influencing the costs of noncompliance. Third parties often enjoy disproportionate capabilities on one or more dimensions. They may be able to exercise coercion, which allows them to physically threaten, sanction, or compel compliance from those who renege on the formal institution. They may engender respect, or even reverence, which endows their decisions with influence. They may control levers of information dissemination, which enables them to advertise or disclose details about members of the group who defect from the formal institutions and about those who respect the institutions. This informational capability can generate reputations and reduce uncertainty about members of a group, which can affect future interactions by creating long-term costs or benefits for actions taken in the present.

The third party plays an important and effective role if its actions focus attention on those who violate the formal institutions and produce pressures for compliance. Not all formal institutions succeed in influencing behavior—many fail to create incentives, constrain behavior, or motivate compliance because the third party lacks either the capability or the willingness to adjudicate violations and disputes or has no ability to enforce its decisions even when it does attempt to adjudicate a dispute. Many governments adopt constitutions and bodies of law that include provisions to protect the rights of their citizens or fairly adjudicate economic disputes, but then they routinely ignore such bodies of law. We like to think that such transgressions occur predominantly in developing or authoritarian states, but we can also find examples of such problems in the more advanced industrialized democracies. For example, shortly after the end of the Civil War, passage of the Fourteenth Amendment to the U.S. Constitution guaranteed equal protection to U.S. citizens regardless of race. Despite this formal rule of law mandating equal protection, U.S. courts and authorities then stood by for almost one hundred years as many states systematically denied African Americans the rights and protections that were available to other citizens.

Reputation

Think about reputation as a mechanism distinct from third-party enforcement of a formal institution. Obviously, a third-party enforcement device—such as labeling some party as reliable or as a scofflaw—can focus attention and generate costs and benefits in terms of reputation. Yet reputations that can affect the likelihood and form of social interactions may also emerge in the absence of a third party, as in decentralized relationships, where parties to a social, political, or economic interaction violate or adhere to the informal rules of a contract or game.

For example, Hasidic Jews dominate the wholesale diamond trade in New York City. Their informal rules ask each trader to be fair and honest and to respect agreements that are consummated by verbal agreement, by a handshake, or by some other symbolic gesture that would be considered weak evidence, at best, in a court of law. Very little cheating occurs, despite the temptation of handling millions and millions of dollars' worth of diamonds; few disputes require resolution. What keeps individuals in this community from cheating and destroying such a system, if the state's courts could not resolve any disputes, given the nature of the contracting mechanism?

A diamond trader's ability to function and thrive depends upon his reputation. If one trader were to cheat another, the cheated trader would quickly inform other traders about the offense. The cheater's reputation would be damaged, and depending upon the severity of the offense, he could be penalized, ostracized, and perhaps forced to leave the diamond trade altogether. This kind of communal discipline occurs through self-enforcement, without resort to a third-party adjudicator and enforcer.

Fear of negative reputation costs can be self-enforcing, can limit cheating, and can protect an informal institution that serves to overcome barriers to cooperation and coordination. Conversely, a good reputation can produce rewards and increasing returns. Developing a reputation for adhering to the rules of the game, even if they are informal rules, helps to lower uncertainty about a party's honesty, reduces transaction costs, and builds trust that can lead to more beneficial interactions. Developing a reputation for fairness and even-handedness, or for being a willing self-enforcer, offers reassurance to other parties in a social interaction that can affect their cost-benefit calculations and condition their choices. This status-enhancing effect holds, whether it involves an informal or a formal institution.

Status Quo and Embedded Interests

Preferences for the status quo and embedded interests both operate to promote institutional stickiness. In a world of uncertainty, people often "prefer the devil they know to the devil they don't know," which simply means that the opportunity to alter or reject a current institution balances the consequences of the current institutional arrangement against the potential implications of a new institutional arrangement. Given that we live in a world of uncertainty, we cannot completely anticipate the consequences of new institutional arrangements; some unknowns remain.

If we are somewhat dissatisfied with current institutional arrangements but also very unsure about the outcome of new ones, we may defend the current arrangements in order to manage our apprehensions of the unknown. In such cases, our willingness to defend the status quo depends upon the extent of our dissatisfaction with the current rules, our estimation of potential benefits from changing the rules of the game, and our uncertainty about attaining the anticipated outcome. The prospect for institutional change increases along with our dissatisfaction with current arrangements, everything else being held constant. The greater the expected gains from institutional change, all else being held constant, the greater the likelihood of such change. But the greater the uncertainty or the lower the expected gains from change in the institutional context, the greater the likelihood of our maintaining the status quo, even if we are relatively dissatisfied with it.

Let's quickly consider how embedded interests work to maintain the status quo and to promote institutional durability independent of uncertainty. Most institutions that resolve difficult cooperation problems are not neutral in terms of the distribution of their effects—they create relative winners and losers in societies. As such, the design of institutions can become the target of political competition. From this perspective, formal or informal institutions are social constructs that reflect preferences about institutional design based on the different capabilities of societal actors and their ability and willingness to exert influence, and these different capabilities can affect the long-term efficacy of an institution. Those who profit from a particular institution can use their resources to promote the viability of that institution and to resist institutional change. The strength of their resistance to institutional change may depend on the size of the gains the status quo arrangement produces for those winners and the expected distributional consequences of institutional change. For example, warlords in the Sudan—those with disproportionate power in their society—have maintained social practices and political institutional arrangements that promote civil conflict, ethnic violence, famine, and starvation, and so damage the collective welfare of their society. It is hard to believe that local political leaders would resist institutional change amid such human tragedy, yet the warlords have adhered stubbornly to status quo arrangements as they seek to maintain their position of influence and continue to reward particular interests at the expense of the larger society.

The willingness of embedded interests to resist institutional change does not preclude such change, for those damaged by the status quo may willingly expend resources to promote change. This opposition of interests may lead to conflict and competition over institutional design. However, those benefiting from the current arrangements may have used the status quo to expand their capabilities, whereas the relative losers may have suffered losses in capabilities—which suggests that, over time, the embedded interests (the winners) are likely to gain in ability to defend the status quo. All else being equal, this likelihood contributes to institutional durability.

The Shadow of the Future

All of the previously mentioned mechanisms that can contribute to institutional durability implicitly assume that people care about the future. Many human interactions take place between individuals, groups, and states that are likely to interact again and again. How people value such future interactions can affect how they behave in their current dealings. Those who live expressly for today—Carpe diem!—and care little about tomorrow are essentially playing a one-shot game, in which they will likely seek to obtain their best possible outcome even if it damages social welfare, hurts their reputation, and risks ostracism from similar interactions in the future. After all, these people put little value or weight on the future or on the long-term consequences of their choices. Their actions may sound excessively self-centered and egomaniacal, yet the conditions of society can create incentives for such behavior. If a society is a violent and chaotic place, where people cheat, steal, and kill without regard for the broader community and its long-term interests, it makes sense for others to shorten their time horizons and take aggressive actions themselves. In such situations, many people will act to ensure the short-term survival and well-being of their family and friends, even if their actions damage society further. In failing states, this logic creates a downward spiral of degenerating social, economic, and political conditions.

However, if people in a society find a means to extend their time horizons, boosting their interest and valuation of the future, the possibility of constructing bargains and institutions that guide current social interactions in order to protect future interactions increases. The greater the likelihood of repeated interactions in the future, the greater the incentives and prospects for constructing and maintaining institutions for overcoming barriers to cooperation, reducing transaction costs, and making social relations more stable and predictable. This dynamic is more than simply an economic calculation about future gains, for repeated interaction contributes to familiarity, which aids understanding and reduces uncertainty—good or bad—about the parties involved in the relationship. With greater familiarity, parties involved in social interactions can design institutions and contracts that take advantage of their different strengths, which can enhance cooperation, and manage their weaknesses, which can damage cooperation. The knowledge that comes from repeated interactions can assist in designing institutions and rules that are robust in the face of pressures to defect.

Familiarity can also activate informal social pressures and build social networks that generate incentives to play by the rules. If productive, more frequent interactions build social momentum and trust that can produce slack or flexibility in social relations—a willingness to forgive or overlook some behavior that seems outside the rules of the game. Rather than allowing a single transgression to destroy the institution or relationship, other parties may give it a second chance, or even more. With repeated interactions, people develop expectations about the other parties. Behavior that deviates from such expectations may be unacceptable, but if it is unusual, familiarity may help to identify it as an aberration, and the other parties may then be willing to wait and see if it is repeated. Absent familiarity, such behavior might immediately undermine the social interaction and damage the institution built to promote that interaction.

Of course, successful institutions are *endogenous*—are themselves causal—to increasing the "shadow of the future." Causality runs both ways and is mutually reinforcing—again, our cycling metaphor from chapter 8. An increasing shadow of the future improves the likelihood of institutional success, and institutional success increases the shadow of the future. Absent such an awareness of and concern for the future, even the most coercive enforcement mechanisms cannot prevent institutional failure and societal dysfunction. If people do not or cannot extend their time horizons, their incentives are often to opt for behavior that is damaging to themselves and to their societies—a social trap that creates a vicious cycle.

Distributional Implications of Institutions

Institutions affect distributional outcomes in society. They produce relative winners and losers, which creates the potential for boundaries within society and the formation of interests along such boundaries. Consequently, institutions and institutional design become targets of political competition wherein power asymmetries influence, perhaps dictate, institutional design so as to advance particular distributional outcomes that favor some interests over others. Many institutional economists argue that because institutions reduce transaction costs and the uncertainties involved in exchange relations, they emerge in order to enhance efficiency. This is a functional argument—an explanation for a phenomenon based upon its consequences. But enhanced efficiency may simply be a secondary or unintended result of institutional design that is intended to produce distributional advantage for some groups versus others.

In a social trap with great uncertainty, many different institutions can structure incentives, promote a better equilibrium, and improve efficiency and social outcomes. In such situations, a variety of institutional arrangements may lower transaction costs and improve social efficiency. But who benefits most, who benefits least, or who loses can shift across the variations in institutional arrangements. Individuals and groups may disagree over variations in institutional arrangements even if every variation improves social outcomes, as they produce different gains and loses at the individual level. The creation of an institution can itself be a social trap.

Hence, institutions are not politically or normatively neutral—not even institutions that improve social outcomes. The rules of electoral systems, regulatory arrangements, administrative law, and judicial rights become targets of political competition as they affect who wins or loses, and who may have greater or lesser influence over future policy discussions and institutional design. In political competition, winning at time t is often endogenous to winning at times $t + 1$, $t + 2$, and so on, as winning often helps to build capabilities and resources that will prove useful in future political and policy struggles.

Some political scientists use this view of institutional design and creation as a reason to downplay the importance of institutions for understanding social activity. They argue that if a society's institutions merely reflect the distribution of power in a society, we need only examine that power distribution in order to understand social outcomes—that is, institutions are unnecessary or secondary independent variables. Perhaps, but if institutions merely reflect the distribution of capabilities and influence in society, we would expect institutional change to closely correspond to societal shifts in power. The fact that societies are dynamic provides leverage for examining the relationship between power and institutional makeup. Societal distributions of wealth, resources, and power change, but institutional change lags behind. This disconnect between the distribution of influence in society and institutional change argues against looking only at the distribution of power. Institutions are sticky; effective ones span such changes in the distribution of influence to provide some durable structure to expectations.

Moreover, an institution can take on a life of its own, beyond what its designers envisioned, and create unanticipated by-products. Policy environments are uncertain. Policymakers may be motivated to resolve or manage a dilemma, but due to uncertainty they cannot anticipate all contingencies—especially given that many of those contingencies will appear only in the future and in the context of future change. If policymakers could anticipate all future possibilities, there would be no uncertainty to influence decisions.

For example, the policymakers who created the European Court of Justice (ECJ) never envisioned the extent to which the court would intervene in national polities to establish new rights and expectations across the EU. Yet through their rulings, the justices of the ECJ extended its mandate and reach beyond the boundaries anticipated by its creators. Individual member states of the EU have at one time or another become disgruntled by ECJ rulings that interfere in their domestic arenas and force governments to shift state-society bargains. Today, significantly reining in the institutional reach of the ECJ and returning to the intentions of its designers would require members of the EU to risk destroying the ECJ and endangering the cooperation that underpins the EU. An unwillingness to take such risks provides some insulation for the ECJ to continue to expand its mandate.

Origins of Institutions

Institutions may be consciously designed and created, but they may also emerge without conscious design as a consequence of human activity that becomes regularized, generating expectations that influence future activity. Encountering uncertainty and risk, policymakers attempt to rationally design institutions to constrain some human behavior and create incentives for other human activity. Policymakers embark on the writing of constitutions, bodies of law and statutes, and regulations and administrative guidelines with conscious intent to steer, motivate, and engineer human activity, but conflict in the process of writing such rules may cloud their rational intentions. Difficult cooperation problems rarely engender universal agreement over an institutional solution, especially given the likely prospects of distributional consequences of different rules, and so institutional design often incorporates compromise that muddies intentions and distorts intended incentives. Nevertheless, these rules are ex ante attempts at rational institutional design with an objective of conditioning human activity. Of course, the success of institutions is more than simply a matter of their construction, but also of their subsequent acceptance, interpretation, and enforcement by society.

To have any chance at rationally designing a successful institution requires a keen understanding of society, the preferences and capabilities of different groups and individuals in society, the legacy of past institutional arrangements, the potential for interaction with other formal and informal institutions, and an ability to anticipate the consequences of a variety of hypothetical institutional arrangements. This is a formidable list of requirements, but policymakers who attempt to design an ideal institution without such understanding are doomed to failure, often quashing expectations and undermining confidence in the governments that have adopted the institution. The world is littered with examples of such failures, despite good intentions. Policymakers at international development organizations as well as private consultants have counseled governments of developing and transitional states in the design of new institutions that are intended to advance the transition toward more effective political economies. Often, they have simply transplanted institutions that worked in some of the advanced industrialized states (e.g., the Washington Consensus) to new arenas. More often than not, these institutions fail in their new environment or require substantial alteration before they can produce significant benefits.

Even with clear knowledge of society, the different interests in society and their preferences, and the path contingency of previous institutional arrangements, policymakers require substantial luck in designing an institution that works as anticipated. As thorough and diligent as a group of intelligent policymakers may be, they cannot anticipate all contingencies. Institutions that appear well-designed beforehand can lead to unintended consequences that either instill greater confidence in the institution, undermine it, or transform it to another purpose. Successful institutional design requires some luck and some art to accompany good social science engineering, if it is to create incentives that actually lead to the intended outcome.

Many institutions and institutional changes—particularly informal ones—emerge from a far less deliberate process. As people interact, patterns may emerge that affect expectations about their future activity. These patterns often emerge incrementally, as small changes and frequent interactions add up over time to create a significant transformation in human activity. These patterns can reduce uncertainty, stabilize expectations, and create incentives to make some choices versus others. If so, they have intermediated the calculus of decision makers and imposed an independent effect upon those calculations. If such patterns and expectations become firmer and more extensive in their reach across larger portions of society, they begin to have the effect of becoming rules of the game. Sometimes policymakers build formal institutions upon the foundations of such informal institutions and established patterns of activity, and this correspondence between formal and informal practices often produces the most effective and durable formal institutions. For example, according to Nicholas Katzenbach, the U.S. attorney general in the Johnson administration, successful international law consists of the codification of existing practices.

Institutions as Devices to Overcome the Time Inconsistency Dilemma

As an ex ante agreement or bargain about future cooperation and interactions, an institution can help to overcome the time inconsistency dilemma that hampers policymakers. This problem reflects the temptation that policymakers face to defect on long-term commitments to policies that benefit society in an effort to realize short-term political gains. A successful institution creates expectations about behavior that can limit this latitude and tie the hands of policymakers by increasing the costs of reneging on the agreement. Defecting from an institution that has gained traction and durability and has succeeded in establishing expectations and conditioning behavior is generally far more costly than changing policy or reneging in a social exchange that does not have institutional status. The development of reputation and value in the institution creates an investment in maintaining the rules of the game, which increases the cost of reneging on the institution. Violating the institution is thus more than a one-shot expense, for it tears at the investment that went into building the institution.

Policymakers, faced with the temptation to defect on an agreement in order to enhance their short-term political survival, can design institutions to intentionally increase the costs of defection from long-term social bargains. Effectively, they use institutional design to attempt to tie their own hands so they will not succumb to short-term pressures to violate these long-term commitments. For example, policymakers face continual pressures to manage the economy—to promote growth or encourage price stability. Workers often want an expanding economy and job creation, while holders of capital worry about inflationary expansion that could eat away at the value of their assets. Such pressures become especially acute at election time or other crises of political survival, and politicians are then sorely tempted to use monetary policy to appeal to these interests even if they are likely to produce policy that undermines expectations and creates risks that may damage economic activity in the long term.

Ideally, we want monetary policy that limits economic volatility, avoiding swings between too much inflation and too little economic stimulus. Such economic engineering is extremely difficult, as economies are complex and their causal mechanisms remain somewhat mysterious. But the difficulties of such engineering are compounded when politicians seek to manage monetary policy for short-term gains. We can look around the world and find political economies suffering under excessive inflation, languishing with low, even negative, real growth as they bounce from one extreme to another. Economic actors find such environments discouraging because they cannot estimate their risks or calculate an expected rate of return. If they have alternatives, they will avoid such environments. Perversely, policymakers' efforts to ensure their political survival by responding to constituent pressures can do severe damage to a political economy's long-term prospects—another social trap.

Many states have enacted laws that, if enforced, create independent central banks to manage monetary policy. These are government organizations, but their enabling legislation seeks to provide central bankers with some insulation from political pressures. To be successful at creating and maintaining a relatively autonomous central bank, policymakers must develop institutions and strategies that limit their ability to manipulate monetary policy for short-term political gain and allow the central bankers to manage monetary policy with a long-term view as to what is best for society. Effectively, politicians must tie their hands and transfer responsibility for monetary policy to more insulated policymakers. A host of strategies can help to limit the ability of politicians to renege on their commitments to an autonomous central bank and relatively apolitical monetary policy. Elected officials may appoint professional bankers and economists with specialized skills and knowledge that provides them with some insulation from political pressure. Central bankers may serve terms of longer duration than those of elected officials, or their terms in office may be staggered to avoid overlap with elections and political terms. They may be protected from being fired by politicians or insulated from the budgetary mechanisms of the government, which would prevent other policymakers from pressuring the central bank through manipulation of the budget or by threats of dismissal.

These strategies to limit the ability of politicians to interfere with the activities of central bankers are examples of institutional design that is intended to make a unit of government less responsive to political pressures—to protect a policy arena from democratic influence. Ironically, the Washington Consensus prescribes an independent central bank to manage monetary policy at a time of democratic expansion. The desire to construct institutions that encourage democratic responsiveness and, at the same time, insulate politicians from socially perverse short-term pressures poses interesting tensions and challenges for policymakers. We can find examples of similar institutions—such as the construction of an independent judiciary with lifetime tenure, in order to insulate the law from short-term temptations for politicians to interfere in court proceedings. Many quasi-independent regulatory agencies in various countries are also constructed to overcome the time inconsistency problem. If such institutional devices succeed, they make short-term actions harmonious or consistent with long-term objectives. They increase the shadow of the future by tying the present to future goals.

IMPORTANT INSTITUTIONAL CONSIDERATIONS

Examples of institutions dot the landscape of domestic and global affairs. We have already examined rules of the game that play significant roles in our political and economic lives and history. The informal law of the market, when unimpeded, forces individuals to respond to the pressures of comparative advantage (another institution) as it creates incentives to either continue or change their productive activities. The Corn Law, a rule that intervened in market exchange, protected British agricultural producers and created incentives that allowed them to continue engaging in inefficient agricultural production instead of finding more socially productive outlets. The institution of most-favored-nation status (MFN) promoted the expansion of trade during the 1800s and again in the post–World War II era. The break-down in domestic and global economic activity was advanced by the adoption of informal and formal beggar-thy-neighbor rules. A cooperative set of rules and interactions broke down as the emergence of an "anything goes" rule created incentives for policymakers to raise trade barriers and engage in competitive currency devaluations.

Negotiators at Bretton Woods designed a monetary system around a set of institutions that defined when a currency was incorrectly valued and how a government could adjust its exchange rate. The Smithsonian Agreement shifted those rules, but only marginally. Perhaps as influential as the formal institutions of the Bretton Woods and Smithsonian monetary system, the adherence of governments to informal practices of restraint contributed to the success of postwar monetary arrangements. An institutional change, the Second Amend-ment to the IMF Articles of Agreement, eliminated the role of gold as a reserve asset, legal-ized floating exchange rates, and encouraged a stable system of exchange rates to replace the Bretton Woods system of stable exchange rates.

Containment depended upon formal and informal rules between the Western democra-cies about what should and should not be exported to the Eastern bloc political economies. Since World War II, the system of global capitalism has been extended by the adoption and creation of new institutions built upon previous institutions. Much institutional develop-ment is path-contingent, but much uncertainty also remains. Incentives are not always con-sistent with global capitalism, and governments often implement polices that produce bar-riers to cooperation and risk for market exchange. Path contingency is not inevitable, as inconsistencies in policymaking occur frequently. We place much of the blame for such out-comes upon the problems of political and economic market failure and social traps.

We can look at institutional arrangements within and across states in order to discover how they affect policy outcomes, create or mitigate social traps, and influence the nature of politics and the resolution of cooperation and coordination problems. As a beginning, we can construct a broad framework of institutional considerations to assist us in examining human activity and recognizing differences in policy outcomes from one national arena to another. We will quickly consider institutional variations in regime type, electoral systems, structure of government and relationships between components of governments, and social institutions. With respect to our interest in global affairs, such institutional considerations are important for distinguishing different national approaches toward the processes of glob-alization, but they also help us to understand differences in domestic politics.

Regime Type

At the most basic level, we classify regimes as either authoritarian or democratic. The rules of the game in democratic regimes accept, even encourage, involvement by a broader range of society in the affairs of governance than do the rules in authoritarian regimes. Usually, this democratic inclusiveness creates more varied demands on policymakers than are likely to be made in authoritarian regimes, and it can complicate the lives and decision processes of policymakers—more constituents to please to ensure political survival, and more who can be angered. But this broader base also creates the possibility for countervailing interests to emerge and advance their cases in policy debates. These pressures can work against each other, thus constraining policymakers from moving too far in one direction or another. As a consequence of needing to appeal to constituents for reelection, democratic leaders must be more conscious of the implications of their policy choices for a broader range of society. Independent of other institutional considerations, simply having a broader swath of diverse and mobilized interests involved in policy debates can both limit policy mobility and arbitrariness and promote compromise. Policymakers are likely to discover that their options are more limited when they are faced with a wider range of constituencies. Trying to please more people and constituencies limits their actions and often produces compromise outcomes that sit between the preferences of different groups—essentially taking the average or splitting the difference.

Authoritarian leaders, while still facing constraints, rely upon much narrower constituencies for their political survival, and there are fewer societal checks and balances to limit their policy flexibility. In successful democratic regimes, the rules of the game are embedded in bodies of formal law and informal practice, and changing those rules usually involves following established procedures that increase transparency and accountability to society. Authoritarian leaders, however, often enjoy greater unilateral influence over the rules of the game and can change those rules with less recourse to established practices and procedures. These leaders are usually more able to arbitrarily replace members of their governments or to redesign their governments than are the leaders of democratic regimes.

Democracies usually enjoy more established and transparent rules of transition or regime change. In successful democracies, elections occur at predictable intervals and the shifting of the reins of power is accomplished with regularity and established procedures. This regularity contributes to greater stability of expectations as one regime hands over governing power and responsibilities to another. Economic and social actors generally prefer such stability to wider variations that can constrain planning ahead far into the future. Even less successful democracies tend to limit such variations, as they attempt to hold elections at predictable intervals and through established procedures. Such electoral processes may be corrupted, but they are still more transparent and predictable than regime change in authoritarian states.

The rules of transition and regime change in authoritarian governments are far less transparent and predictable. The lines of succession are often ad hoc, which creates uncertainty as leaders become vulnerable due to processes such as aging, increasing societal rejection, or elite discomfort. Sometimes an authoritarian leader succeeds at stepping down and transferring power to another family member or a hand-picked successor, but often regime change in authoritarian states takes place as a consequence of a coup or an episode of social disruption, sometimes violent. With the exception of monarchical succession, neither process is embedded in established procedures or rules that domestic and foreign observers can understand and anticipate. Lacking transparency and predictability, regime change in authoritarian states generates greater uncertainty and risk to economic and social actors than does regime change in democratic states. Even if some authoritarian rulers wield the reins of power wisely and productively for their societies, there is no guarantee that their successors will be as wise and productive. This lack of certainty is also true in democratic regimes, but the ability of constituents to reject a leader at the polls and gain greater access to policymakers works to constrain policymakers, good or bad. Deficient policymakers in democratic societies burden their societies less than do similarly deficient leaders in authoritarian regimes.

Electoral Systems

Electoral rules and systems vary from one democracy to another, as do the pathways of ascension to office in authoritarian regimes. Such variations in rules and processes can influence the nature of politics and policies within states and, consequently, between states in the global arena. Let's focus on the electoral rules of democratic regimes, because they tend to be more transparent and durable than the means of ascension and succession in authoritarian states. They are more likely to constitute institutional arrangements than are the ad hoc transfers of power that often characterize authoritarian states. Some democratic polities elect their governments by a plurality rule, while many others use some form of a proportional electoral rule.

Only the leading vote-getter is elected to office under a plurality or winner-take-all rule. We considered such a system and some of its implications for politics in chapter 6. Some plurality rules require that the winner receive a majority and not simply a plurality of the votes cast. Iran has such a rule for election of its president, and Louisiana uses such a rule for its statewide elected offices. In elections contested by more than two candidates, such majority rules sometimes lead to a run-off election between the top two vote-getters when none of the candidates has received a majority of the votes cast in the first round. But most plurality electoral systems—most notably that of the United States—elect the candidate who simply receives the most votes. In such systems, a candidate may receive 49.9 percent of the vote yet fail to gain office. The term *winner-take-all* is apropos, as such systems potentially ignore the interests of those citizens who voted for the losing candidate even if they make up a significant portion of the electorate—the electoral process ensures that the winning candidate must pay attention to the voters who elected her and can choose to ignore the concerns of those whose candidate lost. These electoral losers must worry about minority rights even if they make up almost 50 percent of the electorate.

Politicians in polities with proportional electoral rules (including most West European democracies) gain office if they surpass an established threshold or proportion of the total vote—for example, a 10 percent threshold. This means that particular parts of an electorate or special interests can obtain representation in the legislature even if their proportion of the vote is relatively small. Minority candidates can target a specific issue or portion of the political spectrum and still gain office even while ignoring the preferences of the majority. This type of electoral system offers a greater likelihood that minority interests will be better represented through the electoral process than does a plurality system. Proportional election rules can enable them to advance their agenda, trade votes, wheel and deal, and participate in governing coalitions, whereas in a winner-take-all system, they would be left on the sideline. In highly fragmented proportional governments, a small minority party can wield unusual influence and extract substantial concessions from far larger parties by providing the necessary votes to ensure a governing coalition. In proportional systems, larger parties may face substantial risk if they ignore the smaller groups that are often ignored in a winner-take-all system.

In proportional systems, voters often select their candidates from a party list—they are essentially voting for the party attached to the candidate's name. This process reinforces party unity and ideological attachment to a party, which helps to limit the "cult of personality" or candidate-centered campaigns that can dominate in winner-take-all systems such as the United States. Recognizing that voters are supporting a party more than a specific candidate, some proportional systems allow the transfer of votes to other candidates on the party list, if one or more candidates exceed the threshold necessary for election. This device, known as a single-vote, transferable system, also helps to strengthen party cohesion, as the success of candidates depends upon the success of their parties. Other proportional systems are single-vote, non-transferable. A variety of other plausible proportional systems reflect the efforts of policymakers to structure electoral systems to engineer particular types of outcomes and to overcome barriers to such outcomes. As such, electoral rules, like other institutions, are also targets of political competition.

Differences in electoral institutions, from plurality to proportional systems, can affect party cohesion, determining whether politics and parties will converge on centrist policies and the median voter, or whether parties and politicians can be successful away from the center and the median voter. Differences in electoral rules influence whether a political arena can support three or more stable political parties or will inevitably converge on a two-party system. Consequently, electoral rules prescribe the nature of political competition in a society, as well as the manner in which interests will organize, and the type of coalition-building we should expect in legislatures and among interest groups.

For example, the winner-take-all electoral rule discussed in chapter 6 pushes political campaigns, political advertising and rhetoric, and electoral competition toward the political center as defined by the median voter in an election. This pressure works against the success of relatively extremist candidates and parties and rewards those who can move to the center. Of course, we are still assuming that politicians want to win and then to remain in office. Voters will vote for the party or candidate closest to their preferences, yet, even in a population with strong disagreements and a distribution of voters away from the middle, the median voter will dictate the long-term outcomes of an electoral process under a plurality rule, for politicians and parties must appeal to this voter in order to win. Their poor prospects for electoral reward force extremist elements to choose between supporting more centrist candidates and assisting the victory of a candidate who is even more distant on the political spectrum. Parties and candidates will converge, thus removing extremist debates and issues from the electoral agenda and possibly constraining the winner of an election from pushing such policies once elected if she worries about her electoral future. This centripetal effect makes it difficult, if not impossible, for a third party to emerge and remain viable over an extended period.

Proportional electoral institutions enable a wider range of interests to gain political power and representation. Allowing access to electoral office based upon a prescribed proportion of the vote, even if not a plurality, allows more specialized interests to hold to their policy positions, not moving to the center, and yet remaining viable in the electoral arena. A more diverse range of societal interests can populate a legislature, influence a legislative calendar and agenda, and produce unpredictable coalitions as interests trade their votes to advance their particularistic objectives. Because electoral rules are likely to affect the organization of a legislature and government, which produces differences in political agendas and coalition politics from one political arena to another, this institutional design has implications for the nature of political discourse and interest group activity in the broader society. In global affairs, such variations in electoral rules can contribute to state-by-state differences in policy debates over trade, immigration, national security, capital mobility, and economic policy, as well as willingness to cooperate and coordinate in the global arena.

Structure of Government

Relationships between components of governments are strongly structured by institutions. In most states, constitutions provide the working plans for the structure of government. Constitutions, as institutions, influence the organization of authority in a state, assign responsibilities, help to define how the game of politics will be played between government authorities, and consequently serve to structure political activity throughout society. A government's form affects how it and its society functions. Is the legislative arm separate from the executive arm of government; is the judiciary independent, or are judges responsive to societal pressures or influence from other parts of government; does a government have a federal or nonfederal structure, which affects the lines of authority between national and local governments; are regulatory agencies exposed to political pressures, or are they relatively autonomous; is the civil service based on meritocracy and professionalism or on patronage; and how responsive must bureaucracies be to their political masters?

Relationships between executive and legislative functions fall into two broad categories in democratic systems: presidential and parliamentary. In presidential systems, the executive functions of government are separated by design from the legislative functions. The executive and members of the legislature seek election independently of each other. Their electoral hopes are clearly linked by issues, but voters have the opportunity to vote for members of one party to hold legislative office and for another party to hold executive office. This separation of electoral fortunes creates an opportunity for divided government, wherein different parties hold the reins of power in the legislature and the executive.

Even without divided government, the need to seek election independently of the other branch of government creates a wedge between the legislative and executive functions of government. Separating legislative and executive electoral outcomes introduces differing incentives that may not overlap between the executive and legislature, even among members of the same party. The executive or members of the legislature may find it useful to disagree or attack each other, even if within the same party. Legislators can undermine the policies of an executive from their party and damage her reelection chances without necessarily hurting their own political survival. In fact, showing a streak of independence from an executive within their own party can sometimes be a good electoral strategy for legislators in a presidential system, but hardly ever in a parliamentary system. The electoral separation of the executive and legislature in a presidential system can thus undercut party cohesion and allow external forces such as political and economic geography, regionalism, and sectoral interests to garner influence through the legislature, even if the executive has a broader national objective.

In parliamentary systems, the executive and legislative functions—and, hence, their fortunes—are tightly linked. The executive is elected as a member of the legislature and usually leads the party that controls the most seats in the legislature (although, with coalition governments in a proportional system, it is conceivable, if unlikely, that a member of another party in the governing coalition could serve as the chief executive). Following an election, the head of state offers the leader of the party that has won control of the legislature the opportunity to form a government. (In most parliamentary systems, the head of state and the head of government are separate roles held by different individuals, whereas in presidential systems these roles are usually combined.) In a parliamentary system, the executive and the head of the dominant party in the legislature are generally the same person.

Moreover, as head of the dominant party in the legislature, the executive appoints legislative members from her party, or from parties that make up a coalition government, to serve as ministers of the different executive bureaucracies (such as Finance or Treasury, Defense, Trade or Commerce, Foreign Affairs, Interior). These ministers make up the executive's cabinet. Again, a minister is an elected member of the legislature who has been asked to run a department in the executive branch. This arrangement gives an elected legislative official, one who is responsive to an electoral base, control over a pool or portfolio of resources to allocate. Ministers can use this pool of resources to feather their electoral nests. In presidential systems, cabinet members are separate from the legislature; they are appointed, not elected, officials. Each cabinet member does control a pool or portfolio of resources, but a larger divide separates these appointed officials from the electoral base. Their political survival depends more on the executive and her reelection than on the legislature and its reelection. This dependence can influence their responsiveness to the electorate and to the executive.

Because the executive is the head of the dominant party in the legislature in parliamentary systems, her electoral fortunes are tightly linked to those of the other members of the legislature from her party, as well as to those of members from the parties of the governing coalition. When the legislature overrides the preferences of the executive—signifying that enough members of the governing coalition have disagreed with the executive to reject her leadership—this action is called a "vote of no confidence," and it usually leads to the fall of the government in a parliamentary system. In presidential systems, legislatures can, and often do, vote against the expressed wishes of the executive without bringing down their governments. In a parliamentary system, a vote of no confidence can lead to a new election, but a new government can also be formed without an election. The dominant party may elect a new party leader, who then forms a new government, or, after an exercise of party discipline, party members may reaffirm their support for the present leader, who then gets to form a government anew. The parliamentary form of government gives the executive far more influence over the legislative agenda and legislative machinations than is exercised by the executive in a presidential system, but it also makes the executive more sensitive to her party's interests and acutely concerned about disagreements among members of her party in the legislature. It increases the importance of party cohesion.

The structure of political systems can also differ in the degree of centralization of authority. Federal systems divide responsibilities and authority between national and regional (state and local) governments. With federalism, regional governments enjoy significant autonomy and powers separate from those of the national government. The national government always holds the primary responsibility for national security, but the allocation of other responsibilities, such as education, economic management, fiscal policy, local policing, and adjudication, can vary from one federal system to another and, over time, within the same system. Such decentralization of responsibilities and authority creates a patchwork of rules and discontinuities both among subnational governments in federal systems and between the subnational governments and the national government.

Federal structures are sometimes considered inefficient in terms of governance because the rules of the game can shift from one subnational authority to the next, from one locality to another. Gray areas and ambiguity inevitably appear. Problems may arise between national and subnational governments over which level of government can exercise authority in particular policy areas and over where policy responsibilities—and blame for policy failures—should fall. Also, private actors can exploit such governmental fragmentation. Economic enterprises considering relocation routinely play one subnational government against another in federal systems, using competition among these regional governments as a bargaining strategy to extract concessions, such as tax abatements or breaks, school improvements, infrastructure investments, or labor concessions. In federal systems, regional governments thus compete for investment, resources, people, and programs. In the best cases of intergovernmental competition, this competition can feed policy innovation and creative destruction in the public sector; in the worst cases, it can increase disparities across regions or promote a race to the bottom, in which the governments sacrifice their ability to manage their local economies and cushion against volatile downturns.

In federal systems, the decentralization of authority provides a check on the exercise of authority. Disagreements between levels of government and across subnational governments can limit policy volatility and mobility, which helps to stabilize expectations. But such disagreements and discontinuities can also produce uncertainty and potential crisis if they create significant intergovernmental conflict. Often, such disputes involve constitutional issues that must be adjudicated by the courts responsible for constitutional questions. Other times, legislative action by the central government helps to manage such disputes by clarifying responsibilities and authority. Occasionally, however, such disputes turn into full-fledged constitutional crises, which can explode and threaten the legitimacy of the mechanisms of government, or even precipitate civil conflict.

Lines of authority are much clearer in nonfederal systems. Authority is more centralized, and subnational governments enjoy far less autonomy from the national government than in federal systems. Regional governments are extensions, or subunits, of the national government. What autonomy they do exercise is more a function of the authority expressly granted to them by the central government, or an unintentional side effect of being out of sight and out of mind. In such systems, private citizens cannot as easily shop around for government concessions, playing one government off against another, for the central government limits and directs such competition.

Let's quickly turn to one other set of considerations related to the institutional structure of government: the degree of independence and professionalism of the judiciary, regulatory agencies, and the bureaucracy. The institutional design of governments can vary in terms of whether members of the judiciary are insulated and relatively independent from societal and political pressures as they adjudicate cases, or are relatively exposed to societal pressures or influence from other parts of government. All judges are part of their societies, and they usually recognize the political and societal limitations on their judicial discretion. Judges generally resolve disputes by seeking a solution that a majority of members of society will find tolerable, but judges who are relatively well shielded by institutional design from political and societal pressures are generally more able to rule consistently—and, hopefully, fairly—than are judges who are less insulated by institutional design. A less insulated judiciary may shift rulings as the winds of politics change, or as different groups become mobilized. Institutional features such as lifetime tenure, required professional training and experience in the law, and nonpartisan election can help to shelter judges from the time inconsistency dilemma that politicians often face.

The same institutional considerations of independence and professionalism apply to regulatory agencies and government bureaucracies. These institutional considerations are important variables to consider as we try to understand why governments do what they do in the global arena. How exposed are the employees of government agencies to political pressures? Do the rules of the game produce a civil service based on meritocracy and professionalism or one that is grounded in patronage and corruption? Does the institutional setup of government create incentives for bureaucracies to be responsive to their political masters, or are the incentives of bureaucrats structured to encourage them to do their jobs as professionals even if political winds blow in another direction? Earlier, we examined such considerations in the context of central banks, but the same questions apply across government agencies.

Social Institutions

Most of this chapter focuses on formal and informal political institutions. We would be negligent, however, if we failed to discuss the importance of social institutions, because they also help to make up the political arena, affect uncertainty and risk in society, and sometimes spill over to influence global affairs. For example, social institutions and practices such as labor-management agreements over work rules and wages shape the rules of the game in workplaces over extended periods. These practices can reduce uncertainty in labor-management relations; constrain dysfunctional conflicts between labor and management; limit such disagreements to proscribed periods and condition the form of conflict; allow economic enterprises to price their labor costs for a specified period; and overcome potential time-inconsistency and social-trap problems that tempt both labor and management.

Following World War II, some societies produced a social bargain, a set of social institutions, called *corporatism.* In corporatist states such as West Germany, labor, capital, and the government arrived at an informal agreement concerning the boundaries and nature of labor-capital conflict, the provision of social welfare goods by the state to cushion workers during dislocations, and the state's commitment to ensure a stable macroeconomic arena to protect the assets of capital. The parties involved in the creation of the informal bargains and institutions of corporatism hoped that by establishing such rules of the game they could avoid the disruptions, political extremism, and violent cleavages that had appeared during the interwar years.

Social institutions, like political institutions, may prove dysfunctional. Many of the labor institutions and social bargains that proved so effective and productive in European states in the postwar period now produce unintended and costly consequences. Today, labor institutions in much of the EU create disproportionately high labor costs for economic enterprise and produce incentives for companies to avoid adding new full-time employees. Many of the labor institutions require a transfer of resources to the state to subsidize social insurance programs for society. Because these costs are generally assessed for each full-time employee, many firms prefer to hire multiple part-time workers rather than individual full-time workers to fill positions. This preference has led to structural stickiness in European labor markets, relatively high unemployment, and a quandary for unions, management, and governments.

Labor bargains in the United States once promoted stability in labor relations and the development of a reliable workforce in many unionized industries, such as automobile and steel manufacturing. But today the durability of such bargains generates significant legacy costs for many of these industries. Many U.S. manufacturers owe significant pension and health-care obligations to their retired, or soon-to-be-retired, workers as a consequence of past labor agreements. In the past, agreements to provide such benefits reduced labor strife, reduced uncertainty in labor-management relations, and contributed to the competitiveness of those companies, but in today's business environment, with its aging population, such obligations detract from competitiveness, as more and more of a companies' revenues are committed to paying such legacy costs. These costs reduce the amount of resources that are available for research and development, physical capital improvements, and worker training.

Social institutions can affect the nature and violence of societal divisions and disagreements. No society is homogenous; group identities and interests fragment all societies—some more virulently than others. In some societies, social institutions have been created or have evolved to mitigate and manage potentially disruptive disagreements across group boundaries. In other states, the absence of social institutions to bridge groups and societal cleavages can reinforce incentives for groups to resort to discriminatory tactics, and even violence.

In the aftermath of the disintegration of the Eastern bloc and the Soviet Union, nongovernmental and governmental organizations have sponsored projects that target the construction of civil society in transitional political economies. Such projects seek to advance the building of strong civil societies, which are characterized by an increasing density of social institutions that promote tolerance and bridge societal divisions. These initiatives are designed to promote stability and reduce uncertainty and risk in social relations, which can spill over to political and economic affairs—domestically and internationally.

Veto Points: Institutional Checks and Balances

Ideally, as social scientists interested in the influence of institutions upon global affairs, we want to examine how institutional differences from one political arena to another may contribute to variations in social outcomes and policies. Do variations in the institutional make-up of political economies provide us with analytic leverage for understanding differences in trade policies, monetary policies, policies regarding the external value of currencies, the ability to attract foreign and domestic investment, the incentives for economic enterprises to take risks on the future and expand their activities or to engage in corrupt practices and extract extralegal rents from economic actors, the capacity of legal arenas to fairly adjudicate disagreements, or a society's proclivity for engaging in extralegal means of government replacement? Or does focusing on too many institutional variations from one society to the next serve to overwhelm the systematic analysis that can lead to useful, generalizable statements about the influence of institutions upon social activity? Does describing too many differences from case to case simply undermine the search for commonality and generalizability by making each case appear to be unique? At some level, each case is unique, but we may find that by focusing upon critical relationships in society we can make statements that often carry across societies—a difference that separates the social sciences from the humanities.

So, when we examine institutions, what are we trying to learn? Simply, we want to understand how the rules of the game constrain, motivate, or condition individual choices and social outcomes. From this perspective, we would like to discover and report whether an institutional environment permits an individual to act without restraint or whether it limits her actions, penalizes her behavior, or counterbalances her individual actions. In effect, we seek to understand the checks and balances in institutional settings. This focus allows us to simplify the description of institutional settings and more easily compare one institutional setting to another. Instead of exploring the variety and nuances of institutional arrangements, we ask whether an institutional environment imposes more or less discipline in the form of checks and balances on policymakers—and how much more or less. Differences in electoral systems, structure of government, and regime type can be boiled down into a simple description of the constraints upon policymakers.

We call such institutionally created checks and balances **veto points** in a political economy. Veto points are instances in which a policymaker faces constraints, checks, or countervailing pressures that limit her ability to unilaterally select a course of action. The fewer the veto points in a political economy, the greater the ability of a policymaker to unilaterally decide policy. Where there are more veto points, a policymaker must build support for policies among a wider range of constituencies. For example, in an authoritarian regime, a policymaker encounters far fewer institutional veto points than does a policymaker in a democratic regime with a federal structure and separation between the executive and the legislature. A system with fewer veto points is conducive to a policymaker unilaterally and arbitrarily shifting course if she so desires—which can feed policy volatility and uncertainty in political economies. Conversely, a policymaker facing multiple veto points or players generally has far less policy flexibility—which limits policy volatility and can reduce uncertainty.

We lose the nuance of institutional differences in such generalized characterizations of political economies, but hopefully we capture important comparable factors that help to explain variations in political behavior. There are limitations to such a summary approach to institutional settings. By definition, institutions are supposedly durable, which means that institutional settings are sticky and do not change quickly overtime. But policies can change, and if policies shift while the institutional setting as characterized by veto points remains the same, we may encounter a problem of assigning causal responsibility to the institutional setting. We can overcome this dilemma by disaggregating the veto points and examining specific institutions to discover whether institutional arrangements are, or are not, influential, but this disaggregation limits comparability and generalizability. The strength of the summary approach comes when comparing across cases. Here, even though the summarization of the institutional setting and institutional checks and balances should vary little within each case, variations across cases can provide leverage that allows us to understand and anticipate the nature of political conflict or cooperation from society to society, the nature of policy volatility from state to state, and the different abilities of societies to overcome social traps and create productive social environments. This comparative process can lead to a fuller understanding of social behavior and provide insights that may help policymakers to design institutional settings that can improve the lot of their societies.

CONCLUSION

Institutions can reduce uncertainty, produce incentives, constrain options, induce equilibrium, influence the shadow of the future, create ex ante bargains over future actions, and affect the time inconsistency problem. Normatively good institutions limit destructive individual actions, extend the shadow of the future, overcome the time inconsistency problem, lead to better equilibria, and help societies to overcome barriers to cooperation and social traps. But dysfunctional institutions can generate perverse incentives that encourage individuals to engage in actions that damage social welfare, lead to poor equilibria, exacerbate the time inconsistency problem, and perpetuate social traps. We have noted that many institutional alternatives exist across political economies. Differences in regime type, electoral systems, structure of government, social bargains and arrangements, and other institutional arrangements create tremendous variation in the nature of institutions and their potential effects across political arenas.

EXERCISES

1. Using the definition of an institution in this chapter, is the WTO an institution? Why or why not?

2. What is the difference between a formal and an informal institution? Give examples of each type, and explain why each fits its respective category.

3. Do formal institutions exist in international affairs, given the definition of a formal institution? Explain.

4. How can an institution be an equilibrium?

5. Give an example of an institution that affects global affairs and helps to overcome the time inconsistency problem. Explain how it promotes time-consistent behavior.

6. Give an example of an institution that shortens the shadow of the future and encourages individuals to act against the well-being of their society. Why does it do this?

Now give an example of an institution that extends the shadow of the future and encourages individuals to make choices that improve long-term social welfare. Why does it do this?

7. Provide an example of an institution that affects global affairs, and discuss the distributional implications of that institution. Who wins and who loses?

8. Explain why institutions may be sticky and durable. Why are many institutions slow to change?

9. Give an example of an informal institution in world affairs and explain why it is an institution.

10. Hypothesize how differences between a winner-take-all electoral system and a proportional electoral system might affect international trade policy. Explain your reasoning.

11. Central bank independence has become a popular institutional topic, explanatory mechanism, and variable in international and comparative political economy. How does central bank independence act as an institution?

FURTHER READING

Calvert, Randall. 1995. "The Rational Choice Theory of Social Institutions: Cooperation, Coordination, and Communication." In *Modern Political Economy: Old Topics, New Directions*, ed. J. Banks and E. Hanushek. New York: Cambridge University Press.

Clague, Christopher, Philip Keefer, Stephen Knack, and Mancur Olson. 1996. "Property and Contract Rights under Democracy and Dictatorship." *Journal of Economic Growth*, June, 243–276.

Cukierman, Alex, Steven Webb, and Bilin Neyapti. 1992. "Measuring the Independence of Central Banks and Its Effect on Policy Outcomes." *World Bank Economic Review* 6 (1): 353–398.

Filippov, Mikhail, Peter C. Ordeshook, and Olga Shvetsova. 2004. *Designing Federalism: A Theory of Self-Sustainable Federal Institutions*. Cambridge: Cambridge University Press.

Garrett, Geoffrey, and Peter Lange. 1995. "Internationalization, Institutions, and Political Change." *International Organization* 49 (4): 627–655.

Knight, Jack. 1992. *Institutions and Social Conflict*. Cambridge: Cambridge University Press.

Maxfield, Sylvia. 1997. *Gatekeepers of Growth*. Princeton, N.J.: Princeton University Press.

North, Douglass C. 1990. *Institutions, Institutional Change, and Economic Performance*. Cambridge: Cambridge University Press.

North, Douglass C., and Barry R. Weingast. 1989. "Constitutions and Commitment: Evolution of Institutions Governing Public Choice in 17th Century England." *Journal of Economic History* 49: 803–832.

Olson, Mancur. 1993. "Dictatorship, Democracy and Development." *American Political Science Review* 87 (3): 567–576.

Schotter, Andrew. 1981. *The Economic Theory of Social Institutions*. Cambridge: Cambridge University Press.

Shepsle, Kenneth A. 1986. "Institutional Equilibrium and Equilibrium Institutions." In *Political Science: The Science of Politics*, ed. Herbert Weisberg. New York: Agathon Press.

Glossary

The chapters in which the terms are defined follow each definition.

absolute advantage   A nation's ability to produce a particular commodity more efficiently than other nations (5)

agenda-setters   Actors whose actions constrain the choices of others and direct them toward a limited menu of choices (4)

anarchy   A characterization of the relations between states in the global arena; the lack of an overarching central authority to resolve disagreements, which creates a social context that is open to competition and cooperation, dispute and disagreement, negotiation and compromise, and, sometimes, violent conflict (3)

arbitrage opportunities   Situations in which an individual can purchase in one market an asset that she believes is systematically overvalued or undervalued and then move it to another market, sell it for a gain, or use it to purchase another asset (7)

asset mobility   The capacity for an asset of production to be easily transferred to another factor of production, such as some workers' ability to switch jobs more easily than other workers or the relative ease of selling a stock portfolio versus selling a factory (14)

asymmetric information   A situation in which one party involved in an exchange knows more about the commodity being exchanged than the other parties do (5)

Atlantic economy   The political economies of western and southern Europe, North America, Australia, and Japan—today the core members of the Organization for Economic Cooperation and Development (OECD) (1)

autarky   A policy that seeks complete isolation from the global economy; self-sufficiency (1)

backward induction   The process of examining a decision in reverse, in order to try to understand the rational calculations that could lead to such a decision (2)

balance of payments   An accounting of all the goods, services, and capital exported and imported across national borders, reflecting a nation's economic interactions with those in other nations (5)

banker's acceptances   Financial instruments that a party to an exchange can obtain from her bank to lower the risk of nonpayment of an obligation across national boundaries; *see* letters of credit (7)

beggar-thy-neighbor policies   The use of trade or monetary policies, such as tariff systems or the exchange-rate system, to promote the welfare of one nation's producers and labor at the expense, and relative impoverishment, of other nations' producers and labor (8)

bilateral trade negotiations   A nation-to-nation reciprocal trade agreement that is undertaken by two sides equally and is binding on both parties (7)

budgetary constraints   Limits on the amount of money or resources that one can spend, which thus affect consumption choices (8)

capital   A factor of production that people construct, or invent, and then use to transform the other factors of production—land and labor—to make them more productive (5)

capital account   A part of the balance-of-payments account that comprises capital inflows and outflows related primarily to investment at home and abroad (5)

capital markets   Financial markets where enterprises and governments issue and trade financial obligations with maturities longer than a year (10)

capital mobility   The ease or difficulty of moving capital across national borders or of transforming one financial asset into another (9)

capital mobility hypothesis   A conjecture that posits an inverse relationship between the mobility of capital and the policy autonomy of government or less mobile assets of production (10)

causality   The direct connection between a cause and an effect; a relationship in which a change in input A brings about a change in outcome B (1)

centralized means of allocation   Distribution mechanisms that are more hierarchical and authoritative than the voluntary, consensual nature of a market (1)

cheap talk   An insincere, empty promise of threat, reward, or commitment (4)

China card   A U.S. diplomatic strategy to normalize relations with China in order to play upon the growing split between China and the Soviet Union (11)

closed-economy models   Approaches to the examination of economic conditions in a society by ignoring economic factors and conditions external to the nation and considering the nation as an isolated entity (1)

collective goods   Public commodities that, if available to one member of a group, must be available to all members of that group (7, 13)

command economies   Systems in which allocation mechanisms are centrally directed via the hierarchical mechanisms of the state, unlike the decentralized organization of economic activity in a market economy; *see* centralized means of allocation (11)

comparative advantage   A nation's ability to produce a particular commodity with a greater margin of efficiency over its trading partners than it enjoys in the production of other commodities; the foundation of modern international trade and the basis for the principle of specialization (5)

competitive markets   Decentralized mechanisms that coordinate the allocation, distribution, and use of the raw materials, labor, and capital that go into economic activity; symmetric and voluntary exchange among nonhierarchical parties (5)

completeness   The quality that defines two alternatives as both comparable and capable of being placed in a hierarchy (2)

compulsion   The exercise of power and hierarchy to shift the incentives of individuals to contribute to the group effort, thus essentially transforming a voluntary exchange into a nonvoluntary exchange of resources in order to obtain a collective good (13)

conditionality   The imposition of restrictions upon the extension of financing pending some change, as when the IMF asks a government to address specific national economic problems that the IMF thinks are contributing to the state's persistent balance-of-payments problems (9)

Condorcet Paradox   A situation in which a voting rule aggregates individual preferences that are complete and transitive, but produces a collective outcome that is intransitive (2)

consumption possibilities   The consumption frontier for a nation; the maximum amount of economic goods that can be utilized in a society (5)

contagion network   A web of transactions and connections that transmits opportunities, dislocations, and risks across societies (10)

containment   The use of military and economic capabilities to encircle, restrict, and challenge the Soviet Union and its sphere of influence (9, 11)

convertibility   A government's practice of exchanging its currency for another currency or reserve asset at the established rate of exchange upon request (7)

costs   The goods that we forgo when we choose to consume a particular item (2)

costs of adjustment   The challenges and dislocations that people and societies confront as they adapt to economic and social change (8)

countercyclical policies   Economic policies that work to oppose and counteract the current global economic trend through the provision of collective goods such as liquidity and low levels of tariffs; *see* procyclical policies (7)

countervailing duties   Legitimate tariffs, sanctioned by WTO rules, that are imposed to penalize foreign producers who have received unfair government subsidies and as a consequence are damaging domestic producers who would otherwise be legitimately competitive (9)

creative destruction   The disciplinary mechanism of competitive markets that forces transformation upon uncompetitive producers, generates waves of structural change, and creates economic advance in society (7)

currency control board   An extremely narrow version of a peg, which tightens the trading band of a currency and limits a government's latitude for responding to political pressures to manipulate money supply and the exchange rate (10)

currency risk   Uncertainty about exchange rates due to the fluctuations of currencies vis-à-vis each other (7)

current account   A part of the balance-of-payments account that comprises the imports and exports of goods, services, and several ancillary items (5)

cycling problems   A category of social dilemmas in which coordination is complicated by the existence of multiple equilibria and the absence of a dominant strategy (12)

dead-weight loss   A pure social inefficiency even though some individuals may benefit, as in a government intervention, such as a quota, that allows domestic producers to keep the consumers' cost from the obstruction of trade (9)

debt forgiveness   A development strategy involving cancellation of the debt burden of developing states, in order to relieve them of the need to send capital abroad to pay off their loans instead of investing in domestic economic activity (9)

decentralized   Economic systems in which consumption, production, and allocation choices are voluntary, are determined by supply and demand, and are coordinated by a price mechanism (1)

default risk   The threat that a borrower or a buyer may renege on payment, either partially or wholly (7)

deflation   A persistent decrease in the level of consumer prices for commodities and services, or a persistent increase in the purchasing power of money because of a reduction in available currency and credit relative to the supply of commodities and services (7)

demand   The market force that represents the aggregation of individual consumption preferences (5)

democratization   The process of extending democratic principles to a formally nondemocratic government system by encouraging free choice in political arenas (5)

dependency   A political economy's reliance on a particular resource, which thus makes the state vulnerable to influence (4)

dependent variable   The phenomenon that social researchers are attempting to explain, a factor that is influenced or caused by an independent variable (1)

détente   The reduction of political-military tensions and improvement of economic relations between the United States and Soviet Union that began in the late 1960s (11)

discount rate   The degree to which we allow the future to influence our current choices; a higher discount rate means that we place less value on the future than we do on the present; *see* shadow of the future (12)

disintermediation   A process in which economic enterprises shift their borrowing away from commercial banks, which guarantee a specific rate of return to savers and intermediate their risks, and toward securitized financial instruments such as bonds and equities, in which the investor accepts the full risk of the loan to a borrower but also can reap a greater reward (10)

divisibility   The interaction of group size with the total amount of a collective good; an individual's willingness to contribute may lessen if the benefit of the collective good decreases with its consumption by an increasing number of group members (13)

dominant strategy   A strategy that a player would select regardless of the actions of other players (2)

dumping   A foreign producer's practice of selling its products below their production costs; a predatory behavior designed to drive competitors out of business and grab market share (9)

economic liberalism   The dominant theoretical framework that underpins our modern global political economy; at its heart is exchange within *competitive markets* (5)

economies of knowledge   The efficiency gained from learning about how to produce a product (3)

economies of scale   The efficiency gained in producing a commodity from the concentration of activities and resources that are required to produce it (3)

efficiency   A comparative gauge of the inputs of land, labor, and capital that go into the production of individual goods or services; an efficient market optimizes the use of the resources that go into economic activity to satisfy the aggregated wants and preferences of the members of society (3, 5)

elasticity (of demand and supply)   The relative changeability in consumer demand or producer supply due to a change in price; inelastic demand or supply is relatively inflexible regardless of price, while elastic demand or supply will change with a change in price (4)

empire   A political entity that incorporates far greater territory under a single political authority than does a modern nation-state (3)

entrepreneurs   People who help to generate collective goods when they act in their private interest (13)

equilibrium   A situation in which activity has stopped and there is no switching of strategies; aside from this quality of stability and its value for predicting and explaining behavior, there is nothing inherently special or attractive about an equilibrium (2)

escape clauses   Special provisions included in the GATT (and now the WTO) organizing treaties that allow governments to temporarily protect their domestic industries—allowing them to escape from the discipline of the market—under special circumstances in order to provide time for adjustment and to ease dislocations (9)

euro markets   Markets trading financial instruments that are denominated in a nation's currency outside the boundaries of that nation (9)

European Monetary System (EMS)   A collective peg monetary arrangement formed in 1979 that targeted ±2.25 percent bands for members of the peg, but allowed some weaker-currency states (such as Italy) a wider, transitional band of 6 percent (10)

European Snake   A collective-currency peg that constrained the trading range of European currencies; it was created in response to fears about post–Bretton Woods flotation and designed to limit exchange-rate volatility (10)

exchange-rate mechanism (ERM)   The mechanism that determines the value of one currency versus another and provides a means of adjustment in the balance-of-payments mechanism (5, 10)

externality   The effect of a transaction on a third party that is not directly involved in the exchange (5)

factor endowment   The distribution of factors of production (land, labor, and capital) in a specific economy; each economy has a different factor endowment based on relative abundance of resources (5)

factor intensities   The different quantities of the factors of production necessary to produce a commodity (5)

factors of production   The inputs to economic production—land, labor, and capital (5)

fallacy of composition   A strategic situation in which the outcome is different than simply the sum of the parts, either greater or less (2, 8)

financial futures markets   Markets in which traders purchase financial instruments in a particular currency and lock in the price of that currency at some future date; such betting on the future value of currencies allows hedging against exchange-rate risk and supplies insurance mechanisms to manage currency risk (10)

financing gap   The difference between the level of domestic investment considered necessary to promote economic growth and the level of domestic savings (9)

fiscal policy   Government tax and expenditure strategy designed to influence investment through the use of fiscal stimulus; countercyclical fiscal policy involves expanding government expenditures and/or reducing taxes during a downturn and reducing government expenditures and/or increasing taxes during an expansion; *see* monetary policy (9)

Fleming-Mundell model   A theory that predicts an inherent tension between currency stability, capital mobility, and monetary policy autonomy (10)

floating-exchange-rate   An exchange-rate mechanism in which a currency's value is determined by market forces, rather than being fixed by a government (8)

foreign direct investment (FDI)   Investment in control of productive facilities overseas—usually defined by an investment that amounts to control of 10 percent or more of a company's equity; *see* portfolio investment (5, 10)

free-riding   A collective action problem in which individuals have no incentive to contribute to the provision of a public good, since they cannot be excluded from consuming that good even if they fail to contribute (5)

free-trade areas   Blocs of states that agree to eliminate tariffs or barriers to trade between member states; GATT (and now the WTO) provide exceptions for such exclusionary principles if they conform to certain requirements, such as not raisings tariffs for nonmembers (9)

functional equality   The principle that, regardless of their abilities, all states attempt to perform similar essential functions; they are equal not in how they perform such functions—only in that they all do attempt to perform them (3)

fundamental disequilibrium   A situation in which a nation's balance-of-payments mechanism fails to adjust in response to economic disturbances—such as inflation, chronic unemployment, stagnation, and so on—that can adversely affect its balance-of-payments position and persist over time; for some reason, the prices of a large number of domestically produced goods and services in a state's tradable sector are overvalued, so that changes in a large number of domestic prices will be required to address the underlying problem (9)

game theory   The systematic study of rational choice in strategic settings (2)

glasnost   Political reforms initiated by Mikhail Gorbachev that helped to unleash individual choice and broader citizen participation in political life of the Soviet Union in the 1980s (5, 11)

global capital   Capital that can move from one nation to another (10)

global capitalism   A particular form of social and economic relations connecting national economies, by which exchange across nations occurs primarily in markets, where consumption choices are voluntary, are determined by supply and demand, and are coordinated by a price mechanism (1)

globalization   The processes by which people in one society become culturally, economically, politically, strategically, and ecologically closer to peoples in geographically distant societies (1)

gold standard   A monetary regime in which governments set their currency values relative to gold (7)

Gresham's Law   An economic precept that specifically states that bad money drives out good money, but generalizes to any market or exchange wherein people encounter difficulties distinguishing between good and bad versions of a commodity (7)

hard currency   Any monetary unit that can readily be used and accepted in international transactions; such currencies are desirable because they are considered likely to hold their value over time and so present relatively little currency risk to the parties of an international transaction (10)

Heckscher-Olin model   An economic framework that states that differences in factor endowments across nations produce comparative advantages (5)

hegemon   A leader who helps to manage seemingly incompatible policy preferences across governments, establishes the rules of the game, and assumes a disproportionate share of the costs of maintaining those rules (8)

hegemonic stability   The situation in which a capable and willing hegemonic state unilaterally provides collective goods to overcome obstacles that hinder cooperation and cross-border market exchange (13)

hierarchy   The structure of the international arena in which nation-states are ranked in terms of their effectiveness and capabilities (3)

hierarchy of preferences   A ranking of preferences along a single dimension based upon self-interest—creating a hierarchy from most to least preferred (2)

hyperinflation   A period of rapid inflation that leaves a country's currency virtually worthless (8)

imperialism   Intrusive political and economic domination in overseas colonial possessions; imperial powers employ the political-military tools of hierarchy, not markets, to manage their colonial possessions and change production structures in their colonies (7)

imperial preferences   A set of economic arrangements whereby a colonial power and its colonies, or former colonies, enjoy privileged access to each other's markets (8)

import substitution   A development strategy that advocates protecting the domestic market for domestic manufacturers in order to enable nascent domestic industries to emerge, gain strength, and eventually become competitive in the global economy (14)

incomplete information   A situation in which parties to an exchange or interaction are not fully informed about the resources and preferences of those engaged in the interaction (5)

independent variables   Factors that, when changed, cause a shift in another factor (the dependent variable) (1)

indifference   The state of impartiality, or lack of preference between alternatives that are equal but still comparable (2)

inflation   A persistent increase in the level of consumer prices for commodities and services or a persistent decline in the purchasing power of money, caused by an increase in available currency and credit beyond the proportion of available goods and services (7)

institutions   The formal and informal "rules of the game," laws, and practices that structure the incentives of individuals (2)

intangible attributes   Resources that are created and transformed by people and contribute to a state's capabilities (4)

international monetary regime   A set of formal and informal rules, conventions, and norms that govern international financial transactions—the monetary and financial relations between states; it specifies what policy instruments governments may use, what those instruments can legitimately target as policy, and when they can be used (7)

interdependence   An assessment of the connections and relations across nations, of the degree to which activities in one nation spill over to influence activities in other nations (3)

intransitive collective outcome   A social preference ordering that does not produce a strict hierarchy of social preferences (2)

invisible hand   An idea proposed by Adam Smith, theorizing that an unseen force guides self-interested individual behavior in competitive markets to promote the welfare of society without deliberate intent (2, 5)

jointness of supply   The characteristic that one person's consumption of a collective good does not restrict its consumption by other members of the group (13)

labor   The effort that men and women put into producing a commodity (5)

labor theory of value   A means of comparing production costs by focusing on the labor cost, or amount of labor time needed to produce a commodity (5)

land   Raw materials and physical resources available in nature, such as arable land, water, and raw materials either animal, vegetable, or mineral (5)

leading currency problem   A dilemma created when the leading currency country, the dominant reserve currency state, encounters a fundamental disequilibrium and contemplates adjusting its exchange rate, which would thereby affect prices throughout the system and potentially unsettle international economic transactions (9)

lender of last resort   A nation or bank that acts countercyclically to ensure an adequate supply of capital during economic crisis; a collective good (7)

letter of conditionality   A letter, signed by a government, that offers commitments to address systemic problems in its domestic economy in exchange for financial assistance from an international organization such as the IMF (10)

letters of credit   Financial instruments that a party to an exchange can obtain from her bank to lower the risk and uncertainty of nonpayment of an obligation across national boundaries; *see* banker's acceptances (7)

liberalism   A form of economic interaction based upon voluntary exchange in market settings, where the consumption and production of goods and services are coordinated by a price mechanism and are not manipulated via the intervention of political actors (1)

liquidity   A measure of how mobile an asset is or how easily it can be exchanged; for example, cash is more liquid than land (7)

Maastricht criteria   A set of macroeconomic convergence goals, established by the Maastricht Treaty (1991), which European governments had to meet by 1997, as they moved to Stage III of European Monetary Union (10)

market access under duress   A countercyclical policy of maintaining relatively open markets for international goods at a time of economic crisis and providing an outlet for foreign economic enterprises to sell their goods in order to counter recessionary trends (7)

market failure   A situation in which market exchange fails to allocate societal resources as efficiently as theoretically possible, so that a society produces and consumes less than the optimal levels of goods and services (5, 12)

Marshall Plan   An economic policy initiative of the Truman administration, designed to promote postwar reconstruction and to provide a bulwark against the rise of domestic communist movements in the Western European states (9)

median voter   The voter who is located exactly in the middle of all the voters arrayed on a political spectrum (6)

mercantilism   A system of political economy prevailing in Europe after the decline of feudalism, based upon the principle that the international flow of capital is good if one's own nation attains a favorable balance of trade when compared to other nations, thereby contributing to the political-military might and position of the nation and its sovereign (1, 7)

methodological individualism   A claim that individuals—not larger units of aggregation such as nations or societies—make choices (2)

model   A simplified intellectual construction that postulates a causal relationship across a set of variables, thus providing a tool for examining similarities across social behavior (1)

monetary policy   Government strategy to manage economic activity in a society by manipulating the supply of money, either expanding it to promote growth during an economic downturn or contracting it to restrain inflation during rapid economic expansion; *see* fiscal policy (9)

money   Any medium of exchange that can store value, serve as a unit of accounting and exchange, and help to create a bond between users of this currency and their state (5)

money markets   Markets that involve the trading of financial instruments that have a maturity of less than one year; these short-term obligations include trading in currencies, currency futures, and options; *see* capital markets (10)

monopoly   A market condition in which a single producer is able to manipulate the price of a commodity by affecting the supply of that commodity in a market (5)

monopsony   A market condition in which a single buyer is able to manipulate the price of a commodity by affecting the demand for that commodity in a market (12)

monopsonists   Single buyers who are able to manipulate the price of a commodity by affecting the demand for that commodity in a market (6)

most-favored-nation status (MFN)   An international trade mechanism that automatically extends to the MFN any trade concession such as a lower tariff barrier that one might grant to another nation (7)

mutually assured destruction (MAD)   The Cold War situation in which both sides had the ability to inflict unacceptable losses upon the other side, even after suffering an initial attack by the other side (11)

Nash equilibrium   A stable equilibrium in a social interaction whereby no actor can improve her payoff by unilaterally selecting another strategy (2)

nation   An abstract form of collective identity or community identification that builds upon a grouping of individuals who share one or more characteristics that help to define who is a member of the specific community and who is not (3)

nation-state   The primary unit of political aggregation in world affairs, combining the collective identity of a *nation* with the legal entity of a *state* (3)

national policy autonomy   The ability of a government to maintain independence in producing political commodities and in forming and enforcing its own policies (3)

neoliberalism   A shift away from Keynesian strategies such as fiscal policies, domestic social protections, controls on capital movements, and collective international management, to place greater emphasis on markets to condition, reward, or penalize economic activity (10)

network externality   A dynamic whereby the previous choices made by policymakers in the system spill over to push convergence of future choices elsewhere in the system; an artifact and a contributor of increasing interdependence (7)

nondiscriminatory trading arrangements or **nondiscrimination principle**   Strategy that seeks to inhibit governments from using trade policy to extend privilege to one country but not to others and to prevent political manipulations that could translate into structural inefficiencies that detract from the economic gains from trade (9)

nonexcludability or **nonexclusion principle**   A characteristic of collective goods indicating that every member of the group must have access to the good regardless of her contribution to the collective effort; examples can be positive, such as military protection, or negative, such as pollution (13)

normative theory   A statement about how we want the world to work, what "ought to be"; *see* positive theory (1)

oligopoly   A market condition in which the actions of a few sellers will materially affect price and have a measurable impact on competitors and consumers (5)

oligopsonists   A cartel of buyers that manipulates price and has a measurable impact on competitors and consumers (6)

oligopsony   A market condition in which the actions of a few buyers will materially affect price and have a measurable impact on competitors and consumers (12)

open-economy models   Political economy models in which connections across national economies become important factors to consider when exploring a nation's economic and social welfare and the politics that surrounds it (1)

Ostpolitik ("Eastern policy")   The policy pursued by West Germany in the 1960s which sought the normalization of relations with East European states (11)

par value   The stated value of a currency with a fixed exchange rate (9)

Pareto optimal   A situation or equilibrium wherein another distribution of resources and efforts cannot benefit one member of society without hurting another and lowering the overall efficiency of the production and consumption of goods, given the mix of preferences in society (6)

path dependence or **path contingency**   A characteristic of decision making in which past choices shape the direction of change and condition future choices (15)

pegging   The process by which a nation sets its currency value relative to another currency or reserve asset (7)

perestroika   The economic reforms introduced by Mikhail Gorbachev that ushered in market mechanisms and pressures to the economy of the Soviet Union in the 1980s (5, 11)

petrodollars   The revenues that accrue to oil-producing states from the sale of oil; much of this revenue is recycled into the global economy either through increased consumption or through bank deposits in Western banks located in the large financial centers, which then loan those petrodollars to borrowers (10)

piggybacking   A mechanism for the provision of collective goods by which established organizations use the organizational structures they have developed to advance specific issues to add new concerns and interests to their agenda (13)

plurality rule   A voting model in which the candidate, policy, or referendum with the most votes wins the election—a winner-take-all system (6)

pooling equilibrium   A dilemma caused by incomplete or asymmetric information whereby consumers face difficulties distinguishing among types—good sellers or good products from bad sellers or bad products; *see* separating equilibrium (5)

portfolio investment   An investment that amounts to less than 10 percent of equity in a firm, which insures that investors cannot exercise any control over the firm; a major component in the capital account that does not create control of an overseas facility; *see* foreign direct investment (5)

positive theory   A model for how the world actually works, "what is," rather than how we might want the world to function; *see* normative theory (1)

power   The tools, the means, to influence outcomes and achieve one's own ends; the ability to prevail and overcome obstacles (4)

power hierarchy   A structure that reflects differences in the capabilities of different policy-makers to employ the tools and strategies of influence as they think about trying to affect the behavior of others (4)

preferences   Statements about individual wants, possibly including material wants as well as social and spiritual wants (2)

price   The cost at which something is obtained; *see* price mechanism (1)

price deflation   *see* deflation (7)

price mechanism   The cost factor that coordinates individual consumption preferences (demand), with producers' activities (the supply of specific goods and services) (5)

price takers   All participants in economic exchange whose actions cannot individually control or manipulate prices; in efficient and competitive markets, all parties to an exchange are price takers and must accept the prices determined by the invisible hand of the price mechanism (5)

prisoner's dilemma   A particular form of a social trap that requires the actors to cooperate and to resist playing their dominant strategies in order to achieve a better collective outcome, although the structure of the interaction pushes each player toward her dominant strategy of noncooperation (12)

procyclical policies   A nation's monetary and fiscal efforts to maintain the current economic trend; *see* countercyclical policies (7)

production possibilities curve   The outer boundary of what an economy could conceivably produce given the resources and preferences of society (5)

productivity gains   Improvements in efficiency that occur when producers discover a means to reduce inputs per unit of production (5)

property rights   Rules defining the ownership of property (1, 2, 5)

realism   The reliance of governments on their own means, rather than on international treaties and law; a self-help strategy for constructing public policies to address a world of what is, not a world of what ought to be (3)

realpolitik   *see* realism (3)

regional trading agreements   Blocs of states that agree to lower or eliminate barriers to trade between members; such agreements combine multiple smaller markets into larger unified markets (9)

rents   Extra contributions above what a good or collective good would cost in an efficient market; an inefficiency that detracts from overall social welfare (12)

representation   The processes and mechanisms in society by which demands and preferences are conveyed from the bottom up (4)

satisficing   The process in which, rather than seeking an optimal outcome, individuals find any outcome above a set threshold to be acceptable; this practice can create an efficiency in the use of resources involved in a decision process (15)

scarcity   The concept that all items we consume—those produced by man and those produced by nature—exist in some finite amount, regardless of the demand for those items; this is a key assumption, as it generates the conditions for competition, cooperation, and conflict over the distribution of resources and opportunities (2)

securitization   The transformation and packaging of financial liabilities into financial instruments such as bonds and stocks that can be sold in financial markets (10)

seignorage   An overexpansion of money supply by issuing more currency so that a government can pay its bills and finance its programs, which creates an inflation tax (10)

selective incentive   An additional benefit beyond the collective good provided to latent group members in order to change their cost-benefit calculation and induce cooperation in the provision of the collective good (13)

self-help system   The idea, influenced by Hobbesian theory, that creatures in a state of nature, without a legitimate central authority to resolve disputes, must rely upon their own means to survive; the global arrangement whereby governments, lacking an overarching central authority, must resort to their own capabilities and tools in order to obtain their preferred ends (3)

self-interest   The notion that people make choices based upon their hierarchy of preferences and their budgetary constraints (2, 5)

sensitivity   A component of a state's power potential reflecting the fact that economies and societies need some resources more than others; a state that is sensitive to the availability of a particular resource is vulnerable to potential manipulation and influence because of it, but less so than a state that is dependent upon such a resource (4)

separating equilibrium   The ability to distinguish among types; a solution to the dilemma created by a pooling equilibrium, in which consumers cannot distinguish good sellers or good products from bad sellers or bad products; *see* pooling equilibrium (5)

shadow of the future   A concept indicating how much we value the future as compared to the present and how the future affects our present choices; *see* discount rate (12)

social choice theory   A body of inquiry that studies aggregation mechanisms in search of voting rules that accurately aggregate the preferences of society's members (6)

social trap   A situation in which what appears to be an individual's maximizing, self-interested choice for obtaining a preferred outcome results in a subpar outcome both for the individual and for the larger group or society; this unexpected outcome occurs because of the structure of interactions of the choices made by multiple individuals (2, 12)

sovereignty   The principle that the government of the state is the supreme legitimate authority within its territorial borders; in terms of international relations, it means that, theoretically, no state can exercise legitimate authority within another state's boundaries (3)

spatial model   A useful visual tool for examining the distribution of preferences (2)

specialization   An economic practice whereby each producer does not attempt to produce the entire range of commodities, but rather produces a commodity or supplies a service in which she has a comparative advantage (3, 5)

spurious   A false association; something that seems to covary with the phenomena of interest, but such covariance is a fluke and not due to any real underlying association (1)

stable equilibrium   A game situation in which a strategy exists for given players whereby the intersection of their choices, their payoffs, is stable and no player can improve her payoff by unilaterally selecting another strategy; *see* Nash equilibrium (2)

Stolper-Samuelson theorem   An extension of the Heckscher-Ohlin model, recognizing that the liberalization of trade will benefit abundant factors of production in an economy (5)

strong currency countries   State economies in which there are relatively small discrepancies between money supplies and reserve assets (8)

structural condition   An event that affects everyone in the community and is not a function of an individual's activities independent of contextual conditions (8)

structurally induced equilibrium   A stable situation in which institutions have intervened to alter incentives and push individuals to select strategies that lead to a particular outcome among the range of possible outcomes (15)

subsidies   Government financial assistance to relatively uncompetitive sectors or industries (9)

substitutability   The prospect that economic enterprises and societies will find new sources of a commodity or substitutes for that commodity at affordable prices (4)

supply   The amount of specific goods and services produced in response to consumer demand (5)

systemic factors   Forces that reside outside the domain of any specific national arena and operate across all national arenas (10)

tangible attributes   Naturally occurring resources or physical assets that can be employed and manipulated by people to advance their agendas (4)

tariffs   Government taxes on imports or exports, increasing the price of goods (9)

testable hypotheses   Assumptions about behavior that can be evaluated with information from the empirical world (1)

time inconsistency problem   A policy dilemma in which the short-term demands upon policymakers are at odds with the long-term welfare of society (8)

tit-for-tat policy reactions   Retaliation in kind against burdens imposed by unilateral changes in another nation's policies (8)

tradable sector   That portion of an economy where domestic producers of goods and services compete with overseas producers, whether in overseas markets or at home (7)

transaction costs   The costs of negotiating, monitoring, and enforcing the terms of an exchange or a contract (5)

transitional political-economies   States that are trying to change the organization of their political, economic, and social relations to allow greater political competition and decentralized economic exchange (11)

transitivity The quality that defines three or more alternatives as comparable and capable of being placed in a hierarchy of preference (2)

Triffin Dilemma A long-term inconsistency between persistent U.S. balance-of-payment deficits in the Bretton Woods system, which created liquidity for the system and led to a growing number of dollars held outside the United States, and the size of U.S. gold reserves, convertibility, and the value of the dollar; recognized by Yale economist Robert Triffin (9)

Truman Doctrine A foreign policy enunciated by President Truman, in which the United States was committed to a strategy of active engagement—"supporting free peoples who are resisting subjugation by armed minorities or by outside pressures" (9)

uncertainty A situation in which decision makers have incomplete information about their world, their possible choices, the preferences and possible choices of others, and how multiple decision makers' choices will interact (5)

unholy trinity A framework that describes the relationship between exchange-rate policy, monetary policy, and capital mobility; governments can obtain two of the three components of the trinity, but not all three at the same time (10)

validity The accuracy of a model or claim (1)

veto points Constraints, checks, or countervailing pressures that affect policymakers' ability to unilaterally select a course of action (15)

voting rule A mechanism that defines the process by which societies decide upon the political commodities they will consume; a wide variety of voting rules are employed around the world (6)

Washington Consensus A policy agenda that places great emphasis upon the corrective pressures of market discipline and seeks to reduce government regulation and intervention in the economy by promoting economic openness in trade and capital movements, liberalization of financial markets, fiscal policies that lead to balanced budgets, anti-inflationary monetary policies, stability in exchange-rate relations, expansion of private enterprise, and a reduction in state-owned enterprises; the name of this system reflects the prominence of Washington, D.C., and the organizations located there, in international economic affairs (9, 10)

weak currency countries State economies in which there are relatively large discrepancies between money supplies and reserve assets (8)

Westphalian state system The modern state system, whereby the government of a state, and by definition a territory, is considered the sole legitimate authority within its territorial boundaries (3)

zero-sum game A situation in which one's gain translates into another's loss (1)

Index

Photo Credits

About the Author

Andrew C. Sobel holds a PhD from the University of Michigan. He is associate professor and director of undergraduate studies in the political science department at Washington University in St. Louis. He is also a resident fellow in the Center for Political Economy at Washington University and serves on the board of the Center for New Institutional Social Sciences. He specializes in the politics of international finance with a focus on domestic explanations of international behavior. His books include *State Institutions, Private Incentives, Global Capital* (1999) and *Domestic Choices, International Markets* (1994). His current research compares globalization in the late 1800s and late 1900s and its relationship to the modern social welfare state, as well as investigates the linkages between democracy and growth.